Dear Students:

There is a saying that "knowledge is power." But for that to be true, knowledge must be based on an objective, independent thought process that tests new information against evidence, assumptions, bias, and other points of view. In other words, in order for you to gain new "knowledge," you must "think through" the related issues and ideas, understand them, satisfy yourself that they are reasonable, and make them a part of your personal knowledge base. Furthermore, you must be willing to re-evaluate that knowledge, and perhaps change it, as new issues and ideas arise.

In business, the saying is true—knowledge *is* power. Those who have it hold a competitive advantage over those who don't. Those who understand business information, and know how to interpret and use it, make the best business decisions.

A company's accounting reports, generated by its integrated accounting system, are a major source of business information. But when reading these reports, you must evaluate the information they contain by looking for supporting evidence, assumptions, and bias, and by considering other points of view. Furthermore, you must know how to *interpret* the information contained in these reports. To do this, you must understand how a company's integrated accounting system develops these reports, and what concepts, principles, and assumptions underlie the accounting information contained in these reports. With this in mind, we designed the two volumes of this book to address all of these issues.

After you graduate, you may work for a company and use its accounting information to make decisions as an "internal user." Or, you may consider investing in a company, or have some other reason to use its accounting information to make decisions as an "external user." Your ability to use the material in this book later to help you make effective business decisions (regardless of your career choice) depends on your making it a part of your own knowledge base. This means that you should "think through" the issues and ideas as you read about them, making sure that you understand them before you read further. This will require some effort on your part. As you read the book, read it critically. Test it in your mind. Does it make sense to you?

To help you learn this material and think about what you are learning, we have placed questions throughout the book, labeled with a "stop light," that we think are worth your time and effort to answer. Each time you encounter one of these questions, stop, think through the question, and answer it honestly. Base your answer on what you have learned in your life experiences, on your knowledge of accounting, business, and the world, and on your own common sense. By pausing in your reading and answering these questions, you will have time to process what you are reading and an opportunity to build new knowledge into your already-existing knowledge base.

Besides answering these questions as you read the book, think about what questions you have, or what else you would like to know about the subject at hand. Pursuing the answers to these questions, in class or otherwise, will help you add to your knowledge base and the quality of your later decisions.

We hope you find this book interesting and fun to read!! We also hope you find it useful in increasing your knowledge of accounting, your appreciation of the power of using accounting information for making business decisions, and your ability to use accounting information for your own business decisions.

ACCOUNTING

INFORMATION FOR BUSINESS DECISIONS

UPDATED 2E, VOLUME II

BILLE M. CUNNINGHAM
University of Missouri – Columbia

LOREN A. NIKOLAI
University of Missouri – Columbia

JOHN D. BAZLEY
University of Missouri – Columbia

THOMSON
™

Australia · Canada · Mexico · Singapore · Spain · United Kingdom · United States

THOMSON
™

Accounting: Information for Business Decisions, Updated 2e Volume II

Billie M. Cunningham, Loren A. Nikolai, and John D. Bazley

Editors:
Sam Ventsam; Jan Holloway

Developmental Editor:
Laureen Ranz

Project Development Manager:
Linda deStefano

Sr. Marketing Coordinators:
Lindsay Annett and Sara Mercurio

Production/Manufacturing Manager:
Donna M. Brown

Production Editorial Manager:
Dan Plofchan

Pre-Media Services Supervisor:
Becki Walker

Rights and Permissions Specialists:
Kalina Hintz, Connee Draper

Cover Image
Getty Images*

Accounting: Information for Business Decisions / Updated 2e Volume II / Billie M. Cunningham, Loren A. Nikolai and John D. Bazley

ISBN 13: 978-0-324-55873-9
ISBN 10: 0-324-55873-2
LCCN: 2007902807

International Divisions List

Asia (Including India):
Thomson Learning
(a division of Thomson Asia Pte Ltd)
5 Shenton Way #01-01
UIC Building
Singapore 068808
Tel: (65) 6410-1200
Fax: (65) 6410-1208

Australia/New Zealand:
Thomson Learning Australia
102 Dodds Street
Southbank, Victoria 3006
Australia

Latin America:
Thomson Learning
Seneca 53
Colonia Polano
11560 Mexico, D.F., Mexico
Tel (525) 281-2906
Fax (525) 281-2656

Canada:
Thomson Nelson
1120 Birchmount Road
Toronto, Ontario
Canada M1K 5G4
Tel (416) 752-9100
Fax (416) 752-8102

UK/Europe/Middle East/Africa:
Thomson Learning
High Holborn House
50-51 Bedford Row
London, WC1R 4LS
United Kingdom
Tel 44 (020) 7067-2500
Fax 44 (020) 7067-2600

Spain (Includes Portugal):
Thomson Paraninfo
Calle Magallanes 25
28015 Madrid
España
Tel 34 (0)91 446-3350
Fax 34 (0)91 445-6218

BRIEF CONTENTS

Brief Contents for Volume II starts on page vi.

VOLUME 1

VOLUME 2

CONTENTS

Table of Contents for Volume II starts on page xiii.

PLANNING IN AN ENTREPRENEURIAL ENVIRONMENT   59

CHAPTER 3

DEVELOPING A BUSINESS PLAN: COST-VOLUME-PROFIT
ANALYSIS   60

CHAPTER 4

DEVELOPING A BUSINESS PLAN: BUDGETING   92

VOLUME 2

CHAPTER 21

REPORTING PROPERTY, PLANT, AND EQUIPMENT, AND INTANGIBLES 718

CHAPTER 24

CORPORATE STOCK AND EARNINGS ISSUES 851

PREFACE

CAUTION:

This textbook, the second of two volumes, has a number of themes that revolve around candy, and this preface is no exception. While this book has a lot of the great accounting ingredients you are used to (and all that you will need), it also "breaks the mold" as it incorporates a number of phrases and terms well known to candy lovers (and we believe that includes accountants) Our intent is that you will get a number of cravings while reading this preface, not the least of which is the desire to devour this book and to share its great taste with your colleagues and your students.

Two Great Courses that Make One Great Text . . .

You may recall hearing different food or beverage products promoting how natural and good they are for you by using the phrases "No artificial colors. No artificial sweeteners." Well, we would like to paraphrase those slightly to convey a similar message that is the initial premise as to why the two volumes of this text for the elementary accounting sequence is natural and good for you: "No artificial separation!"

In the real world, today's students will face an accounting environment where management accounting and financial accounting issues are integrated every day. The traditional—and artificial—separation of these topics in textbooks, however, tends to lead students to a perception that the two areas are unrelated. We also believe that traditional and highly technical "preparer-oriented" accounting textbooks (1) isolate accounting from general business decisions, (2) lose students' interest, and (3) reinforce a common misconception that accounting is best left only to accountants. Therefore, such a separation misses the big picture of an integrated accounting system that provides economic information to all users—which is what the overwhelming majority of your students in introductory accounting will be. Together, both volumes of this textbook thoroughly integrate management accounting and financial accounting topics in a way that is more reflective of the world students will face outside of the classroom.

Sometimes You Feel Like a Debit, Sometimes You Don't . . .

A major focus of this textbook is on *using* management accounting and financial accounting information in various business settings. Therefore, we wrote this book at a "nontechnical" level for *all* business and nonbusiness students—not just those intending to be accounting majors. But, because two of us are heavily involved in teaching intermediate accounting and write an intermediate accounting textbook, we are also aware of the needs of your accounting majors. So we also discuss *accumulating* and *reporting* accounting information. We take a nonprocedural approach by explaining transactions in terms of the accounting equation (and entries into "account columns") and *the effect of these transactions on the financial statements* rather than in terms of debits and credits. But, we realize there is a need in many situations to teach procedures. To that end, we have provided a full chapter-length appendix (Appendix A) on recording, storing, and reporting accounting information. This appendix covers the accounting cycle, from journal entries (using debits and credits) through the post-closing trial balance. We designed it so that you may use it anywhere you see fit in the process of teaching from this book. We assure you that our accounting majors who have used this elementary accounting text are well-prepared to enter our intermediate accounting classes.

Ingredients and Nutritional Information (Key Features of this Text)

An Introduction to Business Approach
Chapters 1 and 10 take an "introduction to business" approach to orient students to the business environment—that is, the operations of a company, the different functions of business, managers' responsibilities, and the types of information, management reports, and financial statements the company's integrated accounting system provides for use in internal and external decision making. These chapters provide students with a basic understanding of business so they

can more effectively envision the context in which accounting information is collected and used, and the types of decisions users make in this context. This approach allows students to see the "big picture" more clearly.

Creative and Critical Thinking

Chapter 2 is unique for accounting textbooks, and we integrate that uniqueness into the rest of the book. It introduces students to creative and critical thinking and demonstrates how they are used in decision making and problem solving. Both volumes of this book emphasize the type of analytical thinking that successful accountants and other business people use in a world that is constantly changing and becoming more complex. We believe that as you use analytical thinking in your decision process regarding this textbook, you will not only decide to adopt this two-volume book, but will also be able to use it in a way that will foster your students' growth.

In keeping with Chapter 2, the remaining chapters introduce students to various aspects of accounting and are designed to help them develop their thinking skills. "STOP" questions throughout the textbook (identified by a "stop light") ask students to take a break from reading, and to think about an issue and/or consider the outcome of a situation. We also ask them *why* they think what they think. The end-of-chapter (EOC) materials include both structured and unstructured questions and problems that emphasize the use of creative and critical thinking skills by the students. Therefore, some of the questions and problems do not have a "correct" answer. The focus is on the approach or process that students use to solve them. With the increasing complexity of business activities, we think our inclusion of creative and critical thinking materials will better prepare students to understand the substantive issues involved in new or unusual business practices.

The Simpler Things

Earlier, we mentioned a "nontechnical" approach. Although we explain identifying, measuring, recording, and reporting of economic information, we discuss these activities at a basic level (increases and decreases in account balances) and do not include a discussion of debit and credit rules and journal entries in the main body of the text. We do emphasize the double-entry accounting system through the use of the accounting equation (Assets = Liabilities + Owners' Equity) and its linkage to the income equation (Income = Revenues − Expenses). We use account columns to record transactions, but we explain the increases or decreases in relation to the accounting equation, rather than as debits and credits. At the same time, we also emphasize the effects of the transactions on a company's financial statements and the impact they have on analysis of the company (e.g., its risk, liquidity, financial flexibility, operating capability). We chose this approach to better help students gain an understanding of the logic of the accounting system and its interrelationships, the effects of transactions on a company's financial statements, and the use of accounting information in decision making without getting them "bogged down" in the mechanics of the system. For those wanting to incorporate the mechanics of the system, as we mentioned earlier, we do provide a thorough coverage of debits, credits, and journal entries in Appendix A.

Because You've Kept Us Apart for Too Long...

We also mentioned earlier that together, both volumes of this book integrate management accounting and financial accounting topics in a way that is more reflective of the world students will face outside of the classroom. In blending our discussion of management accounting and financial accounting, we address several management accounting topics prior to discussing specific financial accounting topics. In large part, a company must plan its activities before it communicates its plans to external users, and it must operate and evaluate its operations (internal decision making) before it communicates the results of its operations to external users. Therefore, in keeping with the "introduction to business" theme and the logical sequencing of business activities, we discuss accounting for planning first, and then for operating and evaluating (controlling)—discussing management accounting and financial accounting where they logically fit into this framework.

For instance, Chapter 3 covers cost-profit-volume (CVP) analysis for planning purposes. After students have an understanding of cost and revenue relationships, we introduce them to budgeting in Chapter 4. The discussion of the master budget includes projected financial statements, which links the coverage back to the financial statements we mentioned in Chapter 1. Chapter 5 then introduces accounting for the operations of a company. Chapters 6 through 8 describe a company's major financial statements and discuss how external users would use these statements to analyze the company.

Besides integrating management accounting and financial accounting topics, both volumes of this book also integrate business issues and values and international issues, where appropriate. This approach reinforces the idea that societal and global issues are not topics that can and should be dealt with separately from the other issues, but rather are an integral and significant part of business in today's world.

Plain—and with Peanuts (Building Block Approach)

This textbook also uses a building-block approach. It begins with starting and operating a small retail candy store—a sole proprietorship—and then progresses through the operations of a more complex company in the form of a candy manufacturer—a corporation. This allows students to learn basic concepts first, and then later to broaden and reinforce those concepts in a more complex setting. Several of the same topics reemerge, but each time they are refined or enhanced by a different company structure, a different type of business, or a different user perspective. For example, because of its location at the beginning of the semester, the Chapter 3 discussion of CVP analysis is simple. We cover it again in greater depth in Chapter 11, after students have a better understanding of costs in a manufacturing setting. Each time we revisit an issue, we discuss the uses of accounting information for both internal and external decision making, as appropriate.

Likewise, we use a building-block approach to arranging the end-of-chapter materials according to levels of learning. To indicate these levels, we have divided the homework into sections on *Testing Your Knowledge*, *Applying Your Knowledge*, and *Making Evaluations*. These categories are arranged so that the answers to questions require students to use increasingly higher-order thinking skills as they move from one category of question to the next. The *Testing Your Knowledge* section includes questions that test students' knowledge of specifics—terminology, specific facts, concepts and principles, classifications, and so forth. The *Applying Your Knowledge* section includes questions, problems, and situations that test students' abilities to translate, interpret, extrapolate, and apply their knowledge. The *Making Evaluations* section includes questions, problems, and cases that not only test students' abilities to apply their knowledge but also their abilities to analyze elements, relationships, and principles, to synthesize a variety of information, and to make judgments based on evidence and accounting criteria.

New and Improved Flavor

In this updated second edition, as a result of our own use of the book and of feedback from other users, we have made both volumes of the book even better. These are the major changes and new features of the updated text.

1. We now illustrate transactions by showing their effect on specific accounts under the accounting equation. This is similar to recording in a computer system and much easier for students to understand. Marginal boxes next to these illustrations detail the effects of the transactions on the components of the affected financial statements.

> **FINANCIAL STATEMENT EFFECTS**
>
> Decreases *net* property, plant, and equipment, and total assets on **balance sheet**. Increases expenses, which decreases net income on **income statement** (and therefore decreases stockholders' equity on **balance sheet**).

2. We included more topics in Chapter 18 in the second volume that are oriented to internal users of accounting information, such as the balanced scorecard, benchmarking, and economic value added.

3. We added a section on E-business in Chapter 10 and expanded the discussion of enterprise resource planning (ERP) systems. In later chapters, for many topics we refer to how a company's ERP system can be used to gather information for business decisions about these topics.

4. Additionally, in Chapter 10 we expanded the section on annual reports to include a discussion of (a) management's reporting on the effectiveness of a corporation's internal control and (b) the related extension of the audit to include an examination of the corporation's internal control over financial reporting.

5. We added more homework related to service companies. This reflects the growing service sector in our economy.

6. We expanded the appendix on the Profession of Accountancy by adding a discussion of current developments in the profession as well as the AICPA core competencies. We also moved the

appendix from the back of the book to Chapter 1, where it is closer to the introduction of the business environment.

7. We moved some topics to chapter appendices to keep them available to those who wish to teach them, but also to allow the chapters to be more focused. These topics include the indirect method cash flow statement (as an appendix to Chapter 8), as well as the periodic inventory system under FIFO, average cost, and LIFO (as an appendix to Chapter 19).

8. We updated the discussion of intangibles in Chapter 21, pension plans in Chapter 22, and stock options and the results of discontinued operations in Chapter 24 to reflect changes in GAAP.

9. We have revised the Summary Surfing section to update the Internet homework.

10. We have revised many "real" company examples in the text, and have also updated all of the "real" company problems in the homework.

We believe these changes enhance the "flavor" of the book and make its topics even more relevant and understandable to our students.

Real-World/World-Wide/Total World:

Life is not a "textbook case." That's why we not only integrate management accounting and financial accounting topics, but also include information about real-world companies as examples for many of these topics. And, we include analyses of the financial information of some of these companies in the text and in the homework materials of many chapters. In conjunction with our Web site, the "Summary Surfing" section of each chapter gives students the opportunity to connect to some of these companies via the Internet for further evaluation.

Because each company's Web site may provide a unique path to its financial information, and each organization's Web site will be unique from each other organization's Web site, we provide helpful "surfing" instructions in the following two sections. You may want to direct your students' attention to these sections.

Suggestions for Navigating (Surfing!) a Company's Web site:

Generally, you can access a company's home page by typing in the name of the company in place of "companyname" in the following generic Web address: http://www."companyname".com. If that fails, you can use a search engine, like Yahoo or Google, to locate the company's home page. After you have accessed a company's home page, you can locate its financial statements, annual reports, and other financial information by finding a link on the home page to "About Us," "Company," "Company Information," "Investors," "Investor Relations," "Investor information", or some combination of these terms.

After clicking on this link, you will be sent to the company's financial information. Many times, you can click on the company's annual report for a specific year to find all of the company's financial statements, notes to its financial statements, and related information. Sometimes, however, the company will show a "condensed" annual report which contains only "summary" financial statements. In this case, if you want complete financial information about the company for a specific year, you will need to find the company's SEC 10-K report for that year. Normally, the company's Web site will reference its 10-K report by providing a link to "SEC Filings." To find the financial statements, after clicking on the link, go to Part 2, Item 8 of the 10-K report.

Suggestions for Navigating (Surfing!) an Organization's Web site:

Generally, you can access an organization's (e.g., AICPA) home page by typing in the name of the organization in place of "organizationname" in the following generic Web address: http://www."organizationname".org. If that fails, you can use a search engine, like Yahoo or Google, to locate the organization's home page. After you have accessed an organization's home page, you will have to search the heading or body of that page, the drop-down menus, or "hot links" for an "entry" into the section of the Web site that is likely to contain the information for which you are looking. You may find that you have to go down several "paths" before you find the proper section. Unfortunately, because organizations' Web sites tend to be less standardized than those of corporations, you may find yourself using the "trial and error" method of finding information on those Web sites.

Serving Suggestions (How to Use this Text)

" . . . a well thought out and very well-planned text. The explanations are easy to read and follow. I could teach myself from this book."
— Rebe Herling, Student

Since we (and others) have used this book in our classes, we thought you might appreciate hearing what we have learned from this experience:

1. **Faculty Preferences:** For years, Hershey's made the Kiss only in plain chocolate. Although they had put almonds in a chocolate bar, they couldn't perfect doing so with a Kiss. Nonetheless, they kept trying, and as you know, succeeded several years ago. It has been a great success since then. You, too, can succeed in integrating the financial and managerial accounting areas for the best taste. For financial accounting faculty, the textbook is so well written (see student quote above) that the management accounting material is not difficult to teach. For management accounting faculty, the book leads with management accounting material and contains fewer financial procedures than traditional ones do, so it is not difficult to teach either. Although change doesn't occur without some effort, we have tried to make this change as easy as possible for both of you by providing a great support package that will help you step into the classroom with minimum effort.

2. **The Transfer Issue:** The two volumes of this book do not form an Oreo cookie. They are not designed so that you can split up the parts and eat them separately. Given that most transfer students will check out the receiving school's policies first, we suggest that receiving schools using our book advise transfer students that they should take their entire accounting sequence at one school or the other, but not half and half. To sending schools using our book, we suggest you give your students similar advice. For your course sequence, we suggest that you devote sufficient time to coverage of Appendix A (the accounting cycle, including debits and credits) so that your students who transfer to another school have an adequate foundation in accounting procedures.

3. **Pedagogy:** We designed the pedagogical features of this book with the purpose of guiding the readers through it in a way that will help them learn the material in the book. Opening introductory questions for each chapter highlight the major topics and pique students' interest, as well as guide their reading. In support of these questions, as we mentioned earlier, "STOP" questions throughout each chapter ask students to pause and answer a question related to what they have just read, which

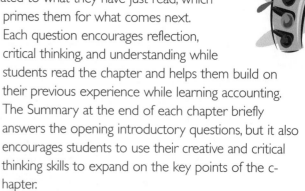

primes them for what comes next. Each question encourages reflection, critical thinking, and understanding while students read the chapter and helps them build on their previous experience while learning accounting. The Summary at the end of each chapter briefly answers the opening introductory questions, but it also encourages students to use their creative and critical thinking skills to expand on the key points of the c-hapter.

Each time we use the accounting equation and account columns in the text to show the effect of a transaction on a company's accounts, we accompany that illustration with a description of the effect of the transaction on the company's financial statements. A marginal box next to the equation details this effect on the components of each of the financial statements affected by the transaction.

We include the financial section of Colgate-Palmolive's annual report in Appendix B (in the second volume of the book). We have homework assignments at the ends of many chapters that ask students questions about the financial information in this annual report.

4. **How to Use the End-of-Chapter Materials:** This book is constructed in a "building block" approach, and so is the homework. We suggest you assign it in the same manner: ask students to test their knowledge first, then apply their knowledge, and finally, after building a strong base of understanding, make evaluations. Each chapter has a Dr. Decisive problem that asks students to apply their new knowledge in a situation closer to one they might be currently experiencing, making accounting a little more personal and relevant for them. In a "Dear Abby" format, students are asked to answer a "problem" mailed in by a reader. We have found it to be a fun way for students to work on teams, where the team constructs an answer to the question or evaluates another team's answer to the question.

DR. DECISIVE

5. **Snickers®:** . . . by chuckling at the joke, the accounting concept it illustrated was planted firmly in my mind." – Lisa Mitchell, Student. The cartoons and photographs in the book are not just for levity. They provide visual enhancements of ideas, as well as humor, and help students apply their knowledge by interpreting cartoons and photos.

6. **Smooth or Crunchy?** Alternative Course: We wrote this book for the elementary accounting sequence, but the very nature of its design has led to its successful use in MBA and Executive MBA/Small Business Programs.

Taste Tested (or "Show-Me")

We know there is always a concern about new editions, but you might have noted that two of us teach in Missouri—the "show-me" state. Having a need to "show ourselves" that the book works, we class-tested it at the University of Missouri-Columbia for eight semesters prior to the first edition. We continue to use both volumes in our elementary course sequence. We used student and instructor feedback (from our institutions and others) to make this two-volume book even better. Here is what we found, and it has been confirmed by other class testers:

- Students liked reading this book.
- The writing style is "user friendly" so that the topics are very understandable.
- The end-of-chapter homework ties in well with the topical coverage in the chapters.
- The Solutions Manual is very clean.
- Instructors found the book to be clear and easy to teach from.

Furthermore, to assure ourselves that the homework and solutions were error-free, we wrote and checked all the homework items and solutions ourselves. In addition, all the solutions were accuracy-checked by graduate students and teaching assistants.

User Feedback

We would love to list all the positive quotes here that we've received from students and instructors who have used the book, but our editors say that would add significantly to the page count and thus to the cost of the book (which our marketing manager advises would result in negative comments from the students). So, we've listed one of each. This should help prove our point as well as illustrate that we have listened to the input of others in all stages of the development of this text.

"[Early in the first semester] I've had three students already tell me that they are really enjoying reading the text!! Wanted to let you know that I've been teaching accounting for 11 years and this is the first time I've ever heard any students make that comment. You should be very proud."
— Instructor, Winthrop University

"I enjoyed studying out of the book because it was written in a manner that is clear and easy to understand. The fact that the examples (Sweet Temptations, Unlimited Decadence) were used throughout the text was very helpful."

— Nathan Troup, Student

Kudos!

THIS BOOK IS A WORK IN PROCESS, AND WE WILL APPRECIATE YOUR FEEDBACK AND SUGGESTIONS FOR IMPROVEMENT AS IT EVOLVES INTO THE THIRD EDITION. BUT IT WOULDN'T HAVE PROGRESSED THIS FAR WITHOUT THE HELP, CREATIVE IDEAS, ENCOURAGEMENT, AND HARD WORK OF NUMEROUS INDIVIDUALS, INCLUDING THE FOLLOWING:

Reviewers

Elizabeth Ammann, Lindenwood University
Janice Benson, University of Wyoming
Kathy Brockway, Kansas State University at Salina
Steven Campbell, University of Idaho
David Collins, Bellarmine University
Lola Dudley, Eastern Illinois University
Jean Hartman, University of St. Thomas
Jerry Kreuze, Western Michigan University
Leonard Long, Bay State College
Tracy Manly, University of Tulsa

Ken Mark, Kansas City Community College
Melanie Middlemist, Colorado State University
Gary Olsen, Carroll College
Keith Patterson, Brigham Young University, Idaho
Franklin Plewa, Idaho State University
James Pofahl, University of Wisconsin, Oshkosh
Alexander Sannella, Rutgers Business School
Cinday Seipel, New Mexico State University
Fred Smith, Kansas State University
John Waters, II, University of Wyoming

Teaching Assistants/Class Testers at the University of Missouri-Columbia

Jaime Bierk
Marcia Bunten
Cassi Costner
Rachel Davis
Carrie Duff
Gwen Ernst
John Faries
Katrinka Goldberg
Stacy Gower
Dave Gusky
Mark Gutwein
Mike Hart
Melissa Kahmann

Tim Koski
Lee Kraft
Shannon Lee
Jennifer Liesmann
Aaron Meinert
Holly Monks
Shannon Mudd
Lynn Nelson
Margaret Ofodile
Susan Parker
Cindy Patterson
Matt Peters
Katrina Pon

Mike Richey
Andrea Romi
Robbie Schoonmaker
Jennifer Seeser
Ken Smith
Dessie Stafford
Tom Stauder
Diane Sturek
Aaron Thorne
Robyn Vogt
Kelly Ward
Michael Weiss
Lisa Wright

Others who made invaluable contributions along the way:

Robin Roberts, University of Central Florida, and **James Stallman,** University of Missouri-Columbia, for significant contributions to earlier versions of several chapters in this book.

Tom Schmidt for his insightful (and inciteful) comments on Chapter 2.

Scott Summers, Brigham Young University, and **Vairam Arunachalam,** University of Missouri-Columbia for their advice on certain database or computer issues.

Jennifer Seeser and **Diane Sturek** for the solutions they developed to the end-of-chapter homework.

Cassi Costner, Herman Eckherle, Kelly Gallagher, Jason Janisse, Heather McWilliams, and **Emily Reinkemeyer** for their accuracy checks of these solutions.

Nathan (N8) Troup for his assistance in the development of certain aspects of the text and ancillaries.

Dana Cunningham for her Chapter 8 photograph.

Bob Hammerschmidt for his Chapter 8 quote.

Anita Blanchar for her meticulous typing of various ancillaries.

Karen Staggs for typing parts of the manuscript.

The thousands of students who endured the class testing of previous editions, especially those students who noticed and reported errors, inconsistencies, and typos in previous versions.

Those who made conscientious efforts toward the production of this book:

Maureen Staudt, Jan Holloway, Sam Ventsam, Laureen Palmisano Ranz our Sr. Developmental Editor, **Dan Plofchan** our Production Editorial Manager, **Nate Anderson, Terry Webster-Isgro, Beth Wolf** our project coordinator, and our compositor, **Integra**.

And thank you to all of the Thomson and Thomson Custom Solutions sales people for their observations, suggestions, and colossal past and future efforts to make this book known to those who dare to change.

Billie M. Cunningham
Loren A. Nikolai
John D. Bazley

ABOUT THE AUTHORS

Billie M. Cunningham

Billie Cunningham is an Adjunct Associate Professor in the School of Accountancy at the University of Missouri-Columbia (MU). She has a wide variety of teaching experience, having taught graduate and/or undergraduate courses at private universities, public universities, and community colleges. She has received several awards for outstanding teaching, including a *2007 Williams-Keepers LLC Teaching Excellence Award in Accountancy,* the MU College of Business *2005-2006 Raymond F. and Mary A. O'Brien Excellence in Teaching Award,* an MU Student-Athlete Advisory Council *2004 Most Inspiring Professor Award, Teacher of the Year, 2000* from the Association of Accounting Students, *Faculty Member of the Year, 2000* from the MU College of Business Student Council, an *Outstanding Faculty Award, 1998* from the Greek Councils of the University of Missouri-Columbia, and the *1995 Exemplary Accounting Educator Award* from the Missouri Association of Accounting Educators. Professor Cunningham has taught at Texas Christian University, University of Dallas, Collin County Community College, and the University of North Texas. She received her B.B.A., M.B.A., and Ph.D. from the University of North Texas. Professor Cunningham has conducted numerous workshops around the country on the use of writing exercises in accounting classes and on incorporating creative and critical thinking strategies into the accounting classroom. She was a coauthor of three previous books: *Accounting: Principles and Applications,* Fifth Edition (1986); *Financial Accounting: Principles and Applications,* Fifth Edition (1986); and *Accounting: Basic Principles,* Fifth Edition (1986); and a contributing author on *Cost Accounting: Principles and Applications,* Fourth Edition (1984) (all with McGraw-Hill Publishing Company).

Professor Cunningham has published articles in professional journals, including *Journal of Accounting Education, Issues in Accounting Education, Accounting Education: A Journal of Theory, Practice and Research, The CPA Journal, Research in Accounting Regulation, Management Accounting, Essays in Economic and Business History, The Community/Junior College Quarterly of Research and Practice Special Edition on College Teaching and Learning,* and *The Community/Junior College Quarterly of Research and Practice.* She received the *Outstanding Article Award* from the Two-Year College Section of the American Accounting Association. In addition, she serves on the Editorial Review Board of *Issues in Accounting Education* and has served as an ad hoc reviewer for *Advances in Accounting*

Education, Journal of Accounting Education, and *Accounting Education: An International Journal.* Professor Cunningham is the faculty advisor for the Association of Accounting Students at MU. She is a member of the American Accounting Association (AAA) and wasChair of the Two-Year College Section and Chair of the Teaching and Curriculum Section. She served on the AAA Accounting Education Advisory Committee and as Vice-President and member of the Executive Committee of the AAA. Professor Cunningham has chaired or served on numerous Federation of Schools of Accountancy committees. She chaired the AICPA Core Competency Framework Best Practices Task Force and served on the AICPA Pre-certificationEducation Executive Committee. In fits of joy, Professor Cunningham sings in her car, dances in her living room, and is an aerobics enthusiast and avid golfer (and we use that term loosely).

Loren A. Nikolai

Loren Nikolai is the Ernst & Young Professor and the Director of the Masters Programs in the School of Accountancy at the University of Missouri-Columbia (MU) where he has taught for over 30 years. He received his B.A. and M.B.A. from St. Cloud State University and his Ph.D. from the University of Minnesota. Professor Nikolai has taught at the University of Wisconsin at Platteville and at the University of North Carolina at Chapel Hill. Professor Nikolai has received an MU Student-Athlete Advisory Council *2004 Most Inspiring Professor Award*, the University of Missouri system-wide *1999 Presidential Award for Outstanding Teaching*, the MU College of Business and Public Administration *1999 Teacher of the Year Award*, the MU Alumni Association *1996 Faculty Award*, the MU College of Business and Public Administration *1994 Accounting Professor of the Year Award*, the Missouri Society of CPAs *1993 Outstanding Accounting Educator of the Year Award*, the MU *1992 Kemper Fellowship for Teaching Excellence*, the St. Cloud State University *1990 Distinguished Alumni Award*, and the Federation of Schools of Accountancy *1989 Faculty Award of Merit*, and was the co-recipient of the *1997 Holstein Creativity Award*. He holds a CPA certificate in the state of Missouri and previously worked for the 3M Company. Professor Nikolai is the lead author of *Intermediate Accounting*, Tenth Edition (2007, South-Western Publishing Company). He was the lead author of two previous textbooks, *Principles of Accounting*, Third Edition (1990) and *Financial Accounting*, Third Edition (1990, PWS-Kent Publishing), and was the coauthor of *Financial Accounting: Concepts and Uses*, Third Edition (1995, South-Western Publishing).

Professor Nikolai has published numerous articles in *The Accounting Review, Journal of Accounting Research, The Accounting Educator's Journal, Journal of Accounting Education, The CPA Journal, Management Accounting, Policy Analysis, Academy of Management Journal, Journal of Business Research*, and other professional journals. He was also lead author of a monograph published by the National Association of Accountants. Professor Nikolai has served as an ad hoc reviewer for *The Accounting Review* and *Issues in Accounting Education*. He has made numerous presentations around the country on curricular and pedagogical issues in accounting education. Professor Nikolai was the Faculty Vice-President of the Beta Alpha Psi chapter at MU for 18 years. He is a member of the American Accounting Association, the American Institute of Certified Public Accountants (AICPA), and the Missouri Society of CPAs (MSCPA). He has served on the AICPA's Accounting and Auditing Practice Analysis Task Force Panel and the Accounting Careers Subcommittee; he has also served on the MSCPA's Relations with Educators, Accounting Careers, and Accounting and Auditing Committees. Professor Nikolai has chaired or served on numerous Federation of Schools of Accountancy (FSA) and American Accounting Association (AAA) committees, was AAA Director of Education for 1985–1987, and was President of the FSA for 1994. Professor Nikolai is married and has two adult children and three grandsons. His family has one cat, and he is an avid basketball player, golfer, and weight lifter.

John D. Bazley

John D. Bazley, Ph.D., CPA, is the John J. Gilbert Professor of Accountancy in the School of Accountancy of the Daniels College of Business at the University of Denver where he has received *the University 1990 Distinguished Teaching Award, the Vernon Loomis Award for Excellence in Advising, the Alumni Award for Faculty Excellence, the Jerome Kesselman Endowment Award for Excellence in Research,* and the *1995 Cecil Puckett Award of the Daniels College of Business.* Professor Bazley earned a B.A. from the University of Bristol in England and an M.S. and Ph.D. from the University of Minnesota. He has taught at the University of North Carolina at Chapel Hill and holds a CPA certificate in Colorado. He has taught national professional development classes for a major CPA firm and was a consultant for another CPA firm. Professor Bazley is co-author of Intermediate Accounting, Tenth Edition (2007, South-Western Publishing). He was also a co-author of *Principles of Accounting and Financial Accounting* (PWS-Kent Publishing Company).

Professor Bazley has published articles in professional journals including *The Accounting Review, Management Accounting, Accounting Horizons, Practical Accountant, Academy of Management Journal, The Journal of Managerial Issues,* and *The International Journal of Accounting,* and was a member of the Editorial Boards of *Issues in Accounting Education* and the *Journal of Managerial Issues.* He was also a co-author of a monograph on environmental accounting published by the National Association of Accountants. He has served as an expert witness for the Securities and Exchange Commission. He has served on numerous committees of The Federation of Schools of Accountancy (including Chair of the Student Lyceum Committee), the American Accounting Association, and the Colorado Society of CPAs (including the Continuing Professional Education Board).

PART 6

MANAGING, REPORTING, AND EVALUATING OPERATIONS IN A CORPORATE ENVIRONMENT

This section consists of five chapters which discuss issues involving a corporation's operating activities. After reading these chapters, you will be able to:

- *understand the relevant costs and revenues in short-term planning decisions*

- *know how to use job order costing and process costing in managing a corporation's manufacturing activities*

- *calculate and use standard costs for direct materials, direct labor, and factory overhead to control a corporation's operations*

- *apply activity-based costing in a corporation's operations*

- *understand how a corporation uses the FIFO, LIFO, or average cost method to report its inventory*

- *use a corporation's inventory and cost of goods sold disclosures for evaluating its operations*

SHORT-TERM PLANNING DECISIONS

"THE ABSENCE OF
ALTERNATIVES
CLEARS THE MIND
MARVELOUSLY."

—HENRY KISSINGER

1. How do relevant costs and revenues contribute to sound decision making?

2. What types of costs and revenues are relevant to decision making?

3. How does a company determine when to drop a product?

4. What is a make-or-buy decision, and what issues does a company consider in this decision?

5. How does a company determine whether to sell a product "as is" or to process it further?

6. What is a product-mix decision, and what issues does a company consider in this decision?

Think about the decisions you have made so far today: what to wear, what to have for breakfast, whether to wash the breakfast dishes right away or wait until later, whether to stop for gas on the way to school or on the way back, what route to take to school, how fast to drive, whether to change lanes, where to park, what route to walk to class . . . whew! Now think about the decisions you made in the last year. They included decisions similar to the ones we have just listed, but they may also have included major decisions, such as where to go to school, what to major in, what career to choose, or even whether to get married. Some of these decisions are easy to make, and others require processing a mind-boggling amount of information and possible outcomes. (What if you consider and weigh all the pertinent factors and still end up in a career that you dislike or married to the wrong person?) Whether decisions affect just today or have long-term effects, organizing and analyzing this information and these possibilities helps the decision-making process.

A company also faces a wide array of decisions, from very simple to extremely complicated. To help a company make sense of the information and possibilities related to business decisions, managers use accounting information as one input in their decision-making processes. In this chapter we discuss the use of accounting information for short-term decisions involving inventory planning.

Both merchandising and manufacturing companies make short-term inventory-planning decisions. However, because of the production function, a manufacturing company faces a larger number and variety of these decisions than does a merchandising company. Some common inventory-planning decisions involve determining answers to the following questions:

1. Should the company drop an unprofitable product?

2. Should the company make or buy a component that becomes a part of a product?

3. Should the company sell a product "as is" or process it further into a different product?

4. Which products should the company advertise?

5. What is the most profitable "product mix" for the company when one of its resources is scarce?

In this chapter, we will emphasize the inventory decisions made by manufacturing companies. But before we look at each of these decisions, we will briefly review decision making, discuss the relevant costs and revenues for decision making, and present the general characteristics or types of information that help managers make better, or more informed, decisions.

DECISION MAKING

Recall from our Chapter 2 discussion of critical thinking that there are several steps in decision making: (1) recognizing the need for a decision (defining the problem), (2) identifying alternative solutions, (3) evaluating the alternative solutions, and (4) making the decision (choosing the best alternative). Although accounting information may be useful in any of these steps, it is particularly helpful in evaluating alternatives (step 3). When a company evaluates each decision alternative, the key question is, "What difference does it make?" One important area where decision alternatives make a difference is in a company's profit. It is important that a company analyze the changes in its costs and revenues caused by each decision alternative so that it understands the profit impact of each alternative. This information can then be weighed against any other considerations that are important to the decision, such as how the alternative affects employees, the community, or the environment.

> **I** How do relevant costs and revenues contribute to sound decision making?

2 What types of costs and revenues are relevant to decision making?

RELEVANT COSTS AND REVENUES

The profit impact of a decision is often one of the most important issues in evaluating decisions like the ones we listed previously. To understand the profit impact of a decision, managers must carefully analyze the costs and revenues that the decision affects—or the *relevant* costs and revenues. **Relevant costs** and **relevant revenues** are *future* costs and revenues that will change as a result of a decision.

It is important to know that a cost or a revenue that is relevant for one decision may not be relevant for another. For example, the temperature outside is relevant for a decision about what to wear today, but is irrelevant for a decision about what classes to take next semester. Likewise, the cost of sugar Unlimited Decadence uses in producing its Darkly Decadent candy bar is relevant for deciding whether to continue producing the candy bar, but is irrelevant for deciding whether the company should make or buy the packaging for the Darkly Decadent candy bar.

An important part of preparing an analysis for a decision is to identify the costs and/or revenues that are relevant to that decision. All relevant costs and revenues should be included in this analysis because incomplete profit information could result in an incorrect decision. Costs and revenues that are *not* relevant to a decision should be omitted from the analysis because they are not helpful in making the decision. Also, if treated improperly, they might result in an incorrect decision.

Determining Relevant Costs and Revenues for a Decision

For a particular decision, a manager must ask two questions to identify the relevant costs and/or revenues: (1) what activities are necessary for the company to carry out the decision? and (2) by how much will the costs and/or revenues be affected if the company undertakes the activities?

As you will see, many inventory decisions involve only costs. Hence, we focus the remaining discussion primarily on identifying relevant costs for an activity. However, the same procedures are used for identifying relevant revenues for an activity.

What Activities Are Necessary for the Company to Carry Out the Decision?

The key to identifying potentially relevant costs is to have a good understanding of the company's activities that are necessary to carry out the decision. Why? Because these activities are the *cause* of all relevant costs. Thus only costs that the company incurs as a *result* of performing these activities can be relevant. Therefore, two large groups of costs can immediately be eliminated from consideration.

First, *no cost incurred prior to making the decision is relevant.* Since the decision must be made before the activities can be carried out, all costs that the company incurs as a result of the activities must be *future* costs. Thus only future costs are relevant. Past costs (sometimes called *sunk* costs) therefore can be eliminated from consideration. Consider the following situation: suppose you are driving to a party at a friend's new house and you make a wrong turn. Now you have a decision to make about what route to take from your present location to your friend's house. (The decision involves an action you will take from *now* into the future.) The fact that you made a wrong turn in the past has nothing to do with the decision alternative (what route to take) that you must choose now. For this decision, the costs of the driving that you have done so far (the mileage) and of the wrong turn (your lost time) are sunk costs. (Whatever decision you make now, you will not regain either the mileage or your lost time.) Similarly, the cost of a machine that a company purchased last year is not relevant to a decision about how the company should use the machine in production this year. (The company already purchased the machine and has incurred this cost whether or not it uses the machine in production this year.)

Suppose it is November and you are trying to decide whether to go to the beach or to a ski resort for Spring Break. Do you think the cost of the swimming suit you bought last year is relevant to that decision? Why or why not? Do you think the cost of a beach hotel or a ski resort condominium is relevant to that same decision? Why or why not?

Second, *future costs that a company will incur for activities that are **not** necessary to carry out the decision are **not** relevant.* These costs relate to other activities that would be undertaken regardless of the outcome of this decision. For example, the cost of sugar to be used in the next year's production of candy bars, although a future cost, is not relevant to Unlimited Decadence's decision to replace an old machine with a new one. This is because the company will use the sugar in the production of candy bars whether it uses the old machine or a new one.

Assuming you have already decided to go somewhere for Spring Break, do you think your March apartment rent or your spring-semester dorm payment is relevant to the decision about whether to go to the beach or to a ski resort? Why or why not?

Remember, the key question in evaluating a decision is, "What difference does it make?" Past costs, as well as future costs associated with activities that are not related to the decision, remain the same no matter what the decision is. For these costs, the answer to the above question is, "It makes no difference." Hence these costs are irrelevant and should not be considered in the analysis.

By How Much Will the Costs and/or Revenues Be Affected If the Company Undertakes the Activities?

The costs that remain for further analysis are the costs required by the decision. Even some of these costs may not be relevant, however. *A specific cost is relevant only if the total amount that the company will incur is affected by the decision.* This fact cannot always be determined until the amounts of the potential relevant costs are estimated, however. Thus the cost-estimation step has two purposes: to provide estimates of relevant costs and to further eliminate irrelevant costs.

For example, suppose Unlimited Decadence is considering two processes to produce the Pure Decadence candy bar. For this decision, it analyzes two potentially relevant costs: direct materials and direct labor. Process 1 requires 2 ounces of one artificial sweetener

Hm-m-m . . . the beach or the mountains? The mountains or the beach? Beach? Mountains? Mountains? Beach? Is there any way to do both?

and 1 hour to produce one case of candy bars. Process 2 requires 4 ounces of a different artificial sweetener and 1.5 hours to produce one case of candy bars. The first artificial sweetener costs $0.60 per ounce, and the second one costs $0.30 per ounce. Direct labor cost is $10 per hour. Are either of these costs relevant to Unlimited Decadence?

The direct materials cost is *not* relevant because the cost of the sweetener to produce a case of candy bars will be $1.20 regardless of which process Unlimited Decadence uses (4 ounces × $0.30 or 2 ounces × $0.60). The direct labor cost, on the other hand, *is* relevant because with Process 1, the labor will cost $10 (1 hour × $10), but the labor will cost $15 (1.5 hours × $10) if Unlimited Decadence uses Process 2. Note that only by estimating these costs do we discover the irrelevance of direct materials cost.

Exhibit 15-1 shows the three-step process by which a manager identifies and separates relevant costs from irrelevant costs. Notice in the first step that we removed all past costs. In the second step, we removed any future costs that are not necessary to carry out the decision. In the third step, we eliminated those costs that would not differ from one decision alternative to another. Then, the only costs left are future costs that a company would incur in different amounts to carry out the decision alternatives. These costs are the relevant costs to include in the decision analysis.

 Which of the following costs are relevant or irrelevant to your decision about whether to go to the beach or to the ski resort? Why?
1. gas for the trip from your college to the beach and from your college to the ski resort
2. the cost of paying your kid brother to feed your fish and pick up your mail
3. the cost of ski rentals
4. the cost of the ski lessons that you took the last time you went skiing
5. the cost of your March car payment

Other Cost (and Revenue) Concepts for Short-Term Decisions

Three additional cost (and revenue) concepts are important for short-term decisions about inventory because they suggest the reason why certain costs (or revenues) might be relevant for a given decision.

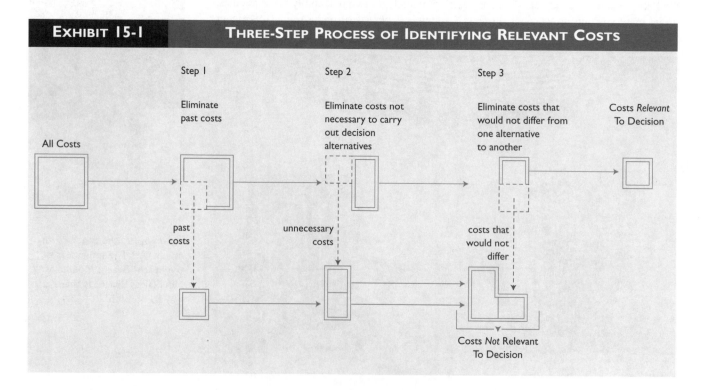

EXHIBIT 15-1   THREE-STEP PROCESS OF IDENTIFYING RELEVANT COSTS

Incremental Costs

In some decisions, one of the alternatives may require activities that a company does not need if it chooses another alternative. In many other decisions, one of the alternatives may require activities at a higher volume than required by another alternative. When either situation occurs, the additional activity usually causes additional costs to be incurred. Cost increases of this type are called *incremental costs*. **Incremental costs** are cost increases resulting from a higher volume of activity or from the performance of an additional activity. They are *always* relevant when the higher volume of activity, or the additional activity, is not necessary for all the alternatives. For example, suppose Unlimited Decadence must decide whether or not to accept a customer's special order for its Darkly Decadent candy bars. The customer wants special packaging with the customer's name displayed prominently on the boxes it has ordered. The incremental costs of the special packaging are relevant because Unlimited Decadence would have to incur these costs only if it accepts the order. The incremental revenues also are relevant because Unlimited Decadence would receive them only if it accepts the order.

Avoidable Costs

In many other short-term inventory decisions, one of the alternatives involves either discontinuing an activity or decreasing its volume. When a company discontinues an activity, or when it decreases its volume, it may reduce certain costs necessary to support that activity or may no longer incur them. **Avoidable costs** are the costs that a company must incur to perform an activity at a given level, but that it can avoid if the company reduces or discontinues the activity. For example, consider **Ford Motor Company**, which decided to consolidate what once were separate operations for cars sold in the United States, Europe, Asia, and South America for the purpose of reducing duplication of effort.[a] As a result of this decision, it planned to cut the number of its suppliers of everything from office supplies to machine tools from 50,000 to 5,000 suppliers over a 4-year period. Ford estimated that this action would reduce its costs (avoidable costs), including ordering and shipping costs, by $1 billion!

 Suppose a company currently makes a part that it uses in one of its products. If it decides to buy that part instead of making it, the cost of the raw materials used in producing that part is an avoidable cost. If the company stops making the part, do you think the depreciation cost of the factory is an avoidable cost? Why or why not?

Opportunity Costs

Performing the activities needed for one of the alternatives in a decision sometimes disrupts a company's other profitable activities or reduces its opportunity to engage in other future profitable activities. If you decide to go snow skiing during Spring Break, you not only must pay for your trip but also must give up the opportunity to work during the break and earn additional money. A company has similar concerns when making production decisions. The profit impact of this disruption or lost opportunity must be included in the decision analysis. This is commonly done by including the *opportunity costs* among the costs to be incurred for that alternative.

 Opportunity costs are the profits that a company forgoes by following a particular course of action. For example, suppose that Unlimited Decadence continuously uses a refining machine to produce Darkly Decadent candy bars. A decision to use the refining machine for a short time to produce Pure Decadence candy bars would cause Unlimited Decadence to decrease production and sales of Darkly Decadent candy bars. The profits that Unlimited Decadence forgoes because of the lost sales of Darkly Decadent candy bars are opportunity costs that it must include in its analysis of whether to use the refining machine to produce Pure Decadence candy bars.

DILBERT® REPRINTED BY PERMISSION OF UNITED FEATURES SYNDICATE, INC.

Illustration of Determining Relevant Costs and Revenues (Special Order)

In this section we show how Unlimited Decadence used the three-step process we described earlier to determine the relevant costs and revenues for a simple inventory decision. Suppose Unlimited Decadence's sales manager returned from a trip to Wyoming, where a movie theater chain offered him $250,000 for 20,000 cases (i.e., $12.50 per case) of Darkly Decadent candy bars. Although tempted to jump at the opportunity to increase sales, Unlimited Decadence's sales manager decided to analyze the decision alternatives first. A quick check with the production supervisor assured the sales manager that the plant had the excess capacity to produce an additional 20,000 cases of Darkly Decadent candy bars without giving up production of other candy bars. Therefore, Unlimited Decadence would not incur an opportunity cost by choosing to accept the offer. Because this offer was below the company's normal $16 per case selling price, the sales manager made an analysis of the relevant costs and revenues before deciding whether or not to accept the offer.

The sales manager asked the company's accountant to provide him with some cost information from the company's records. We show this information in Exhibit 15-2. The sales manager recognized that this data could be misleading because the accountant based the amounts on records of Unlimited Decadence's *past* operations, whereas the decision involved *future* operations. Therefore, before looking at the data, he thought through the decision in the following way:

EXHIBIT 15-2	COST DATA FOR THE WYOMING SALE
Manufacturing costs per unit:	
Direct materials	$ 4.34
Direct labor	6.00
Factory overhead:	
Variable	0.32
Fixed	1.26
Total manufacturing costs	$11.92
Selling costs:	
Advertising	$50,000
Trip to Wyoming	$ 550

Steps 1 and 2

There were only two alternatives to the decision. The company could refuse to accept the offer or could accept it. If Unlimited Decadence refused the offer, it would not engage in cost-incurring activities related to accepting the offer, and it would earn no additional revenue. In other words, Unlimited Decadence would incur no incremental costs or revenues if it did not accept the offer. If it accepted the offer, however, Unlimited Decadence would have to manufacture the 20,000 cases of candy bars and ship them to Wyoming in order to earn the sales revenue. These activities would generate incremental costs and revenues.

Do you agree with the sales manager's conclusion that there were only two alternatives? Can you think of any others?

After looking at the data in Exhibit 15-2, the sales manager penciled in some comments on the projected cost sheet as a result of his thinking in Step 1. Exhibit 15-3 shows the revised data.

By thinking through the activities needed to carry out the decision to accept the offer, the sales manager recognized that two of the listed costs were not relevant. As we show in Exhibit 15-3, he eliminated the cost of the sales manager's trip to Wyoming because it was a past cost (Step 1). He also eliminated advertising because this cost is related to activities that are not necessary to carry out the decision (Step 2). The offer had already been made, so no advertising would be needed. Finally, he recognized that costs related to shipping (incremental costs) would be incurred if the offer was accepted.

Step 3

Next, after deciding what costs he thought might be relevant, he estimated these costs. After obtaining a bid of $6,000 from Hasty Transfer Company to ship the candy bars to Wyoming, he gathered additional information about the manufacturing costs for the candy bars. He found that the past direct materials, direct labor, and factory overhead costs per unit were still good estimates of those costs for the coming year. The total fixed factory overhead would not increase if Unlimited Decadence were to accept the offer and produce 20,000 additional cases of Darkly Decadent candy bars.

With this information, the sales manager eliminated the fixed factory overhead from the analysis (Step 3) because although it would be a future cost incurred to support manufacturing activity, the amount would not be affected by the decision. Having finally identified and estimated all of the relevant costs, the sales manager included the relevant revenue and then made a decision.

The analysis in Exhibit 15-4 clearly shows all the incremental costs and revenues from accepting the order. It shows that accepting the order would result in an increase in company revenues of $250,000 but an increase in company costs of only $219,200. Therefore

EXHIBIT 15-3	COST DATA FOR THE WYOMING SALE (REVISED)

Manufacturing costs per unit:

Direct materials	$ 4.34
Direct labor	6.00
Factory overhead:	
Variable	0.32
Fixed	1.26
Total manufacturing costs	$11.92

Selling costs:

~~Advertising~~	~~$50,000~~	*omit; activity not required*
~~Trip to Wyoming~~	~~$ 550~~	*omit; past cost*
Shipping costs	?	

	EXHIBIT 15-4	RELEVANT COSTS AND REVENUES FOR THE WYOMING SALE

		Accept Offer (20,000 cases)	Reject Offer
Relevant revenues		$250,000	$0
Relevant costs:			
Manufacturing costs:			
Direct materials ($4.34 per case)	$ 86,800		$0
Direct labor ($6 per case)	120,000		0
Variable factory overhead ($0.32 per case)	6,400		0
Total manufacturing costs		$213,200	$0
Shipping costs		6,000	0
Total relevant costs		(219,200)	(0)
Increase in profit		$ 30,800	$0

Unlimited Decadence's profit (before income taxes) would increase by $30,800. Since rejecting the offer would produce no additional profit, the sales manager should have accepted the offer if he based his decision only on the accounting information.

How do you think Unlimited Decadence's regular customers would react to Unlimited Decadence selling Darkly Decadent candy bars to the theater chain in Wyoming at less than its normal selling price? Would there be any opportunity costs for Unlimited Decadence?

Now that we have described and illustrated the steps involved in identifying relevant costs and revenues for decision making, we will discuss several common short-term inventory decisions for a variety of companies. The kinds of decisions we discuss below can sometimes be very complex and can, in some situations, be more properly evaluated as long-term decisions (which we will discuss in Chapter 20). We have made the illustrations relatively simple to emphasize the treatment of relevant costs and revenues in the decisions. For simplicity, we ignore income taxes.

DECIDING WHETHER TO DROP A PRODUCT

3 How does a company determine when to drop a product?

Over its life, a company that sells more than one product will change the mix of specific products it sells. For example, music stores used to sell mostly records and tapes. Now, they sell mostly CDs and DVDs. Part of the change in product mix occurs because a company drops a product from its inventory. The company's managers may decide to drop a product for several reasons. For example, they may decide to drop a product because of changing technology and competition, because it is no longer profitable, because the customers' interest in the product has decreased, because the product is becoming obsolete, because the product has a poor safety record, because new information indicates that the product may harm the environment, or for any combination of reasons. The integrated accounting system helps a company's managers evaluate one factor in the decision to drop a product—the profitability of the product in question.

Ordinarily, products do not become unprofitable overnight. More often there is a gradual decline in profitability. As a company's managers begin to notice a product's decline in profitability, they normally do whatever they can to slow that decline, including reducing prices, increasing advertising, searching for new markets, and/or modifying the product. We do not consider the decisions related to these efforts because they can be very complex. But we *do* consider management accounting information that will highlight the profitability (or the decline in profitability) of individual products. This information helps a company's managers decide whether the company should continue to produce and sell a product when it is profitable or drop it when it is unprofitable. Proper analysis of the company's cost and revenue information also can help the managers avoid decisions that result in either carrying a product too long or dropping it too soon.

The key to evaluating the profit effects of a company's decision to drop a product is to determine the costs that it would not incur (i.e., the avoidable costs) and the revenues that it would not earn if it discontinued production and sale of the product. Avoidable costs are *always* relevant to this evaluation. These costs are the only future costs that the company would *not* incur if it dropped the product. All other costs would be the same in either case.

Once a company's managers determine the avoidable costs, the product profitability component of their decision to drop the product is straightforward. Based on accounting information alone, *a company should drop a product only if the total avoidable costs are more than the revenue it would lose if it dropped the product.* Another way of saying this is that a company should drop a product if the relevant "cost savings" from dropping the product are greater than the relevant "lost revenues." Under this condition, the total company profit will be higher if it drops the product than if it continues to produce and sell the product.

You probably noticed that we said what the best decision would be, *using only the accounting information.* Management accounting information provides useful information to *help* managers make decisions, but it shouldn't be used in a "vacuum." Other issues affect decisions as well, and a company's managers might make decisions that have undesirable consequences if they don't consider all these issues.

For example, in some cases, dropping an unprofitable product might affect sales of another related product. (If movie theaters stopped making and selling popcorn, the sale of soft drinks would surely decrease!) Furthermore, managers should consider the effect on the company's employees of dropping a product. What if dropping an unprofitable product necessitates "laying off" employees?

 In 2001, within days of the terrorist attacks in New York, Washington, D.C., and Pennsylvania, demand for air travel dropped dramatically. Airlines responded by cutting schedules and laying off employees. While most airlines declined to provide their laid-off employees with severance pay, **Continental Airlines** *offered its employees severance pay at a cost of more than $60 million.[b] How do you think Continental Airlines included this cost in its analysis of the decision to cut schedules? How is this analysis similar to that of the decision to cut a product?*

http:www.continental.com

Even if a product turns out to be profitable, the company's managers might consider dropping it for some other reason. For example, if new research indicates that a product is hazardous, the managers would be disregarding the well-being of the company's customers (and perhaps the community in which it manufactures the product) by continuing to produce it.

Management accounting provides an excellent means of determining relevant revenues and costs for particular decisions. By combining this information with other relevant issues, managers can make informed, intelligent decisions. In the following discussion we illustrate how Unlimited Decadence would analyze the relevant costs and revenues for a decision about dropping the Divinely Decadent candy bar.

Suppose the managers at Unlimited Decadence wonder whether the Divinely Decadent candy bar is really a profitable product. The accounting department has assembled preliminary estimates for next year's operations to analyze the expected profitability of the candy bar. We show these estimates in Exhibit 15-5. Unfortunately, this information suggests that Unlimited Decadence would produce and sell the Divinely Decadent candy bar at a $10,900 loss.

© GEORGE HALL/CORBIS

What do you think the avoidable cost would be if an airline dropped a route?

EXHIBIT 15-5 · **EXPECTED PROFIT COMPUTATION**

UNLIMITED DECADENCE CORPORATION
Expected Profit of Divinely Decadent Candy Bars and Other Candy Bars

	Divinely Decadent Candy Bars	Other Candy Bars	Total
Sales revenue	$ 21,647,500	$ 57,984,500	$ 79,632,000
Less variable costs	(15,462,500)	(32,912,500)	(48,375,000)
Contribution margin	$ 6,185,000	$ 25,072,000	$ 31,257,000
Less fixed costs:			
Advertising	$ 1,920,000	$ 2,880,000	$ 4,800,000
Depreciation: Buildings	825,000	1,675,000	2,500,000
Depreciation: Equipment	69,400	990,600	1,060,000
Insurance	128,000	352,000	480,000
Property taxes	302,000	1,062,000	1,364,000
Salaries	351,500	7,048,500	7,400,000
General and administrative	2,600,000	5,100,000	7,700,000
Total fixed costs	$ (6,195,900)	$(19,108,100)	$(25,304,000)
Profit (loss)	$ (10,900)	$ 5,963,900	$ 5,953,000

Notice that the profit computation we show in Exhibit 15-5 separates the variable and fixed costs, and lists the fixed costs so that they can be analyzed individually. The first question the Unlimited Decadence managers should ask is, "Which costs can be avoided if Unlimited Decadence drops the Divinely Decadent candy bar?" The following information about the costs listed in the exhibit is important to Unlimited Decadence's managers.

1. The variable costs for each product are accurate. Therefore, Unlimited Decadence expects the variable costs assigned to the Divinely Decadent candy bars ($15,462,500) to be very close to the actual variable costs incurred. Thus, these variable costs are avoidable costs.

2. The advertising expense of $1,920,000 for the Divinely Decadent candy bars consists of $1,400,000 specifically related to advertising these candy bars and $520,000 allocated to the Divinely Decadent candy bars from general advertising for all company products. Therefore, only the $1,400,000 cost specifically related to the Divinely Decadent candy bars is avoidable. (Unlimited Decadence will continue general advertising for all company products whether or not it drops the Divinely Decadent candy bar.)

3. The depreciation of $825,000 on the portion of the factory buildings that Unlimited Decadence uses to manufacture the Divinely Decadent candy bars is a sunk cost because it is based on the *past* purchase cost of the buildings. It is not relevant to this decision. However, if Unlimited Decadence stops production of the Divinely Decadent candy bar, it will be able to use the space it currently uses for this production to spread out its production facilities for other candy bars. This would improve the efficiency of the production of the other candy bars. Unlimited Decadence estimates that this improved efficiency would increase the profit it earns on the other candy bars by $910,000. If Unlimited Decadence continues to produce the Divinely Decadent candy bars, it will lose this profit increase. Thus, Unlimited Decadence will incur an opportunity cost of $910,000 related to space usage if it continues the production of the Divinely Decadent candy bar.

4. The depreciation of $69,400 on the factory equipment used to produce the Divinely Decadent candy bar is also a sunk cost because it is based on the past purchase

cost of the equipment. It is not relevant to this decision. Because of the age of the equipment, Unlimited Decadence cannot sell it. Furthermore, it cannot use the equipment in the production of other candy bars. Therefore, Unlimited Decadence will give the equipment to a local scrap dealer if it discontinues the production of the Divinely Decadent candy bar.

What if Unlimited Decadence could sell this equipment? Do you think the selling price would be relevant to this decision? If so, how would it affect Unlimited Decadence's profit under each alternative? If not, why not?

5. A discussion with Unlimited Decadence's insurance agent suggests that the company's insurance expense for insurance coverage on equipment and inventories would decrease by $128,000 if Unlimited Decadence discontinues production of the Divinely Decadent candy bar.

6. Unlimited Decadence will be able to avoid the property taxes of $302,000 because of the reduction in the inventory of Divinely Decadent candy bars if it discontinues production of the candy bar.

7. The salaries of $351,500 related to Divinely Decadent candy bar production are for four shift managers and a production superintendent. Unlimited Decadence will lay off all four shift managers if it discontinues production of the Divinely Decadent candy bar. Therefore, their total salaries of $279,000 are avoidable. Instead of laying off the production superintendent, Unlimited Decadence would make her the new manager of the production planning and scheduling department. Her salary ($72,500) is not avoidable. If Unlimited Decadence continues to produce and sell the Divinely Decadent candy bar, the company will need to hire a new manager for production planning and scheduling from outside the company. The personnel department estimates that to hire such a person would cost the company $46,000. This $46,000, therefore, is avoidable if Unlimited Decadence discontinues production of the Divinely Decadent candy bar. Thus, the total avoidable salaries costs are $325,000 ($279,000 + $46,000).

8. Unlimited Decadence does not expect the $2,600,000 of general and administrative expenses allocated to Divinely Decadent candy bar production to be affected by the decision to drop the product. They are not avoidable.

As a result of this analysis, we can show the profit effects of a decision to stop the production and sale of the Divinely Decadent candy bar by comparing the costs that Unlimited Decadence would avoid with the revenues that it would lose. We show this comparison in Exhibit 15-6.

Exhibit 15-6 shows the "cost savings," or relevant costs, of $18,527,500 that Unlimited Decadence would avoid if it dropped the Divinely Decadent candy bar. It also shows the "lost revenues," or relevant revenues, of $21,647,500 that Unlimited Decadence would not earn if it dropped the Divinely Decadent candy bar. Costs that Unlimited Decadence cannot avoid and revenues that it would not lose are not relevant to this decision. Hence, we do not show them in the exhibit. Note that the revenues lost exceed the avoidable costs by $3,120,000. Thus profit would *decrease* by $3,120,000 if Unlimited Decadence discontinued production and sale of the Divinely Decadent candy bar. Based on this information alone, Unlimited Decadence's decision, therefore, would be to continue the production and sales of the Divinely Decadent candy bar.

Suppose Unlimited Decadence learned that its South American supplier of the cocoa beans that give the Divinely Decadent candy bar its distinctive flavor is paying its workers $0.20 an hour to pick the beans. Should Unlimited Decadence drop the Divinely Decadent candy bar? What other alternatives might it consider?

As we show in Exhibit 15-7, we could rearrange the relevant costs and revenues into an income statement format to compute the $6,185,000 contribution margin ($21,647,500 sales revenues lost − $15,462,500 variable costs avoided) that Unlimited Decadence

EXHIBIT 15-6	ANALYSIS FOR THE DECISION TO DROP A PRODUCT

UNLIMITED DECADENCE CORPORATION
Relevant Costs and Revenues for the Decision
to Drop Divinely Decadent Candy Bars

		Stop Production
Avoidable costs:		
Variable costs		$ 15,462,500
Fixed costs		
Advertising	$1,400,000	
Opportunity cost for space usage	910,000	
Insurance	128,000	
Property taxes	302,000	
Salaries	325,000	
Total fixed costs		3,065,000
Total avoidable costs (cost savings)		$ 18,527,500
Sales revenue lost		(21,647,500)
Profit lost		$ (3,120,000)

EXHIBIT 15-7	ALTERNATE ANALYSIS FOR DECISION TO DROP A PRODUCT

		Stop Production
Sales revenue lost		$(21,647,500)
Less: Variable costs avoided		15,462,500
Contribution margin lost		$ (6,185,000)
Less: Avoidable fixed costs (cost savings)		
Advertising	$1,400,000	
Opportunity cost for space usage	910,000	
Insurance	128,000	
Property taxes	302,000	
Salaries	325,000	3,065,000
Profit lost		$ (3,120,000)

would lose if it discontinued the product, and we then can deduct from this amount the $3,065,000 of avoidable fixed costs. The contribution margin that Unlimited Decadence would lose exceeds the avoidable fixed costs by $3,120,000 ($6,185,000 − $3,065,000), confirming that profit would decrease by $3,120,000 if Unlimited Decadence were to discontinue the production and sale of the Divinely Decadent candy bar.

DECIDING WHETHER TO MAKE OR BUY A PART

4 What is a make-or-buy decision, and what issues does a company consider in this decision?

Many products require a manufacturing process to convert basic direct materials into completed products of inventory. These products seldom are produced entirely by one company. For example, think about the many companies involved in the manufacture of automobiles. There are companies that manufacture steel, glass, paint, rubber, plastic, and so on. Other companies use these materials to produce parts such as lights, radios, air conditioners, fuel pumps, and tires. Any company that buys parts from other companies may question whether it would be less costly to produce a part than to purchase it from an outside supplier. That is, the company faces a *make-or-buy decision*.

Many factors affect the make-or-buy decision. If a company must buy the equipment required to manufacture a particular part and must develop the know-how to produce that part, it may be much more costly to make the part than to buy it from the present supplier, but not always. Consider **Aquapore Moisture Systems, Inc.**, based in Phoenix, Arizona. It saved costs by deciding to make a "part," when possible, rather than purchasing it.[c] Aquapore manufactures garden hoses from worn-out tires (the "part"), which it has traditionally purchased from scrap dealers. As a result of a search by its environmental team for opportunities to reduce and recycle waste, the company found more than 30,000 pounds of rubber chunks left over from its hose-manufacturing process. After comparing the relevant costs and revenues, Aquapore decided to purchase a $20,000 machine to grind the rubber chunks into small pieces that it could use to make more hoses. As a result of this decision, the company has virtually no waste from hose production. Furthermore, it has saved about $9,000 a month as a result of lower disposal costs and a reduction in the number of worn-out tires the company has had to buy. Aquapore was so successful that it is now part of Fiskars Corporation, an international company that distributes consumer products around the world.

How do you think the public's knowledge of Aquapore's production methods affects the general perception of the company's environmental consciousness? Do you think this public perception has the potential to affect the company's profits? If so, how and why? If not, why not?

A company can sometimes obtain a short-term cost advantage by making a part. This might occur when the company already has the equipment required for making the part and when it is not fully using that equipment for other production. In this situation, the company might be able to produce the part with little or no incremental costs. This cost advantage may not be long-lasting, however. (What if the company finds that it needs to use the equipment soon for other production?) A decision to make a currently purchased part to obtain a short-term cost advantage may be unwise if the company is likely to reverse the decision in the near future. Valuable business relationships with suppliers might be damaged by a decision to make a part instead of buying it.

Another reason for making a part that a company is currently purchasing involves the issues of quality and supplier reliability. Both of these factors can affect the company's overall costs as well. Poor-quality parts can cause increases in production costs for a company. A company may need to rework products that do not meet minimum quality standards, or may need to replace parts that break during the manufacturing process or after customers purchase the products. Reworking products and replacing parts add to the cost of manufacturing the product. For example, even though Unlimited Decadence doesn't use parts in its products, poor-quality ingredients can have the same effect for it as poor-quality parts have for other manufacturers. Substandard cocoa beans might make it more difficult to refine the chocolate. To overcome this problem, Unlimited Decadence might decide to lengthen the refining process, but this action would also raise the cost of manufacturing the candy bars. Poor-quality parts can also cause customer dissatisfaction with a company's product. This dissatisfaction may lead to a loss of sales (resulting in opportunity costs).

Do you think that Aquapore has an unlimited supply of parts for its garden hoses? Why or why not?

Recently, in an effort to appease customers, **Mazda Corporation** *recalled certain Mazda models to replace faulty seat belts. What specific additional costs do you think Mazda incurred as a result of this measure? What potential liabilities did it try to minimize?*

If the supplier of parts is unreliable, production delays may result that also can cause increases in production costs and lost sales. For example, if late parts cause production delays, the company later may ask its employees to work overtime in order to meet expected product sales. Without the overtime production, the company might temporarily or permanently lose sales if its customers purchase from its competitors. When negotiations with a supplier fail to correct quality and reliability problems, a company may consider producing its own parts.

The decision to make or buy a part involves an analysis of the relevant costs for each alternative. In the following illustration, we show how to consider various activities and their related costs in a make-or-buy decision.

Process Control Company manufactures the electronic control panel that Unlimited Decadence uses to control some of its production processes. Process Control currently purchases 1,000 computer chips per month from an outside supplier at a cost of $5.40 per chip for use in manufacturing the panel. Due to the discontinuation of another product, Process Control has some unused and unsalable machinery that could make as many as 2,000 chips in one production run. Process Control's managers believe the company's employees have the production skills to make the chips and, in fact, that they can make a better-quality chip than is available from Process Control's current supplier. Because of the lower quality of the purchased chip, the company's managers estimate that Process Control currently incurs excess manufacturing costs of $0.60 for each purchased chip used in production. Process Control can avoid this cost by making the higher-quality chip. Exhibit 15-8 shows the relevant cost comparison for the make-or-buy decision.

Notice in Exhibit 15-8 that Process Control's cost study shows no incremental fixed costs related to making or buying the chip. All relevant costs in this situation are variable costs. The comparison shows that making 1,000 chips per month rather than buying them would save Process Control $2,200 ($6,000 − $3,800) per month. A comparison of the per-unit variable costs shows that the company would save $2.20 ($6.00 − $3.80) for each chip made. In this case, based only on the costs of the two alternatives and not considering the other factors that could influence this decision, the company would decide to make as many chips as it needs, up to the maximum that the available machinery can produce.

The decision is not so straightforward, however, if there are some relevant fixed costs involved. Suppose that Process Control does not have the machinery it needs to make the

EXHIBIT 15-8	ANALYSIS FOR THE MAKE-OR-BUY DECISION

PROCESS CONTROL COMPANY
Relevant Costs for the Make-or-Buy Decision

	Make Chip	Buy Chip
Expected monthly requirements (chips)	1,000	1,000
Relevant costs:		
Direct materials	$2,200	
Direct labor	1,050	
Variable overhead	550	
Chip purchase cost		$5,400
Excess manufacturing costs incurred in production of electronic control panels as a result of lower-quality purchased chips	—	600[*]
Total relevant costs	$3,800	$6,000
Relevant costs per unit	$ 3.80	$ 6.00

[*]$0.60 × 1,000

chip, but can lease the machinery for a fixed cost of $2,640 per month. All the other costs remain the same. In this case, the cost of making 1,000 chips is $6,440 ($3,800 + $2,640) per month, and the cost of purchasing 1,000 chips is $6,000 per month. Here, Process Control's manager's would prefer to buy the chip (again, considering this information alone). When fixed costs are involved, the managers should consider the total cost of each *alternative* rather than comparing the total (fixed + variable) costs per *chip*. If it needs more or fewer than 1,000 chips, Process Control's managers may be misled by comparing total costs per chip because fixed costs per chip change when the volume changes, as we discussed in Chapter 11 of Volume 1.

If the number of chips that Process Control needs is likely to change, a different form of analysis is more helpful. The cost of buying the chip is $6.00 per chip purchased. The total cost of making the chip now includes a fixed cost of $2,640 per month and a variable cost of $3.80 per chip made. Exhibit 15-9 shows a graph of the expected costs of both making and buying the chip as the volume needed per month varies.

Note from the graph in Exhibit 15-9 that Process Control's expected total cost of making the chip is higher than the total cost of buying the chip at a volume of 1,000 units. The graph also shows that at a volume below 1,200 units, the total cost of making the chip is always higher, and at a volume above 1,200 units, the total cost of buying the chip is always higher. This form of analysis is useful because it not only helps in making the correct current decision, but also shows the volume level at which the decision would change. Based on this accounting information alone, the correct decision would be to continue buying the chip because the purchase cost at the expected volume of 1,000 chips is less than the cost of making the chips. But remember, the cost difference between the two

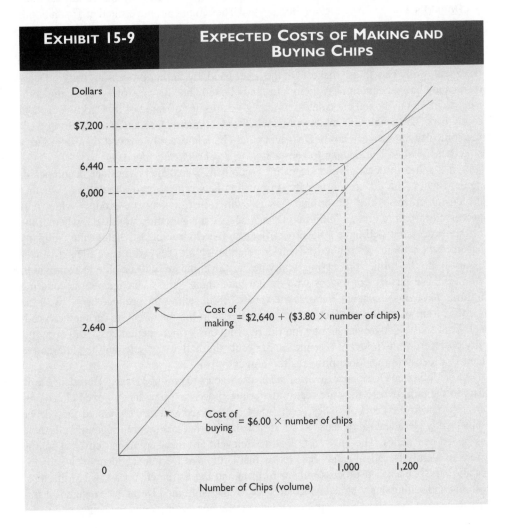

EXHIBIT 15-9	EXPECTED COSTS OF MAKING AND BUYING CHIPS

Cost of making = $2,640 + ($3.80 × number of chips)

Cost of buying = $6.00 × number of chips

alternatives is one of many factors a company's managers consider when deciding whether to make or buy a part.

 Can you think of any alternatives other than continuing to purchase parts from the current supplier or making them? Remembering back to Chapter 10 of Volume 1, what organizational function do you think is responsible for this type of decision? How can accounting information help?

DECIDING WHETHER TO SELL A PRODUCT OR PROCESS IT FURTHER

5 How does a company determine whether to sell a product "as is" or to process it further?

Many companies face the decision of whether to sell a product "as is" or to use it as a direct material in the manufacture of another product. For instance, a meatpacker can sell animal fat "as is" or make soap out of it, a textile mill can sell yarn "as is" or weave cloth out of it, and an oil refinery can sell the kerosene produced in refining oil or process it further to increase gasoline output. (You will make a similar decision when you graduate. Will you take the product of your education—your mind—and sell it to the job market as is, or will you process it further by working toward a more advanced degree?) Consider **Tyson Foods, Incorporated**, which became the dominant leader in the poultry industry by deciding to process chicken further.[d] Instead of just selling whole chickens to grocery stores and restaurant chains, Tyson anticipated the need to have prepared chicken items that need only to be cooked or reheated. For example, Tyson Foods supplied **McDonald's** with its first Chicken McNuggets! These innovations resulted in Tyson Foods possessing a 25 percent share of the poultry market. The corporation is pursuing a similar strategy with pork and fish products.

Now suppose that Unlimited Decadence currently can sell all of the cases of Darkly Decadent candy bars that it makes. On the other hand, by further processing Darkly Decadent candy bars, it can convert them into fancy boxed chocolates. However, for the company to make any boxed chocolates, it must give up sales of some of its Darkly Decadent candy bars. The problem is to determine whether Unlimited Decadence should forgo selling some of the cases of Darkly Decadent candy bars in order to convert them into fancy boxed chocolates. The company faces a *sell-or-process-further decision*.

In a sell-or-process-further decision, a company's managers consider a number of items, such as the difference in company profits between the two alternatives, whether the customers who like the product "as is" will refuse to buy the product when it is processed further (an issue Unlimited Decadence's managers must consider), whether the further processing will have a negative effect on the environment, whether the company has access to employees (either present or potential employees) who have the skills necessary to do the further processing, and whether the company will be able to continue to employ those factory employees who do not have those skills. Management accounting information helps managers compare the "profit" from selling the product "as is" with the "profit" from using the product as a direct material in the manufacture of another product. This analysis involves subtracting the relevant costs (incremental costs and opportunity costs) from the relevant revenues under each alternative and selecting the alternative (sell or process further) that provides the higher "profit."

For Unlimited Decadence, none of the costs it incurs to produce Darkly Decadent candy bars to the point where they are ready for further processing into fancy boxed chocolates are relevant to the decision. These costs must be incurred whether Unlimited Decadence sells Darkly Decadent candy bars "as is," or whether it processes them further and sells them as boxed chocolates. The only costs that are relevant are the incremental costs of selling cases of Darkly Decadent candy bars (costs that Unlimited Decadence incurs if it sells the candy bars, but not if it processes them further) and the incremental costs of further processing and selling fancy boxed chocolates (costs that Unlimited Decadence incurs if it further processes the candy bars into boxed chocolates, but not if it sells the candy bars).

Both the revenue from the sale of Darkly Decadent candy bars (if not processed further) and the revenue from the fancy boxed chocolates (if processed further) are relevant as long as they are different from each other. Next, we show how to consider the relevant costs and revenues in a sell-or-process-further decision.

Unlimited Decadence's managers believe that the company might increase its profits by giving up the sale of some of its Darkly Decadent candy bars to produce and sell higher-priced fancy boxed chocolates. To analyze this alternative, Unlimited Decadence estimates its relevant revenue and cost information. We show this information in Exhibit 15-10.

First, Unlimited Decadence's managers estimate its revenues. They determine that the company would have to give up sales of 31,250 cases of Darkly Decadent candy bars at $16 per case, totaling $500,000, if it processes the candy bars further into fancy boxed chocolates. If it processes the candy bars further, the marketing department estimates that it can sell 200,000 boxes of fancy chocolates at $5 per box, totaling $1,000,000. These are the relevant revenues for this decision that we show in Exhibit 15-10.

Although Unlimited Decadence would not need to expand the factory for the additional processing, it would need to lease new packaging equipment at a fixed cost of $14,000 per year. In addition, Unlimited Decadence would reassign molding equipment it is currently using full-time in the production of other candy bars to this added processing. This reassignment would reduce the production capability slightly for other candy bars. The lost sales for the other candy bars would result in variable opportunity costs of $0.05 per box of fancy chocolates packaged, or a total of $10,000. Furthermore, variable costs of converting the candy bars into boxed chocolates include direct labor and variable overhead costs of $0.40 per box of chocolates, or a total of $80,000. Unlimited Decadence's managers expect delivery costs and the cost of fancy display cartons to cause variable selling costs to be $0.097 for each *box* of chocolates (totaling $19,400) as compared to $0.30 for each *case* of candy bars (totaling $9,375). We show the estimates of these relevant costs for this decision in Exhibit 15-10.

Exhibit 15-10 shows that the difference between the relevant revenue and relevant costs is $385,975 ($876,600 − $490,625) higher under the "process further" alternative

EXHIBIT 15-10	ANALYSIS FOR THE SELL-OR-PROCESS-FURTHER DECISION

UNLIMITED DECADENCE CORPORATION
Relevant Costs and Revenues for the Sell-or-Process-Further Decision

	Sell (as candy bars)	Process Further (into boxed chocolates)
Revenue	$500,000*	$1,000,000†
Relevant costs:		
Fixed leasing costs	—	$14,000
Variable opportunity cost of using fully utilized molding equipment ($0.05 × 200,000)	—	10,000
Variable labor and overhead costs ($0.40 × 200,000)	—	80,000
Variable selling costs	$ 9,375‡	19,400§
Total incremental costs	(9,375)	(123,400)
Difference ("profit")	$490,625	$ 876,600

*31,250 cases × $16
†200,000 boxes × $5
‡31,250 × $0.30
§200,000 × $0.097

than it is under the "sell" alternative. This means that processing candy bars further to make and sell 200,000 boxes of fancy chocolates results in a profit increase of $385,975. This occurs because the increase in revenue of $500,000 ($1,000,000 − $500,000) is $385,975 more than the $114,025 ($123,400 − $9,375) increase in costs. Thus, if Unlimited Decadence's managers only considered the accounting information, their decision should be to further process enough candy bars to satisfy the demand for boxes of fancy chocolates. But, of course, the managers would also consider other factors that might influence this decision.

Notice that we didn't show the manufacturing costs required to produce the candy bars. Unlimited Decadence must incur these costs in the same amount regardless of which alternative it chooses; therefore, these costs are not relevant to the decision.

DECISIONS INVOLVING PRODUCT MIX

6 What is a product-mix decision, and what issues does a company consider in this decision?

Companies that produce and sell several items of inventory face a common problem. They must decide how many units of each product to produce and sell. This is called a *product-mix decision*. For example, **Sara Lee Corporation,** over time, has made some interesting changes its product mix that has included more than 150 brands, from Jimmy Dean sausage to Champion sportswear. In 2005, the company announced that it would focus on the meat and bakery items that are the mainstay of the 66-year-old company. More specifically, the company decided to drop its U.S. apparel items, including Champion sportswear and L'eggs hosiery, and focus on its bakery, meats, and Senseo coffee brand; food service (serving restaurants and food distributors); and international food, beverage, and household products such as Kiwi shoe polish and Sanex shower gels.[e]

 How do you think Sara Lee would be able to analyze its product mix if some of its product costs were in U.S. dollars and some were in euros?

A product-mix decision involves two issues. First, a company can influence the sales volume of each of its products (or a combination of its products) in many ways, such as by sales activities (advertising), promotional campaigns, and the number of sales personnel used for each product. Second, many companies operate with limited productive capacity (for example, with a limited number of machines or a limited amount of time that these machines can be operated) and, as a result, cannot produce as much of every product as they can sell. Thus, the decision about how much to produce and sell of each product can be very complex.

In this section, we illustrate only two very simplified situations, but they should be helpful to you in providing an understanding of how a company uses management accounting information in its product-mix decisions.

Deciding How to Spend Advertising Dollars

The first situation we discuss involves deciding which product a company should advertise. For simplicity, we make the following assumptions:

1. The company currently spends a budgeted amount on advertising for each of several products.

2. The company has added a fixed amount of money to its coming year's advertising budget. The question is, "On which *one* of the several products should the company spend the additional advertising money?"

3. Studies by the marketing department provide reliable estimates of the additional sales volume (units) that would result from spending the additional advertising money on each of the products.

4. The company has enough factory equipment to produce the additional units of any of the products that would be sold as a result of the additional advertising.

In this situation, the company's profit increases if the contribution margin resulting from increased sales is more than the increase in advertising cost. The problem is to choose which product should be advertised so that the largest possible profit increase is obtained. *When the increase in fixed costs* (the additional advertising money is a fixed amount) *does not change between alternatives, the company earns the highest profit from the alternative that produces the largest increase in contribution margin above the increase in fixed costs.* This is the key to the decision. Management accounting information shows the contribution margin per unit for each of the products, while the marketing department information shows the additional sales volume that the advertising would produce. The computation required to evaluate the alternatives simply involves comparing the additional contribution margin for each alternative with the additional advertising cost.

To illustrate, we assume that Unlimited Decadence produces three products—Darkly Decadent candy bars, Pure Decadence candy bars, and Divinely Decadent candy bars—and that it has increased its advertising budget by $200,000. The company plans to spend the entire $200,000 on advertising for one of the candy bars. Exhibit 15-11 shows the contribution margin per unit and the estimated sales volume increases that the advertising would produce for each product. It also shows the calculations that Unlimited Decadence would make to evaluate each alternative.

As you can see in Exhibit 15-11, Unlimited Decadence can increase its profit by spending the additional $200,000 to advertise either Darkly Decadent candy bars or Pure Decadence candy bars. Spending the additional $200,000 to advertise Divinely Decadent candy bars would *decrease* Unlimited Decadence's total profit by $40,000. Unlimited Decadence can obtain the largest profit increase by advertising the Darkly Decadent candy bar. The profit increase would be $180,000. Although the contribution margin *per unit* for Darkly Decadent candy bars is the lowest of the three products, the increase in its sales volume is highest. It is high enough, in fact, to cause an increase in the total contribution margin for Darkly Decadent candy bars that is more than the increase in the total contribution margin of either of the other two products and more than the increase in fixed costs. Thus Unlimited Decadence should spend the additional advertising money on Darkly Decadent candy bars.

EXHIBIT 15-11	ANALYSIS FOR THE PRODUCT-MIX DECISION

UNLIMITED DECADENCE CORPORATION
Analysis of Product-Mix Decision

	Divinely Decadent	Darkly Decadent	Pure Decadence
Selling price per case	$28	$16	$20
Variable costs per case	(20)	(11)	(14)
Contribution margin per case	$ 8	$ 5	$ 6
Sales volume increase resulting from additional advertising (cases)	× 20,000	× 76,000	× 60,000
Additional contribution margin	$160,000	$380,000	$360,000
Additional advertising cost	(200,000)	(200,000)	(200,000)
Increase (decrease) in profit	$ (40,000)	$180,000	$160,000

Deciding How Many Units to Produce

The second situation we discuss involves deciding how many units a company should produce of each of several products. For simplicity, in our discussion of the product-mix decision, we make the following assumptions:

1.   The company's production is limited by a single scarce resource.
2.   The combined customer demand for the company's products exceeds its limited production capacity.

Remember from our discussion in Chapter 11 of Volume 1 that by changing its product mix, a company may also change its total contribution margin.

 How would a change in a company's product mix result in a change in its total contribution margin?

What do we mean by a single scarce resource? Here is an example. As you have been told many times, there are only 24 hours in a day. When we run out of the 24 hours, nothing we do will help us accomplish more in that day. The 24 hours compose our scarce resource and our limit. Similarly, when a company has a limited scarce resource (available machine time, for example), it can manufacture products only until it exhausts the resource. *Therefore, the company earns the highest profit by using up the scarce resource to manufacture the product mix that produces the highest total contribution margin.* In other words, the product-mix decision involves making the most profitable use of this resource. Therefore, the manager must know both the contribution margin per product and how much of the scarce resource the company uses for each of the products. Given this information, the product that makes the most profitable use of the scarce resource is the one that produces the highest contribution margin *per unit of the scarce resource*. The correct decision, using this information alone, is for the company to first produce the product that makes the most profitable use of the scarce resource, until customer demand for the product is satisfied, and then to produce the product that makes the next most profitable use of the resource, and so on until the scarce resource is fully used.

Again, assume Unlimited Decadence produces three products: Divinely Decadent, Darkly Decadent, and Pure Decadence candy bars. Each kind of candy bar uses emulsifiers that are in short supply because of a strike at the supplier's factory. Unlimited Decadence has only 625 pounds (10,000 ounces) of emulsifiers in its inventory and will receive no more for three weeks. So, in this case, emulsifiers are the single scarce resource that will drive our analysis. During this time, Unlimited Decadence's sales managers expect to be able to sell 12,000 cases (units) of Divinely Decadent candy bars, 5,000 cases of Darkly Decadent candy bars, and 15,000 cases of Pure Decadence candy bars. Unlimited Decadence's production and sales managers must decide how many cases of each product to produce and sell during the next three weeks. Exhibit 15-12 shows the contribution margin per case for each product, the direct materials needed for each product, and the contribution margin earned per ounce of emulsifiers.

Notice in Exhibit 15-12 that Divinely Decadent candy bars have the *highest* contribution margin per *unit* ($8 per case). If Unlimited Decadence's managers stopped the analysis here, they would choose to produce only Divinely Decadent candy bars and not make the most profitable decision. The company would run out of emulsifiers, leaving the demand for the other candy bars unmet. Remember that the focus of this decision is on the scarce resource (emulsifiers), and Divinely Decadent candy bars also require the most emulsifiers per case. As a result, they have the *lowest* contribution margin per *ounce* of the scarce emulsifiers of all three candy bars. Darkly Decadent candy bars make the most profitable use of emulsifiers by having the *highest contribution margin per ounce*. Pure Decadence candy bars have the second highest contri-

EXHIBIT 15-12	COMPUTATION OF CONTRIBUTION MARGIN PER UNIT OF A SCARCE RESOURCE

UNLIMITED DECADENCE CORPORATION
Computation of Contribution Margin per Ounce of Emulsifiers

	Divinely Decadent	Darkly Decadent	Pure Decadence
Estimated sales (cases)	12,000	5,000	15,000
Contribution margin per case	$8	$5	$6
Direct materials (emulsifiers) usage per case (ounces)	÷ 3.2	÷ 0.625	÷ 1.25
Contribution margin per ounce of emulsifiers	$2.50	$8	$4.80

bution margin per ounce. Therefore, the company should produce as many cases of Darkly Decadent candy bars as it can until the demand for Darkly Decadent candy bars is satisfied, then produce Pure Decadence candy bars until their demand is satisfied. Finally, the company should produce Divinely Decadent candy bars if any emulsifiers are still available.

In this situation, Unlimited Decadence should use 3,125 ounces (5,000 cases × 0.625) of emulsifiers to produce 5,000 cases of Darkly Decadent candy bars and use the remaining 6,875 ounces (10,000 − 3,125) of emulsifiers to produce 5,500 cases (6,875 ÷ 1.25) of Pure Decadence candy bars. Since demand for Pure Decadence candy bars would not be completely satisfied, Unlimited Decadence would produce no cases of Divinely Decadent candy bars. With this product mix, the total contribution margin would be higher than for any other product mix. For example, if Unlimited Decadence used the 10,000 ounces of emulsifiers to produce 3,125 cases (10,000 ÷ 3.2) of Divinely Decadent candy bars, the total contribution margin would be $25,000 (10,000 ounces × $2.50 per ounce). If it used the emulsifiers to produce 8,000 cases (10,000 ÷ 1.25) of Pure Decadence candy bars, the total contribution margin would be $48,000 (10,000 ounces × $4.80 per ounce). If it used 3,125 ounces of emulsifiers to produce 5,000 cases of Darkly Decadent candy bars and the remaining 6,875 ounces to produce 5,500 cases of Pure Decadence candy bars, however, the total contribution margin would be $58,000 [(3,125 ounces × $8 per ounce) + (6,875 ounces × $4.80 per ounce)]. No other possible mix can earn a higher contribution margin during the three weeks that emulsifiers are in short supply.

 Don't take our word for it. Try to find a mix of candy bars that can produce a higher contribution margin.

In more complicated situations, a company faces many product interdependencies and several scarce resources. For these cases, the company often uses linear programming or some other mathematical programming techniques to determine the optimal product mix. You can study these techniques, which are extensions of what we discussed here, in more advanced courses.

BUSINESS ISSUES AND VALUES

As you may have guessed, some decisions are more straightforward than others. Company managers use accounting information to help them make the types of decisions we discussed in this chapter. But, as we said earlier, managers don't make these decisions using accounting information alone. They also must consider other relevant factors. Consider the decision made by the top managers of **Wal-Mart** several years ago.[f] At that time, Wal-Mart was the nation's largest gun retailer. Yet, that year, the company's managers directed the company's 2,600 stores to stop selling rifles and shotguns to people who had not passed a law-enforcement background check, a step that was criticized by the National Rifle Association. At that time, most background checks were completed within a few hours; 95% were finished within the 72-hour federal limit (under the law, if a gun store didn't receive a background check on a customer within three business days, it could proceed with a sale to the customer). So, Wal-Mart, by making this decision, chose to delay earning revenues on those gun sales by a few hours or a few days, or risked that these customers would go somewhere else to purchase guns more quickly. The 5% of background checks that were not complete within 72 hours were likely to involve buyers whose records showed signs of trouble. Wal-Mart's managers weighed the moral consequences of selling guns to people with felony convictions or other disqualifying factors in their records against the potential loss of revenues and erred on the side of their new "don't know, don't sell" rule. In this case, other relevant factors took precedence over the decision's effect on Wal-Mart's profit.

SUMMARY

At the beginning of the chapter we asked you several questions. During the chapter, we asked you to STOP and answer some additional questions to build your knowledge about specific issues. Be sure you answered these additional questions. Below are the questions from the beginning of the chapter, with a brief summary of the key points relating to the answers. Use your creative and critical thinking skills to expand on these key points to develop more complete answers to the questions and to determine what other questions you have that might lead you to learn more about the issues.

1 How do relevant costs and revenues contribute to sound decision making?

Both merchandising and manufacturing companies make short-term inventory-planning decisions. Regardless of the type of inventory-planning decision these companies make, one factor that they consider is the profit impact of the decision. They can determine the profit impact of the decision by analyzing relevant costs and revenues.

2 What types of costs and revenues are relevant to decision making?

Relevant costs and revenues are future costs and revenues that will change as a result of a decision. If they do not change from one decision alternative to another, costs and revenues are not considered relevant to the decision. They will not sway the decision one way or another. By considering only relevant costs and revenues, managers eliminate the possibility of misusing irrelevant information and thereby making incorrect decisions. To identify relevant costs and revenues, managers first identify the company's activities necessary to carry out the decision and then estimate the costs and/or revenues that are affected by these activities. These costs and revenues can include incremental costs and revenues, avoidable costs, and opportunity costs.

3 How does a company determine when to drop a product?

A company determines when to drop a product by estimating whether the costs that it would not have to incur (i.e., the avoidable costs) would be greater than the revenues that it would not earn if production and sale of the product were discontinued. They would also consider the customer's interest in the product, its safety record, the impact the product has on the environment, and other similar issues.

4 **What is a make-or-buy decision, and what issues does a company consider in this decision?**

In a make-or-buy decision, a company's managers decide whether producing a part would be less costly than purchasing it from an outside supplier. In making this decision, the company's managers compare the relevant incremental costs of producing the part with the relevant costs of purchasing the part. In addition to cost factors, they should consider the quality of the produced part versus the quality of the purchased part, the reliability of the supplier, and the company's desired long-term business relationship with the supplier.

5 **How does a company determine whether to sell a product "as is" or to process it further?**

A company determines whether to sell a product or to process it further by comparing the "profit" from selling the product "as is" with the "profit" from using the product as a direct material in the manufacture of another product. This analysis involves subtracting the relevant costs from the relevant revenues under each alternative, and selecting the alternative (sell or process further) that provides the higher "profit." The company also considers customers' potential responses to the product when it is processed further, the effect on the environment of processing it further, whether the company's current or potential employees have the skills to process it further, whether it will have to layoff employees, and other similar issues.

6 **What is a product-mix decision, and what issues does a company consider in this decision?**

In a product-mix decision, a company decides how many units of each product to produce and sell. In making this decision, a company considers two issues. First, the company considers the impact of activities such as increased advertising on the sales volume of each of its products. Second, the company considers the impact of a limited productive capacity (scarce resource) on the production of each of its products. For the first issue, when the increase in fixed costs (i.e., additional advertising money) does not change among alternatives, the company earns the highest profit from the alternative that produces the largest increase in contribution margin above the increase in fixed costs. For the second issue, the company earns the highest profit by using up the scarce resource to manufacture the product mix that produces the highest contribution margin per unit of scarce resource

KEY TERMS

avoidable costs (p. 499)   relevant costs (p. 496)
incremental costs (p. 499)   relevant revenues (p. 496)
opportunity costs (p. 499)

SUMMARY SURFING

Here is an opportunity to gather information on the Internet about real-world issues related to the topics in this chapter (for suggestions on how to navigate various organizations' Web sites to find the relevant information, see the related discussion in the Preface at the beginning of the book). Answer the following question.

• Go to the **Toyota Motor Corporation** Web site. Find what the company says about its parts and services. How do you think this description affects Toyota's decision about whether to make or but its parts? What would be the pros and cons of making or buying the parts?

INTEGRATED BUSINESS AND ACCOUNTING SITUATIONS

Answer the Following Questions in Your Own Words.

Testing Your Knowledge

15-1   What are relevant costs and relevant revenues?

15-2   Explain why past costs are irrelevant.

15-3   Since past costs are irrelevant in decision making, why do you think keeping past cost records can be helpful in the decision-making process?

15-4   Why should irrelevant costs and revenues be omitted from a decision analysis?

15-5   What is the difference between incremental costs and avoidable costs?

15-6   Under what circumstances is an avoidable manufacturing cost relevant in the make-or-buy decision?

15-7   Under what circumstances is an incremental manufacturing cost relevant in a make-or-buy decision?

15-8   In a decision to make a previously purchased part, think of two incremental costs that might not be avoidable if the decision is reversed a year later. Why would this happen?

15-9   Explain, by using an example, how a fixed cost can be an incremental cost.

15-10   Why might it be valuable to distinguish between relevant fixed costs and relevant variable costs for a short-term decision?

15-11   When are variable costs not relevant in a short-term decision?

15-12   Define an opportunity cost, and give an example of such a cost.

15-13   What two issues are included in a product-mix decision?

Applying Your Knowledge

15-14   Carlos Garcia, who is paid $10 per hour, is the only person who is trained to operate a machine that is critical in the production of bicycle seats. Each bicycle seat has a contribution margin of $4 and requires 1/4 hour of processing time on the machine. Sales of bicycle seats are limited only by scarce time on this machine.

Required: What is the opportunity cost to the company if Carlos becomes sick and leaves work an hour early one day?

15-15   Gorilla Grills has just discontinued its lowest line of high-quality barbecue grills. In its inventory, Gorilla has 40,000 grills that cost $60 per grill to manufacture. At the current selling price of $90, it may take as long as eight years for Gorilla to sell the grills. A foreign buyer has just offered the company $2 million for all the units.

Required: Is the $60-per-unit manufacturing cost relevant in deciding whether or not to accept the offer? List the costs and revenues that you think would be relevant.

15-16   Water Works ended its busy season with an inventory of 15,000 plastic rafts that cost $180,000 to manufacture. The company has two choices. One is that it can store the rafts for six months and sell them for $9 each during the following year. Storage would cost $8,500, and Water Works knows that at least 30% of the rafts would deteriorate during storage. The deteriorated rafts would have no value. The only other alternative is to have a clearance sale now and sell the rafts for $6.20 each. Water Works believes that all of the rafts can be sold if it spends $15,000 to advertise the sale.

Required: Based on this information, prepare an analysis showing the relevant costs and revenues of each alternative, and decide which alternative Water Works should choose.

15-17 On a chilly Saturday morning, Roy Parker bought 30 dozen doughnuts for $72, took 10 gallons of hot coffee, and went to a farm auction. He sold all the coffee and all but 6 dozen of the doughnuts before heading for home late in the afternoon. Knowing that he could not eat 6 dozen donuts himself and that they would be worthless by the next day, he began to consider how he might sell the remaining doughnuts. Only one possibility occurred to him. If he drove across town and left the doughnuts in the lunchroom at the plant where he worked, he was sure that workers on the late shift would be happy to buy the doughnuts. He figured the 8-mile round trip to the plant would cost him about $0.25 per mile. It would take him about an hour to make the trip, and he decided that it would be worthwhile to drive to the plant if he were compensated $10 for his time. Roy believes that workers will "forget" to pay for 1 dozen of the doughnuts.

Required: Prepare an analysis to determine how much Roy would have to charge per doughnut on the doughnuts he sells at the plant to reach his profit goal.

15-18 Happy Apparati Company produces small electrical appliances. The manufacturing costs per unit to produce a small toaster are shown here:

Direct materials	$ 6.50
Direct labor	5.75
Variable overhead	4.25
Fixed overhead	6.00
Total manufacturing cost per unit	$22.50

Variable selling costs to obtain and fill orders normally average $1.50 per unit when Happy sells the toasters to local customers. Recently, however, Happy paid $40,000 to advertise its various products in an international trade magazine. The company has just received an order from a large mail-order merchandising company in Brazil for 700 toasters at a total offering price of $12,000. The merchandising company is willing to pay all shipping charges except the initial packaging, which costs $0.75 per toaster.

Required: Compute the total incremental cost that Happy Apparati would expect to incur if it accepted and filled this order. Should Happy produce and sell the 700 toasters to the Brazilian company?

15-19 Houston Hobby produces several products that are sold by hobby shops across the country. Production of one product, a small model rocket, uses all available machine hours on machine 12A. The rocket, which provides a contribution margin of $2.40 per unit, requires 0.05 machine hours per unit to produce. Houston Hobby would like to use machine 12A in the production of other products. This production would take about 250 hours.

Required: Compute the opportunity cost of using 250 machine hours on machine 12A for other production. If you were a manager at Houston Hobby, how would you use the opportunity cost that you computed?

15-20 Armand Leggitt Company manufactures table legs and chair arms. It owns a lathe that it is not currently using. The lathe, which Armand Leggitt purchased nine years ago for $40,000, has a current book value of $4,000. Armand Leggitt can get $4,800 for the lathe if it sells it now. Armand Leggitt has just received an order for 50,000 table legs; it cannot accept the order unless it keeps the lathe for use in producing the order. If Armand Leggitt keeps the lathe for this purpose, the lathe will have no residual value after the company completes the order. The direct materials, direct labor, and variable overhead costs that Armand Leggitt would incur to produce the order total $49,900. The customer has offered $55,000 for the table legs.

Required: Prepare a schedule to help Armand Leggitt Company determine whether it should accept the order for the table legs.

15-21 The Porter Wagon Company produces sleds, scooters, and wagons. Scooters are not as popular as they used to be, and the company is considering dropping this product. Porter currently sells 5,000 scooters per year for $25 each. Variable manufacturing and selling costs total $17 per scooter. Fixed costs of $45,000 can be avoided if scooters are not produced.

Required: Prepare an analysis to answer each of the following independent questions.
(1) Given this information, by how much would Porter's profit increase if production of scooters is discontinued?

(2) If Porter can increase the sales volume of scooters to 6,000 units per year by spending an additional $10,000 per year on advertising, should Porter continue scooter production?

(3) If Porter can increase the sales volume of scooters to 7,000 per year by reducing its selling price to $20 per scooter, should Porter continue scooter production?

15-22   Buzz Telephone Company manufactures telephones. Buzz currently buys a connector for its phones for $1.80 per unit. Buzz's president asked for cost estimates for making this product and received the following report:

Costs per Unit of Making Connectors	
Direct materials	$0.75
Direct labor	0.30
Variable overhead	0.35
Fixed overhead	0.80
Total manufacturing cost per unit	$2.20

If Buzz makes the connector, production would take place in its machine shop. No additional plant and equipment would be necessary; however, the company would have to hire someone to inspect the connectors before they could be used in producing the company's other products. The inspector's salary would be $15,000 per year.

Required: (1) Compute the incremental costs of making and of buying the connector in quantities of 40,000 units per year. Should the company make the connector or buy it?

(2) Compute the incremental costs of making and of buying the component in quantities of 20,000 units per year. Should the company make the component or buy it?

(3) How many units of the component would have to be produced so that the total costs of making them would be equal to the total costs of buying them?

15-23   Mane Street normally sells 3,000 economy-size bottles of shampoo for $10 per bottle. The cost to manufacture the shampoo is $5.00 per bottle. Further variable processing costs of $4 per bottle for the shampoo would convert it into a shampoo/conditioner, which Mane Street could sell for $16 per bottle. Variable selling costs are $1 per bottle for the shampoo, but for the shampoo/conditioner they would be $2.50 per unit.

Required: Based on this information and assuming that Mane Street can sell 3,000 bottles of shampoo/conditioner, prepare an analysis to answer each of the following questions.

(1) Should Mane Street process the shampoo further into a shampoo/conditioner?

(2) If the selling price per unit of the shampoo/conditioner dropped to $15 per bottle, should Mane Street process the shampoo further into a shampoo/conditioner?

15-24   Uncommon Scents, which makes and sells perfume and body lotion, has $10,000 to spend on advertising. The company has estimated that using the $10,000 to advertise perfume would increase sales of perfume by 5,000 bottles. Uncommon Scents is uncertain how many additional tubes of body lotion it could sell by spending the $10,000, however. The perfume has a contribution margin of $8.50 per bottle, and the body lotion has a contribution margin of $2.00 per tube.

Required: Given this information, prepare an analysis to answer each of the following independent questions.
(1) If spending the $10,000 on body lotion would increase its sales by 4,000 tubes, which product should Uncommon Scents advertise?
(2) If spending the $10,000 on body lotion would increase its sales by 12,000 tubes, which product should Uncommon Scents advertise?
(3) By how many tubes would sales of body lotion have to increase to justify spending the $10,000 on body lotion instead of perfume?

15-25   Light the Night Manufacturing Company can sell a maximum of 4,000 desk lamps and 3,000 floor lamps. Desk lamps have a contribution margin of $6 per lamp and require 2 machine hours to produce. Floor lamps have a contribution margin of $15 per lamp and require 3 machine hours to produce. Light the Night currently has 11,400 machine hours available each month.

Required: Given this information, prepare an analysis to answer each of the following questions.

(1) How many desk lamps and floor lamps should Light the Night produce each month to earn the maximum monthly total contribution margin?

(2) What is the maximum amount Light the Night should pay per month to lease one additional machine, which can be used 360 hours per month?

Making Evaluations

15-26 During a recent 10-year period, the percentage of Americans who drank coffee was constant, at 50%. But the type of coffee that Americans purchased shifted during that time. Growing at a rate of 7%–10% per year, by the end of the 10 years, the number of coffee drinkers who purchased coffee beans rather than ground coffee reached 20%. However, rather than change their product mix to reflect the market, **Kraft Foods**, **Procter & Gamble**, and **Nestlé** cut prices on their Maxwell House, Folgers, and Nescafé coffee. Kraft Foods cut its price per can of Maxwell House ground coffee by $0.30.

Required: What factors and issues do you think Maxwell House weighed in making this decision?

15-27 Show Time Company currently manufactures the hands it uses in the assembly of grandfather clocks. Cost estimates to make each set of hands are as follows:

Direct materials	$8.00 per set
Direct labor	4.00 per set
Variable overhead	2.00 per set
Fixed overhead	13,000 per year

Required: (1) Prepare an analysis to answer each of the following independent questions.

(a) Assume that all variable costs are avoidable and that the company needs 3,000 sets of hands annually. How much of the fixed overhead must be avoidable in order for the company to prefer to buy the sets from an outside supplier at $17 per set instead of continuing to make them?

(b) Assume that all variable costs are avoidable, that the company needs 3,000 sets of hands annually, and that only $6,000 of fixed costs are avoidable. Below what purchase price per set of hands would the company prefer to buy the components from an outside supplier instead of continuing to make them?

(c) Assume that all variable costs are avoidable, that $3,000 of fixed overhead is avoidable, and that the purchase price of a set of hands is $24. Below what number of sets needed would the company prefer to buy the sets of hands from an outside supplier instead of continuing to make them?

(2) Suppose fixed overhead costs include the following:

Rent	$ 5,000
Depreciation, equipment	3,600
Property taxes	300
Foreman's salary	3,000
Routine maintenance	600
Utilities	500
	$13,000

List the fixed costs that you think Show Time could avoid (at least partially) if it purchased sets of hands. What are your reasons for including each of these costs on the list?

15-28 Music, Music, Music Company has just completed a study suggesting that sales of two of its products, sheet music and compact disks, could be increased by spending more on advertising. The following table shows how many additional units of the two products could be sold if advertising for each is increased:

Amount Spent on Advertising Sheet Music	Additional Sales of Sheet Music
$1,000	400 units
2,000	800
3,000	1,100
4,000	1,200

Amount Spent on Advertising CDs	Additional Sales of CDs
$1,000	400 disks
2,000	800
3,000	1,200
4,000	1,600

Sheet music has a contribution margin of $7.00 per unit, and CDs have a contribution margin of $6.00 per unit. The company has a total of $4,000 to spend on additional advertising. The head of marketing, Harry Hill, has asked your boss for a recommendation about how much to spend on advertising for each product in order to increase profit by the greatest amount, and your boss has passed the question on to you.

Required: (1) Compute the increase in the company's profit if the $4,000 is spent on advertising sheet music alone.

(2) Compute the increase in the company's profit if the $4,000 is spent on advertising CDs alone.

(3) Compute the increase in the company's profit if only $3,000 is spent on advertising sheet music alone. How do you explain the difference between this increase in profit and the increase in profit you computed in (1)?

(4) Write a memo to Mr. Hill (sending a copy to your boss) recommending how much additional advertising to spend on each product (up to $4,000 total) in order to increase profit by the greatest amount. Be sure to include the reasoning behind your recommendation.

15-29 Woodchuck Manufacturing produces quality tools for woodworking. Woodchuck has been forced to increase prices by about 40% over the last few years, mostly because of the increased costs of purchased components and other direct materials used in the manufacture of its products. Although Woodchuck will always have a market for its products among craftsmen who appreciate quality, the company is losing much of its business to companies manufacturing low-quality tools. Some of Woodchuck's departments are operating at about half of their usual capacity.

Chuck Woods, the company's founder and president (and your dad's next-door neighbor), would not allow his name to be associated with poor-quality tools. He feels that some price reductions are necessary, however, to keep sales from falling. He is concerned more about providing jobs for his employees than about earning a large profit. If sales fall much further, he will not be able to do either, however. Not a single employee has been laid off, nor has anyone received less than a full paycheck, even though many skilled machinists have pushed brooms and done odd jobs these last few months.

Recently, one of Chuck's foremen suggested that the company attempt to manufacture some of the components currently being purchased. Chuck and his foreman talked at great length, finally choosing to study the possibility of manufacturing a ¾-inch chuck that is used on hand drills, drill presses, and lathes. Everyone was quite excited when it was determined that the kind of equipment needed to manufacture the chuck was owned by the company and was not currently in use. Production would be no problem for the skilled machinists employed by Woodchuck.

It took about a week for Chuck's accountant to find all the information necessary to prepare the report that follows:

Dec. 15

Dear Chuck:

I'm sorry to report that after careful study of the costs of manufacturing ¾-inch chucks, I've concluded that we can't afford to make them. We currently use about 1,000 chucks of this size per month and are now buying them for $6.50 each. The costs to manufacture 1,000 chucks per month would be:

Direct materials	$1,850
Direct labor	1,900
Variable overhead	1,175
Fixed overhead	3,800
Total	$8,725

I'm sorry to bring you this bad news just before the holidays, Chuck. We buy hundreds of other components. Perhaps one of them would be cheaper to make than to buy. I'll be glad to make the cost estimates.

Lief Schmidt

Chuck knows you are studying accounting and has asked your opinion.

Required: Prepare a brief analysis of this situation and write Chuck a letter explaining your recommendation about whether his company should make or buy this component, and whether it also would be worthwhile to consider making rather than buying other components. What other issues should Chuck consider in making his decision?

15-30 Sunnydays Nursery School has been in operation for about five years. The school has never had any trouble filling its limit: 36 children for the morning session, 36 different children for the afternoon session, and 18 children who stay all day and are served a hot lunch. Currently, monthly tuition is $60 for half-day children and $120 for all-day children. The school has a long waiting list of children whose parents want to enroll them for half-days.

All-day children have never been accepted at the school unless their parents qualify for aid under the state's day-care program. Under this program the state pays half of the monthly tuition up to a maximum of $100. New regulations that take effect on January 1 would require accreditation before state funds can be paid under this program. This would require that at least one teacher be certified by the state for teaching at the preschool level. Currently, none of the school's three teachers can qualify for certification.

The director of the school feels that the loss of state funds would pose a serious threat to the school. She believes that a certified teacher could be hired, although this would cost the school $900 per month.

Monthly tuition could be raised to $75 for half-day children and $150 for all-day children. The director is uncertain how this would affect enrollment, however. Alternatively, the school could give up the all-day children who currently receive aid. Several other day-care centers in town (some charging as little as $100 per month) have room to take all of the all-day children.

Monthly operating costs for the school are as follows:

Rent	$ 300
Utilities	160
Salaries	2,400
Insurance	100
Toys and supplies	360
Lunches	378
Total Monthly Cost	$3,698

Toys and supplies are variable at rates of $5 per half-day child per month and $10 per all-day child per month.

Required: (1) What problem does the director have to solve?

(2) Suppose the director has placed you on an advisory committee to make a recommendation about a solution to the problem. With your committee, make a list of possible alternatives that she could consider.

(3) Assume that the director has reviewed all possible choices and has reduced the decision to two possible alternatives: (a) to close the all-day program, not to raise tuition, and not to hire the new teacher; and (b) to keep the all-day program open, to raise tuition, and to hire the new teacher. List the costs and revenues that you think will be relevant in the analysis of these two alternatives and give a reason for including each on the list.

(4) With your committee, make a list of other information you would like to have before advising the director on which of the two alternatives she should choose.

15-31   Midwest Watchamacallits sells Thingamajigs ("Jigs") and Thingamaboppers ("Boppers"). In late April the company found itself with only 1,200 hours of machine time available for the coming month because of the untimely malfunction of an accelerator attached to one of its two operating rod-catch assemblers, which are used in the production of its two products. Although May is not normally a month of high demand, losing one of its two assemblers creates definite problems. Data on the two products are shown here:

	Jigs	Boppers
Selling price per unit	$60	$85
Variable costs per unit	(30)	(40)
Contribution margin per unit	$30	$45
Assembler machine hours per unit	0.25	0.50
Expected May demand (units)	3,200	1,000

Midwest is already committed to pay $2,000 for advertising one (but not both) of the products to increase its demand beyond the estimates shown earlier. The company still has time to select the product to be advertised, however. The marketing department believes that demand for either product could be increased by 200 units with advertising.

Required: Explain how the machine problem would alter the company's advertising decision.

15-32   Pringle Paper Products is considering converting some of its fine writing paper into fancy stationery. The company currently is able to sell all of the fine writing paper it can produce, but it believes that its profit might be improved by giving up some of its fine writing paper sales to produce higher-priced stationery. Although the factory would not have to be expanded for this new processing, new printing equipment would have to be leased for a cost of $19,680 per year. In addition, packaging equipment currently in full-time use in other production would be reassigned to this new processing, thus slightly reducing production capability for another product. The lost sales for this other product would result in opportunity costs of $.02 per box of stationery packaged. Costs of converting the fine writing paper into fancy stationery include direct labor and overhead costs totaling $0.40 per box of stationery. Increased delivery costs and the cost of fancy display cartons are expected to cause variable selling costs to be higher for fancy stationery than for writing paper. The company believes that customer demand will be 10,000 boxes of stationery per year for an indefinite number of years. Pringle estimates that if it does not convert some of its writing paper into fancy stationery, it will earn $50,000 revenue and incur $2,000 in variable selling costs on that writing paper. It also estimates that if it does convert this writing paper into stationery, it will earn $90,000 revenue and incur $5,000 in variable selling costs for the stationery.

Required: (1) Prepare an analysis showing the relevant costs and revenues of each alternative, and decide which alternative should be chosen based on this analysis.
(2) Do you think your decision might change if you knew the manufacturing costs required to produce the fine writing paper? Why or why not?
(3) What if customer demand turns out to be less than 10,000 boxes of stationery per year? At a minimum, how many boxes of stationery must Pringle sell to justify your decision in (1)?

15-33   Yesterday, you received the following letter for your advice column in the local paper:

DR. DECISIVE

Dear Dr. Decisive:

I am a very organized person and prefer to think through things before I do them. My boyfriend, on the other hand, is a real slob and claims that he is just being "spontaneous" when he acts first and thinks later. This is becoming a real problem for us, and I am beginning to wonder what we see in each other. Here's a typical example of how different we are.

Yesterday, I was telling him about my plans for Spring Break and all the decisions my roommate and I are going to have to make. See, my roommate and I are planning to meet some old high school friends at Gulf Shores, Alabama during Spring Break. Classes will be over for Spring Break on a Friday and will not start again until a week from the following Monday.

But I'm not even sure I should go. I'm on a very limited budget. If I don't go, I'll stay on campus, live in the sorority house, and work. I'll have to eat my meals out, though, because my sorority house won't serve meals during the break.

Despite my boyfriend's ridicule of my thoroughness, I have made the following list of choices that my roommate and I have to make:

Transportation:	Car (rent)	Length of stay:	Ten days
	Bus		Five days
	Train		
	Motorhome	Go or not:	Go
	Plane		Stay at
Lodging:	Tent		school
	Motorhome		and work
	Motel		
	Condominium		

Anyway, I need your help. I know there's an organized way of making sense of all of these choices and deciding what to do. My boyfriend says I should just go (that's what he would do). Now that he's made the decision (in his mind), he doesn't want to talk about it any more.

Help!!! How can I make a decision? Is there a process? Maybe when my boyfriend sees your response, he will see the value of being organized.

Call me . . . "Organized, but Undecided."

P.S. Why do you think my boyfriend is so eager for me to go out of town?

Required: Meet with your Dr. Decisive team and write a response to "Organized, but Undecided."

END NOTES

[a]James B. Treece, "Ford: Alex Trotman's Daring Global Strategy," *Business Week,* April 3, 1995, p. 97.
[b]http://abcnews.go.com/sections/world/DailyNews/airline_severances_010925.html
[c]Laura M. Litvan, "Gold from Garbage," *Nation's Business,* July 1995, p. 53.
[d]Thomas Heath, (*Washington Post*), "Tyson Foods Finds Unwelcome Spotlight Blazing upon It," *Des Moines Register*, July 30, 1995, Sec. J, 1, 2.
[e]Mike Colias, "Sara Lee sheds clothing, returns focus to food," *Pittsburgh Tribune-Review,* February 11, 2005. http://www.pittsburghlive.com/x/pittsburghtrib/s_302581.html
[f] http://www.startribune.com/stories/1519/3064082.html

CHAPTER 16

PRODUCT COSTING SYSTEMS IN MANUFACTURING OPERATIONS

"ECONOMIC EFFICIENCY CONSISTS OF MAKING THINGS THAT ARE WORTH MORE THAN THEY COST."

—JOHN MAURICE CLARK

1. How does the way a manufacturing company determines the cost of its inventories and cost of goods sold differ from the way a merchandising company determines them?

2. How does a cost accounting system help a manufacturing company assign costs to its products?

3. Since factory overhead is not a physical part of the product, how does a company include the cost of overhead in the cost of its products?

4. Why is there more than one type of cost accounting system?

5. What is a job order cost accounting system, and how does a company use this system?

6. What is a process cost accounting system, and how does a company use this system?

D id you know that **Hershey Foods Corporation** manufactures more than just candy bars? Hershey Foods Corporation does manufacture candy bars, including the following brands: Hershey's, Reese's, Cacao Reserve, Kissables, Kit Kat, Cadbury's, and Peter Paul, to name a few. But it also manufactures Good & Plenty, Jolly Rancher fruit chews, PayDay, Bubble Yum, Ice Breakers, Twizzlers, baking chocolate, coconut flakes, ice cream topping, and chocolate milk mix.[a]

It costs Hershey Food Corporation a different amount to produce each of these products because the mix of direct materials, the amount and type of direct labor, and the use of factory overhead differ from product to product. To set selling prices high enough to make a desired profit, Hershey must know the cost of each product it manufactures. Moreover, when it makes a sale, Hershey must know the cost of the product it is selling so that it can reduce its Finished Goods Inventory account and increase its Cost of Goods Sold account by that amount. How do you think Hershey determines the cost of each inventory item that it sells? Furthermore, how do you think it determines the costs of its goods-in-process and finished goods inventories?

The process of determining and accumulating the costs of products and activities within a company is called **cost accounting**. Although cost accounting is primarily concerned with determining the cost of producing a product, it may also involve calculating the cost of operating a particular department or the cost of a manufacturing process or marketing technique. In this chapter, we introduce two of the most common types of cost accounting systems that companies use to assign manufacturing costs to products: the job order costing system and the process costing system. In Chapter 17, we will discuss how a company uses standards in its cost accounting system to plan and control its operations. Then, in Chapter 18, we will discuss recent manufacturing developments, the changing information needs of managers in modern manufacturing environments, and a modification of cost accounting systems, called *activity-based costing*.

Although our discussion focuses on manufacturing companies, other companies use cost accounting systems as well. Service companies such as airlines, banks, hospitals, and social service agencies also have developed cost accounting systems by modifying many of the ideas and procedures we describe.

COMMON ELEMENTS OF COST ACCOUNTING SYSTEMS

As we discussed in Chapter 11 of Volume 1, there are three production inputs to the manufacture of a product: direct materials, direct labor, and factory overhead. Exhibit 16-1 (a copy of Exhibit 11-3) shows the relationships among these manufacturing inputs, the manufacturing process, the three inventories, and cost of goods sold for Unlimited Decadence. Take a minute to review these relationships before you read on.

In the cost accounting systems we are about to discuss, the *costs* of the three inputs systematically become the cost of the goods-in-process inventory, the cost of the finished goods inventory, and the cost of goods sold. The company, in essence, "attaches" these three manufacturing costs to the products as it manufactures them, moving the costs with the products as they move from being goods-in-process to finished goods to goods sold. So by the time Hershey finishes manufacturing a batch of Reese's Pieces, it has accumulated the costs of manufacturing them and has assigned these costs to finished goods inventory. When it sells the candy, the manufacturing costs associated with the Reese's Pieces (or "attached to them") become the resulting cost of goods sold. The manufacturing costs associated with the unsold Reese's Pieces remain the costs of the finished goods inventory.

1 How does the way a manufacturing company determines the cost of its inventories and cost of goods sold differ from the way a merchandising company determines them?

2 How does a cost accounting system help a manufacturing company assign costs to its products?

EXHIBIT 16-1   RELATIONSHIPS AMONG MANUFACTURING COST ELEMENTS OF UNLIMITED DECADENCE

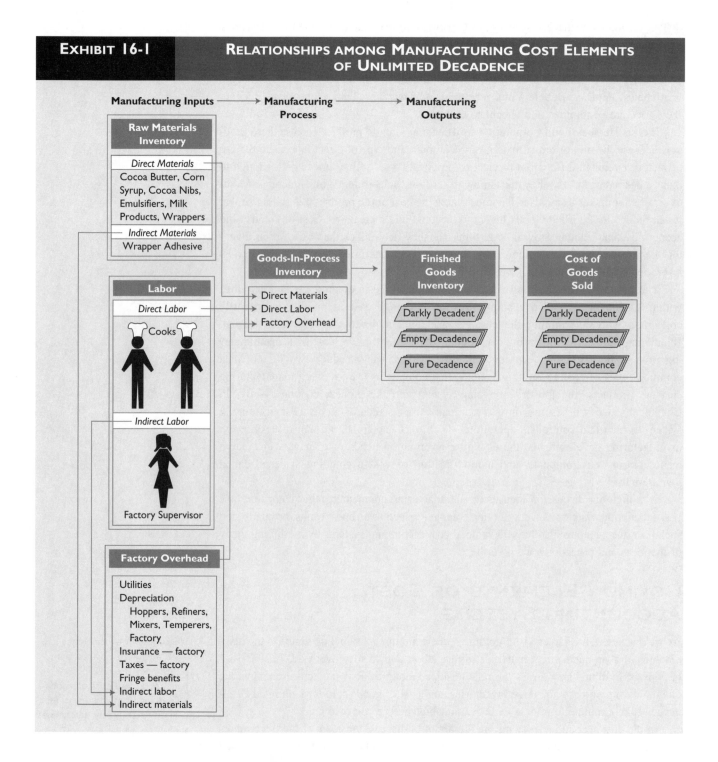

Raw Materials Costs

Remember from Chapter 11 of Volume 1 that raw materials include both direct materials and indirect materials. Since direct materials physically become part of the product and are one of the three production inputs, companies include the cost of direct materials as one of the three manufacturing costs that make up the cost of the finished product. However, it is difficult to associate the cost of indirect materials with individual products, so companies normally include indirect materials costs as part of *factory overhead.*

Labor Costs

Recall that direct labor is the labor of the employees who work with the direct materials to convert or assemble them into the finished products. Companies include the cost of direct labor (usually based on the hourly rate they pay these employees) in the cost of the product as one of the three manufacturing costs. However, they usually include *additional* payroll costs (payroll taxes, pensions, and other fringe benefits associated with these employees) as part of *factory overhead*. Also, since it is difficult to associate the cost of indirect labor with individual products, companies usually include the wages earned by these employees and the additional payroll costs of indirect labor as part of *factory overhead*.

3 Since factory overhead is not a physical part of the product, how does a company include the cost of overhead in the cost of its products?

Factory Overhead Costs

Although factory overhead items are necessary to manufacture a product, they cannot be traced *directly* to each unit produced. However, factory overhead is one of the three production inputs. So, companies include the *total* cost of factory overhead items (including indirect materials and indirect labor) in the cost of the products as one of the three manufacturing costs. As you will see, they then use an allocation process to assign these overhead costs to *individual* products. For example, it would be difficult for Hershey to trace the cost of factory air conditioning to a case of Mounds candy bars. But it *could* allocate a portion of the monthly air-conditioning cost to the Mounds candy bars manufactured that month based on the proportion of the factory's cubic feet that it devotes to manufacturing Mounds candy bars. In that case, if the company uses one-fourth of the factory space to manufacture the Mounds candy bars, it would allocate one-fourth of the air-conditioning cost to these candy bars. Then it could assign this cost to individual cases of Mounds by dividing the allocated cost by the number of cases of Mounds manufactured during the month. Although factory overhead includes a large number and a wide variety of different manufacturing costs, companies normally treat these costs together as a single cost.

THE STRUCTURE OF COST ACCOUNTING SYSTEMS

Manufacturing companies incur costs as they acquire the goods and services they use as inputs to the manufacturing process, and it is relatively easy for these companies to determine the total cost of each *input*. The task of the cost accounting system is to classify the costs incurred according to *activities* performed and then to assign the costs to the product *output* of those activities. As you will see, cost accounting systems classify these costs as products flow through the manufacturing process.

4 Why is there more than one type of cost accounting system?

The Perpetual Inventory System

Most cost accounting systems use a perpetual inventory system to record the costs of the raw materials, goods-in-process, and finished goods inventories. As we described and illustrated in Chapter 6 of Volume 1, in a perpetual inventory system the company keeps a continuous record of the balance in an inventory account. For a merchandising company, this involves increasing the Inventory account for the cost of all merchandise purchases and decreasing this account for the cost of merchandise sold.

A manufacturing company uses the perpetual system for all three inventory accounts. It increases the Raw Materials Inventory account for the cost of the raw materials it purchases and decreases the account for the cost of the raw materials it uses in production. It increases the Goods-in-Process Inventory account for the cost of the *inputs* (direct materials, direct labor, and factory overhead) it uses in production and decreases this account for the cost of the *outputs* (products it completes). It increases the Finished Goods

Inventory account for the cost of the products it completes and decreases the account for the cost of the products it sells.

Does this make sense? Draw a diagram using the accounting equation, arrows, and descriptions to show the perpetual inventory system of a manufacturing company. Label the arrows with a description of the costs they represent. Here's a start:

Assets			=	Liabilities	+	Stockholders' Equity
						Net Income
						Revenues − Expenses
Raw Materials Inventory	Goods-in-Process Inventory	Finished Goods Inventory				?

How Costs Flow through the Accounts

Under the perpetual inventory system, manufacturing costs almost seem as if they flow through the accounts, paralleling the flow of products through the manufacturing process. These costs enter the system as the company incurs them, flowing into the goods-in-process inventory as the company uses direct materials, direct labor, and factory overhead to manufacture products. Once they are in the Goods-in-Process Inventory account, the company assigns, or *applies*, the costs to specific products as manufacturing operations take place.

Exhibit 16-2 is an expansion of Exhibit 16-1 and illustrates how the costs of the inputs "attach" to the candy bars that Unlimited Decadence manufactures. Notice in the bottom half of the exhibit that the "flow" of costs from the cost of the inputs through the cost of goods sold is similar to the physical flow of the candy bars through the manufacturing process. Each numbered arrow from one account to another account matches a numbered arrow in the top half of the exhibit, and represents an entry transferring costs from one account to the next by decreasing one account and increasing the next. *Note also that manufacturing costs become an expense (cost of goods sold) only when Unlimited Decadence sells finished goods inventory.* Before that time, all of these costs are a part of the cost of inventory.

Companies most commonly use one of two kinds of cost accounting systems to assign manufacturing costs to manufactured products: *job order costing* or *process costing* (either of which may be enhanced by *standard costing* and *activity-based costing,* as you will see in later chapters). These cost accounting systems are a practical way for a manufacturing company to get timely information for the following five activities:

1. Planning the company's manufacturing operations

2. Deciding which products to manufacture, what operations to use in their production, how many units of each to produce, and perhaps even what selling prices to charge

3. Evaluating the performance of manufacturing operations, departments, and individual employees

4. Maintaining control over manufacturing costs and discovering ways to reduce costs and improve efficiency

5. Preparing financial statements

How do you think knowing the cost of manufacturing its products helps a company in each of the above five activities?

We will discuss job order costing and process costing systems next, standard costing in Chapter 17, and activity-based costing in Chapter 18. Because job order costing is easiest to understand, we will discuss it first.

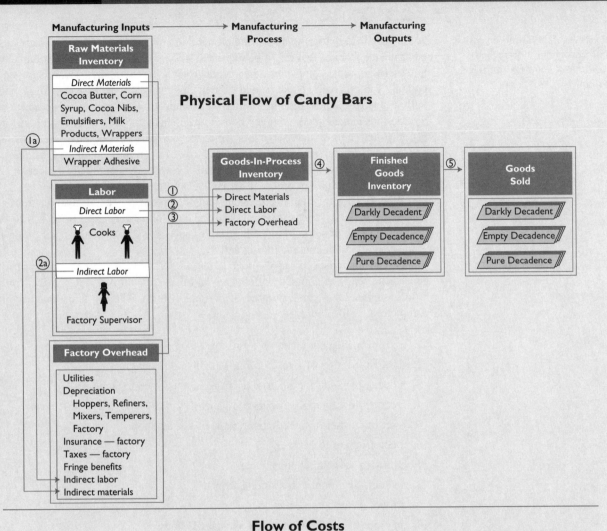

Physical Flow of Candy Bars

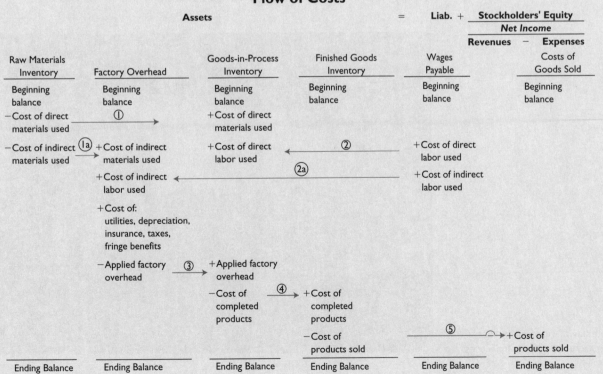

Flow of Costs

JOB ORDER COSTING

5 What is a job order cost accounting system, and how does a company use this system?

Some manufacturing companies make products in a wide variety of sizes and colors, or with other unique features that might be requested by specific customers. For example, in furniture manufacturing, companies might produce sofas in several styles with many upholstery options. Tables, chairs, dressers, and cabinets may vary in type of style, wood, and finish. <u>Sally Industries</u> in Jacksonville, Florida, builds animatronics ("robots")—complete with custom designs and scripted, complex body movements—for theme parks such as <u>Universal Studios</u>' museums, casinos, and fairs. Since they are customized, the robot characters, such as E.T. (the extraterrestrial) on a bicycle, have an enormous number of unique variables such as blinking eyes, rotating wrists, and girth. Similarly, Unlimited Decadence might fill special orders, such as an order for distinctively labeled boxed chocolates.

When a company manufactures one unit of a unique product or manufactures a unique group of products, it treats that unit or group as a **job order**, or "job." (Each of Sally Industries' robots, or sometimes each *group* of robots, is a job order.) A job order may require more than one manufacturing activity.

One characteristic of a job order is that it is easy to determine when the job starts and when it ends. A company often starts a job as a result of a "sales order" from a specific customer for a small number of particular items. The job ends when the order is complete. A "job" could be:

1. a set of mahogany chairs in a furniture factory;
2. the first printing of a textbook in a publishing company;
3. a dozen plows in the plant of a farm-implement manufacturer;
4. a car or truck being serviced at a garage;
5. a set of custom-designed memo pads in a print shop;
6. a construction project;
7. a custom set of kitchen cabinets;
8. an audit by a public accounting firm;
9. a robot for a theme park; or
10. an order of specially sized and packaged candy.

Examples of customized robots manufactured by Sally Industries.

© SALLY INDUSTRIES, INC.

Do you think colleges and universities think of individual courses, like this one, as job orders? Do you think they regard individual students as job orders? Why or why not?

In job order manufacturing, production departments such as machine shops or assembly and finishing departments may perform manufacturing operations on hundreds of different jobs in a month's time. Also, the individual jobs may require manufacturing operations in several production departments. For example, the robots that Sally Industries manufactures go through seven functional areas: mechanical, pneumatic, art, scenic, electronics, programming/audio, and shop administration.[b]

In this kind of manufacturing environment, a company's cost accounting system must determine how much of each department's manufacturing costs to apply to each job on which that department worked. For example, if Sally Industries' art department worked on both E.T. and the Seven Dwarfs, the cost accounting system would determine how much of the art department's costs to apply to E.T. and how much to apply to the Seven Dwarfs. The system would do this for each of the functional areas. The cost accounting system best suited for this situation is known as *job order cost accounting* or *job order costing*. A **job order cost accounting system** keeps track of the costs applied to each job order.

The Job Order Cost Sheet

When a company uses job order costing, the individual job is the key to product or service costing. The company accumulates direct materials, direct labor, and factory overhead costs for each individual job on a *job order cost sheet* or in a computerized job order cost file as it manufactures the job. Throughout our discussion of job order costing, we will illustrate a job order cost sheet. Keep in mind, however, that electronic job order costing systems accumulate costs for jobs in the same way, except that electronic systems use computers. Exhibit 16-3 shows an example of a job order cost sheet for a special order from Sweet Temptations for 250 cases of smaller-sized specially packaged Darkly Decadent candy bars. Unlimited Decadence completed the order on March 12 and will sell this order to Sweet Temptations for $16 per case.[1]

Note how a job order cost sheet has separate columns for the direct materials, direct labor, and factory overhead costs assigned to a job, and a place to summarize these costs after the job is finished. A company's total goods-in-process inventory is the sum of the total accumulated costs of each incomplete job (from the job order cost sheets for each job). When it completes a job, the company takes the total costs assigned to the job (summarized on that job's job order cost sheet) out of the Goods-in-Process Inventory account and adds them to the Finished Goods Inventory account. When the company sells products from finished goods inventory, it takes the costs out of the Finished Goods Inventory account and adds them to the Cost of Goods Sold account. The job order cost sheet for the special order is the source document that Unlimited Decadence uses when it records each of these events in its accounting system. We will discuss each of these issues in the following sections, using selected information from the job order cost sheet in Exhibit 16-3.

How a Company Assigns Raw Materials Costs to Jobs

When a company purchases raw materials, it places them in the raw materials storeroom and records their cost in the Raw Materials Inventory account. For example, Unlimited Decadence would record a credit purchase of sugar costing $639,800 as follows:

---

[1]Because this is a special order, Unlimited Decadence keeps track of the costs of the order (and any other special orders) separately using job order costing. In other production situations, it may use process costing, which we will discuss later in the chapter.

EXHIBIT 16-3	JOB ORDER COST SHEET: UNLIMITED DECADENCE

Job Order Cost Sheet

Product Description _Darkly Decadent Candy Bars_   **Job Order Number** _101_

Notes _Rush Order!!!_   **Units Required** _250 Cases_

Special Sizing and Packaging   **Date Started** _March 10_

    Date Completed _March 12_

		Direct Materials		Direct Labor		Factory Overhead Applied
Date	Request Number	Cost		Labor Ticket Number	Cost	
3-10	541	$ 350		380	$ 84	
				381	96	
				382	96	
				383	84	
				384	90	
				387	96	
				388	72	
				389	96	
3-11	549	735		400	96	
				401	90	
				405	96	
				407	84	
				408	96	
				409	78	
				411	96	
				412	96	
3-12				413	54	
		$ 1,085			$ 1,500	125 hours @ $3.16 = $395

Summary of Costs

Direct Material	$1,085
Direct Labor	1,500
Factory Overhead	395
Total Job Cost	$2,980
Units	250
Cost per Case	$11.92

Assets	=	Liabilities	+	Stockholders' Equity
Raw Materials Inventory		Accounts Payable		
+$639,800		+$639,800		

The company supports the numbers in the Raw Materials Inventory account with records that show the receipts, issues, and current balance for each type of individual raw material item, such as sugar, cocoa beans, and emulsifiers.

The storekeeper, who is responsible for all raw materials kept in the storeroom at the company, must receive a written authorization form, known as a *raw materials requisi-*

EXHIBIT 16-4	RAW MATERIALS REQUISITION: UNLIMITED DECADENCE

Raw Materials Requisition			# _541_	
Item No.	Description	Quantity	Cost per Unit	Cost
885	Sugar	1,000 lbs.	$0.35	$350

Requested for Job Order # _101_
or general factory use _____
by _J. Jones_   **Date** _3/10_

Issued by _T. Hall_
Date _March 10_
Received by _J. Jones_   **Date** _3/10_

tion (or *request*), before issuing raw materials for use in the factory.[2] Unlimited Decadence uses these forms (like the one in Exhibit 16-4) to trace to specific jobs the quantity and cost of *direct* materials it uses in the manufacturing process and to assign these costs directly to those jobs.

Can you think of another reason the storekeeper needs an authorization before releasing raw materials into the factory?

Note that the raw materials requisition we show is for sugar to be used on job order number 101. It gives the information needed (requisition number 541, cost $350, and job order number 101) for the March 10 entry for direct materials on the job order cost sheet we show in Exhibit 16-3.

Unlimited Decadence also can use the information on raw materials requisition forms to assign the total cost of *indirect* materials used to the Factory Overhead account. Exhibit 16-5 shows a summary of Unlimited Decadence's raw materials requisitions for March 10. Notice that two requisitions (numbers 545 and 547) were for indirect materials. Unlimited Decadence will assign these costs to jobs along with other indirect manufacturing costs, as we will discuss later. This form also provides Unlimited Decadence with the information it needs to decrease the Raw Materials Inventory account by the total cost of all raw materials issued and to decrease the individual raw materials records for the cost of each type of raw material (e.g., sugar, cocoa, emulsifiers) issued.

Why do you think companies keep records for each type of raw material that they use?

Thus, raw materials requisitions have several purposes. They:

1. Instruct the storekeeper to issue materials to particular factory departments
2. Transfer responsibility for materials used from the storekeeper to production personnel

---

[2]In some companies, authorized individuals can send electronic requisitions to the storeroom. If production is totally automated, the production system generates and sends an electronic requisition to the storeroom and at the same time updates the accounting records.

EXHIBIT 16-5	RAW MATERIALS REQUISITION SUMMARY: UNLIMITED DECADENCE

Raw Materials Requisition Summary

Direct Materials

Job Order Number	Requisition Number	Department	Amount	Job Order Total
101	541	4	$ 350	$ 350
102	543	3	4,600	
102	544	4	2,100	6,700
103	542	2	4,150	
103	546	3	300	4,450
104	540	2	3,000	3,000
			Total Direct	$14,500

Indirect Materials

	545	4	$40	
	547	3	49	
			Total Indirect	$ 89

Summary for Date	3-10		Total Raw Materials	$14,589

3. Associate the cost of direct materials used with particular jobs, and the cost of indirect materials used with factory overhead

4. Inform the company of the amount by which the Raw Materials Inventory account should be reduced and the Goods-in-Process Inventory and Factory Overhead accounts increased

For example, the total March 10 raw materials requisitions of $14,589 included $14,500 for direct mat erials and $89 for indirect materials. Unlimited Decadence records the issuance of these materials in its accounting system (assuming that it has a beginning balance of $30,200 in its Raw Materials Inventory) as follows:

Assets			=	**Liabilities**	+	**Stockholders' Equity**
Raw Materials Inventory	Goods-in-Process Inventory	Factory Overhead				
Bal $30,200						
−14,589	+$14,500	+$89				
$15,611						

 Notice that we listed factory overhead on the asset side of the equation along with the two inventory accounts. Why do you think we consider factory overhead an asset?

The $14,589 reduction in the raw materials inventory is supported by a total of $14,589 of reductions in the individual raw materials records. The $14,500 increase in goods-in-process inventory is supported by recording appropriate amounts totaling $14,500 on individual job order cost sheets. Recording the $350 cost of sugar from requisition number 541 on the job cost sheet for job order number 101 in Exhibit 16-3 is one example of an entry on an individual job order cost sheet that supports the increase in goods-in-process inventory.

 What do you think happens to the physical direct materials and the accounting for them when the production department doesn't use all of the direct materials issued to it for a particular job? What do you recommend should be done?

How a Company Assigns Factory Labor Costs to Jobs

In a job order cost accounting system, a company also assigns factory labor costs both directly and indirectly to jobs. Recall that direct labor is the labor of employees who work with the raw materials to convert or assemble them into the finished product. The wages earned by machine operators, for example, are direct labor costs of manufacturing candy. The company can trace these direct labor costs to specific jobs on the basis of labor tickets (or computer files) that are kept by the employees and that show the amount of time the employees spent on each specific job. Exhibit 16-6 shows labor ticket #413, from one of Unlimited Decadence's wrapping machine operators on March 12. Note that the $54 cost on this labor ticket is the same $54 that is recorded on the job order cost sheet in Exhibit 16-3 for job order number 101.

A company uses these labor tickets to assign direct labor costs to jobs in the same way that it uses raw materials requisitions to assign direct materials costs to jobs. The time spent on a specific job multiplied by the employees' hourly wage rates gives the direct labor cost to be assigned to that particular job for the manufacturing operation performed by that employee.

The direct assignment of labor costs to specific jobs, however, is only for time spent working on those jobs. The same employees may spend time cleaning and oiling machinery, waiting for work, or making equipment adjustments. The company assigns the wages for this time *indirectly* to jobs by adding them to factory overhead along with other indirect labor costs. The company also normally assigns overtime premiums, the employer's share of payroll taxes, and the cost of fringe benefits, such as vacation pay, to indirect labor.

 Why do you think a company indirectly assigns the cost of time spent on such activities as cleaning and oiling machinery, waiting for work, or making equipment adjustments even though the company considers the same employees to be direct labor?

Recall that indirect labor is labor that is necessary for the operation of the production process but that does not convert or assemble the direct materials into the finished product. Since the costs of this work can't be traced directly to specific jobs (for instance, time spent cleaning and oiling machinery probably benefits all jobs), a company assigns wages paid for supervision, maintenance, materials handling, storekeeping, inspecting, and so on *indirectly* to jobs by adding them to factory overhead first and then "spreading them over" all the jobs. A company records direct and indirect labor costs in a manner similar to that used to record direct and indirect materials costs. For example, suppose Unlimited Decadence's payroll records show that wages of factory personnel for a day total $18,658. If a summary of labor tickets shows that $18,001 is for direct labor on specific jobs and

---

EXHIBIT 16-6	LABOR TICKET: UNLIMITED DECADENCE

Labor Ticket   # _413_

Date _March 12_   Employee Number _2-3-195_

Operation _Wrap & Package Candy_   Department Number _4_

Started _1:00 p.m._   Job Order Number _101_

Completed _5:30 p.m._   Verified by _cfm_

Time	Rate	Amount
4 ½ hours	$12.00	$54.00

$657 is for indirect labor, Unlimited Decadence records these costs in Goods-in-Process Inventory (direct labor) and Factory Overhead (indirect labor) as follows:

Assets		=	Liabilities	+	Stockholders' Equity
Goods-in-Process Inventory	Factory Overhead		Wages Payable		
Bal $14,500	Bal $ 89				
+18,001	+657		+$18,658		
Bal $32,501	$746				

Unlimited Decadence uses the labor tickets to determine the amounts (totaling $18,001) that it assigns to the individual job order cost sheets and to support the $18,001 increase in the goods-in-process inventory. Notice that the accounts also include the amounts (balances) of direct materials ($14,500) and indirect materials ($89) that Unlimited Decadence previously recorded in them.

How a Company Applies (Assigns) Factory Overhead Costs to Jobs: Predetermined Overhead Rate

As you just saw, the amount of direct materials cost a company assigns to a particular job is the specific cost of the direct materials the company used to manufacture the job. This information comes from raw materials requisitions. Similarly, the amount of direct labor cost the company assigns to a job is the specific wages earned by the factory employees for the hours they worked on that job. The hours worked on particular jobs are recorded on labor tickets. Note that a company incurs direct materials costs and direct labor costs because of specific manufacturing activities performed on specific jobs, and that the company easily traces them to particular jobs.

Factory overhead costs are quite different, however. A company incurs almost all factory overhead costs for the general benefit of all manufacturing activity and not specifically because of individual jobs. For example, although all jobs benefit from the use of the building, no individual job can be considered the cause for incurring depreciation on the building. But, because all jobs benefit from the building, the company should assign some of the building's depreciation cost to each job. The same is true for all factory overhead costs. However, individual factory overhead costs cannot be assigned *directly* to a job in the way that the company assigns direct labor and direct materials costs. Instead, the company adds together all factory overhead costs (including indirect materials and indirect labor) and assigns them *indirectly* to jobs in proportion to the amount of manufacturing activity devoted to each job. But what is the measure of manufacturing activity? For this purpose, a company might use direct labor hours, machine hours, or the direct labor cost to measure the manufacturing activity devoted to each job. If the company uses machine hours, for example, a job requiring 10 hours of machine time would have twice as much factory overhead assigned to it as a job requiring 5 hours of machine time. Sally Industries assigns overhead costs to jobs using direct labor hours as its measure of manufacturing activity. This is because producing and *customizing* robots is highly labor-intensive, so the more hours employees log in on a job, the higher are the labor *and* the overhead costs for that job.

This procedure does not assign to each job the exact amount of factory overhead resulting from the manufacture of that job. However, it does assign factory overhead cost roughly in proportion to the factory overhead benefits the individual jobs received, which is a desirable and reasonable result.

 Suppose a company assigned factory overhead costs to jobs by using a procedure that caused it to assign a larger proportion of factory overhead cost to a job than the proportion of factory overhead benefits that the job received. How would this affect the factory overhead costs that the company assigned to other jobs during the same time period? How might this procedure affect managers' decisions about pricing, advertising, or dropping products?

For various reasons, a company may not know the exact amount of factory overhead cost it incurred for manufacturing until the end of the year. For example, the company normally receives a property tax bill or computes depreciation on factory equipment once a year. However, the company usually completes jobs in less than a year. Suppose the company received its property tax bill at the end of the year and assigned the cost of the property taxes to the jobs it was working on at the end of the year. The end-of-year jobs would therefore cost more than those worked on and completed at the beginning of the year. But are they *really* more costly? Didn't the company use the property on which it is paying taxes for *all* of the jobs?

To use a perpetual inventory system with a goods-in-process inventory, a company must be able to include all factory overhead costs in its inventories as it manufactures and completes products. To assign factory overhead costs to individual jobs when manufacturing operations take place or when the company completes jobs, the company estimates the amount of its factory overhead cost for the year and sets an estimated overhead *rate* (cost per direct labor hour, machine hour, or direct labor dollar, for example) at the beginning of the year. Such a rate is called a predetermined overhead rate, and the company uses this rate to *apply* (assign) estimated overhead costs to individual jobs. A company figures its **predetermined overhead rate** at the beginning of a year by dividing the year's budgeted factory overhead cost by the budgeted total volume of manufacturing activity (however it is measured) for the year. For example, suppose that Unlimited Decadence wants to apply factory overhead costs to jobs based on the number of direct labor hours (DLH) worked on each job. If it expects to incur $7,584,000 of factory overhead costs during the year and expects factory employees to work 2,400,000 DLH during that same time period, the predetermined overhead rate is set as follows:

$$\text{Predetermined Overhead Rate} = \frac{\text{Expected factory overhead cost for the year}}{\text{Expected direct labor hours for the year}}$$

$$= \frac{\$7,584,000}{2,400,000 \text{ DLH}}$$

$$= \$3.16 \text{ per DLH}$$

Having determined this rate at the beginning of the year, the company uses it to apply factory overhead costs to jobs throughout the whole year. A job requiring 25 hours of direct labor will have $79 (25 DLH $\times$ $3.16 per DLH) applied to it whether Unlimited Decadence produces it in January or December. Another job requiring 125 direct labor hours will have five times as much factory overhead cost applied (125 DLH $\times$ $3.16 per DLH = $395) as the job requiring 25 hours of direct labor effort.

Unlimited Decadence records the application of factory overhead of $395 to a job requiring 125 direct labor hours during the month (assuming a predetermined overhead rate of $3.16 per DLH) in its accounting system as follows:

Assets		= Liabilities + Stockholders' Equity
Goods-in-Process Inventory	Factory Overhead	
Bal $32,501	Bal $746	
+ 395	− 395	
Bal $32,896	Bal $351	

FINANCIAL STATEMENT EFFECTS
No effect on total current assets and total assets on **balance sheet.**

Unlimited Decadence also applies the factory overhead cost to the specific job, as you can see in the factory overhead column of the job order cost sheet in Exhibit 16-3. Notice that the Goods-in-Process Inventory account also includes the total amounts ($32,501 balance) of direct materials and direct labor costs that Unlimited Decadence recorded in it, and that the Factory Overhead account ($746 balance) also includes the actual indirect material and indirect labor costs that Unlimited Decadence recorded in it.

As Unlimited Decadence incurs *actual* factory overhead costs throughout the year, it adds them to the Factory Overhead account. For instance, in addition to the actual indirect materials and indirect labor that it recorded earlier in the Factory Overhead account, if Unlimited Decadence pays $4,000 for factory utilities, it records this actual cost as follows:

<table>
<tr><td></td><td colspan="2">Assets</td><td>=</td><td>Liabilities</td><td>+</td><td>Stockholders' Equity</td></tr>
<tr><td></td><td>Cash</td><td>Factory
Overhead</td><td></td><td></td><td></td><td></td></tr>
<tr><td></td><td>Bal $56,125</td><td>Bal $ 351</td><td></td><td></td><td></td><td></td></tr>
<tr><td></td><td>− 4,000</td><td>+ 4,000</td><td></td><td></td><td></td><td></td></tr>
<tr><td></td><td>Bal $52,125</td><td>Bal $4,351</td><td></td><td></td><td></td><td></td></tr>
</table>

Notice that the actual factory overhead costs increase the Factory Overhead account and that the *applied* factory overhead costs decrease the account by the amount transferred out of Factory Overhead and into the Goods-in-Process Inventory account.

 If the Factory Overhead account has a positive or negative balance, what do managers know?

How a Company Records the Completion of Jobs

When a company completes a job, it removes the completed products from the factory and takes them to the finished goods storeroom. At the same time, the company computes the cost per unit by dividing the total cost applied on the job order cost sheet by the number of units in the job. Then, the company transfers the job's cost (calculated on the job order cost sheet) from the Goods-in-Process Inventory account into the Finished Goods Inventory account. For example, Unlimited Decadence records the completion of job order #101 ($2,980 = 250 cases × $11.92 per case) as follows:

<table>
<tr><td colspan="2">Assets</td><td>=</td><td>Liabilities</td><td>+</td><td>Stockholders' Equity</td></tr>
<tr><td>Goods-in-Process
Inventory</td><td>Finished Goods
Inventory</td><td></td><td></td><td></td><td></td></tr>
<tr><td>Bal $32,896</td><td></td><td></td><td></td><td></td><td></td></tr>
<tr><td>− 2,980</td><td>+$2,980</td><td></td><td></td><td></td><td></td></tr>
<tr><td>Bal $29,916</td><td></td><td></td><td></td><td></td><td></td></tr>
</table>

Unlimited Decadence then removes the job order cost sheet of the completed job from the goods-in-process supporting records. Notice that the Goods-in-Process Inventory account has a balance of $29,916 representing the costs of the jobs that Unlimited Decadence has not yet completed.

How a Company Records the Sale of Finished Goods

When a company uses a perpetual inventory system for the finished goods inventory, it must make two entries to record a sale. First, it records the revenue from the sale. So, when Unlimited Decadence sells the 250 cases from completed job order #101 to Sweet Temptations on credit at a price of $4,000 (250 × $16 selling price per case), it records the revenue from this sale as follows:

<table>
<tr><td>Assets</td><td>=</td><td>Liabilities</td><td>+</td><td colspan="3">Stockholders' Equity</td></tr>
<tr><td></td><td></td><td></td><td></td><td colspan="3">Net Income</td></tr>
<tr><td></td><td></td><td></td><td></td><td>Revenues</td><td>−</td><td>Expenses</td></tr>
<tr><td>Accounts
Receivable</td><td></td><td></td><td></td><td>Sales
Revenue</td><td></td><td></td></tr>
<tr><td>+$4,000</td><td></td><td></td><td></td><td>+$4,000</td><td></td><td></td></tr>
</table>

Second, the company transfers the cost of the cases that it sells from the Finished Goods Inventory account to the Cost of Goods Sold account by decreasing the Finished

Goods Inventory account and increasing the Cost of Goods Sold account. For example, Unlimited Decadence transfers the $2,980 cost of the 250 cases (250 × $11.92) delivered to Sweet Temptations from its Finished Goods Inventory account[3] to the Cost of Goods Sold account as follows:

Assets	=	Liabilities	+	Stockholders' Equity		
					Net Income	
				Revenues	−	Expenses
						Cost of
Finished Goods						Goods Sold
Inventory						
Bal $2,980						
− 2,980					−	+$2,980
Bal $ 0						

> **FINANCIAL STATEMENT EFFECTS**
>
> Decreases current assets and total assets on *balance sheet*. Increases expenses, which decreases net income on *income statement* (and therefore decreases stockholders' equity on *balance sheet*).

What Happens to Overapplied and Underapplied Overhead?

As we mentioned earlier, by using a predetermined overhead rate to apply factory overhead, a company does not need to wait until the end of the year, when it knows the total *actual* factory overhead cost incurred, to assign overhead costs to jobs. However, the expected factory overhead costs may not equal the actual factory overhead costs for the year. For instance, for various reasons, when a company uses direct labor hours as a measure of manufacturing activity, the number of direct labor hours that factory employees actually work may differ from the expected number of hours. When differences occur, a balance remains in the Factory Overhead account at the end of the year.

 If the company uses machine hours as a measure of manufacturing activity instead of direct labor hours, how might you explain a difference between actual and applied factory overhead costs?

   If the company applies more factory overhead than it actually incurs, the Factory Overhead account will have a negative balance at the end of the year, indicating that the company has "overapplied" factory overhead to the Goods-in-Process Inventory account. If the company actually incurs more factory overhead costs than it applies during the year, the Factory Overhead account will have a positive balance at the end of the year, indicating that the company has "underapplied" factory overhead to the Goods-in-Process account by the amount of the balance. When a company overapplies or underapplies factory overhead, the recorded cost of the year's jobs is too much or too little. As a result, when the jobs are completed and sold, the cost of goods sold recorded in the accounting system will be larger or smaller than the actual cost of goods sold. Fortunately, a company can often estimate its factory overhead costs and activity levels quite accurately. As a result of this accuracy, the amount by which it over- or underapplies factory overhead is seldom very large. In this case, when the amount is small, the company transfers the positive or negative balance of the Factory Overhead account at year-end to the Cost of Goods Sold account. (However, if the amount is large, the company also transfers a portion of it to the Goods-in-Process Inventory and Finished Goods Inventory accounts because their balances are also larger or smaller than the actual costs of the goods-in-process and finished goods inventories.)

   For example, suppose that Unlimited Decadence's factory employees actually worked 2,500,000 direct labor hours and that it actually incurred $7,640,000 of factory overhead costs. Throughout the year Unlimited Decadence incurred and recorded an increase of $7,640,000 in its Factory Overhead account. The company, however, applied factory overhead at a predetermined overhead rate of $3.16 ($7,584,000 ÷ 2,400,000 DLH) on each

---

[3]For simplicity, we only show a $2,980 balance in the Finished Goods Inventory account for the total costs of job order #101. In reality, the Finished Goods Inventory account would have a balance for the costs of *all* the completed jobs that have not yet been sold.

direct labor hour worked. As a result, the total amount that Unlimited Decadence applied by the end of the year (and recorded as a decrease in its Factory Overhead account) is $7,900,000 (2,500,000 DLH × $3.16 per DLH).[4] Thus, Unlimited Decadence *overapplied* its factory overhead by $260,000 ($7,900,000 applied − $7,640,000 incurred). Assume that during the year, Unlimited Decadence sold candy bars costing $50,000,000 (direct materials cost, direct labor cost, and *applied* factory overhead cost) and recorded cost of goods sold of that amount. At the end of the year, Unlimited Decadence will transfer the $260,000 negative balance of the Factory Overhead account to the Cost of Goods Sold account (reducing cost of goods sold), as follows:

Assets	=	Liabilities	+	Stockholders' Equity		
					Net Income	
				Revenues	−	Expenses
Factory						Cost of
Overhead						Goods Sold
+$7,640,000						
− 7,900,000						
Bal $ (260,000)					−	Bal $50,000,000
+ 260,000					−	− 260,000
Bal $ 0					−	Bal $49,740,000

FINANCIAL STATEMENT EFFECTS

Increases current assets and total assets on *balance sheet*. Decreases expenses, which increases net income on *income statement* (and therefore increases stockholders' equity on *balance sheet*).

Note that the entry to Factory Overhead adjusts its balance to zero at the end of the year, indicating that the amount of factory overhead Unlimited Decadence has applied is now equal to its actual factory overhead costs. Since the Factory Overhead account now has a zero balance, Unlimited Decadence can use this account next year to accumulate the factory overhead costs it incurs and applies during that year.

Note also that the entry to Cost of Goods Sold reduces its balance from $50,000,000 to $49,740,000. This makes sense because by overapplying factory overhead by $260,000, Unlimited Decadence initially added more than the actual total of factory overhead to the Goods-in-Process Inventory account. This excess flows to finished goods inventory as Unlimited Decadence completes jobs and to cost of goods sold as it sells them. Thus, when Unlimited Decadence overapplies factory overhead, it also overstates the Cost of Goods Sold account balance. The reduction of that account by $260,000 offsets this overstatement. Similarly, if Unlimited Decadence had underapplied factory overhead (the Factory Overhead account would have a positive balance at year-end), it would have understated the Cost of Goods Sold account balance. To correct for this understatement, Unlimited Decadence would increase the Cost of Goods Sold account (and reduce the Factory Overhead account).

 As a manager, would you prefer that factory overhead be overapplied or underapplied? Why?

You just saw that job order costing systematically moves the costs of manufacturing products through the inventory accounts and into cost of goods sold as the jobs *physically* move through the inventories and then are sold. We next discuss and illustrate the process costing system. As you will see, although this system assigns costs to manufactured products, as does the job order costing system, it accomplishes the task differently.

Application of Job Order Costing in Bidding for a Job

Many different companies use job order costing. For instance, **Van Dyke Tile and Marble Company** of Orlando, Florida, supplies and installs tile and marble for various buildings and facilities. For example, it supplied and installed the tile and marble for the EPCOT

Space Ship Earth at EPCOT Center.

© TIMOTHY O'KEEFE/INDEX STOCK

---

[4]In Chapter 17 we will explain what a company does with the costs associated with the difference between the 2,400,000 expected direct labor hours and the 2,500,000 actual direct labor hours.

Center and the Orlando Airport. Because each installation is different from the others, Van Dyke uses job order costing to determine the amounts to bid on its jobs. In the past, the company used broad written estimates of its costs and added a desired profit margin to those costs to determine the amount of its bid for a job (what Van Dyke would charge its customers for the job). Robert Van Dyke, then president of the company, was concerned because these written estimates involved too much "judgment," and in many cases, the actual costs turned out to be much higher than the estimated costs (so in these cases, the company made less profit than expected). Bob studied the various "generic" job order costing software available for sale, but found that none of them were easily adaptable to the tile and marble business. So over a 10-year period, he wrote and refined job order costing software for the company.

The software stores information such as the costs of each type of tile and marble, and the time and cost it takes to install each type. The software asks the bidder (Van Dyke Tile and Marble) to input answers to a series of questions designed to accumulate the "specs" for the particular job. For instance, the software first asks the bidder to select (from lists) the kind and size of tile to be used and then asks a series of questions that determine the square feet and trim shapes of tile to be installed. It then uses the answers to accumulate estimates of the costs of direct materials (including freight charges) and direct labor (including payroll taxes). The software has reduced the judgment involved in estimating the costs of a job so that the bidder must make a "judgment call" on only one question—"on a scale of 1 to 10 (10 being the most difficult), how difficult is the installation?" Based on the answer to this question, the software adjusts the estimated direct labor hours (and costs) accordingly.

After the software estimates the direct materials and direct labor costs, it then factors in an amount for overhead based on a predetermined rate. This rate is an amount per direct labor hour. By totaling the company's actual overhead cost for each of several years and comparing it to various production costs and activities for those years, Bob found that the changes in overhead most highly correlated with changes in direct labor hours. After estimating the total costs for the job, the software adds in a "profit margin" to determine the total amount to bid for the job. The company has found that the cost estimates from this software, which it uses to determine its "profit margin," are much closer to its actual costs, and hence its actual profit is much closer to its expected profit.

PROCESS COSTING

The job order cost accounting system we discussed in the previous section is well suited for a company that produces unique products in small quantities for customer orders. In some industries, however, companies produce large volumes of identical units of products. In many cases the nature of the products or the high demand for each requires the company to organize the manufacturing operations of each product *separately* to obtain smooth, continuous, and efficient production. For example, **Frito-Lay** produces Lay's Potato Chips in a long, continuous process and Fritos in a separate long, continuous process. Hence, it organizes production so that it works on only one type of product in each process.

Many times production of a product requires only one manufacturing process, but at other times it requires several processes. In these cases the product normally flows from one operation or process to another continuously as the company completes each stage of its production. The company performs manufacturing operations on large quantities of identical units of that product continuously over long periods of time. Examples of such manufacturing can be found in the production of potato chips, paper, flour, some chemicals, cars, and many other products.

The cost accounting system best suited to applying manufacturing costs to a product manufactured in this way is the process cost accounting system. A **process cost accounting system** keeps track of the costs applied to a product as it moves through one or more manufacturing processes. That is, a process cost accounting system uses a manufacturing *process* (like molding, trimming, baking, and painting) rather than an individual job as

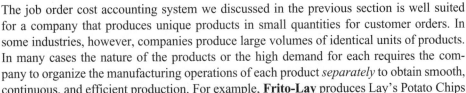 **6** What is a process cost accounting system, and how does a company use this system?

the point of cost accumulation. So, with this system, a company uses raw materials requisitions and labor tickets to trace the quantity and cost of direct materials and direct labor it uses in production to specific *processes* and to apply these costs directly to the processes. As manufacturing takes place, a company adds the direct materials, direct labor, and factory overhead costs of each process to a Goods-in-Process Inventory account set up for that particular process (so molding, trimming, baking, and painting would each have its own Goods-in-Process Inventory account). As products move from process to process, the company transfers the products' costs from the Goods-in-Process Inventory account for the first process to that for the next process, or enters manufacturing costs directly into computer-based systems to accumulate the costs for each manufacturing process. The company uses a *process cost sheet* to assign the manufacturing costs for a particular process to individual products. In the following discussion, we focus on the process cost sheet, but keep in mind that computerized process costing systems accumulate costs similarly. The process cost sheet supports the amounts listed in the Goods-in-Process Inventory account for that process. Since a company using the process cost accounting system manufactures only one type of product (such as Fritos) continuously through a process, it applies the accumulated manufacturing costs of that process to the units of that product (bags of Fritos)—usually at the end of each month.

Process Costing When There Is Only One Process

Sometimes a company manufactures a product completely in a single process. For example, consider Lady MacBeth Company, from whom Unlimited Decadence purchases cleaning supplies. Lady MacBeth manufactures a cleaning solvent in one-gallon bottles by mixing several chemicals in a single mixing process that takes 36 hours. The company applies all of the manufacturing costs it incurs in that mixing process during a month to the bottles of cleaning solvent it manufactures during the month.

As Lady MacBeth incurs these costs, it records them in the same way that we described for job order costing except that the costs are added to the Goods-in-Process Inventory account for the *process* (rather than for the job), as well as to the process cost sheet (rather than to individual job order cost sheets).

When There Is No Beginning or Ending Goods-in-Process Inventory

The simplest process costing situation is when a process has no inventory of unfinished products at either the beginning or the end of a month. In this case, during the month the company starts and completes all of the products it manufactures in that month. It assigns the *average* cost per unit of direct materials, direct labor, and factory overhead to each product it completes. However, in process costing, companies often combine the direct labor cost and the factory overhead cost on the process cost sheet and assign them to units as a single cost element called *conversion cost* (sometimes called *processing cost*) in order to simplify computations. Since this is a common practice, we will use it throughout the remainder of the chapter. **Conversion costs** are the direct labor and factory overhead costs necessary to convert direct materials into a finished product. Thus our discussion of single-process manufacturing involves assigning two cost elements to products: direct materials cost and conversion cost.

 When a company combines direct labor and factory overhead costs, it is applying factory overhead costs the same way it is applying direct labor costs—by direct labor hour. Can you explain why?

For example, suppose that during April, Lady MacBeth Company produced 1,500 bottles of cleaning solvent in a single mixing process. It had no unfinished gallons of solvent at the beginning or end of April. During the month, the company recorded a total of $7,500 [(a) $3,000 of direct materials, (b) $2,000 of direct labor, and (c) $2,500 of applied factory overhead] in the Goods-in-Process Inventory account as follows:

| Assets | | | = Liabilities + Stockholders' Equity |
Raw Materials Inventory	Goods-in-Process Inventory	Factory Overhead	Wages Payable
(a) − $3,000	(a) + $3,000		
	(b) + 2,000		(b) + $2,000
	(c) + 2,500	(c) − $2,500	
	Bal $7,500		

On the process cost sheet, Lady MacBeth treated these costs as two types of manufacturing costs, $3,000 of direct materials and $4,500 ($2,000 + $2,500) of conversion cost, and assigned them to the 1,500 bottles of cleaning solvent, as we show in Exhibit 16-7.

Lady MacBeth recorded the transfer of the $7,500 cost of completed bottles of solvent to finished goods inventory from the goods-in-process inventory at the end of the month as follows:

| Assets | | = Liabilities + Stockholders' Equity |
Goods-in-Process Inventory	Finished Goods Inventory	
Bal $7,500		
− 7,500	+$7,500	
Bal $ 0		

From this total, Lady MacBeth assigned each completed bottle of solvent the same amount of cost ($2.00 per bottle average direct materials cost plus $3.00 per bottle average conversion cost).

It is important to note the steps used in these computations, because with some modification the same steps can be used to handle much more complex situations. The three steps are as follows:

1. Compute the total for each type of manufacturing cost ($3,000 direct materials costs and $4,500 conversion costs)

EXHIBIT 16-7   PROCESS COST SHEET FOR ONE PROCESS (NO BEGINNING OR ENDING INVENTORIES)

LADY MACBETH COMPANY
Process Cost Sheet

	Total Costs Accumulated in Goods-in-Process Inventory		Bottles		Average Costs per Bottle
Direct Materials	$3,000	÷	1,500	=	$2
Conversion	4,500	÷	1,500	=	3
Total	$7,500				

Costs Assigned

To bottles completed and transferred to finished goods inventory
Direct materials	1,500 bottles @ $2	=	$3,000
Conversion	1,500 bottles @ $3	=	4,500
Total Costs Assigned			$7,500

2. Compute the average direct materials cost per product ($2 per gallon) and the average conversion cost per product ($3 per gallon)

3. Assign the total cost to the products by multiplying the number of products times the average costs per product [(1,500 gallons × $2 direct materials costs) + (1,500 gallons × $3 conversion costs) = $7,500 total cost]

But what happens if a process contains unfinished products at the end of a month? We next discuss how a company modifies these steps in such a case.

When There Is Ending Goods-in-Process Inventory

Because manufacturing a product takes time, and because production is continuous, at the end of a month we often find that a particular process has products that are only partially completed. That is, the process has an ending inventory of goods-in-process. When this occurs, the company must modify the cost-assignment procedure so that it assigns costs both to products it completes and transfers out of the process, and to unfinished products left in the process.[5] This modification involves counting the unfinished products as well as those completed and transferred, computing the average costs per unit for all products counted, and assigning costs to all products.

Usually, it is easy to count physical products, regardless of whether they are completed or unfinished. **Ford Motor Company** can count finished cars as they roll off the production line, and it also can count how many cars are still on the production line in different stages of completion. Regarding product costs, the reason for counting the products is to compute an average cost per unit for direct materials and conversion to use in assigning costs to the products involved. However, it doesn't make sense to assign the same amount of cost to unfinished products as to completed products. (Surely, the unfinished products did not cost as much to make, so far, as did the finished products.) So, to assign reasonable costs to products, a company counts its unfinished products and completed products differently.

Suppose at the end of the month, Ford Motor Company's painting department has 100 cars that are half-painted. Do you think the cost of painting these cars so far is as much as the cost of painting other cars that are complete? If so, explain why. If not, what manufacturing costs are left to add to the half-painted cars?

A company that uses the process cost accounting system counts each *completed* product as a whole unit. It counts each *unfinished* product as a part of a whole unit—that part being the estimated percent that the product is complete. For example, Lady Macbeth would count a bottle of solvent that is 80% complete as 80% of a whole bottle. Normally, though, the company does not examine unfinished products individually. Instead, it estimates the average percentage of completion for all unfinished products as a group. It then "counts" the unfinished products by multiplying the total number of unfinished physical products by their average percentage of completion. When physical products in a process are counted this way they are called **equivalent units**. The number of equivalent units in a group of unfinished physical products is the total number of physical products multiplied by their average percentage of completion. A group of 500 completed products that are 100% complete counts as 500 (500 × 100%) equivalent units, whereas a group of 500 unfinished products that are 40% complete counts as 200 (500 × 40%) equivalent units. Thus, Lady MacBeth would count 10 bottles of solvent that are 40% complete (or 40% mixed) as 4 whole bottles (10 × 40%), 300 bottles that are 80% complete as 240 whole bottles (300 × 80%), and so on.

---

[5]To simplify this introductory discussion, we are ignoring the possibility that a third group of units—lost or spoiled units—might also result from the month's operations. Accounting for the costs of spoilage or lost units is complex, and we do not discuss it in this book.

What types of costs must still be incurred to complete these products?

The reason such equivalent unit computations are useful is that they allow a company to assign costs to products in proportion to their percentage of completion. This is desirable because, for example, it is usually fair to assume that the cost incurred to bring 500 products to 40% completion is the same as the cost incurred to complete 200 whole products. Using equivalent units to compute per-unit costs allows a company to assign costs to completed and unfinished products in proportion to the amount of resources each group used.

A company usually does not incur direct materials costs and conversion costs at the same rate, however. The company often adds all direct materials to a process at the beginning of the process, and conversion normally takes place uniformly as the factory employees convert or assemble the direct materials into products. An example of this is **Milliken & Co.**, a leading textile manufacturer in Spartanburg, South Carolina, which adds bolts of fabric completely to a process before dying, bleaching, or other treating occurs. Other examples are in the manufacture of chemicals and in food-processing operations, where all ingredients must be added before mixing, blending, or packaging operations can take place. In these cases, all physical units in the process are 100% complete with regard to direct materials even though their conversion may be only 10% complete. Therefore, these types of companies count equivalent units separately for direct materials and for conversion because *unfinished* products may be at different stages of completion for each respective cost.

In this chapter we always make equivalent unit computations separately for direct materials and for conversion. To simplify these computations, we assume that direct materials are *always* added at the beginning of conversion so that both completed and unfinished products are always 100% complete with regard to direct materials. We also assume that conversion takes place uniformly. Thus, whereas *completed* products are 100% complete with regard to conversion, *unfinished* products are always less than 100% converted.

Let's return to Lady MacBeth Company. Suppose that during July, Lady MacBeth incurred a total of $12,400 in the mixing process and added these costs to the Goods-in-Process Inventory (GIP) account. Lady MacBeth always adds direct materials at the beginning of processing, whereas conversion (mixing) takes place uniformly. Information for the mixing process during July is as follows:

Total Costs Accumulated in Goods-in-Process Inventory (all added during July)		Production Information (physical products)	
Direct materials	$ 7,000	Completed & transferred	1,000
Conversion	5,400	Ending GIP inventory (50% processed)	400
Total	$12,400	Total	1,400

Since 400 unfinished bottles of solvent remain in mixing at the end of July, we must assign the direct materials and conversion costs incurred in July to those bottles as well as to the bottles that Lady MacBeth completed and transferred out of mixing to finished goods inventory. To compute the costs per bottle, we must count the equivalent units for both direct materials and conversion. We show this count in the upper part of the process cost sheet in Exhibit 16-8.

Notice that in the computation of equivalent units for completed bottles of solvent, we count each of the 1,000 *completed* bottles as a full equivalent unit for both direct materials and conversion. We count the ending GIP inventory of 400 *unfinished* bottles, however, as only 200 equivalent units for conversion because the processing of the 400 bottles is only 50% complete. In other words, these bottles have been mixing for 18 of the 36 hours. For direct materials, however, we count each unfinished bottle as a full equivalent unit. This is because Lady MacBeth added all direct materials at the begin-

EXHIBIT 16-8	PROCESS COST SHEET (ENDING INVENTORY)

LADY MACBETH COMPANY
Process Cost Sheet (July)

Equivalent Units

	Physical Units	Equivalent Units for Direct Materials	Equivalent Units for Conversion
Completed and transferred	1,000	1,000	1,000
Ending GIP inventory (50% processed)	400	400	200[a]
Total	1,400	1,400	1,200

[a]400 × 50%

Average Costs per Equivalent Unit

	Total Costs Accumulated in Goods-in-Process Inventory		Equivalent Units		Average Costs per Equivalent Unit
Direct materials	$ 7,000	÷	1,400	=	$5.00
Conversion	5,400	÷	1,200	=	4.50
Total	$12,400				

Costs Assigned

To units completed and transferred to finished goods inventory:			
Direct materials	1,000 equivalent units @ $5.00 = $5,000		
Conversion	1,000 equivalent units @ $4.50 = 4,500	$ 9,500	

To ending (July 31) goods-in-process inventory (unfinished units):			
Direct materials	400 equivalent units @ $5.00 = $2,000		
Conversion	200 equivalent units @ $4.50 = 900	2,900	
Total costs assigned		$12,400	

ning of processing. Thus, although the unfinished bottles are only 50% processed, they are 100% complete with regard to direct materials. We can use the 1,400 equivalent units for direct materials to compute the average direct materials cost per equivalent unit. Similarly, we can use the 1,200 equivalent units for conversion to compute the average conversion cost per equivalent unit. We show these computations in the middle part of the process cost sheet in Exhibit 16-8. To determine the $5.00 average cost per equivalent unit for direct materials, we divide the $7,000 of direct materials costs by the 1,400 equivalent units for direct materials. To determine the $4.50 average cost per equivalent unit for conversion, we divide the $5,400 of conversion costs by the 1,200 equivalent units for conversion.

We now can assign direct materials costs and conversion costs separately to completed and unfinished bottles of solvent based on the average costs per equivalent unit. We can do this for each group (both completed and unfinished bottles of solvent) by multiplying the average costs per equivalent unit by the number of equivalent units in the group. We show these computations in the lower part of the process cost sheet in Exhibit 16-8.

We determine the $9,500 total cost of the units completed and transferred to finished goods inventory in three steps. First, we multiply the 1,000 equivalent units for direct materials by the $5.00 average direct materials cost to determine the $5,000 total direct materials costs for the units transferred. Second, we multiply the 1,000 equivalent units for conversion by the $4.50 average conversion cost to determine the $4,500 total conversion costs for the units transferred. Finally, we combine these two costs to determine the $9,500 total cost of the units transferred.

Next, we determine the $2,900 total cost of the unfinished units in the ending goods-in-process inventory in three steps. First, we multiply the 400 equivalent units for direct materials by the $5.00 average direct materials cost to determine the $2,000 total direct materials costs for the unfinished units. Second, we multiply the 200 equivalent units for conversion by the $4.50 average conversion cost to determine the $900 total conversion costs for the unfinished units. Finally, we combine these two costs to determine the $2,900 total costs of the units transferred.

Notice in this computation that the total costs assigned ($12,400) equals the total costs that accumulated in the Goods-in-Process Inventory account. Based on this cost assignment, we transfer the $9,500 cost of the completed units to the Finished Goods Inventory account from the Goods-in-Process Inventory account as follows:

Assets		=	Liabilities	+	Stockholders' Equity
Goods-in-Process Inventory	Finished Goods Inventory				
Bal $12,400					
− 9,500	+$9,500				
Bal $ 2,900					

> FINANCIAL STATEMENT EFFECTS
>
> No effect on total current assets and total assets on *balance sheet*.

After the preceding entry to transfer the $9,500 cost of completed units to the Finished Goods Inventory account, the ending balance of the Goods-in-Process Inventory account for mixing is $2,900. This is the amount of cost we assigned on the process cost sheet in Exhibit 16-8 to the unfinished bottles of solvent. This will become the cost of the August beginning goods-in-process inventory for the mixing process.

 How does this method compare with the method that we used for a process without a beginning and ending inventory? Are the steps the same? What are the similarities and differences?

When There Are Both Beginning and Ending Balances in Goods-in-Process Inventory

When a company has partially completed products in a process at the beginning of a month, the Goods-in-Process Inventory account for that process has a beginning balance equal to the cost assigned to those units at the end of the previous month. Additional costs incurred during the current month increase this balance. Thus, at the end of the month, the total cost accumulated in the Goods-in-Process Inventory account consists of (1) the beginning inventory balance and (2) additional costs added during the current month.

A company with a beginning balance in its goods-in-process inventory uses one of several methods to determine the amount of the total cost to assign to completed and unfinished products at the end of the month. We show the average cost method because it is both simple and widely used.[6] The **average cost method** assigns the total costs of direct materials and conversion separately to products at the *average* costs per equivalent unit by simply adding the amount of each type of cost in the beginning inventory to the amount of that cost type incurred during the month. The remaining steps are the same as those we discussed earlier.

So let's see what happens to the cost of Lady MacBeth's cleaning solvent in August. Remember that Lady MacBeth ended July with 400 unfinished bottles of cleaning solvent in its goods-in-process inventory, and that it assigned $2,000 direct materials costs and $900 conversion costs to these bottles. During August, Lady MacBeth started 1,200 additional bottles of cleaning solvent. It completed and transferred 1,300 bottles during August and ended August with 300 bottles (60 percent processed) still in process. Lady MacBeth incurred $11,908 of additional costs ($6,000 direct materials and $5,908 conversion) in the mixing process. We add these costs to the Goods-in-Process Inventory account, bringing the balance to $14,808 ($2,900 beginning balance + $11,908) for the mixing process during August as we show below:

Cost Information		Production Information (physical units)	
Costs in beginning inventory (Aug. 1)		Beginning GIP inventory	400
Direct materials	$ 2,000	Added in August	1,200
Conversion	900	Total	1,600
Costs added during August		Completed & transferred	1,300
Direct materials	6,000	Ending GIP inventory (60% processed)	300
Conversion	5,908	Total	1,600
Total	$14,808		

Lady MacBeth must assign the total of $14,808 ($2,000 beginning balance + $6,000 for direct materials and $900 + $5,908 for conversion) to bottles of solvent for August. We show all of the computations needed to assign the $14,808 total costs to Lady MacBeth's Goods-in-Process (GIP) Inventory account and Finished Goods Inventory account at the end of August on the process cost sheet in Exhibit 16-9.

 How does this method compare with the method that we used in the example for a process without a beginning and ending inventory? Are the three steps the same? Be sure to note the similarities and differences.

Note in these computations on the process cost sheet in Exhibit 16-9 that we did not use the number or stage of completion of the *beginning* goods-in-process inventory units. The average cost method does not use this information.

---

[6]Besides the average cost method, a manufacturing company also may use the last-in, first-out (LIFO) or the first-in, first-out (FIFO) methods to apply costs to its inventory. LIFO and FIFO are more complicated, so we don't discuss them here. However, the general idea is the same as the LIFO and FIFO methods that a retail company uses to cost its inventory, as we will discuss in Chapter 19.

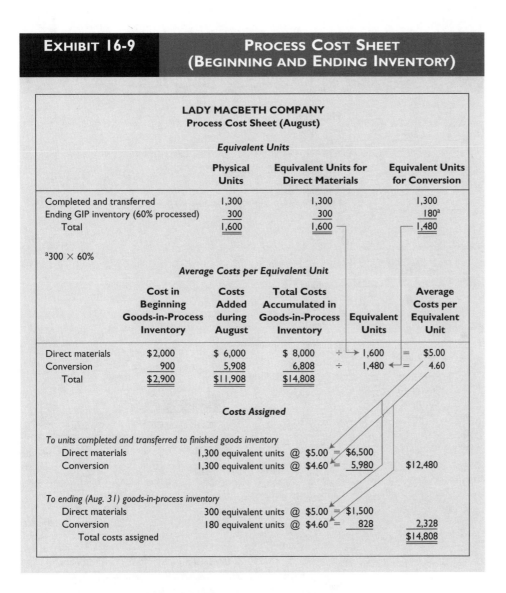

EXHIBIT 16-9	PROCESS COST SHEET (BEGINNING AND ENDING INVENTORY)

LADY MACBETH COMPANY
Process Cost Sheet (August)

Equivalent Units

	Physical Units	Equivalent Units for Direct Materials	Equivalent Units for Conversion
Completed and transferred	1,300	1,300	1,300
Ending GIP inventory (60% processed)	300	300	180[a]
Total	1,600	1,600	1,480

[a]300 × 60%

Average Costs per Equivalent Unit

	Cost in Beginning Goods-in-Process Inventory	Costs Added during August	Total Costs Accumulated in Goods-in-Process Inventory		Equivalent Units		Average Costs per Equivalent Unit
Direct materials	$2,000	$ 6,000	$ 8,000	÷	1,600	=	$5.00
Conversion	900	5,908	6,808	÷	1,480	=	4.60
Total	$2,900	$11,908	$14,808				

Costs Assigned

To units completed and transferred to finished goods inventory
Direct materials	1,300 equivalent units @ $5.00 =	$6,500	
Conversion	1,300 equivalent units @ $4.60 =	5,980	$12,480

To ending (Aug. 31) goods-in-process inventory
Direct materials	300 equivalent units @ $5.00 =	$1,500	
Conversion	180 equivalent units @ $4.60 =	828	2,328
Total costs assigned			$14,808

Process Costing When There Are Multiple Processes

As we mentioned earlier, manufacturing some products involves more than one process. For example, look at Exhibit 16-10, which shows the six conversion processes necessary for Unlimited Decadence to manufacture its Darkly Decadent candy bars. In cases like this, the products transferred out of a process may not be ready for sale but instead may require further conversion in another process. Handling this situation requires very little modification of the steps we illustrated for assigning process costs in single-process manufacturing.

Exhibit 16-11 shows three diagrams of simple arrangements for multiple-process manufacturing. Companies use these and many more complex arrangements in manufacturing a variety of products. The arrows in these diagrams show the flow of products from one process to the next until the products have been converted into finished goods inventory. In these multiple-process situations, manufacturing *costs* flow from one Goods-in-Process Inventory account to the next in a manner corresponding to the flow of products through the processes. As a company completes the conversion of its products, the company removes the costs assigned to them from the last process and transfers them to the Finished Goods Inventory account.

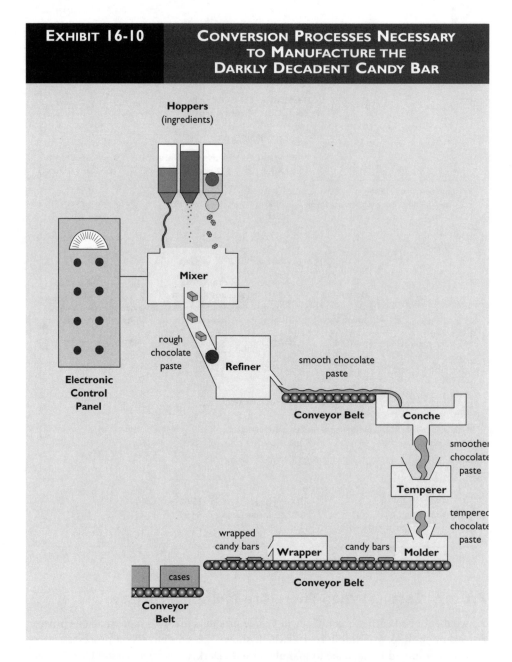

EXHIBIT 16-10   **CONVERSION PROCESSES NECESSARY TO MANUFACTURE THE DARKLY DECADENT CANDY BAR**

Consider the case of Unlimited Decadence's Gluttonous Gooey Gob candy bars, "chewy peanut clusters surrounded by pure milk chocolate, caramel, and marshmallows." Gluttonous Gooey Gobs require conversion in two processes—mixing and molding. Unlimited Decadence assigns costs to mixing the same way it would if Gluttonous Gooey Gobs required only one process—mixing. However, the entry it uses to record the transfer of the costs of the completed Gluttonous Gooey Gobs *out* of the mixing Goods-in-Process Inventory account differs from that made in the single-process case. In the single-process case, the company transfers completed products to finished goods inventory. In this case, however, Unlimited Decadence transfers the completed Gluttonous Gooey Gobs from mixing into molding, where they become goods-in-process inventory for molding. Therefore, Unlimited Decadence transfers the costs assigned to the completely mixed Gluttonous Gooey Gobs from the Mixing Goods-in-Process Inventory account to the Molding Goods-in-Process Inventory account. For example, if

| EXHIBIT 16-11 | FLOW OF UNITS THROUGH MULTIPLE MANUFACTURING PROCESSES |

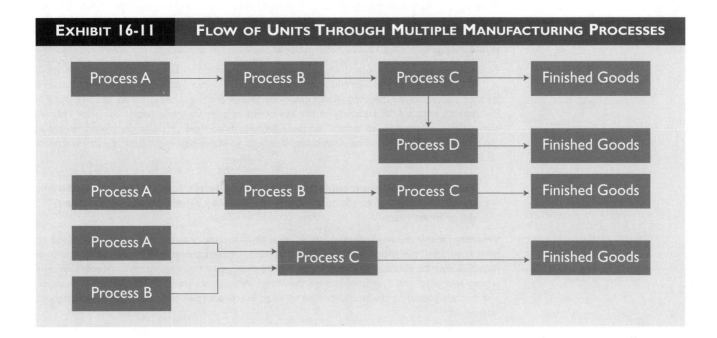

Unlimited Decadence has assigned $1,200 of cost to the Gluttonous Gooey Gobs processed in mixing, when it transfers them from mixing to molding it records the transfer as follows:

Assets		=	Liabilities	+	Stockholders' Equity
Goods-in-Process Inventory	Finished Goods Inventory				
Bal $1,200					
− 1,200	+$1,200				
Bal $ 0					

> **FINANCIAL STATEMENT EFFECTS**
>
> No effect on total current assets and total assets on **balance sheet.**

Unlimited Decadence treats these costs as an additional, separate type of cost, called *prior production cost*, on the process cost sheet for molding. That is, the molding Goods-in-Process account has its own molding conversion costs *as well as* the prior production cost (direct materials and conversion costs) transferred in from the mixing Goods-in-Process account. In addition, Unlimited Decadence makes a separate equivalent units computation on the process cost sheet for prior production costs in the same way it did for the direct materials and conversion costs we discussed earlier.

 In computing equivalent units for prior production costs, what percentage do you think you should use to indicate the percentage of completion?

We have just discussed two popular cost accounting systems: the job order costing system and the process costing system. Each of these systems allows a company to determine and accumulate the costs of its products or activities. In Chapter 17 we will discuss how a company uses standards in its cost accounting system to plan and control its operations. In Chapter 18 we will discuss some recent developments in modern manufacturing philosophies and processes. You will see how these developments have prompted activity-based costing, a modification of the job order and the process costing systems. We will discuss the activity-based costing system and some of its advantages and disadvantages.

SUMMARY

At the beginning of the chapter we asked you several questions. During the chapter, we asked you to STOP and answer some additional questions to build your knowledge about specific issues. Be sure you answered these additional questions. Below are the questions from the beginning of the chapter, with a brief summary of the key points relating to the answers. Use your creative and critical thinking skills to expand on these key points to develop more complete answers to the questions and to determine what other questions you have that might lead you to learn more about the issues.

1 How does the way a manufacturing company determines the cost of its inventories and cost of goods sold differ from the way a merchandising company determines them?

Whereas a merchandising company assigns costs to its inventory and cost of goods sold based on what it paid for the goods, a manufacturing company assigns these costs based on the costs of manufacturing its inventories. These costs include the costs of direct materials, direct labor, and factory overhead, and they flow through the inventory accounts (raw materials, goods-in-process, and finished goods) as the products flow through the production process to the finished goods warehouse.

2 How does a cost accounting system help a manufacturing company assign costs to its products?

A cost accounting system assigns the costs of manufacturing products (direct materials costs, direct labor costs, and factory overhead costs) to the goods-in-process inventory, by job or by process, as the company manufactures the products. Then, as the jobs or processes are completed, it assigns these costs to individual products.

3 Since factory overhead is not a physical part of the product, how does a company include the cost of overhead in the cost of its products?

A company usually assigns factory overhead to products in proportion to the amount of a manufacturing activity, such as direct labor hours, devoted to the manufacture of the products. At the beginning of the year, the company estimates its total annual factory overhead costs and the level of manufacturing activity. Then, it computes a predetermined overhead rate by dividing the estimated costs by the estimated level of activity. As the product is manufactured, the company multiplies the actual level of manufacturing activity (direct labor hours) by the predetermined overhead rate. It adds the resulting amount to the Goods-in-Process Inventory account before determining individual product costs.

4 Why is there more than one type of cost accounting system?

Each cost accounting system is a practical way for a manufacturing company to get timely information about its manufacturing operations, and each is specifically suited for a particular type of manufacturing environment. Job order cost accounting is used by a company that manufactures unique products in small quantities for customer orders. Process costing is better suited for a company that manufactures products, where one manufacturing process, or several processes, continuously produces large volumes of identical units.

5 What is a job order cost accounting system, and how does a company use this system?

In a job order cost accounting system, a company keeps track of its costs to manufacture inventory for each job order. It accumulates the costs of direct materials, direct labor, and factory overhead for each individual job on a job order cost sheet. As a company uses direct materials and direct labor, it adds their costs to the Goods-in-Process Inventory account. As it uses indirect materials and indirect labor, and as it incurs other manufacturing costs, the company adds these costs to the Factory Overhead account. The company then increases the Goods-in-Process Inventory account for the factory overhead by applying overhead based on a predetermined overhead rate. When the job is completed, the company transfers the total costs from the Goods-in-Process Inventory account to the Finished Goods Inventory account. When the units of inventory in the job are sold, the company transfers the costs from the Finished Goods Inventory account to the Cost of Goods Sold account. The company adjusts cost of goods sold for any difference between the actual factory overhead incurred and the factory overhead applied.

 What is a process cost accounting system, and how does a company use this system?

In a process cost accounting system, a company keeps track of its costs to manufacture inventory for each manufacturing process. As manufacturing takes place, the company accumulates the costs of direct materials and conversion (direct labor and factory overhead) for each manufacturing process on a process cost sheet. As a company incurs direct materials and conversion costs in a manufacturing process, it increases the Goods-in-Process Inventory account by the costs of that process. The company then assigns an average cost for direct materials and conversion to each of the units of inventory that flow through that process during the period. To determine the units manufactured for the period, the company counts each completed unit as a whole unit and counts each partially completed unit as an equivalent unit. As units move to the next process, the company transfers the average cost for the prior process out of the Goods-in-Process Inventory account for that process to the Goods-in-Process Inventory account for the next process. After the units of inventory are complete, the total average costs are transferred from the last Goods-in-Process Inventory account to the Finished Goods Inventory account. When units of inventory are sold, the company transfers the average cost per unit sold from the Finished Goods Inventory account to the Cost of Goods Sold account.

KEY TERMS

average cost method *(p. 550)*
conversion costs *(p. 544)*
cost accounting *(p. 527)*
equivalent units *(p. 546)*
job order *(p. 532)*

job order cost accounting system *(p. 533)*
predetermined overhead rate *(p. 539)*
process cost accounting system *(p. 543)*

SUMMARY SURFING

Here is an opportunity to gather information on the Internet about real-world issues related to the topics in this chapter. (For suggestions on how to navigate various companies' Web sites to find their financial statements and other information, see the related discussion in the Preface at the beginning of the book). Answer the following question.

- Go to the **Sally Industry Corporation** Web site. Find the company's description of its production. In order to assign a cost to each of its products, Sally Industry would have to identify specific inputs to its production. What direct labor, and factory overhead costs do you think are part of each product's cost?

INTEGRATED BUSINESS AND ACCOUNTING SITUATIONS

Answer the Following Questions in Your Own Words.

Testing Your Knowledge

16-1   Describe the manufacturing environment for which job order costing is best suited.

16-2   Describe a perpetual inventory system and how it works in a job order costing system.

16-3   How do job order cost sheets support the Goods-in-Process Inventory account in a job order system?

16-4   Explain what it means to apply factory overhead costs.

16-5   What is the purpose of a raw materials requisition (or request)?

16-6   How do you know whether a raw material is a direct material or an indirect material?

16-7   What are the purposes of labor tickets?

16-8   How do you know whether a labor cost is for direct labor or indirect labor? Give two examples of indirect labor.

16-9   Why does a company bother to distinguish direct materials from indirect materials and direct labor from indirect labor?

16-10   Why are factory overhead costs not applied directly to job orders, when the other two manufacturing input costs are applied directly?

16-11   Why does a company predetermine its overhead rate?

16-12   Under what conditions is factory overhead overapplied and underapplied? In either of these cases, why does a company adjust the balance in its Cost of Goods Sold account?

16-13   Describe the manufacturing environment for which process costing is best suited.

16-14   In a process costing system, what are conversion costs and why are they called conversion costs?

16-15   How do process cost sheets support the Goods-in-Process Inventory account in a process costing system?

16-16   In a process costing system, what are prior production costs? How are these costs treated on the process cost sheet?

16-17   Describe, as precisely as you can, how a company computes equivalent units for a group of units in goods-in-process inventory.

16-18   Why does a company compute equivalent units separately for materials and for conversion costs?

Applying Your Knowledge

16-19   During May, Bigg Production Company made a $26,700 credit purchase of raw materials. A summary of raw materials requisitions shows the following raw materials issued into production:

Direct materials for

Job order 101	$17,560
Job order 102	3,030
Job order 104	2,750
Job order 105	1,890
Total direct materials	$25,230
Total indirect materials	1,340
Total raw materials issued	$26,570

Required: (1) Use account columns to record Bigg's purchase of raw materials.
(2) Use account columns to record Bigg's issue of raw materials.

16-20   A summary of labor tickets shows the following labor costs for Bigg Production Company during May:

Direct labor for

Job order 101	(310 hours)	$6,200
Job order 102	(280 hours)	2,800

continued

Job order 104	(200 hours)	2,000
Job order 105	(80 hours)	800
Total direct labor	(870 hours)	$11,800
Total indirect labor		1,325
Total direct and indirect labor		$13,125

Required: Use account columns to record Bigg's direct and indirect labor costs.

16-21 Bigg Production Company could set its predetermined overhead rate based on the year's expected factory overhead cost and either the year's expected direct labor hours or direct labor cost (dollars). Bigg expects this year's factory overhead costs to be $126,000. It also expects that its employees will work 14,000 direct labor hours this year and that this labor will cost $210,000.

Required: (1) What is Bigg's predetermined overhead rate per direct labor hour?
(2) What is Bigg's predetermined overhead rate per direct labor dollar?
(3) Refer to 16-20. How much total overhead would Bigg apply to the job orders in May if it used the predetermined overhead rate per direct labor hour? Use account columns to show how Bigg would apply the factory overhead.
(4) Refer again to 16-20. How much total overhead would Bigg apply to the job orders in May if it used the predetermined overhead rate per direct labor dollar?

16-22 Heavy Metal Products computed its predetermined overhead rate to be $27 per machine hour (with expected overhead costs of $248,400 and with 9,200 expected machine hours for the year).

Required: (1) If actual factory overhead costs were $260,000 and total actual machine hours were 9,500 for the year, by how much did Heavy Metal over- or underapply overhead? Record the actual and applied factory overhead in the Factory Overhead account, and transfer the over- or underapplied overhead to the Cost of Goods Sold account.
(2) What if, instead, actual factory overhead costs were $235,100 and total actual machine hours were 8,900 for the year? Record the actual and applied factory overhead in the Factory Overhead account, and transfer the over- or underapplied overhead to the Cost of Goods Sold account.

16-23 Protez Company produces crankers based on customers' special orders. During October, it started and completed one job order (#89), which contained 80 crankers. The following cost information is available for October:
(1) *Materials Requisitions:* $8,768 direct materials
(2) *Labor Time Cards:* 960 hours of direct labor at $12 per hour
(3) *Factory Overhead:* Factory overhead costs are applied to job orders at a predetermined overhead rate of $6.20 per direct labor hour.

Below is job order cost sheet #89.

Job Order Cost Sheet #89	
Direct Materials	$_____
Direct Labor	_____
Factory Overhead	_____
Total Job Cost	$_____
Units	_____
Cost per Unit	$_____

Required: (1) Complete job order cost sheet #89 for Protez Company.
(2) If Protez Company sold all of the crankers for $600 each, what would be the company's total gross profit?

16-24 Multiple Times Corporation, manufacturer of watches, clocks, and stopwatches, had a balance of $95,420 in its Goods-in-Process Inventory account and the following costs and units on its job cost sheets for its job orders for July:

Job order 16 .... $12,300   (300 stopwatches)
Job order 17 34,100   (1,100 alarm clocks)
Job order 18 6,170   (40 cuckoo clocks)
Job order 19 15,850   (250 sports watches)
Job order 20 27,000   (1,000 standard watches)

Multiple Times completed job orders 16, 17, 18, and 20 during the last week of July. It sold job orders 17 and 18 entirely and 300 watches out of job order 20. Revenues from these credit sales totaled $96,425.

Required: (1) Record the balance in Multiple Times' Goods-in-Process Inventory account during the last week of July (the balance before recording the completion of the job orders). Now record the effect on Multiple Times' accounts of the completion of the job orders during the last week of July.

(2) Record the effect on Multiple Times' accounts of its sales during the last week of July. Determine the ending balance in the Finished Goods Inventory account.

16-25 Woods Custom Furniture Manufacturing worked on a single job order during the entire month of August. It started the job at the beginning of the month and completed and sold the job at the end of the month. The following related events occurred during the month:

(1) Woods made a credit purchase of $18,500 of raw materials.

(2) Woods issued $15,200 of direct materials and $500 of indirect materials into production.

(3) Woods' employees worked 995 direct labor hours at $11.00 per hour. Indirect labor cost Woods $1,700. Woods will pay these wages in September.

(4) The factory returned $110 of direct materials to the storeroom.

(5) Woods' factory overhead, other than indirect labor and materials, amounted to $25,650 as follows:

Depreciation on factory and equipment	$13,500
Insurance (previously paid in advance)	2,200
Property taxes (to be paid in December)	3,600
Other factory overhead (all cash payments)	6,350
Total	$25,650

(6) Woods applied factory overhead at a predetermined overhead rate of $31 per direct labor hour.

(7) Woods completed the job order and transferred it to finished goods inventory.

(8) Woods sold the job order for $105,000 on credit.

Required: Record the effect of each of these events in Woods' accounts.

16-26 On the Border Framing Company began operating on November 1. During November, it began manufacturing a single job order of 5,000 frames. At the end of November, it had not yet completed the frames. During November, it incurred actual factory overhead costs of $7,000. At the end of November, it had a $15,500 balance in its Goods-in-Process Inventory account for this job, consisting of $5,000 of direct materials, $3,000 of direct labor, and $7,500 of applied factory overhead costs for November. During December, On the Border worked only on this job. It completed and sold the job at the end of December. The following events occurred during December:

(1) Direct materials of $10,500 and indirect materials of $500 were used in production.

(2) Employees worked 700 direct labor hours at $10 per hour. The indirect labor cost was $1,250.

(3) Actual factory overhead, other than indirect labor and materials, amounted to $17,000.

(4) Factory overhead was applied at a predetermined overhead rate of $25 per direct labor hour.

(5) The job order was completed and transferred to finished goods inventory.

(6) On the Border sold the 5,000 units in the job for $80,000.

(7) On the Border incurred operating expenses of $18,750 during November and December.

Required: (1) Complete the following job order cost sheet:

Job Order Cost Sheet			
	Beginning December Costs	Costs Added During December	Total Costs
Direct Materials	$5,000	_____	_____
Direct Labor	$3,000	_____	_____
Factory Overhead	$7,500	_____	_____
Total Job Cost			_____
÷ Units			_____
Cost Per Unit			_____

(2) Determine the balances in (a) Finished Goods Inventory and (b) Factory Overhead at the end of December before the job was sold.

(3) Is Factory Overhead underapplied or overapplied, and by how much? What happens to the balance in the Factory Overhead account at the end of the year?

(4) Prepare an income statement for On the Border for the year (November and December).

16-27 PETROIL Refining Company produces one of its products in refining process B.

Required: Compute the number of equivalent units for conversion cost in each of the following groups:

(1) 1,200 completed tanks
(2) 540 tanks (1/3 processed)
(3) 600 tanks (1/2 processed)
(4) 500 tanks (20% processed) and 440 tanks (30% processed)
(5) 400 completed tanks and 100 tanks (75% processed)

16-28 Refer to 16-27.

Required: Compute the number of equivalent units for direct materials cost for each of the five groups, assuming that PETROIL adds direct materials at the beginning of refining process B.

16-29 Suppose that PETROIL Refining Company has no beginning inventory in refining process B in May. During May, it accumulated the following costs in its Goods-in-Process Inventory account:

Direct materials	$2,730
Conversion	3,040
Total	$5,770

PETROIL completed and transferred 400 tanks to the finished goods inventory during May. At the end of May, 250 unfinished tanks were still in process. They were 100% complete for direct materials but only 30% complete for conversion.

Required: (1) Prepare the process cost sheet that PETROIL would use to assign the total direct materials and conversion costs to the completed tanks and to the ending inventory of unfinished tanks.

(2) Record the balance in the Goods-in-Process Inventory account accumulated during May, and then record the transfer of the costs of completed tanks from the goods-in-process inventory to the finished goods inventory.

16-30 Apollo Chemical Company produces procoline in its mixing process. There is no inventory in the mixing process at the beginning of February. Apollo adds direct materials at the beginning of processing. During February, it completed 1,400 bottles of procoline and transferred them from the mixing process to the finished goods inventory. At the end of February, 300 bottles (60% processed) remained in the mixing process. Apollo incurred the following costs in the mixing process during February:

Direct materials	$3,910
Direct labor	1,676
Factory overhead	2,590
Total	$8,176

Required: (1) Prepare the process cost sheet that Apollo would use to assign the direct materials and conversion costs incurred in the mixing process to the completed and unfinished bottles of procoline.

(2) Record the balance in the Goods-in-Process Inventory account accumulated during February, and then record the transfer of the costs of completed bottles of procoline from the goods-in-process inventory to the finished goods inventory.

16-31 Greyson Grinding Company produces an abrasive powder in a grinding process. This process had an inventory at the beginning of June, to which Greyson had assigned the following costs:

Direct materials	$6,700
Conversion	808
Total beginning goods-in-process inventory balance	$7,508

Greyson added the following additional costs to the Goods-in-Process Inventory account during June:

Direct materials	$22,580
Direct labor	14,410
Factory overhead	26,830
Total	$63,820

Greyson added direct materials at the beginning of processing. It completed and transferred 16,000 bags of powder to the finished goods inventory during June. At the end of June, 8,000 bags of powder were unfinished (40% processed).

Required: (1) Prepare the process cost sheet that Greyson would use to assign the total costs accumulated in the Goods-in-Process Inventory account at the end of June to the completed and the unfinished bags of powder.

(2) Record the balance in the Goods-in-Process Inventory account accumulated during June, and then record the transfer of the costs of completed bags of powder from the Goods-in-Process Inventory account to the Finished Goods Inventory account.

16-32 ERIC Industries manufactures dribbits in a single process. It adds direct materials at the beginning of processing. ERIC's cost and production information for the months of July and August is as follows:

Cost Information

	July	August
Costs in beginning GIP inventory		
Direct materials	$ 41,500	$?[a]
Conversion	10,430	?[a]
Costs added during month		
Direct materials	77,300	87,500
Conversion	24,280	39,330
Total	$153,510	$?[a]

[a]To be computed

Production Information (physical units)

	July	August
Beginning GIP inventory	500	300
Added during the month	600	800
Total	1,100	1,100
Completed and transferred	800	900
Ending GIP inventory		
July (30% processed)	300	
August (60% processed)		200
Total	1,100	1,100

Required: (1) Prepare the process cost sheet that ERIC would use to assign the total costs accumulated in the goods-in-process inventory at the end of July to the completed and unfinished units.

(2) Repeat (1) for August.

16-33 The Genuine Products Company manufactures "antique tables" in two processes. First, Genuine Products adds direct materials at the beginning of an assembly process in which the tables are assembled with precut and finished tops and legs. It then transfers the completed tables into an "aging" process in which they are nicked, scratched, and water-spotted by two skilled craftsmen. It adds no new direct materials to the aging process. At the end of the aging process, Genuine Products transfers the tables to the finished goods inventory. Genuine Products has the following cost and production information for the two processes during the month of March:

Cost Information

	Assembly	Aging
Beginning GIP inventory costs:		
Prior production	—	$3,750
Direct materials	$ 860	—
Conversion	240	460
Costs added during March:		
Prior production	—	?ᵃ
Direct materials	11,300	—
Conversion	7,810	3,895
Total	$20,210	?ᵃ

ᵃTo be computed

Production Information (physical units)

	Assembly	Aging
Beginning GIP inventory	40	20
Added	310	320
Total	350	340
Completed and transferred	320	325
Ending GIP inventory		
(50% processed)	60	
(40% processed)		25
Total	380	350

Required: (1) Prepare the process cost sheet that Genuine Products would use to assign the total costs accumulated in each of the two Goods-in-Process Inventory accounts at the end of March to the completed and unfinished tables.

(2) Record the $20,210 balance in the Goods-in-Process Inventory: Assembly account and the $8,105 balance in the Goods-in-Process Inventory: Aging account accumulated during March. Then, record the transfer of the costs of completed tables out of the two Goods-in-Process Inventory accounts at the end of March.

Making Evaluations

16-34   The Machine Shop uses lathes, drill presses, and other metal-working equipment to do machining to customer order. It grinds valves; cuts, drills, and bends sheet metal; and welds. A large portion of The Machine Shop's business is fabrication of machine parts for machine repair work by other companies in the vicinity. The company also often repairs brush hogs and other equipment for local farmers.

Required: What kind of cost accounting system would you recommend that The Machine Shop use? What features of the system that you recommended would be useful to the company, and why would each of these features be useful?

16-35   Chemicals-R-Us operates a large plant in the Midwest. It manufactures several common acids that are in high demand. In fact, several of its acid departments operate 24 hours per day, 7 days a week. Equipment in most of Chemicals' departments is specialized, or customized, for manufacturing specific products. For example, mixing vats and piping are lined for sulfuric acid production. This is not necessary for several other chemicals produced by the company. Chemicals-R-Us keeps a huge storage warehouse near the factory to hold finished chemicals because demand fluctuates greatly and in some months exceeds the company's production capability.

Required: What kind of cost accounting system would you recommend that Chemicals-R-Us use? What characteristics of the company caused you to make your recommendation? What features of the system that you recommended would be useful to the company?

16-36   LUBCO Inc. has opened a new plant to expand production of a compound that is experiencing increased industrial use. You are the production manager of the new plant, which is supposed to be capable of twice the rate of output of the old plant and of a slightly lower processing cost per gallon. Just when you thought things were going great, you received the following memo from Pete Duncan, the vice-president of production for the company:

Dear _____:

What the _____ is going on over there? I put you in charge of the new plant because I thought you could handle it best. But look at the mess your factory is in. The production performance for Compound A62 is erratic. Look at the numbers:

Old Plant

	Cost Incurred	Gallons of Completed Output	Cost per Gallon
January	$240,000	20,000	$12.00
February	240,000	20,000	12.00
March	240,000	20,000	12.00
April	240,000	20,000	12.00
May	240,000	20,000	12.00
June	240,000	20,000	12.00

New Plant

	Cost Incurred	Gallons of Completed Output	Cost per Gallon
January	$441,000	35,000	$12.60
February	487,500	39,000	12.50
March	483,750	43,000	11.25
April	501,200	40,000	12.53
May	500,400	45,000	11.12
June	569,600	40,000	14.24

You've had a production cost per gallon lower than that of the old plant in only two of the six months that the new plant has been operating. And this most recent month is the worst of all. Your per-unit cost is almost 20% higher. If you've got problems, let me know. And if you can't get things turned around soon, I'll come over and run that plant myself.

Pete

Because the vice-president was particularly concerned about cost performance in June, the most recent month, you have gathered the following information for June from your records and those offered by the cost accountant of the old plant.

	Old Plant	New Plant
June production (gallons):	Physical Units	Physical Units
Beginning GIP Inventory	0	0
Started	20,000	48,000
Total	20,000	48,000
Completed	20,000	40,000
Ending GIP Inventory	0	8,000 (75% complete)
Total	20,000	48,000
June costs:		
Direct materials	$200,000	$480,000
Conversion	40,000	90,620
Total	$240,000	$570,620

Required: Write a memo to Pete Duncan describing your assessment of the performance of your new plant relative to that of the old plant.

16-37 Aboveboard Inboard and Outboard Motors is a boat dealership. The company sells new and used boats, and provides repair service as well. Suppose you are the manager of used boat sales. One of your primary sources for used boats is the company's new boat operation, which takes trade-ins. You inspect and make offers on boats traded in. Your cost for each boat includes your offer price plus the parts and labor you purchase from the company's service operation to recondition the boat, an assignment of "overhead," and a sales commission.

You have the following information with which to establish prices for five boats taken in on trade during the second week of August:

Offer Price

Boat A..............................	$ 500
Boat B	1,200
Boat C.............................	900
Boat D	2,100
Boat E..............................	2,300

Parts Requisition Summary

	Requisition	Part	Amount	Total
Boat A	16710	42-21003	$ 21.95	
		42-21004	6.50	
		30-12500	65.35	
		30-12901	4.35	
		30-12911	9.15	$107.30
	16725	5-4100	30.50	30.50
Boat B	16760	42-21103	23.95	
		42-21104	6.50	
		80-65000	13.50	43.95
Boat C	16801	50-81400	43.50	43.50
Boat D	16900	20-92500	1.50	
		80-65300	14.95	16.45
Boat E	16911	30-13100	80.15	
		30-13600	4.90	
		30-13610	9.05	94.10
	16914	95-20200	180.00	180.00

continued

Labor Summary

Mechanic	Boat	Allowed Time	Operation
Repair Shop			
Wu, Lin	A	2 hr	Depth gauge
		1	Starter motor
		1	Tune
		2	Anchor engine
	C	1	Replace light assembly
	D	1	Replace battery connection
Guptil, Ann	B	1	Replace interior light assembly
		1	Change rotor assembly
	E	2	Speed gauge
		3	Overhaul engine
Body Shop			
Austin, Les	B	4	Sand, waterproof bow and stern
	D	1	Touch up, buff

Aboveboard's repair shop charges $35 per hour for labor. Its body shop charges $40 per hour.

You assign "overhead"—which includes your salary, rent, utilities, advertising, insurance, property taxes, and supplies—equally at a predetermined rate to the boats you sell. You estimated this year's total of these indirect costs to be $72,800 and total sales for the year to be 520 used boats.

You pay sales personnel strictly on a commission basis at a rate of 10% of sales revenue from the boats they sell. The dealership wants to earn an average of $50 per used boat sold.

Required: Determine the prices to be charged for the five used boats taken in on trade during the second week of August and discuss the similarities and differences between your pricing computations and the procedures of a job order cost accounting system for a manufacturing company.

16-38   Your boss, Festus B. Thorneapple, stopped by your office today. Among other things, he said:

I know that we apply overhead to jobs in proportion to their relative number of direct labor hours and that we currently allocate overhead at a rate of $60 per direct labor hour. But that bothers me a little. Here's why. I know, for example, that we expect to use 10 direct labor hours and 500 KWH of electricity on the Smith job. And we expect to use 100 direct labor hours and 100 KWH of electricity on the job for Calloway Corp. According to my calculations, that means that we will allocate $600 in overhead costs to the Smith job (10 direct labor hours × $60 per direct labor hour) and $6,000 to the Calloway job (100 direct labor hours × $60 per direct labor hour). The thing that bothers me is that we use much more electricity for the Smith job than for the Calloway job. Since our utility costs are overhead costs, it seems like we should be allocating more overhead costs to the Smith job. I looked at the numbers, and if we applied overhead based on KWH, we would apply overhead at a rate of $11 per KWH, which would change the costs of both jobs.

Anyway, to make a long story short, this made me start wondering whether we are making faulty decisions based on the way we are allocating overhead costs. To start with, how might applying overhead costs based on KWH affect our decisions about what selling prices to charge? Our current policy is to set the selling price at 1.6 times the cost of a job. We have projected that the Smith job will cost $1,800 ($600 factory overhead + $1,000 direct materials + $200 direct labor) and the Calloway job will cost $11,000 ($6,000 factory overhead + $3,000 direct materials + $2,000 direct labor). So, we're planning to sell the Smith job for $2,880 (1.6 × $1,800) and the Calloway job for $17,600 (1.6 × $11,000). If we were to change our method of applying overhead costs from using direct labor hours to using

KWH, how would that affect our decisions about the selling prices to charge for these jobs? When you get a chance, will you please think about this and write me a memo addressing this question?

Required: Write your boss a memo responding to his question.

16-39 Yesterday, you received the following letter for your advice column in the local paper:

DR. DECISIVE

Dear Dr. Decisive:

My roommate and I belong to a service club on campus. Next month, the club is going to hold a bake sale and plans to give the profits to the homeless shelter downtown. We would like to make the largest profit possible, but the members can't agree on how to do that. Even my roommate and I don't agree. She says (and most of the club members agree with her) that the bake sale will make the most profit if each person decides what he or she wants to bake for the sale, gets reimbursed for the cost of the ingredients from the club, and then the club sells everything. She says that's what her high school basketball team did to finance their trips, and they had plenty of money. (I think their parents contributed most of the money for the trips, but that's a different issue.) I am trying to convince the members of the club that what I learned in my accounting class is relevant here: knowing the cost of baking the goods that the club will sell will help the club (1) plan what to bake, (2) decide how many of each type of baked good it wants to sell, (3) decide how much to charge for each item, and (4) make the largest profit.

I know that most of the club members read your column because we try to guess what your answers are going to be before we read your answers. I also think that they pay attention to what you say. So, will you please explain why I am right? My roommate will buy my dinner if you agree with me.

"Correct on Campus"

Required: Meet with your Dr. Decisive Team and write a response to "Correct on Campus."

END NOTES

[a]http://www.hersheys.com/products/.
[b]Thomas L. Barton and Frederick M. Cole, "Accounting for Magic," *Management Accounting*, January 1991, p. 28.

CHAPTER
17

STANDARD COSTS AND VARIANCE ANALYSIS FOR DECISION MAKING

"IDEALISM INCREASES IN DIRECT PROPORTION TO ONE'S DISTANCE FROM THE PROBLEM."

—JOHN GALSWORTHY

1. What is a price standard and a quantity standard, and how does a company compute a standard cost?

2. What is included in a company's direct materials price and quantity standards?

3. When a company compares its actual direct materials costs to its direct materials standards, how does it determine what caused the difference between the two?

4. What is included in a company's direct labor price and quantity standards?

5. When a company compares its actual direct labor costs to its direct labor standards, how does it determine what caused the difference between the two?

6. How does a company use its manufacturing cost variances to control its operations?

What measures do you use to describe your personal level of fitness? Do you use weight? body fat composition? cholesterol levels? triglyceride levels? strength? resting heart rate? blood pressure? Whatever measures you use, you probably compare them against standards, such as the ideal weight for a 21-year-old woman or man, or the average resting heart rate of serious runners, or the range of reasonable blood pressures. If your fitness level is "substandard," perhaps you alter your diet, change your exercise program, or visit with your doctor to get ideas for moving your fitness level closer to the standard—or to control your weight, body fat composition, cholesterol level, and so forth.

A company also tries to measure and control its "fitness." In earlier chapters, we discussed how a company uses ratios, industry averages, and comparisons with competitors' ratios to evaluate its performance. A company also uses its cost accounting system to measure its "fitness." When a company's costs deviate from its standards, the company uses this information to locate problems and fix them or, in other words, to *control* its operations.

In Chapter 16 we discussed cost accounting systems primarily in regard to *product costing*. We described two types of cost accounting systems: job order and process cost accounting systems. Most manufacturing companies use these systems, or some combination of these systems, to assign direct materials, direct labor, and factory overhead costs to the products they make. But they also use the information from these same cost accounting systems to help managers *plan* and *control* company operations.

In this chapter we will emphasize the use of cost accounting systems in controlling a company's operations. Our discussion focuses on the development of *standard costs* and how managers use them to evaluate the manufacturing activities of a company, or the company's manufacturing "fitness."

MORE ABOUT STANDARD COSTS

Remember from our discussion in Chapter 11 of Volume 1 that **standard costs** are the costs that a company *should* incur in performing an activity or producing a product under a given set of planned operating conditions. As you saw in Chapter 12 of Volume 1, standard costs are useful in planning because they aid in the development of budgets. Managers can use standard costs to help them develop, for any level of planned production, raw materials budgets, direct labor budgets, and factory overhead budgets. Managers can also use standard costs of selling activities (such as costs of finished goods warehouse operations, shipping, and delivery) and standard costs of some general and administrative expenses to help them prepare the selling expenses budget and the general and administrative expenses budget.

However, the most valuable use of standard costs is in controlling a company's operations. As you saw in Chapter 12 of Volume 1, managers can use flexible budgeting in their control activities. A "flexible budget" for manufacturing costs shows the standard costs for direct materials, direct labor, and factory overhead at various levels of production. Managers can use this flexible budget information as a benchmark against which to measure the actual costs of production. If an actual production cost is different from the standard cost budgeted for the actual level of production (in other words, if there is a *variance),* one or more of the planned conditions must not have existed. When the actual cost is greater than the standard cost, the variance is *unfavorable.* When the actual cost is less than the standard cost, the variance is *favorable.* By analyzing this unfavorable or favorable variance, managers can determine which of the planned conditions did not exist and decide what changes, if any, to make in the company's operations.

> **1** What is a price standard and a quantity standard, and how does a company compute a standard cost?

Can you think of a situation where it really might not be favorable for the company if the actual cost of some activity is less than the standard cost of that activity?

Recording Standard Costs in the Accounts

When a manufacturing company uses a **standard cost system**, it normally assigns standard costs rather than actual costs to each of its inventory accounts (Raw Materials

Inventory, Goods-in-Process Inventory, and Finished Goods Inventory). This simplifies cost recording by *eliminating* the following tasks:

1. Keeping detailed records of actual costs to support the raw materials inventory; the supporting raw materials inventory records can be kept in *physical quantities* only
2. Recording *actual* costs on job order cost sheets in job order costing
3. Calculating *actual* costs per unit in process costing

By assigning standard costs to inventory accounts, managers avoid assigning different costs to identical units in inventory just because problems (such as inefficient production by a new employee, a machine breakdown, or the use of faulty materials) result in production costs that are higher for some units than for others. Thus, a company that uses a standard cost system does not record in inventory the costs that result from inefficiency in manufacturing operations. Rather, it measures these costs as variances and treats them separately from the costs of inventories. In this chapter, we discuss the calculations of variances for direct materials and direct labor, and in the Appendix to this chapter we discuss the calculations of variances for factory overhead. As we discuss these calculations, we will show you how standard costs affect the inventory accounts.

Manufacturing Cost Standards

To understand variance computations and to know what they mean, you need to understand how a company establishes a standard cost for each product it manufactures. Unlimited Decadence, for example, has a standard cost for each case of candy bars it produces. But as you know, a company calculates the cost of its manufactured products by adding together the costs of its *inputs*—direct materials, direct labor, and factory overhead. (The *cost* of Unlimited Decadence's candy bars is made up of the costs of the ingredients, labor, and overhead that went into manufacturing the candy bars.) These input costs are based on the quantity of inputs for each product and their costs. Therefore, a company establishes the *standard* cost of a unit of product output (e.g., a case of candy bars) by determining two standards for each *input* to the manufacturing process. The two standards for each of these inputs are a price standard and a quantity standard.

A **price standard** is the *cost* that a company should incur to acquire one unit of *input* for a manufacturing process. Examples of price standards include the cost per pound for direct materials and the cost per hour for direct labor. Unlimited Decadence's direct materials purchases budget, which we discussed and illustrated in Chapter 12 of Volume 1, shows that the standard price for a pound of sugar is $0.35. Its direct labor budget shows that the standard cost for labor is $12 per hour.

A **quantity standard** is the *number* of units of an *input* that a company should use to produce one unit of product *output*. For example, Unlimited Decadence uses 4 pounds of sugar and 0.5 hours of direct labor (product input) for each case of Darkly Decadent candy bars it produces (product output). These amounts—4 pounds per case and 0.5 hours per case—are the quantity standards for direct materials and direct labor.

A company determines the **standard cost of an input** *for one unit of product output* by multiplying the quantity standard of the input by its price standard. So at Unlimited Decadence, the standard cost of sugar for one case of Darkly Decadent candy bars is $1.40 (4 pounds × $0.35). The standard cost of labor for a case of Darkly Decadent candy bars is $6 (0.5 hours × $12).

A manufacturing company spends a lot of time and effort designing its products and its manufacturing operations for efficient production. It tries to determine the least costly way of manufacturing each product, while maintaining high product quality, by considering (1) the prices of various types, sizes, and qualities of direct materials, and (2) the expected direct labor and factory overhead costs that would result from using different combinations of direct labor and machine operations. This planning process results in a

EXHIBIT 17-1	STANDARD MANUFACTURING COSTS: CASE OF DARKLY DECADENT CANDY BARS

UNLIMITED DECADENCE
Darkly Decadent Candy Bars

Inputs	Standard Quantity and Price	Standard Cost per Output Unit
Direct materials (sugar)	4 pounds @ $0.35	$ 1.40
Other direct materials	(assumed)	2.94
Direct labor	0.5 DLH @ $12.00	6.00
Factory overhead		
Variable	0.5 DLH @ $0.64	0.32
Fixed	0.5 DLH @ $2.52	1.26
Total standard cost per case		$11.92

set of specific conditions for the production of the company's products. The company determines price and quantity standards for direct materials, direct labor, and factory overhead from these planned conditions.

Exhibit 17-1 shows the standard manufacturing costs for one case of Darkly Decadent candy bars. The planned conditions for the production of these candy bars provide the basis for all of the illustrations and exhibits in this chapter.

Notice in Exhibit 17-1 how we computed the standard costs per case of candy bars by multiplying the quantity standard for each input by its price standard. For example, we determined the $1.40 standard sugar cost of a case of Darkly Decadent candy bars by multiplying the quantity standard (4 pounds per case of Darkly Decadent candy bars) by the price standard ($0.35 per pound of sugar). To simplify the illustration, we show how Unlimited Decadence computed the standard cost of one direct material—sugar. We show a summary figure, $2.94, for the total standard cost of all the other direct materials, although in reality, Unlimited Decadence would have computed the standard cost of each of the direct materials. Also notice that we set the standard factory overhead rates (price standards for factory overhead) separately for variable and fixed overhead ($0.64 per hour variable and $2.52 per hour fixed). We established the quantity standards for fixed and variable factory overhead by determining the number of direct labor hours (DLH) required per case of candy bars under planned operating conditions (0.5 direct labor hours per case). In Chapter 16, under the job order cost accounting system, we applied *total* factory overhead to the cost of a case of candy bars at a rate of $3.16 per direct labor hour.

STANDARD COSTS AND VARIANCES FOR DIRECT MATERIALS

You just learned that a company sets standard costs for each of the direct materials it uses to manufacture its products. But how does it determine the standard costs for direct materials and compute the variances between standard and actual direct materials costs? And how do the standard costs and variances affect its cost accounting system?

2 What is included in a company's direct materials price and quantity standards?

Direct Materials Price and Quantity Standards

Before a company uses standard costs for its direct materials, it first sets its direct materials price and quantity standards.

Direct Materials Price Standard

As we discussed earlier, a **direct materials price standard** shows the *cost* that a company should incur to acquire one unit of a direct material for production. The cost includes two factors: (1) the invoice price (less any expected discounts) to be paid to normal suppliers when the company purchases materials in expected quantities, and (2) any transportation costs the company expects to pay.

Direct Materials Quantity Standard

A **direct materials quantity standard** shows the *amount* of a direct material that a company should use to produce one unit of product. This amount includes three factors: (1) the amount of materials that should end up in each "good" unit[1] of product; (2) an allowance for materials normally lost through various manufacturing operations ("waste"); and (3) an allowance for *normal* amounts of spoiled production ("spoilage"—products that are not "up to snuff" and, therefore, unacceptable for sale). In this way the direct materials quantity standard shows the average (normal) amount of a material that the company should use per unit of product when it performs manufacturing operations under planned conditions.

 Why do you think both direct materials that are normally lost through various manufacturing operations and normal amounts of spoiled production are included in the direct materials quantity standard?

Setting Standards for Direct Materials

Exhibit 17-2 shows the computations of the direct materials price and quantity standards for the sugar used by Unlimited Decadence to produce Darkly Decadent candy bars, the product whose standard cost we showed in Exhibit 17-1.

EXHIBIT 17-2	DIRECT MATERIALS PRICE AND QUANTITY STANDARDS

UNLIMITED DECADENCE
Direct Materials Price and Quantity Standards for Sugar
Case of Darkly Decadent Candy Bars

Price standard (dollars per pound)*
Invoice price	$0.24
Transportation charges	0.11
Standard price per pound	$0.35

Quantity standard (pounds per case)†
Material content per completed unit	3.90 pounds
Allowance for waste in pouring, mixing, refining, molding	0.10 pounds
Standard quantity per case	4.00 pounds

*Materials are purchased in 50-pound bags in multiples of 20. At that quantity the normal supplier charges $0.24 per pound. If purchased in smaller quantities, the price would be $0.25 per pound. The normal supplier offers terms of n/30. Materials are to be shipped by rail from the supplier to St. Louis, where they are to be picked up by a local trucking company and brought to the plant, unloaded, inspected, and stacked in the storeroom at a total cost of $110 for each 20 bags (1,000 pounds) purchased.
†The manufacturing process involves pouring the 50-pound bags of sugar into bins, followed by mixing the sugar with other ingredients, refining the chocolate mix, and molding it into candy bars. During these processes, an average of 1.25 pounds of sugar is lost from each bag (when the sugar is poured into the bins and when chocolate paste is left in the mixing, refining, and molding equipment). Materials lost through pouring, mixing, refining, and molding are hauled away at no charge by a shelter for the homeless.

---

[1] In our later discussion, one unit always refers to one "good" unit.

Notice the conditions that are important in setting the price standard. Price standards are influenced by the type, size, and quality of the required direct materials, but they also are influenced by several other conditions. Planned purchase quantities affect the invoice price. The supplier's terms (n/30) also affect the purchase cost. Finally, both shipping by normal freight carriers and unloading and inspecting in the usual manner determine the transportation cost per pound of material. Together these conditions determine the standard price per pound to make the required sugar available for production.

Many conditions also influenced the determination of the direct materials quantity standard in Exhibit 17-2. For example, the size of the 50-pound bags of sugar (in relation to the size of the desired product) affects the pouring, mixing, refining, and molding operations and determines the resulting sugar content of the product and the allowance for waste. In determining that no allowance for normal spoilage is necessary for this product, Unlimited Decadence also considers the quality of the sugar as well as the proper adjustment of the equipment, the skill level of the laborers, and the condition of the storage areas for the direct materials and candy bars. Careful study of these conditions enables the engineering and production department personnel to determine the standard quantity of direct materials to be budgeted and used per unit of product.

Direct Materials Price and Quantity Variances

A company that uses standard costs for its direct materials compares these standard costs with actual costs by computing a direct materials price variance and a direct materials quantity variance.

Direct Materials Price Variance

When a company purchases direct materials under conditions other than those planned, the cost per direct material unit may differ from the price standard. If this occurs, it causes a direct materials price variance. A **direct materials price variance** is the difference between the standard cost that a company *should have incurred* to acquire the direct materials and the actual cost it *did* incur to acquire the direct materials. The company computes this variance by multiplying the actual number of direct material units *purchased* by the difference between the standard price and the actual price per direct material unit. Companies normally compute direct materials price variances at the time they purchase materials. Unlimited Decadence makes the computation for its sugar[2] as we show next, assuming it purchased (on credit) 1,500,000 pounds of sugar for the production of Darkly Decadent candy bars at an actual cost of $540,000 ($0.36 per pound):

3 When a company compares its actual direct materials costs to its direct materials standards, how does it determine what caused the difference between the two?

How would you determine the standard cost of one batch of brownies?

Direct Materials Price Variance:

Standard purchase cost	1,500,000 lbs. @ $ 0.35	= $ 525,000
− Actual purchase cost	1,500,000 lbs. @ $ 0.36	= (540,000)
Direct materials price variance	1,500,000 lbs. @ $(0.01)	= $ (15,000) unfavorable

In the computation of the direct materials price variance, the standard purchase cost (what the company *should* have paid) is found by multiplying the total actual quantity purchased by the direct materials price standard ($0.35 from Exhibit 17-2). As a result, Unlimited Decadence computes the $15,000 unfavorable direct materials price variance as the difference between the standard and the actual purchase costs ($525,000 − $540,000). Or it can compute the variance by multiplying the actual number of units purchased times the difference between the standard price and the actual price per unit [1,500,000 pounds × ($0.35 − $0.36)]. The direct materials price variance for sugar

---

[2]Unlimited Decadence also computes direct materials price and quantity variances for its other direct materials. We do not show those computations here.

is *unfavorable* because the actual purchase price per unit is higher than the standard price. In other words, the company paid more than it should have paid for the sugar. If the actual purchase price per unit is less than the standard price, the direct materials price variance is *favorable*. We set up all the variance calculations in this chapter so that *a negative number means an unfavorable variance and a positive number means a favorable variance.*

 Do you think a company should always try to pay less than the standard price for its direct materials if it can? Why or why not?

Direct Materials Quantity Variance

When operating conditions that actually occur during production differ from those planned, the actual quantity of direct materials the company uses to produce a given number of products may differ from the standard direct materials quantity budgeted for that number of products. The **standard direct materials quantity budgeted** is the amount of direct materials that *should be used* for the company's actual production level. It is computed by multiplying the actual number of units produced by the direct materials quantity standard per unit. For example, if Unlimited Decadence produces 360,000 cases of Darkly Decadent candy bars, it should use 1,440,000 pounds (360,000 cases produced × 4 pounds per case from Exhibit 17-2) of direct materials (sugar).

The **direct materials quantity variance** is the difference between the standard cost of the quantity of direct materials that a company *should have used* for the actual number of units produced and the standard cost of the quantity of direct materials that it *did* use to produce those units. In other words, a direct materials quantity variance indicates that the company used more or less direct materials for the actual number of units produced than the standard direct materials quantity budgeted for that number of units. We show this computation next, assuming Unlimited Decadence produced 360,000 cases of Darkly Decadent candy bars during the month and used 1,480,000 pounds of direct materials (sugar) in that production:

Direct Materials Quantity Variance:

Standard quantity budgeted at standard price	1,440,000* lbs. @ $0.35	= $ 504,000
−Actual quantity used at standard price	1,480,000 lbs. @ $0.35	= (518,000)
Direct materials quantity variance	(40,000) lbs. @ $0.35	= $ (14,000) unfavorable

*360,000 cases of candy bars × 4 pounds per case = 1,440,000 pounds.

The key to computing the direct materials quantity variance is a correct computation of the standard direct materials quantity budgeted for the actual number of units produced. Remember that the standard direct materials quantity budgeted is computed by multiplying the *actual* number of units produced by the direct materials quantity standard for one unit (360,000 cases of Darkly Decadent candy bars × 4 pounds per case = 1,440,000 pounds). Notice in the computation of the direct materials quantity variance that both the standard direct materials quantity budgeted and the actual direct materials used are multiplied by the $0.35 price standard for the direct materials (sugar). Thus, Unlimited Decadence can compute the direct materials quantity variance by finding the difference between the standard direct materials quantity *budgeted* for the actual number of cases produced and the actual direct materials *used,* and multiplying that difference by the direct materials price standard [e.g., (1,440,000 − 1,480,000) × $0.35]. Notice also that the $14,000 direct materials quantity variance for sugar is *unfavorable* because the actual quantity of direct materials used is more than the standard quantity budgeted for the production of 360,000 cases of Darkly Decadent candy bars. If the actual quantity of direct materials used is less than the standard quantity budgeted for a given output, the direct materials quantity variance is *favorable.*

If a case of Darkly Decadent candy bars requires 4 pounds of sugar, what do you think would cause Unlimited Decadence to use more sugar in the production of these candy bars?

Recording Direct Materials Variances

To assign standard costs to inventories, a company must separate variances from actual costs and record the variances separately in variance accounts. A company records its direct materials price variances at the time it purchases direct materials. Unlimited Decadence records the credit purchase of 1,500,000 pounds of sugar for the production of Darkly Decadent candy bars as follows (this entry relates to the direct materials price variance computation we showed earlier):

Assets	=	Liabilities	+	Stockholders' Equity		
					Net Income	
				Revenues	−	Expenses
Raw Materials Inventory		Accounts Payable				Direct Materials Price Variance
+$525,000		+$540,000				+$15,000

> **FINANCIAL STATEMENT EFFECTS**
>
> Increases current assets and total assets on **balance sheet**. Increases current liabilities and total liabilities on **balance sheet**. Increases unfavorable direct materials price variance (and therefore increases cost of goods sold), which decreases net income on **income statement** (and therefore decreases stockholders' equity on **balance sheet**).

Note that Unlimited Decadence recorded the $540,000 actual purchase cost of the 1,500,000 pounds of sugar (1,500,000 lbs. @ $0.36) as Accounts Payable. (It *does owe* its supplier the actual purchase price of the sugar!) However, it added the $525,000 standard cost of these direct materials (1,500,000 lbs. @ $0.35) to Raw Materials Inventory. Thus *it keeps the Raw Materials Inventory account at standard cost.* The $15,000 unfavorable direct materials price variance (1,500,000 lbs. @ $0.01) is recorded in a separate account entitled Direct Materials Price Variance. Note that all "variance" accounts are "temporary" stockholders' equity accounts. As we briefly discuss later, a company normally closes its variance accounts to its Cost of Goods Sold account (an expense account) at the end of the accounting period. Thus, the rules for recording unfavorable and favorable variances relate to the rules for recording expenses. An unfavorable variance (i.e., more cost than planned) increases cost of goods sold (expense), so *an **unfavorable** variance during the accounting period is **added to** the variance account.* A favorable variance (less cost than planned) decreases cost of goods sold, so it is like a *contra-expense* (we discussed contra accounts in Chapter 13). *A **favorable** variance during the accounting period is **subtracted from** the variance account.*

Why do you think variance accounts affect stockholders' equity? If a company did not use a standard costing system, would its total stockholders' equity be the same as or different from what it would be if the company were using a standard costing system? Why?

A company records its direct materials quantity variances as it *uses* direct materials. Unlimited Decadence records the use of 1,480,000 pounds of sugar to produce 360,000 cases of Darkly Decadent candy bars as follows (this entry relates to the direct materials quantity variance computation we showed earlier):

Assets		=	Liabilities	+	Stockholders' Equity		
						Net Income	
					Revenues	−	Expenses
Raw Materials Inventory	Goods-in-Process Inventory						Direct Materials Quantity Variance
Bal $525,000							
−518,000	+ $504,000						+$14,000
Bal $ 7,000							

> **FINANCIAL STATEMENT EFFECTS**
>
> Decreases current assets and total assets on **balance sheet**. Increases unfavorable direct materials quantity variance (and therefore increases cost of goods sold), which decreases net income on **income statement** (and therefore decreases stockholders' equity on **balance sheet**).

Note that Unlimited Decadence reduced the Raw Materials Inventory account by the $518,000 standard cost of the *actual* sugar used (1,480,000 lbs. @ $0.35). This 1,480,000 pounds is the quantity of sugar that it actually moved out of the raw materials warehouse and into production. However, it added the $504,000 standard cost of the *standard direct materials quantity budgeted* (1,440,000 lbs. @ $0.35) to the Goods-in-Process Inventory account.[3] Thus *it also keeps the Goods-in-Process Inventory account at standard cost.* Note that the $14,000 unfavorable direct materials quantity variance is added to the Direct Materials Quantity Variance account. When Unlimited Decadence closes this variance account, it will increase its Cost of Goods Sold account. Later in this chapter, after we discuss direct labor and factory overhead variances, we will discuss how managers use the direct materials price and quantity variance.

A Diagram of Direct Materials Variance Computations

An illustration of the direct materials variance computations may be helpful in understanding the preceding computations and the amounts appearing in the entries we just described. With prices on the vertical dimension and quantities on the horizontal dimension, actual cost totals, standard cost totals, and variances appear as areas of the rectangles in Exhibit 17-3.

The area of the entire rectangle (actual quantity purchased × actual price) is the $540,000 total actual cost of direct materials purchased (1,500,000 lbs. @ $0.36). The long, thin horizontal rectangle (1) labeled as the direct materials price variance ($15,000 unfavorable) has an area equal to the actual quantity purchased times the difference be-

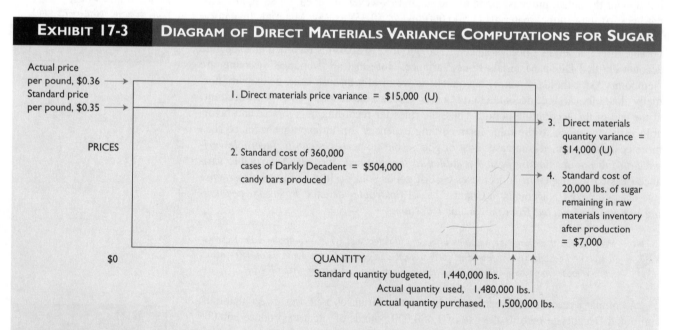

EXHIBIT 17-3   DIAGRAM OF DIRECT MATERIALS VARIANCE COMPUTATIONS FOR SUGAR

1. The direct materials price variance is $0.01 for each pound of sugar purchased. For 1,500,000 pounds purchased, the total unfavorable direct materials price variance is $15,000.
2. The standard cost of sugar for producing cases of Darkly Decadent candy bars is $0.35 per pound. For 360,000 cases, the standard number of pounds budgeted is 1,440,000 for a standard cost of $504,000.
3. But Unlimited Decadence used 40,000 additional pounds of sugar. The standard cost of those extra pounds, at $0.35 per pound, is $14,000 — the unfavorable direct materials quantity variance.
4. The standard cost of 20,000 pounds of sugar remaining in raw materials inventory from the purchase, at $0.35 per pound, is $7,000.

[3]Unlimited Decadence also adds $1,058,400 of standard cost [360,000 cases × $2.94 (from Exhibit 17-1)] for other direct materials to the Goods-in-Process Inventory account. We do not show that entry here.

tween the standard price paid and the actual price [1,500,000 lbs. × ($0.35 − $0.36)]. When the $15,000 unfavorable direct materials price variance is subtracted from the $540,000 total actual purchase cost, the $525,000 remainder represents the standard cost of the actual quantity purchased (1,500,000 lbs. @ $0.35). Note in Exhibit 17-3 that the rectangle (2, 3, and 4) representing this $525,000 remainder is divided into three smaller rectangles. From left to right, the three rectangles represent (2) the $504,000 standard cost of the standard quantity of sugar Unlimited Decadence should have used in manufacturing 360,000 cases (1,440,000 lbs. @ $0.35), (3) the $14,000 unfavorable direct materials quantity variance [(1,440,000 − 1,480,000 lbs.) × $0.35], and (4) the $7,000 standard cost of the 20,000 pounds of unused direct materials (sugar) remaining from this purchase in the raw materials inventory for future use [(1,500,000 − 1,480,000 lbs.) × $0.35].

STANDARD COSTS AND VARIANCES FOR DIRECT LABOR

A company also determines standard costs and computes variances for the direct labor it uses to manufacture its products. This section shows how a company determines standard costs for direct labor, how it computes variances between standard and actual direct labor costs, and how it records the standard direct labor costs and variances in its cost accounting system.

4 What is included in a company's direct labor price and quantity standards?

Direct Labor Price and Quantity Standards

Before a company uses standard costs for its direct labor, it first sets its direct labor price and quantity standards.

Direct Labor Price Standard

A **direct labor price standard** shows the current wage rate that a company should incur per hour for a specific type of direct labor employed in production. Examples of different types of direct labor include machinists, welders, painters, assembly workers, and cooks. For Unlimited Decadence, direct labor includes employees who work as mixers, refiners, molders, and wrappers. Direct labor price standards also may be set to include an allowance for payroll taxes and fringe benefits. Although a company that does not use a standard cost system normally treats these additional payroll costs as factory overhead costs, it is common for a company that *does use* a standard cost system to include such items in its

"We've found the key to productivity. Its
Fred, down in the shop. He makes the stuff."

direct labor price standards. In setting the price standard for each manufacturing operation required to make one unit of product, a company assumes that the operation is performed by a properly trained operator earning the usual wage rate for that operation.

Direct Labor Quantity Standard

A **direct labor quantity standard** shows the amount of direct labor time that a company should use to produce one unit of product. A company sets direct labor quantity standards in a two-step process. First, it carefully studies the time required to perform the direct labor operations needed to produce a product. Then, it allows for *normal* amounts of labor time used for personnel rest breaks, machine adjustments and idle time, and production of normal amounts of spoiled units. A direct labor quantity standard shows the direct labor time the company expects to use per unit when it performs manufacturing operations under planned conditions.

Setting Standards for Direct Labor

Exhibit 17-4 shows the computations of the price and quantity standards for the direct labor used in producing Darkly Decadent candy bars. For simplicity we assume that the same labor rate is earned by all workers in each direct labor operation.

In Exhibit 17-4 the direct labor price standard of $12 per hour includes the basic wage rate of $9.60 in both departments plus payroll tax and fringe benefit allowances that total $2.40. Unlimited Decadence set the quantity standard for direct labor by adding the standard hours per unit of product for the various required labor operations and the normal amounts of rest breaks and machine adjustments. Mixing (0.15 hours) and refining operations (0.25 hours) prepare the direct materials so that they are ready for the molding and wrapping operations (0.1 hours). After the molding and wrapping operations are completed, the cases of Darkly Decadent candy bars are finished. At that time each case should have had a total of 0.5 direct labor hours devoted to it.

Direct Labor Price and Efficiency Variances

A company that uses standard costs for its direct labor compares those standard costs with actual direct labor costs by computing a direct labor price variance and a direct labor efficiency variance.

EXHIBIT 17-4	**DIRECT LABOR PRICE AND QUANTITY STANDARDS**

UNLIMITED DECADENCE
Direct Labor Price and Quantity Standards for
a Case of Darkly Decadent Candy Bars

Price standard (dollars per direct labor hour)*

Basic wage rate	$ 9.60
Payroll taxes (Social Security and unemployment compensation)................	1.44
Fringe benefits (vacation pay, insurance, etc.)	0.96
Standard price (rate) per direct labor hour..	$12.00

Quantity standard (direct labor hours per case)

Mixing operations	0.15 hours
Refining operations..	0.25
Molding and wrapping operations...	0.10
Standard direct labor quantity per case..	0.50 hours

*We assume in this exhibit that payroll taxes total 15% of the basic wage rate. We assume fringe benefits to be 10% of the basic wage rate. We use these rates for simplicity.

Direct Labor Price Variance

The **direct labor price variance** is the difference between the cost that a company *should have incurred* for the actual number of labor hours worked [at the standard direct labor price (rate) per hour] and the actual direct labor cost it *did* incur for the number of actual labor hours worked. It is also known as the direct labor *rate* variance. The direct labor price (rate) variance shows how much of the difference between the standard and actual direct labor costs can be explained by the difference between the standard and actual labor rates. A company computes the direct labor price variance by multiplying the actual direct labor hours worked by the difference between the direct labor price standard and the actual direct labor price per hour. We show this computation next, assuming 182,000 direct labor hours were worked (to produce 360,000 cases of Darkly Decadent candy bars) at a total direct labor cost of $2,165,800 ($11.90 per hour):

Direct Labor Price Variance:

Actual hours at standard price	182,000 hours @ $12.00 =	$ 2,184,000
−Actual direct labor cost	182,000 hours @ $11.90 =	(2,165,800)
Direct labor price variance	182,000 hours @ $ 0.10 =	$ 18,200 favorable

Note that we computed the direct labor cost that Unlimited Decadence should have incurred for the actual number of hours worked by multiplying the actual number of hours times the direct labor price standard ($12.00 from Exhibit 17-4). As a result, we can compute the $18,200 favorable direct labor price variance as the difference between the standard direct labor cost and the actual direct labor cost ($2,184,000 − $2,165,800) or by multiplying the actual number of hours worked by the difference between the standard price and the actual price (rate) per hour [182,000 hours × ($12.00 − $11.90)]. This direct labor price variance is *favorable* because the actual direct labor rate per hour is less than the direct labor price standard. If the actual rate per hour exceeds the standard rate, the direct labor price variance is *unfavorable*.

 Can you think of a situation where a favorable direct labor price variance may actually be unfavorable for a company? Why would this be the case?

Direct Labor Efficiency Variance

When actual operating conditions during production differ from the planned conditions, the total actual direct labor hours that a company's employees work may differ from the standard direct labor hours budgeted for the number of products manufactured. Here, the **standard direct labor hours budgeted** is the number of direct labor hours that *should be used* for the company's actual production level. A company computes the standard direct labor hours budgeted by multiplying the actual number of units produced by the standard direct labor hours per unit (the direct labor quantity standard). For example, when Unlimited Decadence produces 360,000 cases of Darkly Decadent candy bars, it should use 180,000 direct labor hours (360,000 cases produced × 0.5 standard direct labor hours per case from Exhibit 17-4).

The **direct labor efficiency variance** is the difference between the standard cost of the direct labor hours that a company *should have used* for the actual number of units produced and the standard cost of the direct labor hours that it *did* use to produce those units.[4] In other words, a direct labor efficiency variance indicates that the *actual* direct labor hours that the company's employees worked on the actual number of units produced were more or less than the standard direct labor hours *budgeted* for that number of units. We illustrate the computation next, assuming Unlimited Decadence produced 360,000

5 When a company compares its actual direct labor costs to its direct labor standards, how does it determine what caused the difference between the two?

---

[4]The direct labor efficiency variance is sometimes called the direct labor quantity variance because its computation is similar to the direct materials quantity variance. However, employees may react negatively to being thought of as a quantity rather than as efficient contributors to the company's activities. Hence, we refer to the variance as the direct labor efficiency variance.

cases of Darkly Decadent candy bars during the month and its employees worked 182,000 actual direct labor hours:

Direct Labor Efficiency Variance:

Standard hours budgeted at standard price	180,000 hours[*] @ $12.00 =	$ 2,160,000
−Actual hours at standard price	182,000 hours @ $12.00 =	(2,184,000)
Direct labor efficiency variance	(2,000) hours @ $12.00 =	$ (24,000) unfavorable

[*]360,000 cases of candy bars × 0.5 hours per unit = 180,000 hours.

The key to computing the direct labor efficiency variance is a correct computation of the standard direct labor hours budgeted for the actual number of units produced. Remember that a company computes the standard direct labor hours budgeted by multiplying the *actual* number of units produced by the direct labor quantity standard for one unit (360,000 cases × 0.5 hours per case = 180,000 standard direct labor hours budgeted). This means that employees of Unlimited Decadence should have worked 180,000 direct labor hours when they produced 360,000 cases of Darkly Decadent candy bars. Notice in the efficiency variance computation that both the standard direct labor hours budgeted and the actual direct labor hours are multiplied by the $12.00 price standard. Thus the $24,000 unfavorable direct labor efficiency variance can be computed by finding the difference between the standard direct labor hours budgeted (for the actual number of cases produced) and the actual direct labor hours worked, and multiplying that difference by the direct labor price standard [e.g., (180,000 − 182,000) × $12]. Notice also that the $24,000 direct labor efficiency variance is *unfavorable* because the employees actually worked more hours than the standard direct labor hours budgeted for the production of 360,000 cases of Darkly Decadent candy bars. If the actual direct labor hours worked are less than the standard direct labor hours budgeted for a given output, the direct labor efficiency variance is *favorable*.

 Can you think of a situation where a favorable direct labor efficiency variance may actually be unfavorable for the company? Why would this be the case?

Recording Direct Labor Variances

A company records both the direct labor price variance and the direct labor efficiency variance at the time production takes place. In a standard cost system, a company adds the standard cost of direct labor to the Goods-in-Process Inventory account. Unlimited Decadence records the use of 182,000 direct labor hours for the production of 360,000 cases of Darkly Decadent candy bars as follows (this entry relates to the computations of both the direct labor price variance and the direct labor efficiency variance we showed earlier):

<table>
<tr><td>Assets</td><td>=</td><td>Liabilities</td><td>+</td><td colspan="4" align="center">Stockholders' Equity</td></tr>
<tr><td></td><td></td><td></td><td></td><td colspan="4" align="center">Net Income</td></tr>
<tr><td></td><td></td><td></td><td></td><td align="center">Revenues</td><td>−</td><td colspan="2" align="center">Expenses</td></tr>
<tr><td>Goods-in-Process Inventory</td><td></td><td>Wages Payable</td><td></td><td></td><td></td><td>Direct Labor Price Variance</td><td>Direct Labor Efficiency Variance</td></tr>
<tr><td>Bal $1,562,400[*]
+2,160,000</td><td></td><td>+$2,165,800</td><td></td><td></td><td>−</td><td>−$18,200</td><td>+$24,000</td></tr>
<tr><td>Bal $3,722,400</td><td></td><td></td><td></td><td></td><td></td><td></td><td></td></tr>
</table>

[*]Standard costs for sugar ($504,000 = 360,000 cases × $1.40) and for direct materials other than sugar ($1,058,400 = 360,000 cases × $2.94) from Exhibit 17-1.

Note that Unlimited Decadence recorded the actual direct labor cost incurred (182,000 hours @ $11.90 = $2,165,800) as Wages Payable. However, it added the $2,160,000 standard cost for 360,000 cases of Darkly Decadent candy bars (180,000 standard direct labor hours budgeted @ $12 per hour) to the Goods-in-Process Inventory account to keep that account at standard cost. (Notice it includes the standard costs for direct materials we recorded earlier.) Also note that it recorded the $18,200 favorable direct labor

---

FINANCIAL STATEMENT EFFECTS

Increases current assets and total assets on *balance sheet*. Increases current liabilities and total liabilities on *balance sheet*. Decreases direct labor price variance, increases direct labor efficiency variance [and therefore increases (net) cost of goods sold], which decreases net income on *income statement* (and therefore decreases stockholders' equity on *balance sheet*).

EXHIBIT 17-5	DIAGRAM OF DIRECT LABOR VARIANCE COMPUTATIONS

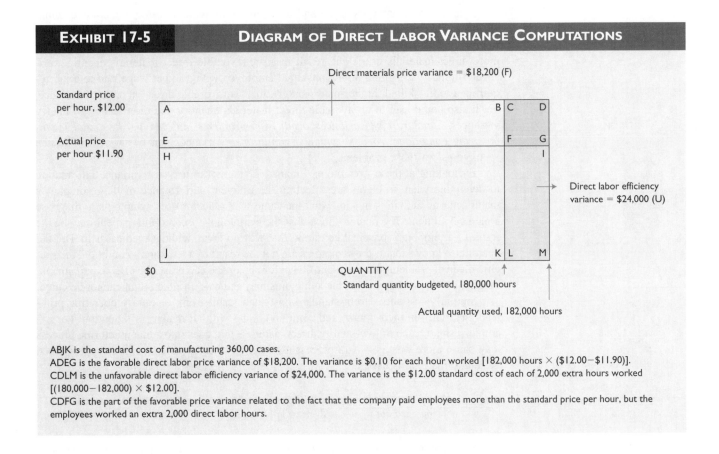

ABJK is the standard cost of manufacturing 360,00 cases.
ADEG is the favorable direct labor price variance of $18,200. The variance is $0.10 for each hour worked [182,000 hours × ($12.00−$11.90)].
CDLM is the unfavorable direct labor efficiency variance of $24,000. The variance is the $12.00 standard cost of each of 2,000 extra hours worked [(180,000−182,000) × $12.00].
CDFG is the part of the favorable price variance related to the fact that the company paid employees more than the standard price per hour, but the employees worked an extra 2,000 direct labor hours.

price variance and the $24,000 unfavorable direct labor efficiency variance in separate variance accounts. When Unlimited Decadence closes these variance accounts, the net effect will be to increase its Cost of Goods Sold account by $5,800 ($24,000 − $18,200).

A Diagram of Direct Labor Price Variance Computations

Exhibit 17-5 shows the preceding direct labor variance computations and the amounts appearing in the entries we just described. As in Exhibit 17-3, prices are on the vertical dimension and quantities are on the horizontal dimension. Actual cost totals, standard cost totals, and variances appear as areas of the rectangles. The area of rectangle ABJK is the $2,160,000 standard cost of the quantity of labor Unlimited Decadence *should have used* in manufacturing 360,000 cases of Darkly Decadent candy bars (180,000 hours @ $12.00 per hour). The area of rectangle HIJM is the $2,265,800 actual cost of the labor Unlimited Decadence *actually* used to manufacture 360,000 cases (182,000 hours @ $11.90 per hour). Note that there is a $5,800 ($2,160,000 − $2,165,800) unfavorable total variance. The area of rectangle ADEG is the $18,200 favorable direct labor price variance [182,000 hours × ($12.00 − $11.90)], caused by the fact that the actual price was less than the standard price. The area of rectangle CDLM is the $24,000 unfavorable direct labor efficiency variance [(180,000 hours − 182,000 hours) × $12], caused by the fact that the company used more direct labor hours than it planned to use to manufacture 360,000 cases.

USING MANUFACTURING COST VARIANCES TO CONTROL OPERATIONS

The standard costs are the costs that a company expects to incur when its manufacturing operations are running as smoothly as its managers have planned. When problems occur in these operations, however, variances arise. If a machine is out of adjustment, it can

6 How does a company use its manufacturing cost variances to control its operations?

cause more direct materials usage and result in an unfavorable direct materials quantity variance. The purchase of a less-expensive grade of material than needed for the production of a product causes a favorable direct materials price variance, but it also could cause more direct materials usage and result in an unfavorable direct materials quantity variance. Similarly, assigning a new unskilled employee with a lower wage rate to a job requiring a more-skilled, higher-paid worker causes a favorable direct labor price variance, but it also could lead to unfavorable direct materials quantity and direct labor efficiency variances. *Standard cost variances result from problems that change the actual manufacturing conditions from the planned conditions.* Variances can be thought of as the "symptoms" of those problems.

By looking at these "symptoms," managers attempt to use cost variance information to determine what problems are affecting the efficient performance of their company's manufacturing activities in somewhat the same way a doctor uses symptoms to diagnose a medical ailment. The doctor knows that the symptoms observed in a patient may be the result of a temporary physical condition that will go away without medical help. But the doctor also knows that if the symptoms are not the result of a temporary condition, the specific medical problem must be identified before he or she can prescribe effective treatment. Finally, the doctor knows that the symptoms may indicate an illness that cannot be cured.

Similarly, variances from standard costs can result from temporary operating problems that will run their course and come to an end without managers' attention. For example, a small batch of low-quality direct materials that goes into a manufacturing process may cause more waste or extra processing time, but these problems will disappear when the faulty material is used up.

 What circumstances might cause managers to decide to scrap the low-quality direct materials and not try to use them up in production?

Variances can also be caused by uncontrollable changes in operating conditions, such as labor rate changes resulting from a new union contract or changes in direct materials prices. However, variances may result from operating problems that, if identified, can be corrected so that future operations will be more efficient.

To make variance computations more helpful to managers in identifying specific problems, management accountants follow three general rules:

1. They try to measure variances as quickly as they can after the variances occur.
2. They try to measure variances in as much detail as is helpful in pinpointing specific problems.
3. They try to report variances to managers who are in a position to identify and correct the problems that are likely to have caused the variances.

Measuring Variances Quickly

Variances should be measured as quickly as possible after they occur so that managers can recognize problems early and correct them before they cause too much damage. Although the variance computations we showed for Unlimited Decadence were based on a period of a month, many companies compute variances weekly or even daily to help identify problems more quickly. Two practices followed by many companies in computing direct materials variances provide an excellent example of how management accountants attempt to follow this general rule.

Direct materials price variances can be computed either as materials are purchased or as they are used. Most companies compute direct materials price variances at the time of purchase (as we did in our computation) because these variances are caused by problems arising at the time of purchase. To wait until materials are used (perhaps months after purchase) would delay recognition and correction of those problems.

Direct materials quantity variances also can be computed quickly after they occur. Many companies allow the storekeeper to issue only the standard amount of direct materials required for a given amount of products when the materials requisition is presented. If this amount of materials is not enough to complete production, an additional materials requisition must be presented before more direct materials are issued. This practice ensures that there is a document indicating that an unfavorable direct materials quantity variance is occurring. The supervisors of production operations can then be alerted.

Measuring Variances in Detail

The reason for measuring variances in detail is that these detailed variance computations provide better clues to help managers identify specific problems. We have already discussed some examples of the kinds of detailed computations that are helpful. Rather than computing a single total manufacturing cost variance, for example, we discussed computations of separate variances for two of the inputs to the manufacturing process (direct materials and direct labor). In addition, we described price and quantity variance computations for direct materials and direct labor.

Recall our illustration of the direct labor efficiency variance. The production of Darkly Decadent candy bars required direct labor hours to be worked in mixing, refining, and molding and wrapping operations (see Exhibit 17-4). Using the direct labor quantity standard (0.5 DLH per case) computed in Exhibit 17-4, we determined that 180,000 standard direct labor hours were budgeted to produce 360,000 cases (360,000 × 0.5). We subtracted the 182,000 actual direct labor hours worked from these standard direct labor hours budgeted and multiplied the excess hours (2,000) by the $12 direct labor price standard to compute the overall $24,000 unfavorable direct labor efficiency variance. However, it is more helpful for identifying the problem(s) causing that variance if a company measures the excess labor hours worked in each individual operation or each production department. Then the company can compute the direct labor efficiency variances for the individual operations or departments and correct any problems causing these variances.

For example, recall that the production process includes mixing, refining, and molding and wrapping. Suppose that of the total 182,000 actual direct labor hours, 55,250 actual direct labor hours were worked in mixing, 89,650 actual direct labor hours were worked in refining, and 37,100 actual direct labor hours were worked in molding and wrapping. Exhibit 17-4 shows that the direct labor quantity standard is 0.15 hours in mixing, 0.25 hours in refining, and 0.10 hours in molding and wrapping. Thus the standard direct labor hours budgeted for 360,000 cases is 54,000 hours (360,000 × 0.15) in mixing, 90,000 hours (360,000 × 0.25) in refining, and 36,000 hours (360,000 × 0.10) in molding and wrapping operations. Unlimited Decadence can compute the direct labor efficiency variance for each operation, as we show here:

Direct Labor Efficiency Variances:

Mixing [(54,000 − 55,250) × $12]	$(15,000) unfavorable
Refining [(90,000 − 89,650) × $12]	4,200 favorable
Molding and wrapping [(36,000 − 37,100) × $12]	(13,200) unfavorable
Total unfavorable variance	$(24,000)

Note in this computation that the direct labor efficiency variances for mixing ($15,000) and for molding and wrapping ($13,200) are unfavorable because the actual direct labor hours are more than the standard direct labor hours budgeted. In refining, however, the $4,200 direct labor efficiency variance is favorable. The value of this more detailed direct labor efficiency variance computation is that it helps focus managers' attention on individual operations or departments. In this way, operations that are inefficient can be found. Operations that are especially efficient also can be recognized. Investigations of the causes of both unfavorable and favorable variances can often help improve the efficiency of future operations.

Reporting Variances

To be useful, manufacturing cost variance information must be communicated to managers who can correct problems in the manufacturing operations by the actions they take or the decisions they make. By measuring variances in enough detail to separate variances incurred in different operations or departments, or during different work shifts in the same department, a company can provide various managers with reports showing the variances that result from the operations for which they are responsible. These reports can help the managers identify and correct their departments' operating problems.

Reporting favorable variances to managers is just as important as reporting unfavorable variances. Favorable variances normally indicate that performance of manufacturing activities was better than planned and may indicate opportunities for continued good performance. The company can reward employees who have done a particularly good job and can share with other employees new or innovative production methods that may have caused the favorable variances. *Favorable* variances, however, are not always good. They sometimes can result from potentially serious problems. For example, the $4,200 favorable direct labor efficiency variance computed for the refining operations could be an indication of employees' hasty and sloppy processing, which might lead to customer dissatisfaction and lost sales. Thus, both unfavorable and favorable variances may be indications of potential trouble. So, it is important that managers understand what caused the unfavorable and favorable variances.

Of course, not all manufacturing cost variances deserve managers' attention. Some variances result from minor problems that are not long-lasting and not serious enough for managers to incur the cost of investigating the problems. Other variances may quickly be recognized as resulting from permanent and uncontrollable changes in operating conditions, suggesting the need for revision of the price or quantity standards. For example, a direct labor price variance may be caused by increased wage rates resulting from a new union contract. A company should note this change in conditions and revise the direct labor price standard.

By considering the absolute or relative size of variances, managers direct their attention to the operations that are most likely to benefit from attention. That is, the detailed variance analysis can enable managers to use the principle of *management by exception.* Variance computations are especially helpful when they are computed quickly after they occur and are reported to the managers who can take corrective action.

THE FLEXIBILITY OF VARIANCES

Although variance analysis is a technique developed and used by manufacturing companies, it is flexible enough to be used for other purposes. For example, a company's sales managers may notice a variance between budgeted sales and actual sales. By doing a variance analysis similar to one we described in this chapter, the managers would be able to identify the portion of the variance that is due to a difference between the actual and the budgeted sales price, and the part that is due to the fact that the company sold more or fewer products than it planned to sell. They also would be able to identify how much of the difference between actual and budgeted sales is due to a difference in sales mix. This type of analysis allows managers to focus on specific questions, the answers to which will help them improve the company's performance. Some questions that they might ask include: Why were sales lower than expected? Were lower sales a result of the economy, or were they a consequence of something the company did, or did not do? What can the company do to improve the volume of sales? Why did the sales mix change? Should the company change its marketing to emphasize different products? Why were sales prices different? Did they affect the volume of sales?

Variance analysis also is used by managers of other types of organizations. Take Old Rosebud, for example.[a] Old Rosebud is a 400-acre farm in the Kentucky Bluegrass that specializes in boarding thoroughbred horses. In evaluating its operations, Old Rosebud

What are some of the variable costs per day to board each of these horses?

uses four variances: a sales volume variance [(budgeted boarding days − actual boarding days) × the budgeted daily contribution margin per mare]; a sales price variance [(budgeted boarding rate − actual boarding rate) × actual boarding days]; a variable cost variance [(budgeted variable costs per mare per day − actual variable costs per mare per day) × actual boarding days]; and a fixed cost variance (budgeted fixed costs − actual fixed costs). To get the most meaningful information from its variance analysis, Old Rosebud computes a variable cost variance for each variable cost individually.

During one year, variance analysis helped Old Rosebud's managers discover that sales volume had decreased significantly because of an economic downturn that caused a decline in breeding activities, which in turn decreased the demand for thoroughbred horse boarding (which showed up in the unfavorable sales volume variance). But surprisingly, the biggest problem for the company concerned *price*. The unfavorable sales price variance was almost twice as large as the sales volume variance! In an effort to attract boarders from its competitors, Old Rosebud had lowered boarding prices. What Old Rosebud discovered through its analysis was that at the volume of boarding days that it had achieved in that year, *if it had not lowered its boarding rates* it would have earned six times more income than it actually achieved!

How are Old Rosebud's variances similar to and different from those that we discussed earlier in the chapter?

BUSINESS ISSUES AND VALUES

Earlier we mentioned that variances help managers locate problems as soon as possible so that they can begin to correct them. Many companies use variances to locate the manager who has responsibility in the area in which the problem is occurring. But though this is useful for assigning responsibility for *fixing* a problem, companies must use special care in assigning responsibility for the *cause* of the problem. For example, suppose a company has an unfavorable direct materials quantity variance. There are several possible causes of this type of unfavorable variance:

1. Maybe a machine was out of alignment, causing it to produce bad parts. If so, the production department probably had to produce that part again with different direct materials (using at least twice the standard amount of materials). Perhaps this is the

production manager's responsibility. Maybe the machine should have been aligned more often. Or maybe it was one unique incident that a proper alignment schedule could not have prevented.

2. Maybe new, inexperienced employees were being trained during the time period in which the variances occurred. The learning mistakes of these "trainees" may have caused the variance. In this case, perhaps the variance was uncontrollable, but the variance would still point to the production manager.

3. Maybe a messy factory floor was interfering with clean operations and causing the factory workers to make mistakes. Again, the production manager has responsibility for the factory floor.

So, at first glance, it looks as though the production manager has responsibility for fixing the problem and *may have* responsibility for causing the problem. But what if the cause of the problem is that the purchasing department decided to purchase direct materials from a new supplier, and these materials were of a lower quality than those purchased from the original supplier? It is possible that the new direct materials didn't hold up as well in the production process, causing more materials to have been used in order to get "good" products. If so, then the responsibility for causing and fixing the problem belongs to the purchasing manager. Incorrectly identifying the responsibility for a problem can delay the correction of the problem. Furthermore, holding managers responsible for correcting problems over which they have no control may lead to severe morale problems.

Variances point to problems and to *possible* causes of problems. To solve the problems, managers must know the causes, and to do that, they must use their creative thinking skills to identify alternate possible causes. This process will help ensure that the problem is addressed quickly and directly.

SUMMARY OF DIRECT MATERIALS AND DIRECT LABOR VARIANCE COMPUTATIONS

Exhibit 17-6 shows, in equation form, the computations of the variances we have discussed. Note the similarity between the direct materials variance computations and the direct labor variance computations.

EXHIBIT 17-6	**SUMMARY OF DIRECT MATERIALS AND DIRECT LABOR VARIANCE COMPUTATIONS**			
Direct materials price variance	=	Actual direct materials units purchased	×	(Standard price per unit of direct materials − Actual price per unit of direct materials)
Direct materials quantity variance	=	(Standard direct materials quantity budgeted for actual units produced − Actual direct materials used)	×	Direct materials price standard
Direct labor price variance	=	Actual direct labor hours worked	×	(Standard direct labor price per hour − Actual direct labor price per hour)
Direct labor efficiency variance	=	(Standard direct labor hours budgeted for actual units produced − Actual direct labor hours worked)	×	Direct labor price standard

SUMMARY

At the beginning of the chapter we asked you several questions. During the chapter, we asked you to STOP and answer some other questions to build your knowledge about specific issues. Be sure you answered these additional questions. Below are the questions from the beginning of the chapter, with a brief summary of the key points relating to the answers. Use your creative and critical thinking skills to expand on these key points to develop more complete answers to the questions and to determine what other questions you have that might lead you to learn more about the issues.

1 What is a price standard and a quantity standard, and how does a company compute a standard cost?

A price standard is the *cost* that a company should incur to acquire one unit of *input* for a manufacturing process. A quantity standard is the *number of units* of an input that a company should use to produce one unit of product in a manufacturing process. A company determines the standard cost of an input for one unit of product output by multiplying the quantity standard of the input by its price standard.

2 What is included in a company's direct materials price and quantity standards?

A direct materials price standard includes two factors: (1) the invoice price (less any expected discounts) to be paid to normal suppliers when the company purchases materials in expected quantities; and (2) any transportation costs the company expects to pay. A direct materials quantity standard includes three factors: (1) the actual amount of materials that should end up in each "good" unit of product; (2) allowances for materials normally lost through various manufacturing operations; and (3) allowances for normal amounts of spoiled production (products that are not "up to snuff" and, therefore, are unacceptable for sale). The direct materials quantity standards show the average (normal) quantity of materials that the company should use per unit of product when it performs manufacturing operations under the planned conditions.

3 When a company compares its actual direct materials costs to its direct materials standards, how does it determine what caused the difference between the two?

A company uses direct materials variances to help it determine the causes of differences between actual and standard direct materials costs. A direct materials price variance is the difference between the cost that the company *should have incurred* (at the standard price) to acquire the direct materials and the actual cost it *did* incur to acquire direct materials. A company computes this variance by multiplying the actual number of direct material units *purchased* by the difference between the standard price and the actual price per direct material unit. Companies normally compute direct materials price variances at the time they purchase materials. The direct materials quantity variance is the difference between the standard cost of the quantity of direct materials that a company *should have used* for the actual number of units produced and the standard cost of the direct materials that it *did* use to produce those units.

4 What is included in a company's direct labor price and quantity standards?

A direct labor price standard shows the current hourly wage rate that a company should incur for a specific type of direct labor employed in production. Direct labor price standards also may be set to include an allowance for payroll taxes and fringe benefits. A direct labor quantity standard shows the amount of direct labor time that a company should use to produce one unit of product. A company sets direct labor quantity standards in a two-step process. First, it carefully studies the time required to perform the direct labor operations needed to produce a product. Then, it allows for normal amounts of labor time used for personnel rest breaks, machine adjustments and idle time, and production of normal amounts of spoiled units.

5 When a company compares its actual direct labor costs to its direct labor standards, how does it determine what caused the difference between the two?

A company uses direct labor variances to help it determine the causes of differences between actual and standard direct labor costs. A direct labor price variance is the difference between the cost that a company should have incurred for the actual number of labor hours worked [at the standard direct labor price (rate) per hour] and the actual direct labor cost it did incur for the number of actual labor hours worked. A company computes this direct labor price variance by multiplying the actual direct labor hours worked by the difference between the direct labor price standard and the actual direct labor price per hour. The direct labor efficiency variance is the difference between the standard cost of the direct labor hours that a company *should have used* for the actual number of units produced and the standard cost of the direct labor hours that it *did* use to produce those units. In other words, the *actual* direct labor hours that the company's employees worked on the actual number of units produced were more or less than the standard direct labor hours *budgeted* for that number of units.

How does a company use its manufacturing cost variances to control its operations?

Managers attempt to use cost variance information to determine what problems are affecting the efficient performance of their company's manufacturing activities. To make variance computations more helpful to managers in identifying specific problems, management accountants try to measure variances as quickly as they can after the variances occur, to measure variances in as much detail as is helpful in pinpointing specific problems, and to report variances to managers who are in a position to identify and correct the problems that are likely to have caused the variances.

KEY TERMS

direct labor efficiency variance *(p. 577)*
direct labor price standard *(p. 575)*
direct labor price variance *(p. 577)*
direct labor quantity standard *(p. 576)*
direct materials price standard *(p. 570)*
direct materials price variance *(p. 571)*
direct materials quantity standard *(p. 570)*
direct materials quantity variance *(p. 572)*
price standard *(p. 568)*

quantity standard *(p. 568)*
standard costs *(p. 567)*
standard cost system *(p. 567)*
standard cost of an input for one unit of product output *(p. 568)*
standard direct labor hours budgeted *(p. 577)*
standard direct materials quantity budgeted *(p. 572)*

APPENDIX

Standard Costs and Variances for Factory Overhead

In the chapter we discussed how a company sets the standard costs and variances for its direct materials and direct labor. We focused on direct materials and direct labor because their costs and variance computations are more straightforward than those of factory overhead. Both direct materials costs and direct labor costs are variable costs, and these costs are relatively easy to assign to the company's products. On the other hand, there is a large variety of factory overhead costs that are made up of both variable and fixed costs. These costs are initially applied to the company's products based on estimates. These factors make calculating factory overhead variances a little more challenging.

Factory overhead includes all manufacturing costs other than direct materials and direct labor costs. As we discussed in Chapter 16, it includes the costs of items such as indirect materials, indirect labor, and utilities, as well as maintenance, depreciation, insurance, and property taxes on factory plant and equipment. Because of the large number and variety of these costs, a company typically combines them and applies them to units of product as a single cost element, *factory overhead* (or simply *overhead*), through the use of predetermined overhead rates. As we discussed in Chapter 16, the company commonly determines these rates prior to production. It then *applies* factory overhead to Goods-in-Process Inventory in an amount equal to the predetermined rate multiplied by the number of direct labor hours (or machine hours or other measure of activity) worked in production.

Factory Overhead Price and Quantity Standards

Before a company uses standard costs for its factory overhead, it first sets its factory overhead price and quantity standards.

Factory Overhead Price Standards

The **price standards for factory overhead** are the standard predetermined overhead rates. A company often establishes separate rates for variable and fixed factory overhead. The variable factory overhead rate is the sum of all the standard variable overhead costs per unit of product. The company computes its fixed factory overhead rate by determining the budgeted amount of annual fixed factory overhead and dividing that amount by the estimated annual volume of manufacturing activity (measured in standard direct labor hours, machine hours, or other measure of activity).[5]

Factory Overhead Quantity Standard

The **quantity standard for factory overhead** is the volume of production activity (direct labor hours, machine hours, or other measure of activity) that *should be used* to produce one unit of product. If a company uses direct labor hours to apply factory overhead, the quantity standard for overhead is the same as the quantity standard for direct labor. If it uses machine hours or some other measure of activity for overhead application, it must determine a separate quantity standard showing the budgeted machine hours (or other activity) required to produce one unit of product. Although a company may use several measures of activity for budgeting and applying factory overhead, the most commonly used measure is standard direct labor hours. Unlimited Decadence uses standard direct labor hours for budgeting and applying factory overhead.

Setting Standards for Factory Overhead

Exhibit 17-7 shows the computation of standard factory overhead rates at three volumes (expressed in standard direct labor hours) using overhead costs from the flexible overhead budget in that exhibit.

Notice in Exhibit 17-7 that the fixed factory overhead budget is $504,000 per month (or $6,048,000 per year) at each of the three volumes shown. This is because Unlimited Decadence does not expect fixed overhead costs to be affected by changes in the volume (all of these volumes are within the relevant range of activity). As a result, however, *the fixed factory overhead rate per standard direct labor hour depends on the volume of standard direct labor hours used to compute the rate.* Note that the fixed factory overhead rate is a different amount at each of the three volumes. Hence, the total factory overhead rate is different at each volume as well. Thus, if a company expects monthly production volumes to fluctuate and computes the monthly fixed overhead rate based on each month's volume, the fixed overhead (and total overhead) rates will also fluctuate.

It is usually not desirable to allow fixed factory overhead rates to change because of fluctuating production volume.

Why do you think it is not desirable to allow fixed factory overhead rates to change because of changes in production volume?

To avoid this problem, a company usually computes its standard fixed overhead rate using a volume that reflects the normal activity or practical capacity of its manufacturing operations. **Normal activity** is the average of the company's expected annual production volumes, usually computed for three to five years into the future. It is closely related to the average sales volume expected over that future period.

Why do you think expected annual production volumes and expected average sales volumes are closely related?

Practical capacity is the volume of activity at which the company's manufacturing facilities are capable of operating per year under *practical* conditions, allowing for usual levels of efficiency.

---

[5]In Chapter 18 we will discuss activity-based costing, which uses additional measures of activity to apply factory overhead.

EXHIBIT 17-7	FLEXIBLE OVERHEAD BUDGET AND RATE COMPUTATION

UNLIMITED DECADENCE
Flexible Factory Overhead Budget for Darkly Decadent Candy Bar

Volume (cases per month)	360,000	400,000	440,000
Volume (standard direct labor hours)	180,000	200,000*	220,000
Factory overhead costs:			
Variable:			
Indirect labor ($0.12/case)	$ 43,200	$ 48,000	$ 52,800
Indirect materials ($0.08/case)	28,800	32,000	35,200
Utilities ($0.05/case)	18,000	20,000	22,000
Other variable overhead ($0.07/case)	25,200	28,000	30,800
Total variable overhead ($ 0.32/case)	$115,200	$128,000	$140,800
Fixed:			
Supervisory salaries	$114,000	$114,000	$114,000
Depreciation of plant and equipment	150,000	150,000	150,000
Other fixed overhead	240,000	240,000	240,000
Total fixed overhead	$504,000	$504,000	$504,000
Total factory overhead	$619,200	$632,000	$644,800

Standard Overhead Rate Computations at Each Volume

	180,000 Standard Direct Labor Hours	200,000 Standard Direct Labor Hours	220,000 Standard Direct Labor Hours
Variable	$\dfrac{\$115,200}{180,000 \text{ DLH}} = \$0.64/\text{DLH}$	$\dfrac{\$128,000}{200,000 \text{ DLH}} = \$0.64/\text{DLH}$	$\dfrac{\$140,800}{220,000 \text{ DLH}} = \$0.64/\text{DLH}$
Fixed	$\dfrac{\$504,000}{180,000 \text{ DLH}} = \$2.80/\text{DLH}$	$\dfrac{\$504,000}{200,000 \text{ DLH}} = \$2.52/\text{DLH}$	$\dfrac{\$504,000}{220,000 \text{ DLH}} = \$2.29/\text{DLH}$
Total	$\dfrac{\$619,200}{180,000 \text{ DLH}} = \$3.44/\text{DLH}$	$\dfrac{\$632,000}{200,000 \text{ DLH}} = \$3.16/\text{DLH}$	$\dfrac{\$644,800}{220,000 \text{ DLH}} = \$2.93/\text{DLH}$

*Recall that the quantity standard for direct labor is 0.5 hours per case. Thus the standard direct labor hours budgeted for a unit volume of 400,000 units is 200,000 hours (400,000 units × 0.5 hours per case).

It is closely related to the physical size of the manufacturing facilities, which typically does not change much from year to year. Computing the fixed factory overhead rate using the overhead budget at either normal activity or practical capacity provides stability to the fixed factory overhead rate (and therefore to the total overhead rate), which would not exist if a company used the expected monthly or annual production volume.

Variable factory overhead rates are not influenced by the volume chosen for the rate computation. The reason is that the total budgeted variable factory overhead cost varies directly in proportion to volume. Thus a company uses the standard variable overhead rate to budget variable overhead cost regardless of the volume at which it is computed. Observe in Exhibit 17-7 that the standard variable overhead rate for producing Darkly Decadent candy bars is $0.64 per standard direct labor hour at each of the three volumes.

Throughout our discussion of factory overhead variances we assume that normal activity for Unlimited Decadence is 4,800,000 cases of Darkly Decadent candy bars (2,400,000 standard direct labor hours) per year and that the company used that volume to set its standard predetermined fixed overhead rates. Unlimited Decadence's predetermined overhead rates are as follows:

Variable overhead rate	=	$0.64 per standard direct labor hour
Fixed overhead rate	=	2.52 per standard direct labor hour
		($6,048,000 ÷ 2,400,000 DLH)
Total overhead rate	=	$3.16 per standard direct labor hour

Applying Factory Overhead Costs in a Standard Cost System

Overhead application is slightly different when a company uses a standard cost system instead of an actual cost system (as we discussed in Chapter 16). When a company does not have a standard cost system but applies factory overhead using a predetermined overhead rate per direct labor hour, it computes the amount applied by multiplying the *actual direct labor hours worked* by the predetermined overhead rate. When a company uses a standard cost system, however, it computes the amount of factory overhead applied by multiplying the *standard direct labor hours budgeted* for the actual number of units produced by the standard predetermined overhead rate. (The number of standard direct labor hours budgeted for factory overhead costs is the *same* as the number of standard direct labor hours budgeted for direct labor costs.) For example, suppose that employees of a company with a predetermined overhead rate of $3 per direct labor hour actually work 105 hours to produce 50 units that should have taken 2 standard direct labor hours per unit to produce. If the company is *not* using a standard cost system, it will apply $315 (105 actual hours × $3 per hour) of factory overhead to those units. If it *is* using a standard cost system, however, it will apply only $300 [100 (50 units × 2 hours) standard direct labor hours *budgeted* × $3 per hour] to those units.

Factory Overhead Variances

Factory overhead variances arise when the actual amount of factory overhead cost incurred during a period differs from the amount of factory overhead cost applied.

Total Overhead Variance

The **total overhead variance** is the difference between total factory overhead cost *applied* and total actual factory overhead cost *incurred* in a standard cost system. The computation of the $56,600 unfavorable total overhead variance experienced by Unlimited Decadence during a month when Unlimited Decadence produced 360,000 cases of Darkly Decadent candy bars and incurred actual factory overhead costs of $625,400 is as follows:

Total Overhead Variance:

Total overhead cost applied	
(180,000 standard direct labor hours budgeted @ $3.16)	$568,800
−Total overhead cost incurred	(625,400)
Total overhead variance	$ (56,600) unfavorable

Note in this computation that Unlimited Decadence multiplies the *standard direct labor hours budgeted* to produce 360,000 cases of Darkly Decadent candy bars (360,000 cases × 0.5 standard direct labor hours per case = 180,000 hours) by the total predetermined overhead rate ($3.16 per hour) to compute the $568,800 total overhead cost applied. It subtracts the $625,400 total actual overhead cost incurred to compute the $56,600 unfavorable total overhead variance. When the total actual overhead cost incurred is more than the total overhead cost applied, as in the preceding computation, the total overhead variance is *unfavorable*. When the amount incurred is less than the amount applied, the total overhead variance is *favorable*.

To improve managers' understanding of the reasons why the total overhead variance occurred, companies usually divide the total overhead variance into at least two separate overhead variances. Next, we will discuss two of these overhead variances that together make up the total overhead variance: the overhead budget variance and the fixed overhead volume variance.

Overhead Budget Variance

The **overhead budget variance** is the difference between the total overhead *budgeted* and the total actual overhead *incurred*. The total overhead budgeted is the amount of factory overhead cost that a company *should* incur to produce a given number of units under planned operating conditions. A company computes the total overhead budgeted by multiplying the standard direct labor hours budgeted for the actual number of units produced by the variable overhead rate, and then adding the result to the budgeted fixed overhead. When the company incurs actual total factory overhead costs that exceed the total overhead budgeted, the overhead budget variance is *unfavorable*. Incurring lower costs than budgeted results in a *favorable* budget variance.

Does this make sense? What is the difference between the overhead budget variance and the total overhead variance?

Next, we show the computation of the $6,200 unfavorable overhead budget variance for the month when Unlimited Decadence produced 360,000 cases of Darkly Decadent candy bars. Unlimited Decadence computes the total overhead budgeted by first multiplying the 180,000 standard direct labor hours budgeted by the $0.64 variable overhead rate to determine the $115,200 budgeted variable overhead cost. It adds this amount to the $504,000 budgeted fixed overhead cost to determine the $619,200 total overhead budgeted. It subtracts the $625,400 total actual overhead cost incurred (that we used in the total overhead variance computation) to determine the $6,200 unfavorable overhead budget variance.

Overhead Budget Variance:
Total overhead budgeted (based on 180,000 standard direct labor hours budgeted):

Variable (180,000 hours @ $0.64)	$115,200	
Fixed	504,000	$619,200
−Total actual overhead cost incurred		(625,400)
Overhead budget variance		$ (6,200) unfavorable

The overhead budget variance arises when the actual costs of the individual overhead items differ from those budgeted. To provide useful control information, a company normally reports the overhead budget variance *item by item* so that its managers can judge which items need attention. We show such a breakdown of the overhead budget variance in Exhibit 17-8. For this illustration, we assumed the actual amounts incurred, whereas we took the budgeted amounts from Exhibit 17-7.

In Exhibit 17-8 five of the seven overhead items in the overhead budget variance report show unfavorable variances. Indirect labor and indirect materials, in particular, show very large unfavorable variances relative to their budgeted amounts. Together they make up over 80 percent [($2,600 + $2,400) ÷ $6,200] of the total unfavorable overhead budget variance. By directing the attention of Unlimited Decadence's managers to these two items, the overhead budget variance report enables them to use the management-by-exception principle.

How do you think knowing the indirect labor and indirect materials variances would enable managers to use the management-by-exception principle?

Fixed Overhead Volume Variance

The **fixed overhead volume variance** is the difference between the amount of *applied* fixed overhead and the amount of *budgeted* fixed overhead. A company computes this variance by sub-

EXHIBIT 17-8	OVERHEAD BUDGET VARIANCE REPORT

UNLIMITED DECADENCE
Overhead Budget Variance Report

	Budgeted Overhead at 180,000 Standard Direct Labor Hours Budgeted	Actual Overhead Costs Incurred	Overhead Budget Variance
Indirect labor	$ 43,200	$ 45,800	$ (2,600) unfavorable
Indirect materials	28,800	31,200	(2,400) unfavorable
Utilities	18,000	18,400	(400) unfavorable
Other variable overhead	25,200	25,050	150 favorable
Supervisory salaries	114,000	114,500	(500) unfavorable
Depreciation of plant and equipment	150,000	150,000	0
Other fixed overhead	240,000	240,450	(450) unfavorable
Total	$619,200	$625,400	$ (6,200) unfavorable

tracting the total budgeted fixed overhead cost from the amount of applied fixed overhead cost (standard direct labor hours budgeted for the actual number of units produced multiplied by the standard fixed overhead rate per hour). It is *unfavorable* when the budgeted fixed overhead is more than the applied fixed overhead and *favorable* when the budgeted fixed overhead is less than the applied fixed overhead.

 Does this make sense to you? Why do you think the fixed overhead volume variance is unfavorable when the budgeted fixed overhead is more than the applied fixed overhead?

The fixed overhead volume variance arises solely because of the difference between the way fixed overhead is applied and the way it is budgeted. A company *applies* fixed overhead by multiplying the predetermined fixed overhead rate by the standard direct labor hours budgeted for the actual number of units produced. (So when the volume of production changes, the total amount of fixed overhead applied changes.) However, a company *budgets* total fixed overhead at the total amount it expects to incur regardless of its production volume.

Unlimited Decadence expected to incur total fixed overhead costs of $504,000 per month (see Exhibit 17-7), or $6,048,000 per year. Recall that the company used a normal activity of 200,000 standard direct labor hours per month (2,400,000 per year) to compute its standard fixed overhead rate of $2.52 per standard direct labor hour. It applied fixed overhead at this rate. During the month when Unlimited Decadence produced 360,000 cases, the number of standard direct labor hours budgeted for that output was 180,000 direct labor hours (360,000 × 0.5). At this volume, Unlimited Decadence *applied* $453,600 (180,000 standard direct labor hours budgeted × $2.52 per standard direct labor hour) of fixed overhead to that output. The amount of fixed overhead *budgeted*, however, was $504,000. The fixed overhead volume variance is computed as follows:

Fixed Overhead Volume Variance:

Fixed overhead applied (180,000 standard direct labor hours budgeted at $2.52 per hour)	$453,600
−Fixed overhead budgeted	(504,000)
Fixed overhead volume variance	$ (50,400) unfavorable

Exhibit 17-9 shows both the amount of fixed overhead that Unlimited Decadence would apply at various levels of standard direct labor hours and the amount of fixed overhead budgeted. It also shows the $50,400 unfavorable fixed overhead volume variance we computed earlier.

Notice in Exhibit 17-9 that for all volumes *below* the normal activity of 200,000 standard direct labor hours, the amount of fixed overhead applied is less than the amount budgeted. This results in an *unfavorable* fixed overhead volume variance. Remember that fixed costs do not change as a result of changes in volume. A company underapplies fixed overhead when the actual volume of production output is less than normal activity and requires fewer standard direct labor hours than does normal activity. The company has achieved less than a normal product output with the same fixed costs, and the fixed overhead applied is less than that budgeted—an *unfavorable* condition. For all volumes *above* normal activity, the company has achieved more than a normal product output with the same fixed costs. The amount of fixed overhead applied is more than the amount budgeted, and this results in a *favorable* fixed overhead volume variance. A company overapplies fixed overhead when the actual volume of production is greater than normal activity and requires more standard direct labor hours than does normal activity. In this case, the amount of fixed overhead applied is more than that budgeted—a *favorable* condition. For example, if Unlimited Decadence had produced 420,000 cases, 210,000 standard direct labor hours (420,000 cases × 0.5 hours per case) would have been budgeted for that volume of production. Applied fixed overhead would be $529,200 (210,000 standard direct labor hours budgeted × $2.52 per hour). But the fixed overhead cost should not have changed because Unlimited Decadence produced more cases than it expected to produce. The fixed overhead cost (the amount budgeted) would still be $504,000. In this case the fixed overhead volume variance would be $25,200 favorable ($529,200 applied − $504,000 budgeted). We also show this variance in Exhibit 17-9.

The only time that a company will *not* have a fixed overhead volume variance (that is, its volume variance will be zero) is when the number of standard direct labor hours used to apply fixed overhead to actual product output (the standard direct labor hours budgeted) is *exactly equal* to

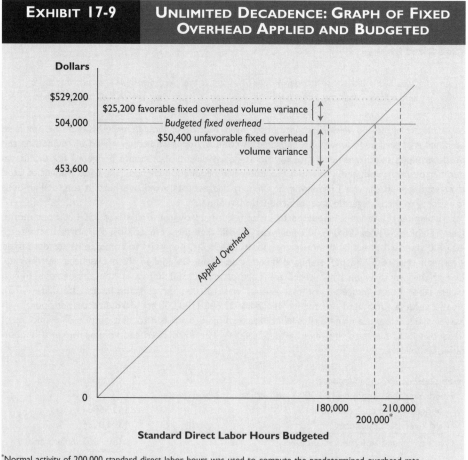

| EXHIBIT 17-9 | UNLIMITED DECADENCE: GRAPH OF FIXED OVERHEAD APPLIED AND BUDGETED |

*Normal activity of 200,000 standard direct labor hours was used to compute the predetermined overhead rate.

the production volume (the normal activity) the company used to compute its fixed overhead rate. Note in Exhibit 17-9 that when the standard direct labor hours budgeted are 200,000, the normal activity level that Unlimited Decadence used to compute its predetermined overhead rates, the amount of fixed overhead applied equals the amount budgeted ($504,000) and the fixed overhead volume variance is zero.

It is important to understand that *there can never be a "variable" overhead volume variance*. The reason is that variable overhead is applied in the same way it is budgeted: at a constant rate per standard direct labor hour. For a month when Unlimited Decadence produces 360,000 cases of Darkly Decadent candy bars (for which 180,000 standard direct labor hours are budgeted), its variable overhead budget is $115,200 (see Exhibit 17-7). This is the same amount that would be applied in that month. The amount of variable overhead budgeted for a given production volume (in units) equals the amount of variable overhead applied to the units produced. For Unlimited Decadence, the variable overhead rate is $0.64 per standard direct labor hour. The amount of variable overhead budgeted and applied is $115,200 (180,000 standard direct labor hours budgeted × $0.64 per hour).

A company applies variable overhead by multiplying the variable overhead rate per standard direct labor hour by the standard direct labor hours budgeted for the actual number of units produced. Therefore, the company can compute the fixed overhead volume variance as the difference between the *total* overhead budgeted and the total overhead applied (using the standard direct labor hours budgeted for the number of units produced). When the fixed overhead volume variance is added to the overhead budget variance, the sum is the total overhead variance. Notice in the following table how the overhead variances relate to one another as differences between the total overhead *incurred, budgeted,* and *applied*.

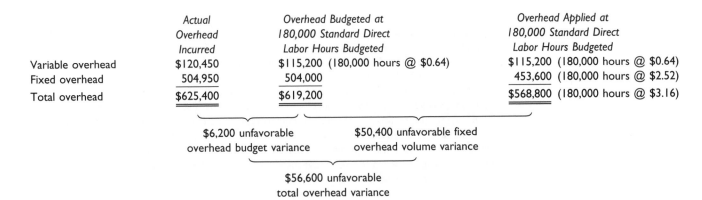

	Actual Overhead Incurred	Overhead Budgeted at 180,000 Standard Direct Labor Hours Budgeted	Overhead Applied at 180,000 Standard Direct Labor Hours Budgeted
Variable overhead	$120,450	$115,200 (180,000 hours @ $0.64)	$115,200 (180,000 hours @ $0.64)
Fixed overhead	504,950	504,000	453,600 (180,000 hours @ $2.52)
Total overhead	$625,400	$619,200	$568,800 (180,000 hours @ $3.16)

$6,200 unfavorable overhead budget variance

$50,400 unfavorable fixed overhead volume variance

$56,600 unfavorable total overhead variance

The fixed overhead volume variance shows that the volume of units produced in a period was more or less than the volume used to set the predetermined standard overhead rate. This difference in production volume could have resulted from a sales volume that was higher or lower than expected (so the company would have had to adjust its volume of production). An unfavorable fixed overhead volume variance could be a symptom of an inefficiency or problem in the manufacturing process.

To complete our discussion of overhead variance computations, in Exhibit 17-10 we show graphically how the fixed factory overhead volume variance and the overhead budget variance together make up the total overhead variance. In this exhibit we show both the total overhead

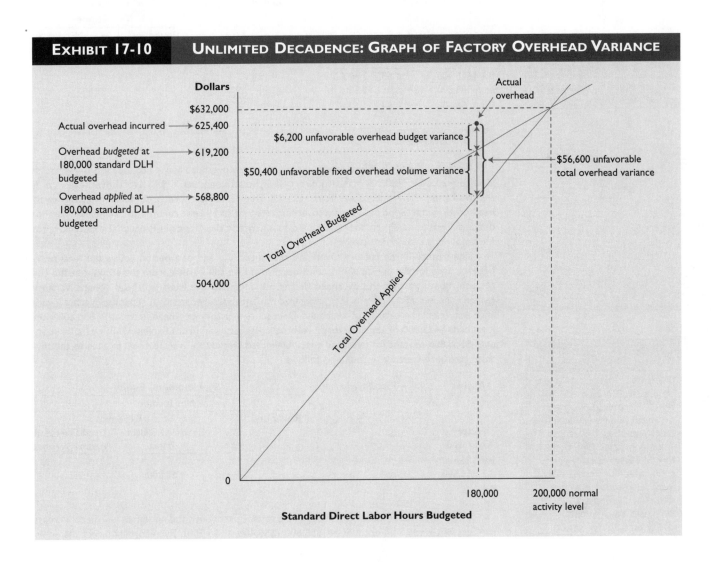

EXHIBIT 17-10   UNLIMITED DECADENCE: GRAPH OF FACTORY OVERHEAD VARIANCE

budgeted and the total overhead applied at various levels of standard direct labor hours budgeted. We also show the actual overhead incurred. We show the overhead budget variance, the fixed overhead volume variance, and the total overhead variance for the month when Unlimited Decadence produced 360,000 cases of Darkly Decadent candy bars (when 180,000 standard direct labor hours were budgeted).

Note in Exhibit 17-10 how we add the $6,200 unfavorable overhead budget variance and the $50,400 unfavorable fixed overhead volume variance to show the $56,600 unfavorable total overhead variance. Note also that the $50,400 unfavorable fixed overhead volume variance appears as the difference between the total overhead *budgeted* and the total overhead *applied* using the 180,000 standard direct labor hours budgeted. The $56,600 unfavorable total overhead variance appears as the difference between the actual overhead incurred and the total overhead applied at 180,000 standard direct labor hours.

Recording Factory Overhead Variances

As we discussed in Chapter 16, a company records the factory overhead costs it actually *incurred* as increases in the Factory Overhead account. The company records the factory overhead costs it *applied* (at standard) as decreases in the Factory Overhead account (and increases in the Goods-in-Process Inventory account). To understand the application of standard factory overhead costs, recall that Unlimited Decadence applied $568,800 of standard factory overhead (from Exhibit 17-10). It records the application as follows:

Assets		=	Liabilities	+	Stockholders' Equity		
					Net Income		
					Revenues	−	Expenses
Factory Overhead	Goods-in-Process Inventory						
Bal $625,400	Bal $3,722,400*						
−568,800	+ 568,800						
Bal $ 56,600	Bal $4,291,200						

*Standard costs for sugar ($504,000) plus standard costs for other direct materials ($1,058,400) plus standard costs for direct labor ($2,160,000).

Note that the $568,800 standard amount of factory overhead applied to the Goods-in-Process Inventory account (180,000 standard direct labor hours budgeted × $3.16 total overhead rate) is removed from the Factory Overhead account. Thus, a company records *standard* factory overhead costs in the Goods-in-Process Inventory account just like it records the standard costs for direct materials and direct labor (which we summarize in the Goods-in-Process account above for the amounts we recorded earlier).

The balance in the Factory Overhead account at the end of a period equals the total overhead variance for the period. Companies usually remove this balance from the account at the end of each month so that the overhead budget variance and the fixed overhead volume variance (which together make up the total overhead variance) are recorded in separate overhead variance accounts. The balance of Unlimited Decadence's factory overhead account is $56,600 after it records $625,400 of actual factory overhead costs incurred (from Exhibit 17–8) and after it applies $568,800 of standard overhead costs. Unlimited Decadence transfers this balance to the separate overhead variance accounts as follows:

Assets	=	Liabilities	+	Stockholders' Equity			
				Net Income			
				Revenues	−	**Expenses**	
Factory Overhead						Overhead Budget Variance	Fixed Overhead Volume Variance
Bal $56,600							
−56,600					−	+$6,200	+$50,400
Bal $ 0							

When Unlimited Decadence closes these variance accounts, the net effect will be to increase its Cost of Goods Sold account by $56,600 ($50,400 + $6,200). By recording direct materials, direct labor, and factory overhead as we illustrated in this chapter, Unlimited Decadence records the $4,291,200 standard manufacturing cost of producing 360,000 cases of Darkly Decadent candy bars in its Goods-in-Process Inventory account. This standard cost consists of $1,562,400 standard direct materials cost ($504,000 for sugar and $1,058,400 for other direct materials), $2,160,000 standard direct labor cost, and $568,800 standard factory overhead cost. Although we do not show it here, Unlimited Decadence transfers the $4,291,200 standard cost of completed cases of Darkly Decadent candy bars ($11.92 per case from Exhibit 17-1 for the 360,000 cases) from the Goods-in-Process Inventory account to the Finished Goods Inventory account when it completes the units. As it sells the candy bars, it removes this standard cost from the Finished Goods Inventory account and adds it to the Cost of Goods Sold account. So, in addition to the three inventory accounts, the Cost of Goods Sold account is also recorded at standard cost.

At the end of an accounting period for which a company prepares financial statements, its variance accounts for factory overhead will have balances. If the company's standards reflect current planned conditions, these balances will be small. A company normally transfers these variance account balances at the end of the period to its Cost of Goods Sold account, as we discussed earlier. Transferring these variance balances to Cost of Goods Sold causes the expense to reflect actual costs rather than standard costs, so that the company reports its actual net income on its income statement. If the total (net) amount of these variances is not small, a more complicated procedure is required. This procedure is beyond the scope of this book.

Summary of Factory Overhead Variance Computations

Exhibit 17-11 shows, in equation form, the computations of the factory overhead variances we have discussed.

EXHIBIT 17-11	SUMMARY OF FACTORY OVERHEAD VARIANCE COMPUTATIONS

$$\text{Total overhead variance} = \left(\begin{array}{c}\text{Standard direct labor}\\\text{hours budgeted for}\\\text{actual units produced}\end{array} \times \begin{array}{c}\text{Standard total}\\\text{overhead rate per}\\\text{direct labor hour}\end{array}\right) - \begin{array}{c}\text{Actual total}\\\text{overhead cost}\\\text{incurred}\end{array}$$

$$\text{Overhead budget variance} = \left[\begin{array}{c}\text{Total budgeted}\\\text{fixed overhead}\end{array} + \left(\begin{array}{c}\text{Standard direct labor}\\\text{hours budgeted for}\\\text{actual units produced}\end{array} \times \begin{array}{c}\text{Standard variable}\\\text{overhead rate per}\\\text{direct labor hour}\end{array}\right)\right] - \begin{array}{c}\text{Actual total}\\\text{overhead}\\\text{cost incurred}\end{array}$$

$$\text{Fixed overhead volume variance} = \left(\begin{array}{c}\text{Standard direct labor}\\\text{hours budgeted for}\\\text{actual units produced}\end{array} \times \begin{array}{c}\text{Standard fixed}\\\text{overhead rate per}\\\text{direct labor hour}\end{array}\right) - \begin{array}{c}\text{Total budgeted}\\\text{fixed overhead}\end{array}$$

SUMMARY SURFING

Here is an opportunity to gather information on the Internet about real-world issues related to the topics in this chapter (for suggestions on how to navigate various companies' Web sites to find their financial statements and other information, see the related discussion in the Preface at the beginning of the book). Answer the following question.

- Go to the **Hershey Foods Corporation** website. Find a recipe for Hot Cocoa. What is the direct materials quantity standard for Hot Cocoa? How would you determine the direct materials and direct labor quantity standards, and the direct materials and direct labor price standards?

INTEGRATED BUSINESS AND ACCOUNTING SITUATIONS

Answer the Following Questions in Your Own Words.

Testing Your Knowledge

17-1 What is a standard cost system?

17-2 What is the difference between a price standard and a quantity standard?

17-3 How does a company compute the standard cost of an input per unit of output in its manufacturing operations?

17-4 What costs are included in a direct materials price standard?

17-5 What amounts are included in a direct materials quantity standard?

17-6 Distinguish between a direct materials price variance and a direct materials quantity variance.

17-7 Why is a direct materials price variance usually computed at the time of purchase?

17-8 How does a company record the purchase of direct materials (on credit) in a standard cost system?

17-9 How does a company record the use of direct materials in a standard cost system?

17-10 What does a direct labor price standard include?

17-11 What amount does a direct labor quantity standard include?

17-12 Distinguish between a direct labor price variance and a direct labor efficiency variance.

17-13 How does a company record wages for direct labor in a standard cost system?

17-14 What rules do management accountants follow to make variance computations more helpful?

17-15 Why is it useful for managers to have a "breakdown" of the standard cost variances for individual operations or departments?

17-16 Should managers investigate all variances to identify the problems causing them? Briefly discuss.

17-17 (Appendix) What are the price standards for factory overhead?

17-18 (Appendix) What is the quantity standard for factory overhead?

17-19 (Appendix) Distinguish between an overhead budget variance and a fixed overhead volume variance.

17-20 (Appendix) Explain how a company records the actual factory overhead incurred and the factory overhead applied.

17-21 (Appendix) What is the balance in a company's factory overhead account at the end of the period, and how does the company remove this balance?

Applying Your Knowledge

17-22 The Morgan Company plans to purchase material X in 5-gallon drums (1,000 at a time) at an invoice price of $20 per drum and to take a 2% cash discount by paying for the material within 10 days. Freight and receiving costs for a shipment of 1,000 drums should total $900. During April, a rush order for one of Morgan's products caused an emergency cash purchase of 1,000 gallons of material X from an alternate supplier. The alternate supplier delivered the material the next day, charging Morgan $4,500 with no cash discount. Freight and receiving costs totaled $180.

Required: (1) Compute the direct materials price standard (per gallon) for material X.
(2) Compute the direct materials price variance related to the emergency purchase.

17-23 The Melton Company has set the standard direct materials cost for one of its products at $11.60 per unit (4 pounds per unit @ $2.90 per pound). During March, Melton purchased 4,100 pounds of this direct material on credit at a total cost of $12,050 and used 3,700 pounds to produce 930 units of product.

Required: (1) Compute Melton's direct materials price and quantity variances for March.
(2) Record (a) the purchase of this direct material and (b) the use of this direct material.

17-24 Playtime Products makes large dollhouses. The standard cost of the carpet used for their construction is $9.60 per dollhouse (6 square feet @ $1.60 per square foot). During September, Playtime paid $27,160 to purchase carpet, half of which was used to produce dollhouses during that month. Direct materials variances related to the purchase and use of this carpet during September were as follows:

Direct materials price variance   = $(2,040) unfavorable
Direct materials quantity variance = $1,840 favorable

Required: Compute the following related amounts: (1) the number of square feet of carpet material purchased in September, and (2) the number of dollhouses produced in September.

17-25 Foster Furniture uses a standard cost system. One model of sofa has a standard direct labor cost of $111 (10 hours per sofa @ $11.10 per hour). During the first week of October, Foster manufactured 15 of these sofas. Because of illness, one of the regular employees was replaced during that week by a new, untrained employee. Employees worked a total of 157 direct labor hours at an average labor cost of $10.80 per hour on the sofas. The direct labor price variance and the direct labor efficiency variance for the production of the sofas resulted from substituting the untrained employee for the regular skilled worker.

Required: (1) Compute the direct labor price variance and the direct labor efficiency variance.
(2) How much extra direct labor cost was incurred in the production of the sofas because of the substitution of the untrained employee?

17-26 The Morristown Manufacturing Company incurred $88,000 of direct labor cost in its machine shop during the month of June. This cost was the result of 5,910 direct labor hours worked to produce 2,000 units of product. The direct labor quantity standard is 3 direct labor hours per unit, and the direct labor price standard is $15 per direct labor hour.

Required: (1) Compute the direct labor price variance.
(2) Compute the standard direct labor hours budgeted.
(3) Compute the direct labor efficiency variance.
(4) Record the wages incurred for direct labor.

17-27 The SpitShine Company produced 5,400 gallons of brass polish in January. The direct labor quantity standard for this polish is 0.4 hours per gallon, and the direct labor price standard is $12 per hour. During January, the following direct labor variances were recorded:

Direct labor price variance   = $(1,744) unfavorable
Direct labor efficiency variance = $(240) unfavorable

Required: Compute the following related amounts: (1) the actual direct labor hours worked during January and (2) the average actual wage rate paid per direct labor hour in January.

17-28 (Some Appendix) The Pierless Paint Company produces an exterior house paint known as Pierpont 163. Two direct materials are combined in the manufacture of this paint: pier and pont. Pierpont 163 is sold in 1-gallon cans, the standard costs of which are shown here:

Standard cost per gallon: Pierpont 163

stand.

Material pier:	0.8 gallons @ $4.00 per gallon	$3.20
Material pont:	0.4 pounds @ $0.60 per pound...	0.24
Direct labor:	0.01 hours @ $10.00 per hour..	0.10
Variable overhead:	0.01 direct labor hours @ $8.00 per hour*	0.08
Fixed overhead:	0.01 direct labor hours @ $22.00 per hour*	0.22
	Total standard cost per gallon	$3.84

*Overhead rates were computed at normal activity of 2,000 standard direct labor hours per month.

Inventory records last month show:

Actual

Item	Beginning Inventory	Purchases	Ending Inventory
Material pier	80,000 gallons	126,000 gallons @ $3.80 per gallon	30,000 gallons
Material pont	35,000 pounds	135,000 pounds @ $0.62 per pound	90,000 pounds

Additional production information from last month:
Gallons of Pierpont 163 produced: .... 212,000 gallons
Actual direct labor cost (2,170 direct labor hours @ $9.80 per hour): $21,266
Actual overhead costs:.. $63,565

Required: Compute the following variances:

(1) Direct materials price and quantity variances for (a) material pier and (b) material pont
(2) Direct labor price and efficiency variances
(3) (Appendix) Overhead budget variance
(4) (Appendix) Fixed overhead volume variance

17-29 (Some Appendix) The Hammond Manufacturing Company produces Yagis. Standard costs per Yagi are as follows:

Stand

	Standard Cost per Yagi
Direct materials:	
Aluminum tubing (144 feet @ $0.40 per foot)	$ 57.60
Hardware (1 package @ $5.00 per package)...	5.00
Direct labor (3 direct labor hours @ $9.60 per hour)................................	28.80
Factory overhead:	
Variable (3 direct labor hours @ $2.00 per hour)	6.00
Fixed (3 direct labor hours @ $4.00 per hour)	12.00
Standard manufacturing cost per Yagi..	$109.40

Factory overhead is budgeted and applied on the basis of standard direct labor hours. The overhead rates were set at a practical capacity of 5,600 standard direct labor hours per year.

Actual production and cost data from last year:

Actual

Yagis produced:	1,350
Aluminum tubing purchased (on credit):	280,000 feet @ $0.42 per foot = $117,600
Aluminum tubing used:	196,400 feet
Hardware purchased (on credit):	1,360 packages @ $4.95 per package = $6,732
Packages of hardware used:	1,360 packages
Direct labor cost:	4,130 direct labor hours @ $9.70 per hour = $40,061
Total factory overhead cost:	$32,050 (assume all was paid in cash except for depreciation of $4,500 on equipment)

Required: (1) Calculate the direct materials price and quantity variances for each direct material.

(2) Calculate the direct labor price and efficiency variances.

(3) Record (a) the purchase and use of the raw materials and (b) the wages incurred for direct labor.

(4) (Appendix) Calculate the overhead budget variance.

(5) (Appendix) Calculate the fixed overhead volume variance.

(6) (Appendix) Record (c) the factory overhead incurred and applied and (d) the overhead budget variance and the fixed overhead volume variance.

17-30 (Appendix) The Roberts Company produces product X, which is in high demand. Mr. Roberts, the owner, believes that three or four times as many units could be sold as his five employees are capable of making. Direct materials and direct labor quantity standards and price standards are as follows:

Direct materials quantity standard	1.3 pounds per unit
Direct labor quantity standard	9 hours per unit
Direct materials price standard	$10 per pound
Direct labor price standard	$12 per hour

Factory overhead is budgeted and applied on the basis of standard direct labor hours. Practical capacity is 10,000 standard direct labor hours. The factory overhead budget at practical capacity shows $45,000 of variable overhead and $18,000 of fixed overhead.

Required: (1) Compute the standard variable and fixed overhead rates per direct labor hour based on the budget at practical capacity.

(2) Compute the standard direct materials, direct labor, variable overhead, and fixed overhead costs per unit of product X.

17-31 (Appendix) Refer to 17-30. At the beginning of this year the Roberts Company leased a new machine—for $4,500 per year—that would allow production of a unit of product X out of 1 pound of direct materials in 5 direct labor hours. Mr. Roberts was so happy with the efficiency of this new machine that he raised the labor rate he paid his employees to $13 per hour. This change did not affect the total variable overhead budgeted at practical capacity.

Required: (1) Revise the quantity and price standards for direct materials, direct labor, and factory overhead so that they reflect the expected changes resulting from the new machine.

(2) Compute the revised total standard cost per unit of product X.

17-32 (Appendix) Hugland Company budgets its factory overhead on the basis of a normal activity of 100,000 standard direct labor hours (DLH) per year. It estimates that its variable factory overhead is $4 per DLH and its fixed factory overhead is $600,000 per year. Hugland applies its factory overhead using a predetermined rate based on the preceding information. Hugland has a direct labor quantity standard of 2 hours per unit of product. During the current year, Hugland produced 48,000 units of product and incurred actual factory overhead costs of $990,000.

Required: Compute Hugland's (1) predetermined overhead rate, (2) total overhead variance, (3) overhead budget variance, and (4) fixed overhead volume variance.

17-33 (Appendix) The total annual factory overhead budget of the Reynolds Company is given by the following cost equation:

$$\text{Total overhead cost budgeted} = \$78,000 + \$3.50X$$
$$\textit{where } X = \text{standard direct labor hours}$$

The Reynolds Company has a practical capacity of 20,000 standard direct labor hours, but it expects to operate at a normal activity level of 15,000 standard direct labor hours. The direct labor quantity standard is 5 hours per unit of product. Last year the company produced 2,400 units and incurred $124,900 of actual overhead costs.

Required: (1) Using the factory overhead budget at *practical* capacity, (a) compute the variable and fixed overhead rates per direct labor hour; (b) compute the overhead budget variance; and (c) compute the fixed overhead volume variance.

(2) Using the factory overhead budget at *normal* activity, repeat all the computations required in (1).

(3) Discuss the similarities and differences between your computations in (1) and (2).

17-34 (Appendix) The Brimestone Company produces several products. The company's factory overhead rates were previously determined at its normal activity of 90,000 units (180,000 standard direct labor hours budgeted) per year, as shown here:

	Factory Overhead Budget at 90,000 Units (180,000 standard direct labor hours budgeted)	Standard Factory Overhead Rates per Hour
Variable	$360,000	$2
Fixed	540,000	3
Total	$900,000	$5

This year, 82,500 units were produced and actual factory overhead totaled $802,500 (all of which was paid in cash except depreciation of $300,000 on factory and equipment).

Required: (1) Compute (a) the total overhead variance, (b) the overhead budget variance, and (c) the fixed overhead volume variance.

(2) Prepare entries in the accounts of Brimestone to record (a) factory overhead incurred and (b) factory overhead applied.

(3) Prepare the entry in the accounts of Brimestone to record the overhead budget variance and the fixed overhead volume variance.

17-35 (Appendix) The Sanford Corporation produces a single product and uses a standard cost system. Fixed and variable overhead costs are applied to this product on a standard machine hour basis. Sanford uses its normal activity of 100,000 standard machine hours to set its standard overhead rates. Summary data from Sanford's flexible budget are as follows:

Standard Machine Hours per Year	Total Overhead Costs Budgeted per Year
80,000	$124,000
90,000	132,000
100,000	140,000
110,000	148,000

The standard machine hour requirement for Sanford's product is 2 machine hours per unit. Last year 45,000 units were produced, and actual overhead costs were $132,800.

Required: (1) Compute the fixed and variable overhead rates per standard machine hour. (*Hint:* Total overhead cost is a *mixed* cost that can be separated into fixed and variable components.)

(2) Compute the amount of fixed overhead cost *budgeted* at 80,000, 90,000, 100,000, and 110,000 standard machine hours, respectively.

(3) Compute the amount of fixed overhead cost *applied* at 80,000, 90,000, 100,000, and 110,000 standard machine hours, respectively.

(4) Compute last year's fixed overhead volume variance.

(5) Draw two lines, one representing the amount of fixed overhead *budgeted* and the other representing the amount of fixed overhead *applied*, on a graph using the vertical axis to measure dollars and the horizontal axis to measure standard machine hours. On this graph, show the fixed overhead volume variance computed in (4).

(6) Compute last year's overhead budget variance.

17-36 (Appendix) The Glover Company produces Product A, for which the following standards have been set:

Direct materials (3 pounds @ $2.50 per pound)..	$ 7.50
Direct labor (1 hour @ $12.20 per hour)..	12.20
Total factory overhead (1 direct labor hour @ $7 per hour)	7.00
Standard manufacturing cost per unit of A...	$26.70

The fixed factory overhead rate was determined from the fixed factory overhead budget of $76,000 at a normal activity of 20,000 standard direct labor hours (20,000 units of Product A) per month.

Actual data recorded during April:

Units of Product A produced	13,000
Direct materials purchased..	100,000 pounds @ $2.47 per pound
Direct materials used	39,620 pounds
Direct labor cost..	13,025 hours @ $12.48 per hour
Total factory overhead cost..	$125,000

Required: (1) Compute the following:
  (a) Fixed factory overhead rate per standard direct labor hour
  (b) Variable factory overhead rate per standard direct labor hour
  (c) Direct materials price and quantity variances
  (d) Direct labor price and efficiency variances
  (e) Overhead budget variance
  (f) Fixed overhead volume variance

(2) Using dollars on the vertical axis and standard direct labor hours budgeted on the horizontal axis, graph the amount of total factory overhead budgeted and total factory overhead applied as standard direct labor hours vary. Clearly show the fixed factory overhead volume variance and the overhead budget variance for April on this graph.

Making Evaluations

17-37 The Oldtown Clock Company makes walnut veneer clocks that look like antiques. A new clock to be manufactured requires a veneer strip 6 inches wide and 18 inches long. Oldtown's supplier of walnut veneer will sell veneer in 6-inch-wide strips that are 8 feet long for $12.50 per strip. The supplier is also willing to sell Oldtown 6-inch-wide strips in 6-foot lengths at a price of $9.60 per strip.

The veneer strips must be carefully cut by hand into 18-inch lengths in Oldtown's cutting department. Each 6-inch cut across the strip should take 3 minutes. Direct labor rates in the cutting department are $16.00 per hour. No other manufacturing costs are affected by the company's choice of buying 6- or 8-foot strips. The odd-sized pieces of veneer that are left after cutting have no value.

Required: (1) Assuming the veneer strips are purchased in 6-foot lengths, compute the expected direct materials cost of the veneer and the expected direct labor cost that would be incurred per clock in the cutting department.

(2) Assuming the veneer strips are purchased in 8-foot lengths, compute the expected direct materials cost of the veneer and the expected direct labor cost that would be incurred per clock in the cutting department.

(3) Considering your answers to (1) and (2), should Oldtown purchase the veneer strips in 6- or 8-foot lengths?

(4) Assuming the veneer strips are purchased in 6-foot lengths, determine (for the veneer strips and for veneer cutting operations) the following: (a) the direct materials quantity standard (in feet per clock); (b) the direct materials price standard per foot; and (c) the direct labor quantity standard (in hours per clock).

17-38 The Ranger Company produces Ringos. The president of the company has recently been puzzled by apparent problems causing direct labor price variances that she cannot identify. You are asked to help the president understand the source of the direct labor price variance. The president informs you that 7 direct labor hours at $12 per hour should be worked to produce each Ringo and that the standard direct labor cost totals $84 per Ringo. During April, 700 Ringos were produced, 4,900 direct labor hours were worked, and direct labor cost incurred was $59,374.

Required: (1) Given the preceding information, compute the direct labor price and efficiency variances.

(2) Suppose on further investigation you discover that 990 of the 4,900 direct labor hours were worked in Ranger's Sanding Department and the rest in the Painting Department. Furthermore you discover that production of each Ringo should require the following:

Sanding Department: 2 direct labor hours @ $11.00 per hour =	$22.00
Painting Department: 5 direct labor hours @ $12.40 per hour =	62.00
Total direct labor cost per Ringo	$84.00

You also discover that during April, $10,890 of the direct labor cost was incurred in the Sanding Department and $48,484 in the Painting Department. Given this additional information, compute the direct labor price and efficiency variances for the Sanding Department and the Painting Department separately.

(3) Based on the results obtained in (1) and (2), what would you tell the president about the direct labor price variance?

17-39 The Cozyhome Company makes doghouses. These houses are built in two departments. Department A cuts ¾-inch plywood into two shapes (1 and 2) and paints the pieces with quick-drying paint. Doghouses are assembled in Department B using three pieces of shape 1 and two pieces of shape 2. Direct labor quantity standards for the operations of these two departments are shown here:

Department A : Cutting and painting	
Shape 1	0.21 hours per piece
Shape 2	0.25 hours per piece
Department B: Assembly	
Assembly	1 direct labor hour per doghouse

On August 18, actual production was as follows:

Department A:	
Pieces of shape 1:	80 cut and painted
Pieces of shape 2:	40 cut and painted
Department B:	
Doghouses:	20 assembled

Three laborers worked 8 hours each in Department A and three laborers worked 8 hours each in Department B. All workers earn $15.00 per hour. At the beginning of the day, six pieces of shape 1 but no pieces of shape 2 were ready for assembly.

Required: (1) Compute the standard direct labor cost of one doghouse.

(2) Compute the standard direct labor hours budgeted in Departments A and B for the work done in the Cozyhome shop on August 18.

(3) Compute the direct labor efficiency variances occurring in each of the departments.

(4) Write a brief report on the direct labor performance of the two departments and include a suggestion on how, in the future, managers might avoid the problem that occurred on August 18.

17-40 Missouri Briar Company is a manufacturer of corncob pipes. The company has grown rapidly over the past 10 years. Originally a small supplier of cheaply made pipes for novelty and souvenir shops, the company now supplies large quantities of high-quality pipes to pipe shops throughout the country. Several grades of pipes are sold. The best pipes—Grade A—smoke more sweetly than the finest imported briar pipes. Demand continues to grow. Profit seems to have leveled off over the past two years, however. Pipe production does not seem to be as efficient as it used to be.

Producing a pipe involves several distinctly different operations that require special labor skills. Production starts with "rough cobbing," in which seasoned cobs are cut and drilled. Next comes a critical "sorting" operation, in which the cut and drilled cobs are sorted by quality and shape and sent to different departments set up to produce different grades of pipes.

In these departments, "plugging," "stemming," and "finishing" operations are performed. More skill is required, and a great deal more time is taken in the production of Grade A pipes than in the production of Grade B or Grade C pipes. "Final grading" is the last operation performed. It is an inspection process aimed at maintaining quality. Grade A pipes that do not pass inspection are downgraded and sold as Grade B or C pipes. Grade B pipes that do not pass inspection are downgraded and sold as Grade C pipes. Grade C pipes that do not pass inspection are sold as novelties.

During the last two years Alex Hrechko, the president of Missouri Briar Company, has noticed that the average direct materials and direct labor cost per pipe have increased considerably, although he is not sure why. Alex is worried that things are out of control.

Some data from the last three years are presented in the following table:

	2006 Average Direct Costs Per Pipe			2007 Average Direct Costs Per Pipe			2008 Average Direct Costs Per Pipe		
	Pipes Produced	Materials	Labor	Pipes Produced	Materials	Labor	Pipes Produced	Materials	Labor
Grade A	20,000	$0.90	$1.20	20,000	$0.95	$1.30	21,250	$1.00	$1.45
Grade B	30,000	0.86	1.10	31,000	0.89	1.23	33,750	0.94	1.40
Grade C	40,000	0.85	1.00	46,000	0.88	1.14	53,750	0.93	1.35
Novelty	10,000	0.84	0.95	13,000	0.87	1.10	16,250	0.91	1.30
Total	100,000			110,000			125,000		

Required: Discuss in what ways the data given in the table are deficient for evaluating the performance of the company's manufacturing operations. Also discuss how a standard cost system could improve the president's ability to control the manufacturing operations of his company.

17-41 Carmen A., the supervisor of purchasing operations, is responsible for buying needed materials at the most favorable delivered prices for the Long Manufacturing Company. She is evaluated on the basis of net materials price variances each month. Harlan D., the production supervisor, is responsible for producing the company's products in the desired quantities, attaining appropriate quality standards, and meeting the production schedules that have been adopted. He is evaluated on the basis of net direct materials quantity variances for all materials used each month as well as direct labor efficiency and overhead budget variances.

During January, Carmen obtained a 30% quantity discount off a slightly lower than standard price for a one year's supply of dingers from a new supplier. Normally, dingers are purchased in much smaller quantities. Dingers are critical to the quality of several of the company's products and to the efficiency of direct materials and direct labor usage in several manufacturing processes. The dingers purchased by Carmen in January are of inferior quality.

Required: Discuss the effects that the January purchase of inferior dingers will have on the performance evaluation of both Carmen A. and Harlan D. and the likely effects on company profit. Suggest a way to change the performance evaluation system so that it might be more fair to the individuals involved and might improve company profitability as well.

17-42 (Some Appendix) ". . . and Roy, you know as well as anyone else that while our sales volume is down, we've got to cut costs. Your department's unit costs are up 2% this June. We just can't have any more of this or I'll have to find someone who can keep the costs down." Roy Lilley, a production department manager for the JJS Company, left the meeting room very upset. He had just been severely criticized by the production supervisor because of inefficiency in his department. The basis for that criticism was the following report:

DEPARTMENT 40-00 (ROY LILLEY)
COST REPORT: MAY AND JUNE

	May	June
Production (units)	20,000	16,000
Direct labor hours	4,000	3,100
Costs:		
Direct materials	$10,000	$ 8,400
Direct labor	30,000	22,000
Factory overhead	40,000	34,875
Total	$80,000	$65,275
Cost per unit	$ 4.00	$ 4.08

Roy felt that something was wrong. It seemed to him that his department had worked harder than any of the others to keep costs down. This same episode occurred last summer too, and Roy had almost quit his job because of it.

The cost accounting system used by the JJS Company applies all costs incurred each month to the units produced. Actual total overhead costs, for example, are computed at the end of the month and assigned to the month's production at an actual rate per direct labor hour. In May, total overhead costs had been $100,000 while 10,000 actual direct labor hours were worked in the factory. In June, overhead costs were $90,000 while direct labor hours had dropped to 8,000.

Required: Discuss how useful the cost report is in judging the performance of Roy Lilley's department during June. Also discuss how a standard cost system could be used to prepare another performance report for Department 40-00, one that would be more useful to Roy Lilley and to the production supervisor.

17-43 (Some Appendix) Bill C., the supervisor of purchasing operations, is responsible for buying needed materials for the Short Manufacturing Company at the most favorable delivered prices. He is evaluated on the basis of net materials price variances each month. Peggie C., the production supervisor, is responsible for producing the company's products in the desired quantities, attaining appropriate quality standards, and meeting the production schedules that have been adopted. She is evaluated on the basis of net direct materials quantity variances for all materials used each month as well as direct labor efficiency and overhead budget variances.

During February the company's sales manager, Toni C., landed two huge orders for one of the company's products. These two orders were obtained because Toni promised the customers almost immediate delivery; she would not have obtained the orders otherwise. Toni C. is evaluated on the basis of total sales dollars from orders she obtains. In fact, she receives a fixed percentage sales commission based on her sales dollars.

To obtain enough direct materials for the production required, Bill C. placed rush orders with the company's regular supplier and with several other suppliers at above standard prices. He also made special and costly shipping arrangements in order to have direct materials available in time for production.

Peggie C. used several old machines that had been previously taken out of production because they were inefficient, and she employed several inexperienced machine operators in order to complete production in time to meet the deadlines she was given.

Required: Discuss how Toni C.'s promises of "almost immediate delivery" will affect her own performance evaluation and those of Bill C. and Peggie C. Also discuss the likely effects that her promises will have on company profit. Suggest ways to change the performance evaluation system so that it might be more fair to the individuals involved and might improve company profitability as well.

17-44 Yesterday, you received the following letter for your advice column in the local paper:

DR. DECISIVE

Dear Dr. Decisive:

My roommate and I bought a new desk for our room and thought we could just load it up in his truck, carry it up to our room, and use it. WRONG! As it turned out, there was *some assembly required*. In the middle of our "assembly," we discovered that we were two screws short of what we needed. Well, as if this wasn't bad enough, my roommate, the accounting major, started thinking about standards. He told me that this desk didn't have the standard amount of direct materials included with it. Then he started mumbling about variances and how there were favorable and unfavorable variances (the direct materials variance was favorable for the company that sold us the desk but was unfavorable for us, or something like that). Anyway, one thing led to another, and the next thing I knew we were arguing about whether a favorable variance is always favorable for the company. I think the answer is yes. Otherwise, why would a variance be called favorable? My roommate says I'm wrong, and besides, I'm on his *unfavorable* side right now because it was my idea to buy the desk. I think if you say I'm right, he will see both the favorable and the unfavorable side of me. Please help settle our dispute.

"Two-Sided"

Meet with your Dr. Decisive team and write a response to "Two-Sided."

END NOTE

[a]Hans Sprohge and John Talbott, "Applications in Accounting: New Applications for Variance Analysis," *Journal of Accountancy*, April 1989, 137–141.

CHAPTER 18

MODERN DEVELOPMENTS IN MANAGING OPERATIONS

"A GREAT WIND IS BLOWING AND THAT GIVES YOU EITHER IMAGINATION OR A HEADACHE."

—CATHERINE THE GREAT

1. How has the global economy caused companies to become more competitive?

2. How can an accounting system help a company identify strategies that will enhance its ability to compete in the long run?

3. As part of its efforts to become more competitive, how can a company measure quality and the costs of quality?

4. How does just-in-time production help a company reduce its costs, operate more efficiently, and control quality?

5. How have improved technology and factory layouts helped companies become more competitive?

6. When a company uses activity-based costing, what three stages does it follow to allocate factory overhead costs to products?

7. How does activity-based costing improve managers' decisions?

Suppose that you have always had an interest in running competitively. When you were little and raced the other kids, you consistently won. Suppose also that as you grew up, you competed in school track-and-field events and won state track meets, and that you recently won a national track-and-field competition that makes you eligible to run in the Olympics. How will you evaluate your chances of winning in the Olympics? And how will you prepare to win? Remember, the people you will be competing against also have won school track-and-field events and other track meets, and have proven themselves to be the best in their own countries. Furthermore, some of them have practiced in environments that are different from (and maybe better than) yours; they are perhaps aware of more successful running techniques than you use, and they may wear more technologically advanced running shoes than you do. With this in mind, as you look for ways to improve your performance, you might practice in an environment similar to that of the Olympic venue, hire an additional coach known for his or her innovative techniques, search for ways to run more efficiently (to eliminate the wasted motion that adds to your time), and learn more about the best available running shoes.

Today, companies face a similar situation. Many no longer compete only in their own countries; world competition has become commonplace. Even companies that are well-established in their own countries cannot afford to be complacent about their success because other companies in the same country, as well as those in other countries, are eager to win the competition for customers by using improved technology, by selling high-quality products at lower prices, and by meeting shorter delivery schedules. Consequently, to make themselves more competitive, many companies have adopted a Japanese philosophy called *kaizen*, or continuous improvement. These companies consistently strive for higher-quality products and services, more efficient operations, and lower costs.

Here's what can happen when a company focuses on improvement. In an effort to improve its operations, **Alexander Doll Company**, a New York City manufacturer of collectible dolls, set up a team of employees to evaluate its production line.[a] At the time, production was spread out over three floors, which caused extra handling that not only damaged the dolls but also wasted time. Furthermore, the factory scheduled production so that the dolls moved from process to process in batches. This batch processing caused a collection, or "log jam," of dolls before each process as batches of dolls waited their turn while the process finished a previous batch. By combining all the operations at one location (on one floor) and by processing the dolls continuously, rather than in batches, Alexander Doll Company achieved dramatic improvements.

For instance, the distance each doll traveled through the production process went down from 630 to 40 feet, and the time to complete a doll dropped from 90 days to 90 *minutes*! The production area decreased from 2,010 to 980 square feet, and the average productivity per person per day increased from 8 to 25 dolls. Even with this substantial betterment, the company plans to continue to make improvements. Managers of companies like Alexander Doll Company have found that better information obtained from their companies' accounting systems supports their ability to continuously improve their companies in these areas.

Do you suppose Alexander Doll Company uses a job order or a process cost accounting system? Why?

EFFECTS OF MODERN DEVELOPMENTS ON COMPETITION

As we discussed in Chapter 2, many factors affect the current business environment, but global competition, alone, has forced companies to reassess everything from operations to customer service. This additional competition has accelerated the rate of technological advances, allowing companies to produce and sell a wider assortment of products and services. Because of the increasing rate of technological change, many products and services appeal to customers for shorter periods of time before more-advanced products and services capture their attention. Advances in communication and transportation have provided customers with worldwide product information and greater access to these products.

How has the global economy caused companies to become more competitive?

Global competition not only has *contributed* to the rate of change in the business environment but is a *part* of that change. Now, instead of just trying to maintain their share of customers or to gain customers by successfully competing against companies in their own countries, companies also must defend or increase their share of customers by competing with companies from other countries.

A company can use numerous strategies to make itself more competitive, including the following:

1. Selling a better (higher-quality) product than that offered by any of its competitors
2. Responding to customer needs and wants, and providing superior customer service
3. Reducing the amount of time between receiving a customer's order and delivering the product
4. Selling a product equal in quality to that of its competitors but at a lower price

Along with the philosophy of continuous improvement, several other management philosophies and production techniques have emerged that help a company implement these strategies and compete more effectively. Next, we will discuss several of these philosophies and techniques, including the balanced scorecard, benchmarking, total quality management, just-in-time strategies, improved technology and factory layout, and activity-based costing. As you will see in this chapter, a company's accounting system can be reconfigured to support these philosophies and techniques.

THE BALANCED SCORECARD

2 How can an accounting system help a company identify strategies that will enhance its ability to compete in the long run?

A company's accounting system provides financial measures that help internal users manage the company's activities. These measures report on the results of the company's *past* activities, and because of the timing of the reporting, lag behind the activities. In the rapidly changing business environment, measures of past activities may not provide sufficient information to help managers plan strategies to make the company more competitive in its long-term future. In a more balanced approach, a company's accounting system [perhaps through its enterprise resource planning (ERP) system] retains the financial measures of the company's past performance. But it also supplements them with both leading indicators of the activities that will drive the company's *future* financial performance and by lagging measures of the success of these activities in moving the company toward its goals. This approach is often referred to as the **balanced scorecard**.

The balanced scorecard approach links competitive strategies with specific measures of the success of the strategies. *It focuses on causes and effects.* In other words, the balanced scorecard answers questions such as: What goal (or effect) do the company's managers hope to achieve, and what actions must they take to achieve that goal? Then after they begin to implement the strategies, how can they measure whether they are, in fact, achieving the desired goal?

A company's managers can begin using the balanced scorecard approach by first viewing the company's performance from four perspectives: the stockholders' perspective, the customers' perspective, the internal business perspective, and the perspective of innovation and learning. The balanced scorecard provides the information from these perspectives that managers use to help them identify four sets of strategic objectives for the company:

- Financial objectives
- Customer-related objectives
- Objectives for internal business processes
- Objectives for innovation and learning

A company's managers specify *financial objectives* by determining the answers to broad questions such as the following: What are the expectations of the company's stockholders about the future success of the company? What do they think are acceptable levels of growth and profitability for the company, and how much risk are the stockholders willing to take? Based on the answers to the previous questions—the financial objectives—the managers can determine the company's customer-related objectives.

The company's *customer-related objectives* address how the company will achieve the levels of growth, profitability, and risk specified in the company's financial objectives. In other words, to achieve these levels, what must the company do to create value and differentiate its product for its existing customers, and to attract new customers?

The answers to these questions direct how the company should prioritize its *internal business processes objectives*. The internal business processes objectives derive from the answers to the following questions: In what areas must the company excel—product quality? on-time delivery? throughput time from customer order to delivery of the product? The answers to questions like these become the company's objectives for internal business processes.

Finally, to accomplish all this, the company's managers must determine how the company should support the change, innovation, and growth necessary to achieve these objectives. It must develop *objectives for innovation and learning* within the company. Exhibit 18-1 illustrates the cascading relationships of the four sets of strategic objectives.

Once the company's managers have identified objectives for the company, they must determine the overall strategies that will allow them to achieve each of the objectives. For example, if one of the company's objectives is to increase profitability for its stockholders, its strategies could include establishing a new market in another geographical area, increasing customers in existing markets, and/or increasing sales to existing customers. Strategies might also include reducing expenses by controlling product quality, by reducing the size of inventories, and by utilizing property and equipment more efficiently. We will discuss total quality management, just-in-time strategies involving inventories, and improved technology and factory layout—all strategies for reducing costs—later in this chapter.

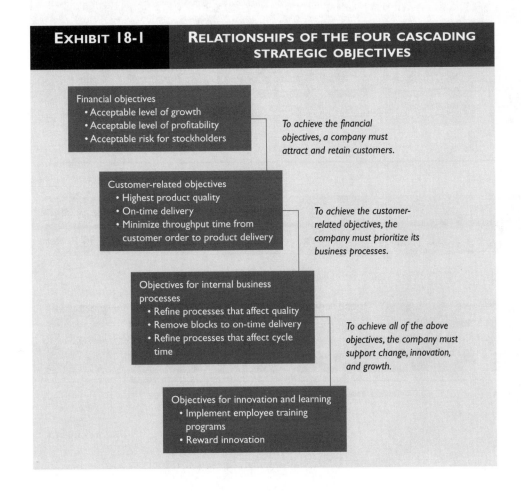

EXHIBIT 18-1   RELATIONSHIPS OF THE FOUR CASCADING STRATEGIC OBJECTIVES

Financial objectives
• Acceptable level of growth
• Acceptable level of profitability
• Acceptable risk for stockholders

To achieve the financial objectives, a company must attract and retain customers.

Customer-related objectives
• Highest product quality
• On-time delivery
• Minimize throughput time from customer order to product delivery

To achieve the customer-related objectives, the company must prioritize its business processes.

Objectives for internal business processes
• Refine processes that affect quality
• Remove blocks to on-time delivery
• Refine processes that affect cycle time

To achieve all of the above objectives, the company must support change, innovation, and growth.

Objectives for innovation and learning
• Implement employee training programs
• Reward innovation

All of the strategies that result from the balanced scorecard approach are critical elements for achieving goal congruence among the company's departments and employees. These strategies are important because they become reference points for the department managers and employees to use in determining their own, more specific strategies for achieving the company's objectives.

In order to achieve these specific strategies, the managers of a company that uses the balanced scorecard approach should set up both performance driver measurements (leading indicators of the company's future performance) and outcome measurements (lagging indicators of the company's past or current performance) that link to the objectives in a "cause-and-effect" manner. For example, the top part of Exhibit 18-2 shows *from right to left* the thought sequence that a company's managers should go through to determine the strategies that they must implement in order for the company to achieve its broad objectives. For instance, if one of the broad objectives of the company is to improve profitability for its stockholders, managers might accomplish this by increasing sales (among other strategies). To increase sales, managers might need to improve the satisfaction of the company's customers. One way to accomplish this is by arranging for faster delivery of the company's product.

 What are some ways the company might speed up the delivery of its product to customers?

The company's managers would continue this backward process—first looking at improvements from the perspective of the company's financial objectives, then from the customers' perspective, the internal business processes perspective, and then, finally, from the perspective of innovations and learning.

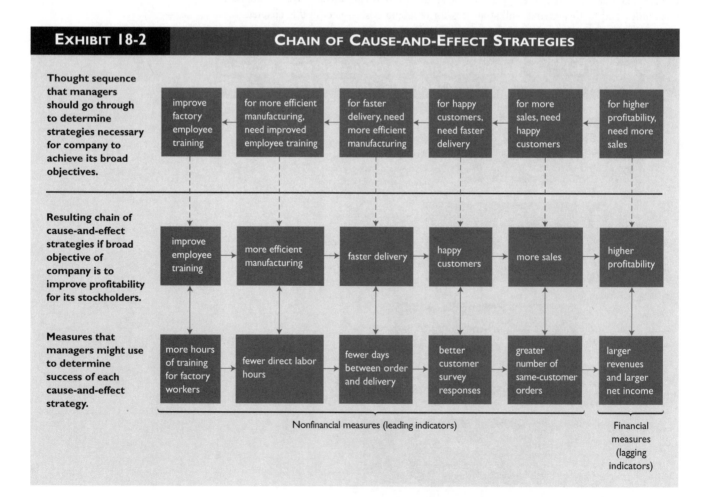

EXHIBIT 18-2   **CHAIN OF CAUSE-AND-EFFECT STRATEGIES**

Thought sequence that managers should go through to determine strategies necessary for company to achieve its broad objectives.

improve factory employee training ← for more efficient manufacturing, need improved employee training ← for faster delivery, need more efficient manufacturing ← for happy customers, need faster delivery ← for more sales, need happy customers ← for higher profitability, need more sales

Resulting chain of cause-and-effect strategies if broad objective of company is to improve profitability for its stockholders.

improve employee training → more efficient manufacturing → faster delivery → happy customers → more sales → higher profitability

Measures that managers might use to determine success of each cause-and-effect strategy.

more hours of training for factory workers → fewer direct labor hours → fewer days between order and delivery → better customer survey responses → greater number of same-customer orders → larger revenues and larger net income

Nonfinancial measures (leading indicators)   Financial measures (lagging indicators)

The middle part of Exhibit 18-2 shows the resulting chain of cause-and-effect strategies, from left to right, if the broad objective of the company is to improve profitability for its stockholders. The bottom part of Exhibit 18-2 shows examples of measurements that managers might use to measure the success of each cause-and-effect strategy.

The leading indicators (measurements) provide information about whether activities are in place that should help the company implement a strategy successfully. The lagging indicators reveal, after the fact, whether the strategies resulted in enhanced financial performance for the company.

BENCHMARKING

The balanced scorecard helps a company link its competitive strategies with the success of those strategies, allowing the company to continually improve its operations. The basis of comparison is the company's own past performance. **Benchmarking**, on the other hand, allows the company to compare its operations against its most successful competitors by measuring its own practices against the best practices (benchmarks) occurring in the industry in which it operates. Many industry trade associations conduct surveys of their member companies regarding the practices of those companies and then make the results of those surveys available to their members. For example, the National Confectioners Association (NCA) may attempt to investigate new market trends regarding sugar-reduced and sugar-free products, or how companies are successfully reducing or replacing trans fats. Based on surveys, the NCA may establish glycemic indexes and other nutritional benchmarks. Other examples of areas that the NCA might investigate are product shelf lives, or the quality of chocolate bars made with cocoa from a particular region of the world. Unlimited Decadence, if it were a member of this organization, would be able to see where its practices rank against the best practices in the industry.

THE ISSUE OF QUALITY

Because providing better-quality products or services to its customers gives a company a "leg up" on its competition, managers are giving the issue of quality increasing attention and using it as a selling point for their companies' products. For example, **Leisure Life Limited**, a manufacturer of small boats, includes the following paragraph in its sales brochures:

3 As part of its efforts to become more competitive, how can a company measure quality and the costs of quality?

> Every Leisure Life Limited boat must pass a rigorous test of nearly 100 quality checks during assembly and before shipping. . . . Our boats have earned the reputation of being the highest quality in the industry, and for good reason. Compare the quality of design, construction, and attention to detail of any Leisure Life Limited boat against any other small boat and you will agree that our reputation is well deserved.

As more companies export their products to other countries as a means of expanding their set of customers, they may choose to adopt **ISO 9000**, a set of quality standards set up by the **International Organization for Standardization**, a consortium of European countries. They may adopt these standards not only because they agree with them, but also because many large potential customers in Europe *require* that their suppliers adhere to these standards. Both Leisure Life's statement of quality and ISO 9000 are consistent with a management philosophy called *total quality management,* which we will discuss next.

Total Quality Management

Total quality management (TQM) is a management philosophy or approach that focuses on a company's customers. These customers can be consumers—what we normally picture as the customers of the company. But the "customers" may also exist *inside* the company. Departments or divisions may serve all or some of the employees of other departments or divisions of the company. For example, if a company has an employee cafeteria, the employees of the company who eat lunch in the cafeteria are the cafeteria's customers.

Under the TQM philosophy, all employees of the company work as a team with their external and internal customers, as well as with their suppliers, to foster continuous improvement in the company to meet or exceed the expectations of the customers. The ideal is 100 percent quality rather than, say, 95 percent quality. (Think about it. If you take 120 credit hours during your undergraduate program, that's about 1,800 actual hours spent in the classroom. Do you want 5 percent, or 90 of those hours, filled with misinformation? How would you know which 90 of the 1,800 hours contained misinformation? Perhaps worse yet, when you are ill do you want 5 percent of your doctor's education to be filled with misinformation?) Exhibit 18-3 illustrates the potential magnitude of less than 100 percent quality.

 How do you think including its suppliers on the team helps a company meet or exceed its customers' expectations?

The atmosphere of continuous improvement must be supported by an information system that provides continuous feedback to help all employees perform better. When this feedback is available, employees can measure information about the activities of the company against benchmarks and can take corrective action when necessary. As you will see next, one important component of TQM and the measurement of quality is the integrated accounting system. This integrated accounting system may be part of a company's *enterprise resource planning system* (ERP). As we discussed in Chapter 10 of Volume 1, under an ERP system, a company stores information in an electronic "data warehouse." Managers can "data mine" the information in this data warehouse to extract useful information for TQM, as we discuss in the following sections.

EXHIBIT 18-3	WHAT 99.9 PERCENT QUALITY ACHIEVES (OR DOESN'T ACHIEVE)

Strive for Perfection—OR ELSE!*
If 99.9 percent is good enough, then . . .

- Two million documents will be lost by the IRS this year.
- 811,000 faulty rolls of 35mm film will be loaded this year.
- 22,000 checks will be deducted from the wrong bank accounts in the next 60 minutes.
- 1,314 phone calls will be misplaced by telecommunications services every minute.
- 12 babies will be given the wrong parents each day.
- 268,500 defective tires will be shipped this year.
- 14,208 defective personal computers will be shipped this year.
- 103,260 income tax returns will be processed incorrectly this year.
- 2,488,200 books will be shipped in the next 12 months with the wrong cover.
- 5,517,200 cases of soft drinks produced in the next 12 months will be flatter than a bad tire.
- Two plane landings daily at O'Hare International Airport in Chicago will be unsafe.
- 3,056 copies of tomorrow's *Wall Street Journal* will be missing one of the three sections.
- 18,322 pieces of mail will be mishandled in the next hour.
- 291 pacemaker operations will be performed incorrectly this year.
- 880,000 credit cards in circulation will turn out to have incorrect cardholder information on their magnetic strips.
- $9,690 will be spent today, tomorrow, next Thursday, and every day in the future on defective, often unsafe sporting equipment.
- 55 malfunctioning automatic teller machines will be installed in the next 12 months.
- 20,000 incorrect drug prescriptions will be written in the next 12 months.
- 114,500 mismatched pairs of shoes will be shipped this year.
- $761,900 will be spent in the next 12 months on tapes and compact discs that won't play.
- 107 incorrect medical procedures will be performed by the end of the day today.
- 315 entries in *Webster's Third New International Dictionary of the English Language* will turn out to be misspelled.

*InSight, Syncrude Canada Ltd., Communications Division

How Can the Integrated Accounting System Measure Quality?

Have you ever purchased a product that didn't measure up to your expectations of quality? What did you do about it? If the company from whom you purchased the product is "lucky," *it* will notice the problem before you do, recall the product, and fix or replace it. Or if *you* notice the problem first, you will return it for warranty work or replacement. In those cases, the company can "make it right" and perhaps maintain your goodwill. But if, instead, the company is "unlucky," and you decide to harbor a grudge and never purchase a product from that company again, the company stands to lose more than the cost of the warranty work or replacement—it stands to lose all of your future business (and perhaps the future business of all the people you tell about your experience with that product). The costs of flaws in products that reach the customers are called **external failure costs**. These costs occur *after* the product leaves the company. Since managers are focused on continuous improvement, including the reduction of external failure costs, they are usually interested in monitoring both the cost of external failures and the number of those failures.

For example, recently, **Cane Creek Cycling Components**, of Fletcher, North Carolina, recalled about 7,700 Thudbuster bicycle suspension seat posts because the cradle for the seat could break and put riders at risk of injury (ouch!).[b] Independent bicycle dealers sold the seat posts for about $140 each. If Cane Creek refunded the sales price for each of these bicycles, its measurable external failure cost would be $1,078,000. As we discussed in previous chapters, some companies use a Warranty Expense account and a Sales Returns and Allowances account to help them keep track of some of their external failure costs. An integrated accounting system most useful to managers measures the *number* of warranty repairs, product replacements, and product recalls as well as all their costs (costs of raw materials, labor, overhead, and shipping), and you can be sure Cane Creek's internal records contain this information as well.

 How do you think the integrated accounting system could measure the cost of losing future business or the cost of customer ill will?

Because of the risk of losing or alienating their customers, companies prefer to catch product defects *before* their products leave the company, or to prevent defects altogether. The

"**We jacked up our prices to insure that you receive the same quality and service in the future.**"

Do you think price is always related to quality?

costs of catching product defects inside the company are called **appraisal costs.** The salaries of product inspectors and equipment testers, and the costs of materials used in the inspecting and testing processes, are examples of appraisal costs that the accounting system captures and communicates. The integrated accounting system also captures and communicates the number of inspections and tests conducted, at what point (or points) in the production process they are conducted, and how many defects the inspectors and testers find.

The costs of reworking defective products after the inspectors and testers find the defects (the wages of factory employees who rework the defective products, the cost of replacement parts and materials, and overhead costs) and the amount of time that the factory is "down" while employees trace and fix the cause of the defects are called **internal failure costs.** The integrated accounting system provides information about these costs as well as the number of defective products reworked. For instance, earlier in the book we used the Purchases Returns and Allowances account to help keep track of some of these internal failures.

 What do you think are the similarities between internal and external failure costs? How do these costs differ from each other?

Companies can minimize external failure costs, appraisal costs, and internal failure costs by preventing defects from occurring in the first place. The costs of preventing flaws and defects are called **prevention costs**. These costs include employee training costs (for example, salaries of trainers, salaries of employees during their training time, and costs of training facilities). A case in point is **Taco Inc.**, a Cranston, Rhode Island, manufacturer of heating and cooling equipment.[c] As part of its employee-training program, one of Taco's managers teaches a class on the ISO 9000 international quality standards. Taco Inc.'s prevention costs include the manager's salary while teaching the class, the salaries of the employees while taking the class, and the costs of the Taco Learning Center (consisting of two classrooms, a computer lab room, a library, and a conference room). Prevention costs also include equipment maintenance costs (wages of maintenance employees and costs of indirect materials).

 Why do you think equipment maintenance costs are considered to be prevention costs?

The integrated accounting system provides information about training and equipment maintenance costs, as well as other information that managers might want to know about prevention costs. This information includes, for instance, the number of employees trained, the number of training seminars, the number of machines maintained, and the number of maintenance orders over a specified time period.

 If you were the president of a company, which of the four costs of quality could you most easily justify? Why?

But what if a company wants to take quality a step further and not just reduce defects, but manufacture a higher-quality product than it has previously manufactured? Many times, a higher-quality product costs more to manufacture than does one of lower quality. To keep its profit the same, a company trying to increase the quality of its product would have to raise selling prices (or sell more units) to make up the difference in cost, or would have to lower other costs. Otherwise, it would end up with less profit.

In the past, managers tried to balance the value of the increased quality against the related increase in costs—the increase in quality might not be worth the additional costs of a higher-quality product if the company's customers seemed satisfied with the current level of product quality. Now, however, managers realize that a competitor of the company may succeed at providing a better product without raising prices or incurring higher costs, or may manage to sell an equal-quality product at a lower price. Furthermore, the competitor may shorten the time it needs to deliver high-quality products to customers.

As companies have learned, one way a competitor can manufacture higher-quality products without raising prices or incurring higher costs is by reducing other costs enough to cover the increased costs of manufacturing a higher-quality product. The competitor can sell an equal-quality product at a lower price by reducing the costs of manufacturing the product without reducing quality.

A company can reduce its product costs, as well as the amount of time between the customer order and the delivery of the product, by eliminating or reducing inefficiencies in its production process and by using improved technology. One way a company can reduce inefficiencies is by identifying those activities that are not adding value to its products or services and then minimizing or eliminating those activities. By "adding value," we mean making products or services more valuable to customers. For example, consider the following categories of manufacturing activities: production, inspection, transfer, idle time, and storage. Of these categories, only production activities add value to the products.

Although inspection activities are necessary to ensure that products meet a specified level of quality, they do not give the customer a higher level of quality; instead, they help the company maintain the expected level of quality. Transfer activities simply move products from one part of the factory to another. Idle time is factory time not used for production and includes setup time, "log jam" or queue time that occurs when products are waiting behind other products for processing, maintenance time, and repair time. Storage activities involve warehousing products between the time of their manufacture and the time of their sale or delivery. It is only the conversion of raw materials and parts into finished products that adds value to products. Many companies have found that changing from traditional production strategies to just-in-time production strategies has helped them reduce these inefficiencies.

JUST-IN-TIME (JIT) STRATEGIES FOR MANUFACTURING COMPANIES

Many companies use **just-in-time strategies** to reduce costs by reducing or eliminating inventories, streamlining the factory and increasing operational efficiencies, and controlling quality. The approach to production these companies use differs from that of traditional manufacturing companies.

Traditional manufacturing companies (in this case, those other than JIT-oriented companies) base their production and inventory orders on forecasts of demand for their products. Think back to our Chapter 12 discussion of a manufacturing company's budgets. Remember that we based Unlimited Decadence's production budget on predicted sales. That is, Unlimited Decadence planned to produce in any given month enough candy bars so that the combination of its production and its beginning inventory for the month would cover that month's predicted sales as well as one-half of the following month's predicted sales. Based on its sales budget, Unlimited Decadence planned to build up inventories of finished goods in anticipation of future sales, and also to have extra inventory on hand in case it underestimated sales. Its production budget influenced production scheduling as well as planned orders of raw materials, as shown in its raw materials purchases budget. Based on the production budget (which was based on forecasted sales), Unlimited Decadence planned to build up its raw materials inventory in anticipation of future production. So, in traditional manufacturing, the sales forecast "pushes" the products through the production process. Hence, we could call the production process in a traditional factory **push-through production**.

The practice of building up inventories can cause companies to operate inefficiently. For example, inventory ties up resources such as cash (which a company doesn't get back until it sells the inventory and collects the related receivables), floor space, and labor, keeping the company from using these resources for other purposes. By minimizing inventories, companies also minimize this kind of inefficiency and the costs associated with it.

4 How does just-in-time production help a company reduce its costs, operate more efficiently, and control quality?

What costs do you think are associated with tying up cash, floor space, and labor?

Unlike traditional companies, companies that use JIT strategies minimize their inventories. Suppliers deliver materials and parts to these companies just in time for production of the orders placed by the company's customers, so there is no buildup (or there is minimal buildup) of raw materials inventories. Goods-in-process inventory moves through production just in time for the next process, so incomplete products don't build up after one process while waiting to enter the next process (which they may do in a conventional factory). When these companies complete orders, they deliver the orders directly to their customers rather than to the storeroom or warehouse, avoiding a buildup of finished goods inventories. In these companies, production is based on customers' orders rather than on a forecast of what customers *might* order. So, customers' orders "pull" the products through the production process, from the customers' orders backward through the production process to the purchase of raw materials. Because of this characteristic, production in a JIT factory is called **pull-through production**. Exhibit 18-4 illustrates push-through and pull-through production. In the exhibit, you can see that pull-through production even *looks* more efficient than push-through production.

Notice in the JIT portion of Exhibit 18-4 that there is no finished goods inventory. This is usually the case because a company that uses a JIT system ordinarily ships its finished products to its customers immediately after manufacturing the products. In this situation, the company may choose to record its product costs (for direct materials, direct labor, and factory overhead) *directly* in its Cost of Goods Sold account. Under this system, if the company does have a finished goods inventory on hand at the end of its accounting period, the company "backs out" the costs of the products still on hand from its Cost of Goods Sold account, and records these costs in a Finished Goods Inventory account. This method and variations of this method are sometimes referred to as **back-flush costing**.

 Notice that we said that a company using JIT strategies minimizes its inventories. Why do you think the company doesn't just eliminate its inventories altogether?

Along with inventory buildups, another source of inefficiency in the production process is numerous setup times. A company that manufactures a variety of products may use some of the same machines for different products. For example, Unlimited Decadence could use the hoppers, mixer, refiner, conche, temperer, molder, and wrapper in different combinations to manufacture most of its candy bars. Many times, when a company uses a machine for manufacturing more than one product, workers on the production line must set the machine up differently for each product. For the Unlimited Decadence factory to mold a candy bar in a unique shape, the molder would need to be set up to produce candy bars in that shape. So each time production switched from a candy bar with one shape to one with a different shape, the machine setup would take time away from production and would occupy labor so that it could not be used productively somewhere else. The more setups a company has, the longer will be the total production time. In trying to eliminate inefficiencies and costs, a company that has a JIT factory also tries to minimize setup times. As you will see later in this chapter, manufacturing technology has improved setup times for a company that takes advantage of this technology.

A company using JIT production also reduces inefficiencies and costs in its factory by minimizing **product defect rates**, the percentage of defective products manufactured. Besides bringing production to a grinding halt while employees locate and fix the problem that caused the defects, product defects also slow delivery times because of the production delays. (Remember, the company maintains zero or minimal finished goods inventories, so it can't deliver "spare" products when the factory shuts down.) Furthermore, defects can raise the costs of inspecting the products if, as a result of these defects, the company decides to make more regular inspections. Defects also can raise the costs of production because of the additional costs of correcting the defects.

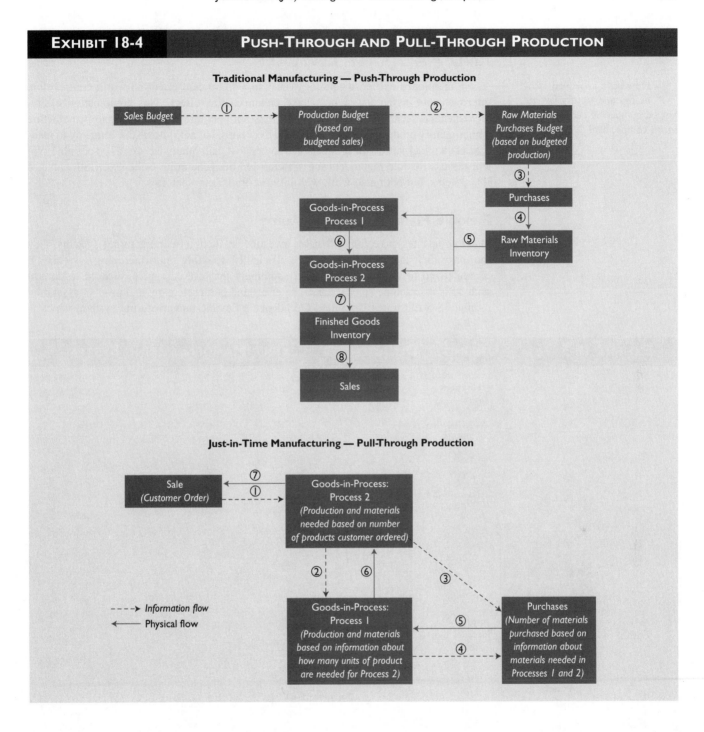

EXHIBIT 18-4   **PUSH-THROUGH AND PULL-THROUGH PRODUCTION**

Traditional Manufacturing — Push-Through Production

Just-in-Time Manufacturing — Pull-Through Production

- - - -> Information flow
← Physical flow

One way a company minimizes its product defect rates is by choosing, and closely working with, a supplier that emphasizes quality. This way the company can be assured that it makes its products with high-quality raw materials and parts. In addition, the company can minimize its product defect rates by training its factory employees to detect product defects and by emphasizing regular equipment maintenance and ongoing defect prevention. Many companies also take advantage of advances in technology and improve their factory layouts to minimize their defect rates.

If a company has a philosophy of continuous improvement and is able to reduce inefficiencies in its factory, how do you think that will affect the company's standard costs? Why?

THE EFFECT OF IMPROVED TECHNOLOGY AND FACTORY LAYOUT

5 How have improved technology and factory layouts helped companies become more competitive?

As we mentioned earlier, technology has had a significant effect on world competition. Improvements in factory layouts have enhanced this effect. This combination of improvements in technology and factory layouts not only allows a company to manufacture higher-quality products and minimize its defect rates, but also allows the company to manufacture a wider variety of products at a lower cost than otherwise would be possible. We will discuss flexible manufacturing systems and manufacturing cells next. Both enhance JIT systems, but both also work well in more-traditional factories.

Flexible Manufacturing Systems

Many companies have found that by investing in flexible manufacturing systems, they can make their factories operate more efficiently. **Flexible manufacturing systems** are computerized networks of automated equipment that use computer software to control such tasks as machine setups, direct materials and parts selection, and product assembly. Exhibit 18-5 illustrates Unlimited Decadence's flexible manufacturing system, which is

EXHIBIT 18-5   UNLIMITED DECADENCE'S FLEXIBLE MANUFACTURING SYSTEM

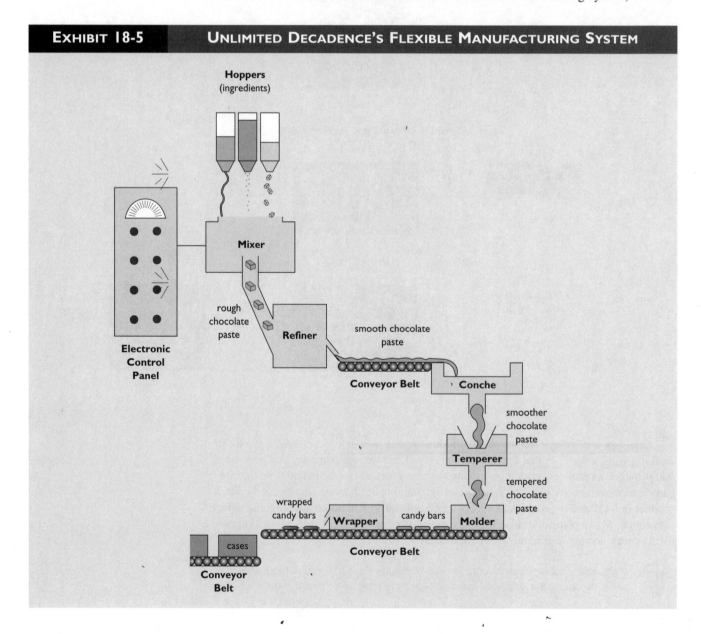

run by an electronic control panel. The control panel selects the ingredient mix for each type of candy bar that Unlimited Decadence produces with this system, designates the amount of time each machine spends on each type of candy bar, monitors the temperature and candy density, and directs the packaging of each type of candy bar. Furthermore, it causes adjustments to be made to the production process when any of these variables deviate from an acceptable range of values.

A company that manufactures a wide variety of products stands to benefit the most from flexible manufacturing systems; since the equipment is automated, setup costs are almost zero. Computers drive each setup, and many times the setup involves merely using different software rather than requiring a physical change in the machinery. So each setup takes less time, causes lower labor costs, and results in fewer mistakes than when employees must make physical changes in the machinery for each setup.

In many flexible manufacturing systems, computer software also drives the selection and delivery of parts and materials needed for current production. Some companies have computer-driven robots that select parts and materials and that either deliver them to the production area or put the parts on a computerized belt that will deliver the parts to the production area. As part of their ERP systems, some companies using JIT production have computer systems "networked" to their suppliers' computers. With this arrangement, the computer that is running production can order parts and other raw materials electronically from suppliers so that they will arrive at the factory just in time for production. After the parts and materials arrive in the production area, computer-driven machinery assembles them into products.

 How do you think switching from a traditional factory to a flexible manufacturing system would affect the costs of materials, labor, and overhead relative to each other? Why?

When **Fuji Electric**, a Japanese manufacturer of electronic machinery, changed from a traditional manufacturing system to a flexible manufacturing system, Fuji improved its ability to compete.[d] Now Fuji's factory is automated and uses information in bar codes on its products, read by automated scanners, to direct machine setups, materials and parts selection, and product assembly. Currently it takes 24 hours, on average, from the time a customer places an order until Fuji delivers that order. It used to take three days. Additionally, Fuji now uses one-third as many factory workers, keeps about one-third less inventory on hand, and produces three times the variety of products it did when it used a traditional system!

Fuji's experience demonstrates that, besides reducing labor costs by using automated equipment instead of labor, flexible manufacturing systems make factories more efficient by reducing setup times and overall production times. Producing each type of product doesn't require a separate production line; the same machines can be used to manufacture a greater assortment of products. Keep in mind, however, that although converting to a flexible manufacturing system reduces some costs, it may increase other costs, including equipment costs and any interest the company must pay on money borrowed to acquire the equipment. Managers must consider these cost tradeoffs when deciding whether to convert to a flexible system. We will discuss equipment purchase decisions (capital budgeting decisions) in Chapter 20.

Manufacturing Cells

Many companies have found that by reconfiguring the layouts of their factories, they can improve manufacturing efficiency. In a traditional factory, products move through the factory from process to process until they are completed. Typically, a company groups together, in an area of the factory called a *department* or *process,* those machines that perform similar tasks. For instance, a candy factory might have a pulverizing department, a mixing department, a refining department, a

Is this a traditional factory layout or a manufacturing cell layout?

© EYEWIRE/GETTY IMAGES

conching department, a tempering department, a molding department, and a wrapping packaging department. Specialized employees, assigned to a process or department, perform a specific task on each product that moves through that department or process. Other employees maintain the factory equipment and may even specialize in maintaining particular types of equipment. Products may travel a considerable distance across the factory to get from process to process.

When a company reconfigures its factory to use manufacturing cells, it moves its machines from processes or departments to *cells*. Each cell is responsible for manufacturing a specific product, or "family" of products, and is made up of the machines needed to manufacture that product or family. The company assigns workers to each cell and trains them to operate and maintain *all* the machines in the cell (a much more interesting job than just doing one particular task day after day). These employees also are responsible for making decisions about production in their cells (like whether to shut down production in the cell when a product flaw or defect is discovered)—decisions that production supervisors in a traditional factory typically make. Products move from machine to machine (process to process) within the cell until they are finished. Exhibit 18-6 shows how Unlimited Decadence might organize its factory under a traditional layout and one with manufacturing cells.

 How do you think Exhibit 18-6 would be different if the factory using manufacturing cells was a JIT factory?

Manufacturing cells are more efficient than the traditional factory layout because products don't need to travel as far to get from process to process. Labor costs may be reduced because employees are able to perform a greater variety of tasks. (There is less need for specialized employees who are limited to doing a few tasks, who do only those tasks when needed, and who may have idle time when their specialty is not needed.) Furthermore, employee morale may be better in a factory that uses manufacturing cells. Also, because of the employees' greater involvement in total production (including making decisions that traditionally would have been a manager's decision), employees take more pride in their work, tend to take "ownership" in their work, and are more inclined to do quality work.

ACTIVITY-BASED COSTING

In today's competitive world market, a company needs accurate and timely cost information to compete effectively. As we have been discussing, one way a company competes is by minimizing costs and inefficiencies in its operations. To do this, the company's managers must know which of its activities create value for its customers and which do not. Then they can manage costs by becoming more efficient in performing value-adding activities and by working to eliminate, or minimize, non-value-adding activities. Managing costs requires a good understanding of which activities, or factors related to these activities, cause the company to incur costs.

For planning, operating, and evaluating decisions, the managers of a company need good estimates of product and service costs based on realistic assumptions. But as factories have become more automated, there are fewer direct labor costs and what appear to be more fixed factory overhead costs. Both job order costing and process costing, using direct labor hours or machine hours to allocate factory overhead costs, assume that all overhead costs result from one type of activity (such as direct labor or machine usage). But if you think about it, some overhead costs may have nothing to do with direct labor or machine usage. For example, air-conditioning costs may be more directly related to the number of cubic feet in the factory than they are related to either direct labor or machine usage. Numerous factors can cause a company to incur overhead costs, such as purchase orders, machine setups, inspections, and floor space occupied. So, more

EXHIBIT 18-6	UNLIMITED DECADENCE: TRADITIONAL FACTORY VS. MANUFACTURING CELLS

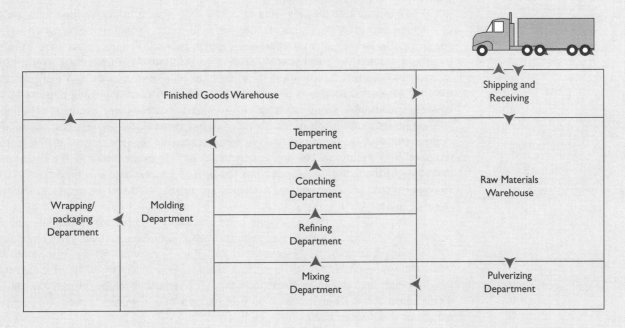

Traditional Factory

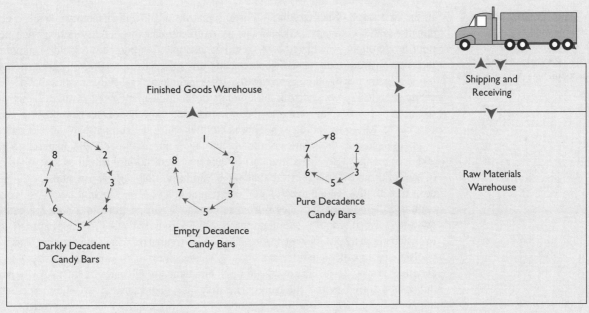

Factory with Manufacturing Cells

1	Pulverizing	4	Refining	7	Molding
2	Mixing	5	Conching	8	Wrapping/Packaging
3	Refining	6	Tempering		

traditional methods of determining product and service costs may no longer provide relevant information. Activity-based costing, however, enhances the results of job order costing and process costing by providing companies with more precise cost information that results from taking into account these numerous factors in the allocation of factory overhead.

A manufacturing company uses activity-based costing in conjunction with job order costing and process costing. Under both job order costing and process costing, a company allocates its factory overhead costs to individual units of product. Conventional job order costing and process costing both follow a multiple-stage overhead-allocation process that allocates overhead costs to jobs or processes, and then allocates the costs of jobs or processes to units of the product. A company using **activity-based costing** also follows a multiple-stage process to allocate factory overhead to units of product under either a job order cost accounting system or a process cost accounting system. However, as we will discuss in the next section, the first stage is different from that used in conventional costing. Furthermore, the stages are based on the assumption that many of the factory overhead costs (both fixed and variable overhead costs) that a company incurs are the result of activities not related to direct labor hours. (In fact, some of these costs may stay the same as direct labor hours increase or decrease, and so may *appear to be* fixed costs. Other costs may appear to vary with direct labor hours, perhaps because the company separated mixed costs into fixed and variable components by using direct labor hours as its measure of volume.) As you will see, this more realistic assumption provides a more precise measurement of the true cost of a manufactured product than does the assumption that all overhead costs *are* directly related to direct labor hours. Knowing the true cost of each of a company's products helps its managers make better decisions.

Three-Stage Allocation Process

In the first stage of activity-based costing, instead of allocating factory overhead costs to departments, a company allocates factory overhead costs to activity pools. Each **activity pool** is a grouping of related activities. For example, the company would accumulate the factory overhead costs related to purchasing raw materials in a *pool for purchasing activities.* The activities of purchasing raw materials include several sub-activities that involve locating suppliers, processing purchase orders, receiving shipments of inventory, transporting the newly received inventory to the raw materials warehouse, and processing accounts payable related to the purchases. These activities cause the company to incur certain overhead costs, such as the salaries of the purchasing agents, dock receivers, materials handlers, and accounts payable clerks; the cost of supplies used in these activities; and depreciation of the forklifts that transport the materials. Similarly, the company would accumulate the costs of activities related to setting up equipment in a *pool for machine setups;* it would accumulate the costs of activities related to conducting inspections in a *pool for quality inspections;* and it would accumulate the costs of activities related to shipping merchandise to customers in a *pool for order shipments.* The activities on which the company bases these pools are often called **cost drivers** because they each drive, or cause the company to incur, certain overhead costs. The overhead costs the company allocates to each activity pool are the costs incurred by the company as a result of engaging in the activities represented by the pool. Exhibit 18-7 lists some examples of cost drivers. As each cost driver (e.g., number of purchase orders, number of direct labor hours) increases, the company can expect its related costs in the cost pool to increase. So the costs in the cost pool are variable costs and vary in proportion to the increases or decreases in the cost driver.

In the second stage of activity-based costing, the company assigns the factory overhead costs accumulated in each activity pool to jobs (or processes) based on the relative number of activities (*driver units*) needed to complete the jobs (or processes). For example, if a company has only two processes, one needing three setups and the other needing seven setups, the company will allocate the total costs accumulated in the machine setup

6   When a company uses activity-based costing, what three stages does it follow to allocate factory overhead costs to products?

| | EXHIBIT 18-7 | EXAMPLES OF COST DRIVERS |

Number of direct labor hours
Number of purchase orders
Number of material movements
Number of products reworked
Number of employees
Number of square feet of floor space

Number of machine hours
Number of deliveries
Number of inspections
Number of hours of training time
Number of part types
Number of machine setups

pool to the two processes in a three-to-seven ratio. So if the machine setup pool contains costs totaling $10,000, the company will allocate $3,000 (3/10 × $10,000) to the first process and $7,000 (7/10 × $10,000) to the second process.

In the third stage, the company assigns the total factory overhead costs allocated to each job (or process) equally to the individual units of product in the job (or process). So if each process in the above example had 500 units, the company would assign each unit in the first process a setup cost of $6 ($3,000 ÷ 500 units) and each unit in the second process a setup cost of $14 ($7,000 ÷ 500 units). Exhibit 18-8 illustrates the three-stage allocation process that Unlimited Decadence uses in activity-based costing.

Computations of Predetermined Factory Overhead Rate

As we showed in Chapter 17, Unlimited Decadence uses direct labor hours as a means of allocating factory overhead costs to products. But direct labor hours don't drive all its overhead costs and probably don't reflect the amount of each activity used by different products. For instance, Unlimited Decadence uses 10 ingredients in its Darkly Decadent candy bars. In ordering these ingredients, it must process 10 purchase orders (one for each ingredient). It must process these purchase orders regardless of whether or not its factory is totally automated (whether or not it has *any* direct labor hours). The salaries of the employees who process these orders are considered to be indirect labor costs, which are part of factory overhead. So in this case, overhead costs should increase for each purchase order processed. If Unlimited Decadence's factory were totally automated, it could not allocate these factory overhead costs to its products based on direct labor hours because there would be no direct labor hours! But even if a company does have direct labor in its factory, if it uses direct labor hours to allocate all factory overhead costs to products, it may distort the individual costs (such as the costs of processing purchase orders) included in the total cost of each of its products. Here's how this can happen.

Traditional Approach

Suppose that Unlimited Decadence plans to produce and sell two products (the Darkly Decadent candy bar and the Pure Decadence candy bar) during the coming year. The production and sales volume of the Pure Decadence candy bar will be relatively low compared to that of the Darkly Decadent candy bar. Assume that the normal activity of Unlimited Decadence is a production volume of 5,000,000 cases of Darkly Decadent candy bars and 1,000,000 cases of Pure Decadence candy bars. Each case of Darkly Decadent candy bars takes 0.5 direct labor hours (DLH) to produce. Each case of Pure Decadence candy bars takes 0.75 direct labor hours. At normal activity, employees of Unlimited Decadence must work 3,250,000 direct labor hours (DLH), computed as follows:

Darkly Decadent candy bars (5,000,000 cases × 0.5 DLH) = 2,500,000 DLH
Pure Decadence candy bars (1,000,000 cases × 0.75 DLH) = 750,000 DLH
Total direct labor hours = 3,250,000 DLH

Assume Unlimited Decadence estimates that its variable factory overhead will be $0.64 per direct labor hour and its total fixed factory overhead costs will be $8,320,000

EXHIBIT 18-8

THREE-STAGE ALLOCATION PROCESS USED BY UNLIMITED DECADENCE FOR ACTIVITY-BASED COSTING

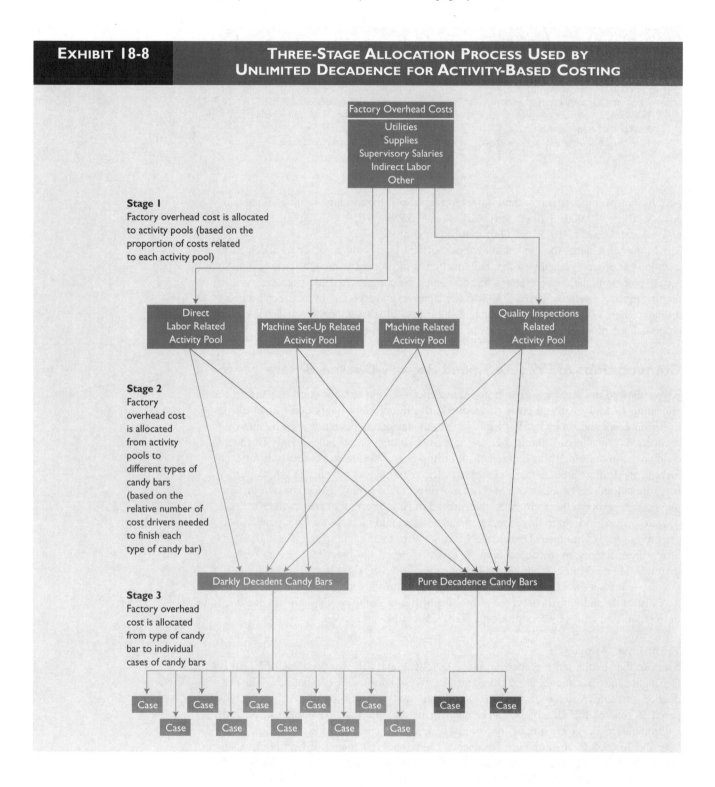

at its normal activity level.[1] If it uses direct labor hours as a basis for applying factory overhead costs to the two products, its *predetermined overhead rate* will be $3.20 per direct labor hour, computed as follows:

---

[1]The total factory overhead costs and the direct labor hours given here are different from those in Chapters 12 of Volume 1 and 17 because there, for simplicity, we assumed that Unlimited Decadence was producing only one type of candy bar.

$$\text{Predetermined Overhead Rate} = \frac{\text{Total Variable Overhead Costs} + \text{Total Fixed Overhead Costs}}{\text{Total Direct Labor Hours}}$$

$$= \frac{\$0.64\ (3{,}250{,}000\ \text{DLH}) + \$8{,}320{,}000}{3{,}250{,}000\ \text{DLH}}$$

$$= \frac{\$2{,}080{,}000 + \$8{,}320{,}000}{3{,}250{,}000\ \text{DLH}}$$

$$= \frac{\$10{,}400{,}000}{3{,}250{,}000\ \text{DLH}}$$

$$= \$3.20\ \text{per DLH}$$

Note that this $3.20 rate includes $0.64 per direct labor hour of variable overhead costs and $2.56 per direct labor hour ($8,320,000/3,250,000 DLH) of fixed overhead costs. Using this $3.20 rate to assign factory overhead to each case of candy bars, Unlimited Decadence would assign the following overhead costs to each case of candy bars:

Darkly Decadent candy bars ($3.20×0.5 DLH)................ $1.60 per case

Pure Decadence candy bars ($3.20×0.75 DLH).............. $2.40 per case

So at its normal activity level, Unlimited Decadence would apply the total overhead costs to the two types of candy bars as follows:

Darkly Decadent candy bars ($1.60 × 5,000,000 cases) =	$ 8,000,000
Pure Decadence candy bars ($2.40 × 1,000,000 cases) =	2,400,000
Total factory overhead applied:	$10,400,000

However, using this method of allocating factory overhead costs to products doesn't take into account the effect that other activities—such as setups, machine hours, and inspections—have on overhead costs.

Activity-Based Costing Approach

Suppose Unlimited Decadence decides to use activity-based costing to assign factory overhead costs to the two types of candy bars. It does so because it has observed that many of the factory overhead costs it incurs result from activities unrelated to direct labor hours. It has also observed that the proportion of these activities needed to produce the various candy bars is different than the proportion of direct labor hours needed to produce these candy bars. For example, the production of Pure Decadence candy bars is done in smaller batches than the Darkly Decadent candy bars. Therefore, production of Pure Decadence candy bars requires more machine setups than production of Darkly Decadent candy bars. Furthermore, since Pure Decadence candy bars are of higher quality, their production requires a longer use of the mixer, refiner, conche, and temperer machines. In addition, to ensure the higher quality, more inspections are made during the production process. As we discuss later, activity-based costing is more expensive to use, but Unlimited Decadence's managers think that it will provide more accurate overhead cost allocations to the two candy bars. Using activity-based costing, the managers will reexamine all of its overhead costs to see how it can better associate changes in these costs with various cost drivers. It may find that some overhead costs still vary with direct labor hours, that some costs vary with other cost drivers, and that some costs are still fixed.

For example, suppose that Unlimited Decadence identifies the activity pools and their related cost drivers in total and for each type of candy bar (remember, Unlimited Decadence is producing five times as many cases of Darkly Decadent as Pure Decadence candy bars) as follows:

Activity Pool/Cost Driver	Expected Number of Activities (Driver Units)		
	Darkly Decadent	Pure Decadence	Total Driver Units
Direct labor related activities/			
direct labor hours (DLH)	2,500,000 DLH	750,000 DLH	3,250,000 DLH
Machine setup related activities/			
machine setups (MS)	232,000 MS	568,000 MS	800,000 MS
Machine related activities/			
machine hours (MH)	3,000,000 MH	1,000,000 MH	4,000,000 MH
Quality inspections related activities/			
inspections (IN)	600,000 IN	400,000 IN	1,000,000 IN
General factory	(not associated with an identifiable cost driver)		

And suppose, also, that Unlimited Decadence has been able to trace $3,900,000 of its factory overhead costs (its previous $2,080,000 variable overhead costs and $1,820,000 of its previous fixed overhead costs) to these cost pools. It also has been able to determine the cost per activity (driver unit), as we show in the following schedule.

Activity Pool	(a) Traceable Costs	(b) Total Driver Units	(a) ÷ (b) Rate per Driver Unit
Direct labor related	$ 650,000	3,250,000	$0.20 per DLH
Machine setup related	800,000	800,000	$1.00 per MS
Machine related	1,320,000	4,000,000	$0.33 per MH
Quality inspections related	1,130,000	1,000,000	$1.13 per IN
Total variable (traceable) costs	$3,900,000		

Unlimited Decadence would allocate the $3,900,000 variable (traceable) overhead costs in the activity pools and the remaining $6,500,000 fixed overhead costs ($8,320,000 previous fixed overhead costs − $1,820,000) to the two types of candy bars, as we show in the following schedule.

	Darkly Decadent		Pure Decadence		Total Amount
	Driver Units	Amount	Driver Units	Amount	
Variable overhead:					
Direct labor related					
(at $0.20 per DLH)	2,500,000 DLH	$ 500,000	750,000 DLH	$ 150,000	$ 650,000
Machine setup related					
(at $1.00 per MS)	232,000 MS	232,000	568,000 MS	568,000	800,000
Machine related					
(at $0.33 per MH)	3,000,000 MH	990,000	1,000,000 MH	330,000	1,320,000
Quality inspections					
related (at $1.13 per IN)	600,000 IN	678,000	400,000 IN	452,000	1,130,000
Total variable overhead costs		$2,400,000		$1,500,000	$3,900,000
Variable overhead cost per case		$0.48[*]		$1.50[†]	
Fixed overhead cost per case		1.00[‡]		1.50[§]	
Total overhead cost per case		$1.48		$3.00	

[*]$2,400,000 total variable overhead costs ÷ 5,000,000 cases of Darkly Decadent candy bars
[†]$1,500,000 total variable overhead costs ÷ 1,000,000 cases of Pure Decadence candy bars
[‡]$6,500,000 fixed overhead costs ÷ 3,250,000 DLH = $2; $2 × 0.5 DLH
[§]$6,500,000 fixed overhead costs ÷ 3,250,000 DLH = $2; $2 × 0.75 DLH

Note that Unlimited Decadence calculated the variable overhead cost per case for each type of candy bar ($0.48 for the Darkly Decadent candy bar and $1.50 for the Pure Decadence candy bar) by dividing the total variable (traceable) overhead costs by the normal production of that candy bar. It determined the fixed overhead cost per case in the same manner as it had earlier. First, it calculated a $2 fixed overhead rate per direct labor hour by dividing the total remaining fixed overhead costs ($6,500,000) by the total direct labor hours (3,250,000). It then applied the overhead to each case of candy bars based on the number of direct labor hours needed to produce a case of each candy bar. Unlimited Decadence then added the $0.48 variable overhead cost per case and the $1.00 fixed overhead cost per case to determine the $1.48 total overhead cost per case for the Darkly Decadent candy bars. Thus, $1.48 is the *predetermined overhead rate* for each case of Darkly Decadent candy bars. It added the $1.50 variable overhead cost per case and the $1.50 fixed overhead cost per case to determine the $3.00 total overhead cost per case for the Pure Decadence candy bar. Thus, $3.00 is the *predetermined overhead rate* for each case of Pure Decadence candy bars.

So, using activity-based costing, Unlimited Decadence would apply $1.48 of factory overhead costs to each case of Darkly Decadent candy bars and $3.00 to each case of Pure Decadence candy bars, as follows:

Darkly Decadent candy bars ($1.48 × 5,000,000 cases) =	$ 7,400,000
Pure Decadence candy bars ($3.00 × 1,000,000 cases) =	3,000,000
Total factory overhead applied	$10,400,000

Recall that, using only direct labor hours to allocate overhead costs, Unlimited Decadence allocated $1.60 of factory overhead costs (totaling $8,000,000) to each case of Darkly Decadent candy bars and $2.40 of factory overhead costs (totaling $2,400,000) to each case of Pure Decadence candy bars. Using activity-based costing has caused Unlimited Decadence to "rethink" the overhead costs of each of its products. As it expected, Unlimited Decadence has determined that some of its variable overhead costs continue to vary with direct labor hours, but that other variable overhead costs vary with the cost drivers of machine setups, machine hours, and quality inspections. It also has discovered that some of the overhead costs that it had assumed were fixed are instead variable costs.

For decision-making purposes, the managers of a company may express, for each activity pool, the total number of driver units required for each product on an "average per unit" basis. Thus, for instance, since the normal activity of Unlimited Decadence for Pure Decadence candy bars is 1,000,000 cases, these candy bars require the following average driver units per case for each activity pool:

Activity Pool	Average Number of Driver Units per Case
Direct labor related.............................	0.75 DLH per case (750,000 total driver units ÷ 1,000,000 cases)
Machine setup related.........................	0.568 MS per case (568,000 ÷ 1,000,000)
Machine related....................................	1.00 MH per case (1,000,000 ÷ 1,000,000)
Quality inspections related...............	0.40 IN per case (400,000 ÷ 1,000,000)

If a company uses this approach, the managers determine its variable cost per unit of product by multiplying the average number of driver units per unit of product by the rate per driver unit for each activity pool. Unlimited Decadence would compute its $1.50 variable cost per case of Pure Decadence candy bars as follows:

Average Number of Driver Units per Case	Rate per Driver Unit	Variable Cost per Case
0.75 DLH	$0.20 per DLH	$0.15
0.568 MS	1.00 per MS	0.568
1.00 MH	0.33 per MH	0.33
0.40 IN	1.13 per IN	0.452
Variable cost per case		$1.50

This approach enables the managers to more easily see, for each activity pool, how a change in the average number of driver units per unit of product would affect the variable cost of that unit. For instance, if Unlimited Decadence increased its machine hours from 1 to 2 to produce a case of Pure Decadence candy bars, the variable cost per case for machine hours would increase from \$0.33 (1 MH × \$0.33) to \$0.66 (2 MH × \$0.33), and the total variable cost per case would increase to \$1.83 (\$1.50 + an additional \$0.33).

 Does this make sense to you? Try this approach with the Darkly Decadent candy bars. Did you get \$0.48 variable overhead cost per case?

For cost management purposes, the managers of a company may also periodically measure the average consumption (use) of cost driver units per unit of product. This measurement helps them assess the progress the company is making in its attempt to continuously improve the efficiency of its manufacturing activities. For example, managing product quality by preventing product defects might reduce the need for frequent inspections, which might reduce costs. For Unlimited Decadence, reducing the number of inspections per case of Pure Decadence candy bars from 0.40 IN per case to 0.10 IN per case would reduce variable costs per case by \$0.339 [(0.40 − 0.10) × \$1.13] even though the cost per inspection would remain at \$1.13.

Activity-Based Costing for Service Companies

In our discussion of activity-based costing so far, we focused on the assignment of factory overhead to the units manufactured in a manufacturing company. Service companies also have "overhead" and also may use activity-based costing to assign this overhead to the services that they provide. A service company that uses activity-based costing goes through the same three-stage allocation process that we discussed for a manufacturing company. Namely, a service company (1) allocates its overhead costs to activity pools based on cost drivers, (2) assigns the overhead costs accumulated in each pool to jobs based on the relative number of activities needed to complete the jobs, and (3) assigns the total overhead costs in each job to the individual units in the job. However, a service company defines "overhead costs," "jobs," and "units" differently than does a manufacturing company. A service company might be, for instance, an auto repair shop, a bank, a hospital, or a CPA firm. Here, we briefly discuss the similarities and differences between the assignment of overhead for service companies and manufacturing companies, using these four service companies as examples.

Stage One

In the first stage, a service company assigns its overhead costs to activity pools. But, what are its "overhead costs"? Some kinds of overhead costs are incurred by both service companies and manufacturing companies; for example, utilities, insurance, and depreciation. However, there are distinct differences in the cost elements of a service company as compared to a manufacturing company. Since a service company does not manufacture a product, it does not have direct materials and direct labor as we defined them for a manufacturing company. It may have materials directly related to providing the service, however. These might include auto repair parts, deposit slips, prescription drugs, or audit working papers. It will also have the labor that worked directly on the service provided to the customer. So, the wages and salaries paid to an auto mechanic, a teller, a nurse, or an auditor may be considered direct labor. As you can see, what one service company thinks is its "direct materials" and "direct labor" may be much different from that of another service company. As a result, since the remaining costs of operating a service company are its "overhead," these types of costs are also likely to differ from one service company to another. For instance, as significant overhead costs, an auto repair shop would have machine lubricant costs while a bank would have security costs. A hospital would have food costs, while a CPA firm would have secretarial costs. Hence, the overhead costs that service companies allocate to their activity pools are likely to be more heterogeneous than those of manufacturing companies.

A service company has some cost drivers that are similar to those of a manufacturing company. For instance, a service company might use the number of direct labor hours, employees, square feet of floor space, or hours of training time as its cost drivers. However, it might also use other cost drivers such as numbers of repair parts orders, checking accounts, patient days, or number of audit hours. Each service company must identify the cost drivers appropriate for its type of overhead activity.

Stage Two

In the second stage, a service company assigns the overhead costs in each activity pool to the jobs based on the relative number of activities used to complete each job. (Generally, service companies think of their operations as relating to discrete jobs rather than processes.) Here, jobs don't involve the manufacture of a product, but rather the completion of a service. For instance, for an auto repair shop, a job might be the replacement of an engine while for a bank, a job might involve granting a car loan to a customer. For a hospital, a job might involve surgery and hospital care for a patient while for a CPA firm, a job might be an audit "engagement." Whichever way a service company defines its jobs, it assigns its overhead costs in each activity pool to each job using that activity pool in proportion to the relative use of the activities by each job.

For example, suppose a hospital creates an activity pool for its general care activity, including costs such as maintenance, housekeeping, dietary, and laundry. Using patient days as the cost driver (because the costs in this pool tend to increase with the level of hospital occupancy), the hospital can calculate a predetermined overhead rate per patient day. Then, by multiplying that predetermined rate by the number of days individual patients stay in the hospital, the hospital can calculate and assign its general care costs to those patients in proportion to their length of stay.

Stage Three

The third stage of the overhead allocation process, where a service company assigns the total overhead costs for each job to the units in the job, generally is very simple. In most cases the job involves one customer, so the customer is the "unit." Therefore, the total overhead costs are assigned to the customer of the engine repair, the car loan, the surgery and hospital care, or the audit engagement. Although service companies may have more heterogeneous overhead costs than manufacturing companies, the objective is still the same in activity-based costing. The goal is to assign overhead costs to jobs in a fair and equitable manner.

Activity-Based Costing and Managers' Decisions

The more precise information provided by activity-based costing can help managers make better decisions. For instance, when managers add the total factory overhead cost per unit to the per-unit costs of direct materials and direct labor to determine the unit cost for a product, they have a better idea of the true product cost. This is because they were able to trace costs to the activities that affect these costs. With this more precise product cost information, managers can make better decisions about setting normal selling prices. Activity-based costing has also led to activity-based management. **Activity-based management** involves managing a company's activities to increase its customers' satisfaction and to increase its profits, either through increased revenues or reduced costs. So, activity-based costing information may be used in activity-based management for making better decisions about what price to charge a customer for a special order, whether to drop a product, whether to make or buy a part, whether to sell a product or process it further, and what to set as the product mix, as well as for making better decisions involving cost-volume-profit analysis.

7 How does activity-based costing improve managers' decisions?

In these decisions, however, managers must be careful in how they analyze costs. For instance, in some decisions, the *total* overhead cost per unit (variable overhead cost per unit + fixed overhead cost per unit) is not applicable because the fixed cost *per unit* depends on the production level. Under activity-based costing, Unlimited Decadence was able to identify—with several activity pools—some of what it had previously assumed were fixed overhead costs, so that these costs were recognized to be variable costs. This change reduced its total fixed overhead costs. The remaining fixed overhead costs, however, *still are fixed in total*. Therefore, the $1.00 fixed overhead cost per case of Darkly Decadent candy bars and the $1.50 fixed overhead cost per case of Pure Decadence candy bars apply only at Unlimited Decadence's normal activity level of 5,000,000 cases of Darkly Decadent candy bars and 1,000,000 cases of Pure Decadence candy bars. Furthermore, even if a company's production volume doesn't change, these per-unit costs may not be relevant for certain decisions. The point is that the managers of a company using activity-based costing make decisions in the same way that managers of other companies make decisions—by considering the *relevant* costs (both fixed and variable) and revenues that will change as a result of the decision, as we discussed in Chapter 15.

Let's consider the impact of activity-based costing on managers' decisions involving cost-volume-profit (C-V-P) analysis. In Chapter 11 of Volume 1, in our discussion of C-V-P analysis, we said that in the coming year, Unlimited Decadence planned to produce and sell Darkly Decadent candy bars for $16 per case and Pure Decadence candy bars for $20 per case. The variable costs per case were $11 and $14, respectively. These variable costs included costs for direct materials, direct labor, and variable factory overhead (allocated based on direct labor hours), along with other nonmanufacturing variable costs. With contribution margins of $5 per case for Darkly Decadent candy bars and $6 per case for Pure Decadence candy bars, and with total fixed costs (both manufacturing and nonmanufacturing) of $24,800,000, we determined that when the sales mix was 5 cases of Darkly Decadent candy bars to 1 case of Pure Decadence candy bars, Unlimited Decadence would need to sell 4,000,000 cases of Darkly Decadent candy bars and 800,000 cases of Pure Decadence candy bars to break even, as we show in the following schedule.

Sales revenue:		
Cases of Darkly Decadent candy bars	$64,000,000	
(4,000,000 cases @ $16 per case)		
Cases of Pure Decadence candy bars	16,000,000	
(800,000 cases @ $20 per case)		
Total sales revenue		$80,000,000
Less: Variable costs:		
Cases of Darkly Decadent candy bars	$44,000,000	
(4,000,000 cases @ $11 per case)		
Cases of Pure Decadence candy bars	11,200,000	
(800,000 cases @ $14 per case)		
Total variable cost		(55,200,000)
Total contribution margin		$24,800,000
Less: Total fixed cost		(24,800,000)
Profit		$ 0.00

The more precise overhead cost allocation of activity-based costing shifts $1,820,000 of the $24,800,000 total fixed cost to variable costs, decreasing the total fixed costs to $22,980,000. Thus, the variable costs for Darkly Decadent candy bars increase by $0.16 [$0.48 new variable overhead cost per unit − ($0.64 old variable overhead cost per DLH × 0.5 DLH per unit)], from $11 to $11.16 per case, and the contribution margin decreases to $4.84 per case ($16 selling price − $11.16). The variable costs for Pure Decadence candy bars increase by $1.02 [$1.50 − ($0.64 × 0.75 DLH)], from $14 to $15.02 per case, and the contribution margin decreases to $4.98 per case ($20 selling price − $15.02).

If Unlimited Decadence recomputed the break-even point (assuming the same sales mix) using the variable costs and fixed costs determined by activity-based costing, its break-even sales volume would change, as follows:

$$\text{Break-even point} \atop \text{(in "units")} = \frac{\text{Total fixed costs}}{\text{Contribution margin per "unit"}}$$

$$= \frac{\$22,980,000}{(\$4.84 \times 5 \text{ cases}) + (\$4.98 \times 1 \text{ case})}$$

$$= \frac{\$22,980,000}{\$29.18}$$

$$= 787,526 \text{ "units" (rounded up)}$$

Since there are five cases of Darkly Decadent candy bars and one case of Pure Decadence candy bars in every "unit" of sales mix, Unlimited Decadence would need to sell 3,937,630 cases of Darkly Decadent candy bars (787,526 × 5 cases) and 787,526 cases of Pure Decadence candy bars (787,526 × 1 case) to break even. In other words, with the current sales mix, sales price, and recomputed variable costs, contribution margins, and total fixed costs, Unlimited Decadence would need to sell less of each kind of candy bar in order to break even, as we show in the schedule below.

Sales revenue:
Cases of Darkly Decadent candy bars	$63,002,080	
(3,937,630 cases @ $16 per case)		
Cases of Pure Decadence candy bars	15,750,520	
(787,526 cases @ $20 per case)		
Total sales revenue		$78,752,600
Less: Variable costs:		
Cases of Darkly Decadent candy bars	$43,943,960*	
(3,937,630 cases @ $11.16 per case)		
Cases of Pure Decadence candy bars	11,828,640	
(787,526 cases @ $15.02 per case)		
Total variable cost		(55,772,600)
Total contribution margin		$22,980,000
Less: Total fixed cost		(22,980,000)
Profit		$ 0.00

*Rounded to balance, since we previously rounded the number of "units"

For Unlimited Decadence to achieve a desired pretax income of $5,400,000, using direct labor hours to allocate overhead costs, we determined in Chapter 11 that it would need to sell 4,870,970 cases of Darkly Decadent candy bars and 974,194 cases of Pure Decadence candy bars. However, using activity-based costing, Unlimited Decadence would need to sell 4,862,920 (972,584 × 5) cases of Darkly Decadent candy bars and 972,584 cases of Pure Decadence candy bars to earn $5,400,000 of pretax income, as follows:

$$\text{"Unit" sales to earn \$5,400,000} \atop \text{pretax income} = \frac{\text{Total fixed costs} + \text{Desired pretax income}}{\text{Contribution margin per "unit"}}$$

$$= \frac{\$22,980,000 + \$5,400,000}{\$29.18}$$

$$= 972,584 \text{ "units" (rounded up)}$$

So, with the current sales mix, Unlimited Decadence would need to sell less of each kind of candy bar to earn its desired profit.

Suppose Unlimited Decadence determined that it would need to sell more of each kind of candy bar to earn its desired profit. Do you think that should affect its decision about whether to use activity-based costing? Why or why not?

What if Unlimited Decadence decided to change its sales mix? Activity-based costing shows that the contribution margin is lower for both Darkly Decadent candy bars and Pure Decadence candy bars. However, the contribution margin for Pure Decadence candy bars is *significantly* lower (from $6 to $4.98) than Unlimited Decadence had planned when it had based its overhead allocation on direct labor hours. Therefore, Unlimited Decadence should carefully consider these decreased contribution margins when deciding whether to change its sales mix.

 How many cases of each type of candy bar do you think Unlimited Decadence would need to sell to earn a pretax income of $5,400,000 if its sales mix changed to 3 cases of Darkly Decadent candy bars for every 4 cases of Pure Decadence candy bars? Do you think Unlimited Decadence should try to achieve this sales mix? What other questions might you ask before you make this decision?

As we mentioned earlier, other management decisions of a company can be affected by the use of activity-based costing. For example, a switch to activity-based costing caused the automotive division of **Slade Manufacturing** to raise selling prices on some of its products.[e] This decision resulted in $1.2 million in additional revenues. Clearly, managers must know product costs in order to make these decisions. Keep in mind, how-ever, that managers need to know more than product costs to make these decisions. As we discussed in Chapter 2 of Volume 1, decision makers should gather *all* the relevant facts before identifying and evaluating alternative solutions to problems and then making decisions. Consider the following decision about whether or not to try to meet a customer's expectations.

BUSINESS ISSUES AND VALUES: CAN SATISFYING CUSTOMERS BE A BAD DECISION?

In our previous discussion about TQM, we said that companies with this philosophy fostered continuous improvement to meet or exceed their customers' expectations. However, there is a major difference between fostering continuous improvement to meet or exceed the expectations of the customers and meeting *unreasonable* demands of customers. After trimming down production to make its operations more efficient, a company must evaluate whether the revenues it will earn from satisfying its customers is greater than the costs of meeting all its customers expectations, and then must decide whether to continue to try to meet these expectations. Remember, the overall goal of a company is to earn a profit, so decisions must be made with that in mind. Activity-based costing can help the managers of a company isolate which customers cannot be satisfied profitably.

But profit should not be the sole criterion for making a decision about a customer. For example, a company may want to retain a customer even though it may not be profitable to do so. If the customer is new, the company may think that satisfying this customer may lead to a long-term *profitable* relationship. Other unprofitable customers may provide other benefits to the company, such as leading-edge insights into technology or industry trends, or the ability to give the company credibility that helps it attract other customers. So with this additional information, the company should be able to evaluate the advantages and disadvantages of trying to keep this type of customer happy and should then make a decision.

Of course, the managers of a company can make good decisions only if they have good information to support those decisions. Consequently, each company should choose a cost accounting system that supports its information needs.

CHOOSING WHICH COST ACCOUNTING SYSTEM TO USE

A company should choose the cost accounting system (job order costing, process costing, or one of these systems enhanced by activity-based costing) that best meets its particular needs. However, a cost accounting system can be expensive to set up and operate. For example, under activity-based costing, identifying cost drivers and allocating overhead costs to products based on these cost drivers can be both time-consuming and expensive. Thus, a company also must consider whether the benefits gained from the information that the accounting system communicates exceed the costs of getting that information. Many companies have chosen *not* to use activity-based costing because of the expense of obtaining the information they would need in operating that system. As you saw earlier, both the ability of a particular cost accounting system to provide needed information and the cost of operating that system depend largely on the way a company organizes its manufacturing operations and the nature and variety of the products it produces.

Modern manufacturing systems with features such as computer control of manufacturing operations, robotics, quickly adjustable multipurpose machinery, tight quality control, and minimum (if not zero) inventory levels present a challenge to management accountants because one cost accounting system alone may not suit a company's needs. Therefore, companies with such modern manufacturing operations may create hybrid costing systems by adapting many of the product costing techniques we described in this and previous chapters. Such systems might be described as partly job order costing systems, partly process costing systems, and partly activity-based costing systems. These companies also may develop new techniques, such as incorporating cost accounting systems within enterprise resource planning (ERP) systems. The important requirement is that a company's cost accounting system meet the information needs of its managers and employees.

SUMMARY

At the beginning of the chapter we asked you several questions. During the chapter, we asked you to STOP and answer some other questions to build your knowledge about specific issues. Be sure you answered these additional questions. Below are the questions from the beginning of the chapter, with a brief summary of the key points relating to the answers. Use your creative and critical thinking skills to expand on these key points to develop more complete answers to the questions and to determine what other questions you have that might lead you to learn more about the issues.

1   How has the global economy caused companies to become more competitive?

Instead of just competing against companies in their own countries, companies must also compete against companies from other countries. The additional competition of the global economy has accelerated the rate of technological advances, allowing companies to produce and sell a wider assortment of products and services. Many of these products and services appeal to customers for shorter periods of time because more-advanced products and services soon capture their attention. Advances in communication and transportation have provided customers with worldwide product information and greater access to these products.

2   How can an accounting system help a company identify strategies that will enhance its ability to compete in the long run?

By retaining the financial measures of a company's past performance and supplementing them with leading indicators of, and measures of, the activities that will drive the company's *future* financial performance, an accounting system can provide the information that a company's managers need to be able to identify strategies that will enhance the company's ability to compete in the long run. This approach is often referred to as the *balanced scorecard*. The balanced scorecard approach links competitive strategies with specific measures of the success of the strategies. *It focuses on causes and effects. Benchmarking,* on the other hand, allows the company to compare its operations against its most successful competitors by measuring its own practices against the best practices (benchmarks) occurring in the industry in which it operates.

3   As part of its efforts to become more competitive, how can a company measure quality and the costs of quality?

A company can measure external failure costs by counting the number and measuring the costs of warranty repairs, product replacements, and product recalls. It can measure appraisal costs by counting the number of inspections and tests conducted, noting where in the production process they are conducted, and counting how many defects the inspectors and testers find. It also can measure the salaries of product inspectors and equipment testers, and the costs of materials used in the inspecting and testing processes. A company can measure internal failure costs by assessing the number of defective products reworked, the costs of reworking defective products, and the amount of time that the factory is "down" while employees trace and fix the cause of the product defects. It can measure prevention costs by tallying employee training costs and equipment maintenance costs, and by counting the numbers of employees trained, training seminars given, machines maintained, and maintenance orders taken.

4   How does just-in-time production help a company reduce its costs, operate more efficiently, and control quality?

A company using just-in-time production reduces its costs and operates more efficiently by minimizing inventory levels and, therefore, tying up less cash, floor space, and labor. It also minimizes the number of setup times. It controls quality by minimizing product defect rates. It accomplishes this by choosing, and closely working with, a supplier that emphasizes quality, by training its factory employees to detect product defects, by emphasizing regular equipment maintenance and ongoing defect prevention, and by taking advantage of advances in technology and improving factory layouts.

5   How have improved technology and factory layouts helped companies become more competitive?

Improvements in technology and factory layouts allow companies to manufacture higher-quality products and minimize their defect rates, and also to manufacture a wider variety of products at a lower cost than otherwise would be possible. Flexible manufacturing systems minimize setup and production times. Manufacturing cells minimize the time that products spend moving from process to process, and also minimize labor costs. These improvements allow companies to sell higher-quality products at lower prices.

6   When a company uses activity-based costing, what three stages does it follow to allocate factory overhead costs to products?

In the first stage, a company allocates its factory overhead costs to activity pools, or groupings of costs of related activities. In the second stage, it assigns the factory overhead costs accumulated in each activity pool to jobs or processes based on the relative number of activities (driver units) needed to complete the jobs or processes. In the third stage, the company assigns the total factory overhead costs allocated to each job or process equally to the individual units of product resulting from that job or process.

7   How does activity-based costing improve managers' decisions?

Activity-based costing helps managers better understand not only the behavior of a company's factory overhead costs, but also what company activities drive that behavior. So in making a decision, a manager can more precisely predict the cost effects of any particular decision alternative. Without activity-based costing, some costs may appear to be fixed and therefore managers may assume that these costs will not change from one decision alternative to another. Or, managers may assume that a variable cost varies with direct labor hours when, in reality, it does not. But when a company uses activity-based costing, managers see that some "fixed" costs, in fact, may vary with specific company activities and some variable costs may vary with some measure of volume other than direct labor hours. They also see that these costs may be different from one decision alternative to another. This insight helps managers make better decisions because they can better see the effects that different decision alternatives have on costs, and because they can better determine which costs are relevant for those decisions.

KEY TERMS

activity-based costing (p. 622)
activity-based management (p. 629)
activity pool (p. 622)
appraisal costs (p. 614)
back-flush costing (p. 616)
balanced scorecard (p. 608)
benchmarking (p. 611)
cost drivers (p. 622)
external failure costs (p. 613)

flexible manufacturing systems (p. 618)
internal failure costs (p. 614)
ISO 9000 (p. 611)
just-in-time strategies (p. 615)
prevention costs (p. 614)
product defect rates (p. 616)
pull-through production (p. 616)
push-through production (p. 615)
total quality management (TQM) (p. 611)

SUMMARY SURFING

Here is an opportunity to gather information on the Internet about real-world issues related to the topics in this chapter (for suggestions on how to navigate various organizations' Web sites to find the relevant information, see the related discussion in the Preface at the beginning of the book). Answer the following question.

- Go to the **American Society for Quality's** Web site and search for a benchmarking overview. What is the step-by-step process involved with benchmarking?

INTEGRATED BUSINESS AND ACCOUNTING SITUATIONS

Answer the Following Questions in Your Own Words.

Testing Your Knowledge

18-1   List two strategies a company might use to make itself more competitive.

18-2   What is the balanced scorecard approach?

18-3   When using the balanced scorecard approach, what are the four perspectives from which a company's managers view the company's performance?

18-4   What is the difference between leading indicators and lagging indicators in the balanced scorecard approach?

18-5   What is benchmarking? How does benchmarking add to the information provided by the balanced scorecard approach?

18-6   Briefly explain TQM.

18-7   What are external failure costs? Give two examples. What accounts might be used to keep track of these costs?

18-8   What is the relationship between appraisal costs and internal failure costs?

18-9   What are prevention costs, and what costs do they help minimize?

18-10   Explain the difference between push-through production and pull-through production.

18-11   Briefly explain how JIT production and inventory work.

18-12   Briefly explain how a flexible manufacturing system works.

18-13   Briefly explain how a company uses manufacturing cells.

18-14   Briefly explain the three stages of activity-based costing.

18-15   Briefly explain what is meant by a "cost driver" in activity-based costing.

Applying Your Knowledge

18-16   Curl-Up-and-Dry Corporation manufactures hair dryers, curling irons, and hot rollers. As part of its "new" image, Curl-Up is placing special emphasis on quality products. To initiate the company's quality-improvement program, Buzz Whitehair has gathered together the following list of items from the integrated accounting system related to quality and asked you to help him organize it so that he can determine what quality improvements to make. The following items relate to last month's activities:
(a) Scheduled maintenance performed on eight casing machines
(b) $31,545 paid to product inspectors
(c) 56 warranty repairs done
(d) $45,650 paid to employees in training
(e) Factory down 10 hours for unscheduled repairs after inspectors found product defects
(f) Raw materials costing $11,575 were used to repair recalled products
(g) Found 210 product defects
(h) Spent $500 on materials used in testing hair dryers
(i) Spent $310 shipping replacements for broken hair appliances still under warranty
(j) Held 12 training seminars around the country

Required: For each item in the list, indicate whether it is (a) an external failure cost or measure, (b) an appraisal cost or measure, (c) an internal failure cost or measure, or (d) a prevention cost or measure.

18-17   Thun Company produces two products, Tweeters and Woofers, and uses activity-based costing. The company's normal activity level is 100,000 units of Tweeters and 80,000 units of Woofers. It has developed the following "activity" information for these products.

Cost Drivers	Expected Number of Activities (Driver Units)		
	Tweeters	Woofers	Total
Purchase orders (PO)	60,000	30,000	90,000
Direct labor hours (DLH)	40,000	8,000	48,000

It has $76,800 of fixed factory overhead costs that are not associated with an identifiable cost driver. It traces its $183,600 total variable overhead costs to the following activity pools related to the previous cost drivers:

Activity Pool	Traceable Costs
Purchase related..	$126,000
Direct labor related......................................	57,600

Thun assigns its fixed factory overhead costs to units based on 48,000 direct labor hours. It takes 0.4 direct labor hours to produce a unit of Tweeters and 0.1 direct labor hours to produce a unit of Woofers.

Required: Determine Thun's total overhead cost per unit of each product.

18-18   Brandt Company uses activity-based costing. The company produces Flims and Flams (microscopic parts used in rocket engines), and its normal activity level is 40,000 cases of Flims and 100,000 cases of Flams. Brandt has $511,200 total factory overhead cost at this expected production volume. It traces its $341,200 total variable factory overhead costs to two activity pools as follows: direct labor related, $197,200; inspection related, $144,000. In regard to these activity pools, Brandt expects to use 68,000 direct labor hours (DLH), of which 8,000 are for Flims and 60,000 are for Flams. It expects the factory to conduct 80,000 inspections (IN), of which 20,000 are for Flims and 60,000 are for Flams.

Brandt has $170,000 of fixed factory overhead costs that are not traceable to an identifiable cost driver. It assigns these costs to cases based on 68,000 direct labor hours. It takes 0.2 direct labor hours to produce a case of Flims and 0.6 direct labor hours to produce a case of Flams.

Required: (1) Determine Brandt's total overhead cost per case of Flims and per case of Flams.

(2) Assuming Brandt produces 40,000 cases of Flims and 100,000 cases of Flams during the coming year, apply its factory overhead to each case of the products.

18-19 Demolition Derby produces two products, Igniters and Blasters, and its normal activity is 300,000 cartons of Igniters and 100,000 cartons of Blasters. It uses activity-based costing, and has developed the following "activity" information for these products.

Cost Drivers	Expected Number of Activities (Driver Units)		
	Igniters	Blasters	Total
Direct labor hours (DLH)	60,000	40,000	100,000
Square feet of floor space (SF)	600,000	200,000	800,000
Material moves (MM)	350,000	50,000	400,000

Demolition Derby has $300,000 of fixed factory overhead costs that are not associated with an identifiable cost driver. It traces its $1,200,000 total variable factory overhead costs to its activity pools related to the previous cost drivers as follows: direct labor related, $600,000; floor space related, $200,000; and material moves related, $400,000. Demolition Derby assigns its fixed factory overhead costs to cartons based on 100,000 direct labor hours. It takes 0.2 direct labor hours to produce a carton of Igniters and 0.4 direct labor hours to produce a carton of Blasters.

Required: (1) Determine Demolition Derby's total overhead cost per carton of each product.

(2) For each activity pool, determine the average driver units per carton of Blasters. Verify the total variable overhead cost per carton of Blasters, which you computed in (1).

18-20 Toga Toga Company produces two products, Greek Letters and Roman Numerals, and uses activity-based costing. The normal activity for Toga Toga Company is 400,000 sets of Greek Letters and 200,000 sets of Roman Numerals. It has developed the following partially completed schedules of "activity" information for these products:

Activity Pool	Traceable Cost	Total Driver Units	Rate per Driver Unit
Direct labor related	$ (a)	300,000 DLH	$2.00/DLH
Machine set-up related	300,000	600,000 MS	(b)
Purchase related	560,000	(c) PO	$1.40/PO
Total variable O/H costs	$ (d)		

Variable Overhead	Greek Letters		Roman Numerals		Total Amount
	Driver Units	Amount	Driver Units	Amount	
$2.00 per DLH	(e)	$480,000	(f)	$ (g)	$ (h)
$0.50 per MS	500,000 MS	(i)	100,000 MS	50,000	300,000
$1.40 per PO	300,000 PO	420,000	100,000 PO	140,000	560,000
Total variable O/H costs		$ (j)		$310,000	$ (k)
Variable overhead cost per set		$ (l)		$ (m)	
Fixed overhead cost per set		(n)		(o)	
Total overhead cost per set		$ (p)		$ (q)	

Toga Toga Company has $450,000 of fixed factory overhead costs that are not associated with an identifiable cost driver. It assigns its fixed factory overhead costs to sets based on 300,000 direct labor hours. It takes 0.6 direct labor hours to produce a set of Greek Letters and 0.3 direct labor hours to produce a set of Roman Numerals.

Required: Determine the missing amounts (a) through (q) in Toga Toga's schedules.

18-21   Color Me Pink Company produces two products, Crayons and Markers. Its normal activity is 600,000 boxes of Crayons and 200,000 boxes of Markers. Color Me Pink uses activity-based costing and has developed the following "activity" information for these products.

Cost Drivers	Expected Number of Activities (Driver Units)		
	Crayons	Markers	Total
Machine hours (MH)	160,000	40,000	200,000
Direct labor hours (DLH)	300,000	160,000	460,000
Color changes (CC)	1,200,000	400,000	1,600,000

Color Me Pink traces its $2,785,000 total variable factory overhead costs to the following activity pools:

Activity Pool	Traceable Costs
Machine hours related....................................	$1,000,000
Direct labor related.......................................	345,000
Color change related......................................	1,440,000

Color Me Pink has $920,000 of fixed factory overhead costs that are not traceable to an identifiable cost driver and assigns these costs to boxes based on 460,000 direct labor hours. It takes 0.5 direct labor hours to produce a box of Crayons and 0.8 direct labor hours to produce a box of Markers.

Required: (1) Determine Color Me Pink's total overhead cost per box of Crayons and per unit of Markers.
(2) For each activity pool, determine the average driver units per box of Markers. Verify the total variable overhead cost per box of Markers, which you computed in (1).

18-22   Blapp Company manufactures both Prangs and Floppers. It uses activity-based costing to assign its manufacturing costs, and has developed the following "normal activity" information related to its activity pools:

Product	Production (Units)
Prangs	500,000
Floppers	500,000

Driver Units (Expected Number of Activities)

	Cost Drivers			
Product	Purchase Orders (PO)	Square Feet of Floor Space (FS)	Direct Labor Hours (DLH)	Reworks (R)
Prangs	300,000	200,000	200,000	100,000
Floppers	150,000	200,000	300,000	150,000
Total driver units	450,000	400,000	500,000	250,000

Blapp has $2,925,000 of total factory overhead costs at its expected production volume. It traces its $2,325,000 total variable overhead costs to the activity pools related to the previous cost drivers as follows: purchase related, $450,000; floor space related, $1,200,000; direct labor related, $400,000; and rework related, $275,000. Blapp has $600,000 of fixed factory overhead costs that are not associated with an identifiable cost driver. It assigns these costs to units based on 500,000 direct labor hours. It takes 0.4 direct labor hours to produce a unit of Prangs and 0.6 direct labor hours to produce a unit of Floppers.

Required: (1) Determine Blapp's total overhead cost per unit of Prangs and per unit of Floppers.

(2) Assuming Blapp produces 500,000 Prangs and 500,000 Floppers during the coming year, apply its factory overhead to each unit of the products.

18-23 Rough Razor Company produces two types of razors, Cutters and Slicers, and uses activity-based costing. Rough Razor has a normal activity of 450,000 cases of Cutters and 600,000 cases of Slicers. It has developed the following "activity" information for these products.

	Expected Number of Activities (Driver Units)		
Cost Drivers	Cutters	Slicers	Total
Purchase orders (PO)	60,000	20,000	80,000
Machine setups (MS)	50,000	100,000	150,000
Inspections (IN)	20,000	80,000	100,000
Direct labor hours (DLH)	90,000	180,000	270,000

Rough Razor traces its $898,000 total variable overhead costs to the following activity pools related to the previous cost drivers:

Activity Pool	Traceable Costs
Purchase related	$336,000
Machine setup related	315,000
Inspection related	85,000
Direct labor related	162,000

Rough Razor has $405,000 of fixed factory overhead costs that are not associated with an identifiable cost driver. It assigns these costs to cases based on 270,000 direct labor hours. It takes 0.2 direct labor hours to produce a case of Cutters and 0.3 direct labor hours to produce a case of Slicers.

Required: Determine Rough Razor's total overhead cost per case of Cutters and per case of Slicers.

18-24 Ted Marks has built a new facility and is planning to start a "senior citizens" home called Marks Retirement Home. Based on market research, he expects to have 100 percent occupancy when he opens. He expects to have 50 "moderate-care" residents and 100 "low-care" residents. Moderate-care residents will be housed two to a room and will require more nursing care. Low-care residents will be housed in separate rooms. All residents will be served three meals a day.

Ted has asked for your help in using activity-based costing to determine the costs of providing services to each type of resident. He will use this cost information to determine how much to charge each resident. Ted has identified three activity pools and the related cost drivers, as follows:

Activity Pool	Cost Driver
Food-related activities	# of meals served
Lodging-related activities	Square feet
Nursing care	# of nursing hours

Ted has also developed the following monthly cost and driver unit estimates.

Activity Pool	Traceable Total Costs	Total Driver Units	=	Moderate-Care Driver Units	+	Low-Care Driver Units
Food-related	$ 60,750	13,500 meals		4,500 meals		9,000 meals
Lodging-related	18,750	37,500 square feet		7,500 sq. feet		30,000 sq. feet
Nursing care	25,200	720 hours		480 hours		240 hours
O/H costs	$104,700					

Ted also estimates that $50,400 of monthly fixed overhead costs are not traceable to an identifiable cost driver and wants to assign these costs to residents based on the 720 estimated nursing hours per month.

Required: (1) Determine Marks' monthly total overhead cost per moderate-care resident and low-care resident.

(2) Assuming Ted wants to charge residents at a rate twice the estimated monthly overhead cost, determine the annual fee that Marks Retirement Home should charge each type of resident.

18-25 Glenda's Gourmet Groceries specializes in selling high-quality food items and has three departments: Meats, Produce, and Canned Goods. Glenda has prepared the following income statements and profit margin ratios for the current year, both in total and broken down by each department.

	Total	Meats	Produce	Canned Goods
Sales revenue	$600,000	$300,000	$200,000	$100,000
Cost of goods sold	(280,000)	(120,000)	(100,000)	(60,000)
Gross profit	$320,000	$180,000	$100,000	$ 40,000
Overhead costs	(210,000)	(105,000)	(70,000)	(35,000)
Profit	$110,000	$ 75,000	$ 30,000	$ 5,000
Profit margin	18.33%	25%	15%	5%

When preparing the above income statements, Glenda allocated the "overhead costs" to each department based on that department's revenues as a percentage of the total sales revenue.

Glenda is concerned that the way that overhead costs are allocated to each department does not provide a "fair" measure of each department's profit margin. She has asked you to apply activity-based costing principles to determine a more accurate amount of overhead costs for each department so that she can more fairly determine each department's profit margin. You have determined that $180,000 of the $210,000 overhead costs is traceable to departments, and that the remaining $30,000 should continue to be allocated to each department based on that department's revenues as a percentage of the total sales revenue. You have also identified three activity pools, along with the total traceable overhead costs as well as the type of driver units and total driver units for each activity pool, as follows:

Activity Pool	Traceable Total Costs	Total Driver Units
Purchasing	$ 49,000	3,500 Purchase orders (PO)
Preparation	76,000	5,000 Cuts (C)
Stocking	55,000	4,000 Stocking hours (SH)
	$180,000	

You have also been able to identify how many driver units apply to each department as follows:

Activity Pool	Meats Driver Units	Produce Driver Units	Canned Goods Driver Units
Purchasing	1,000 PO	2,000 PO	500 PO
Preparation	2,800 C	1,900 C	300 C
Stocking	600 SH	1,800 SH	1,600 SH

Required: (1) Using activity-based costing principles, determine the total overhead costs to allocate to each department.

(2) Prepare a total income statement and revised income statements for each department, based on your findings in (1).

(3) Compute revised profit margins for each department.

Making Evaluations

18-26. Squander Management Corporation has the overall goal of improving its profitability by manufacturing a higher-quality product. Because of your reputation as a creative thinker, you have been "tapped" by the company's managers to use the balanced scorecard approach to develop an initial list of cause-and-effect strategies and measurements that will help the company achieve its goal and measure whether it is successful.

Required: Develop a chart similar to that in Exhibit 18-2 to present to the company's managers.

18-27. Behemoth Vehicles manufactures SUVs and trucks, and would like to benchmark its products against those of other companies. It has turned to you to help it organize its benchmarking process. What advice would you give Behemoth in response to the following questions?

Required: (1) What aspects of the SUVs and trucks would you recommend that Behemoth benchmark?
(2) To whom should Behemoth compare its SUVs and trucks?

18-28. Refer to 18-16. Suppose that after helping Buzz organize his list, you get the following voice-mail message from Buzz: "Thanks for your help in organizing my list of quality items. You used four categories of costs and other measures of quality to organize the list, and I'm hoping you can help me figure out how to use these categories to help the company get the most 'bang' for its 'buck.' Curl-Up-and-Dry's annual budget meeting is coming up next month, and I want to be sure to balance the resources allocated to each of these categories to ensure the maximum quality improvement for the company. But it seems like the four categories you used are interrelated. When I go to the meeting, I want to recommend that we focus on, and allocate more money to, one of the four costs of quality. I also want to be able to justify my recommendation. Which category do you think we should focus on, and how will the focus on that one category affect the costs and other measures of quality in the other categories?"

Required: Write Buzz a memo outlining your recommendation and how you think the focus you recommend will affect the other costs and measures of quality.

18-29. Night Light Inc. manufactures a popular type of dorm room lamp. College students claim that this lamp, alone, has saved thousands of friendships because it allows one person to study with books and papers completely illuminated while other students sleep in blissful darkness. However, Night Light recently has suffered a public relations nightmare. Lately, it has experienced an unprecedented high number of warranty repairs and product recalls. And worse, because of the popularity of the lamp, the newspapers have been illuminating the public about this development. It seems no one has been left in the dark. After a lengthy investigation into the cause of the problem, a lightbulb went off in the production manager's head. It seems that a faulty part from a supplier had caused most of the warranty and recall problems. Dwight, the production manager (and also your cousin), has come to you for some consulting services.

Required: Write Dwight a memo recommending alternative courses of action that his company might take to get the product and the company's reputation turned around.

18-30. Jones Company has just asked Smith Company to sell it 100 Sprackets for $80 per unit. Smith normally sells Sprackets for $84 each. Smith produces and sells several products, and prices each product at 200% of the product's cost. Smith Company's cost of producing Sprackets under its traditional costing system is based on the following information:

Direct materials... 4 parts @ $2.50 per part
Direct labor.. 2 DLH @ $12 per hour
Total factory overhead................................. $4 per DLH

Smith's controller says, "There is no way we can accept this order; it would not be profitable. We need to sell our products for at least 200% of our cost in order to cover our selling and administrative expenses, and earn a reasonable profit. We would earn only about 190% of our cost on this order." Smith's factory accountant says, "Yes, we should accept Jones' order. If we accept the order, we will make more than 200%."

Smith's factory accountants and engineers have been working on installing activity-based costing in its factory. Below are its variable factory overhead rates for the activity pools used in producing Sprackets.

Rate per Driver Unit	Average Driver Units per Spracket
Direct labor related (at $0.25/DLH)..	2 DLH
Machine setup related (at $0.40/setup).......................................	4 setups
Quality inspections related (at $0.50/inspection)	3 inspections

Because Smith has identified more factory overhead costs as being variable under activity-based costing, each product has different variable costs per unit and its fixed overhead rate has been reduced from $2.10 per DLH to $0.80 per DLH.

Required: (1) Compute the cost per Spracket that Smith's controller must be using to justify his comment.

(2) Compute the cost per Spracket that Smith's factory accountant must be using to justify her comment.

(3) Discuss who is "right" and what accounts for the difference in the costs and selling prices per Spracket.

18-31   Fritz Company manufactures and sells various products. The president of Fritz comes to you (the chief factory accountant) with a concern. She says, "I am concerned about how well our Plappers are selling. Our Plappers are just as good as the next company's, but we are losing sales, and I've determined this is because our $130 selling price per unit is too high. But based on our cost accounting system, we have to sell our products at a gross profit of at least 40% of our selling price in order to cover our selling and administrative expenses. Based on the following costs from our system, we can't afford to reduce our selling price, so perhaps we should drop this product from our product line. Check this out for me."

Direct materials (2 parts at $5 per part)................................	$10
Direct labor (4 DLH at $14 per hour)....................................	56
Total factory overhead ($3 per DLH)	12
Total cost per Plapper...	$78

You have been working with engineers to design and implement activity-based costing in the company's factory. You have found that some factory overhead costs that you previously assumed were fixed are instead variable costs. Based on your findings, you have developed several activity pools and have found that each product has variable costs per unit different from what you previously assumed. The rate per driver unit and the average driver units per Plapper for each activity pool in regard to Fritz Company's variable factory overhead are as follows:

Rate per Driver Unit	Average Driver Units per Plapper
Direct labor related (at $0.50/DLH)..	4 DLH
Material movement related (at $0.20/movement)......................................	5 movements
Machine hours related (at $0.60/machine hour)	2 machine hours
Inspection related (at $0.40/inspection)..	6 inspections

Under activity-based costing, Fritz Company's fixed factory overhead rate is reduced from $1 per direct labor hour (under the old costing system) to $0.60 per direct labor hour.

Required: (1) Based on Fritz Company's traditional costing approach, prove that it is earning a 40% gross profit rate on its sales of Plappers.

(2) Based on the new activity-based costing approach, determine what selling price Fritz Company could charge for Plappers to obtain its target gross profit. Write the president a short memo explaining your findings and making a recommendation.

18-32   Paller Metal Products uses activity-based costing and currently manufactures Component X for use in one of its products. Ople Company has approached the president of Paller with an offer to sell Component X to Paller at a price of $14 per unit for all the units that

Paller needs in production. The units would be sold on credit (terms 2/10, n/30) to Paller and would be shipped from Ople's factory FOB shipping point, with the shipping costs being $0.50 per unit. The president sends you (the factory accountant) an e-mail that says:

> I want to know whether or not to accept this offer. I have started to analyze our costs and have developed, based on our cost records, the following schedule for Component X (CompX). I don't know much about activity-based costing, so I didn't fill in the cost for the variable factory overhead.

CompX

Direct materials... $7
Direct labor (0.4 DLH × $15) 6
Variable factory overhead.. ?
Fixed factory overhead (0.4 DLH × $5) 2
　　　Total Cost per Unit.. $?

Analyze our costs to produce CompX, complete the schedule (showing supporting calculations), and make a recommendation to me as soon as possible.

Under its activity-based costing system, Paller allocates its variable factory overhead to activity pools. CompX goes through three of these activity pools. Paller's cost records indicate that the average driver units for CompX in each activity pool and the rate per driver unit are as follows:

Activity Pool/Cost Driver	Average Driver Units per CompX	Rate per Driver Unit
Direct labor related/Direct labor hours (DLH)	1.00 DLH	$0.50/DLH
Setup related/Number of setups (SU)	0.80 SU	$0.35/SU
Inspection related/Number of inspections (IN)	0.40 IN	$0.60/IN

You determine that Paller's total fixed factory overhead costs will not change if it discontinues manufacturing CompX.

Required: Prepare a memo to the president in response to his e-mail.

18-33　Yardguard Company manufactures and sells a variety of "home improvement" products. One product, a lawn mower, is in such high demand that the company has operated both of the departments it uses to produce mowers at the departments' maximum capacity for several years. The company expects to be able to sell all of the mowers it can produce for many years at $180 per mower. The major reason for the popularity of the Yardguard mower is its quiet and reliable engine. Engines are manufactured in Department A. Mower housing, engine mounting, and testing of the mowers take place in Department B. Yardguard uses activity-based costing to assign variable factory overhead to its products. Cost information relating to mower manufacturing in the two departments is as follows:

	Department A	Department B
Expected production	25,000 engines	25,000 mowers
Variable manufacturing costs per unit:		
Direct materials	$17	$21*
Direct labor	10	13
Variable factory overhead	?†	16
Fixed factory overhead	$24 per engine	$ 8 per mower
Selling and administrative costs		
Variable: $20 per mower sold		
Fixed:　$300,000		

*Excluding engines
†Mowers go through three activity pools (purchase related, materials movement related, and inspection related) for the assignment of variable factory overhead in Department A. The rate per driver unit is $5 per purchase order, $3 per materials movement, and $2 per inspection. The average driver units per engine are 0.4 purchase orders, 1.0 materials movement, and 0.5 inspections.

Yardguard recently has been offered $75 per engine for 5,000 engines for the coming year and must decide whether or not to accept the offer. If the company accepts this offer, it will produce and sell only 20,000 mowers. In this case, the company's total fixed factory overhead costs for each department will not change. The controller of Yardguard has asked you, a management accountant for the company, to prepare an analysis of this offer.

Required: (1) Write the controller a memo that recommends whether or not to accept the offer for 5,000 engines. Include in the memo (a) a schedule of the pretax profit Yardguard would earn by *not* accepting the offer, and (b) a schedule of the pretax profit Yardguard would earn by accepting the offer.
(2) What minimum price per engine would make the offer acceptable?

18-34 Altus Company produces and sells two products, Hinkels and Quirts. During the coming year, its normal activity level of production is 400,000 cases of Hinkels and 100,000 cases of Quirts. Each case of Hinkels requires 0.6 DLH, and each case of Quirts requires 0.8 DLH. Altus has been budgeting and applying its factory overhead on the basis of 320,000 standard direct labor hours (DLH). Based on this activity level, Altus has computed its estimated total variable factory costs to be $1,280,000 and its total fixed factory overhead costs to be $1,520,000. Its standard costs for direct labor and direct materials for a case of each product are as follows:

	Hinkels	Quirts
Direct labor	$6	$ 8
Direct materials	5	10

At this activity level, Altus has no nonfactory variable costs, and it estimates its nonfactory fixed costs to be $2,000,000. Altus expects to sell each case of Hinkels for $21 and each case of Quirts for $30, and desires to earn a pretax income of $300,000.

Required: (1) Compute Altus Company's (a) variable factory overhead cost per direct labor hour and (b) fixed factory overhead cost per direct labor hour.
(2) Compute Altus Company's total cost per case of (a) Hinkels and (b) Quirts.
(3) Compute Altus Company's break-even point in "units" and in cases of Hinkels and Quirts.
(4) Compute the volume (in "units" and in cases of Hinkels and Quirts) that Altus Company must produce and sell to achieve its desired pretax income.

Now suppose that Altus Company uses activity-based costing to budget and apply its factory overhead at its normal activity level (400,000 cases of Hinkels and 100,000 cases of Quirts). Based on an analysis by its management accountants and engineers, Altus has identified several activity pools and their related cost drivers. It also has recognized that $1,000,000 of factory overhead costs that it previously considered to be fixed costs are variable costs. Thus, it traced its $2,280,000 total variable factory overhead costs to these cost pools and computed a rate per driver for each activity pool as follows:

Activity Pool/Cost Driver	Traceable Costs	Total Driver Units	Rate per Driver Unit
Purchase related/Purchase orders (PO)	$ 440,000	200,000	$2.20/PO
Material move related/Material moves (MM)	615,000	150,000	4.10/MM
Machine related/Machine hours (MH)	265,000	100,000	2.65/MH
Direct labor related/Direct labor hours (DLH)	960,000	320,000	3.00/DL
Total variable (traceable) costs	$2,280,000		

Altus has determined that at its normal activity level, Hinkels and Quirts will use the following number of driver units in each activity pool:

	Number of Driver Units	
Cost Driver	Hinkels	Quirts
PO	150,000	50,000
MM	110,000	40,000
MH	60,000	40,000
DLH	240,000	80,000

Altus has $520,000 fixed factory overheads that are not associated with an identifiable cost driver. It assigns these costs to cases based on 320,000 direct labor hours.

Required: (5) Using activity-based costing, determine Altus Company's total factory overhead cost per case of (a) Hinkels and (b) Quirts.

(6) Using activity-based costing, compute Altus Company's total cost per case of (a) Hinkels and (b) Quirts.

(7) Using activity-based costing, compute Altus Company's break-even point in "units" and in cases of Hinkels and Quirts.

(8) Using activity-based costing, compute the volume (in "units" and in cases of Hinkels and Quirts) that Altus Company must produce and sell to achieve its desired pretax income.

(9) Explain why Altus Company's total cost per case in (6) differs from that in (2).

(10) Explain why Altus Company's volumes needed to reach its break-even point and earn its desired pretax income in (7) and (8) are lower than the volumes needed to reach its break-even point and earn its desired pretax income in (3) and (4).

18-35 Jim Q is the president of Kluger Company, a medium-sized manufacturing company that sells a variety of products. The company has been in business for many years and has had a history of increasing production, sales, and profits. Jim's compensation arrangement states that he receives a salary plus a bonus based on the company's performance. The bonus is 10 percent of the amount by which the company's actual profit exceeds its target profit for the year. In computing its "profit," the company disregards income taxes and Jim's bonus. The company uses C-V-P analysis to determine the production and sales units needed to achieve its yearly target profit. The "units" that the company produces and sells are based on a constant product mix of all its products. The company also uses traditional flexible budgeting based on normal activity to determine its variable and fixed costs. During the past year, the company had a target profit of $1.2 million, based on estimated total fixed costs of $6 million, an estimated $0.60 contribution margin per unit, and a planned production (and sales) volume of 12 million units. During that year, its actual production (and sales) volume also was 12 million units. For the coming year, the company has used the same estimates, except that it has set its target profit at $1.8 million based on planned production (and sales) of 13 million units.

You are a management accountant who just started working for Kluger. You are knowledgeable about activity-based costing and have done some fairly extensive studies about the company's factory overhead. You have determined that many of the factory overhead costs that the company has always considered to be fixed do, in fact, vary with different cost drivers. You have set up several activity pools based on these cost drivers and, as a result of applying activity-based costing, have found a very high correlation between Kluger's estimated and actual variable factory overhead costs, as well as its estimated and actual fixed overhead costs, over the past several years. Based on these findings, you are confident that the company's contribution margin is $0.50 per unit and that its total fixed costs are $4 million.

One day, you meet Jim Q in the lunchroom and he says, "Do you have any ideas about how we can better manage our factory costs?" You respond that you would like to implement activity-based costing in the factory. He says, "I've studied activity-based costing, and I don't think it would help the company. Setting up all these activity pools is too much work, costs too much, and doesn't give us any better information than we had before. Let's just stay with the traditional flexible budgeting that we use now." You are surprised by Jim's response and go back to your office to think about what he said.

Required: (1) Draw a graph of Kluger's total estimated fixed costs and contribution margin for last year under traditional flexible budgeting (TFB). Label the lines on your graph.

(2) On the same graph that you drew in (1), draw Kluger's total estimated fixed costs and total contribution margin under activity-based costing (ABC). Label the new lines on your graph.

(3) Using the graph, briefly explain why Jim Q may prefer traditional flexible budgeting.

(4) How could Jim's compensation arrangement be changed so that he might be more receptive to implementing activity-based costing? Give an illustration for this past year and for the coming year.

18-36 Yesterday, you received the following letter for your advice column in the local paper:

DR. DECISIVE

Dear Dr. Decisive:

My sister and my best friend are dating, which has its good points and its bad points. One of the bad points is that sometimes I get caught in the middle of their disagreements. For example, last night, a newspaper article about a local manufacturing company started the most recent debate. According to the article, the company is losing competitive ground. The company has a traditional factory and, until recently, has been a leader in its industry. Since it is a mainstay of our community, its predicament has been the talk of the town.

Anyway, my sister and my best friend were trying to "solve" this company's problem, and started talking about TQM, JIT, flexible manufacturing systems, and manufacturing cells. My sister, who has always been fascinated by machinery and processes, said that a company that uses total quality management, flexible manufacturing systems, and manufacturing cells is using just-in-time manufacturing. In fact, she thinks they are all one and the same. My friend (who has never been in a factory in his life) says that a company can have total quality management, flexible manufacturing systems, and manufacturing cells and not be using just-in-time manufacturing.

Well, to get to the point, my problem is that I sided with my sister, and my best friend is acting like my *EX*-best friend. I think he'll come around, though, when he sees that you agree with my sister and me. Please hurry!!! My sister will always be my sister, but your answer may be just in time to save my friendship.

"Stuck in the Middle"

Required: Meet with your Dr. Decisive team and write a response to "Stuck in the Middle."

END NOTES

[a]Roberta Maynard, "A Company Is Turned Around through Japanese Principles," *Nation's Business*, February 1996, 9.
[b]http://www.canecreek.com/site/product/seatpost/recall/recall.html
[c]Michael Barrier, "Closing the Skills Gap," *Nation's Business*, March 1996, 27.
[d]Thomas A. Stewart, "Brace for Japan's Hot New Strategy," *Fortune*, September 21, 1992, 62ff.
[e]Robin Cooper, Robert S. Kaplan, Lawrence S. Maisel, Eileen Morrissey, and Ronald M. Oehm, "From ABC to ABM," *Management Accounting*, November 1992, 55.

REPORTING INVENTORY

CHAPTER 19

"I THINK THERE IS A WORLD MARKET FOR MAYBE 5 COMPUTERS."

—THOMAS WATSON, CHAIRMAN OF IBM, 1943

1. How does a company determine the costs and amounts of inventory that it includes in the inventory reported on its balance sheet?

2. What alternative cost flow assumptions may a company use for determining its cost of goods sold and ending inventory?

3. How do alternative cost flow assumptions affect a company's financial statements?

4. How do a company's inventory and cost of goods sold disclosures help a user evaluate the company?

5. How does a company apply the lower-of-cost-or-market method to report the inventory on its balance sheet?

6. What methods may a company use to estimate its cost of goods sold and inventory?

On **Hershey Foods**' (maker of "Reese's Peanut Butter Cups") December 31, 2005 balance sheet, the company shows that it owns $610.3 million of inventory—14.2 percent of its $4,295 million total assets. On February 28, 2006, **Rocky Mountain Chocolate Factory**'s balance sheet total for inventory was $2.9 million. Given that its total assets were about $19.1 million, 15.4 percent of Rocky Mountain's assets were inventory. These dollar amounts of current assets shown on Hershey Foods' and Rocky Mountain's balance sheets result from prior budgeting, purchasing, and inventory management decisions as well as the accounting methods used to keep track of inventory.

There are various ways to understand the meaning of these disclosures. For example, if Hershey manufactures one piece of candy for an average cost of three cents, its inventory account balance held the dollar equivalent of over 20 billion pieces! Hershey Foods' $610.3 million in inventory is over 210 times greater than Rocky Mountain Chocolate Factory's $2.9 million. Should you conclude that Hershey manufactures about 210 times the amount of candy produced by Rocky Mountain? Another way to think about these amounts is to think about the business operations that create them. For example, a company's inventory results from acquiring and manufacturing items that are available for sale to its customers. In their respective income statements, Hershey Foods reported cost of sales of $2,966 million and accounts payable of $168 million. Rocky Mountain Chocolate Factory reported cost of sales of $14.0 million and accounts payable of $1.1 million. So Hershey Foods' cost of sales was 4.9 times its inventory and 17.7 times its accounts payable, while Rocky Mountain Chocolate Factory's was 4.8 and 12.7 times, respectively.

Can you conclude whether Hershey Foods or Rocky Mountain Chocolate Factory is better at managing its inventory? What factors besides these amounts on the balance sheets and income statements of the two companies should you consider?

A company uses the term **inventory** to describe its assets that are (1) ready for sale, (2) being produced for sale, or (3) ready for use in a production process. So when you walk into a **Wal-Mart** store, everything you see on the shelves, as well as the goods in the warehouse, is inventory. If you visited a **Ford** factory, the completed cars waiting for shipment, the partially completed cars on the production line, and the parts waiting to be added to the cars are inventory. So you can see that inventory is an important asset for both retail and manufacturing companies.

Retail companies often refer to their inventory as *merchandise inventory*. They purchase this inventory for resale from wholesalers or directly from manufacturers. As we discussed in earlier chapters, manufacturers have several types of inventory because they make their products. Their inventories include *raw materials inventory, goods-in-process inventory* (sometimes called *work-in-process* inventory), and *finished goods inventory*. Remember, merchandise inventory for a retailer and finished goods inventory for a manufacturer are essentially equivalent because they both are products ready to be sold to customers. For simplicity, in this chapter our inventory calculations use the merchandise inventory of a retailer, but in our evaluation discussion, we include both retail and manufacturing companies. As we discussed briefly in Chapter 7 of Volume 1, a company reports inventory as a component of current assets on its balance sheet at the cost it incurred to buy or manufacture the inventory.

Does the fact that a company reports inventory at its historical cost affect the usefulness of this balance sheet information? How?

In previous chapters we discussed several issues regarding inventories. In Chapter 6 of Volume 1, we discussed the differences between the perpetual and the periodic inventory systems. Recall that a company uses the **perpetual inventory system** to keep a continuous record of the cost of inventory on hand and the cost of inventory sold. It uses a **periodic inventory system** when it does *not* need to keep a continuous record of the inventory on hand and sold. Instead, it determines the inventory on hand by a physical count at the end of the accounting period. In this chapter, we use the perpetual inventory system. We discuss the periodic inventory system in the Appendix to the chapter.

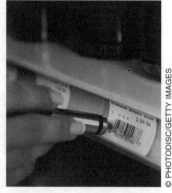

How do bar codes help a company monitor its inventory?

In Chapter 9 of Volume 1, we briefly discussed simple controls for the ordering, accepting, and storing of inventory. We also explained the specific identification method of accounting for inventory. Under the **specific identification method**, a company assigns a specific cost (what it paid for that specific unit) to each unit of inventory it sells and to each unit that it holds in its ending inventory.

In Chapters 15 through 18, we explained how a company's managers use accounting information to help them make decisions regarding inventory planning, inventory operations, and inventory control. The inventory planning issues we discussed for a manufacturing company included using relevant revenues and costs for making decisions such as whether to make or buy a product or part of a product, and whether to sell a product as is or process it further. The inventory operations issues involved using job order and process costing for manufactured inventory, as well as activity-based costing and just-in-time inventory systems. The inventory control issues dealt with standard costs and the use of variance analysis to control manufacturing operations. In this chapter, we explain how a company reports its inventory and cost of goods sold on the financial statements it includes in its annual report. We discuss how a company records the acquisition of inventory, computes cost of goods sold, records cost of goods sold, and related issues. We also describe how a company's inventory and cost of goods sold disclosures help external users assess the company's liquidity, profitability, and operating capability.

 If you prepared a personal balance sheet, what would you include as inventory? Why?

REPORTING INVENTORY ON THE BALANCE SHEET

Let's assume that you decide to start a T-shirt business on campus and that you form a corporation with your parents and yourself as shareholders. You have an agreement with a wholesale company that will supply shirts with your designs printed on them. Now suppose you purchase 500 shirts with a special design on them to sell at the homecoming football game. You pay $6 per shirt but intend to sell them for $15 each. When you have the boxes of shirts, what value should you assign to them? Should it be $6 per shirt because that is what you paid for them? Or since you designed a creative homecoming message on the shirts, should the value be higher, say $10 a shirt? Or since you are very confident that you can sell all the shirts, is the $15 selling price the best value? Or because you have agreed to pay a commission of $1 per shirt to the students who sell them, is $14 a shirt perhaps best?

 Can you think of another value that might be appropriate? If you decide to use the cost, what costs in addition to the $6 cost of the shirt might you include in the cost of inventory?

The alternatives we considered in assigning a value to the inventory of shirts show why managers and external users, in order to make informed business decisions, need to understand how a company accounts for and reports on its inventory. In our T-shirt example we did not apply any accounting rules to help decide what value to use. A company using GAAP, however, is required to base its inventory reporting on two accounting concepts we introduced earlier in the book—the *historical cost concept* and the *matching principle*. Let's review these concepts.

Recall that the historical cost concept states that a company records its transactions on the basis of the dollars exchanged (in other words, the cost) in the transaction. Once the company records a transaction, it usually retains the *cost* involved in the transaction in its accounting records. So your company would report the T-shirts at $6 per shirt under GAAP.

Some accounting and business experts express concerns about the usefulness of historical costs for inventory. They say, "Since the manufacturing activities of a company like Ford add value to the product, we should record that added value and report the inventory at an amount higher than the cost." In other words, they question the *relevance* of presenting this historical cost amount. Supporters of the historical cost concept argue that until the company has a transaction with a buyer at an agreed price, there is insufficient evidence to support any other value than the cost. They say, "Companies earn a profit by selling, not by manufacturing items or putting them on the shelves." So they argue that cost *is* the relevant value.

 To whom might the $15 selling price be relevant?

Supporters of historical cost also argue that the *reliability* of historical costs and GAAP's emphasis on *conservatism* (which we discuss later in the chapter) outweigh any potential increase in relevance that would be gained from using any other measure of value, such as the selling price.

In essence, GAAP supporters say, "If we report inventory at the selling price (or any amount above the cost), then we also have to record the profit before we sell the item—after all, the balance sheet has to balance. But profit doesn't occur until we sell the inventory at a specified price. Everyone thinks they can sell their inventory at a desired price, but it doesn't always happen!"

 Which accounts do you think would be affected, and how would they be affected, if a company records its inventory at more than it paid for its inventory?

Until someone actually buys the T-shirt for $15, we are not sure how reliable that dollar amount is. Assume, for example, that you recorded the inventory in your records at $15 per shirt and that your parents, as investors, made a business decision based on your $15 estimate. Now suppose that on the day of the homecoming game, it rained and game attendance was low, so you decided to sell shirts for only $10 at halftime. Then your income would be $5 less per shirt. So, the company's investors would have been hurt by the estimate you recorded. With historical cost accounting, at least external users "know what they are getting." For example, if we polled ten accountants, all ten would conclude that the historical cost was $6 per shirt, and all ten would report the same income and asset amounts. If a company recorded inventory at its selling price rather than at its historical cost, those same ten accountants would probably differ in their estimates of the selling price of the shirts, and would therefore report different income and asset amounts.

 Whose side do you take on this discussion—the supporters or the critics of the historical cost concept? Explain your position.

The matching principle states that to determine its net income for an accounting period, a company computes the total expenses involved in earning the revenues of the period and deducts them from the revenues earned in that period. Therefore, a company reports the inventory expense, usually known as **cost of goods sold** or **cost of sales**, in the period in which it sells the item and reports the revenue from the sale. For example, Unlimited Decadence reports the cost of the chocolates it sells to Sweet Temptations in the same period in which it reports the revenue from the sales.

So, the historical cost concept and the matching principle provide the basis for how a company accounts for inventory and reports it in the company's financial statements. In this chapter we will address five important issues: (1) computing the historical cost and the amount of inventory, (2) using alternative inventory cost flow assumptions, (3) using a company's inventory and cost of goods sold disclosures for evaluation, (4) using the lower-of-cost-or-market rule, and (5) estimating the cost of inventory and the cost of goods sold.

COMPUTING THE HISTORICAL COST AND THE AMOUNT OF INVENTORY

The cost of each unit of inventory includes all the costs incurred to bring the item to its existing condition and location. Thus the cost of inventory includes the purchase price (less any purchases discounts), sales tax, applicable transportation costs, insurance, customs duties, and similar costs. When a cost, such as the cost of ordering the inventory, is difficult to associate with a particular inventory item, many companies record it as a general and administrative expense. A company determines the cost of each unit of inventory by reviewing the source documents (e.g., invoices) it uses to record the purchase of the inventory.

When a company takes a physical inventory, it counts the units of inventory in its stores and warehouses (and factories). The company also may own additional units of inventory that are in transit. **In transit** means that a freight company is in the process of delivering the inventory from the selling company to the buying company. The company (the buyer or the seller) that has economic control over the items in transit includes them in its inventory. Typically, economic control transfers at the same time legal ownership transfers.

A company may buy or sell inventory under terms of FOB (free on board) shipping point or FOB destination. **FOB shipping point** means that the selling company transfers ownership to the buyer at the place of sale (shipping point)—that is, *before* the inventory is in transit. The selling company excludes these items in transit from its inventory; the buying company includes them in its inventory. The buying company is responsible for any transportation costs incurred to deliver the items, and includes those costs as a cost of its inventory (rather than immediately recording them as an expense). **FOB destination** means that the selling company transfers ownership to the buyer at the place of delivery (after transit is completed). The selling company includes these items in transit in its inventory until delivery takes place; the buyer excludes them. In this case, the selling company is responsible for any transportation costs incurred to deliver the items and includes those costs in its selling expenses.

I How does a company determine the costs and amounts of inventory that it includes in the inventory reported on its balance sheet?

Why do you think the selling company includes transportation costs on the income statement, whereas the buying company includes transportation costs on the balance sheet?

© ERNEST H. ROBL

What do you think is the inventory in this picture? On whose balance sheet do you think it is recorded?

USING ALTERNATIVE INVENTORY COST FLOW ASSUMPTIONS

2 What alternative cost flow assumptions may a company use for determining its cost of goods sold and ending inventory?

Once a company has determined the number of units in its ending inventory and the cost of the units it purchased during the period, it must determine how to allocate the total cost of these units (the cost of goods available for sale) between the ending inventory (balance sheet) and the cost of goods sold (income statement). The following diagram shows this relationship:

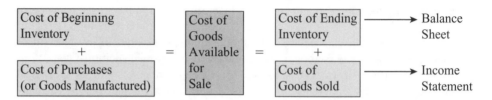

If the cost of each unit of inventory is the same during the period, the company simply allocates these costs to ending inventory and cost of goods sold according to how many units it has left and how many it has sold. It is more difficult to determine which costs a company includes in the ending inventory and which costs it includes in the cost of goods sold when the costs it incurred to acquire the units changed during the period. Such changes are common in the current economic environment. GAAP allows a company to choose one of four alternative cost flow assumptions to allocate its cost of goods available for sale between ending inventory and cost of goods sold:

1. Specific identification
2. First-in, first-out (FIFO)
3. Average cost
4. Last-in, first-out (LIFO)

A company must disclose in its annual report the method it uses, and it must use that method consistently every year. Since we discussed the specific identification method in Chapter 6, in this chapter we will focus on the FIFO, average cost, and LIFO methods. We will discuss each of the methods for Granola Goodies Company, using the information in Exhibit 19-1. For simplicity, we use a month rather than the more common quarterly or annual accounting period used by actual companies.

The company has a beginning inventory (1,000 units) of $5,000 and makes two purchases (500 and 900 units) during January for a total cost of $8,150 ($2,750 +

EXHIBIT 19-1	GRANOLA GOODIES COMPANY: INVENTORY INFORMATION		
Beginning inventory, January 1	1,000	units @ $5.00 per unit	$ 5,000
January 7 sale	(400)	units	
January 12 purchase	500	units @ $5.50 per unit	2,750
January 20 sale	(700)	units	
January 24 purchase	900	units @ $6.00 per unit	5,400
January 26 sale	(200)	units	
Cost of goods available for sale			$13,150
Ending inventory, January 31	1,100	units	

Notes: 1. The units are sold for $13 per unit.
      2. Granola Goodies Company uses the perpetual inventory system.
      3. 2,400 (1,000 + 500 + 900) units are available for sale during January.

$5,400). During the month it sold 1,300 (400, 700, and 200) units. Therefore it must divide its cost of goods available for sale (for its 2,400 units available) of $13,150 ($5,000 + $8,150) between the 1,300 units it sold (the cost of goods sold) and its ending inventory of 1,100 units. For illustration purposes, we assume that Granola Goodies Company uses the *perpetual inventory system*. (In the chapter Appendix, we discuss how each of the cost flow assumptions is applied under the periodic inventory system.) Under the perpetual system, the company records the cost of goods sold each time it sells a unit, and updates its inventory account each time the physical inventory changes (each time it makes a purchase or a sale). Note that we assume the company makes only three sales during the month.

When the costs to acquire the inventory have changed during the period, each of the inventory cost flow assumptions produces different amounts for the cost of goods sold and the ending inventory balance. It is important to understand that these *cost* flow assumptions may *not* be related to the actual *physical* flow of the goods in inventory. Typically a company will use a FIFO physical flow of its inventory to reduce the risk of obsolescence, but may still use any of the cost flow assumptions to allocate its cost of goods available for sale between ending inventory and cost of goods sold.

First-In, First-Out

When a company uses the **first-in, first-out (FIFO)** cost flow assumption, it includes the *earliest (first)* costs it incurred in the cost of goods sold as it sells its products, leaving the *latest* costs in ending inventory. (In other words, the company *assumes* that it sells the inventory in the same order as it purchased it—*even if it may not actually sell the inventory in the same order.*) Under the FIFO cost flow assumption, Granola Goodies Company computes the cost of goods sold to be $6,650 and the ending inventory to be $6,500, as we show in Exhibit 19-2. The exhibit has two parts: the upper part shows a diagram of the "flow" of costs; the lower part shows schedules computing the cost of goods sold and the ending inventory.

The company sold 1,300 units. Using the FIFO cost flow assumption, the company moves the first costs it incurred into cost of goods sold first. The most recent costs it incurred remain in inventory. Therefore, the 400 units sold on January 7 have a cost of $5 per unit from the beginning inventory. After the sale, the cost of 600 units from the beginning inventory remain in inventory. On January 12, the company purchased 500 units at $5.50 per unit. For the January 20 sale of 700 units, 600 units have a cost of $5 per unit from the beginning inventory and 100 units have a cost of $5.50 from the January 12 purchase. After this sale, the cost of 400 units from the January 12 purchase remains in the Inventory account. On January 24, the company purchased 900 units at $6 per unit. For the January 26 sale, the 200 units have a cost of $5.50 from the January 12 purchase. This leaves the cost of the other 200 units from the January 12 purchase in the Inventory account. The cost of the ending inventory includes the cost of these 200 units remaining from the January 12 purchase ($1,100), as well as the cost of the 900 units the company purchased on January 24 ($5,400). So the total cost of the 1,100 units in ending inventory is $6,500.

Average Cost

When a company uses the average cost flow assumption under the perpetual inventory system, it must compute an average cost per unit after each purchase and then assign this new average cost to items sold until the next purchase (when it computes another new average cost). This method is called the **moving average** cost flow assumption; because this method involves tedious calculations, we will not discuss it further. However, we show the computations for the average cost method under the periodic inventory system in the chapter Appendix.

EXHIBIT 19-2 — **GRANOLA GOODIES COMPANY: FIRST-IN, FIRST-OUT COST FLOW ASSUMPTION**

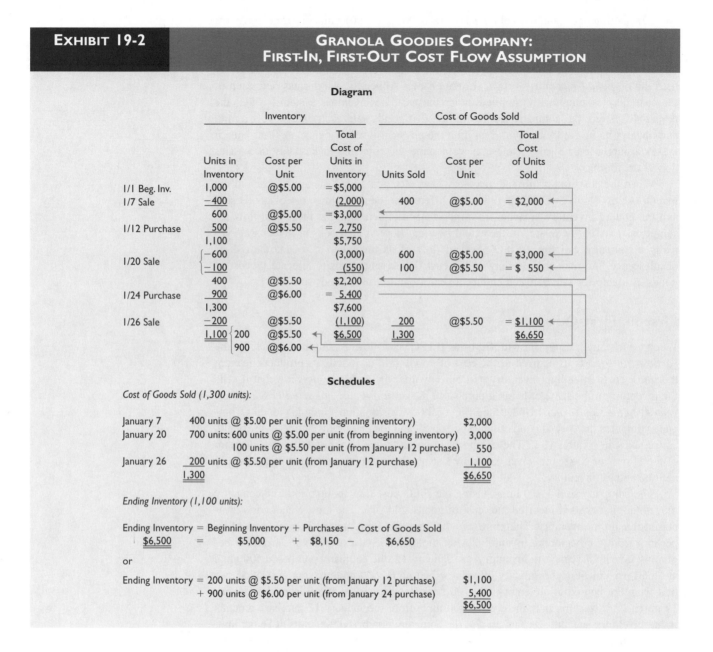

Last-In, First-Out

When a company uses the **last-in, first-out (LIFO)** cost flow assumption, it includes the *latest (last)* costs it incurred before a sale in its cost of goods sold and the earliest costs (part or all of which are costs it incurred in previous periods) in ending inventory. (In other words, it *assumes* that the order in which it sells the inventory items is the reverse of the order in which it purchased them. Remember, however, that these *cost* assumptions are not necessarily the same as the actual *physical* flows of the inventory.) Under the LIFO cost flow assumption, Granola Goodies Company computes the cost of goods sold to be $6,950 and the ending inventory to be $6,200, as we show in Exhibit 19-3. Again, this exhibit has two parts: the upper part shows a diagram of the "flow" of costs; the lower part shows schedules computing the cost of goods sold and the ending inventory.

The company sold 1,300 units. Using the LIFO cost flow assumption, the company moves the most recent costs it incurred to purchase inventory into cost of goods sold first. The earliest costs it incurred remain in the Inventory account. The 400 units sold on Jan-

| EXHIBIT 19-3 | GRANOLA GOODIES COMPANY:
LAST-IN, FIRST-OUT COST FLOW ASSUMPTION |

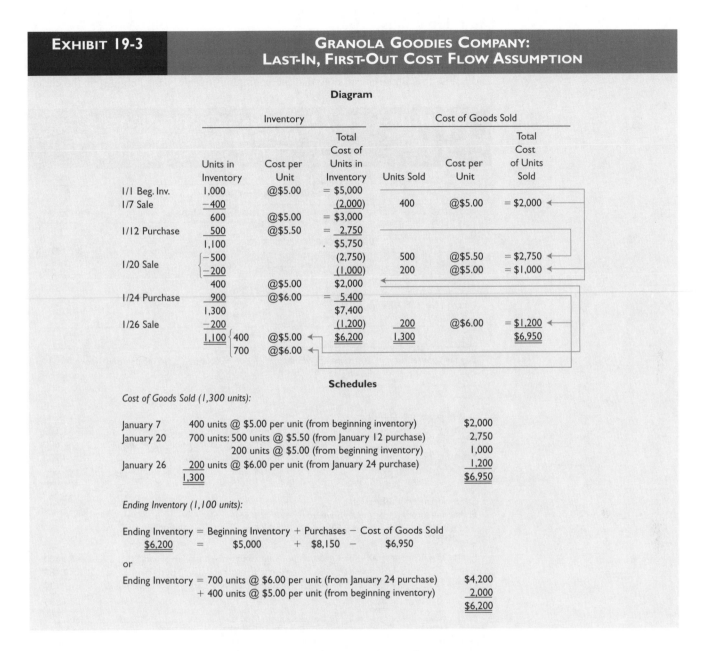

Diagram

	Inventory			Cost of Goods Sold		
	Units in Inventory	Cost per Unit	Total Cost of Units in Inventory	Units Sold	Cost per Unit	Total Cost of Units Sold
1/1 Beg. Inv.	1,000	@$5.00	= $5,000			
1/7 Sale	−400		(2,000)	400	@$5.00	= $2,000
	600	@$5.00	= $3,000			
1/12 Purchase	500	@$5.50	= 2,750			
	1,100		$5,750			
1/20 Sale	−500		(2,750)	500	@$5.50	= $2,750
	−200		(1,000)	200	@$5.00	= $1,000
	400	@$5.00	$2,000			
1/24 Purchase	900	@$6.00	= 5,400			
	1,300		$7,400			
1/26 Sale	−200		(1,200)	200	@$6.00	= $1,200
	1,100 {400	@$5.00	$6,200	1,300		$6,950
	{700	@$6.00				

Schedules

Cost of Goods Sold (1,300 units):

January 7	400 units @ $5.00 per unit (from beginning inventory)	$2,000
January 20	700 units: 500 units @ $5.50 (from January 12 purchase)	2,750
	200 units @ $5.00 (from beginning inventory)	1,000
January 26	200 units @ $6.00 per unit (from January 24 purchase)	1,200
	1,300	$6,950

Ending Inventory (1,100 units):

Ending Inventory = Beginning Inventory + Purchases − Cost of Goods Sold
$6,200   = $5,000   + $8,150   − $6,950

or

Ending Inventory = 700 units @ $6.00 per unit (from January 24 purchase) $4,200
+ 400 units @ $5.00 per unit (from beginning inventory)   2,000
$6,200

uary 7 have a cost of $5 per unit from the beginning inventory. On January 12, the company purchased 500 units at $5.50 per unit. For the January 20 sale of 700 units, the first 500 of these units have a cost of $5.50 per unit from the January 12 purchase, and the remaining 200 units have a cost of $5 from the beginning inventory. (Remember that we are *assuming* that the most recent units purchased are sold first, even though that may not be the case.) On January 24, the company purchased 900 units at $6 per unit. For the January 26 sale, the 200 units sold have a cost of $6 per unit from the January 24 purchase. The cost of the ending inventory, then, includes the cost of the remaining 700 units from the January 24 purchase and the cost of 400 units from January's beginning inventory. So, the total cost of the 1,100 units in ending inventory ($6,200) includes the cost of 400 units remaining from the beginning inventory ($2,000) plus the cost of 700 units remaining from the purchase on January 24 ($4,200).

Do you think a large retail company could apply the average or the LIFO cost flow assumption under the perpetual inventory method? Why or why not?

Additional Illustration

Exhibit 19-4 continues the Granola Goodies Company inventory system example through February so that we can give you another illustration of the differences between FIFO and LIFO. It is important to note that the beginning inventory for February is the ending

EXHIBIT 19-4	GRANOLA GOODIES COMPANY: ENDING INVENTORY AND COST OF GOODS SOLD FOR FEBRUARY

Additional Information

	Units	Purchases
Beginning Inventory, February 1	1,100 units	
February 7 purchase	400 units @ $6.20 per unit	$2,480
February 15 sale	(300) units	
February 19 purchase	800 units @ $6.40 per unit	$5,120
February 24 sale	(700) units	
Ending inventory, February 28	1,300 units	

First-In, First-Out

Beginning Inventory = 200 units @ $5.50 per unit + 900 units @ $6.00 per unit (from
Exhibit 19-2)
= $6,500

Cost of goods sold (1,000 units)

February 15	300 units: 200 units @ $5.50 per unit (from beginning inventory)	$1,100	
	100 units @ $6.00 per unit (from beginning inventory)	600	
February 24	700 units @ $6.00 per unit (from beginning inventory)	4,200	
	1,000	$5,900	

Ending Inventory (1,300 units)

Ending Inventory = Beginning Inventory + Purchases − Cost of Goods Sold
$8,200 = $6,500 + $7,600 − $5,900

or

Ending Inventory = 100 units @ $6.00 per unit (from beginning inventory)	$ 600
+ 400 units @ $6.20 per unit (from February 7 purchase)	2,480
+ 800 units @ $6.40 per unit (from February 19 purchase)	5,120
1,300	$8,200

Last-In, First-Out

Beginning Inventory = 700 units @ $6.00 per unit + 400 units @ $5.00 per unit (from
Exhibit 19-3)
= $6,200

Cost of Goods Sold (1,000 units)

February 15	300 units @ $6.20 per unit (from February 7 purchase)	$1,860
February 24	700 units @ $6.40 per unit (from February 19 purchase)	4,480
	1,000	$6,340

Ending Inventory (1,300 units)

Ending Inventory = Beginning Inventory + Purchases − Cost of Goods Sold
$7,460 = $6,200 + $7,600 − $6,340

or

Ending Inventory = 100 units @ $6.40 per unit (from February 19 purchase)	$ 640
+ 100 units @ $6.20 per unit (from February 7 purchase)	620
+ 1,100 units (from beginning inventory)	6,200
1,300	$7,460

inventory for January and that, therefore, the amounts for the two cost flow assumptions differ. The calculations otherwise follow the same procedures as for January.

EFFECTS OF THE TWO ALTERNATIVES

As you just saw, the FIFO and LIFO cost flow assumptions affect a company's financial statements differently. We will discuss the advantages and disadvantages of these assumptions in this section.

3 How do alternative cost flow assumptions affect a company's financial statements?

Effects on the Financial Statements

The choice made by managers to adopt the FIFO or the LIFO cost flow assumption for a company affects both the company's income statement and balance sheet. If costs are *rising*, cost of goods sold is lower under FIFO because the first costs moved into cost of goods sold are the earliest (lower) costs. Since cost of goods sold is lower, gross profit (sales − cost of goods sold) is higher and net income is higher. Under LIFO, the most recent (higher) costs are moved into cost of goods sold first, making it higher than the cost of goods sold under FIFO. Therefore, the gross profit and net income under LIFO are lower than under FIFO. If costs are *falling,* the relationships between FIFO and LIFO are reversed.[1] Using the Granola Goodies Company example, the following comparative ending inventory and gross profit figures result from selling 1,300 units for $16,900 in *January* (assuming a selling price of $13 per unit):

	FIFO		LIFO	
Sales		$16,900		$16,900
Cost of goods available for sale	$13,150		$13,150	
Ending inventory	(6,500)		(6,200)	
Cost of goods sold		(6,650)		(6,950)
Gross profit		$10,250		$ 9,950

Since Granola Goodies is experiencing rising costs, you can see that under FIFO, its ending inventory is highest, its cost of goods sold is lowest, and therefore its gross profit is highest. In contrast, LIFO results in the lowest ending inventory, the highest cost of goods sold, and therefore the lowest gross profit. It is often said that FIFO takes a balance sheet approach by reporting the inventory at the cost of the company's most recent purchases, a cost that is close to its replacement cost. The **replacement cost** is the cost (including any transportation costs ordinarily incurred) that a company would have to pay at the balance sheet date to purchase (replace) an item of inventory (based on purchasing inventory in normal quantities from the usual suppliers). Although FIFO reports ending inventory at close to replacement cost, it understates cost of goods sold when costs are rising because cost of goods sold is *not* close to the amount the company paid for its most recent purchases. In contrast, since LIFO includes the most recent costs in cost of goods sold first, it takes an income statement approach by matching the most recent costs against revenues. However LIFO understates ending inventory because the cost of the ending inventory is *not* close to the amount the company paid for its most recent purchases.

Note that we made a simplifying assumption in the Granola Goodies Company example for January and that this assumption has made the differences less than they might otherwise be. We assumed that the beginning inventory consisted of 1,000 units at $5 under both methods. Recall, however, that the beginning inventory of the period is the ending inventory of the previous period. Therefore the use of each method in the previous period (assuming costs changed) means that the beginning inventory would differ under each of the alternatives, just as the ending inventory for January differs under each method.

---

[1]Although we do not show the calculations in the chapter, whether costs are rising or falling, the average cost amounts would be between those of FIFO and LIFO (but would typically be much closer to the FIFO amount).

You can see this relationship in the calculations for February (Exhibit 19-4), in which the beginning inventory is different in all three situations. This factor can become very significant when a company uses the LIFO cost flow assumption. If the number of units in a company's inventory increases during each period, it carries over the costs in the beginning inventory for each period. Therefore, a company using LIFO builds up *layers* of costs in its inventory.

To understand this, look back at Exhibit 19-4. The February ending LIFO inventory for Granola Goodies of $7,460 includes four layers of cost: $5, $6.00, $6.20, and $6.40 per unit. As years pass, however, these costs will become very outdated. For example, many companies adopted LIFO in the late 1930s and others during the period of high inflation in the middle of the 1970s. The inventories they report in today's balance sheets include elements of costs from many years ago that usually bear little or no relationship to the costs of the current period or to the costs that will be incurred to replace the inventory. Therefore, users say that the LIFO inventory cost in the balance sheet is *not relevant*.

 Do you think the LIFO cost of goods sold is relevant? Why or why not?

Income Measurement

At this point, you may be having some difficulty understanding LIFO. It may seem to be a counter-intuitive method, and we have just said that the LIFO inventory cost in the balance sheet is not relevant. So the next issue is very important. Many users of financial statements argue that LIFO results in a better measure of income when costs are rising. To understand this point, consider Granola Goodies Company in *January*. If the company uses the FIFO method, it will be selling units for $13 and, for 1,100 of the units, recording cost of goods sold of $5 per unit and a gross profit of $8 per unit during January. The company must replace the inventory during the month by paying $5.50 or $6 per unit, however, so the company must use $0.50 or $1 more of the gross profit to buy the replacement units of this inventory. Therefore, only $7.50 or $7 represents the real gross profit of Granola Goodies Company (the amount of the gross profit that is left to cover the company's operating costs after it replaces the inventory it sold). A **holding gain** (or **inventory profit**) is the artificial profit that results when a company records cost of goods sold at an historical cost that is lower than the replacement cost of the units sold. In this example, the holding gain is $0.50 or $1 per unit sold. Since the holding gain cannot be distributed to the owners as dividends without reducing the ability of the company to replace the units of inventory sold, many users argue that the holding gain should be excluded from the calculation of income.

 Why do you think inventory profit is called a "holding gain"?

Impact of Tax Rules

Why would the managers of a company select LIFO for financial reporting when it results in lower reported income? *If the company is a corporation, LIFO is allowed for income tax purposes only if LIFO is also used for the financial statements.* (Any of the other methods may be used for calculating corporate taxable income, regardless of which method is used for financial reporting.) And why would managers of a company select LIFO for income tax purposes? If we assume rising costs, the use of LIFO results in lower taxable income (because of higher cost of goods sold) and consequently in the payment of less income taxes. For instance, according to their recent annual reports, three major U.S. companies—**ExxonMobil**, **General Motors**, and **General Electric**—have together saved over $6 billion in taxes by using LIFO instead of FIFO. This tax saving is a very strong, practical argument in favor of LIFO because companies using LIFO avoid cash payments for income taxes and therefore have more cash available than they otherwise would for such things as paying employees, investing in property and equipment, reducing liabilities, or paying dividends.

 Do you think you pay less when you purchase a car because the manufacturer uses LIFO?

Managers' Selection of an Inventory Cost Flow Assumption

If the managers of a company expect that the costs of acquiring inventory will increase in the future, then we should expect them to select LIFO because of the lower income taxes that the company will have to pay. Of course, the income the company reports in its financial statements also will be lower. Reporting a lower income, however, does not mean that the company's stock price goes down. There is much evidence that investors understand how LIFO affects net income and that the stock price of a company is *not* lower because the company reports a lower income under LIFO. Instead, the stock price should be higher because the company pays less taxes. Alternatively, if the managers expect that the costs of acquiring inventory will *decrease* in the future, then we should expect them to select FIFO (or average cost) because the company would again pay lower income taxes.

Although the managers are able to select one of the four (including specific identification) cost flow assumptions to account for a company's inventory, once they make the selection, they are required by GAAP to consistently apply that method from period to period. If the managers make a change, they must disclose the effects of the change (the difference between what net income would have been under the old method, and what it is under the new method) in the company's annual report. Managers also may select more than one method by using a different cost flow assumption for different types of inventory. For example, if a retail company is selling clothing that has rising costs and computers that have falling costs, the company may select LIFO for the clothing and FIFO for the computers.

 If costs are decreasing, explain how the two methods would affect a company's inventory, cost of goods sold, and gross profit.

Disclosure in the Financial Statements

A company reports its inventory in the current assets section of its balance sheet, usually immediately after receivables. It discloses its inventory cost flow assumption (FIFO or LIFO) and its method of valuing the inventory (we will discuss these methods later in the chapter) usually in a note to the financial statements. It deducts cost of goods sold from net sales on its income statement to determine gross profit. It includes the cash paid to purchase or manufacture inventory in the cash flows from operating activities on its cash flow statement.

USING INVENTORY AND COST OF GOODS SOLD DISCLOSURES FOR EVALUATION

Up to this point in the chapter we have focused on reporting inventory and cost of goods sold. Understanding these issues provides the foundation needed to learn how external users study a company's inventory and cost of goods sold disclosures to help them evaluate its *liquidity, profitability,* and *operating capability* (efficiency)—measures of how well a company uses its assets to generate revenue and cash flows.

Investors and creditors evaluate inventory and cost of goods sold, like other parts of the financial statements, by performing *intra*company and *inter*company analysis, through the use of horizontal analysis, vertical analysis, and ratio analysis. We will discuss intracompany analysis first, followed by intercompany analysis. We will use **Intel Corporation**'s

4 How do a company's inventory and cost of goods sold disclosures help a user evaluate the company?

2005 annual report to provide the information we need to explain intracompany analysis. Intel primarily manufactures and sells computer chips and is classified as part of the electronics components industry. We selected Intel because inventory is very important to electronics manufacturers. (We will also discuss Intel's property, plant, and equipment in Chapter 21.)

 Would you expect Intel to use the FIFO or LIFO cost flow assumption? Why?

Intracompany Analysis of Inventory: Intel Corporation

Exhibit 19-5 presents information taken from Intel's 2005 annual report—its balance sheets, income statements, and notes. Since we discussed liquidity, including the current and quick ratios, in Chapter 7 of Volume 1, we do not repeat that discussion here. However, recall that liquidity is a measure of how quickly an asset can be turned into cash and that the *current ratio* (current assets divided by current liabilities) and the *quick ratio* (quick assets divided by current liabilities) are used to evaluate a company's liquidity.

EXHIBIT 19-5	INVENTORY DISCLOSURES: INTEL

Consolidated Balance Sheets (in part)

December 31, 2005 and December 25, 2004

(In millions)	2005	2004
Assets		
Current assets:		
Cash and cash equivalents	$ 7,324	$ 8,407
Short-term investments	3,990	5,654
Trading assets	1,458	3,111
Accounts receivable, net of allowance for doubtful accounts of $64 ($43 in 2004)	3,914	2,999
Inventories	3,126 ←	→ 2,621
Deferred tax assets	1,149	979
Other current assets	233	287
Total current assets	**$21,194**	**$24,058**

Consolidated Statements of Income (in part)

Two years ended December 31, 2005 and December 25, 2004

(In millions)	2005	2004
Net revenue	$38,826	$34,209
Cost of sales	15,777	14,463

Notes (in part)

Inventories. Inventory cost is computed on a currently adjusted standard basis (which approximates actual cost on an average or first-in, first-out basis). Inventory is determined to be saleable based on a demand forecast within a specific time horizon, generally six months or less. Inventory in excess of saleable amounts is not valued, and the remaining inventory is valued at the lower of cost or market. Inventories at fiscal year-ends were as follows:

(In millions)	2005	2004
Raw materials	$ 409	$ 388
Work in process	1,662	1,418
Finished goods	1,055	815
Total	**$3,126**	**$2,621**

Compute the quick and current ratios for Intel on December 31, 2005 and December 25, 2004, if the current liabilities are $9,234 million and $8,006 million for these dates respectively. How has the company's liquidity changed?

More information can be gained by analyzing the information disclosed on Intel's financial statements. The balance sheet shows that Intel's inventory increased by $505 million ($3,126 − $2,621) in 2005 because Intel purchased and manufactured more inventory than it sold. The income statement shows that during 2005, the company had cost of goods sold of $15,777 million. Using just the information from these two financial statements, we can figure out the total cost incurred (in millions) by Intel to acquire (manufacture or purchase) inventory in 2005 as follows:

$$\text{Beginning Inventory} + \text{Cost of Inventory Acquired} - \text{Ending Inventory} = \text{Cost of Goods Sold}$$

or

$$\$2,621 + \text{Cost of Inventory Acquired} - \$3,126 = \$15,777$$

Therefore, Cost of Inventory Acquired = $15,777 + $3,126 − $2,621
= $16,282

Comparing the cost of inventory acquired in a given year with that of previous years will enable you to understand how a company's manufacturing (or purchasing) activities have increased (or decreased).

What was the cost of inventory acquired in 2004 if the beginning inventory was $2,519 million?

Now we discuss two questions about inventory and cost of goods sold.

Question #1: Does Intel Sell Its Inventory Profitably?

We discussed profitability, including the gross profit percentage, in Chapter 6 of Volume 1. A variation of the gross profit percentage is the cost of goods sold (cost of sales) as a percentage of net sales (net revenue), which we compute for Intel as follows (in millions):

	2005	2004
Cost of goods sold	$\dfrac{\$15,777}{\$38,826} = 40.6\%$	$\dfrac{\$14,463}{\$34,209} = 42.3\%$
Net sales		

Thus we see that Intel's costs compared with selling prices have decreased by 1.7% from 2004 to 2005. Therefore, its gross profit percentage has increased in 2005.

Another comparison we can make is to see if the company's increase in inventory affected its sales. In 2005 Intel increased its inventory by $505 million whereas its sales increased by $4,617 ($38,826 − $34,209); a good result! By comparison, in 2004 Intel increased its inventory by $102 million while increasing its sales by $4,068; an even better result!

Why do you think that Intel increased its inventory by 19.3% in 2005 while its sales increased by 13.5%?

Question #2: Does Intel Use Its Inventory Efficiently?

We discussed the inventory turnover ratio (cost of goods sold divided by average inventory) in Chapter 7 of Volume 1 as a means of evaluating operating capability (efficiency). We do not repeat that discussion here but instead look at this ratio and related issues that arise when we compare two (or more) companies. Since Intel does *not* use LIFO, we do

not need to make any adjustments. However, for a company using LIFO, the lower ending inventory cost (assuming rising costs) affects the computation and evaluation of current assets, working capital, and any financial ratios that include inventory, thereby
reducing comparability between it and other companies.

*Compute the inventory turnover ratio, and the inventory turnover in days, for Intel in
2005. How do these compare with the amounts for 2004 if the inventory at the beginning of 2004 was $2,519 million?*

Intercompany Analysis within an Industry

One limitation of intracompany analysis is that it fails to provide an external comparison
of the company's performance. Do we know how well Intel is performing relative to other
companies in the electronics components industry? *Intercompany analysis* provides this
relative analysis. We discussed intercompany comparisons of liquidity in Chapter 14 of
Volume 1. Here, we focus our discussion on those special issues, related to evaluating
operating capability (efficiency), that are raised by the use of alternative cost flow assumptions. In Chapter 21 we will discuss the comparison of Intel to industry norms using property, plant, and equipment.

   Listed below are three alternatives that may exist when comparing companies that
have significant amounts of inventory. For this discussion, we will assume a comparison
of just two companies and will treat the FIFO and average cost methods as interchange-
able, since they are not likely to result in materially different amounts.

*Why do you think that the FIFO and the average cost methods are not likely to result in
materially different amounts? Do you think that the LIFO and the average cost methods
are likely to differ materially? Why or why not?*

Alternative #1: Both Companies Use the FIFO or the Average
Cost Flow Assumption

When you are comparing two companies that use the FIFO or average cost flow assumption
(such as Intel), you have the simplest situation. The ending inventory amounts of the companies are comparable because they are the latest costs of the period. Although the cost
of goods sold amounts are based on the earliest costs of the period, including the costs of
the beginning inventories, these amounts should be comparable (unless the companies
have very different inventory turnovers and significant changes in their costs).

*Why do you think that different inventory turnovers and significant changes in costs would
affect the comparability of the cost of goods sold for two companies?*

Alternative #2: Both Companies Use the LIFO Cost Flow Assumption

When you are comparing two companies that use the LIFO cost flow assumption, you might
think that you have another simple situation. But be careful! Since cost of goods sold is
computed from the latest costs of the period, the two cost of goods sold amounts are comparable (again assuming similar inventory turnovers). However, the ending inventory
amounts of the two companies are *not* comparable because they are the earliest costs. As
we discussed previously in the chapter, the inventory under LIFO is made up of "layers"
of costs from periods since the company adopted LIFO. Therefore, a company that adopted
LIFO in 1975 would have a very different inventory cost from that of a company that adopted
LIFO in 1990, even if their physical inventories are exactly the same. Also, two companies
that adopted LIFO in the same year would not have comparable ending inventory costs because each company would have added layers of different amounts in each period.

   To overcome these limitations of comparing the LIFO balance sheet amounts, companies must disclose the costs of their ending inventories under an alternative, more com-

parable, cost flow assumption, such as FIFO, average, current, or replacement cost. Fortunately, you don't have to worry about the distinction between these titles—for our purposes, they all mean the same because the amounts are unlikely to be significantly different. Therefore, you can think of them all as being the same as the FIFO inventory value. We will refer to them as **non-LIFO** amounts. Also, rather than disclose the amounts directly, companies often disclose the *difference* between the LIFO and the non-LIFO ending inventory amounts. Sometimes they call this difference the **LIFO reserve**.

 How might this discussion affect your computation of the inventory turnover ratio?

Since the inventory turnover ratio uses the (average) inventory for the year, the ratio computations are not relevant (or comparable) when they are based on LIFO inventory values. Therefore, it is preferable to base the ratio on the non-LIFO cost of the inventory disclosed rather than the LIFO amount reported on the balance sheet.

Exhibit 19-6 shows the inventory amounts and related disclosures for **Winnebago**. If we use the nonrelevant "LIFO cost" amounts on the balance sheets, we would compute the inventory turnover ratio for 2005 (the fiscal year ending August 27, 2005) as follows:

$$\text{Inventory Turnover} = \frac{\text{Cost of Goods Sold}}{\text{Average Inventory}}$$

$$= \frac{\$854{,}997}{(\$120{,}655 + \$130{,}733) \div 2}$$

$$= \underline{6.80}$$

 Why do you think that Winnebago uses a year-end in August instead of the more commonly used December 31?

Using the preferable non-LIFO (replacement cost) amounts shown in Note 4, we compute the inventory turnover ratio as follows:

$$\text{Inventory Turnover} = \frac{\text{Cost of Goods Sold}}{\text{Average Inventory}}$$

$$= \frac{\$854{,}997}{(\$152{,}116 + \$157{,}925) \div 2}$$

$$= \underline{5.52}$$

Is this vehicle "inventory" or "property and equipment"?

© LAYNE KENNEDY/CORBIS

Dividing these two ratios into 365 days gives the inventory turnover as 53.7 days and 66.1 days, respectively. While a 12 day difference is significant for Winnebago, the difference may be more or less significant for other companies you analyze and for intercompany comparisons.

 *Do you think that **General Motors** and **Ford** would have the same inventory turnover ratio amounts if they were equally efficient? Why or why not?*

Alternative #3: One Company Uses FIFO/Average While the Other Uses LIFO

The most complex situation arises when the two companies you are comparing use different cost flow assumptions. This should not happen too often because, as we discussed earlier, managers should choose a cost flow assumption based on the expected cost changes in that industry. Since users normally make comparisons within an industry, companies within that industry will generally select the same cost flow assumption.

In this situation, we again use the disclosures made by Winnebago. But this time we use the company's disclosures to convert the LIFO beginning and ending inventory

EXHIBIT 19-6	INVENTORY DISCLOSURES: WINNEBAGO INDUSTRIES

Consolidated Balance Sheets (in part)

(dollars in thousands)	August 27, 2005	August 28, 2004
Assets		
Current assets:		
Cash and cash equivalents	$ 19,484	$ 24,445
Short-term investments	$ 93,100	$ 51,100
Receivables, less allowance for doubtful accounts		
($270 and $161, respectively)	40,910	46,112
Inventories	120,655	130,733
Prepaid expenses and other assets	4,333	4,814
Deferred income taxes	9,610	12,865
Total current assets	$288,092	$270,069

Consolidated Statements of Income (in part)

	Year Ended		
(in thousands, except per share data)	August 27, 2005	August 28, 2004	August 30, 2003
Net revenues	$991,975	$1,114,154	$845,210
Cost of goods sold	854,997	951,985	731,832
Gross profit	$136,978	$162,169	$113,378
Operating expenses:			
Selling	19,936	20,764	19,753
General and administrative	18,787	30,607	16,331
Total operating expenses	38,723	51,371	36,084
Operating income	$ 98,255	$ 110,798	$ 77,294

Notes to Consolidated Financial Statements (in part)
Note 1 (in part)
Inventories. Inventories are valued at the lower of cost or market, with cost being determined by using the last-in, first-out (LIFO) method and market defined as net realizable value.

Note 4: Inventories. Inventories consist of the following:

(dollars in thousands)	August 27, 2005	August 28, 2004
Finished goods	$ 67,998	$ 58,913
Work-in-process	45,657	47,337
Raw materials	38,461	51,675
	$152,116	$157,925
LIFO reserve	(31,461)	(27,192)
	$120,655	$130,733

The above value of inventories, before reduction for the LIFO reserve, approximates replacement cost at the respective dates.

amounts, as well as the cost of goods sold amount, to non-LIFO amounts. We illustrate this conversion in Exhibit 19-7 using Winnebago's disclosures given in Exhibit 19-6. First, we take the LIFO information from Winnebago's balance sheet, income statement, and notes, and compute the cost of inventory acquired during the year ($844,919) following

| EXHIBIT 19-7 | COMPUTATION OF NON-LIFO AMOUNTS FOR WINNEBAGO | | | |

(in thousands)

	Beginning Inventory	+	Cost of Inventory Acquired	−	Ending Inventory	=	Cost of Goods Sold
LIFO	$ 130,733 (1)	+	$844,919 (3)	−	$ 120,655 (1)	=	$854,997 (2)
LIFO reserve	27,192 (4)			−	31,461 (4)	=	(4,269) (3)
Non-LIFO	$157,925 (4)	+	$844,919 (5)	−	$152,116 (4)	=	$850,728 (3)

(1) Balance sheet information
(2) Income statement information
(3) Calculated amount
(4) Note 4 disclosures from Winnebago; may be presented in the balance sheet instead
(5) Amount is the same under either method

the procedures we discussed earlier. This cost is the same under any inventory cost flow assumption. Then we add the $27,192 and $31,461 LIFO reserve amounts to the LIFO beginning inventory and ending inventory, respectively, and subtract the $4,269 difference in the reserve from the LIFO cost of goods sold. This results in the $157,925 non-LIFO beginning inventory, the $152,116 non-LIFO ending inventory, and the $850,728 non-LIFO cost of goods sold. We now have the non-LIFO amounts of ending inventory and cost of goods sold, which are necessary for us to compare two companies using different inventory cost flow assumptions. Note that we can convert only a LIFO company to non-LIFO and not the other way around, because non-LIFO companies are not required to make disclosures of LIFO amounts.

You must be careful when you use this approach. If the LIFO reserve *increases* during the year, then the non-LIFO cost of goods sold is *lower* than the LIFO amount. Alternatively, if the LIFO reserve *decreases* during the year, then the non-LIFO cost of goods sold is *higher* than the LIFO amount. For Winnebago, the LIFO reserve increased during 2005 and therefore its non-LIFO cost of goods sold is *lower* than the LIFO amount.

In Exhibit 19-7, did the difference between the cost of goods sold amounts move in the direction (increase or decrease) that you would expect? Why or why not?

So you see that for any ratio that uses inventory or cost of goods sold to measure liquidity, profitability, or operating efficiency, you need to understand which cost flow assumption the company is using. You also need to consider whether to use the financial statement amounts or to modify them by using the additional information disclosed.

Business Issues and Values

Earlier we said that there should not be many situations in which two companies in the same industry use different cost flow assumptions, because managers should choose a cost flow assumption based on the expected cost changes in that industry. However, look at the following recent disclosures for **Coca-Cola** and **PepsiCo**:

Coca-Cola
"Inventories consist primarily of raw materials, supplies, concentrates and syrups, and are valued at the lower of cost or market. We determine cost on the basis of average cost or first-in, first-out methods."

PepsiCo

"Inventories are valued at the lower of cost or market. Cost is determined using the average, first-in, first-out (FIFO) or last-in, first-out (LIFO) methods."

 Do you consider these two companies to be in the same industry? Have the two companies made different choices for their primary cost flow assumptions? Why do you think the managers made the choices that they did?

U.S. companies usually don't use LIFO for their international operations (and non-U.S. companies usually don't use LIFO) because they cannot use it for income tax reporting in those other countries. Therefore, when a U.S. company with international operations, such as **General Motors**, experiences rising costs, it will overstate income because it includes holding gains in income. Similarly, a non-U.S. company with rising inventory costs will overstate its income if it doesn't use LIFO.

While companies must disclose the inventory method(s) they use, most do not provide the reasons for their choice(s). **General Mills** provides an interesting exception. It used to state (in part), "We generally use LIFO as the preferred method of valuing inventory because we believe that it is a better match with current revenues. However, FIFO is used for most foreign operations, where LIFO is not recognized for income tax purposes and the operations often lack the staff to accurately handle LIFO complexities." Unfortunately, it now provides a less useful disclosure.

When a company using LIFO reduces the physical quantity of inventory from the beginning of the year to the end of the year, it has a **LIFO liquidation**. Then the company includes lower costs from previous periods in its cost of goods sold and reports a **LIFO liquidation profit**—the extra profit that results from reporting a lower cost of goods sold than it would have if it had not had a LIFO liquidation. Companies are required to disclose this LIFO liquidation profit. For example, **General Electric** reported LIFO liquidation profits of $8 million, $6 million, and $4 million in three consecutive years. Whereas a reduction in inventory quantities may be caused by managers making sound decisions, such as developing more-efficient inventory management, it also can be caused by managers deliberately reducing inventory quantities (a company reducing its beginning inventory by selling more inventory than it purchased) to "increase" profit.

 Explain whether you think it is desirable for a company's income to be influenced by managers' choices, rather than just from economic transactions and events.

USING THE LOWER-OF-COST-OR-MARKET METHOD

4 How does a company apply the lower-of-cost-or-market method to report the inventory on its balance sheet?

The GAAP requirement that companies report their inventories at historical cost (under any one of the four alternative cost flow assumptions) is modified in one situation. When the market value of a company's inventory falls below its cost, the company is required to reduce, or "write down," the inventory to that market value. This is called the **lower-of-cost-or-market (LCM) method.** The company reports the inventory at the lower market value on its balance sheet and includes the corresponding "loss" on its income statement (typically by increasing cost of goods sold).

The use of the term *market value* here may lead to confusion. You should understand that *market value* refers to the cost to the company of replacing the item of inventory and *not* to the selling price the company charges its customers. As we discussed earlier, the replacement cost is the cost (including any transportation costs ordinarily incurred) that a company would have to pay at the balance sheet date to purchase (replace) an item of inventory (based on purchasing inventory in normal quantities from the usual suppliers). A decline in the replacement cost of the inventory is the result of declining costs for the supplier of the inventory.

For example, suppose that Cane Candy Company has 100 boxes of candy for which it paid $50 per box. If the replacement cost declines to $40 per box, the company includes the inventory on its balance sheet at $40 per box because the $50 cost is an overstatement of the resource—inventory—that the company will use to generate future revenues. The company has lost $10 per unit (which it reports on its income statement) by owning the inventory while its cost declined. If the company had delayed the purchase, it could have acquired the inventory for only $40 per unit.

The lower-of-cost-or-market method is an example of applying the conservatism principle. The **conservatism principle** holds that a company should apply GAAP in such a way that there is little chance that it will overstate assets or income. Therefore, companies record a loss (or an increase in an expense) when there is evidence of a loss, whereas they must wait to record a gain (or an increase in a revenue) until an actual transaction occurs. This principle does *not* mean that a company should understate its assets or income; rather, it states that when there is a doubt about the likely effect of an accounting method, the company should report the more conservative amount. The rationale for the conservatism principle is that the users of financial statements are least likely to be misled if a company uses the least favorable valuation; conservatism also tends to offset the optimistic view of the company's managers. Many users disagree with the conservatism principle, however, because they believe that accounting should strive to obtain the best valuation, with a bias neither toward nor against conservatism. Furthermore, since the long-term income of the company is the same whether conservatism is applied or not, reducing its income or asset values in the current period will result in higher income in the future than the company would otherwise report. Therefore, conservatism may be unfair to present stockholders and biased in favor of prospective stockholders because of the lower valuation. Nevertheless, the conservatism principle has affected several accounting practices, including the lower-of-cost-or-market method.

How do you think conservatism could be unfair to present shareholders?

Another argument in favor of the lower-of-cost-or-market method is based on the assumption that the relationship between cost and selling price remains fairly constant. That is, it is common for companies to set their selling prices at a certain percentage (called the *markup*) above the cost of the inventory. For example, if a company normally sells for $100 units that cost $50, the markup is 100% of cost. If the replacement cost of the inventory drops to $40, the company would write down its inventory to this $40 cost and record a $10 loss. We might expect the company to reduce the selling price to $80, thus maintaining its 100% markup on this cost. Use of the lower-of-cost-or-market method thus separates the loss on holding the inventory ($10) from the gross profit that results from selling the inventory ($80 − $40). Also note that the company records the loss associated with the decline in value in the period of the decline, not in the period in which the inventory is ultimately sold.

Whose side do you take on this discussion—the supporters or the critics of the conservatism principle? Explain your position.

A company often applies the lower-of-cost-or-market method to its entire inventory. First, the company computes the total cost of all the units in its ending inventory. Second, it computes the total replacement cost (market) of these units. Finally, the company reports the lower of the two totals as inventory on its balance sheet. If the company reports the lower replacement cost as its inventory, it also reports the difference between the total cost and this lower total replacement cost as an increase in the cost of goods sold on its income statement.

To understand the importance of the lower-of-cost-or-market method, consider that **Cisco Systems** recently wrote down its third quarter inventory by $2.36 billion—almost twice as much as the inventory of $1.2 billion that Cisco reported in the third quarter of the previous year!

Would you expect the replacement cost of the inventory to be less than the actual cost of the inventory for a company that uses FIFO? one that uses average cost? one that uses LIFO? Explain why.

ESTIMATING THE COST OF INVENTORY AND THE COST OF GOODS SOLD

6 What methods may a company use to estimate its cost of goods sold and inventory?

Sometimes a company needs to estimate the cost of its inventory. If a company has a loss of inventory in a fire or theft, or if the inventory accounting records are destroyed, it may need to estimate its loss. Also, if a company is using the periodic inventory system (which we discuss in the chapter appendix), managers may estimate the cost of the inventory during the year so that they can prepare the internal (e.g., monthly) financial statements without incurring the cost of taking a physical inventory. Companies often use one of two methods to estimate the cost of inventory. Companies use the gross profit method in the special situations just described, whereas retailing companies such as supermarkets and department stores routinely use the retail inventory method for preparing financial statements.

Gross Profit Method

A company uses the **gross profit method** to estimate the cost of its inventory by first determining the historic gross profit percentage (gross profit ÷ net sales) based on the income statements of previous periods. It then multiplies its net sales of the current period by the historic gross profit rate to determine its estimated current gross profit. Next, it subtracts the estimated current gross profit from the net sales to determine the estimated cost of goods sold. Finally, it subtracts the estimated cost of goods sold from the cost of goods available for sale to determine its estimate of the ending inventory.

For example, suppose that the beginning inventory of Watson Company for the current period is $12,000, net purchases are $48,000, and net sales are $70,000. If the historic gross profit rate based on the company's income statements of previous periods is 40%, we can estimate the ending inventory of the current period in four steps as follows:

Step 1: Estimate the current gross profit

$$\text{Gross Profit} = \text{Net Sales} \times \text{Historic Gross Profit Percentage}$$
$$= \$70,000 \times 40\%$$
$$= \$28,000$$

© J. L. BULCOA/GETTY IMAGES

What kind of evidence do you think an insurance company would want to see supporting this company's inventory fire loss claim?

DILBERT® REPRINTED BY PERMISSION OF UNITED FEATURES SYNDICATE, INC.

Step 2: Estimate the cost of goods sold

$$\begin{aligned}
\text{Cost of Goods Sold} &= \text{Net Sales} - \text{Gross Profit} \\
&= \$70,000 - \$28,000 \\
&= \$42,000
\end{aligned}$$

Step 3: Determine the actual cost of goods available for sale

$$\begin{aligned}
\text{Cost of Goods Available for Sale} &= \text{Beginning Inventory} + \text{Net Purchases} \\
&= \$12,000 + \$48,000 \\
&= \$60,000
\end{aligned}$$

Step 4: Estimate the ending inventory

$$\begin{aligned}
\text{Ending Inventory} &= \text{Cost of Goods Available for Sale} - \text{Cost of Goods Sold} \\
&= \$60,000 - \$42,000 \\
&= \underline{\underline{\$18,000}}
\end{aligned}$$

We illustrate these relationships in income statement format as follows (Steps 1–4 are listed in parentheses):

Net sales		$70,000	(100%)
Cost of goods sold:			
Beginning inventory	$12,000		
Net purchases	48,000		
Cost of goods available for sale (actual) (3)	$60,000		
Less: Ending inventory (estimated) (4)	(18,000)		
Cost of goods sold (estimated)	(2)	(42,000)	(60%)
Gross Profit (estimated)	(1)	$28,000	(40%)

The accuracy of the gross profit method depends on the reasonableness of the historic gross profit percentage. Since the percentage is based on the gross profit and net sales relationships of past periods, it is an accurate estimate of the gross profit rate of the current period only if the gross profit relationships have not changed. If a company knows that conditions have changed, it should adjust the gross profit percentage so that the estimated cost of the ending inventory will be more accurate.

If a company uses the gross profit method to estimate a casualty loss (e.g., loss from fire), it calculates the amount of the loss by subtracting the cost of any salvaged inventory from the cost of the inventory it estimates that it had on hand before the casualty.

Retail Inventory Method

Retail companies generally find it easier and less expensive to base their inventory accounting system on the retail value of their inventory. They mark their merchandise and put it on display at the retail price. During the physical inventory, it is easier to count the inventory at retail prices than to identify the cost of each item. The *cost* of the inventory must be included in the financial statements, however.

A company uses the **retail inventory method** to estimate the cost of its inventory by multiplying the retail value of the ending inventory by the cost-to-retail ratio of the current period (this method approximates the average cost flow assumption). To apply this method, the company completes the following steps:

1. Compute the total goods available for sale (beginning inventory plus net purchases) at *both* cost and retail value (selling price). The company must keep detailed records of the beginning inventory and the net purchases at both cost and retail prices to compute these amounts.

2. Compute a cost-to-retail ratio by dividing the cost of the goods available for sale by the retail value of the goods available for sale.

3. Compute the ending inventory at retail by subtracting the net sales for the period from the retail value of the goods available for sale.

4. Compute the ending inventory at cost by multiplying the ending inventory at retail by the cost-to-retail ratio.

We illustrate these steps for the retail inventory method in the following example, using the same cost and sales information from the gross profit method and assuming the retail amounts (Steps 1 through 4 are listed in parentheses):

	Cost	Retail	
Beginning inventory	$12,000	$ 20,000	
Purchases (net)	48,000	80,000	
Goods available for sale	$60,000	$100,000	(1)
Cost-to-retail ratio $\dfrac{\$ 60,000}{\$100,000} = 0.60$			(2)
Less: Sales (net)		(70,000)	
Ending inventory at retail		$ 30,000	(3)
Ending inventory at cost (0.60 × $30,000)	$18,000		(4)

Watson Company had goods with a retail value of $100,000 available for sale during the period and made net sales of $70,000. Therefore the retail value of the ending inventory is $30,000. Since the company's costs are 60% of the retail value, the cost of the ending inventory is $18,000. Watson Company reports this cost on its ending balance sheet.

Note that the retail inventory method is an estimating procedure and is useful for quarterly financial statements. It does not eliminate the need for taking a periodic physical inventory, however, especially at the end of the fiscal year. For example, if Watson Company takes a physical inventory and finds that the retail value of the inventory is $29,000, the cost of the inventory it reports on the balance sheet is $17,400 (0.60 × $29,000) because this amount is more accurate than the $18,000 we computed earlier. The company adds the difference of $600 to its cost of goods sold on its income statement for the period.

 Why would a company's accounting system report a quantity of inventory that differs from the physical count?

Summary of Estimating Methods

The gross profit method and the retail inventory method are similar because they both estimate the cost of inventory by using a profit percentage. However, the retail inventory method is more sensitive to price changes because it uses a current period estimate of the profit percentage, whereas the gross profit method uses an estimate based on past periods. We can summarize the two methods as follows:

Gross Profit Method	Retail Inventory Method
Cost of goods available for sale Less: Cost of goods sold [sales × (1 − gross profit rate)]	Retail value of goods available for sale Less: Sales (net)
	Ending inventory at retail × Cost-to-retail ratio
Ending inventory at cost	Ending inventory at cost

SUMMARY

At the beginning of the chapter we asked you several questions. During the chapter, we asked you to STOP and answer some additional questions to build your knowledge about specific issues. Be sure you answered these additional questions. Below are the questions from the beginning of the chapter, with a brief summary of the key points relating to the answers. Use your creative and critical thinking skills to expand on these key points to develop more complete answers to the questions and to determine what other questions you have that might lead you to learn more about the issues.

1 **How does a company determine the costs and amounts of inventory that it includes in the inventory amount reported on its balance sheet?**

The cost of each unit of inventory includes all the costs incurred to bring the item to its existing condition and location. Thus the cost of inventory includes the purchase price (less any purchases discounts), sales tax, applicable transportation costs, insurance, customs duties, and similar costs. When a cost, such as the cost of ordering the inventory, is difficult to associate with a particular inventory item, many companies record it as a general and administrative expense. When a company takes a physical inventory, it counts the units of inventory in its stores and warehouses (and factories). The company also counts any additional units of inventory that it owns that are in transit. A company may buy or sell inventory under terms of FOB (free on board) shipping point or FOB destination. FOB shipping point means that the selling company transfers ownership to the buyer at the place of sale (shipping point)—that is, before the inventory is in transit. The selling company excludes these items in transit from its inventory while the buying company includes them in its inventory. The buying company is responsible for any transportation costs incurred to deliver the items and includes these costs as a cost of its inventory (rather than immediately recording them as an expense). FOB destination means that the selling company transfers ownership to the buyer at the place of delivery—that is, after transit is completed. The selling company includes these items in transit in its inventory until delivery takes place, and the buyer excludes them. In this case, the selling company is responsible for any transportation costs incurred to deliver the items and includes these costs in its selling expenses.

2 **What alternative cost flow assumptions may a company use for determining its cost of goods sold and ending inventory?**

A company may use the FIFO, the average, or the LIFO cost flow assumption, as well as the specific identification method. When a company uses the first-in, first-out (FIFO) cost flow assumption, it includes the earliest (first) costs it incurred in the cost of goods sold and the latest costs in the ending inventory. That is, the first costs it incurred are the first costs it includes as costs of the units sold. When a company uses the average cost flow assumption, it allocates an average cost per unit to both the ending inventory and the cost of goods sold. When a company uses the last-in, first-out (LIFO) cost flow assumption, it includes the latest (last) costs incurred in its cost of goods sold and the earliest costs (part or all of which are costs it incurred in previous periods) in the ending inventory.

 3 **How do alternative cost flow assumptions affect a company's financial statements?**

The choice made by managers to adopt the FIFO or the LIFO cost flow assumption has an effect on both the income statement and the balance sheet. If costs are rising, gross profit (sales − cost of goods sold), income, and ending inventory are higher under FIFO and lower under LIFO. Ending inventory is higher under FIFO and lower under LIFO because under LIFO the oldest costs remain in this inventory. The average cost amounts are between those of FIFO and LIFO. If costs are falling, the relationships are reversed. Many users of financial statements argue that LIFO results in a better measure of income when costs are rising and that holding gains should be excluded from income. If the company is a corporation in the United States, LIFO is allowed for income tax purposes only if it is also used for the financial statements. If costs are rising, the use of LIFO results in lower taxable income and, consequently, in the payment of less income taxes; therefore the company has more cash available than it otherwise would for such things as paying employees, investing in property and equipment, reducing liabilities, or paying dividends. If the managers of a company expect that the costs of acquiring inventory will increase in the future, then they should select LIFO because of the lower income taxes that the company will have to pay. Alternatively, if the managers expect that the costs of acquiring inventory will decrease in the future, then they should select FIFO or average cost because the company would pay lower income taxes.

 4 **How do a company's inventory and cost of goods sold disclosures help a user evaluate the company?**

As with other parts of financial statements, a user evaluates inventory and cost of goods sold by performing intracompany and intercompany analysis, through the use of horizontal analysis, vertical analysis, and ratio analysis. For any ratio that uses inventory or cost of goods sold to measure liquidity, profitability, or operating efficiency, a user needs to understand which cost flow assumption the company is using. For a company using LIFO, the lower ending inventory cost (assuming rising costs) affects the computation and evaluation of current assets, working capital, and any financial ratios that include inventory, thereby reducing comparability between it and other companies. The use of alternative cost flow assumptions raises special issues related to evaluating liquidity, profitability, and operating capability (efficiency). Three alternatives may exist when comparing companies that have significant amounts of inventory: (1) both companies use the FIFO or the average cost flow assumption, (2) both companies use the LIFO cost flow assumption, and (3) one company uses the FIFO or the average cost flow assumption while the other uses the LIFO cost flow assumption. The user needs to consider whether to use the financial statement amounts or to modify them by using the additional information disclosed.

 5 **How does a company apply the lower-of-cost-or-market method to report the inventory on its balance sheet?**

When the market value of a company's inventory falls below its cost, the company reduces, or "writes down," the inventory to that market value. The company reports the inventory at the lower market value on its balance sheet and includes the corresponding loss on its income statement (typically by increasing cost of goods sold). The market value is the cost of replacing the inventory item.

 6 **What methods may a company use to estimate its cost of goods sold and inventory?**

A company uses the gross profit method if it has a loss of inventory in a fire or theft, or if the accounting records are destroyed, and it needs to estimate its loss. Also, if a company is using the periodic inventory system, managers may use the gross profit method to estimate the cost of the inventory during the year so that they can prepare the internal (e.g., monthly) financial statements without incurring the cost of taking a physical inventory. A company uses the gross profit method to estimate the cost of its inventory by first determining the historic gross profit percentage (gross profit ÷ net sales) based on the income statements of previous periods. It then multiplies its net sales of the current period by the historic gross profit percentage to determine its estimated current gross profit. Next, it subtracts the estimated current gross profit from the net sales to determine the estimated cost of goods sold. Finally, it subtracts the estimated cost of goods sold from the cost of goods available for sale to determine its estimate of the ending inventory.

Retailing companies such as supermarkets and department stores routinely use the retail inventory method for preparing financial statements. They complete the following steps: (1) compute the total goods available for sale (beginning inventory plus net purchases) at *both* cost and retail value (selling price), (2) compute a cost-to-retail ratio by dividing the cost of the goods available for sale by the retail value of the goods available for sale, (3) compute the ending inventory at retail by subtracting the net sales for the period from the retail value of the goods available for sale, and (4) compute the ending inventory at cost by multiplying the ending inventory at retail by the cost-to-retail ratio.

KEY TERMS

conservatism principle *(p. 667)*
cost of goods sold or **cost of sales** *(p. 650)*
first-in, first-out (FIFO) *(p. 653)*
FOB destination *(p. 651)*
FOB shipping point *(p. 651)*
gross profit method *(p. 668)*
holding gain or **inventory profit** *(p. 658)*
in transit *(p. 651)*
inventory *(p. 648)*
last-in, first-out (LIFO) *(p. 654)*
LIFO liquidation *(p. 666)*

LIFO liquidation profit *(p. 666)*
LIFO reserve *(p. 663)*
lower-of-cost-or-market (LCM) method *(p. 666)*
moving average *(p. 653)*
non-LIFO *(p. 663)*
periodic inventory system *(p. 648)*
perpetual inventory system *(p. 648)*
replacement cost *(p. 657)*
retail inventory method *(p. 670)*
specific identification method *(p. 649)*

APPENDIX

The Periodic Inventory System

In the illustrations of inventory cost flow assumptions in the chapter, we assumed the use of the *perpetual* inventory system. In that system, a company computes the cost of goods sold and the inventory balance as each sale is made. When a company uses the *periodic* inventory system, it does not keep track of the cost of each unit it sells. At the end of the period, it first counts the number of units in its ending inventory (by taking a physical inventory) and then determines the number of units sold by subtracting the number of units in the ending inventory from the number of units available for sale. It next computes the *cost* of the ending inventory using either FIFO, average cost, or LIFO. We discuss each of these cost flow assumptions in the following sections. It then computes the cost of goods sold at the end of the period by subtracting the cost of the ending inventory from the total cost of goods available for sale for the period.

First-In, First-Out (Periodic)

When a company uses the FIFO cost flow assumption, it includes the earliest (first) costs it incurred in cost of goods sold. The most recent (last) costs it incurred remain in ending inventory. On January 31, Granola Goodies Company has an ending inventory of 1,100 units. As we show in Exhibit 19-8, the company computes the cost of the 1,100 units in the ending inventory to be $6,500, consisting of the most recent costs incurred, which are the cost of the 900 units from the January 24 purchase ($5,400) and the cost of 200 units from the January 12 purchase ($1,100). It computes the $6,650 cost of goods sold by subtracting the $6,500 ending inventory from the $13,150 ($5,000 + $8,150) cost of goods available for sale. The cost of goods sold (for the 1,300 units sold) includes the earliest costs—the cost of the 1,000 units in beginning inventory ($5,000) plus the cost of 300 units from the January 12 purchase ($1,650). Note that, when the company uses FIFO, the cost of goods sold and the cost of the ending inventory are the same amounts

EXHIBIT 19-8	GRANOLA GOODIES COMPANY: FIRST-IN, FIRST-OUT COST FLOW ASSUMPTION (PERIODIC INVENTORY SYSTEM)

Inventory Information

Beginning inventory, January 1	1,000 units @ $5.00 per unit	$ 5,000
January 12 purchase	500 units @ $5.50 per unit	2,750
January 24 purchase	900 units @ $6.00 per unit	5,400
Cost of goods available for sale in January	2,400 units	$13,150
Ending inventory, January 31*	(1,300) units	
Sales during January	1,100 units	

Calculations

Ending Inventory (1,100 units):

900 units @ $6.00 per unit (from January 24 purchase)..	$5,400
200 units @ $5.50 per unit (from January 12 purchase)..	1,100
1,100	$6,500

Cost of Goods Sold (1,300 units):

Cost of Goods Sold = Beginning Inventory + Purchases − Ending Inventory
  $6,650   = $5,000   + $8,150   − $6,500

or

Cost of Goods Sold = 1,000 units @ $5.00 per unit (from beginning inventory).............	$5,000
+300 units @ $5.50 per unit (from January 12 purchase)...........	1,650
	$6,650

*Based on physical inventory

under both the perpetual and periodic inventory systems, as we show in Exhibits 19-2 and 19-8. This will always be true when a company uses FIFO because it always includes in the ending inventory the latest costs that it incurred to acquire inventory.

Average Cost (Periodic)

When a company uses the **average cost** flow assumption, it allocates the average cost per unit for the period to both the ending inventory and the cost of goods sold. That is, it combines the costs of all the units available for sale, computes the average cost, and assigns the resulting average cost to the units in both the ending inventory and the cost of goods sold. As we show in Exhibit 19-9, Granola Goodies Company computes its average cost per unit of $5.48 (rounded) by dividing the total cost of goods available for sale ($13,150) by the number of units available for sale during the period (2,400, which includes the 1,000 units in the beginning inventory plus the 1,400 units purchased).

The company computes the cost of the ending inventory balance to be $6,028 for the 1,100 units remaining on hand at the average cost of $5.48 per unit and computes the cost of goods sold to be $7,122, which includes the 1,300 units sold at the average cost of $5.48 per unit (adjusted for a $2 rounding error).

Last-In, First-Out (Periodic)

When a company uses the LIFO cost flow assumption, it includes the most recent (last) costs it incurred in cost of goods sold. The earliest (first) costs it incurred remain in ending inventory. Granola Goodies Company has an ending inventory of 1,100 units. As we show in Exhibit 19-10,

EXHIBIT 19-9	GRANOLA GOODIES COMPANY: AVERAGE COST FLOW ASSUMPTION (PERIODIC INVENTORY SYSTEM)

Average Cost per Unit = Cost of Goods Available for Sale ÷ Number of Units Available for Sale
                      = $13,150 ÷ 2,400
                      = $5.48 per Unit (rounded)

Ending Inventory (1,100 units):

Ending Inventory   = Number of Units × Average Cost per Unit
                     = 1,100 × $5.48
                     = $6,028

Cost of Goods Sold (1,300 units):

Cost of Goods Sold	=	Beginning Inventory	+	Purchases	−	Ending Inventory
$7,122	=	$5,000	+	$8,150	−	$6,028

or

Cost of Goods Sold   = Number of Units Sold × Average Cost per Unit
                     = 1,300 × $5.48 = $7,122 (adjusted for $2 rounding error)

under LIFO, the company computes the cost of the 1,100 units in ending inventory to be $5,550, consisting of the earliest costs incurred, which are the cost of the entire beginning inventory ($5,000) and the cost of 100 units from the January 12 purchase ($550). It computes the $7,600 cost of goods sold by subtracting the $5,550 ending inventory from the $13,150 cost of goods available for sale. The $7,600 cost of goods sold (for the 1,300 units sold) includes the latest costs—the cost of the units from the January 24 purchase ($5,400) and the cost of 400 units from the January 12 purchase ($2,200).

Note that the cost of goods sold and the ending inventory under the LIFO perpetual method ($6,950 and $6,200, as we show in Exhibit 19-3) differ from those under the LIFO periodic method ($7,600 and $5,550, as we show in Exhibit 19-10). The differences result from the assumptions each makes about the timing of the sales. Under the perpetual system, the company computes the cost of goods sold when each sale is made and therefore includes the cost(s) of the *most recent purchase(s) at that time*. Under the periodic system, the company treats the whole accounting

EXHIBIT 19-10	GRANOLA GOODIES COMPANY: LAST-IN, FIRST-OUT COST FLOW ASSUMPTION (PERIODIC INVENTORY SYSTEM)

Ending Inventory (1,100 units):

1,000 units @ $5.00 per unit (from beginning inventory)..	$5,000
100 units @ $5.50 per unit (from January 12 purchase)...	550
1,100	$5,550

Cost of Goods Sold (1,300 units):

Cost of Goods Sold	=	Beginning Inventory	+	Purchases	−	Ending Inventory
$7,600	=	$5,000	+	$8,150	−	$5,550

or

Cost of Goods Sold = 900 units @ $6.00 per unit (from January 24 purchase)	$5,400
+ 400 units @ $5.50 per unit (from January 12 purchase)	2,200
	$7,600

period (a month in this example) as a single unit, and assumes that all the sales are made after all the purchases. Under this assumption, it computes the cost of goods sold after recording the cost of all the units purchased during the period. Therefore, the cost of goods sold always includes the costs of the *latest purchases of the period*. For example, Granola Goodies' first sale occurs on January 7, and under the *perpetual* system the company assumes that the cost of goods sold for those units is taken from the beginning inventory of $5.00 per unit since that is the only inventory on hand at the time of the sale. Under the *periodic* system, however, since the number of units purchased exceeds the number of units sold for the month, the company includes none of the cost of the beginning inventory in the cost of goods sold. Instead, it takes the cost of the 1,300 units sold from the cost of the most recent purchases (January 24 and January 12) of the period.

SUMMARY SURFING

Here is an opportunity to gather information on the Internet about real-world issues related to the topics in this chapter (for suggestions on how to navigate various companies' Web sites to find their financial statements and other information, see the related discussion in the Preface at the beginning of the book). Answer the following questions.

- Go to the **Procter & Gamble Company** Web site. Find the company's most recent financial statements and related notes. How much does Procter & Gamble report as inventories for the current year? What accounting method or methods does the company use for its inventories? Now go to the **Colgate-Palmolive** Web site. Find the company's most recent financial statements and related notes. How much does Colgate-Palmolive report as inventories for the current year? What accounting method or methods does the company use for its inventories? Evaluate the comparability of the information disclosed by the two companies.

- Go to the **JCPenney Company** Web site. Find the company's most recent financial statements and related notes. By how much would JCPenney's inventory be different in the most recent year if it used non-LIFO? By how much would JCPenney's cost of goods sold be different in the most recent year if it used non-LIFO?

INTEGRATED BUSINESS AND ACCOUNTING SITUATIONS

Answer the Following Questions in Your Own Words.

Testing Your Knowledge

19-1   What three types of assets may a company include in its inventory?

19-2   What is the difference between merchandise inventory and finished goods inventory?

19-3   Company X purchases inventory under terms FOB destination from Company Y, and the goods are still in transit. Which company includes the goods in its inventory? Why? How would your answers change if the purchase had been made under terms FOB shipping point?

19-4   Explain which costs are included in cost of goods sold and ending inventory under the (a) FIFO, (b) average cost, and (c) LIFO cost flow assumptions.

19-5   Explain the impact of FIFO and LIFO on a company's income statement and balance sheet if costs are rising.

19-6   Where does a company report its ending inventory and its inventory cost flow assumption in its financial statements?

19-7   Explain the difference between intracompany and intercompany analysis.

19-8   Explain what is meant by a *LIFO liquidation profit*.

19-9   Explain what is meant by the lower-of-cost-or-market (LCM) method.

19-10   Under the LCM method, what does "market value" mean?

19-11   How does a company use the gross profit method to estimate its ending inventory?

19-12   How does a company use the retail inventory method to estimate its ending inventory?

19-13   (Appendix). What is the difference between the perpetual and the periodic inventory methods?

Applying Your Knowledge

19-14   The Schulte Tape Company has a beginning inventory for May of $2,500 (250 tapes at $10 each) and makes the following purchases and sales of tapes during May:

May	5	Purchases	150 tapes @ $11 = $1,650
	12	Sales	160 tapes
	22	Purchases	150 tapes @ $12 = 1,800
	25	Sales	90 tapes

Required: Compute the cost of goods sold and the ending inventory for May if the company uses the following:
   (1) The perpetual inventory system and the FIFO cost flow assumption
   (2) The perpetual inventory system and the LIFO cost flow assumption

19-15   The Gomez Folding Chair Company has 400 chairs (at $15 each) in its beginning inventory for July. It makes the following purchases and sales of chairs during July:

Date	Purchases	Sales
July 6	200 chairs @ $16 each	
14		220 chairs @ $30 each
21	140 chairs @ $17 each	
29		100 chairs @ $31 each

Required: Compute the cost of goods sold and the ending inventory for July if the company uses the following:
   (1) The perpetual inventory system and the FIFO cost flow assumption
   (2) The perpetual inventory system and the LIFO cost flow assumption

19-16   The Russell Video Company had 200 videos in its April 1 inventory. It uses the perpetual inventory system and made the following purchases and sales of videos during April and May.

April	9	Purchases	20 videos for $15 each
	17	Sales	30 videos
	24	Purchases	50 videos for $16 each
	26	Sales	20 videos
May	8	Sales	30 videos
	15	Purchases	70 videos for $17 each
	22	Sales	50 videos

The FIFO and the LIFO costs of the videos in the April 1 inventory were $12 and $8, respectively.

Required: (1) Compute the cost of goods sold and the ending inventory for each month if the company uses the following:
   (a) The FIFO cost flow assumption
   (b) The LIFO cost flow assumption
   (2) Which cost flow assumption provides the more realistic balance sheet amount for ending inventory? Why? Which provides the more realistic measure of income? Why?

19-17 The Caldwell Company had 50 electric motors in its November 1 inventory. The company uses the perpetual inventory system and made the following purchases and sales of electric motors during November and December.

Nov. 12	Sales...	40 electric motors
20	Purchases	100 electric motors for $65 each
29	Sales...	80 electric motors
Dec. 4	Purchases	100 electric motors for $75 each
10	Purchases	50 electric motors for $80 each
16	Sales...	140 electric motors

The FIFO and the LIFO costs of the electric motors in the November 1 inventory were $64 and $50, respectively.

Required: (1) Compute the cost of goods sold and the ending inventory for each month if the company uses the following:
   (a) The FIFO cost flow assumption
   (b) The LIFO cost flow assumption
   (2) Which cost flow assumption provides the more realistic balance sheet amount for ending inventory? Why? Which provides the more realistic measure of income? Why?

19-18 The Brabham Kite Company had the following FIFO costs and replacement costs of kites for its ending inventory.

Item #	Number of Units	Unit Cost	Unit Replacement Cost
804	100	$10	$11
603	150	12	10
331	320	8	6
928	70	20	22

Required: (1) Compute the value of the ending inventory under the lower-of-cost-or-market method.
   (2) How are the company's financial statements affected by the application of the lower-of-cost-or-market method?
   (3) Show how the ending inventory would be reported on the company's balance sheet.

19-19 The Seaman Company's ending inventory of vacuum cleaner parts included the following items:

Item #	Number of Units	Unit Cost (FIFO)	Unit Replacement Cost
A12B	50	$100	$90
L15C	150	76	82
P27X	200	60	55
W08S	400	10	9

Required: (1) Compute the value of the ending inventory under the lower-of-cost-or-market method.
   (2) Show how the ending inventory would be reported on the company's balance sheet.
   (3) If, at the end of the next year, none of the items in inventory has a market value below cost, how will the income statement for that year be affected by the application of the lower-of-cost-or-market method in this year?

19-20 On March 31, Ireland Peat Company needs to estimate its ending inventory for preparation of its first quarter's financial statements. The following information is available:

Inventory, January 1................................	$40,000
Purchases (net)...	40,000
Sales (net)	85,000

A study of past income statements indicates that a gross profit percentage of 25% of net sales is appropriate.

Required: Compute the cost of goods sold and the ending inventory.

19-21   On September 1, a fire destroyed all but $5,000 of Redster Company's inventory. The following information is available from the company's accounting records:

Inventory, January 1 .... $ 24,000
Purchases (net), January 1 through August 31 67,000
Sales (net), January 1 through August 31 100,000

Based on recent history, Redster's gross profit has averaged 30% of net sales.

Required: Compute the estimated loss of inventory from the fire.

19-22   Lotus Tire Company estimates its ending inventory for its quarterly financial statements by using the gross profit method. The following information is available from its accounting records:

	First Quarter	Second Quarter
Inventory, Jan. 1	$30,000	
Purchases	38,000	$50,000
Purchases returns	3,000	5,000
Sales	70,000	80,000
Sales returns	3,000	2,000

The company uses a gross profit percentage of 30% of net sales.

Required: (1) Compute the cost of goods sold and the ending inventory for each quarter.
(2) How would your answer for the second quarter change if the company's gross profit percentage dropped to 28% for that quarter?

19-23   Scheckter Department Store uses the retail inventory method. At the end of the first quarter, the following information is available:

	Cost	Retail
Inventory, Jan. 1	$15,000	$18,000
Purchases	47,000	86,000
Purchases returns	3,000	4,000
Sales		90,000
Sales returns		5,000

Required: (1) Compute the cost of goods sold and the gross profit for the first quarter.
(2) If the company took a physical inventory at the end of the first quarter and the retail value was $14,000, what is the cost of the ending inventory?
(3) What may have caused the difference in the answers for (1) and (2)?

19-24   Burris Department Store uses the retail inventory method. At the end of the first quarter, the following information is available:

	Cost	Retail
Inventory, Jan. 1	$ 5,000	$ 9,000
Purchases	35,000	68,000
Purchases returns	2,000	3,000
Sales		70,000
Sales returns		2,000

Required: (1) Compute the cost of goods sold and the gross profit for the first quarter.
(2) If the company took a physical inventory at the end of the first quarter and the retail value was $5,000, what is the cost of the ending inventory?
(3) What may have caused the difference in the answers for (1) and (2)?

19-25   (Appendix). Use the information in 19-14.

Required: Compute the ending inventory and the cost of goods sold if the company uses the following:
(1) The periodic inventory system and the FIFO cost flow assumption.
(2) The periodic inventory system and the LIFO cost flow assumption.

19-26 (Appendix). Use the information in 19-15.

Required: Compute the ending inventory and the cost of goods sold if the company uses the following:
        (1) The periodic inventory system and the FIFO cost flow assumption.
        (2) The periodic inventory system and the LIFO cost flow assumption.

19-27 (Appendix). The Ginther Power Tool Company had 100 air compressors in its January 1 inventory. It uses the periodic inventory system and made the following purchases of air compressors during January and February.

January 10	50 air compressors for $100 each
20	40 air compressors for $102 each
February 5	20 air compressors for $104 each
18	70 air compressors for $108 each

Sales during January and February were 80 air compressors and 100 air compressors, respectively. The FIFO, the average, and the LIFO costs of the air compressors in the January 1 inventory were $97, $95, and $62, respectively.

Required: (1) Compute the ending inventory and the cost of goods sold for each month if the company uses the following:
        (a) The FIFO cost flow assumption
        (b) The average cost flow assumption
        (c) The LIFO cost flow assumption
     (2) Which cost flow assumption provides the most realistic balance sheet amount for ending inventory? Why? Which provides the most realistic measure of income? Why?

19-28 (Appendix). The Johnson Watch Company had 300 watches in its July 1 inventory. The company uses the periodic inventory system and made the following purchases of watches during July and August.

July 8	40 watches for $20 each
27	100 watches for $21 each
Aug. 18	50 watches for $22 each
24	60 watches for $23 each

Sales during July and August were 200 watches and 150 watches, respectively. The FIFO, the average, and the LIFO costs of the watches in the July 1 inventory were $19, $18, and $13, respectively.

Required: (1) Compute the ending inventory and the cost of goods sold for each month if the company uses the following:
        (a) The FIFO cost flow assumption
        (b) The average cost flow assumption
        (c) The LIFO cost flow assumption
     (2) Which cost flow assumption provides the most realistic balance sheet amount for ending inventory? Why? Which provides the most realistic measure of income? Why?

Making Evaluations

19-29 Birkin Company uses the FIFO inventory cost flow assumption. It includes the following amounts in the company's financial statements:

Inventory, January 1	$100,000
Purchases	300,000
Cost of goods sold	250,000
Inventory, December 31	150,000

The company sells only one product, and purchases and sales are made evenly throughout the year. The replacement cost of the inventory at January 1 and December 31 is $125,000 and $187,500, respectively. The cost of the company's purchases was 25% higher at the end of the year than at the beginning.

Required: The owner of Birkin Company asks you to analyze the preceding information and tell her the following:

(1) How much would the cost of goods sold be if it was computed on the basis of the average replacement cost for the period?

(2) What is the amount of the holding gain (inventory profit) included in the income computed on a FIFO basis?

(3) Did the number of units in inventory increase or decrease during the year?

19-30 **Coca-Cola** disclosed the following in its 2005 annual report:

Inventories: Inventories consist primarily of raw materials, supplies, concentrates and syrups, and are valued at the lower of cost or market. We determine cost on the basis of average cost or first-in, first-out methods.

PepsiCo disclosed the following in its 2005 annual report (in millions):

Inventories: Inventories are valued at the lower of cost or market. Cost is determined using the average, first-in, first-out (FIFO) or last-in, first-out (LIFO) methods.

Year-end	2005	2004
Raw materials	$ 738	$ 665
Work-in-process	112	156
Finished goods	843	720
	$1,693	$1,541

Approximately 17% in 2005 and 15% in 2004 of the inventory cost was computed using the LIFO method. The differences between the LIFO and FIFO methods of valuing these inventories were not material.

Required: (1) Why do you think that Coca-Cola and PepsiCo use different cost flow assumptions?

(2) Why do you think that PepsiCo uses all three cost flow assumptions?

(3) Is there anything you find surprising about PepsiCo's disclosures?

19-31 **Crown Holdings** disclosed the following in its 2005 annual report (amounts in millions):

Year ended December 31	2005	2004
Cost of products sold	$5,759	$5,463

Inventory Valuation: Inventories are stated at the lower of cost or market, with cost for U.S. inventories principally determined under the last-in, first-out (LIFO) method. Non-U.S. inventories are principally determined under the average cost method.

Inventories:

	2005	2004
Finished goods	$281	$ 307
Work in process	101	111
Raw materials and supplies	428	476
	$810	$894

Approximately 20% of worldwide productive inventories at December 31, 2005 and 2004 were stated on the LIFO method of inventory valuation. Had average cost (which approximates replacement cost) been applied to such inventories at December 31, 2005 and 2004, total inventories would have been $51 and $43 higher, respectively.

Required: (1) Why do you think that Crown Holdings uses different cost flow assumptions?

(2) Explain why a user might want to convert Crown Holdings' inventory and cost of goods sold to non-LIFO amounts.

(3) Compute the amounts of Crown Holdings' beginning and ending inventory for 2005, and its 2005 cost of goods sold under a non-LIFO method.

(4) Compute Crown Holdings' inventory turnover ratio for 2005 (a) using the LIFO amounts and (b) the non-LIFO amounts.

(5) What is the cumulative effect on Crown Holdings' cost of goods sold of using LIFO?

19-32 The **Sherwin-Williams Company** disclosed the following in its 2005 annual report (in thousands):

Year ended December 31	2005	2004
Cost of goods sold	$4,110,296	$3,412,378

December 31	2005	2004	2003
Inventories			
Finished goods	$686,913	$651,095	$552,657
Work in process and raw materials	121,631	121,757	85,580
	$808,544	$772,852	$638,237

Inventories: Inventories were stated at the lower of cost or market with cost determined principally on the last-in, first-out (LIFO) method. The following presents the effect on inventories, net income and net income per common share had the company used the first-in, first-out (FIFO) inventory valuation method adjusted for income taxes at the statutory rate and assuming no other adjustments. This information is presented to enable the reader to make comparisons with companies using the FIFO method of inventory valuation.

	2005	2004
Percentage of total inventories on LIFO	89%	81%
Excess of FIFO over LIFO	$187,425	$125,212
Decrease in net income due to LIFO	(40,855)	(18,580)
Decrease in net income per share due to LIFO	(.29)	(.13)

Required: (1) Why do you think Sherwin-Williams use the LIFO method?

(2) Explain why a user might want to convert Sherwin-Williams' inventory and cost of goods sold to non-LIFO amounts.

(3) Compute the amounts of Sherwin-Williams' beginning and ending inventory for 2005 and its 2005 cost of goods sold under a non-LIFO method. Why is your answer for the difference in the LIFO and non-LIFO cost of goods amounts different than the income effect disclosed by the company?

(4) Compute Sherwin-Williams' inventory turnover ratio for 2005 (a) using the LIFO amounts and (b) the non-LIFO amounts.

(5) What is the cumulative effect on Sherwin-Williams' cost of goods sold of using LIFO?

19-33 When Janet Guthrie arrived at her dress shop on the morning of June 15, 2008, she found that thieves had broken in overnight and stolen much of her merchandise. The agent of Alright Insurance Company agreed to visit in the afternoon and promised he would write a check for the amount of the loss if she could verify it. Janet took a physical inventory of the merchandise not stolen and determined that its cost was $2,000. Janet needs to make an estimate of the loss so that she can collect the insurance money and buy new merchandise. She asks for your help, and you agree to look at her accounting records. She tells you that the store has been in business since January 1, 2007, and that she does not use the retail method of accounting for inventory. You obtain the following information:

Inventory, January 1, 2007	$ 7,000
Purchases, 2007	49,000
Purchases, 2008	33,000
Sales (net), 2007	80,000
Sales (net), 2008	50,000
Purchases returns, 2007	4,000

Purchases returns, 2008	2,500
Inventory, January 1, 2008	16,000
Physical inventory after theft.............................	2,000

Required: How much would you recommend that Janet settle for with the insurance company? What is the major assumption underlying your answer?

19-34 Use the financial section of the 2005 annual report for **Colgate-Palmolive** in Appendix B to answer the following questions.

Required: (1) Why do you think that Colgate-Palmolive uses different cost flow assumptions?

(2) Explain why a user might want to convert Colgate-Palmolive's inventory and cost of goods sold to non-LIFO amounts.

(3) Compute the amounts of Colgate-Palmolive's beginning and ending inventory for 2005, and its 2005 cost of goods sold under a non-LIFO method.

(4) Compute Colgate-Palmolive's inventory turnover ratio for 2005 (a) using the LIFO amounts and (b) the non-LIFO amounts.

(5) What is the cumulative effect on Colgate-Palmolive's cost of goods sold of using LIFO?

(6) What is a LIFO liquidation and what was its effect on Colgate-Palmolive's income statement in 2005?

19-35 Yesterday, you received the following letter for your advice column in the local paper:

DR. DECISIVE

Dear Dr. Decisive:

I think I must be losing my mind! I have just been looking over some annual reports with my girlfriend. I was trying to impress her with my knowledge. But then I started to explain to her about inventory, cost of goods sold, and such measures of performance as gross profit and inventory turnover. I got lost trying to explain why some companies use one method, other similar companies use a different method, and others use *three* different methods. Is all this just to help keep accountants in jobs? My girlfriend made sense when she said, "When I go in a clothing store, I just pick the one that is on top of the pile, but when I buy food I always look for the package with the latest expiration date. Is there an accountant watching me through the security camera to check which I buy?"

Call me "Inventory-ily Impaired."

Required: Meet with your Dr. Decisive team and write a response to "Inventory-ily Impaired."

PART 7

MANAGING, REPORTING, AND EVALUATING NONCURRENT ASSETS IN A CORPORATE ENVIRONMENT

CHAPTER 20
CAPITAL EXPENDITURE DECISIONS

CHAPTER 21
REPORTING PROPERTY, PLANT, AND EQUIPMENT, AND INTANGIBLES

This section consists of two chapters that discuss issues involving a corporation's noncurrent assets. After reading these chapters, you will be able to:

- *Understand the time value of money and the present value of future cash flows*

- *Compute the net present value of a capital expenditure proposal*

- *Know how to make a capital investment decision*

- *Explain how a corporation values and reports property, plant, and equipment, and intangible assets on its financial statements*

- *Understand how different depreciation methods affect a corporation's financial statements*

- *Use a corporation's noncurrent asset information in intracompany and intercompany analyses*

CAPITAL EXPENDITURE DECISIONS

1   What is a capital expenditure, and what are the four steps in a capital expenditure decision?

2   What does a company include in the initial cost of a capital expenditure proposal?

3   What are the relevant costs of a capital expenditure proposal, and how do operating income, depreciation, and ending cash flows affect these costs?

4   How does a company determine the rate of return it requires on a capital expenditure proposal?

5   How does a company use the net present value method to evaluate a capital expenditure proposal?

6   What is the difference between the payback method and the average rate of return on investment method for evaluating a capital expenditure proposal?

7   How does a company decide which capital expenditure proposal to accept when it has several proposals that accomplish the same thing, or when it cannot obtain sufficient cash to make all of its desired investments?

Have you ever purchased, or considered purchasing, a car? If so, you probably considered how the car looked, how much power it had, how comfortable it was, how it performed on the road, and how it compared with other cars. More importantly, you most certainly weighed, not only the price of the car, but also how much the payments would be and when you would make them (including payments for upkeep and repairs). Furthermore, you probably considered how well the car would retain its value and what its potential value would be when you are ready to sell it. A company makes a similar decision when it invests in property and equipment and in certain long-term projects.

In this chapter we will discuss a company's long-term decision making involving capital expenditures. Like the decision to purchase a car, a capital expenditure decision involves considering related cash receipts and payments that occur at different times, perhaps over several years. Therefore, in this type of decision making, a manager must understand such issues as how to estimate cash receipts and payments, what cash receipts and payments are relevant to the decision to make a capital expenditure, and what steps must be completed in the process of making the decision. Many of these issues are the same as those we discussed in Chapter 15 on short-term decision making. As you will see, however, a key difference between the two types of decisions is that for long-term decision making, the manager needs to consider the time value of money and therefore must have an understanding of present value computations.

CAPITAL EXPENDITURE DECISIONS

A **capital expenditure** decision is a long-term decision in which a company determines whether or not to make an investment (cash payment) at the time of the decision in order to obtain future net cash receipts totaling more than the investment. The future net cash receipts related to the investment provide a "return" on the investment. This "return" is what makes a company want to make a capital expenditure (investment).

Most companies have a large number and a wide variety of investment (capital expenditure) opportunities each year. They can expand factory or office size, replace old equipment, purchase additional new equipment, introduce new products, increase inventories, start an employee training program, or engage in a special advertising campaign, to name a few. These opportunities or "projects" come to the attention of a company's managers in the form of *proposals* to invest cash. Because these proposals involve estimating future cash receipts and payments over several years, capital expenditure decisions are sometimes referred to as *capital budgeting* decisions.

What is a capital expenditure, and what are the four steps in a capital expenditure decision?

Other than the purchase of a car, can you think of any personal capital expenditure decisions you have made or will make? What cash receipts and payments are related to those decisions?

MAKING A CAPITAL EXPENDITURE DECISION

As a general rule, *a capital expenditure proposal is acceptable to a company when its return on investment is greater than the cost to the company of providing the cash to make the investment.* Therefore, to determine whether a capital expenditure proposal is acceptable, a company must complete four steps. First, the company must estimate the initial cash payment needed to make the investment. Second, the company must estimate the future cash receipts and payments (cash flows) expected from the investment, and the time period over which it expects these future cash receipts and payments to occur. Third, the company must determine its cost of providing the cash to make the investment. Finally, the company must determine whether the estimated future cash flows will provide it a return that is sufficient (after adjusting for the time value of money) to cover the cost of providing the cash to make the investment. If the cash flows of a proposal will produce a return on investment that is higher than the cost of providing the cash to make the investment, the difference contributes to the long-term "profitability" of the company. This makes the proposal acceptable for the company. If the return on investment will be less than the cost, the proposal is undesirable and should be rejected. We will discuss each of the preceding steps in the following sections.

Estimating the Initial Cash Payment

2 What does a company include in the initial cost of a capital expenditure proposal?

Whenever a company makes a capital expenditure decision, one of the first questions it asks is, "What is this going to cost?" The question may be broken down into two parts: (1) the initial cost and (2) the cost(s) incurred in later years. We will discuss any costs incurred in later years in the estimated future cash receipts and payments section of this chapter. The **initial cost** is the expected cash payment to be made to put the proposal into operation. In other words, it is the capital that the company must expend (the *capital expenditure*) to make the investment.

For instance, a company may be deciding whether or not it should invest in a new machine that it will use for six years. A vendor has quoted a price of $10,000 for the machine. The company expects to pay transportation costs of $800 to get the machine to its factory, and costs of $400 for installing the machine. The estimated initial cost of this capital expenditure proposal is $11,200, computed as follows:

Cost of machine	$10,000
Transportation costs	800
Installation costs	400
Estimated initial cost	$11,200

This $11,200 is the estimated cash payment that the company must make to put the machine into operation (the initial cash payment). In some cases, a capital expenditure proposal may require the investment of additional *working capital*. For instance, a new piece of equipment may require an investment in additional raw materials inventory. In this case, for capital expenditure decision making, the additional cost of the investment in raw materials inventory should be included in the estimated initial cost of the equipment. However, with just-in-time inventory systems, additional investments in inventory may not be necessary.

 Why do you think additional investments in inventory may not be necessary with a just-in-time inventory system?

You may think that determining the estimated initial costs of a proposed capital expenditure is easier than estimating expected future cash flows because initial costs are incurred at the present time and therefore are more "definite" and "accurate." In many situations this is true, but not always. In some cases initial costs involve the use of estimates that are not very precise and that include large numbers. For instance, take the example of a company that is considering a capital expenditure to build a new 100,000-square-foot factory. What is the initial cost of the factory? The estimated initial cost includes the cost of construction, the cost of all the equipment that goes into the factory, training costs for the employees, and many other costs. A contractor may give a "rough estimate" of the cost of construction but is not likely to spend much time on the estimate if the company is only considering building the factory. The U.S. government does print estimated "per-foot" costs of construction, but they are just that—estimates. And these estimates vary from city to city and by type of construction. So determining the initial cost of this type of capital expenditure can rely heavily on estimates. Nonetheless, a good estimate is better than a guess!

Estimating Future Cash Flows

The expected future net cash receipts help to provide the return on an investment. As we show in the following diagram, these net future cash receipts may come in three forms:

(1) future cash receipts only, (2) future cash receipts that are more than future cash payments, or (3) savings of future cash payments.

The return from some investments comes from future cash receipts only. An example of this is when a company buys stocks or bonds of another company to receive dividends or interest. The dividends or interest received plus the eventual selling price of the securities (all cash receipts) provide a return when they are more than the amount initially invested in the securities.

In other cases, both future cash receipts and payments affect the return from the investment. For example, suppose Unlimited Decadence invests in additional equipment to be able to produce and sell more cases of Darkly Decadent candy bars. If the cash receipts from increased sales are more than the cash payments for increased production and selling costs, the increase in the *net* cash receipts (the difference between the future cash receipts and cash payments) provides a return on the investment when it is more than the amount that Unlimited Decadence initially invested in the additional equipment.

Finally, some investments do not involve increasing future cash receipts, but instead involve *reducing future cash payments*. The effect on a company's cash, however, is the same. The benefit received by the decrease in future cash payments also can provide a return on the investment. For example, suppose that a local newspaper invests $3,000 today in an employee training program that is expected to save $1,000 in payments for labor costs each year for five years. This investment has the same expected return for the newspaper as would investing $3,000 to increase cash receipts from sales of advertising space in the paper by $1,000 each year for five years.

Estimating Relevant Cash Flows

Whether you are dealing with future cash receipts only, net future cash receipts, or savings in future cash payments, it is important to identify the expected relevant cash flows and to estimate the number of years over which these cash flows will occur. **Relevant cash flows** are future cash flows that differ, either in *amount* or in *timing*, as a result of accepting a capital expenditure proposal. That is, relevant cash flows are (1) the expected *additional* future cash flows (either future receipts or payments) over and above a company's existing cash flows, or (2) the expected *savings* in future cash payments. Relevant cash flows may be either *variable* or *fixed* cash flows. Again, the key is whether there is a change to the company's cash flows as a result of accepting the proposal. The reason that cash flows differing in amount or in timing are relevant is that they affect the company's long-term profitability.

Capital expenditure decisions involve whether or not to make a long-term investment: to buy a machine or not to buy it, to expand the size of the factory or not to expand it, to introduce a new product or not to introduce it, and so on. We refer to alternatives such as *not* buying the machine, *not* expanding the size of the factory, or *not* introducing the new product as the *"do-nothing"* alternative. Choosing the do-nothing alternative does not change a company's cash flows. On the other hand, choosing to accept a capital expenditure proposal—whether it is to buy a new machine, expand the size of the factory, or introduce a new product—*does* cause changes in the company's cash flows. In evaluating a capital expenditure proposal, *it is useful to think of the do-nothing alternative as having zero cash flows and the capital expenditure proposal as having cash flows equal*

3 What are the relevant costs of a capital expenditure proposal, and how do operating income, depreciation, and ending cash flows affect these costs?

*to the **changes** it causes.* This approach helps you focus on the relevant cash flows from the proposal.

Deciding what cash flows are relevant for a capital expenditure decision is similar to deciding what costs are relevant for a short-term decision. Cash receipts and payments that occurred *prior* to the capital expenditure decision are irrelevant because they cannot be affected by the decision. They are *sunk costs*. Cash flows that result from activities *not* required for any of the decision alternatives also cannot be relevant (even if they are future cash flows) because selecting any of the alternatives will not affect them. To be relevant to a particular capital expenditure decision, cash flows must

1. occur in the future,

2. result from activities that are required by the proposal, and

3. cause a change in the company's existing cash flows.

Operating Income and Annual Cash Flows

When a company estimates its relevant future cash flows from a capital expenditure proposal, it uses the "best" available information for its predictions. Frequently, the best available information is its expected future additional operating revenues and/or expenses. Most revenues and expenses of a company result in related cash receipts and payments of the same amounts at approximately the same points in time. For example, a company usually collects cash from credit sales very soon after the sales occur. Similarly, a company normally pays salaries to employees soon after the employees earn them. As a result, cash receipts from accounts receivable and cash payments for salaries payable in a year are likely to be about the same as the sales revenue and salaries expense for the year. Of course, sometimes large differences occur. For example, sometimes a company prepays expenses for several years. In this case the company considers the amount of the cash payment and the year in which it makes the payment rather than the annual expense.

Treatment of Depreciation

Depreciation is another expense for which the related cash flows occur in different years and in different amounts than the expense. For example, if Unlimited Decadence plans to purchase a machine for $1,000 cash and use the machine until it sells it at the end of 10 years for the estimated residual value of $100, the yearly "straight-line" depreciation expense for each of the 10 years will be $90 [($1,000 − $100) ÷ 10]. Since it plans to pay cash for the machine on the date of purchase, Unlimited Decadence would make no cash payments for the machine in any of those years, however.

The planned purchase and the resale of this machine involve only two relevant cash flows. The first is the cash payment of $1,000 to purchase the machine. The second is the $100 cash receipt at the end of year 10. A capital expenditure analysis should focus on the amounts and timing of these cash flows and *not* on the $90 yearly depreciation expense. It is important to understand that we are not ignoring this major cost; we are simply treating it in a different way.[1]

 Even though depreciation is not a cash flow, it affects a corporation's income tax payments. How do you think depreciation expense would affect a corporation's income tax payments over the life of the related asset?

Ending Cash Flows

A capital expenditure proposal may have some relevant cash flows occurring at the end of the project's life. For instance, in the example we just presented for depreciation, there was a cash receipt (the residual value) at the end of the machine's life. Another example

---

[1]The depreciation that a company includes on its tax return provides yearly cash savings in income taxes. However, for simplicity, we do not consider these cash flows in this chapter.

relates to the earlier discussion of the possibility of investing in additional working capital (e.g., inventory) at the beginning of a project. If this occurs, the company will "recover" the working capital at the end of the project (when the company sells the final items of inventory), and will treat this "recovery" as a cash receipt. Not all proposals have cash receipts at the end of the project's life. In fact, in some cases there will be an additional cash payment. For instance, it is sometimes necessary to pay someone to haul off fully depreciated and used-up factory equipment.

When a company decides to accept a capital expenditure proposal, it stores the information it used to analyze the proposal in its integrated accounting system. Later, then, it may use the information in its accounting process. For instance, suppose that based on a capital expenditure analysis, a company decides to purchase a new machine. As the company uses this machine, it retrieves the information about the machine's estimated life and estimated residual value from its integrated accounting system for use in its depreciation expense calculations, as you will see in Chapter 21.

Determining the Required Return on Investment

For any capital expenditure proposal, the question arises as to the company's required return on the investment. The required return is equal to the cost of providing cash for the investment, and is expressed as a percentage rate. For instance, a 15% rate means that the cost is 15 cents per year for every dollar invested. A company's financial position improves as a result of accepting a capital expenditure proposal only when the proposal provides a return on investment that is higher than the cost of providing the cash for the investment (in this case, greater than 15%).

4 How does a company determine the rate of return it requires on a capital expenditure proposal?

The rate that measures the cost to a company of providing cash for investments is called the company's *cost of capital.* A company's **cost of capital** is the weighted-average cost (rate of return) it must pay to all sources of capital. Remember, a company receives its capital from short-term borrowing (e.g., issuing notes payable), long-term borrowing (e.g., issuing bonds payable), and stockholders (e.g., selling stock). Each of these creditor and stockholder groups demands a "return on its investment" in the form of interest, dividends, or increased market value. The key to determining a company's cost of capital is to combine these returns into an "average" return.

There are several ways a company may compute its average cost of capital. One simple way is to determine the return demanded by each group and then weight this rate by the proportion of the company's total capital that the group has provided. For instance, suppose a company's total capital consists of 40% liabilities and 60% stockholders' equity. The liabilities pay an interest rate of 8%, and stockholders expect a return of 12%. In this example, the company's weighted average cost of capital is 10.4%, computed as follows:

	Proportion of equity		Required return		
Debt	40%	×	8%	=	3.2%
Stockholders' equity	60%	×	12%	=	7.2%
Cost of capital					10.4%

A company's cost of capital is the *cutoff rate* used to distinguish between acceptable and unacceptable capital expenditure proposals. In other words, the return on the proposed capital expenditure must be equal to or greater than the company's cost of capital to be acceptable. In this example, the return must be equal to or greater than 10.4%. In this book we are not concerned with computing a company's cost of capital. We stress that a proper cutoff rate must be set and used consistently in evaluating whether capital expenditure proposals will benefit a company. Throughout the rest of this chapter and in the homework, we will refer to this cutoff rate as the company's **required rate of return**.

Determining Acceptable Capital Expenditure Proposals

*The return on an investment comes from the receipt of future **net** cash receipts that total more than the investment.* For example, if a $100 investment provides a net cash receipt of $121 two years later, the investment earns a return. The receipt of $121 can be thought of as the sum of (1) a return *of* the investment ($100), plus (2) a return *on* the investment ($21). Regarding a capital expenditure proposal, the question is whether the expected return *on* the investment is high enough to make the investment acceptable. An *acceptable* rate of return on a capital expenditure proposal is one that is *equal to* or *higher than* the company's required rate of return. An *unacceptable* rate of return is *lower* than the required rate of return, in which case the proposal should be rejected.

A company may use several methods to analyze whether the rate of return on a capital expenditure proposal is acceptable. We will discuss three: (1) the net present value method, (2) the payback method, and (3) the average rate of return on investment method. Before we discuss these methods, however, you need to understand the concept of the time value of money and the computation of "present value."

THE TIME VALUE OF MONEY AND PRESENT VALUE

Since capital expenditure decisions involve cash payments and cash receipts occurring at different times, often over several years, a manager must consider the time value of money in these decisions. *No analysis that ignores the time value of money can provide a sound basis for making capital expenditure decisions.*

To understand the time value of money, consider whether you would rather receive $1 today or $1 next year. Your answer should be that you would rather receive $1 today because a dollar held today is worth more than a dollar received a year from now. If you received $1 today and put it in an interest-bearing account, you would have more than $1 a year from now. If you waited until next year to receive $1, you would have only $1 a year from now. The difference between the two amounts is *interest*, which reflects the *time value of money*.

To illustrate the time value of money, suppose that you have $100 on January 1, 2007, and can invest it at 10%. This money will grow over the next three years as shown in the following table:

Year	Amount at Beginning of the Year	Interest at 10%	Amount at End of the Year
2007	$100	$10.00	$110.00
2008	110	11.00	121.00
2009	121	12.10	133.10

Therefore you would rather have $100 today than $100 in one year because the $100 today grows to $110 in one year. Alternatively, the table shows that the following amounts, given the 10% interest rate and their respective dates, have *equivalent* values:

- $100 at the beginning of 2007
- $110 at the end of 2007 (beginning of 2008)
- $121 at the end of 2008 (beginning of 2009)
- $133.10 at the end of 2009 (beginning of 2010)

 Why do you think these four amounts are equivalent?

Since these amounts have equivalent values, if you were asked which amount you wanted to receive on the respective date, you would be indifferent about the four alternatives, given the 10% rate.

THE FAR SIDE® BY GARY LARSON

Einstein discovers that time is actually money.

It is important to know that the dollar amounts have a time and an interest rate attached to them. Whenever you are considering the time value of money, you must always know the date at which the dollar amount is measured and the appropriate interest rate. A dollar received or paid in 2007 does not have the same value as a dollar received or paid in 2008.

Definition of Present Value

There is an important term that is widely used whenever the time value of money is being considered. The **present value** is the value today of a certain amount of dollars paid or received in the future. Either the payor or the receiver of money can use the present value concept.[2] In the preceding example, $100 is the present value at the beginning of 2007 of $133.10 to be paid or received at the end of 2009 when the interest rate is 10%.

The concept underlying present value is compound interest. **Compound interest** is interest that accrues on both the principal and the past (unpaid) interest. Thus during 2007, interest of 10% accrues on the principal of $100, making a total of $110 at the end of 2007. In 2008, interest of 10% accrues on the $110 (the principal *and* the 2007 interest). The interest amounts to $11 for 2008. Similarly, in 2009, interest of $12.10 is accrued on $121 ($100 + $10 + $11) so that the total amount is $133.10 at the end of 2009.

The computation of a present value is necessary in many situations. In this chapter, we will use present value computations in evaluating capital expenditure proposals. In later chapters, we will use present value computations in accounting for items such as investments in bonds, bonds payable, leases, and mortgages. As you will see, formulas and tables simplify present value computations.

---

[2]Another concept sometimes used is future value. The **future value** is the value at a future date of a certain amount of dollars paid or received today. Since present value is more commonly used, for simplicity we do not discuss future value in this book.

Present Value Formulas and Tables

Formulas or tables may be used instead of preparing year-by-year calculations of present values. But first you must understand that there are two types of future cash flows, a single amount and an annuity.

Present Value of a Single Future Amount

A single future **amount** is a one-time future cash flow. For example, if Unlimited Decadence plans to use a mixing machine for three years and then sell it, the cash it will receive from the sale is a single future amount. The general relationship between the present value and a future amount is shown in the following equation:

$$PV = \frac{FA}{(1 + i)^n}$$

where:

PV = Present value
FA = Future amount
i = Interest rate
n = Number of periods

Using the same example of 10% and three years, if the future amount of $133.10 is known, the present value is calculated as follows:

$$PV = \frac{FA}{(1 + i)^n}$$

$$= \frac{\$133.10}{(1 + 0.10)^3}$$

$$= \frac{\$133.10}{1.331}$$

$$= \underline{\underline{\$100}}$$

A table can simplify the calculation process even more. Table 20-1 at the end of this chapter is entitled Present Value of $1 Due in n Periods, but you can use it to figure the present value of any single future amount. With information from the table, you can compute a present value by using the following simple formula:

$$PV = FA \times \text{Present Value of \$1 Factor}$$

A **factor** is a decimal amount in the table. If you look up the factor for 10% and three periods in Table 20-1,[3] you will find that it is 0.7513. This represents the present value of *$1* received or paid at the end of three years. The present value of *$133.10* received or paid at the end of three years, using a 10% interest rate, is 133.10 times the present value of $1. Another way of saying this is that the present value of $133.10 is $133.10 times the 0.7513 factor, as follows:

$$PV = FA \times \text{Present Value of \$1 Factor for 3 Periods at 10\%}$$
$$= \$133.10 \times 0.7513$$
$$= \underline{\underline{\$100}}$$

 What do you think the present value of $10 received or paid at the end of three years is, using a 10% interest rate?

---

[3]The factors in Table 20-1 were computed using the equation for the present value of $1 factor shown at the beginning of Table 20-1.

The process of converting a future amount to a present value is known as *discounting*, and the rate used is often called the **discount rate.** Thus, we can say that the $133.10 future amount is discounted to the $100 present value by multiplying it by the 0.7513 present value of $1 factor for three periods at the 10% discount rate.

Present Value of an Annuity

In many situations we are not concerned with the present value of a single future amount but with the present value of an annuity. An **annuity** is a series of *equal* periodic future cash flows. These cash flows may be either received or paid. For example, if on January 1 Unlimited Decadence purchased a new mixing machine that will require $200 of maintenance at the end of each of the next three years, the three $200 payments are an annuity. In this book we will assume that the first cash flow in an annuity occurs at the *end* of the first year. Thus, if an annual annuity begins on January 1, 2008, the first cash flow occurs on December 31, 2008.

We could compute the present value on January 1, 2008 of a three-year $200 annuity at 10% by treating it as three separate single future amounts and using Table 20-1, but there is an easier way. Instead of using Table 20-1, we will use Table 20-2 at the end of the chapter.

 How would you compute the present value for the preceding example using Table 20-1?

Table 20-2 is entitled Present Value of an Annuity of $1 per Period, but you can use it to compute the present value of an annuity of any amount. The present value is computed using the following simple formula:

$$PV \text{ of an Annuity} = \frac{\text{Periodic Amount of}}{\text{an Annuity}} \times \frac{\text{Present Value of}}{\text{an Annuity Factor}}$$

If you look up the factor for 10% and three periods in Table 20-2,[4] you will find that it is 2.4869. This is the present value of *$1* received or paid at the end of each of the next three years using a 10% discount rate. Therefore, you can compute the present value of an annuity of $200 received or paid at the end of each year for the next three years using a 10% discount rate as follows:

$$
\begin{aligned}
PV \text{ of Annuity} &= \text{Annuity} \times \text{Present Value of Annuity Factor for 3 Periods at 10\%} \\
&= \$200 \times 2.4869 \\
&= \underline{\underline{\$497.38}}
\end{aligned}
$$

Another way of saying this is that the annuity of $200 received or paid at the end of each year for the next three years is discounted to a present value of $497.38.

Many calculators have the capacity to compute the present value of a single future amount and the present value of an annuity. The calculation process follows exactly the same concepts that we discussed earlier. These calculators use equations to determine each factor whenever a calculation is made. If you use a calculator to make your present value computations, you may find an occasional "rounding" error between your answer and what is shown in this book. That is because the calculator does not round its factors, whereas the factors in Tables 20-1 and 20-2 are rounded to four decimal places.

Present Value Examples

In making capital expenditure decisions, you may need to compute both the present value of a single future amount and the present value of an annuity. To help you better understand these computations, we provide the following examples.

---

[4]The factors in Table 20-2 were computed using the equation for the present value of an annuity factor, shown at the beginning of Table 20-2. The factor in Table 20-2 for a given year and interest rate also may be computed by summing the factors in Table 20-1 for each year prior to and including the given year for that interest rate.

Example 1
Compute the present value of a $100 cash receipt at the end of 5 years if the interest rate is 12%.

Present Value = Future Amount × Present Value of $1 Factor
= $100 × 0.5674
= $56.74 (receipt)

Example 2
Compute the present value of cash receipts of $300 at the ends of years 1, 2, and 3 if the interest rate is 14%.

Present Value = Annuity × Present Value of Annuity Factor
= $300 × 2.3216
= $696.48 (receipt)

Example 3
Compute the present value of a $200 cash receipt at the ends of years 1 and 2, and a $300 cash receipt at the end of year 3, if the interest rate is 10%.

Present Value = ($200 × 1.7355) + ($300 × 0.7513)
= $572.49 (receipt)

Example 4
Compute the present value of a $500 cash receipt at the end of 10 years together with a $300 cash payment at the end of 2 years, if the interest rate is 8%.

Present Value = ($500 × 0.4632) − ($300 × 0.8573)
= ($25.59) (net payment)

Example 5
Compute the present value of a $500 cash receipt at the end of each year for 5 years, together with a $200 cash payment at the end of each year for 5 years, if the interest rate is 12%.

Present Value = ($500 − $200) × 3.6048
= $1,081.44 (net receipt)

If you used a calculator to solve the examples, your answers might be a few cents different from those shown because of rounding errors. Also, in Examples 3, 4, and 5 there are other ways to compute the present value of the cash receipts and payments, but all result in the same present value that we computed in each example.

 What is another way of computing the present value for Example 3?

A dramatic example of the time value of money involves the 1989 spill of crude oil in Alaska's Prince William Sound by the oil tanker *Exxon Valdez*. In December 2006, after several appeals, **Exxon Corporation**, the owner of the tanker that spilled 11 million gallons of oil into the Sound, was ordered to pay $2.5 billion for damages to the Sound and in government fines. (The original judgment in 1994 was $5 billion, to be paid over a 10-year period—the largest amount that had been assessed for an environmental violation at that time. Furthermore, these payments would be tax deductible in the years that Exxon paid them.) Although Exxon intends to appeal this most recent judgment, compare the full $2.5 billion that Exxon Corporation could pay at the time of the fine, with the present value of the net payments (payments minus related tax deductions) of $1.215 billion that Exxon could make. By extending its payments over the next 10 years, Exxon could reduce its actual costs to less than half of the assessed damages and fine.

Now that you understand the time value of money and what we mean by present value, we can now discuss how a company makes capital expenditure decisions. As we mentioned earlier, a company has the choice of using one or more of several approaches to evaluating capital expenditure proposals. We will begin our discussion with the net present value method.

NET PRESENT VALUE METHOD

The net present value method is one approach to evaluating whether or not to undertake a capital expenditure proposal. It considers the time value of money and involves a three-step process:

5 How does a company use the net present value method to evaluate a capital expenditure proposal?

1. Determine the initial expected cash payment (investment) required to implement the capital expenditure proposal
2. Determine the present value of the expected future net cash receipts from the capital expenditure proposal
3. Determine the net present value by subtracting the amount of Step 1 from the amount of Step 2

Step 1 involves determining the expected cash payment (investment) needed to put the proposal into operation. This investment is already stated at its present value, since it takes place at the present time, just before putting the project into operation.[5] Step 2 involves first estimating the expected future cash receipts and payments (and the length of time over which the company expects these cash receipts and payments to occur), as we discussed earlier. It then involves discounting the expected future *net* cash receipts (future cash receipts minus future cash payments) for each year to their present value using the company's required rate of return (its cost of capital).

Step 3 involves computing the net present value. The **net present value** of a capital expenditure proposal is the present value of the expected future net cash receipts and payments minus the expected initial cash payment (investment). When the net present value is zero or positive, the capital expenditure proposal is acceptable because the project will earn at least the company's required rate of return. When the net present value is negative, the capital expenditure proposal is *not* acceptable because it will earn

[5]Another way of looking at this is to consider that the initial investment takes place in time period *zero*, which always has a present value factor of 1.0, regardless of the discount rate. Some books will multiply the initial cash payment by 1.0 to determine the present value. Since we consider this approach to be extra work to get the same result, we do not use it in this book.

less than the company's required rate of return.[6] We can summarize these decision rules as follows:

When the net present value is:	The decision rule is:
Zero	Acceptable; rate of return on the proposal is *equal to* the required rate of return
Positive	Acceptable; rate of return on the proposal is *greater than* the required rate of return
Negative	Not acceptable; rate of return on the proposal is *less than* the required rate of return

We will illustrate the net present value method with two examples.

Capital Expenditure Proposal: Build New Factory

In the first example, Unlimited Decadence is considering building a new factory. The new factory will be 100,000 square feet. Construction costs are estimated to be $70 per square foot, or a total of $7,000,000 (100,000 × $70). Equipment, installation, and training costs are expected to be $1,920,000. The company estimates that the new factory will be used for 12 years, after which it (and the equipment) will be sold for $1,000,000 (the residual value). Therefore, it computes its expected depreciation on the factory and equipment to be $660,000 per year. The factory is expected to increase the company's operating revenues by $8,000,000 per year and to increase its operating expenses (including depreciation) by $6,660,000 per year. Unlimited Decadence's required rate of return is 14 percent. Should Unlimited Decadence build this factory?

To analyze this capital expenditure proposal, Unlimited Decadence first determines the expected initial cost of the investment. In this case, the initial cost is $8,920,000 ($7,000,000 + $1,920,000). The company then determines the amounts and timing of its expected additional future cash flows. In this example, Unlimited Decadence estimates it will have $8,000,000 additional cash *receipts* from operations in years 1 through 12. The company estimates it will have $6,000,000 additional cash *payments* for operations in years 1 through 12. (Note that although Unlimited Decadence estimated that operating expenses would be $6,660,000 per year, it *excludes* the $660,000 depreciation from the analysis because the depreciation does not involve a yearly cash payment.) Therefore, its expected future *net* operating cash receipts are $2,000,000 per year for years 1 through 12. Unlimited Decadence also estimates that it will have a $1,000,000 cash receipt from the residual value at the end of year 12.

Since the company's required rate of return is 14 percent, it uses this percentage as the discount rate to compute the present value of the future cash flows. We show the computation of the net present value of building this factory in Exhibit 20-1. Unlimited Decadence computed the present value of its expected future cash flows first. Note that Unlimited Decadence listed each type of cash flow along with the year(s) during which it expects the cash flow to occur and the future amount of the cash flow. It then multiplied each future amount by the appropriate present value factor for the 14% required rate of return.

The net operating cash receipts are an annuity because they occur in the same amounts each year. The present value factor of an annuity for 12 years at 14% comes from Table 20-2 at the end of this chapter; it is 5.6603. The present value of the net operating cash receipts is $11,320,600. Since the $1,000,000 residual value is a single cash receipt at the end of year 12, the 0.2076 present value factor comes from Table 20-1 at the end of the chapter. The present value of the residual value, then, is $207,600.

---

[6]Some companies use a "time-adjusted rate of return" method. This method determines (by trial and error) the *rate* that, when used to discount the cash flows from the proposal, gives a net present value of *zero*. Then a company knows exactly what rate of return a proposal will earn. We use the net present value method because it is an easier approach and shows acceptable proposals with rates of return that are equal to or greater than the required rate of return.

EXHIBIT 20-1	CAPITAL EXPENDITURE PROPOSAL: BUILD NEW FACTORY

Present Value of Expected Future Net Cash Receipts

Type	Years	Future Amount	×	14% Discount Factor	=	Present Value
Net operating cash receipts	1-12	$2,000,000*		5.6603[†]		$11,320,600
Residual value	12	1,000,000		0.2076[‡]		207,600
Present value of expected future net cash receipts						$11,528,200

Expected Investment (Initial Cash Payments)

Type	Amount
Factory (100,000 sq. ft. × $70/sq. ft.)...	$7,000,000
Equipment, installation, training	1,920,000
Initial investment..	(8,920,000)
Net present value	$ 2,608,200

Decision: Project is acceptable.

*$8,000,000 operating receipts − $6,000,000 operating payments
[†]From Table 20-2 (annuity), n = 12, i = 14%
[‡]From Table 20-1 (single amount), n = 12, i = 14%

The sum of the two present values of the future cash flows is the $11,528,200 present value of the expected future net cash receipts. This amount minus the $8,920,000 expected initial investment results in the $2,608,200 *positive* net present value. The capital expenditure proposal to build the new factory is acceptable because it has a positive net present value. This means that the rate of return on the proposal is *greater than* the 14% rate of return that Unlimited Decadence requires on its capital expenditures.

Capital Expenditure Proposal: Purchase Wrapper Machine

Now assume that Unlimited Decadence is considering replacing its existing "wrapper" machine with a new improved one. In addition to wrapping the candy bars, the new wrapper machine also would count and box the candy bars. Currently, this counting and boxing must be done by an employee. The new machine costs $30,000 to buy, and installation costs are expected to be $500. The old machine could be sold for $400.

Unlimited Decadence expects to use the new machine for four years, after which it can sell the machine for $1,000 (the residual value). The new machine will not increase production. However, because the machine does the counting and boxing, Unlimited Decadence estimates that the new machine will save $10,000 per year in employee labor costs. Unlimited Decadence's required rate of return is 14%. Should it purchase the new wrapper machine?

The expected initial cost of the investment is $30,100, which is the $30,000 cost of the new machine plus the $500 installation cost less the $400 received from the residual value of the old machine. The future cash flows consist of expected "savings" in cash payments of $10,000 each year for four years (remember, these are treated like cash receipts) and a $1,000 cash receipt from the residual value at the end of year 4.

Unlimited Decadence used its 14% required rate of return as the discount rate to compute the present value of its expected future cash flows. We show the computations of the net present value of purchasing the wrapper machine in Exhibit 20-2.

| | EXHIBIT 20-2 | CAPITAL EXPENDITURE PROPOSAL: PURCHASE WRAPPER MACHINE |

Present Value of Expected Future Net Cash Receipts

Type	Years	Future Amount	×	14% Discount Factor	=	Present Value
Savings in wages	1-4	$10,000		2.9137*		$29,137
Residual value	4	1,000		0.5921†		592
Present value of expected future net cash receipts						$29,729

Expected Investment (Initial Cash Payments)

Type	Amount
Cost of machine	$30,000
Installation and testing	500
Less: Residual value of old machine	(400)
Present value of initial investment	(30,100)
Net present value	$ (371)

Decision: Project is *not* acceptable.

*From Table 20-2 (annuity), n = 4, i = 14%
†From Table 20-1 (single amount), n = 4, i = 14%

The present value of the future net cash receipts totals $29,729. It consists of two present values: the $29,137 present value of the $10,000 annuity from the savings in labor costs for each of years 1 through 4 and the $592 present value of the new machine's $1,000 residual value received at the end of year 4.

Unlimited Decadence subtracted the $30,100 initial investment from the $29,729 to determine the *negative* net present value of $371. The capital expenditure proposal to purchase a new wrapper machine is *not* acceptable because it has a negative net present value. This means that the rate of return on the project is *less than* the 14% rate of return that Unlimited Decadence requires on its capital expenditures.

ALTERNATIVE METHODS FOR EVALUATING CAPITAL EXPENDITURE PROPOSALS

In addition to the net present value method, there are several other methods a company might use to evaluate a capital expenditure proposal. We will discuss two: (1) the payback method and (2) the average rate of return on investment method.

Payback Method

6 What is the difference between the payback method and the average rate of return on investment method for evaluating a capital expenditure proposal?

The payback method evaluates a capital expenditure proposal based on the payback period. The **payback period** is the length of time required for a return *of* the initial investment. That is, it is the length of time needed for the future net cash receipts to "pay back" the initial cash payment for the capital expenditure.

To illustrate, we will use the previous example in which Unlimited Decadence was considering whether to purchase a wrapper machine. The initial investment was $30,100, and the expected future net cash receipts were $10,000 in years 1 through 4 and $1,000 at the end of year 4. The following schedule shows how Unlimited Decadence computed the payback period:

	Amount to Pay Back at Beginning of Year	Net Annual Cash Receipts Expected	Total Amount Paid Back at Year-End	Amount Left to Pay Back at Year-End
Year 1	$30,100	$10,000	$10,000	$20,100
Year 2	20,100	10,000	20,000	10,100
Year 3	10,100	10,000	30,000	100
Year 4	100	11,000	30,100	—

The schedule shows that $30,000 of the investment would be paid back by the end of Year 3. Since only $100 of the investment would remain unpaid at the beginning of year 4, and $11,000 of net cash receipts are expected in Year 4, the $100 would be paid back in 0.009 years ($100 ÷ $11,000), or after a little more than 3 days (0.009 × 365 days) of Year 4. Thus the payback period is 3.009 years.

Sometimes a company will use the payback period computation to determine whether a capital expenditure proposal is acceptable. It does this by setting a maximum payback period for acceptable proposals. A capital expenditure proposal with a payback period longer than the maximum period would not be acceptable. In addition, a company also might use the payback period to judge whether one capital expenditure proposal is better than another. The company would judge the proposal with the shorter payback period to be better.

Unfortunately, the payback period is *not* a good measure for either purpose. There is no objective way to determine an appropriate payback period. Hence, setting a maximum payback period is arbitrary. A project may have a short payback period for a return *of* the investment and be considered an acceptable proposal. However, the project may provide no return *on* the investment. Therefore, such a project would not contribute to the overall profitability of the company and thus the company should not consider it acceptable.

 Think of a numerical example to illustrate a project that has a short payback period but no return on the investment.

Another project may have a payback period longer than the maximum payback period and be judged to be unacceptable under this method. However, the project may provide a large return *on* the investment later in the project's life and thus may be considered acceptable under another method. *The problem with the payback method is that the payback period focuses on the return of the investment and completely ignores the return on the investment.* The payback period computation, by itself, cannot provide a sound basis for making capital expenditure decisions.

Average Rate of Return on Investment Method

Another approach that a company sometimes will use in making capital expenditure decisions is the average rate of return on investment method. The **average rate of return on investment** is the average return *on* the investment per year, per dollar invested. It is usually expressed as a percentage per year. The company compares this percentage per year for a proposal against its minimum required rate of return to determine whether the proposal is acceptable.

A company computes the average rate of return on investment by dividing the total estimated net cash receipts from an investment (the return on investment) by the number of years over which the cash will be received times the dollars invested. Since this is a "mouthful," we show the computation in equation form on the following page. In this equation, the total estimated net cash receipts is the numerator and is equal to the total cash receipts minus the total cash payments (including the initial investment).

$$\text{Average Rate of Return on Investment} = \frac{\text{Total Cash Receipts} - \text{Total Cash Payments}}{\text{Years} \times \text{Investment}}$$

To understand this method, consider Unlimited Decadence's proposal for purchasing a wrapper machine, which we discussed earlier. The average rate of return for this proposal is 9.1%, computed as follows:

$$\begin{aligned} \text{Average Rate} \\ \text{of Return on} \\ \text{Investment} \end{aligned} = \frac{(\$10,000 + \$10,000 + \$10,000 + \$10,000 + \$1,000) - \$30,100}{4 \times \$30,100}$$

$$= \frac{\$10,900}{\$120,400}$$

$$= \underline{9.1\%}$$

Since 9.1% is less than Unlimited Decadence's minimum required rate of return of 14%, the method shows that the proposal is unacceptable.

In contrast to the payback period computation, the average rate of return *does* consider the return *on* investment. The average rate of return on investment method, however, does not provide a good basis for making capital investment decisions. The reason is that *the average rate of return on investment method does not consider the time value of money*. For a proposal that has cash flows occurring late in the life of the project, the "averaging" process may lead a company to erroneously accept a capital expenditure proposal that will not contribute to its profitability.

 Given what you have learned about present value analysis, how do you think the averaging process might lead a company to accept a proposal that has cash flows occurring late in the life of the project, so that the project would not contribute to its profitability?

Although companies sometimes use the payback method and the average rate of return on investment method to evaluate capital expenditure proposals, these methods do not consider the return on investment, do not account for the time value of money, or both. Therefore, they should not be used *by themselves* for capital expenditure decisions. Some companies use these methods in conjunction with the net present value method to help screen potentially acceptable proposals and to provide supporting analyses.

 What additional information do you think a combination of the three methods could provide that a company would not get using the net present value method alone?

SELECTING ALTERNATIVE PROPOSALS FOR INVESTMENT

7 How does a company decide which capital expenditure proposal to accept when it has several proposals that accomplish the same thing, or when it cannot obtain sufficient cash to make all of its desired investments?

Capital expenditure decisions would be much easier if a company could invest in all proposals that it identified as being acceptable. This is not always possible, however. Consider the following two situations in which a company must select between two or more proposals that it has identified as being acceptable.

Mutually Exclusive Capital Expenditure Proposals

Capital expenditure proposals often arise because of alternative ways a company has to perform an activity, do a job, or provide a service. Sometimes there are several alternatives. In this situation, the capital investment alternatives are called *mutually exclusive*. **Mutually exclusive capital expenditure proposals** are proposals that accomplish the same thing, so that when one proposal is selected, the others are not. For example, a company might be considering air conditioning its offices. Although several makes and models of air conditioners may be available, each with a different set of cash flows, one is enough to do the job.

A company evaluating mutually exclusive capital expenditure proposals completes a two-step process. In the first step, the company analyzes each proposal to determine whether or not it is acceptable. The company does this analysis using the net present value method we discussed earlier. If more than one proposal is acceptable (i.e, has a positive net present value), a second step is necessary. In the second step, the company selects one of the acceptable alternatives by *choosing the proposal with the highest positive net present value*. When the company selects a proposal in this way, the analysis in the first step provides the information needed for the second step.

For example, suppose that Unlimited Decadence is considering replacing a "mixer" machine with a new, improved one. There are three different mixer machines on the market, only one of which can be selected. All have the same life and cost about the same, but each would provide different savings in electricity, labor costs, and so on. As the first step in analyzing these mutually exclusive proposals, Unlimited Decadence prepared a net present value analysis for each proposal. Below are the resulting net present values for each machine:

Machine	Net Present Value
A...	$6,300
B...	(2,200)
C...	4,700

In this situation, Unlimited Decadence would eliminate Machine B after the first step because it has a negative net present value. In the second step, it would select Machine A because Machine A has a higher positive net present value than Machine C.[7]

Occasionally, a company considers several mutually exclusive capital expenditure proposals with the requirement that it *must* select one proposal. That is, the alternative of not investing at all is not an available choice. This might happen, for instance, when a company must obtain equipment or facilities to comply with a law. When one of the capital expenditure proposals must be accepted, *the best proposal is the one with the highest (most positive) net present value, even if that net present value is negative*.

Suppose, for example, that a recently established safety ordinance requires that Unlimited Decadence add additional lights to its factory parking lot. The additional lights require a cash payment, although they will provide no cash receipts. Normally, Unlimited Decadence would not make such a capital expenditure because it would result in a negative net present value. Because of the new law, however, *not* investing in additional lights is an unacceptable alternative. If several proposals for additional lighting would comply with the safety ordinance, Unlimited Decadence would choose the proposal with the *least negative* net present value.

Capital Rationing

The previous analyses identified acceptable capital expenditure proposals. If a company has enough cash available, all acceptable capital expenditures could be made (including one selected from each set of mutually exclusive proposals). Sometimes, however, a company finds itself with a larger number of acceptable capital expenditure proposals than it can finance. When this occurs, the company must make its capital expenditure decisions in a situation known as *capital rationing*. **Capital rationing** occurs when a company

---

[7]Choosing the better alternative may be more complicated when the mutually exclusive capital expenditure proposals require a different amount of investment or when the numbers of years over which they affect the company's cash flows differ. We do not discuss procedures to handle such situations in this book.

cannot obtain sufficient cash to make all of the investments that it would like to make. A difficult decision arises when this happens. The company must choose which of the acceptable proposals to invest in, which to delay until sufficient funds become available, and which to forget altogether, if necessary.

Many approaches to handling this problem have been suggested. A detailed study of these approaches is beyond the scope of this book. However, we will discuss the general idea for one approach. This approach involves looking at the acceptable capital expenditure proposals to find all the possible combinations that do not require a larger total investment of cash than is available. Under this approach, *a company chooses the combination of capital expenditure proposals that provides the highest total net present value for the total investment available.*

For example, suppose that Unlimited Decadence has $200,000 cash available for capital expenditures during the current budget period and has the following three proposals that are acceptable because of their positive net present values:

Proposal	Initial Investment Required	Net Present Value
A	$200,000	$120,000
B	110,000	80,000
C	90,000	50,000

Unlimited Decadence could accept capital expenditure proposal A, which would use the entire $200,000 cash available for investment. Or it could undertake both proposals B and C with the $200,000 cash available. In this case, Unlimited Decadence should select proposals B and C because together they provide a higher total net present value of $130,000 ($80,000 + $50,000) than proposal A's $120,000 net present value.

BUSINESS ISSUES AND VALUES

Although the methods we discussed seem to be relatively easy to implement through tables and formulas, not all capital expenditure proposals are easy to quantify. For example, consider the decision about whether to invest in an employee fitness program. Corporations such as **Johnson & Johnson**, **PepsiCo**, **IBM**, and **Kimberly-Clark** have invested in wellness programs with facilities alone costing between $1.8 million and $11 million. On top of the costs of the facilities, these corporations added the costs of the salaries and benefits for fitness center employees, health screenings, and incentives for employees. **General Dynamics C4 Systems** reimburses up to $250 per year for each employee's own membership in a fitness facility or program where an on-site facility is not available. But how do these corporations measure the benefits of their programs, and how far into the future do they have to go before they start seeing these benefits? Companies have been able to measure such factors as the percentage decline in employee smoking and the decline in insurance claims of employees who quit smoking, the average number of insurance claims for exercisers versus nonexercisers, rates of absenteeism for smokers versus nonsmokers and exercisers versus nonexercisers, and reductions in insurance costs. However, many of these factors can't be measured for years after the initial investment, and some other factors can't be quantified at all. For example, the increase in employee morale from company fitness programs is harder to measure but no less important.

In making capital expenditure decisions, companies need to consider *all* the relevant factors, including the difficult-to-measure ones. Otherwise, in cases like this, a company might put an arbitrary limit on the time horizon of the project (and therefore not see the long-term benefits of the project) or might not consider the nonquantifiable benefits of the project. Thus, the company might decide against a capital expenditure that is actually in its best interests.

If you were deciding whether or not to purchase an exercise bike, what costs and benefits would you consider?

© PHOTODISC/GETTY IMAGES

SUMMARY

At the beginning of the chapter we asked you several questions. During the chapter, we asked you to STOP and answer several additional questions to build your knowledge about specific issues. Be sure you answered these additional questions. Below are the questions from the beginning of the chapter, along with a brief summary of the key points relating to the answers. Use your creative and critical thinking skills to expand on these key points to develop more complete answers to the questions and to determine what other questions you have that might lead you to learn more about the issues.

1 **What is a capital expenditure, and what are the four steps in a capital expenditure decision?**

A capital expenditure is a long-term investment (cash payment) made by a company in order for it to obtain future net cash receipts totaling more than the investment. In making a capital expenditure decision, a company completes four steps. First, the company must determine the expected initial cash payment needed to make the investment. Second, the company must estimate the future cash receipts and payments (cash flows) expected from the investment and the time period over which it expects these future cash receipts and payments to occur . Third, the company must determine its cost of providing the cash to make the investment. Finally, the company must determine whether the estimated future cash flows will provide a return that is sufficient (after adjusting for the time value of money) to cover the cost of providing the cash to make the investment.

2 **What does a company include in the initial cost of a capital expenditure proposal?**

The initial cost of a capital expenditure proposal is the expected cash payment necessary to put the proposal into operation. In other words, it is the capital that the company must expend to make the investment. It includes such items as the cost of an asset, transportation costs, and installation costs.

3 **What are the relevant costs of a capital expenditure proposal, and how do operating income, depreciation, and ending cash flows affect these costs?**

The relevant costs of a capital expenditure proposal are future cash flows that differ, either in amount or in timing, as a result of accepting a capital expenditure proposal. That is, relevant costs are (1) the additional future cash flows (either receipts or payments) to a company's existing cash flows, or (2) the savings in future cash payments. Frequently, the best available information to use in predicting these relevant costs is the expected future additional operating revenues and/or expenses. Most revenues and expenses of a company (the company's operating income) result in related cash receipts and payments of the same amounts at approximately the same points in time. But depreciation is an expense for which the related cash flows occur in different years and in different amounts than the expense, so a company does not consider depreciation expense when it predicts relevant cash flows. A company considers ending cash flows related to the capital expenditure to be relevant costs.

4 **How does a company determine the rate of return it requires on a capital expenditure proposal?**

The rate of return that a company requires on a capital expenditure proposal is the cost to the company of providing the cash for the investment. It is the weighted-average cost the company must pay to all its sources of capital. This rate of return is called the company's cost of capital.

5 **How does a company use the net present value method to evaluate a capital expenditure proposal?**

A company evaluates a capital expenditure proposal using the net present value method by considering the time value of money in a three-step process. Step 1 involves determining the expected cash payment needed to put the proposal into operation (the investment). This investment is already stated at its present value, since it takes place at the present time, just prior to putting the project into operation. Step 2 involves first estimating the expected future cash receipts and payments (and the length of time over which the company expects these cash receipts and payments to occur). It then involves discounting the expected future *net* cash receipts (future cash receipts minus future cash payments) for each year to their present values using the company's required rate of return (its cost of capital). Step 3 involves computing the net present value, by subtracting the initial cash payment (from Step 1) from the present value of the expected future net cash receipts and payments (from Step 2). When the net present value is zero or positive, the capital expenditure proposal is acceptable. When the net present value is negative, the capital expenditure proposal is not acceptable because it will earn less than the company's required rate of return.

6 **What is the difference between the payback method and the average rate of return on investment method for evaluating a capital expenditure proposal?**

A company using the payback method evaluates a capital expenditure proposal based on the length of time required for a return of the initial investment. A company using the average rate of return on investment method compares a company's average return on the investment per year, per dollar invested, against the company's minimum required rate of return to determine whether the proposal is acceptable.

7 **How does a company decide which capital expenditure proposal to accept when it has several proposals that accomplish the same thing, or when it cannot obtain sufficient cash to make all of its desired investments?**

A company evaluating several proposals that accomplish the same thing (called *mutually exclusive proposals*) completes a two-step process. In the first step, the company analyzes each proposal to determine whether or not it is acceptable. The company does this analysis using the net present value method. If more than one proposal is acceptable (i.e,. has a positive net present value), a second step is necessary. In the second step, the company selects one of the acceptable alternatives by choosing the proposal with the highest positive net present value. One approach to deciding which capital expenditure proposal to accept when a company cannot obtain sufficient cash to make all of its desired investments (called *capital rationing*) involves looking at the acceptable capital expenditure proposals to find all possible combinations of proposals that do not require a larger total investment of cash than is available. A company chooses the combination of capital expenditure proposals that provides the highest total net present value for the total investment available.

KEY TERMS

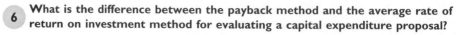

amount *(p. 694)*
annuity *(p. 695)*
average rate of return on investment
  (p. 701)
capital expenditure *(p. 687)*
capital rationing *(p. 703)*
compound interest *(p. 693)*
cost of capital *(p. 691)*
discount rate *(p. 695)*
factor *(p. 694)*

future value *(p. 692)*
initial cost *(p. 688)*
mutually exclusive capital expenditure
  proposals *(p. 702)*
net present value *(p. 699)*
payback period *(p. 700)*
present value *(p. 697)*
relevant cash flows *(p. 689)*
required rate of return *(p. 691)*

SUMMARY SURFING

Here is an opportunity to gather information on the Internet about real-world issues related to the topics in this chapter (for suggestions on how to navigate various companies' Web sites to find their financial statements and other information, see the related discussion in the Preface at the beginning of the book). Answer the following question.

- Go to the **Gold's Gym Enterprises, Inc.** website. Then click on *About Gold's* and then on *Gold's Story*. What future cash receipts and cash payments do you think its managers considered in deciding whether Gold's Gym should invest in "The Mecca of Body Building"?

INTEGRATED BUSINESS AND ACCOUNTING SITUATIONS

Answer the Following Questions in Your Own Words.

Testing Your Knowledge

20-1 What is a capital expenditure decision? Give three examples of capital expenditure opportunities.

20-2 When is a capital expenditure proposal acceptable to a company?

20-3 What four steps must a company complete to determine whether or not a capital expenditure proposal is acceptable?

20-4 What is the initial cost of a capital expenditure proposal? Give three examples of items included in the initial cost of purchasing a machine.

20-5 Identify three forms of expected net future cash receipts.

20-6 What are relevant cash flows? How are cash inflows and outflows that occurred prior to a capital expenditure decision included in relevant cash flows?

20-7 Briefly discuss how depreciation expense on a machine is treated in a capital expenditure analysis.

20-8 What is a company's cost of capital? How does it relate to the required rate of return on a capital expenditure?

20-9 What is an acceptable rate of return on a capital expenditure proposal?

20-10 What is meant by the term *the time value of money*?

20-11 What is the relationship between present value and compound interest?

20-12 Explain how to compute the present value of a future amount.

20-13 Explain how to compute the present value of an annuity.

20-14 Define the net present value of a capital expenditure proposal. Identify what amount of net present value indicates an acceptable (unacceptable) proposal.

20-15 Define the term *payback period*. Why is the payback period a poor measure for determining whether a capital expenditure proposal is acceptable?

20-16 Briefly explain why the average rate of return on investment method is better than the payback method in judging whether a capital expenditure proposal is acceptable. Does your answer mean that the average rate of return on investment method is a good method for making capital investment decisions?

20-17 What are mutually exclusive capital expenditure proposals? Give an example.

20-18 Define the term *capital rationing*. Identify an investment approach that a company could use in a capital rationing situation.

Applying Your Knowledge

20-19 The following are four sets of cash flows:
(a) A single $500 cash inflow at the end of year 5.
(b) A series of $100 cash inflows at the end of years 1, 2, 3, 4, and 5.

(c) A cash inflow of $300 at the end of year 3 and a cash inflow of $400 at the end of year 5.

(d) A series of cash outflows of $60 at the end of years 1 through 10.

Required: Determine the present value of each of the sets of cash flows using a discount rate of 12%.

20-20 The following are four sets of cash flows:

(a) A single $300 cash inflow at the end of year 5.

(b) A series of $600 cash inflows at the end of years 1, 2, 3, 4, and 5.

(c) A cash inflow of $400 at the end of year 3 and a cash inflow of $500 at the end of year 5.

(d) A series of cash outflows of $80 at the end of years 1 through 10.

Required: Determine the present value of each of the sets of cash flows using a discount rate of 10%.

20-21 The following are two *independent* questions.

(a) The Delta Company sells a new type of pecan shelling machine that it claims will save a constant amount of labor costs at a particular company each year for 10 years. Delta suggests that this savings would have a present value (at 16%) of $19,332.80 to the company. What is the amount of the annual labor cost savings being claimed?

(b) The Sigma Company sells a small mechanical apparatus with a complicated solid-state control unit that attaches to an automobile's carburetor. Sigma claims the apparatus will save the average car owner $100 per year in gasoline bills that should be worth over $800 (present value) to the owner using a discount rate of 10%. If the apparatus can save $100 per year, how many years would it have to be used for the present value of the savings to exceed $800?

Required: Prepare an analysis to answer each of the questions.

20-22 Tom Hammond is considering investing $5,600 in a tract of farmland a group of his friends is planning to buy. His share of the expected selling price of the land after five years would be $9,600.

Required: (1) Compute the net present value of the land investment, assuming a 12% required rate of return.
(2) Should Tom make the investment? Why or why not?

20-23 The McKenzie Company is considering buying a machine that would increase the company's cash receipts by $2,200 per year for five years. Operation of the machine would increase the company's cash payments by $100 in each of the first two years, $200 in the third and fourth years, and $300 in the fifth year. The machine would cost $6,000 and would have a residual value of $500 at the end of the fifth year.

Required: (1) Assuming a 16% required rate of return, compute the net present value of the machine investment being considered by McKenzie Company.
(2) Should McKenzie Company make the investment? Why or why not?

20-24 Carmichael Radio Company, a distributor of radio towers and antennas, is considering buying the entire inventory of West Tower Company, which manufactures extremely large, heavy-duty towers, and which is going out of business. These towers would cost $250,000 delivered to Carmichael's warehouse. Carmichael plans to sell these towers to special customers. Carmichael's required rate of return is 20%.

Required: Compute the net present value of Carmichael's investment for *each* of the following assumed patterns of cash inflows that could result from the sale of these towers.

(1) Cash inflows of $100,000 each year for 6 years.
(2) Cash inflows of $60,000 each year for 8 years.
(3) Cash inflows of $200,000 during the first year, $100,000 in each of the second and third years, and $50,000 in each of the fourth and fifth years.

20-25 Bowler Company is considering purchasing a packaging machine for $20,000 that will have a residual value of $200 after 10 years. It would be depreciated using the straight-line method. The machine would reduce labor costs in the shipping department by $8,000 per year. Experience with such machines suggests that finished goods that could be sold for $3,200 would be ruined each year by the packaging machine. Ownership of the machine also would increase property taxes and insurance (paid annually) by $300 per year. Bowler's required rate of return is 20%.

Required: (1) Prepare an analysis to determine whether the purchase of this machine is an acceptable capital expenditure for Bowler.

(2) What is the highest price Bowler should be willing to pay for the packaging machine?

20-26 Keeler Company is considering purchasing an overhead conveyor system for $200,000 that will have a residual value of $3,000 after eight years. This conveyor system would be depreciated on a straight-line basis. The conveyor system would reduce labor costs in the shipping department by $60,000 per year. Experience with such systems indicates that $7,000 would be spent each year on maintenance to keep it operating properly. Ownership of the new conveyor system also would increase property taxes and insurance by $2,000 per year. Keeler's required rate of return is 16%.

Required: (1) Prepare an analysis to determine whether the purchase of this over-head conveyor system is an acceptable capital expenditure for Keeler.

(2) What is the highest price Keeler should be willing to pay for the over-head conveyor system?

20-27 A company is considering the following three capital expenditure proposals:

(a) Proposal A—An investment of $10,000 promising cash receipts of $3,600 per year for 5 years.

(b) Proposal B—An investment of $10,000 promising a single cash receipt of $20,000 after 5 years.

(c) Proposal C—An investment of $10,000 promising a cash receipt of $2,000 each year for 4 years and $12,000 in the fifth year.

Required: (1) Prepare an analysis to determine the acceptability of each of the capital expenditure proposals, assuming a 16% minimum required rate of return.

(2) If only one of the three proposals can be selected for investment, which one should it be? Write a brief justification for your selection.

20-28 A company is considering the following three capital expenditure proposals:

(a) Proposal A—An investment of $12,000 promising cash receipts of $2,700 per year for 20 years.

(b) Proposal B—An investment of $12,000 promising a single cash receipt of $390,000 after 20 years.

(c) Proposal C—An investment of $12,000 promising a cash receipt of $2,300 each year for 19 years and $45,000 in the 20th year.

Required: (1) Prepare an analysis to determine the acceptability of each of the capital expenditure proposals, assuming a 20% minimum required rate of return.

(2) If only one of the three proposals can be selected for investment, which one should it be? Write a brief justification for your selection.

20-29 A company is considering the following investment proposals:

(a) $12,000 invested in a savings account that pays $240 (in cash) quarterly.

(b) $12,000 invested in a delivery van, which would reduce delivery expenses so that cash payments are decreased by $1,200 per year for 10 years.

(c) $12,000 invested in land, for which real estate taxes of $100 would be paid each year. The company expects to be able to sell the land after 8 years for $25,000.

Required: Compute the payback period for each of the proposals.

20-30 Refer to 20-23.

Required: Compute the payback period of McKenzie Company for this machine.

20-31 Refer to 20-23.

Required: Compute the average rate of return on investment for the machine being considered by McKenzie Company.

20-32 Refer to 20-22.

Required: Compute the average rate of return on Tom Hammond's land investment.

20-33 Merimac Company can accept either capital expenditure proposal A or B (but not both), or it can reject both proposals. Proposal A requires an investment of $700 and promises increased net cash inflows of $220 for each of the next five years. Proposal B requires an investment of $700 and promises increased net cash inflows of $230 per year for the next four years and $100 in the fifth year. The company's required rate of return is 20%.

Required: (1) Prepare an analysis to determine which (if either) of the proposals should be selected for investment.
(2) How would your answer to (1) be altered if one of the two proposals must be selected?

20-34 The Mosely Company has identified the following capital expenditure proposals as acceptable. Only $50,000 is available for investment, however.

Investment Proposal	Required Investment	Net Present Value
A	$10,000	$ 4,000
B	20,000	12,000
C	10,000	5,000
D	30,000	16,000
E	10,000	7,000
F	20,000	13,000

Required: Determine the combination of proposals to be selected.

Making Evaluations

20-35 The Greenville Manufacturing Company is considering replacing an old machine that cost the company $80,000 five years ago. This machine could be used for 10 more years, at which time it would have no residual value. If it were sold now, net receipts from its disposal would be $25,000. The old machine requires four operators to run it, each earning $28,000 per year.

The new machine, which costs $145,000, has an estimated life of 10 years and a residual value of $6,000 at the end of that time. The new machine requires only three operators, each earning $30,000 per year. Actual direct materials costs would be slightly less with the new machine because materials waste (currently $4,000 per year) could be cut in half.

Maintenance on the old machine, which currently runs approximately $3,000 per year, would be decreased by 40% with the new machine. At present, power costs are $20,000 per year. The new machine would require 5% less power. Greenville estimates that the revenues associated with the product produced by the old machine, $150,000 per year, would not be changed by purchasing the new machine. Greenville's required rate of return is 20%.

Required: (1) Prepare a schedule of the relevant cash flows for this capital expenditure proposal to replace the old machine. Indicate any cash flows that are not relevant, and explain why they are not relevant.
(2) Compute the net present value of the proposal. Is this proposal acceptable?
(3) What maximum amount should Greenville be willing to pay for the new machine?

20-36 Several years ago, Dane Company signed a contract to supply 5,000 units of a special product each year to one of its customers at a price of $20 per unit. This contract, which runs for five more years, is noncancelable.

Dane is currently producing the product with an old machine that can be kept running for five more years if $12,000 of maintenance cost per year is incurred. Other operating costs to produce this product with the old machine (excluding maintenance) total $60,000 per year. The old machine has no residual value now and will have none after the contract is fulfilled.

East Company has recently offered to sell Dane 5,000 units of this product per year over the next five years for $14 per unit. Dane had almost decided to accept this offer from East as the best possible way to satisfy its contract when a new machine capable of producing the 5,000 units each year for $56,000 total cash operating costs per year became available. This new machine would cost $55,000 and would have a residual value of $10,000 after five years. Dane's required rate of return is 16%.

Required: (1) Is purchasing 5,000 units of the product per year from East Company preferable to producing them on the old machine? Explain.

(2) By computing the net present value of this proposal, determine the acceptability of the capital expenditure proposal to buy the new machine.

(3) If East Company withdraws its offer to supply the units, would your answer to (2) change? Explain, supporting your explanation with computations if necessary.

20-37 Porter Paper Company has just been ordered by the court to install a pollution-control device on the exhaust system of one of its production processes. The company's required rate of return is 20%. Two devices are available on the market.

Device A costs $20,000 and is expected to last 12 years, after which it would have a zero residual value. It costs $600 per year to operate and maintain.

Device B costs $12,000 and would last only six years, after which it would have a residual value of $1,000. If device B is purchased, Porter would have to replace it in six years. The second unit would have an expected cost at that time of $18,000. The second unit would also be expected to have a residual value of $1,000 at the end of its six-year life. Both the first and second unit of device B cost $800 per year to operate and maintain.

Required: (1) By computing the net present value of the investment for each of the devices, determine which pollution-control device Porter should purchase.

(2) How much *per year* would the court have to fine Porter for ignoring the order to ensure that it would be less expensive (in terms of present value of costs) for the company to comply with the court order by purchasing one of the devices?

(3) Suppose the court fine is less than the cost of complying with the court order. What else should Porter Paper consider as it decides what to do?

20-38 Wayne Industries is considering introducing a new product. Wayne believes it can sell 32,000 units of this product per year for 10 years at a price of $9 per unit. Wayne estimates that the cost of producing the product would be $3 per unit. Additional production costs of $75,000 would be required during the first year, however, while the production department became familiar with the techniques required to produce the new product. Cash payments for advertising this product are expected to be $50,000 per year. Variable selling costs are expected to be about $2 per unit sold.

Wayne Industries has already spent $300,000 on research and development of this product. If the new product is introduced, an additional $220,000 would have to be invested immediately to obtain the additional plant and equipment necessary for production. This additional plant and equipment would have a residual value of $100,000 after 10 years. Wayne's required rate of return is 20%.

Required: (1) Prepare a schedule of the relevant annual net cash flows for this capital expenditure proposal to introduce this new product.

(2) Compute the net present value of the proposal.

(3) Discuss whether Wayne should accept this proposal.

20-39 Midus Muffin Shops, a chain of fast-food shops serving breakfast 24 hours a day, is considering opening a shop in Danville. The shop could be opened in one of two ways, either by building the shop between a west-side shopping center and Danville's small college campus or by buying a vacant building on the edge of the downtown business district. The expected investment required in either case is $100,000. An extensive analysis of the potential of these two locations, however, suggests that the expected cash inflows and outflows from their operations would be very different.

The downtown location would have a much greater volume of customers than the west-side location for at least five years. Furthermore, this volume would be concentrated between 6 a.m. and 11:30 p.m., allowing considerable savings in wages during the early-morning hours. The volume of the west-side location would be smaller and more uniform throughout the day and night.

The costs of upkeep for the new west-side building should be considerably less than for the older building downtown, however. Furthermore, an interstate highway currently under construction 100 miles to the north is expected eventually to come through Danville within three blocks of the west-side location after five or more years, increasing the potential volume of customers to that shop by a considerable amount.

Required: Assume that you are a consultant to Midus and have been assigned to make a recommendation to the company about what to do in Danville. Write the president of Midus a memo describing the approach that should be used to make this decision, listing the important factors that you expect to influence the decision, and requesting specific information that you will need to evaluate the decision alternatives.

20-40   Mary T. lives with her mother and is an administrative secretary for a large architectural company in a small midwestern city. She earns $25,000 per year. She dreams of being an architect, however. Salaries for new architects in her company start at $40,000 per year. Mary has been accepted at several universities. Because she is bright and ambitious, she believes she can graduate in four years (including summer school) unless she works part-time, in which case she would need five years to graduate. She has been looking at college catalogues for several months, calculating the total costs for tuition, fees, room and board, books and supplies, and so on. She has tabulated these costs and ruled out all but one school because of the high out-of-state tuition. She has estimated the following costs per year of attending the state university:

Tuition and fees	$3,800
Room and board..	3,500
Books and supplies....................................	500
Automobile..	600
Clothes	400
Miscellaneous	200
Annual Cost	$9,000

Although it seems like a lot of money, Mary believes her total cost over four years ($36,000) would be paid back before she finishes her first year working as an architect. Before she resigns from her job, she comes to you for your opinion.

Required: Write Mary a letter describing how she should evaluate this decision. Make some tentative calculations using any of the preceding information that you feel is relevant and assuming any additional information that is necessary to demonstrate how she should consider the monetary aspects of her decision. Disregard income taxes.

20-41   Yesterday, Sandy received a note from her father, who is now 45 years old, asking for advice in starting his plans for retirement. The pertinent parts of that note are as follows:

. . . and you know how much your mom and I like to travel. I was thinking that my pension from the company plus social security wouldn't be enough to allow us much travel during those years while we're still young enough to be active. Assuming our health continues, we'd like to supplement our retirement income 'til we're about 75. I thought you might be able to clear my thinking a bit since you're taking those business classes at the university.

It isn't investment advice that I'm asking for. You know that I'll just put anything I save in certificates of deposit at the Community Saving and Loan. I think I should be able to average about 6% interest per year there. The main things I'm having trouble thinking about are whether I should start saving now or wait 'til you finish school, and whether to retire at 55, 60, or 65.

Incidentally, your Grandpa just told me that he put $25,000 in U.S. savings bonds in my name when he sold the drugstore. I was 20 years old then. They've probably earned only about 4% per year, so I doubt whether they will help much. What do you think?

Someone at work told me that if I had a certain amount of money saved when I retired, I could withdraw about 9% of that amount every year for 20 years before the money ran out. Could that be possible? By my reckoning that would be 180% of what I started with. If it's true, maybe I could retire at 55 after all. I'd like your explanation, though, before I rely on that idea.

Required: Assuming that you are Sandy, write a note to your dad to answer his questions in order to help him begin his retirement planning. (Ignore income tax considerations.)

20-42 Miss Priss Cosmetics currently reimburses its forty saleswomen for the use of their personal automobiles for the business. Terri K., company sales manager, has been trying without success to persuade the company to buy a number of cars to be used by her sales staff in the future, however. Terri's assistant has estimated the costs of operating company-owned automobiles an expected 30,000 miles per year on the basis of accounting records for automobiles used by company executives. The cost estimates in comparison with average mileage reimbursements are as follows:

Comparisons of Annual Costs of Company Automobiles with Annual Mileage Reimbursements

Company-Owned Car

Gas and oil	$1,800
Tires	300
Maintenance	400
Insurance and property taxes	500
Licenses, parking, tolls, etc.	200
Washing and waxing	100
Depreciation ($16,500 − $1,500) ÷ 3 years	5,000
Total Annual Operating Costs	$8,300

Mileage Reimbursement

30,000 @ $0.30	$9,000

The company is currently paying $0.30 per mile on an average of 30,000 miles driven by each saleswoman, and the sales manager believes that considerable savings are possible if the company buys cars to be used by sales personnel. She was recently questioned by John Q., the company's financial vice-president, about high costs in her department at a recent managers' meeting. Straining to keep her temper, she responded that if the company weren't so tight, it could save $28,000 per year by buying automobiles for the sales staff instead of paying that high mileage rate. She had the annual cost comparison to show him if he challenged her on her statement.

At previous meetings, Terri had emphasized that a fleet of clean new cars with the company name on them would improve the company image and increase brand-name recognition, both factors leading to increased future sales. She emphasized that this would be especially true given that many of the sales routes would be lengthened next year to an average of 36,000 miles per year and would include areas where the company's products had not previously been sold. Terri had repeatedly been told that it would be too expensive for the company to buy cars for the sales staff to use, which is why she had instructed her assistant to prepare the cost comparison shown above.

Required: (1) Assume that Miss Priss Cosmetics has a cost of capital of 10% and that you are the company's financial vice-president. Write the sales manager a brief memo explaining why it would not be desirable for the company to buy cars for her staff in spite of the annual costs estimated by her assistant. Ignore the lengthening of sales routes and the possibility that sales might be increased.

(2) Now assume that you are the sales manager. Write the financial vice-president a memo describing how the analysis in (1) would be affected by (a) longer sales routes and (b) possible sales increases due to an improved company image and name recognition.

20-43   Yesterday, you received the following letter for your advice column in the local paper:

DR. DECISIVE

Dear Dr. Decisive:

Last weekend, my roommate (let's just call him "Crunch") and I were visiting my father. Crunch and my father have a lot in common—Crunch is a varsity football player (left tackle), and Dad is a diehard football fan. Anyway, Crunch and I were looking through one of Dad's billions of football scrapbooks and came across an article describing the contracts of two NFL quarterbacks. Well, a good weekend got better because we were soon in the middle of one of our famous friendly debates. We couldn't (and still can't) agree on which quarterback got the better deal. According to the article, each quarterback received a six-year contract. "Lightning Z" would earn a total of $45 million, or an average of $7.5 million per year, and "Zinger B" would earn a total of $40.5 million, or an average of $6.75 million per year. So, the article said that, based on annual average salaries, "Lightning Z" was the higher-paid player. I agree with the article—it's an obvious conclusion—but Crunch disagrees with me.

According to the contracts, here's how each was supposed to be paid:

Year	Lightning Z	Zinger B
2006	$ 3 million	$13 million
2007	$10 million	$ 8.325 million
2008	$ 8.275 million	$ 7.675 million
2009	$ 6.55 million	$ 6.75 million
2010	$ 7.825 million	$ 3 million
2011	$ 9.35 million	$ 1.75 million
Total	$45 million	$40.5 million

Before contract negotiations, Lightning Z was about to enter the last year of a previous contract in which he was supposed to earn $4.5 million in 2006. To negotiate a better contract in later years, and to help his team, he "gave up" $1.5 million in salary in 2006. (This gave his team enough room below the salary cap to hire a top draft pick in 2006.) Zinger B negotiated a $10 million signing bonus (which he received at the beginning of 2006) as part of his $13 million 2006 salary.

You can see that even after giving up $1.5 million in 2006, Lightning Z is clearly getting the better deal. Crunch says Zinger B has the better deal because he is getting more money "up front."

Please help me convince Crunch that even though he knows his football (and is quite good at playing football), I'm right about this. A lot is riding on this. Whoever loses (and your answer is the deciding factor) must buy the winner two tickets to the next Chiefs game. I'm still trying to decide whom to take with me (maybe Crunch, maybe not).

"Undecided"

Required: Meet with your Dr. Decisive team and write a response to "Undecided."

END NOTES

[a]"Court Cuts Exxon Spill Award", Columbia Daily Tribune, Saturday, December 23, 2006, 8A.
[b]http://www.gdc4s.com/careers/benefits.cfm#Fitness_Program

TABLE 20-1

Present Value of $1 Due in n Periods

$$Factor = \frac{1}{(1 + i)^n}$$

(n) Period	1%	2%	3%	4%	5%	6%	7%	8%	9%	10%	12%	14%	15%	16%	18%	20%	24%
1	.9901	.9804	.9709	.9615	.9524	.9434	.9346	.9259	.9174	.9091	.8929	.8772	.8696	.8621	.8475	.8333	.8065
2	.9803	.9612	.9426	.9246	.9070	.8900	.8734	.8573	.8417	.8264	.7972	.7695	.7561	.7432	.7182	.6944	.6504
3	.9706	.9423	.9151	.8890	.8638	.8396	.8163	.7938	.7722	.7513	.7118	.6750	.6575	.6407	.6086	.5787	.5245
4	.9610	.9238	.8885	.8548	.8227	.7921	.7629	.7350	.7084	.6830	.6355	.5921	.5718	.5523	.5158	.4823	.4230
5	.9515	.9057	.8626	.8219	.7835	.7473	.7130	.6806	.6499	.6209	.5674	.5194	.4972	.4761	.4371	.4019	.3411
6	.9420	.8880	.8375	.7903	.7462	.7050	.6663	.6302	.5963	.5645	.5066	.4556	.4323	.4104	.3704	.3349	.2751
7	.9327	.8706	.8131	.7599	.7107	.6651	.6227	.5835	.5470	.5132	.4523	.3996	.3759	.3538	.3139	.2791	.2218
8	.9235	.8535	.7894	.7307	.6768	.6274	.5820	.5403	.5019	.4665	.4039	.3506	.3269	.3050	.2660	.2326	.1789
9	.9143	.8368	.7664	.7026	.6446	.5919	.5439	.5002	.4604	.4241	.3606	.3075	.2843	.2630	.2255	.1938	.1443
10	.9053	.8203	.7441	.6756	.6139	.5584	.5083	.4632	.4224	.3855	.3220	.2697	.2472	.2267	.1911	.1615	.1164
11	.8963	.8043	.7224	.6496	.5847	.5268	.4751	.4289	.3875	.3505	.2875	.2366	.2149	.1954	.1619	.1346	.0938
12	.8874	.7885	.7014	.6246	.5568	.4970	.4440	.3971	.3555	.3186	.2567	.2076	.1869	.1685	.1372	.1122	.0757
13	.8787	.7730	.6810	.6006	.5303	.4688	.4150	.3677	.3262	.2897	.2292	.1821	.1625	.1452	.1163	.0935	.0610
14	.8700	.7579	.6611	.5775	.5051	.4423	.3878	.3405	.2992	.2633	.2046	.1597	.1413	.1252	.0985	.0779	.0492
15	.8613	.7430	.6419	.5553	.4810	.4173	.3624	.3152	.2745	.2394	.1827	.1401	.1229	.1079	.0835	.0649	.0397
16	.8528	.7284	.6232	.5339	.4581	.3936	.3387	.2919	.2519	.2176	.1631	.1229	.1069	.0930	.0708	.0541	.0320
17	.8444	.7142	.6050	.5134	.4363	.3714	.3166	.2703	.2311	.1978	.1456	.1078	.0929	.0802	.0600	.0451	.0258
18	.8360	.7002	.5874	.4936	.4155	.3503	.2959	.2502	.2120	.1799	.1300	.0946	.0808	.0691	.0508	.0376	.0208
19	.8277	.6864	.5703	.4746	.3957	.3305	.2765	.2317	.1945	.1635	.1161	.0829	.0703	.0596	.0431	.0313	.0168
20	.8195	.6730	.5537	.4564	.3769	.3118	.2584	.2145	.1784	.1486	.1037	.0728	.0611	.0514	.0365	.0261	.0135
21	.8114	.6598	.5375	.4388	.3589	.2942	.2415	.1987	.1637	.1351	.0926	.0638	.0531	.0443	.0309	.0217	.0109
22	.8034	.6468	.5219	.4220	.3418	.2775	.2257	.1839	.1502	.1228	.0826	.0560	.0462	.0382	.0262	.0181	.0088
23	.7954	.6342	.5067	.4057	.3256	.2618	.2109	.1703	.1378	.1117	.0738	.0491	.0402	.0329	.0222	.0151	.0071
24	.7876	.6217	.4919	.3901	.3101	.2470	.1971	.1577	.1264	.1015	.0659	.0431	.0349	.0284	.0188	.0126	.0057
25	.7798	.6095	.4776	.3751	.2953	.2330	.1842	.1460	.1160	.0923	.0588	.0378	.0304	.0245	.0160	.0105	.0046
26	.7720	.5976	.4637	.3607	.2812	.2198	.1722	.1352	.1064	.0839	.0525	.0331	.0264	.0211	.0135	.0087	.0037
27	.7644	.5859	.4502	.3468	.2678	.2074	.1609	.1252	.0976	.0763	.0469	.0291	.0230	.0182	.0115	.0073	.0030
28	.7568	.5744	.4371	.3335	.2551	.1956	.1504	.1159	.0895	.0693	.0419	.0255	.0200	.0157	.0097	.0061	.0024
29	.7493	.5631	.4243	.3207	.2429	.1846	.1406	.1073	.0822	.0630	.0374	.0224	.0174	.0135	.0082	.0051	.0020
30	.7419	.5521	.4120	.3083	.2314	.1741	.1314	.0994	.0754	.0573	.0334	.0196	.0151	.0116	.0070	.0042	.0016

TABLE 20-2

Present Value of an Annuity of $1 per Period

$$\text{Factor} = \frac{1 - \frac{1}{(1 + i)^n}}{i}$$

(n) Number of Periods	1%	2%	3%	4%	5%	6%	7%	8%	9%	10%	12%	14%	15%	16%	18%	20%	24%
1	0.9901	0.9804	0.9709	0.9615	0.9524	0.9434	0.9346	0.9259	0.9174	0.9091	0.8929	0.8772	0.8696	0.8621	0.8475	0.8333	0.8065
2	1.9704	1.9416	1.9135	1.8861	1.8594	1.8334	1.8080	1.7833	1.7591	1.7355	1.6901	1.6467	1.6257	1.6052	1.5656	1.5278	1.4568
3	2.9410	2.8839	2.8286	2.7751	2.7232	2.6730	2.6243	2.5771	2.5313	2.4869	2.4018	2.3216	2.2832	2.2459	2.1743	2.1065	1.9813
4	3.9020	3.8077	3.7171	3.6299	3.5460	3.4651	3.3872	3.3121	3.2397	3.1699	3.0373	2.9137	2.8550	2.7982	2.6901	2.5887	2.4043
5	4.8534	4.7135	4.5797	4.4518	4.3295	4.2124	4.1002	3.9927	3.8897	3.7908	3.6048	3.4331	3.3522	3.2743	3.1272	2.9906	2.7454
6	5.7955	5.6014	5.4172	5.2421	5.0757	4.9173	4.7665	4.6229	4.4859	4.3553	4.1114	3.8887	3.7845	3.6847	3.4976	3.3255	3.0205
7	6.7282	6.4720	6.2303	6.0021	5.7864	5.5824	5.3893	5.2064	5.0330	4.8684	4.5638	4.2883	4.1604	4.0386	3.8115	3.6046	3.2423
8	7.6517	7.3255	7.0197	6.7327	6.4632	6.2098	5.9713	5.7466	5.5348	5.3349	4.9676	4.6389	4.4873	4.3436	4.0776	3.8372	3.4212
9	8.5660	8.1622	7.7861	7.4353	7.1078	6.8017	6.5152	6.2469	5.9952	5.7590	5.3282	4.9464	4.7716	4.6065	4.3030	4.0310	3.5655
10	9.4713	8.9826	8.5302	8.1109	7.7217	7.3601	7.0236	6.7101	6.4177	6.1446	5.6502	5.2161	5.0188	4.8332	4.4941	4.1925	3.6819
11	10.3676	9.7868	9.2526	8.7605	8.3064	7.8869	7.4987	7.1390	6.8052	6.4951	5.9377	5.4527	5.2337	5.0286	4.6560	4.3271	3.7757
12	11.2551	10.5753	9.9540	9.3851	8.8633	8.3838	7.9427	7.5361	7.1607	6.8137	6.1944	5.6603	5.4206	5.1971	4.7932	4.4392	3.8514
13	12.1337	11.3484	10.6350	9.9856	9.3936	8.8527	8.3577	7.9038	7.4869	7.1034	6.4235	5.8424	5.5831	5.3423	4.9095	4.5327	3.9124
14	13.0037	12.1062	11.2961	10.5631	9.8986	9.2950	8.7455	8.2442	7.7862	7.3667	6.6282	6.0021	5.7245	5.4675	5.0081	4.6106	3.9616
15	13.8651	12.8493	11.9379	11.1184	10.3797	9.7122	9.1079	8.5595	8.0607	7.6061	6.8109	6.1422	5.8474	5.5755	5.0916	4.6755	4.0013
16	14.7179	13.5777	12.5611	11.6523	10.8378	10.1059	9.4466	8.8514	8.3126	7.8237	6.9740	6.2651	5.9542	5.6685	5.1624	4.7296	4.0333
17	15.5623	14.2919	13.1661	12.1657	11.2741	10.4773	9.7632	9.1216	8.5436	8.0216	7.1196	6.3729	6.0472	5.7487	5.2223	4.7746	4.0591
18	16.3983	14.9920	13.7535	12.6593	11.6896	10.8276	10.0591	9.3719	8.7556	8.2014	7.2497	6.4674	6.1280	5.8178	5.2732	4.8122	4.0799
19	17.2260	15.6785	14.3238	13.1339	12.0853	11.1581	10.3356	9.6036	8.9501	8.3649	7.3658	6.5504	6.1982	5.8775	5.3162	4.8435	4.0967
20	18.0456	16.3514	14.8775	13.5903	12.4622	11.4699	10.5940	9.8181	9.1285	8.5136	7.4694	6.6231	6.2593	5.9288	5.3527	4.8696	4.1103
21	18.8570	17.0112	15.4150	14.0292	12.8212	11.7641	10.8355	10.0168	9.2922	8.6487	7.5620	6.6870	6.3125	5.9731	5.3837	4.8913	4.1212
22	19.6604	17.6580	15.9369	14.4511	13.1630	12.0416	11.0612	10.2007	9.4424	8.7715	7.6446	6.7429	6.3587	6.0113	5.4099	4.9094	4.1300
23	20.4558	18.2922	16.4436	14.8568	13.4886	12.3034	11.2722	10.3711	9.5802	8.8832	7.7184	6.7921	6.3988	6.0442	5.4321	4.9245	4.1371
24	21.2434	18.9139	16.9355	15.2470	13.7986	12.5504	11.4693	10.5288	9.7066	8.9847	7.7843	6.8351	6.4338	6.0726	5.4509	4.9371	4.1428
25	22.0232	19.5235	17.4131	15.6221	14.0939	12.7834	11.6536	10.6748	9.8226	9.0770	7.8431	6.8729	6.4641	6.0971	5.4669	4.9476	4.1474
26	22.7952	20.1210	17.8768	15.9828	14.3752	13.0032	11.8258	10.8100	9.9290	9.1609	7.8957	6.9061	6.4906	6.1182	5.4804	4.9563	4.1511
27	23.5596	20.7069	18.3270	16.3296	14.6430	13.2105	11.9867	10.9352	10.0266	9.2372	7.9426	6.9352	6.5135	6.1364	5.4919	4.9636	4.1542
28	24.3164	21.2813	18.7641	16.6631	14.8981	13.4062	12.1371	11.0511	10.1161	9.3066	7.9844	6.9607	6.5335	6.1520	5.5016	4.9697	4.1566
29	25.0658	21.8444	19.1885	16.9837	15.1411	13.5907	12.2777	11.1584	10.1983	9.3696	8.0218	6.9830	6.5509	6.1656	5.5098	4.9747	4.1585
30	25.8077	22.3965	19.6004	17.2920	15.3725	13.7648	12.4090	11.2578	10.2737	9.4269	8.0552	7.0027	6.5660	6.1772	5.5168	4.9789	4.1601

CHAPTER 21

REPORTING PROPERTY, PLANT, AND EQUIPMENT, AND INTANGIBLES

"SOMETHING RARE AND REMARKABLE IS GOING ON, AS COMPANIES BUY EQUIPMENT AT FIERCE RATES. THE BENEFITS COULD BE ENORMOUS."

— JOSEPH SPIERS

1. What types of assets does a company include in its property, plant, and equipment, and how does the company compute its historical costs?

2. Why does a company depreciate its property, plant, and equipment, and what are the causes of depreciation?

3. How does a company calculate its depreciation expense, and why does it compute depreciation expense differently for financial reporting than for income taxes?

4. How does a company evaluate the impairment of its property, plant, and equipment?

5. How does a company record and report the disposal of property, plant, and equipment?

6. How do external users evaluate information about a company's property, plant, and equipment?

7. What are intangible assets and natural resource assets, and what does a company report about them?

On **Hershey Foods**' (maker of "Caramello Candy Bars") December 31, 2005 balance sheet, the company shows that it owns $1,659 million (net) in property, plant, and equipment—39 percent of its total assets. On **Rocky Mountain Chocolate Factory's** February 28, 2006 balance sheet, its property, plant, and equipment was $6.7 million (net). Given that its total assets were about $19 million, 35 percent of Rocky Mountain's assets are included in property, plant, and equipment. These dollar amounts of current assets shown on Hershey Foods' and Rocky Mountain's balance sheets result from prior capital budgeting decisions as well as the accounting methods the companies used to keep track of property, plant, and equipment.

There are various ways to understand the meaning of these disclosures. For example, if Hershey manufactures one piece of candy for an average cost of three cents, its property, plant, and equipment asset account balances held the dollar equivalent of over 55 billion pieces! Hershey Foods' $1,659 million in property, plant, and equipment is almost 248 times greater than Rocky Mountain Chocolate Factory's $6.7 million. Should you conclude that Hershey has physical assets that are about 248 times larger than those of Rocky Mountain? Another way to think about these amounts is to think about how the assets are used. For example, the assets included in property, plant, and equipment are purchased to manufacture and sell the company's products, as well as to support the activities of the company's managers. In their respective financial statements, Hershey Foods reported revenue (net sales) of $4,836 million, depreciation expense of $200 million, and purchases of property, plant, and equipment of $181 million. Rocky Mountain Chocolate Factory reported revenue of $28.1 million, depreciation expense of $799 thousand, and purchases of property, plant, and equipment of $1.3 million. So Hershey Foods' revenue was 2.9 times its property, plant, and equipment (net) and 26.7 times its purchases of property, plant, and equipment, while Rocky Mountain Chocolate Factory's was 4.2 and 21.6 times, respectively.

Can you conclude whether Hershey Foods or Rocky Mountain Chocolate Factory is better at managing its property, plant, and equipment? What factors besides these amounts on the balance sheets, income statements, and cash flow statements of the two companies should you consider?

© PHOTODISC/GETTY IMAGES

What long-term assets can you identify in this picture?

A company uses the term **property, plant, and equipment** to describe all of the physical (tangible), long-term assets it uses in its operations. So when you walk into a **Wal-Mart** store, the land, building, and equipment (including its cash registers as well as shelves) are property, plant, and equipment. If you visited a **Ford** factory, the land, building, and manufacturing machinery are property, plant, and equipment. If you visited either company's head office, the land, building, and equipment (including computers and office furniture) are property, plant, and equipment. As we discussed briefly in Chapter 7 of Volume 1, a company reports these assets in a separate section of the balance sheet, often called *property, plant, and equipment*; *long-term* assets; or *fixed* assets. It reports land at its original cost because of the assumption that the land does not get used up, but it reports the other property, plant, and equipment assets at their cost, less their accumulated depreciation.

In Chapter 19, we explained how companies report on inventory and how external users use a company's disclosures of inventory and cost of goods sold for evaluation. In this chapter, we explain how companies report on their property, plant, and equipment and depreciation expense in the financial statements included in their annual reports. Because many companies also have intangible assets and/or natural resource assets, we also discuss the accounting issues related to these assets.

ISSUES INVOLVED IN REPORTING PROPERTY, PLANT, AND EQUIPMENT

1 What types of assets does a company include in its property, plant, and equipment, and how does the company compute its historical costs?

Make a list of a few long-term assets you own. Your list may include your watch or jewelry, a computer, a car, etc. Next, use your best judgment to write down a dollar value for each asset. How did you decide which value to use? Did you have any problems deciding what value to assign? Write down why you chose the values you selected for each of your assets.

Exhibit 21-1 shows the list for Jennifer Book, a business student. In addition to writing her list, Jennifer explained why she had some difficulty deciding the dollar values to assign to her assets. Perhaps your difficulties were similar to hers. Let's examine the problems she encountered assigning values.

EXHIBIT 21-1	JENNIFER BOOK'S LIST OF FOUR ASSETS SHE OWNS AND SOME ISSUES WITH ASSIGNING DOLLAR VALUES TO THEM	
Asset	**Value**	**Issues in Deciding Dollar Value**
Computer	$800	I paid about $2,000 for the computer when I bought it two years ago. But I'm sure I couldn't sell it for that amount today. The way computers get outdated so fast, I figure it is worth less than half of what I paid for it.
Clothes	$0	Even though I paid about $2,500 for them, I will give them away when they wear out or are out of style. Therefore, I don't see that I should give them any value.
Car	$12,000	I bought the car two years ago for $18,000, but I am not going to sell it for another 4 years, so the "blue book" value doesn't seem relevant to me. Since I have owned the car for one-third of the time I plan to own it, I assigned a value of $12,000.
Wedding ring	$600	This is the amount my husband and I paid for the ring three years ago. I think it is worth much more than $600 now, but I am not sure how much more. I saw a ring like mine in a jewelry store for $1,100, but you know stores charge a huge markup. Of course, I really only paid for half of it.

As we show in Exhibit 21-1, Jennifer lists her computer, clothes, car, and wedding ring as some of her long-term assets. We see that Jennifer has doubts about the appropriate dollar values to list for her assets. For example, even though she purchased the computer two years ago for $2,000, she knows that she could not sell it for that amount today. She has used the computer a lot, and technology has improved substantially since her purchase. She concludes that $800 is the best value to list. For her clothes, she decides to list them at $0 because she knows that she won't sell them—eventually she will give them to a charity. However, for her car, which she bought two years ago for $18,000 and plans to keep for another four years, she lists the value at $12,000—two-thirds of its original cost. "I am not going to sell the car for another 4 years, so the 'blue book' value doesn't seem relevant to me," she says. The $600 Jennifer lists for her wedding ring represents the amount she and her husband paid for the ring at the time of the purchase— the ring's dollar value at the time she acquired the asset. Although Jennifer decided to write down $600, she expresses some concerns about it. She thinks the ring is worth more than $600 today (although she has no intention of selling it) because she saw a similar ring selling for $1,100. On the other hand, she points out that she purchased the ring jointly with her husband and so has only $300 invested in the ring.

Do you agree with Jennifer's decisions? Was she consistent in her approach to valuing the assets? Why or why not? Did you have valuation problems similar to Jennifer's? Do you think that a long-term asset you own is worth more than its original cost, but do not know its value? Or, on the other hand, do you have a long-term asset that you think is no longer worth what you paid for it, but you do not know what amount to write down?

The difficulties that Jennifer had in assigning dollar values for long-term assets illustrate why financial statement users, in order to make informed business decisions, need to understand how companies account for and report on property, plant, and equipment. Notice that Jennifer did not use any accounting rules to help her decide. A company, however, is required to use GAAP, which for property, plant, and equipment is based on two accounting concepts we introduced earlier in the book—the *historical cost concept* and the *matching principle*. Let's review these concepts.

Recall that the historical cost concept states that a company records its transactions on the basis of the dollars it exchanged (in other words, the cost) in the transaction. Once a company records a transaction, it usually retains the *cost* involved in the transaction in its accounting records. For instance, in 2000, Unlimited Decadence paid $35,000 for 10 acres of land on which to build its headquarters. At the end of 2008, real estate professionals estimate that the land has a market value greater than $85,000. Under the historical cost concept, Unlimited Decadence continues to show the land on its 2008 ending balance sheet at $35,000.

Which accounts would be affected, and how would they be affected, if a company records its property, plant, and equipment at more than the company paid for them?

Many accounting and business experts express concerns about the usefulness of the historical cost concept. They ask, "How does including the $35,000 cost of the land in Unlimited Decadence's 2008 ending balance sheet help investors and creditors make business decisions?" In other words, they question the *relevance* of presenting this historical cost amount. Supporters of the historical cost concept argue that if the company has no intention of selling the asset, then the market value is *not* relevant. Since Unlimited Decadence has no intention of selling its headquarters building and the land underneath it, the $85,000 is not relevant.

To whom might the market value be relevant?

Supporters of historical cost also argue that the *reliability* of historical costs and GAAP's emphasis on *conservatism* outweigh any potential increase in relevance that might be gained from using the market value. In essence, GAAP supporters say, "We know that Unlimited Decadence paid $35,000 for its land. Until someone actually buys the land from Unlimited Decadence for $85,000, we are not sure how reliable that dollar amount is. If an investor made a business decision based on the $85,000 estimate and the land was later sold for only $50,000, that investor might have been hurt by our estimate. With historical cost accounting, at least external users know what information they are getting." Also we know that all accountants would conclude that the historical cost was $35,000, whereas they probably would differ in their estimates of the market value.

 Whose side do you take on this discussion—the supporters or the critics of the historical cost concept? Explain your position.

The matching principle states that to determine its net income for an accounting period, a company computes the total expenses involved in earning the revenues of the period and deducts them from the revenues earned in that period. Because property, plant, and equipment provide benefits every period that they are used and because they have a finite life, a company includes a portion of their cost as an expense in its measurement of net income for each accounting period that the company benefits from their use. For example, Unlimited Decadence owns machines that wrap its candy bars after they are produced. Each accounting period in which it uses a candy-wrapping machine, it matches a portion of the cost of the machine against the revenues it recorded during the period. Recall from Chapter 5 of Volume 1 that the part of the cost of property, plant, and equipment that a company allocates as an expense to each accounting period in which the company uses the asset is called **depreciation expense**. The recording of depreciation expense is an end-of-period adjustment. Also recall from Chapter 7 of Volume 1 that **accumulated depreciation** is the total depreciation recorded on an asset to date, and that the **book value** of an asset, or **net asset value**, is the cost of the asset less its accumulated depreciation.

So, the historical cost concept and the matching principle provide the basis for how a company accounts for property, plant, and equipment and reports on them in its financial statements. In the next sections we will address seven important issues: (1) computing the historical cost of property, plant, and equipment; (2) the reasons for depreciating property, plant, and equipment; (3) calculating depreciation expense for both financial reporting and income taxes; (4) recording the impairment of property, plant, and equipment, (5) disposing of property, plant, and equipment; (6) reporting property, plant, and equipment and depreciation expense in a company's annual report; and (7) using information about a company's property, plant, and equipment and depreciation expense to evaluate its operations.

COMPUTING THE COST OF PROPERTY, PLANT, AND EQUIPMENT

The total cost of an asset classified as property, plant, and equipment includes all the costs a company incurs to acquire the asset *and* to get it ready for use. These costs may include the invoice price (less any cash discounts), sales taxes, transportation charges, and installation costs.

 Do you think that this principle is the same as the one that we discussed in Chapter 19 for recording inventory? Why or why not?

For instance, suppose that Unlimited Decadence purchases a vertical agitator machine with a contract price of $40,000 on terms of 2/10, n/30. The company incurs sales tax of 7%, transportation costs of $1,500, and installation costs of $1,200. The company deducts the cash discount of $800 (2% × $40,000) and pays the net invoice price of $39,200 ($40,000 − $800). Given this information, we can calculate the cost[1] of the machine as follows:

---

[1]The discount should be deducted from the cost of the machine whether or not it is taken. If it is not taken, the amount of the discount not taken is treated as interest expense.

Contract price..	$40,000
Sales tax..	2,800
Transportation costs	1,500
Installation costs	1,200
Less: Cash discounts available..................................	(800)
Acquisition cost	$44,700

Note that although these costs may be incurred at various times, Unlimited Decadence includes in the cost of the machine all the costs to acquire the asset and get it ready for its intended use because they are necessary for the machine to be able to produce the benefits for which it was purchased. Since Unlimited Decadence will benefit from using the machine over its intended life, it allocates the cost of the machine as an expense over its life, and *not* in the period in which it acquired the machine. Therefore, Unlimited Decadence records the machine as an item of property, plant, and equipment at $44,700. It reports the cash paid as a cash outflow for an investing activity on its cash flow statement.

 Assume you are starting a typing service in your home. You purchase new computer equipment and supplies to start the company. Listed below are the types of costs you incurred while setting up the computer equipment. Would you categorize each cost as (a) a cost that is part of the acquisition cost of the computer equipment, (b) a cost that is an expense of the current period for the company, or (c) neither (a) nor (b)? Why?

1. Purchase price of the computer
2. Purchase price of the printer
3. Purchase price of the computer and printer cables
4. Purchase price of three boxes of paper
5. Charges for delivery and setup of the computer equipment
6. Purchase price of the pizza eaten while setting up the computer equipment
7. Charges for delivery of the pizza
8. Costs of installing special electrical outlets for the computer equipment
9. Cost of replacing the lamp that was broken during the delivery

REASONS FOR DEPRECIATING PROPERTY, PLANT, AND EQUIPMENT

The assets a company includes in its property, plant, and equipment provide it with benefits for more than one year. As we stated earlier in the chapter, the *matching* principle requires that a company match the expenses involved in obtaining the revenues of the period against the revenues it recorded in that accounting period. Unlimited Decadence expects its vertical agitator machine to last three years. Each year, this machine mixes ingredients for the candy that Unlimited Decadence sells. Therefore, each year, Unlimited Decadence matches part of the machine's historical cost against the revenue produced by the sale of the candy that this machine helped manufacture that year.

2 Why does a company depreciate its property, plant, and equipment, and what are the causes of depreciation?

Causes of Depreciation

Think more about the long-term assets you may personally own. Assume you own a car and a computer. What factors cause these particular assets to depreciate? The number of miles you drive your car each year and how hard you drive it are the most likely factors that determine how many years it will last. On the other hand, a computer's life is more likely to be limited by technological innovations (e.g., you want a faster, more powerful computer to run new software).

A company's property, plant, and equipment depreciate for two primary reasons: (1) physical causes and (2) functional causes, as we illustrate in Exhibit 21-2 on the following page. **Physical causes** include wear and tear due to *use,* deterioration and decay caused by the passage of *time,* and damage and destruction. For example, Unlimited Decadence's vertical agitator machine may have parts that break or wear out. **Functional causes** limit the life of the asset, even though the physical life is not exhausted. An asset is made obsolete because new

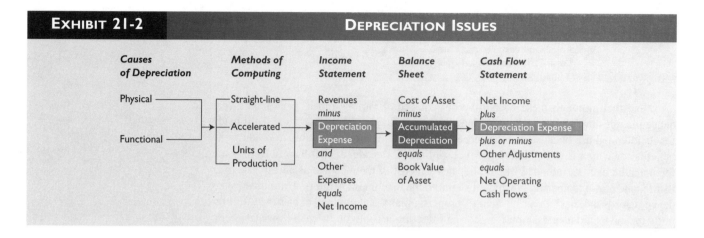

EXHIBIT 21-2   **DEPRECIATION ISSUES**

Causes of Depreciation	Methods of Computing	Income Statement	Balance Sheet	Cash Flow Statement
Physical	Straight-line	Revenues *minus*	Cost of Asset *minus*	Net Income *plus*
Functional	Accelerated	Depreciation Expense *and* Other Expenses *equals* Net Income	Accumulated Depreciation *equals* Book Value of Asset	Depreciation Expense *plus or minus* Other Adjustments *equals* Net Operating Cash Flows
	Units of Production			

technology is introduced or because the asset is no longer suitable for the company's operations even though it still may be physically sound. So, depreciation on a car tends to be from physical causes (but may be from functional causes if you want to purchase a new car to be "cool"), whereas depreciation on a computer tends to be from functional causes.

Think about the assets you own. What would be the primary cause for each type of asset to depreciate?

Service Life and Residual Value

There are three factors involved in the calculation of the depreciation amount: (1) the **cost** of the asset; (2) the **estimated service life** of the asset, which is the life over which a company expects the asset to be useful; and (3) the **estimated residual value** of the asset, which is the cash the company estimates it will receive from the sale or disposal of the asset at the end of its estimated service life. The service life often is referred to as the *economic life,* and the residual value as the *salvage value.*

A company's managers must estimate the service life and the residual value when the company acquires the asset. They do this by analyzing how the physical and functional causes of depreciation will affect the asset. The managers' estimate of the service life also directly affects the estimate of the residual value. In some cases, managers will plan to keep the asset until its physical life is exhausted. In this case, the estimated residual value will be close to zero. Alternatively, managers may plan to dispose of the asset well before its physical life is exhausted. In this situation, the estimated residual value may be relatively large. For example, airlines often sell planes long before the end of their physical lives. Although managers sometimes find it difficult to estimate the service life and the residual value of an asset, they must make realistic estimates using the best information available. Because of the difficulty of estimating the residual value, many companies use an arbitrary amount, such as 10 percent of the cost. The company's estimates of an asset's useful life and residual value affect the amount of depreciation it records for the asset. The estimates of the service life and residual value should be consistent with the estimates the company used in the capital expenditure decisions that we discussed in Chapter 20.

Think of an asset you own. Identify the residual values and service lives that you could select. Would other people with the same asset use the same amounts?

Depreciation Is an Allocation of Cost, Not a Valuation

A company does not record depreciation in an attempt to estimate the value of an asset. By that, we mean that depreciating an asset is not an attempt to estimate the market value of an asset *during* its life. Depreciation involves matching the acquisition (historical) cost of the asset, as an expense, against the revenue it helps to earn. Therefore, it is only at the time of acquisition and at the end of the life of an asset (if the original estimate of the residual value is accurate) that the book value (the cost of the asset less the accumulated depreciation) is equal to its market value. During the life of the asset, the book value is the *cost* of the remaining benefits that the company expects to obtain from the asset, and *not* the value of those benefits.

Systematic and Rational Allocation of Costs

Since precisely measuring the benefits that a particular asset provides is usually impossible, the underlying principle is that a company matches the depreciation expense in a "systematic and rational" manner against its revenue. **Systematic** means that the calculation follows a formula and is not determined in an arbitrary manner. As you will see, the straight-line method and the alternative methods, which we will discuss later in the chapter, are systematic. **Rational** means that the amount of the depreciation relates to the benefits that the asset produces in any period. Thus, managers should use the *straight-line method* when it is likely that the asset will produce equal benefits each period over its life. Using this method, the company records an equal depreciation amount each period and matches this expense against the benefits (revenues) each period. An *accelerated depreciation method* records the highest amount of depreciation in the first year of the asset's life and lesser amounts in each subsequent year. Therefore, managers should use an accelerated method when the asset produces benefits that are highest early in the life of the asset and when the benefits decline in each succeeding period. Managers may select different depreciation methods for different types of assets because the patterns of benefits generated by each type of asset vary.

 Can you think of an asset for which accelerated depreciation is appropriate? Explain why.

CALCULATING DEPRECIATION EXPENSE

Earlier, we discussed why GAAP requires that a company record property, plant, and equipment in its accounting records at historical cost (GAAP's requirements for relevant and reliable information) and why a company depreciates property, plant, and equipment (GAAP's requirement that costs be matched as expenses against revenues they helped to earn). In the next sections, we will focus on how a company determines the specific amounts that it records as depreciation. This understanding will help you analyze the reporting of property, plant, and equipment in financial statements. To illustrate depreciation expense, first we will briefly discuss the straight-line method of depreciation. Then we will explain an accelerated depreciation method that some companies use.

3 How does a company calculate its depreciation expense, and why does it compute depreciation expense differently for financial reporting than for income taxes?

Straight-Line Depreciation

A company using the **straight-line method** computes depreciation expense by allocating the cost of an asset, less its estimated residual value, equally to each period of the asset's estimated service life. This is the simplest and most commonly used way that companies calculate depreciation. The straight-line method is appropriate when the company expects to use the asset approximately equally in each period. If the benefits are equal in each period, the total *remaining* benefits decline equally each period. This pattern of depreciation occurs, for example, when physical deterioration and decay occur at a steady rate over the life of the asset. Then a company records an equal amount of depreciation expense each period by using the straight-line method. The amount of the straight-line depreciation is computed as follows.

$$\text{Depreciation per Year} = \frac{(\text{Cost} - \text{Estimated Residual Value})}{\text{Estimated Service Life}}$$

The cost less the residual value is known as the **depreciable cost**. It is the estimated total portion of the acquisition cost that the company will allocate to depreciation expense over its service life. Sometimes a company may express depreciation in terms of a rate per year. For straight-line depreciation, a company computes this rate by dividing 100% by the estimated life.

For example, suppose that Unlimited Decadence buys a blending machine (that it uses to mix ingredients) for $25,000 on January 1, 2008, and estimates that it will sell the machine for $2,500 (the residual value) after using it for 5 years (the service life). Unlimited Decadence computes the straight-line depreciation expense as follows:

$$\text{Depreciation per Year} = \frac{(\$25,000 - \$2,500)}{5 \text{ years}}$$
$$= \$4,500$$

The $22,500 depreciable cost of the blending machine is the acquisition cost of $25,000 less the $2,500 residual value. This $22,500 is allocated equally to each year of the asset's 5-year life, or at the rate of $4,500 per year. The straight-line rate is 20% (100% ÷ 5). So Unlimited Decadence could also compute the straight-line depreciation expense by multiplying the depreciable cost by the straight-line rate ($22,500 × 20% = $4,500).

Companies generally record depreciation in their accounting records as an end-of-period adjustment. If a company prepares financial statements only on an annual basis, the end-of-period depreciation adjustment records depreciation expense for the entire year. If a company prepares financial statements every quarter, it records depreciation expense each quarter only for that quarterly period. Accumulated depreciation shows the total depreciation that the company has recorded as of the end of the period (including the depreciation recorded for the same asset in previous periods).

Unlimited Decadence records the annual depreciation expense we just calculated for its blending machine in its accounting records at December 31, 2008, as follows:

	Assets		=	Liabilities	+	Stockholders' Equity		
							Net Income	
						Revenues	−	Expenses
		Accumulated Depreciation:						Depreciation Expense:
	Blending Machine	Blending Machine						Blending Machine
	Bal $25,000	− Bal $ 0						
		− +4,500					−	+$4,500
	Bal $25,000	− Bal $4,500						

FINANCIAL STATEMENT EFFECTS

Decreases *net* property, plant, and equipment, and total assets on **balance sheet.** Increases expenses, which decreases net income on *income statement* (and therefore decreases stockholders' equity on *balance sheet*).

In Chapter 7 of Volume 1, when we first explained accumulated depreciation, we subtracted the amount directly in the asset account. Here we record it in a separate account so that it is easier for managers to know both the cost and the accumulated depreciation of an asset, and to prepare the company's annual report which requires the disclosure of both amounts. Accumulated Depreciation is a *contra*-account—the company records increases in the account and subtracts the balance from the related asset account (Blending Machine) to compute the book value of the asset. This is why we show a minus sign (−) in the column to the left of the Accumulated Depreciation account. For example, on its December 31, 2008 balance sheet, Unlimited Decadence would report the $20,500 book value of its blending machine as follows:

Property, Plant, and Equipment
Blending Machine.. $25,000
Less: Accumulated depreciation................................ (4,500)
$20,500

A company should keep separate asset, depreciation expense, and accumulated depreciation accounts for each type of asset. Separate asset and accumulated depreciation accounts allow users to easily check the historical cost and accumulated depreciation for each type of asset, and are needed for the disclosures we will discuss later. We show a summary of the annual straight-line depreciation expense, the accumulated depreciation, and the book value over the life of Unlimited Decadence's blending machine in the top part of Exhibit 21-3.

In the lower part of Exhibit 21-3, we also use our blending machine example to help explain the relationships among the historical cost of an asset, accumulated depreciation, and book value. First, keep in mind that the blending machine's historical cost, $25,000, does not change during its service life. This follows GAAP's reliance on the historical cost concept. Second, note that when Unlimited Decadence places the blending machine into service at the start of 2008, accumulated depreciation equals $0. At the end of each year, Unlimited Decadence records annual depreciation expense of $4,500 and increases the blending machine's accumulated depreciation by this $4,500. By the end of the fifth year of the blending machine's service life (year 2012), accumulated depreciation totals $22,500 ($4,500 annual depreciation expense × 5 years), and the book value is $2,500, the estimated residual value. Note also how the book value of the blending machine changes over

EXHIBIT 21-3	STRAIGHT-LINE DEPRECIATION: UNLIMITED DECADENCE'S BLENDING MACHINE

Straight-Line Depreciation Schedule:
Blending Machine

Year	Depreciation Expense	Accumulated Depreciation	Book Value at the End of the Year
2008	$4,500	$ 4,500	$20,500
2009	4,500	9,000	16,000
2010	4,500	13,500	11,500
2011	4,500	18,000	7,000
2012	4,500	22,500	2,500

- ■ Depreciation Expense for the Year
- ■ Accumulated Depreciation at End of the Year (EOY)
- ☐ Book Value at End of the Year (EOY)

its service life. At the start of 2008, the $25,000 historical cost of the blending machine and its book value are equal. Then the blending machine's book value declines by $4,500 each year as a result of the recording of depreciation expense and accumulated depreciation. At the end of 2012, Unlimited Decadence's blending machine has been fully depreciated so that its book value ($2,500) equals its estimated residual value.

 If a company purchases a used asset, do you think it starts with a balance in Accumulated Depreciation? Why or why not?

Partial Period Depreciation

In the previous example, Unlimited Decadence purchased the blending machine on January 1, 2008, so we computed a full year of depreciation. But companies do not always purchase property, plant, and equipment on the first day of the year! So how does a company compute depreciation expense when it buys an asset during the year?

A common approach is to compute depreciation expense to the nearest whole month. Thus, if Unlimited Decadence purchased the blending machine on April 3, 2008, it would compute the depreciation expense for 2008 based on 9 months to be $3,375 ($4,500 × 9/12). Then in 2009 through 2012, its depreciation expense would be $4,500 per year. Finally, it would use the machine through the first three months of 2013. So the depreciation expense for 2013 for this machine would be $1,125 ($4,500 × 3/12), and the book value would be $2,500 on April 1, 2013.

Accelerated Depreciation Methods

In 2004, over 97 percent of U.S. companies used straight-line depreciation for at least *some* of their assets. So, not all companies use the straight-line method. GAAP allows a company's managers to choose among several additional methods, including (1) the double-declining-balance method, (2) the sum-of-the-years'-digits method, and (3) the units-of-production method. Double declining balance and sum of the years' digits are two **accelerated depreciation methods**, which record the highest depreciation in the first year of an asset's service life and lower depreciation in subsequent years. We will discuss the units-of-production method later in the chapter.

Double-Declining-Balance Method

A company using the **double-declining-balance method** computes depreciation expense by multiplying the book value of an asset at the beginning of the period by twice the straight-line rate. The double-declining depreciation rate is computed by dividing 200% by the asset's estimated life. Note that the double-declining-balance method uses twice the *rate* that is used for the straight-line method (*not* twice the amount). In addition, the residual value is *not* considered in the calculation of the depreciation expense under the double-declining-balance method. A company using this method bases its depreciation calculation on the asset's book value rather than its depreciable cost. However, the asset is not depreciated below the estimated residual value. In other words, its book value must not drop below its residual value. Using the double-declining-balance method, a company computes the depreciation expense as follows:

$$\text{Depreciation per Year} = \frac{200\%}{\text{Estimated Service Life}} \times \text{Book Value at the Beginning of the Year}$$

Here's how Unlimited Decadence would compute depreciation expense for its blending machine if it used the double-declining-balance method. Recall that Unlimited Decadence purchased the blending machine at the beginning of 2008 for $25,000, and that the machine had an estimated residual value of $2,500 and an estimated service life of 5 years. Since the asset has a life of 5 years, the double-declining-balance depreciation rate is 40%

(200% ÷ 5) per year. Unlimited Decadence would calculate the depreciation expense each year as follows:

**Double-Declining-Balance Depreciation Schedule:
Blending Machine**

Year	Book Value at the Beginning of the Year	Depreciation Calculation	Depreciation Expense	Accumulated Depreciation	Book Value at the End of the Year
2008	$25,000	40% × $25,000	$10,000	$10,000	$15,000
2009	15,000	40% × 15,000	6,000	16,000	9,000
2010	9,000	40% × 9,000	3,600	19,600	5,400
2011	5,400	40% × 5,400	2,160	21,760	3,240
2012	3,240		740*	22,500	2,500

*40% × $3,240 = $1,296, but depreciation expense is limited to $740 so that the asset's book value equals its $2,500 estimated residual value.

Note that Unlimited Decadence bases the calculation of the depreciation in the first year on the total acquisition cost of $25,000 and *not* on the acquisition cost less the estimated residual value. In the year 2012, it must make a modification to the usual calculations because a company should *not* depreciate the asset below its estimated residual value. Therefore, in 2012, Unlimited Decadence records depreciation expense of only $740 (instead of 40% × $3,240, or $1,296). This $740 is exactly the amount of depreciation expense needed to reduce the book value to $2,500 at the end of the year so that the book value is equal to the estimated residual value.

During the first year of the blending machine's useful life, would the straight-line method or the double-declining-balance method cause Unlimited Decadence to report the higher net income? the higher total assets? the higher stockholders' equity? Would this be true during the last year of the blending machine's useful life? Why or why not?

Sum-of-the-Years'-Digits Method

GAAP allows a company's managers to select another accelerated depreciation method called the sum-of-the-years'-digits method. The **sum-of-the-years'-digits method** computes depreciation expense by multiplying the depreciable cost (cost − residual value) of an asset by a fraction that declines each year.[2] The declining fraction that is used depends on the length of the asset's useful life. Because few companies use the sum-of-the-years'-digits method and because its effects on a company's financial statements are similar to those of the double-declining-balance method, we do not go through the detailed calculations of this method.

COMPARISON OF DEPRECIATION METHODS

Now that we have discussed the straight-line and accelerated methods of depreciation allowed by GAAP, let's compare the effects of each type of method on a company's financial statements. In Exhibit 21-4, we graph the amount of depreciation expense incurred each year of the blending machine's useful life unde the straight-line and the double-declining-balance methods. This exhibit shows that the amount of depreciation expense that Unlimited Decadence records each year for its blending machine depends on which depreciation method the company selects.

In Exhibit 21-5, we show how the blending machine's book value changes during the five years of its useful life for each of the two depreciation methods. Notice that at the start of the machine's useful life, its book value is the same under each method ($25,000).

---

[2]The numerator of the fraction changes each year and is the years' digits, used in reverse order. So for an asset with a 5-year life, the numerator is 5 in the first year, 4 in the second year, and so on. The denominator is the sum of the years' digits [i.e., (1 + 2 + 3 + 4 + 5)], or [n(n + 1) ÷ 2]. So for a 5-year asset, the denominator is 15 [i.e., (5 × 6) ÷ 2]. Therefore, the fractions (or rates) for a 5-year asset are $^5/_{15}$, $^4/_{15}$, $^3/_{15}$, $^2/_{15}$, and $^1/_{15}$.

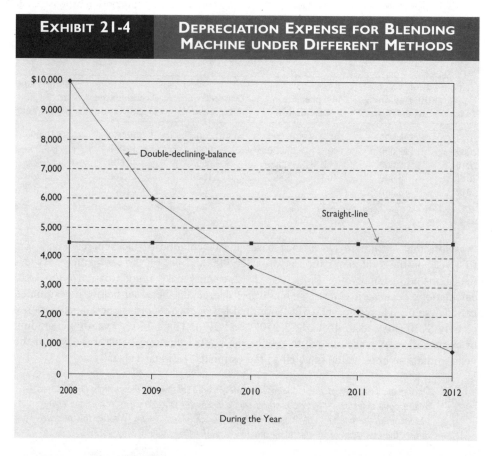

EXHIBIT 21-4   DEPRECIATION EXPENSE FOR BLENDING MACHINE UNDER DIFFERENT METHODS

During the Year

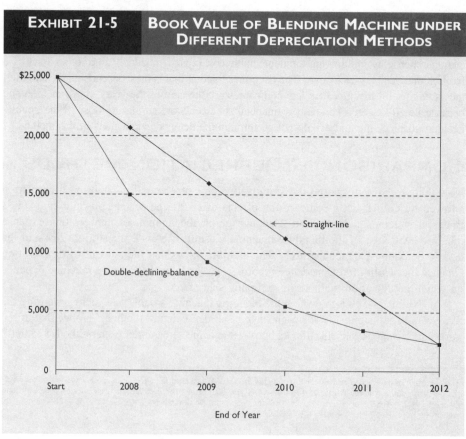

EXHIBIT 21-5   BOOK VALUE OF BLENDING MACHINE UNDER DIFFERENT DEPRECIATION METHODS

End of Year

The $25,000 is the machine's acquisition cost. The decline in book value each year results from the recording of annual depreciation expense and accumulated depreciation. The ending book values are the same for both methods and equal the asset's actual residual value if the company's managers have correctly estimated the residual value and the service life.

 If you were a manager for Unlimited Decadence, which depreciation method would you choose? Why?

DEPRECIATION AND INCOME TAXES

As we explained earlier, under GAAP, a corporation deducts depreciation expense from revenues as part of its calculation of net income. It also deducts depreciation expense in reporting *taxable* income on its income tax return. But because the depreciation rules under GAAP differ from those for computing income taxes, the amounts of depreciation expense in any year for financial reporting and for income tax reporting are different. These amounts are different because financial reporting and the Internal Revenue Code have different objectives. An objective of GAAP is to prepare income statements that fairly present the income-producing activities of the company and that are useful to decision makers. In contrast, two objectives, among others, of the Internal Revenue Code are to obtain revenue for the operation of the federal government and to provide investment incentives for certain kinds of business activity.

The managers of a corporation have a responsibility to the stockholders to minimize the income taxes paid by the corporation without violating the law. Therefore, it is desirable for a corporation to record, for income tax purposes, as much depreciation as possible early in the life of an asset. Higher depreciation in the early years of an asset's life reduces the corporation's taxable income in those years, thereby reducing the income taxes paid in those years. To accomplish this, companies use an accelerated depreciation method acceptable under the Internal Revenue Code—the **Modified Accelerated Cost Recovery System (MACRS)**—for income tax purposes.

 If the total depreciation for both methods is the same over the life of the asset, why do managers consider the use of MACRS to be advantageous?

There are three major ways in which MACRS depreciation is different from GAAP depreciation: (1) MACRS defines the *tax life* of the asset, (2) MACRS uses *no residual value,* and (3) MACRS specifies a depreciation percentage for each year. In contrast, for GAAP depreciation, managers estimate the *service life* and the *residual value* of the asset and select a method based on the matching principle.

Companies frequently disclose the use of different methods. For example, in a note to **Wal-Mart**'s 2006 financial statements, the corporation explains that its financial statement and tax depreciation methods are different, as follows:

> **Depreciation . . .** Depreciation . . . for financial statement purposes is provided on the straight-line method over the estimated useful lives of the various assets. For income tax purposes, accelerated methods of depreciation are used . . .

Exhibit 21-6 shows MACRS depreciation (except for buildings) as a percentage of the cost of an asset for each of the tax lives. Buildings are depreciated under the straight-line method over either 27.5 years (residential buildings) or 39 years (nonresidential buildings). Three longtime users of MACRS—**General Motors**, **ExxonMobil**, and **General Electric**—have together saved over $21.7 billion in taxes by using MACRS rather than straight-line depreciation for taxes, thereby lowering taxable income.

 Do you think you pay less when you purchase a car because the car manufacturer uses MACRS for its income taxes?

| EXHIBIT 21-6 | PERCENTAGE OF AN ASSET'S COST USED TO COMPUTE MACRS DEPRECIATION | | | | |

Year of Life	Tax Life of Asset in Years*					
	3	5	7	10	15	20
1	33.33%	20.00%	14.29%	10.00%	5.00%	3.750%
2	44.45	32.00	24.49	18.00	9.50	7.219
3	14.81	19.20	17.49	14.40	8.55	6.677
4	7.41	11.52	12.49	11.52	7.70	6.177
5		11.52	8.93	9.22	6.93	5.713
6		5.76	8.92	7.37	6.23	5.285
7			8.93	6.55	5.90	4.888
8			4.46	6.55	5.90	4.522
9				6.56	5.91	4.462
10				6.55	5.90	4.461
11				3.28	5.91	4.462
12					5.90	4.461
13					5.91	4.462
14					5.90	4.461
15					5.91	4.462
16					2.95	4.461
17						4.462
18						4.461
19						4.462
20						4.461
21						2.231

*The percentages are based on the half-year convention—depreciation for half a year is recorded in the year of acquisition and in the final year of depreciation for tax purposes. The percentages are also based on a change to the straight-line method in the period in which the straight-line depreciation exceeds the amount calculated under the accelerated method.

SUBSEQUENT EXPENDITURES

After purchasing an asset, a company often makes additional expenditures on the asset during its economic life. The company classifies these costs as either capital expenditures or operating expenditures. A **capital expenditure** is a cost that increases the benefits the company will obtain from an asset. An **operating expenditure** is a cost that only maintains the benefits that the company originally expected from the asset.

 If you own a car, which of your costs would you classify as capital expenditures? operating expenditures?

A *capital* expenditure increases the benefits to be obtained from an asset either by significantly increasing the usefulness of the asset or by extending its life. Examples of capital expenditures (often called *renewals* and *betterments*) include additions, improvements, and unusual repairs such as adding a new wing to a building, installing additional insulation, or repairing a boiler in such an extensive way that its life is extended. A company records a capital expenditure as an addition to the cost of the asset. The company includes the additional cost in the calculation of the depreciation expense it records over the remaining life of the asset.

The major item of *operating* expenditures is routine repair and maintenance costs. For example, if a company buys a delivery truck that it expects to use for 150,000 miles, it knows that it will have to perform repairs and maintenance during that time. Thus, each routine repair merely maintains the ability of the truck to last for 150,000 miles and does not extend the asset's life or increase its usefulness. A company records an operating expenditure (sometimes called a *revenue expenditure*) as an expense when incurred.

It is important for a company to record an additional cost correctly as a capital or operating expenditure. Managers must use good judgment. An error in classification may have a significant effect on the company's financial statements. For example, suppose a company incorrectly records the cost of adding a new wing to a building as a repairs expense. As a result, the company overstates the repairs expense on its income statement and understates net income in the period of the expenditure. Also, it understates the asset—Building—on its balance sheet and therefore understates depreciation expense (thereby overstating net income) in each period for the rest of the life of the asset.

Or suppose a company incorrectly records routine repairs to machinery as an increase in the machinery account. Then, it understates the repairs expense on its income statement and overstates net income. It overstates the asset—Machinery—on its balance sheet and therefore overstates depreciation expense (thereby understating net income) for the rest of the life of the asset. You can see that the correct classification of subsequent expenditures is important for measuring a company's net income, which affects a user's evaluation of the company's performance.

Explain which of the two errors may be more likely to occur.

IMPAIRMENT OF PROPERTY, PLANT, AND EQUIPMENT

Recall that an asset of a company is an economic resource that will provide future benefits to the company, and that the company reports its property, plant, and equipment at book value (historical cost − accumulated depreciation). The future economic benefits that the property, plant, and equipment will provide are the expected net operating cash flows that the company will receive from using the assets in its operations. But what if the market value of these assets is less than their book value? In this case, these assets may not provide sufficient future net operating cash flows to "recover" the book value. Then it may be argued that the book value is *not* a good measure of the cost of the expected future benefits. So an asset is **impaired** when the expected future net operating cash flows are less than the book value of the asset.

Under GAAP, a company must review its property, plant, and equipment assets (and certain identifiable intangible assets discussed later in the chapter) to see if they are impaired. Impairment exists whenever events or changes in circumstances indicate that the book value of the assets may not be recoverable through the net operating cash flows that the company will receive from those assets. Examples of events or changes in circumstances that indicate that assets may be impaired include a significant decrease in the market value of the assets, a significant change in the way the assets are used, a significant change in the business or regulatory environment, a current period operating loss, or a negative cash flow from operating activities. In making this review, a company may look at each individual asset or at groups of related assets (e.g., a production line or a factory).

4 How does a company evaluate the impairment of its property, plant, and equipment?

Why does each of the examples indicate that the company may not be able to generate net operating cash inflows that equal or exceed the book value of the asset?

If the book value of an asset is not recoverable through the future net operating cash flows expected from that asset, then a company must reduce the book value of that asset and record an impairment loss. For each property, plant, and equipment asset, a company computes the impairment loss as the difference between the asset's book value and its lower market value. The market value is the amount at which the asset could be bought or sold in a current transaction between willing parties. However, market prices frequently will not be available for a used asset. Therefore, a company may use the present value of the estimated future net operating cash flows generated by the asset as a measure of its market value. The discount rate that a company uses to determine the present value is the rate of return that the company would require for a similar investment with similar risks. For example, this could be the rate the company used to evaluate capital budgeting projects, as we discussed in Chapter 20. When the company records the impairment loss, it reduces the asset's book value to the lower market value. It reports the impairment loss on the income statement as part of income from continuing operations, and reports the new (reduced) book value on the ending balance sheet. The reduced book value (i.e., market value) becomes the new "cost" of the asset, and the company uses this new cost to compute the depreciation over the remaining life of the asset. Once a company has written an asset down, if the market value subsequently increases, the company may not write it back up.

 Is the impairment of property, plant, and equipment similar to the lower-of-cost-or-market method for inventory? Why or why not?

To understand an impairment loss, suppose that Unlimited Decadence determines that a building and some machinery are impaired and that their market value of $2 million is $500,000 less than the book value of $2.5 million. Unlimited Decadence reduces the book value of the property, plant, and equipment assets that it reports on its balance sheet from $2.5 million to $2 million. It also reports a loss of $500,000 in income from continuing operations on its income statement. Unlimited Decadence will depreciate the new "cost" of $2 million over the remaining useful life of the assets.

EXTERNAL USER PERSPECTIVE: EVALUATION OF GAAP FOR ASSET IMPAIRMENT

GAAP for an asset impairment is intended to enhance the usefulness of a company's financial statements by requiring the company to report the loss when it is incurred and to show the lower market value of its productive assets. The information is more relevant because the company reports the loss in current income, and because the asset amount shows the lower market value of the company's investment, thereby helping users assess

Suppose you are a passenger on this plane and are reading American Airlines' annual report. What do you think the company means when it refers to its airplanes as "impaired"? Should you get off the plane immediately?

COURTESY OF AMERICAN AIRLINES

the *return on investment*, *operating capability*, and *risk* of the company. The information also improves comparability across companies.

These principles do allow significant flexibility for a company's managers, however. For example, they do not require that a company review its assets for impairment on a regular basis, because that would be very costly. Also, estimating future net operating cash flows is subjective. For example, the company could use current or expected cost and volume information. Furthermore, the discount rate used to calculate the present value of those cash flows is a management choice. Also note that the reduction in the asset's book value will "guarantee" future profits because of the reduced depreciation expense in future periods.

To illustrate asset impairment, in 2005, **Calpine** (a major North American power company) reported a $5.5 billion loss due to reductions in the value of its power plants and energy projects. In 2004, **DIRECTV** wrote off $1.7 billion, primarily related to the abandonment of satellites it had not yet launched.

 Do you think that the reporting of impairment losses creates both relevant and reliable information? Why or why not?

DISPOSING OF PROPERTY, PLANT, AND EQUIPMENT

Although property, plant, and equipment lasts longer than one year, it doesn't last forever. At some point, Unlimited Decadence's blending machine will stop blending and its vertical agitator will stop shaking. After a few years, even if the machines are still functioning, newer models may make the current ones obsolete. Even though Unlimited Decadence might be able to continue using the machine, it may be difficult to compete with companies that upgrade their machines.

When a company disposes of a depreciable asset, one of three things happens: (1) the asset is sold for an amount equal to its book value at the date of disposal; (2) the asset is sold for an amount greater or less than its book value on that date, in which case the company records a gain or loss; or (3) the asset is traded for another asset.

Regardless of the reason for the disposal, a company records and reports depreciation expense for the current period up to the date of disposal. For example, if Unlimited Decadence starts its fiscal year on January 1 and sells its blending machine on July 30, 2011, it reports depreciation expense on the machine for seven months in its 2011 income statement. The blending machine had not been fully depreciated at the start of 2011, and it was used to help Unlimited Decadence earn income during the first seven months of the year.

Then, when a company disposes of the property, plant, and equipment, it removes the balances in both the specific asset account and the related accumulated depreciation account from its accounting records. Disposals range from the very simple, where there is no cash involved and the book value is zero, to more complex transactions in which the company receives cash and reports a gain or loss on the disposal because the actual selling price of the asset is not equal to its book value. A company usually reports any gain or loss in the "other items" section of its income statement, as we discussed in Chapter 10 of Volume 1. (This is similar to the procedure a company uses to record the impairment of an asset.)

To illustrate a disposal involving the sale of an asset, we assume that Unlimited Decadence sells office equipment for $1,500. The equipment had originally cost $10,000 and has a current book value of $1,000 (accumulated depreciation is $9,000). Therefore, Unlimited Decadence reports a gain of $500 (the cash received of $1,500 − the book value of $1,000). Based on this information, Unlimited Decadence records the sale as follows.

5 How does a company record and report the disposal of property, plant, and equipment?

Assets		= Liabilities +	Stockholders' Equity
			Net Income
			Revenues – Expenses
			(Gains) (Losses)
		Accumulated Depreciation:	
	Office	Office	Gain on Sale of
Cash	Equipment	Equipment	Equipment
+$1,500	–$10,000	– –$9,000	+$500

 If Unlimited Decadence sold the equipment for $800 instead, how would it record the sale?

When a company trades in an old asset for a new asset, it pays cash for the difference between the market value of the new asset and the market value of the old asset traded in. The company records the new asset at its market value (cost), reduces its cash for the amount paid, and removes the cost and accumulated depreciation of the old asset from its accounting records. The company also records a gain or loss for the difference between the market value of the old asset and its book value. The company reports the gain or loss in the "other items" section of its income statement and the cash received as a cash inflow from an investing activity on its cash flow statement.

For instance, assume Unlimited Decadence purchases a new machine that has a market value of $7,000—by paying $5,000 cash and trading in an old machine with a market value of $2,000. The old machine has a book value of $3,000 ($11,000 cost – $8,000 accumulated depreciation). In this case, Unlimited Decadence records the new equipment at $7,000, reduces cash by $5,000, eliminates the cost of $11,000 and the $8,000 accumulated depreciation on the old machine, and records a $1,000 loss ($2,000 market value of the old equipment – $3,000 book value of the old equipment).

REPORTING PROPERTY, PLANT, AND EQUIPMENT, AND DEPRECIATION EXPENSE

We have used the title Property, Plant, and Equipment in this chapter because it is the title most companies use in their balance sheets. You may come across titles such as Plant and Machinery, Land and Buildings, Fixed Assets, or for a retail company, Property and Equipment. For example, **Intel Corporation** uses the term "Property, Plant and Equipment" and **Deere & Company** uses "Property and Equipment," even though both are manufacturing companies.

The types and extent of property, plant, and equipment information reported in companies' annual reports vary from one company to another. However, GAAP requires all companies to disclose the following items in their financial statements or in the notes accompanying these statements:

1. Depreciation expense for the period

2. Balances of major classes of depreciable assets by nature (such as buildings or equipment) or function (such as candy manufacturing or transportation) on the balance sheet date

3. Accumulated depreciation, either by major classes of assets or in total, on the balance sheet date

4. A general description of the method or methods used in computing depreciation with respect to the major classes of depreciable assets, and how these methods differ from those used for income taxes

We show PepsiCo's property, plant, and equipment disclosures on December 31, 2005, in Exhibit 21-7.

EXHIBIT 21-7	DISCLOSURES OF PROPERTY, PLANT, AND EQUIPMENT: PEPSICO

Consolidated Balance Sheet (in part)

(in millions except per share amount)
PepsiCo, Inc. and Subsidiaries
December 31, 2005 and December 25, 2004

	2005	2004
Property, Plant and Equipment, net	$8,681	$8,149

Notes to Consolidated Financial Statements (in part)

Note 4 (in part) – Property, Plant and Equipment.
Depreciation is recognized on a straight-line basis over an asset's estimated useful life. Land is not depreciated and construction in progress is not depreciated until ready for service. ... Useful lives are periodically evaluated to determine whether events or circumstances have occurred which indicate the need for revision.

	Average Useful Life	2005	2004
Land and improvements	10–30 yrs.	$ 685	$ 646
Buildings and improvements	20–44	3,736	3,605
Machinery and equipment, including fleet and software	5–15	11,658	10,950
Construction in progress		1,066	729
		17,145	15,930
Accumulated depreciation		(8,464)	(7,781)
		$ 8,681	$ 8,149

Depreciation expense was $1,103 million in 2005, $1,062 million in 2004, and $1,020 million in 2003.

Examine PepsiCo's disclosures. Find where it makes each required disclosure. What other important information did PepsiCo disclose? Why do you think PepsiCo made these disclosures? What do the disclosures tell you about PepsiCo's management decisions concerning property, plant, and equipment? What additional disclosures do you think might be useful?

Although we have used the term "depreciation expense" throughout the chapter, a manufacturing company includes some of that "expense" as part of the cost of the inventory that it manufactures, as we discussed in Chapter 16. Many companies also use a "functional" classification for their expenses. In this case, the company allocates the depreciation expense among its functional classifications, such as cost of goods sold, selling, and general and administrative expenses.

PROPERTY, PLANT, AND EQUIPMENT, AND THE CASH FLOW STATEMENT

A company reports the cash it paid for purchases of property, plant, and equipment as a cash outflow in the cash flows from investing activities section of its cash flow statement. A company reports the cash it received from the sale of property, plant, and equipment as a cash inflow in the cash flows from investing activities section of its cash flow statement. If a company uses the indirect method of computing its net cash provided by operating activities (which we discussed in the appendix to Chapter 8 of Volume 1), it adds back depreciation expense to its net income because depreciation is a noncash expense that was subtracted from revenue in calculating the net income. Under the indirect method, a company also subtracts (adds) gains (losses) on sales of property, plant, and equipment from (to) its net income because it included these gains and losses in calculating the net income but they did not affect its cash flows from operating activities.

USING INFORMATION ABOUT PROPERTY, PLANT, AND EQUIPMENT, AND DEPRECIATION EXPENSE

6 How do external users evaluate information about a company's property, plant, and equipment?

Up to this point in the chapter we have focused on reporting property, plant, and equipment. These issues provide the foundation you need for understanding how external users use a company's property, plant, and equipment disclosures to help them evaluate its operating capability and operating efficiency. A company's **operating capability** is its ability to maintain its level of physical output. For instance, external users evaluate Unlimited Decadence's disclosures to help them determine if it can maintain or increase the number of chocolates it produces and sells. **Operating efficiency** refers to how well a company uses its assets to generate revenue.

As with other parts of financial statements, external users use property, plant, and equipment for evaluation by performing intracompany and intercompany analysis—through the use of horizontal analysis, vertical analysis, and ratio analysis. We will discuss intracompany analysis first, followed by intercompany analysis. We use **Intel Corporation's** 2005 annual report to provide the information we need to explain intracompany analysis. We selected Intel because property, plant, and equipment are very important to "electronic computer" manufacturers and because Intel provides a substantial amount of information in its annual report.

Intracompany Analysis of Property, Plant, and Equipment: Intel Corporation

Exhibit 21-8 presents property, plant, and equipment information taken from Intel's 2005 Annual Report—its balance sheet, income statement, and cash flow statement. Intel's financial statements provide more information than just the net changes in its property, plant, and equipment. You can get more detailed information by analyzing the property, plant, and equipment information on the balance sheet *and* on the cash flow statement. The operating activities section of its cash flow statement reveals that Intel recorded $4,345 million in (straight-line) depreciation expense during 2005. (Remember that depreciation is not a cash flow but is added to net income on the cash flow statement because it is a noncash expense used in computing net income.) The cash flows from investing activities section of Intel's cash flow statement shows that during 2005 the company added $5,818 million of new property, plant, and equipment. Using the information from these two financial statements, we can determine the total dollar changes that occurred for Intel's property, plant, and equipment accounts during 2005. We show these calculations in Exhibit 21-9.

 Analyze Exhibit 21-9. Can you explain each item included in Intel's Property, Plant, and Equipment and Accumulated Depreciation accounts?

After Exhibit 21-9 are three specific questions that relate to Intel Corporation's operating capability and efficiency. You can ask these same three questions (as well as others) when using information about any company's property, plant, and equipment for intracompany analysis. Under each question, we explain how financial analysis helps external users answer these questions.

EXHIBIT 21-8	SELECTED FINANCIAL INFORMATION: INTEL

Financial Statement Information Taken from Intel's 2005 Annual Report Relating to Property, Plant, and Equipment

Balance Sheet Information

December 31, 2005 and December 25, 2004

(In millions)	2005	2004
Property, plant and equipment:		
Land and buildings	$13,938	$13,277
Machinery and equipment	27,297	24,561
Construction in progress	2,897	1,995
	44,132	39,833
Less accumulated depreciation	(27,021)	(24,065)
Property, plant and equipment, net	17,111	15,768
Total assets	$48,314	$48,143

Income Statement Information

Two years ended December 31, 2005

(In millions)	2005	2004
Net revenues	$38,826	$34,209
Cost of sales	15,777	14,463
Research and development	5,145	4,778
Marketing, general and administrative	5,688	4,659
Other (listed) expenses	126	179
Operating costs and expenses	26,736	24,079
Operating income	$12,090	$10,130

Cash Flow Statement Information

Two years ended December 31, 2005

(In millions)	2005	2004
Cash and cash equivalents, beginning of year	$ 8,407	$ 7,971
Cash flows provided by (used for) operating activities:		
Net income	8,664	7,516
Adjustments to reconcile net income to net cash provided by (used for) operating activities (in part):		
Depreciation	4,345	4,590
Cash flows provided by (used for) investing activities:		
Additions to property, plant, and equipment	(5,818)	(3,843)

Question #1: Does Intel Own Enough Property, Plant, and Equipment to Maintain Production or Increase the Amount of Electronic Components Above What It Produced Last Year?

To answer this question, we first examine Intel's comparative balance sheets to see how its property, plant, and equipment changed from the end of the previous year (2004) to the end of the current year (2005). From the balance sheet information provided in Exhibit 21-8 we see that the company's ending 2004 net property, plant, and equipment

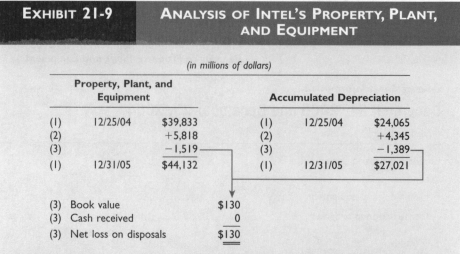

EXHIBIT 21-9	**ANALYSIS OF INTEL'S PROPERTY, PLANT, AND EQUIPMENT**

(in millions of dollars)

	Property, Plant, and Equipment				Accumulated Depreciation	
(1)	12/25/04	$39,833		(1)	12/25/04	$24,065
(2)		+5,818		(2)		+4,345
(3)		−1,519		(3)		−1,389
(1)	12/31/05	$44,132		(1)	12/31/05	$27,021

(3)	Book value	$130
(3)	Cash received	0
(3)	Net loss on disposals	$130

(1) The beginning and ending balances for Property, Plant, and Equipment and Accumulated Depreciation are taken from Intel's balance sheets.

(2) The increases in Property, Plant, and Equipment (due to $5,818 additions) and Accumulated Depreciation (due to $4,345 depreciation expense) are taken from Intel's cash flow statement.

(3) From the information provided in (1) and (2), we calculated the $1,519 decrease in Property, Plant, and Equipment and the $1,389 decrease in Accumulated Depreciation. These decreases indicate that Intel must have sold some property, plant, and equipment. Because Intel did not disclose any cash inflow from selling the Property, Plant, and Equipment, we know that the company must have incurred a loss on the sale. The loss ($130) is equal to the difference between the book value of the property, plant, and equipment it sold ($1,519 cost − $1,389 accumulated depreciation) and the cash received ($0).

balance was $15,768 million and its 2005 net balance was $17,111 million (a big company!). So, Intel's dollar amount of property, plant, and equipment (net) increased by $1,343 million ($17,111 million − $15,768 million). That is an 8.5% ($1,343 million ÷ $15,768 million) increase from the end of 2004 to the end of 2005. At the end of 2005, Intel has invested 35% ($17,111 ÷ $48,314) of its total assets in property, plant, and equipment (net), as compared with 33% ($15,768 ÷ $48,143) at the end of 2004. Intel's increase ($1,343) in property, plant, and equipment (net) during 2005 and the increase in property, plant, and equipment as a proportion of total assets provide evidence that Intel can increase its production (operating capability) during the coming year.

We present additional information from Intel's annual report in Exhibit 21-10. This exhibit also provides information useful in answering questions #1 and #2. The top bar graph in Exhibit 21-10 shows Intel's capital additions over the past 10 years, while the bottom bar graph shows Intel's net revenues over the past 10 years.

 Study these two bar graphs. What information, in addition to that provided in Intel's financial statements, do the bar graphs provide? How useful is this additional information?

Question #2: Does Intel's 2005 Increased Investment in Property, Plant, and Equipment Produce Significant Increases in Net Revenue?

We learned from our analysis in Exhibit 21-9 that Intel increased its investment in property, plant, and equipment during 2005 by $4,299 ($5,818 purchased − $1,519 sold). Another analysis will help determine if this increased investment in property, plant, and equipment was converted into increased revenue for Intel. According to Intel's income statement, net revenues for 2004 were $34,209 million. In 2005, its net revenues totaled $38,826 million, a $4,617 million increase from 2004. Thus net revenues increased from 2004 to 2005 by 13.5% ($4,617 ÷ $34,209). So Intel's 8.5% increase in property, plant, and equipment (net) in 2005 (from the answer to Question 1) helped produce a significant increase in its 2005 net revenues.

EXHIBIT 21-10	SELECTED ANNUAL REPORT INFORMATION: INTEL CORP.

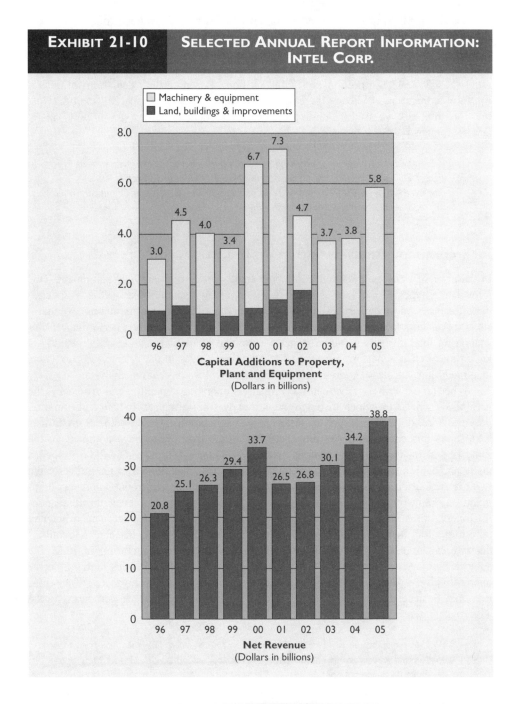

Capital Additions to Property,
Plant and Equipment
(Dollars in billions)

Net Revenue
(Dollars in billions)

 Describe a situation in which a company's financial statements indicate that the company may have a problem maintaining operating capability. Specifically, what trends in property, plant, and equipment and sales revenue would signal this problem?

Question #3: Does Intel Use Its Property and Equipment Efficiently?

A common way that external users evaluate how efficiently a company is using its property, plant, and equipment is to relate property, plant, and equipment to revenues. They do this by calculating a property, plant, and equipment efficiency ratio as follows:

$$\text{Property, Plant, and Equipment Efficiency Ratio} = \frac{\text{Net Revenues}}{\text{Average Net Property, Plant, and Equipement}}$$

The higher the ratio, the larger the dollar amount of net revenue produced by each dollar invested in net property, plant, and equipment. In 2004, Intel's ratio was 2.17 ($34,209 million ÷ $15,768 million). On average, every dollar Intel had invested in net property, plant, and equipment generated $2.17 in net revenue during 2004. For 2005, the ratio was 2.27 ($38,826 million ÷ $17,111 million). Based on the calculations of this ratio, Intel's operating efficiency increased significantly in 2005 compared to 2004. (Note that for simplicity we used the ending rather than average amount of net property, plant, and equipment.)

Is the number of employees who work for a company relevant to an analysis of its efficiency? Do you think that the revenue-per-employee and the gross-fixed-assets-per-employee would be useful measures of its efficiency? Can you think of an industry where the ratios would be high? Which ones? Why?

Intercompany Analysis within an Industry

In the prior sections, you learned a lot about Intel's property, plant, and equipment. This information indicated that Intel is increasing its operating capability, as well as its operating efficiency. As we have stated in earlier chapters, one limitation of intracompany analysis is that it fails to provide an external comparison of the company's performance. Our analysis of Intel gives us "positive signals" as to its performance each year, but we do not know how well it is performing relative to other companies in the "electronic computers manufacturing" industry. *Inter*company analysis provides this relative analysis.

When an external user evaluates a company's operating capability and efficiency, the user needs a basis on which to judge the company's performance. Industry information provides a good initial measure of performance expectations. The investor or creditor is asking, "Is this company performing better or worse than the average company in the same line of business?" For example, Exhibit 21-11 shows the average 2005 property, plant, and equipment efficiency ratios for four industries. The 2005 average ratios for the two manufacturing industries shown – candy products and the electronic computers manufacturing industry – are 6.0-to-1 and 13.9-to-1, respectively. However, the retail confectionery stores industry has a higher 2005 property, plant, and equipment efficiency ratio of 6.9-to-1 than the related manufacturing industry, most likely because the retail industry uses less property, plant, and equipment than does the manufacturing industry. The advertising agencies industry has a much higher ratio because companies in that industry operate with even less property, plant, and equipment. Thus, a company with a 6-to-1 ratio may be acceptable in the candy products industry but would be viewed poorly in the advertising agencies industry.

Why do you think the two manufacturing industries have such different ratios from those of the retail grocery stores and advertising agencies industries? Why do advertising agencies have the highest ratio?

In the previous section we calculated Intel Corporation's 2005 property, plant, and equipment efficiency ratio to be 2.27. Now we can incorporate electronic computers manufacturing industry information into our evaluation. In addition to seeing that Intel's ratio strenghtened from 2004 to 2005, from 2.17 (or 2.17 to 1) to 2.27, we now see that Intel's ratio is also well below the industry average of 13.9.

What does this tell us about Intel's operating capability and efficiency? One interpretation is that Intel is not operating as efficiently as many other companies in this industry. However, because this ratio relies on historical cost amounts for property, plant, and equipment, users of this ratio need to interpret a below-industry average ratio carefully. For example, Intel's relatively low ratio may be because Intel uses modern, more costly property, plant, and equipment that has not been depreciated much. Recall that the net property, plant, and equipment of Intel is about 35% of its total assets at the end of

| EXHIBIT 21-11 | PROPERTY, PLANT, AND EQUIPMENT EFFICIENCY RATIOS: FOUR INDUSTRIES |

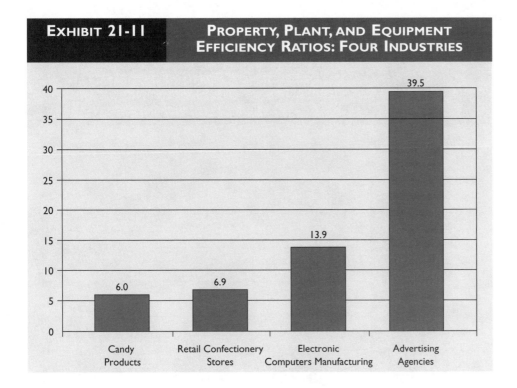

2005. The industry average is only 20%. Therefore, it appears that Intel is more "capital intensive" than many other companies in this industry; that is, it needs more property, plant, and equipment to conduct its business. Also remember that Intel's property, plant, and equipment net balance increased 8.5% from the end of 2004 to the end of 2005. These facts might suggest that Intel's relatively low ratio is also due to the company's significant investment in new property, plant, and equipment. Also, the ratio may be affected by the age of the assets as we discuss later.

 Can you think of another reason why Intel's ratio may be lower than the industry average?

Intercompany Comparisons with Major Competitors

Our comparison of Intel's operating capability and performance with the average level of performance for the industry raised questions about Intel's performance. Although industry data is a good place to start making intercompany comparisons, the evaluation should not stop there. Industry averages show a composite performance measure of many different companies. A clearer picture of Intel's relative operating capability and efficiency may be obtained by comparing Intel with its major competitors.

Exhibit 21-12 on the following page shows the 2005 property, plant, and equipment efficiency ratio for the electronic computers manufacturing industry, for Intel, and for two of its largest competitors—**AMD Corporation** and **National Semiconductor Corporation**. By singling out Intel's major competitors, we see that the largest companies in this industry all have property, plant, and equipment efficiency ratios well below the 13.9 industry average. Therefore the industry average may not be representative of the operations of these particular companies. For example, these large companies may produce different types of products or may rely more on high-tech equipment and less on skilled labor to produce their products.

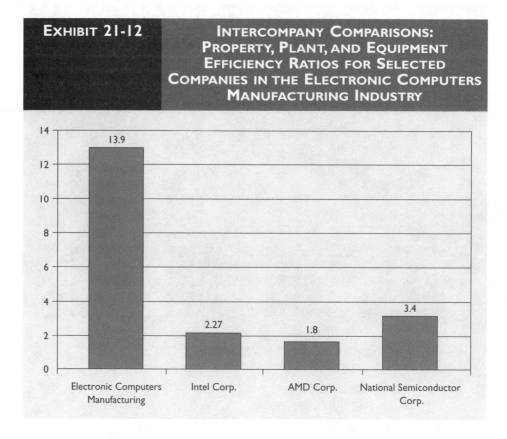

EXHIBIT 21-12

INTERCOMPANY COMPARISONS: PROPERTY, PLANT, AND EQUIPMENT EFFICIENCY RATIOS FOR SELECTED COMPANIES IN THE ELECTRONIC COMPUTERS MANUFACTURING INDUSTRY

Do you think that __General Motors__, __Ford__, and __DaimlerChrysler__ would have the same ratios if they were equally efficient? Why or why not?

We do not repeat this extensive discussion of intercompany analysis in other chapters. However, you should think about how you would perform this analysis for inventories in Chapter 19 and for other topics in the remaining chapters of this book.

Estimating the Average Age and the Average Life of Property, Plant, and Equipment

Two additional issues related to analyzing a company's property, plant, and equipment involve estimating the average age and the average life of these assets. The average age is important because the older a company's property, plant, and equipment, the less likely it is that the company will be able to maintain its *operating capability* in the future. Also, the average age may affect a user's evaluation of a company's *profitability* over time, or in comparison to another company.

The average life of a company's property, plant, and equipment is important because it affects the company's *profitability* through its depreciation expense. The longer the life, the lower is the depreciation expense and the higher the net income. Similarly, the shorter the life, the higher is the depreciation expense and the lower the net income.

Unfortunately, companies do not provide useful disclosures of the average age and the average life of their property, plant, and equipment. (They are required to disclose the lives for each category of property, plant, and equipment, but these disclosures are usually too vague to be useful.) So, if a user wants to analyze a company's property, plant, and equipment to help evaluate the company's operating capability and profitability, the user must estimate the average age and average life of these assets. In the following sections, we explain how to make these estimates assuming that a company uses the straight-line depreciation method. This is a reasonable assumption because most companies use this method.

Average Age

To compute the average age of a company's property, plant, and equipment, you need to think about the balance in accumulated depreciation. This balance represents the lifetime depreciation that the company has recorded on the property, plant, and equipment that it currently owns. Also remember that under the straight-line depreciation method a company's accumulated depreciation increases by approximately the same amount each year. Therefore the average age of a company's property, plant, and equipment may be computed as follows:

$$\text{Average Age} = \text{Accumulated Depreciation} \div \text{Annual Depreciation Expense}$$

Companies are required to disclose both the accumulated depreciation and the annual depreciation expense. However, since a company is only required to disclose a single amount of accumulated depreciation, a user can only calculate a single average age for all of the company's property, plant, and equipment. Also a company typically buys and sells assets every year, so this calculation will only result in an approximate measure of the average age. Using Intel's disclosures shown in Exhibit 21-8, we can estimate the average age of its property, plant, and equipment at the end of 2005 to be 6.2 years ($27,021 accumulated depreciation at the end of 2005 ÷ $4,345 depreciation expense for 2005). As we would expect for a technologically advanced company, its property, plant, and equipment is not very old.

A user may use the average age of a company's property, plant, and equipment to evaluate its operating capability in two ways. First, as an intracompany comparison, the user can calculate the average age at the end of each year for several years to determine whether the average age has changed over time. If the average age is increasing, this may indicate that the company's operating capability is decreasing because it is using older assets in its operations. If the average age is decreasing, this may indicate that the company's operating capability is increasing because it is using newer assets in its operations. Second, as an intercompany comparison, the user can compare the average age of the company's property, plant, and equipment to that of its competitors. If the average age of a company's property, plant, and equipment is higher than its competitors, this may indicate that the company has less operating capability. And if the average age of its property, plant, and equipment is lower than its competitors, the company may have more operating capability.

Average Life

To compute the estimated average life that a company's managers have decided to use to calculate depreciation expense for its property, plant, and equipment, you use the formula for the calculation of depreciation (assuming use of the straight-line method):

$$\text{Annual Depreciation Expense} = \frac{\text{Cost} - \text{Residual Value}}{\text{Estimated Life}}$$

Therefore,

$$\text{Estimated Life} = \frac{\text{Cost} - \text{Residual Value}}{\text{Annual Depreciation Expense}}$$

Companies are required to disclose both the cost of their property, plant, and equipment and the annual depreciation expense. So a user must estimate the residual value in order to compute the estimated life. As we mentioned earlier in the chapter, many companies use an arbitrary residual value such as zero or 10%, and either would be a reasonable assumption to make for most companies. However, either assumption would not be as reasonable for a company that has major investments in nonmanufacturing real-estate assets (such as office buildings), or for a company in an industry where assets are often sold well before the end of their useful lives (such as a major airline). It is also appropriate to subtract the cost of any land and construction in process (partially completed buildings) from the cost of the property, plant, and equipment, since neither is depreciated. As with the estimated average age of a company's property, plant, and equipment, the user must understand that this calculation provides an approximation of the estimated life used by the company to calculate its depreciation expense. Using Intel's disclosures shown in Exhibit 21-8, we estimate that its managers decided that the average useful life of its property, plant, and equipment (assuming a zero residual value) is 9.5 years [($44,132 cost − $2,897 construction in progress = $41,235 adjusted cost) ÷ $4,345 depreciation expense for 2005]. As we would expect for a technologically based company, its property, plant, and equipment does not have a very long useful life.

A user may use this estimate of the average life of a company's property, plant, and equipment to evaluate its operating capability by assessing whether the average life seems reasonable for the company, or whether the average life used by the company is significantly different from that used by its competitors. Furthermore, the user can assess how the average life used affected the company's profitability. If the user thinks the average life used by the company is too long (or too short), the user can re-compute the company's annual depreciation expense to determine how the change in depreciation expense affects the company's income. For example, suppose a user thought that the average life Intel's managers used was too short and wanted to know what effect an increase of 20% in the average life of Intel's property, plant, and equipment would have on its 2005 operating income. Since we computed the average life to be 9.5 years, a 20% increase would result in a revised average life of 11.4 years. Dividing the $41,235 adjusted cost (that we computed earlier) by this 11.4 average life results in a revised depreciation expense of $3,617 ($41,235 ÷ 11.4), which is $728 less than the $4,345 actual 2005 depreciation expense. So with a 20% longer life assigned to its property, plant, and equipment, Intel's 2005 operating income would have been 6% higher ($728 ÷ $12,090 operating income, from Exhibit 21-8).

By changing the average life of a company's property, plant, and equipment to one that is more reasonable, or to one that is closer to the average life used by a competitor, a user can also re-compute the company's return on assets. The numerator will change because of the revised depreciation expense as we just computed, and the denominator will change by the revised accumulated depreciation. Then the user may have a better comparison of the profitability of the two companies.

Compute the estimated average age and average life of Colgate-Palmolive's property, plant, and equipment using the information in Appendix B.

Why do you think the SEC requires companies to disclose more than GAAP requires?

Disclosures in SEC Filings

A company must disclose more information about property, plant, and equipment in its annual 10-K filing with the Securities and Exchange Commission than GAAP requires. SEC requirements indicate that investors and creditors may want more than the historical cost amounts provided in the financial statements in order to make their business decisions. A company's managers also may discuss activities related to property, plant, and equipment in the letter to shareholders or the management's discussion and analysis section of the company's 10-K report. The 10-K report also often contains other types of statistical data that can be used to help external users assess a company's outlook for the future.

In Exhibit 21-13, we show *selected* information from the 10-K report that **Rocky Mountain Chocolate Factory, Inc.,** submitted to the SEC for the year ended February 28, 2006. This report included financial statements, management's discussion and analysis, and other information.

Study Exhibit 21-13. What does this information tell you about Rocky Mountain's activities related to property, plant, and equipment? How would you use the information?

EXHIBIT 21-13	SELECTED FINANCIAL INFORMATION: ROCKY MOUNTAIN CHOCOLATE FACTORY

	For the Years Ended February 28	
CASH FLOW STATEMENT (in part)	2006	2005
Cash Flows from Investing Activities		
Purchase of property and equipment	$ (1,300,314)	$(1,406,698)

NOTES TO FINANCIAL STATEMENTS (in part)

Property and Equipment: Property and equipment are recorded at cost. Depreciation and amortization are computed using the straight-line method based upon the estimated useful lives of the assets which range from five to thirty-nine years. Leasehold improvements are amortized on the straight-line method over the lives of the respective leases or the service lives of the improvements, whichever is shorter.

The Company reviews its long-lived assets through analysis of estimated fair value, including identifiable intangible assets, whenever events or changes indicate the carrying amount of such assets may not be recoverable. The Company's policy is to review the recoverability of all assets, at a minimum, on an annual basis.

	February 28, 2006	February 28, 2005
Property and Equipment—At Cost		
Land	$ 513,618	$ 513,618
Building	4,705,242	3,962,051
Machinery and equipment	6,252,011	7,553,261
Furniture and fixtures	817,137	611,930
Leasehold improvements	641,637	484,385
Transportation equipment	331,640	180,723
Construction in progress	—	527,658
	$13,261,285	$13,833,626
Less accumulated depreciation	6,562,681	7,707,645
Property and equipment, net	$ 6,698,604	$ 6,125,981

Store Concept

The Company seeks to establish a fun and inviting atmosphere in its Rocky Mountain Chocolate Factory store locations. Unlike most other confectionery stores, each Rocky Mountain Chocolate Factory store prepares certain products, including fudge and caramel apples, in the store. Customers can observe store personnel making fudge from start to finish, including the mixing of ingredients in old-fashioned copper kettles and the cooling of the fudge on large marble tables, and are often invited to sample the store's products. The Company believes that an average of approximately 40% of the revenues of franchised stores are generated by sales of products prepared on the premises. The Company believes the in-store preparation and aroma of its products enhance the ambiance at Rocky Mountain Chocolate Factory stores, are fun and entertaining for its customers and convey an image of freshness and homemade quality.

Properties

The Company's manufacturing operations and corporate headquarters are located at its 53,000 square foot manufacturing facility, which it owns in Durango, Colorado. During fiscal 2006, the Company's factory produced approximately 2.5 million pounds of chocolate candies, an increase of 11.0% from the approximately 2.2 million pounds produced in fiscal 2005. The factory has the capacity to produce approximately 3.5 million pounds per year. In January 1998, the Company acquired a two-acre parcel adjacent to its factory to ensure the availability of adequate space to expand the factory as volume demands.

As of March 31, 2006, all of the 9 Company-owned stores were occupied pursuant to non-cancelable leases of five to ten years having varying expiration dates, from August 2006 to January 2011, some of which contain optional five-year renewal rights. The Company does not deem any individual store lease to be significant in relation to its overall operations.

The Company acts as primary lessee of some franchised store premises, which it then subleases to franchisees, but the majority of existing locations are leased by the franchisee directly. Current Company policy is not to act as primary lessee on any further franchised locations. At March 31, 2006, the Company was the primary lessee at 35 of its 301 franchised stores. The subleases for such stores are on the same terms as the Company's leases of the premises.

Business Issues and Values

The *actual* net cost of a company's property, plant, and equipment asset is the difference between the purchase price of the asset and the actual residual value. This net cost is not known with certainty until the company disposes of the asset. Meanwhile, the managers of the company must make important decisions regarding the allocation of the *estimated* net cost as an expense to each accounting period. For depreciation expense, they must estimate the pattern of benefits (to decide which method to use), the life of the asset, and the residual value. In addition, to determine any impairment loss, they must compute the market value, probably by discounting the future cash flows the asset is estimated to generate.

Each of these decisions allows for considerable flexibility, and if the managers' estimates are in error, a company *could* report a depreciation amount each year that is quite different from the "correct" amount. So the flexibility may sometimes cause reporting problems for the company and interpretation problems for users. For example, if managers underestimate the annual depreciation expense early in the life of the asset, the company will report income amounts that are too high in those years. To offset this early underestimate of depreciation expense, the managers will, in later years, need to increase the annual depreciation expense, or the company will report a loss on the sale of the asset. (With lower accumulated depreciation, the book value of the asset will be higher than expected at the end of its service life.) In either case, the company will report an income amount that is too low in those years. Since these potential effects extend over the lives of the assets, it may be many years before external users (and the managers) are aware of the misstated income. Therefore, ratios involving income and property, plant, and equipment assets will be misleading during those years, perhaps causing users to make misguided decisions. Furthermore, unethical managers might deliberately *understate* the annual depreciation expense (by overstating the estimated life and/or the residual value) in order to *overstate* annual income and any related ratios. Such a manipulation of income is, of course, a violation of accounting principles and could result in legal sanctions against the managers.

INTANGIBLE ASSETS

7 What are intangible assets and natural resource assets, and what does a company report about them?

Up to this point in the chapter, we have focused on managing, reporting, and evaluating a company's property, plant, and equipment. All types of property, plant, and equipment (land, buildings, machines, etc.) have at least two things in common—they have useful lives longer than one year, and they are *tangible*. Tangible means "having a physical substance" (i.e., they can be seen or touched). Many companies also have another category of long-term assets called *intangible assets*. **Intangible assets** are a company's long-term assets that do *not* have physical substance. These assets have value to a company because they provide it with specific *legal rights* or *economic benefits*. For example, some companies own intangible assets such as patents, copyrights, trademarks and tradenames, franchises, and computer software. Unlimited Decadence Corporation (if it were a real corporation) would own the tradenames (i.e., the exclusive legal right to use a name or symbol) for the words "Unlimited Decadence," "Empty Decadence," and "Pure Decadence." No other company could use these labels without its approval.

 In Exhibit 12-12 of Volume 1, why do you think that Unlimited Decadence doesn't show any intangible assets on its balance sheet?

Intangible assets are similar to a company's tangible assets of property, plant, and equipment in several respects: they have an expected life of more than one year; they derive their value from their ability to help provide revenue for the company; and the company records their cost as an expense in the periods in which it receives their benefits. However, intangible assets generally have five characteristics that make them different from tangible assets:

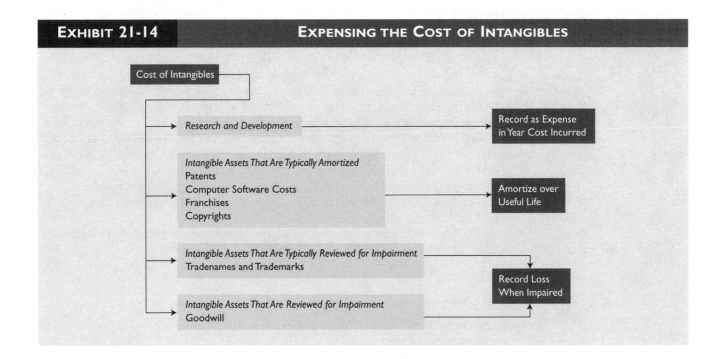

EXHIBIT 21-14 — **EXPENSING THE COST OF INTANGIBLES**

1. They do not have a physical substance but usually result from legal rights.
2. There is generally a higher degree of uncertainty regarding their future benefits.
3. Their value is subject to wider fluctuations because it may depend on competitive conditions.
4. They may have value only to a particular company.
5. They may have expected lives that are very difficult to determine.

As with property, plant, and equipment, a company initially records an intangible asset at its acquisition cost. For some intangibles, the company then allocates this cost as an expense over the asset's useful life. This expense is called **amortization expense** rather than depreciation expense, even though the matching concept underlies both expenses. However, for other intangibles the company does *not* amortize their cost, but instead reviews them for impairment, as we discuss later in the chapter. We summarize these issues in Exhibit 21-14. Before we explain each type of intangible asset mentioned earlier, we will discuss accounting for research and development costs because this accounting may affect the dollar amounts that a company includes in its financial statements as intangible assets. We will discuss amortization expense and impairment in a later section.

Research and Development Costs

Many companies engage in research and development (R&D) to improve their products or services. Expenditures on R&D by technologically oriented companies may be a major part of their total costs each period. In 2005, Intel Corporation incurred $5,145 million in R&D costs, which was over 15% of its operating expenses.

Research is aimed at the discovery of new knowledge intended for use in developing a new or improved product or process. **Development** is the translation of research into a plan or design for a new or improved product or process. The costs included in R&D are those for items such as materials, depreciation on assets used in R&D projects, the salaries of R&D employees, and a reasonable allocation of general and administrative costs.

Each year many companies spend large amounts of money on R&D because they expect to receive total future benefits that exceed the total costs incurred. However, not all R&D projects are successful. Some projects of a company will be unsuccessful (the costs will exceed the benefits), and others will be successful (the benefits will exceed the costs). But overall, the company's managers must expect the total benefits to exceed the total costs. If a company expects benefits to exist for many periods in the future, it could be argued that the company should record the cost of acquiring these benefits as an asset. However, most projects do not provide benefits that exceed costs. For example, one recent study reported that only 1 out of every 20 to 25 ideas becomes a successful product and that only 1 of every 10 to 15 new products becomes a hit. Therefore, because of the uncertainty of the success of each R&D project, GAAP requires a company to *record all R&D costs as an expense when it incurs them*. This uncertainty is why Intel includes its total R&D costs of $5,145 million in its 2005 income statement as an operating expense.

Usually, increases in a company's expenses are viewed negatively because they reduce net income. Do you think this is true for R&D costs? Why or why not?

Patents

A **patent** is an exclusive right granted by the U.S. government (or the government of another country) giving the owner of an invention the control of its manufacture or sale for 20 years from the date of the patent application. The owner of a patent cannot renew it, but may extend its effective life by obtaining a new patent on modifications and improvements to the original invention. Alternatively, competition may make its *useful* life much less than 20 years. As a general rule, a company records the costs of obtaining a patent in an intangible asset account entitled Patents. Recall, however, that a company records as an expense all the R&D costs associated with the internal development of an invention. Therefore, the costs that a company records as an asset for a patent primarily are the costs of processing the patent application and any legal costs incurred, which may be relatively small. For example, **IBM** had nearly 32,000 patents in 2005 yet reported only $15 million of patents and trademarks (out of $105,748 million of assets) on its balance sheet because they primarily were internally developed. Alternatively, if a company purchases a patent from another company, it records the entire acquisition cost as an asset.

If a company develops its own invention, it does not show the costs of development as an asset on its balance sheet. However, if a company purchases a patent from another company, it shows the entire purchase price as an intangible asset. Do you think GAAP is treating this issue fairly? Why would GAAP require patents to be accounted for in these ways?

Copyrights

A **copyright** is an exclusive right granted by the U.S. government (or the government of another country) to publish or sell literary or artistic products for the life of the author plus an additional 70 years. Copyrights cover such items as books, music, and films.

Are you allowed to make copies of this book and sell them to your friends? Why or why not?

As with patents, a company records the costs of *obtaining* the copyright in an intangible asset account called Copyrights. The costs of *producing* the copyrighted item are accounted for separately. For example, a film company accounts for the costs of producing a film separately from the copyright on the film. Therefore, the film company records another asset for these costs, entitled, for example, Film Production.

FROM THE WALL STREET JOURNAL. REPRINTED BY PERMISSION OF CARTOON FEATURES SYNDICATE.

"I believe in truth in advertising, *too,* Hargreave. . . but I *don't* think we should call our new video game 'gimme your quarter!'"

Trademarks and Tradenames

A **trademark** or **tradename** is an exclusive right granted by the U.S. government (or the government of another country) to use a name or symbol for product identification. Pepsi, FritoLay, Tropicana, Quaker, and Gatorade for example, are all tradenames owned by PepsiCo. Rocky Mountain Chocolate Factory disclosed in its 10-K report:

> The trade name "Rocky Mountain Chocolate Factory®," the phrases "The Peak of Perfection in Handmade Chocolates®" and "America's Chocolatier®," "World's Chocolatier™" as well as all other trademarks, service marks, symbols, slogans, emblems, logos and designs used in the Rocky Mountain Chocolate Factory system, are proprietary rights of the Company. All of the foregoing are believed to be of material importance to the Company's business. The registration for the trademark "Rocky Mountain Chocolate Factory" has been granted in the United States and Canada. Applications have also been filed to register the Rocky Mountain Chocolate Factory trademark and/or obtained in certain foreign countries. The Company has not attempted to obtain patent protection for the proprietary recipes developed by the Company's master candy-maker and is relying upon its ability to maintain the confidentiality of those recipes.

The right to a trademark or tradename lasts for 20 years and is renewable indefinitely as long as the company uses the trademark or tradename continuously. Again, a company records only the costs directly associated with obtaining the trademark or tradename, in an intangible asset account. The company records the costs of promoting the name and producing the product separately, as marketing expense and inventory, respectively.

For many companies, trademarks and tradenames are one of their most valuable assets. Yet, as we mentioned, GAAP allows companies that have internally developed valuable trademarks to show only the direct costs of obtaining their trademarks (e.g., filing fees). For instance, since Unlimited Decadence internally developed its tradenames, it does not report an intangible asset on its balance sheet. As with patents, if a company purchases an established trademark from another company, it reports the trademark as an intangible asset at the purchase price.

Franchises

A **franchise** is an agreement entered into by two parties. For a fee, one party (the franchisor) gives the other party (the franchisee) rights to perform certain functions or sell certain products or services over the legal life of the franchise, all of which is specified in the franchise agreement. In addition, the franchisor may agree to provide certain services to the franchisee. For example, many McDonald's restaurants are locally owned and operated under a franchise agreement with the **McDonald's Corporation**. As with other intangibles, a franchisee records the cost it incurred to acquire the franchise as an intangible asset.

 What kinds of services do you think that McDonald's provides to its franchisees?

Computer Software Costs

A company that designs *software for sale* (rather than for its own information systems) incurs three types of costs associated with the software. First, **software production costs** are the costs of designing, coding, testing, and preparing documentation and training materials. The company includes these costs in R&D expense until it establishes the technological feasibility of the product. The company establishes *technological feasibility* either on the date of the completion of a detailed program design or, in its absence, on the completion of a working model of the product. After this date, the company records all additional software production costs as an intangible asset until the product is available for sale to customers. After the product is ready for sale, the company records any software production costs incurred as an expense. We summarize the accounting for software production costs as follows:

We will discuss the rules for the amortization of intangibles later. However, there is a special rule for computer software costs. The amortization expense is the greater of the following amounts: (1) the cost of the intangible asset multiplied by the ratio of *current* gross revenues from the software to the estimated *total* amount of gross revenues from the software, or (2) the straight-line method. The company amortizes the intangible asset for the software production costs over the expected life of the product, which will typically be a relatively short period, such as five years, because of technological change.

Generally, as a result, companies assign most computer software production costs to an expense because, for many companies, technological feasibility occurs after they complete the detailed logic of the program and begin coding. For many companies, software may be a significant, or perhaps the only, revenue-producing "asset" of a company. As the U.S. economy moves toward intangible outputs and creative processes, one may argue that accounting should accommodate this transition by allowing companies to record the results of creative processes as assets when future cash inflows are probable.

The second category of computer software costs is the **unit cost** of producing the software, such as costs of the disks and the duplication of the software, packaging, documentation, and training materials. The company reports these unit costs as inventory and then as cost of goods sold when it reports the related revenue. The third category of computer software costs is the **maintenance and customer-support costs** that the company incurs after it releases the software. It records these costs as an expense when it incurs them.

 *Do you think these rules would cause a computer software company, such as **Microsoft**, to have a low or high gross profit percentage?*

A different set of rules apply to the costs of software that a company develops for *internal use,* such as an airline's computer reservation system or a company's management information system. A company records the costs that it incurs in the preliminary stage of development as an expense. The company starts to record software costs as an asset when managers authorize and commit to funding a computer software project and (1) it is probable that the project will be completed and (2) the software will be used to perform the function intended. The company then amortizes the asset using the straight-line method over the estimated useful life of the software, unless another method provides better matching. The company adds the costs for upgrades and enhancements of the software to the asset, whereas it records the costs incurred for maintaining the software as an expense. It also records the training costs for using the software as an expense. The company must also record any impairment, as we discussed earlier.

Goodwill

Goodwill is another intangible asset that may appear on a company's balance sheet. Goodwill is often called "excess of cost over net assets of acquired companies." A company records goodwill when it purchases another company or a significant portion of another company at a price greater than the market value of the other company's *net* assets (assets minus liabilities). In this situation, the company first records each of the identifiable net assets at its market value. Then, it records **goodwill** as an intangible asset at the difference between the purchase price the company paid and the market value of the identifiable net assets it acquired.

Why would a purchasing company be willing to pay the owners of the purchased company more than the market value of its identifiable net assets? The reason is that companies do not record some "assets" under GAAP. For example, Unlimited Decadence has established a reputation for high-quality products, innovative marketing, and dedicated employees. These characteristics make Unlimited Decadence more valuable than the sum of its recorded net assets. If another company decides to buy Unlimited Decadence, it is also buying Unlimited Decadence's reputation. Therefore, the company should be willing to pay more than just the market value of the net assets that Unlimited Decadence includes on its balance sheet.

Amortization and Impairment of Intangibles

A company separates the intangible assets that we discussed above into three categories to determine whether or not to record an expense and how to review them for impairment. The three categories are: (1) intangible assets with a limited life, (2) intangible assets with an indefinite life, and (3) goodwill.

Intangible Assets with a Limited Life Are Amortized

Intangible assets (such as a patent) that have a limited life (e.g., a legal life) are amortized over the expected life of the benefits they produce. Amortization expense is the allocation of a portion of the acquisition cost of an intangible asset as an expense. Therefore, it is exactly the same concept as depreciation expense, with only a change in the title.

A company amortizes the cost of an intangible with a limited life over its expected *service* life and not necessarily over its legal life. For example, although a patent has a maximum legal life of 20 years, its expected service life may be less than 20 years. A company allocates the cost of the patent as an expense over the lesser of the two periods, its actual service life or its legal life of 20 years. As with depreciation, a company selects the amortization method based on the expected pattern of benefits the intangible asset will produce, except that if the company cannot reliably determine the pattern, it must use the straight-line method. Since it is unlikely that an intangible asset will have a residual value, we do not use one in this chapter. Intangible assets that are amortized are also reviewed for impairment, as we discussed earlier in the chapter for property, plant, and equipment.

The recording of amortization expense is the same as the recording of depreciation expense, except for the different titles. For example, suppose a company has a patent which cost $20,000 and has an estimated life of 10 years. It records the $2,000 annual amortization on this patent as follows:

	Assets			=	**Liabilities**	+	**Stockholders' Equity**		
								Net Income	
							Revenues	−	**Expenses**
	Patent		Accumulated Amortization: Patent						Amortization Expense: Patent
	Bal $20,000	−	Bal $ 0						
			+2,000					−	+$2,000
	Bal $20,000	−	Bal $2,000						

Intangible Assets with an Indefinite Life Are Not Amortized

Some intangibles, such as trademarks and tradenames, have a potentially indefinite life. An intangible with an indefinite life is not amortized (until its life is no longer considered to be indefinite), but is reviewed for impairment. A company must review such intangibles for impairment annually and when events or circumstances occur that indicate the intangible may be impaired. The company records and reports an impairment loss when the fair value of the asset is less than the book value. The amount of the impairment loss is the difference between the fair value and the book value, and is usually reported in the "other items" section of the company's income statement.

Goodwill Impairment

Before 2002, goodwill was amortized over its useful life, not to exceed 40 years. Most companies used the maximum life of 40 years. Beginning in 2002, goodwill is not amortized. Instead it is reviewed for impairment annually. This issue is related to the acquisition of one company by another company, which we discuss more fully in Chapter 23.

Income Tax Rules for Amortization of Intangibles

The rules for computing a company's income taxes may require different treatment of the amortization of intangibles than GAAP. For income taxes, most intangible assets are amortized over their expected lives. However, for those assets that have an indefinite life or for which there is no evidence of a decline in value, such as goodwill, the amortization period is 15 years.

Reporting a Company's Intangible Assets

Companies usually list their intangible assets on the balance sheet in a separate section called Intangibles, which is often presented below Property, Plant, and Equipment. Intangible assets are reported at either cost, cost less the accumulated amortization, or fair value if the intangible has been impaired. Exhibit 21-15 shows how Colgate-Palmolive reports its intangible assets on its balance sheet and the related disclosures in the notes.

Using Information about Intangible Assets for Evaluation

GAAP for intangibles reflects a concern that a company report relevant and reliable amounts for its assets. External users should understand that the market value of a company's intangible asset is often much greater than the book value that the company reports on its balance sheet. Further, as we explained earlier, external users must be aware that many companies possess a tremendous amount of "goodwill" that they do not show on their

EXHIBIT 21-15	DISCLOSURE OF INTANGIBLES: COLGATE-PALMOLIVE

Consolidated Balance Sheet (in part)

(in millions except per share amount)
Colgate-Palmolive Company
December 31, 2005 and December 31, 2004

	2005	2004
ASSETS		
Goodwill	$1,845.7	$1,891.7
Other intangible assests, net	783.2	832.4

5. Goodwill and Other Intangible Assets

The net carrying value of Goodwill as of December 31, 2005 and 2004 by segment is as follows:

	2005	2004
Oral, Personal and Home Care		
North America	$ 276.6	$ 276.9
Latin America	539.1	502.0
Europe	843.8	936.5
Asia/Africa	171.2	161.3
Total Oral, Personal and Home Care	1,830.7	1,876.7
Pet Nutrition	15.0	15.0
Total Goodwill	$1,845.7	$1,891.7

Other intangible assets as of December 31, 2005 and 2004 are comprised of the following:

	2005			2004		
	Gross Carrying Amount	Accumulated Amortization	Net	Gross Carrying Amount	Accumulated Amortization	Net
Trademarks	$418.5	$(158.2)	$260.3	$432.1	$(147.0)	$285.1
Other finite life intangible assets	11.9	(10.6)	1.3	10.2	(8.4)	1.8
Indefinite life intangible assets	521.6	—	521.6	545.5	—	545.5
Total Other intangible assets	$952.0	$(168.8)	$783.2	$987.8	$(155.4)	$832.4

The changes in the net carrying amounts of Goodwill and Other intangible assets during 2005 are mainly due to the impact of foreign currency translation adjustments.

Amortization expense of the above trademarks and other finite life intangible assets was $15.6 for the year ended December 31, 2005. Annual estimated amortization expense for each of the next five years is expected to approximate $16.

balance sheets because they did not purchase it. Thus, we can make the distinction between the costs of *internally developed* goodwill, which a company records as an expense as incurred, and the costs of *purchased* goodwill, which a company records as an asset.

Intracompany and intercompany analyses of intangibles should take this into consideration. Therefore, external users should not rely solely on the annual reports of a company and its competitors. They should use additional sources of information when evaluating intangibles. One CPA went so far as to say, "GAAP is of little use to financial analysts studying brand names because the only time these assets are shown at their true market value is when a company is acquired." However, some countries, such as Great Britain, allow companies to report internally developed intangibles on their balance sheets.

In the following table, we show *Business Week's* list of the five most valuable brands in the world in 2005. Note that none of these brands are reported as assets on the companies' balance sheets, for the reasons we discussed earlier. We also show the total assets reported on each company's 2005 balance sheet.

Company	2005 Brand Value (in billions of dollars)	Total Assets in 2005 Balance Sheet (in billions of dollars)
Coca-Cola	$67.525	$ 29.427
Microsoft	59.941	70.815
IBM	53.376	105.748
General Electric	46.996	673.342
Intel	35.588	48.314

As you can see, the companies' brand values are very significant and would affect how a user would evaluate each of these companies. Stock market studies of companies that own visible brand names have found that the stock prices for these companies do reflect the market value of the brand names. Using these higher values in ratios, such as return on assets, will reduce the apparent profitability of the company.

 Do you consider the cost of your education to be an asset or an expense? Why?

Business Issues and Values: Accounting for Intangibles

For some companies, intangibles are perhaps their most important "asset." Many companies develop reputations for exceptionally reliable products, good customer service, high-quality research and development, and good management. For example, Coca-Cola's strength might be said to rely heavily on the secret formula for its syrup, its tradename, and its image among consumers, which is developed and maintained through advertising and promotion. Similarly, General Electric's strength might be said to rely heavily on its technological ability and its marketing and customer service skills. None of these items appears as an asset on the balance sheet of Coca-Cola or GE, because either the accounting rules require that the costs are recorded as expenses (e.g., advertising, R&D, and employee training), the intangible was internally developed so long ago that it is fully amortized (e.g., a tradename), or the intangible was internally developed and the cost that could be recorded as an asset was not material (e.g., the cost of filing for a patent). Also, service companies and companies that produce computer software rely almost entirely on their employees to generate revenue, yet record no asset related to their skills and talents. This "intellectual capital" is not recorded as an asset.

Therefore, many companies today have "intangibles" that have a significant value, but are not reported as assets on the balance sheet. These "intangibles" are often referred to as "internally developed goodwill." The costs associated with these items are recorded as an expense in the period that they are incurred. No asset is recorded, because there has been no transaction with another entity to establish the value of the asset as there has been when purchased goodwill is recorded. So it is important to distinguish such "internally developed goodwill" from the *purchased* goodwill that we discussed earlier in the chapter and discuss in more detail in Chapter 23.

It is reasonable to argue that certain intangible assets should not be amortized, because there is no evidence of a limited life, just as land is not depreciated. For example, an NFL franchise does not appear to have a limited life or a decline in value at this time, and therefore perhaps should not be amortized. Such intangibles are not amortized, but are reviewed for impairment annually.

Since goodwill is not amortized beginning in 2002, the income of a company that has made acquisitions is higher beginning in 2002 (except in periods when a company records and reports goodwill impairment). For example, when AOL acquired TimeWarner, the transaction resulted in $150 billion of goodwill. Before 2002, **AOL Time Warner** amortized this goodwill over a 40-year life, so its goodwill amortization was $3.75 billion per year. Beginning in 2002, under the new rules it no longer amortizes the goodwill and therefore its income before income taxes is increased by $3.75 billion per year. However, also under the new rules, AOL Time Warner decided in 2002 to report an impairment loss on the goodwill of $56 billion. So a user must analyze AOL Time Warner's performance in the last few years very carefully.

Can you think of another company whose total market value exceeds the market value of its net assets because of each of the above "intangible" items? What factors do you think could affect the lives of the "assets" that compose goodwill?

Remember, GAAP applies to financial reporting in the United States. Under International Accounting Standards, intangibles must be amortized over a maximum of 20 years. Also, in some countries, including Great Britain, goodwill may be "written off" immediately by reducing stockholders' equity. These differences make it more difficult to compare U.S. companies with non-U.S. companies.

NATURAL RESOURCE ASSETS

In addition to property, plant, and equipment and intangible assets, some companies have natural resource assets (sometimes called *wasting assets*). A **natural resource asset** is an asset that is used up as it is extracted, mined, dug up, or chopped down. Examples of natural resource assets are oil, coal, gravel, and timber. A company usually reports its natural resource assets in a separate section of the balance sheet. They may appear above or below property, plant, and equipment, depending on the relative importance of the two categories of assets to the particular company. A company accounts for these assets in the same manner as it accounts for its other categories of physical, long-term assets. That is, it records the cost as an asset and then allocates that cost as an expense over the expected service life of the asset. **Depletion expense** is the portion of the cost (less the estimated residual value) of a natural resource asset that a company allocates as an expense to each accounting period over the asset's service life. Thus, we see that companies use three different titles—**depreciation** for property, plant, and equipment, **amortization** for intangible assets, and **depletion** for natural resource assets—for the single concept of the allocation of the cost of an asset as an expense against the benefits (revenues) the asset produces. Companies often compute depletion expense using the units-of-production (or activity) method.

UNITS-OF-PRODUCTION METHOD

A company uses the **units-of-production method** to compute depletion expense based on the amount of a natural resource asset that is used up (activity level). That is, the company allocates the depletable cost (cost minus estimated residual value) as an expense each year based on the actual production and sale of the natural resource for that year. This method is appropriate because it results in an equal depletion expense for every unit sold. For example, suppose that Deep Pit Mine Company purchased a copper mine for $10 million and estimates that the mine will produce 10,000 tons of copper. (We will ignore the residual value in this example.) Deep Pit computes the depletion *rate* on the basis of the total estimated number of tons (lifetime activity level), as follows:

$$\text{Depletion Rate} = \frac{\text{Cost} - \text{Estimated Residual Value}}{\text{Total Estimated Lifetime Activity Level}}$$

$$= \frac{\$10 \text{ million} - \$0}{10,000 \text{ tons}}$$

$$= \underline{\underline{\$1,000 \text{ per ton}}}$$

Then it computes the depletion expense for the year by multiplying the depletion rate times the number of tons mined and sold during the year. For example, assume that Deep Pit mined and sold 500 tons of copper in 2008. Under the units-of-production method, the company calculates its annual depletion expense as follows:

$$\text{Depletion Expense} = \text{Rate per Ton} \times \text{Actual Number of Tons Mined and Sold}$$
$$= \$1,000 \times 500$$
$$= \underline{\underline{\$500,000}}$$

The company records the $500,000 as an increase in the depletion expense and as a decrease directly in the asset (Copper Mine) account to reduce its book value. The company reports the book value of the natural resource asset on its balance sheet. Because estimating the expected production of a natural resource asset is difficult, a company may revise its expected production after several years as a result of new geological information. As a result, it then calculates a new depletion rate by dividing the remaining book value (less any estimated residual value) by the remaining estimated production.

Although in this example we illustrate depletion of a mine using the units-of-production method, the managers of a company may apply the method to other assets. For instance, Unlimited Decadence could have based the depreciation of its blending machine (which we discussed earlier in the chapter) on the number of pounds of ingredients processed by the machine each accounting period or on the number of hours it operates. When compared with the straight-line method, the activity method produces a constant depreciation rate per *unit* (pound of ingredients sold, for Unlimited Decadence), but the total depreciation expense will vary per *year* as the activity level (number of pounds sold) varies.

SUMMARY

At the beginning of the chapter we asked you several questions. During the chapter, we asked you to STOP and answer some additional questions to build your knowledge about specific issues. Be sure you answered these additional questions. Below are the questions from the beginning of the chapter, with a brief summary of the key points relating to the answers. Use your creative and critical thinking skills to expand on these key points to develop more complete answers to the questions and to determine what other questions you have that might lead you to learn more about the issues.

1 What types of assets does a company include in its property, plant, and equipment, and how does the company compute its historical costs?

A company includes all of the physical (tangible), long-term assets it uses in its operations in property, plant, and equipment, including land, building, machinery, and equipment. The total cost of an asset classified as property, plant, and equipment includes all the costs a company incurs to acquire the asset and to get it ready for use. These costs may include the invoice price (less any cash discounts), sales taxes, transportation charges, and installation costs.

2 Why does a company depreciate its property, plant, and equipment, and what are the causes of depreciation?

The assets a company includes in its property, plant, and equipment provide it with benefits for more than one year. A company depreciates property, plant, and equipment because the matching principle requires that the company match the expenses involved in obtaining the revenues of the period against the revenues it recorded in that accounting period. A company's property, plant, and equipment depreciate for two primary reasons: (1) physical causes and (2) functional causes. Physical causes include wear and tear due to use, deterioration and decay caused by the passage of time, and damage and destruction. Functional causes limit the life of the asset, even though the physical life is not exhausted. An asset is made obsolete because new technology is introduced or because the asset is no longer suitable for the company's operations even though it still may be physically sound.

3 How does a company calculate its depreciation expense, and why does it compute depreciation expense differently for financial reporting than for income taxes?

A company may use the straight-line method to compute depreciation expense by allocating the cost of an asset, less its estimated residual value, equally to each period of the asset's estimated service life. The straight-line method is appropriate when the company expects to use the asset approximately equally each period. A company also may use the following: (1) the double-declining-balance method, (2) the sum-of-the-years'-digits method, and (3) the units-of-production method. The double-declining-balance method and the sum-of-the-years'-digits method are two accelerated depreciation methods. A company using the double-declining-balance method computes depreciation expense by multiplying the book value of an asset at the beginning of the period by twice the straight-line rate. A company using the units-of-production method allocates the cost of an asset, less its estimated residual value, equally to each unit produced by that asset.

In any year, the depreciation expense a company records for financial reporting differs from the amount it records for income tax reporting because the rules are different: financial reporting and the Internal Revenue Code have different objectives. An objective of GAAP is to prepare income statements that fairly present the income-producing activities of the company and that are useful to decision makers. In contrast, two objectives, among others, of the Internal Revenue Code are to obtain revenue for the operation of the federal government and to provide certain kinds of investment incentives for business activity. Companies use the Modified Accelerated Cost Recovery System (MACRS) of depreciating assets for income tax purposes. MACRS depreciation is different from GAAP depreciation because (1) MACRS defines the tax *life*, (2) MACRS uses *no residual value*, and (3) MACRS specifies a depreciation percentage for each year. In contrast, for GAAP depreciation, managers estimate the service life and the residual value of the asset, and select a method based on the matching principle.

4 How does a company evaluate the impairment of its property, plant, and equipment?

A company must review its property, plant, and equipment assets (and certain identifiable intangible assets) for impairment whenever events or changes in circumstances indicate that the book value of the assets may not be recoverable through the net cash flows that the company will receive from those assets. Examples of such events or changes in circumstances include a significant decrease in the market value of the assets, a significant change in the way the assets are used, a significant change in the business or regulatory environment, a current period operating loss, or a negative cash flow from operating activities. If the book value of an asset is not recoverable through the future net operating cash flows expected from that asset, then a company records an impairment loss. The impairment loss is computed as the difference between the asset's book value and its lower market value. The market value may be computed by discounting the expected future net operating cash flows to their present value using the company's applicable discount rate.

5 How does a company record and report the disposal of property, plant, and equipment?

When a company disposes of property, plant, and equipment, regardless of the reason for the disposal, it records depreciation expense for the current period up to the date of disposal. Then, the company removes the balances in the asset account and in the related accumulated depreciation account from its accounting records. Disposals range from the very simple, in which there is no cash involved and the book value is zero, to more complex transactions in which the company receives cash and reports a gain or loss on the disposal because the actual selling price is not equal to the book value.

6 How do external users evaluate information about a company's property, plant, and equipment?

External users use information about a company's property, plant, and equipment and depreciation expense to help evaluate its operating capability and operating efficiency. A company's operating capability is its ability to maintain its level of physical output. Operating efficiency refers to how well a company uses its assets to generate revenue. External users make their evaluations by performing intracompany and intercompany analysis—through the use of horizontal analysis, vertical analysis, and ratio analysis.

7 What are intangible assets and natural resource assets, and what does a company report about them?

Intangible assets are long-term assets that do not have a physical substance. These assets have value to a company because they provide specific legal rights or economic benefits. Intangible assets include patents, copyrights, trademarks and tradenames, franchises, computer software costs, and goodwill. A company reports its intangible assets that have a limited life on its balance sheet at their cost less accumulated amortization and reviews them for impairment in the same way as property, plant, and equipment. It reports the amortization expense for these intangible assets on its income statement. Amortization expense is the portion of the acquisition cost of an intangible asset that a company allocates as an expense to each accounting period over the asset's service life. Intangibles that have an indefinite life, as well as goodwill, are not amortized, but are reviewed for impairment annually.

A natural resource asset is an asset that is used up as it is extracted, mined, dug up, or chopped down. Examples of natural resource assets are oil, coal, gravel, and timber. A company reports the book value of its natural resource assets on its balance sheet and reports depletion expense for these assets on its income statement. Depletion expense is the portion of the cost (less the estimated residual value) of a natural resource asset that a company allocates as an expense to each accounting period over the asset's service life. A company often computes depletion expense using the units-of-production (or activity) method. Under the units-of-production method, the company computes a depletion rate and then multiplies the rate by the number of units mined and sold during the year to determine the depletion expense.

KEY TERMS

accelerated depreciation methods (p. 728)
accumulated depreciation (p. 722)
amortization (p. 757)
amortization expense (p. 749)
book value (p. 722)
capital expenditure (p. 732)
copyright (p. 750)
cost (p. 724)
depreciable cost (p. 724)
depreciation (p. 757)
depreciation expense (p. 722)
depletion (p. 757)
depletion expense (p. 757)
development (p. 749)
double-declining-balance method (p. 728)
estimated residual value (p. 724)
estimated service life (p. 724)
franchise (p. 750)
functional causes (p. 722)
goodwill (p. 752)
impaired (p. 733)

intangible assets (p. 748)
maintenance and customer-support costs (p. 752)
Modified Accelerated Cost Recovery System (MACRS) (p. 731)
natural resource asset (p. 757)
net asset value (p. 722)
operating capability (p. 738)
operating efficiency (p. 738)
operating expenditure (p. 732)
patent (p. 750)
physical causes (p. 722)
property, plant, and equipment (p. 719)
rational (p. 724)
research (p. 749)
software production costs (p. 752)
straight-line method (p. 724)
sum-of-the-years'-digits method (p. 729)
systematic (p. 724)
trademark or tradename (p. 750)
unit cost (p. 752)
units-of-production method (p. 756)

SUMMARY SURFING

Here is an opportunity to gather information on the Internet about real-world issues related to the topics in this chapter (for suggestions on how to navigate various companies' Web sites to find their financial statements and other information, see the related discussion in the Preface at the beginning of the book). Answer the following questions.

• Go to the **Intrawest Corporation** Web site. Find the company's most recent financial statements and related notes. Do you agree with the lives and method used by Intrawest for its properties assets? By how much would the lives have to be different for you to believe there would be a material impact on its financial statements?

• Go to the **Procter & Gamble Company** Web site. Find the company's most recent financial statements and related notes. How much property, plant, and equipment does Procter & Gamble report for the current year? What depreciation method or methods does the company use? How much was the company's research and development cost? Now click on **Colgate-Palmolive**. Find the company's financial statements and related notes. How much property, plant, and equipment does Colgate-Palmolive report for the current year? What depreciation method or methods does the company use? How much was the company's research and development cost? Evaluate the comparability of the information disclosed by the two companies.

INTEGRATED BUSINESS AND ACCOUNTING SITUATIONS

Answer the Following Questions in Your Own Words.

Testing Your Knowledge

21-1 What does a company include in its property, plant, and equipment?

21-2 At what amount does a company report each of its property, plant, and equipment assets?

21-3 Explain the difference between depreciation expense and accumulated depreciation. What is the book value of an asset?

21-4 What costs does a company include in the total cost of a machine it acquires?

21-5 Why does a company depreciate a building?

21-6 Explain what is meant by the (a) physical causes and (b) functional causes of depreciation.

21-7 Identify the three factors involved in the calculation of depreciation.

21-8 What do we mean when we say that depreciation expense is matched against revenue in a "systematic and rational" manner?

21-9 Explain how a company computes straight-line depreciation expense.

21-10 Explain how a company computes double-declining-balance depreciation expense.

21-11 Identify the three ways in which MACRS depreciation for income taxes is different from GAAP depreciation.

21-12 What is a capital expenditure, and how is it accounted for? What is an operating expenditure, and how it is accounted for?

21-13 When a property, plant, and equipment asset is impaired, how does a company compute the amount of an impairment loss?

21-14 How does a company account for the disposal of a machine that it has been using in its operations?

21-15 Explain how a company accounts for the trade-in of a used asset for a new asset.

21-16 What items of information does GAAP require that a company disclose about its property, plant, and equipment? How does a company report its property, plant, and equipment transactions on its cash flow statement?

21-17 What are intangible assets? Give three examples.

21-18 What are research and development, and how does a company record its research and development costs?

21-19 Explain the difference between a patent, a copyright, and a trademark or tradename.

21-20 What are the three types of computer software costs for a company that designs software for sale, and how does the company account for them?

21-21   What is goodwill, and what is it frequently called on a company's balance sheet?

21-22   What is amortization expense, and how is it computed?

21-23   What is depletion expense, and how is it computed under the units-of-production method?

Applying Your Knowledge

21-24   The Young Outdoor Clothing company owned the following assets at the end of its accounting period:
  (a) Land on which it had built a warehouse
  (b) Land on which it is planning to build a new store two years from now
  (c) A retail store
  (d) Shelving used for the display of products
  (e) Old cash registers that were replaced by point-of-sale systems and will be sold next year
  (f) Goods held for sale in a warehouse

  Required: Which of the assets are the company's property, plant, and equipment? Explain your reasoning.

21-25   Hawkins Publishing Company acquired a new copying machine. The machine had a contract price of $8,000 and was purchased on terms of 2/10, n/30. The bill was paid within 10 days. The sales tax rate is 6% on the contract price. Delivery costs paid by the company were $200. Modifications to the room in which the copier was installed were $150, of which $20 was the result of damage caused by an accident. After a month of use, a service representative repaired damage caused by an employee unfamiliar with the machine, at a cost of $50.

  Required: What is the cost of the copying machine? Justify any item(s) you did not include.

21-26   Jackson Company purchased a milling machine on January 1, 2008 for $120,000. The machine had an expected life of 10 years and a residual value of $4,000.

  Required: (1) Compute the depreciation for 2008 and 2009 under each of the following methods: (a) straight line and (b) double declining balance.
  (2) Show how the company would report the book value of the machine on its December 31, 2009 balance sheet under each method.

21-27   On January 1, 2008, Desmond Photo Developing Company purchased a machine for printing pictures. The cost of the machine was $80,000, and the estimated life and residual value are five years and $10,000 respectively.

  Required: (1) Compute the depreciation expense for 2008 and 2009 under each of the following methods: (a) straight line and (b) double declining balance.
  (2) Show how Desmond would report the book value of the machine on its December 31, 2009 balance sheet under each method.

21-28   The Mingus Ice Cream Company purchased a delivery truck on January 1, 2008 for $80,000. The company expected the truck to be driven for 100,000 miles and then sold for $12,000 at the end of 2011. The truck was driven 20,000 miles in 2008.

  Required: Compute the depreciation for 2008 under each of the following methods: (1) straight line and (2) units of production (miles driven).

21-29   The Tatum Tax Service Company purchased a computer system on January 1, 2008 for $50,000. The company expected the computer system to be used for four years and have a residual value of $6,000.

  Required: Prepare a depreciation schedule for the life of the asset under each of the following methods: (1) straight line and (2) double declining balance.

21-30   The Prentiss Poster Company purchased a printing machine for $18,000 on April 2, 2008. The company estimated the life and residual value of the machine as four years and $2,000, respectively. The company uses the straight-line depreciation method, and its fiscal year ends December 31. The company sells the machine on March 31, 2012.

Required: Compute the depreciation expense, accumulated depreciation, and book value for each fiscal year over the life of the machine.

21-31 The Paul Cleaning Company purchased an industrial cleaning machine on January 1, 2008 for $30,000. The machine had an expected life of five years, a residual value of zero, and a life of three years under the Modified Accelerated Cost Recovery System for income taxes.

Required: For each year of the machine's service life, compute the depreciation expense reported (a) on the company's financial statements (using the straight-line method) and (b) on the company's income tax returns.

21-32 The following events occurred for a company during the year:
(a) Installed a solar energy collector in a warehouse
(b) Installed a hydraulic lift door in a delivery truck
(c) Put a new roof on a warehouse
(d) Painted a new advertising logo on the fleet of company trucks
(e) Redecorated offices
(f) Repaired a company car involved in an accident; the car was not covered by insurance

Required: Classify the preceding items as capital expenditures or operating expenditures. Explain your reasoning.

21-33 The Brooks Legal Services Company paid for the following items with cash during 2008:
(a) Installation of energy-efficient windows in offices, $8,500
(b) Overhaul of machine to extend its original life by three years, $1,000
(c) Replacement of dead trees on landscaping around office building, $700
(d) Repainting of all offices, $1,000
(e) Installation of facilities for handicapped employees in office building, $4,900
(f) Replacement of tires on company trucks, $5,300

Required: Prepare entries to record the preceding transactions. Explain your reason for how you recorded each item.

21-34 On December 31, 2008, Franklin Company has an asset that is impaired. The machine cost $100,000 on January 1, 2005, and has accumulated depreciation of $40,000 at the end of 2008. The company estimates that the machine will produce net cash inflows of $13,000 each year for the next four years, and the company uses a discount rate of 12%.

Required: (1) Compute the impairment loss on the machine.
(2) Prepare the entry to record the impairment loss.

21-35 Brown Hydraulic Engineering Company owns a machine that originally cost $25,000. The accumulated depreciation account now has a balance of $18,000.

Required: Prepare entries to record the disposal of the machine if it is sold for cash in the amount of: (1) $7,000, (2) $1,000, or (3) $12,000.

21-36 The Snowdon Mining Company purchased a machine for $80,000 on January 1, 2005. The company depreciates the asset using the straight-line method over five years to a zero residual value. On December 31, 2008, the company sells the machine.

Required: Prepare entries to record the disposal of the machine if it is sold for cash in the amount of: (1) $16,000, (2) $11,000, and (3) $17,000. Assume the company has recorded depreciation expense for 2008.

21-37 Scafell Die Cutting Company owns a machine that originally cost $70,000 and currently has accumulated depreciation of $52,000. The company trades in the machine to a dealer on a new model, which has a selling price (market value of) $90,000. The old machine has a market value of $15,000, so Scafell pays $75,000 in the exchange.

Required: (1) What is the amount at which Scafell records the new machine?

(2) What is the gain or loss that Scafell records on the trade-in of the old machine?

(3) How would your answer to (2) change if Scafell pays only $70,000 in the exchange?

21-38 The Everest Sweater Company reports the following items in its financial statements for 2008 and 2009.

	2008	2009
Sales	$67,000	$73,000
Sales returns	2,000	3,000
Property, plant, and equipment	26,000	32,000
Accumulated depreciation	7,000	10,000

Required: Compute the property, plant, and equipment efficiency ratio for 2008 and 2009. For simplicity, use the ending amounts of net property, plant, and equipment in your ratios. Evaluate your results.

21-39 The Larsone Company uses the straight-line method with no residual value to depreciate its property, plant, and equipment. On its 2008 income statement, Larsone reported depreciation expense of $15,000 and net income of $20,000. On its December 31, 2008 balance sheet, Larsone reported the following amounts:

Property, plant, and equipment	$150,000
Less: Accumulated depreciation	(30,000)
Property, plant, and equipment (net)	$120,000

Required: (1) Compute the average age of Larsone's property, plant, and equipment.

(2) Compute the average life of Larsone's property, plant, and equipment.

(3) If a user decides the average life of Larsone's assets should be 2 years shorter, compute Larsone's revised depreciation expense for 2008.

(4) Compute Larsone's return on assets for 2008 (a) using its reported amounts, and (b) using the 2-year shorter life. Use the ending amount of property, plant, and equipment (net) as the total assets and ignore income taxes.

21-40 The Noyce Company was involved in the following transactions:

(a) Purchased a patent from another company

(b) Developed a design for a new type of machine for use in its production process

(c) Purchased a franchise for exclusive regional sale of a product

(d) Obtained a trademark on a new product

(e) Developed an advertising campaign for a new product

(f) Purchased another company for more than the market value of its identifiable net assets

Required: (1) Explain whether the company should record an intangible asset for each of the preceding items. If not, how would it record each item?

(2) For each item recorded as an intangible asset, indicate whether the company would typically amortize the asset.

21-41 The Nevis Company owns the following intangible assets at the beginning of the year:

(a) A new patent purchased for $34,000

(b) A copyright purchased for $16,000

(c) A trademark purchased for $35,000

(d) A franchise purchased for $55,000

The company amortizes intangible assets with a limited life using the straight-line method over 10 years.

Required: Record the Nevis Company's amortization expense for the year.

21-42 The Skiddaw Company purchased land for $22 million in 2008. The company expects to be able to mine 2 million tons of molybdenum from this land over the next 20 years, at which time the residual value will be zero. During 2008, the company mined and sold 60,000 tons; during 2009, it mined and sold 80,000 tons.

Required: Compute the depletion expense for 2008 and 2009.

21-43 The Bonnington Company purchased a coal mine for $1.4 million in 2008. The company expected to be able to mine 500,000 tons of coal from this mine over the next 10 years, after which it expected to sell the land for $200,000. During 2008, the company mined and sold 20,000 tons of coal. Early in 2009, the company revised its estimate of the total remaining tons to be mined to 580,000 tons. During 2009, the company mined and sold 40,000 tons.

Required: Record the depletion expense for 2008 and 2009.

Making Evaluations

21-44 Coltrane Corporation is a newly formed company and has purchased a building, office equipment, a machine to be used in production, and three company cars. The company is considering which depreciation method to select for each asset for financial reporting. The president wants to report the highest possible net income and pay the lowest possible income taxes. He also argues that the building is unlikely to go down in value in the next five years, so there is no need to depreciate it for that time. He wants to "save the depreciation" until later in the life of the building, when the value will go down. The chief accountant agrees that it is possible to minimize the payment of income taxes, but argues that it is incorrect to select a depreciation method in order to maximize net income or to relate to the value of the asset. She also points out that the value of the cars decreases significantly as soon as they are driven away from the dealer.

Required: (1) Evaluate the correctness of each argument.
(2) Which depreciation method do you think the chief accountant will likely suggest for each asset? Explain your reasoning.

21-45 Ten years ago, Davis Corporation purchased some equipment for $200,000. The company is depreciating the equipment on a straight-line basis to a zero residual value for financial reporting purposes, and is using MACRS for income taxes. Davis is now about to replace the equipment. The income tax rate has been 40%. The president is shocked to find out that the company does not have enough cash available to replace the equipment because the purchase price has doubled. The president lends the company enough money to buy the new equipment but says, "Now we will record twice as much depreciation as before so that we don't have this problem again."

Required: (1) Considering only the preceding facts, by how much do you think the cash balance of the company will have changed over the life of the equipment?
(2) Can the company implement the president's proposed depreciation policy? Do you agree that it would be more desirable?

21-46 Charlotte Parker is considering purchasing either Gordon Company or Rollins Company. Both companies started business five years ago, and at that time, each company purchased property, plant, and equipment for $110,000 and decided to depreciate the assets over 10 years with no residual value. Gordon Company uses straight-line depreciation, and Rollins Company uses double-declining-balance depreciation. The two companies have very similar products and reputations, and their total assets (other than property, plant, and equipment) and total liabilities on their balance sheets are very similar.

Required: (1) Compute the book value of the property, plant, and equipment for each company at the end of five years.
(2) Which company represents the more desirable purchase? Explain your reasoning. Ignore income taxes.
(3) Would your answer to (2) change if income taxes are considered and both companies are corporations?

21-47 **Pfizer** reported that its depreciable property and equipment at December 31, 2005 had a cost of $26,617 million and accumulated depreciation of $9,527 million. The company uses the straight-line depreciation method. Assume that the average life of the assets is 10 years.

Required: (1) What is the average age of the assets on December 31, 2005? Round your answer to the nearest whole year.

(2) If the company used the double-declining-balance method instead, what would be the amount of accumulated depreciation of December 31, 2005? Round each of your calculations to the nearest million, and the depreciation percentage to the nearest whole number.

(3) How much depreciation expense would be recorded in 2006 under the straight-line and double-declining-balance methods, respectively?

(4) Explain whether you agree with Pfizer's use of the straight-line method.

21-48 **Wal-Mart** disclosed the following in its annual report for its fiscal year ending January 31, 2006 (in millions):

Property and Equipment at cost	2006	2005
Land	$16,643	$ 14,472
Buildings and improvements	56,163	46,574
Fixtures and equipment	22,750	21,461
Transportation equipment	1,746	1,530
	$97,302	$ 84,037
Less: Accumulated depreciation	21,427	18,637
Property and equipment, net	$75,875	$ 65,400

Cash flows from operating activities	2006	2005
Net income	$11,231	$10,267
Adjustments to reconcile net income to net cash provided by operating activities		
Depreciation and amortization	4,717	4,264

Cash flows from investing activities		
Payments for property and equipment	$(14,563)	$(12,893)

Wal-Mart uses the straight-line depreciation method. Assume that the amortization is not material and that all acquisitions of property and equipment were cash transactions.

Required: (1) Compute the estimated average age of the depreciable property and equipment for the year ended January 31, 2006. Round your answer to the nearest whole year.

(2) Compute the estimated average life of the depreciable property and equipment for the year ended January 31, 2006. Round your answer to the nearest whole year.

(3) In evaluating Wal-Mart's property and equipment, why would you want to estimate the average age and the average life of these assets? What else might you want to know?

(4) Evaluate how Wal-Mart's management of its property and equipment has changed for the year ended January 31, 2006, as compared to the previous year.

21-49 **Yum! Brands** disclosed the following in its 2005 annual report (in millions):

Property, Plant and Equipment, net	Dec. 31 2005	Dec. 25 2004
Land	$ 567	$ 617
Buildings and improvements	3,094	2,957
Capital leases, primarily buildings	126	146
Machinery and equipment	2,399	2,337
	$ 6,186	$ 6,057
Accumulated depreciation and amortization	(2,830)	(2,618)
	$ 3,356	$ 3,439

Depreciation and amortization expense related to property, plant and equipment was $459 million and $434 million in 2005 and 2004, respectively.

continued

	For year ended	
	Dec. 31 2005	Dec. 25 2004
Cash flows from investing activities		
Capital spending	$(609)	$(645)
Sales of property, plant and equipment	81	52

Yum! Brands uses the straight-line depreciation method (assume that amortization is not material). Assume that capital spending is for the purchase of property, plant, and equipment, and that these purchases were cash transactions.

Required: (1) Why is the company using straight-line depreciation?

    (2) Compute the estimated average age and average life of the property, plant, and equipment at the end of 2005. Round your answer to the nearest whole year.

    (3) Compute the gain or loss on the sale of the property, plant, and equipment in 2005.

    (4) If the company consistently had (a) gains or (b) losses on the sales of property, plant, and equipment, explain what you would conclude.

    (5) Evaluate how **Yum! Brands'** management of its property, plant, and equipment has changed in 2005 compared to 2004.

21-50 **Eastman Chemical Company** disclosed the following in its 2005 annual report (in millions):

Properties at Cost	Dec. 31, 2005	Dec. 31, 2004
Balance at beginning of year	$9,628	$9,861
Capital expenditures	343	248
Deductions	(374)	(481)
Balance at end of year	$9,597	$9,628

Accumulated Depreciation	Dec. 31, 2005	Dec. 31, 2004
Balance at beginning of year	$6,436	$6,442
Provision for depreciation	287	302
Fixed asset impairments	9	134
Deductions	(297)	(442)
Balance at end of year	$6,435	$6,436

Cash Flow Statement	2005	2004
Proceeds from sales of fixed assets	$50	$127

Required: (1) Recreate the entries to record the transactions that affected Properties at Cost and Accumulated Depreciation during 2005. Assume that all acquisitions and sales of property, plant, and equipment were cash transactions.

    (2) If Eastman Chemical Company used a longer estimated life, explain whether its gain or loss on the sale of property, plant, and equipment would be larger or smaller.

21-51 Use the financial section of the 2005 annual report for **Colgate-Palmolive** in Appendix B to answer the following questions.

Required: If GAAP allowed the company to record research and development costs and advertising costs as an asset, and amortize them over three years, would the effects on the 2005 income before income taxes and ending total assets be material? Assume that the costs were incurred at the beginning of each year.

21-52 **PepsiCo** disclosed in its 2005 annual report that it amortizes brands and other identifiable intangibles with a limited life on a straight-line basis over their estimated useful lives of three to forty years. It also disclosed the following amounts (in millions):

Intangible Assets	2005	2004
Amortizable intangible assets, net	$ 530	$ 598
Goodwill	4,088	3,909
Other nonamortizable intangible assets	1,086	933

Amortization expense was $150 and $147 in 2005 and 2004, respectively. The accumulated amortization on the amortizable intangible assets was $781 and $635 at December 31, 2005 and 2004, respectively.

Required: For requirements (2) and (3), assume the company had no disposals of intangibles during 2005.

(1) Why does the company use the straight-line amortization method?

(2) Compute the average age of the amortizable intangibles at the end of 2005.

(3) Compute the average estimated life of the amortizable intangibles at the end of 2005.

(4) Explain whether PepsiCo purchased or sold intangibles in 2005.

21-53   The **Walt Disney Company** uses the following depreciation and amortization policies (in part):

Note 1 (excerpts)

Film and Television Costs   Film and television costs include capitalizable direct negative costs, production overhead, interest, development costs and acquired production costs and are stated at the lower of cost, less accumulated amortization, or fair value. Acquired programming costs for the Company's television and cable/satellite networks are stated at the lower of cost, less accumulated amortization, or net realizable value. Acquired television broadcast program licenses and rights are recorded when the license period begins and the program is available for use. Marketing, distribution, and general and administrative costs are expensed as incurred.

Film and television production and participation costs are expensed based on the ratio of the current period's gross revenues to estimated remaining total gross revenues from all sources on an individual production basis. Television network series costs and multiyear sports rights are charged to expense based on the ratio of the current period's gross revenues to estimated remaining total gross revenues from such programs or on a straight-line basis, as appropriate. Estimated remaining gross revenue for film productions includes revenue that will be earned within ten years of the date of the initial theatrical release. For television network series, we include revenues that will be earned within ten years of the delivery of the first episode, or if still in production, five years from the date of delivery of the most recent episode, if later. For acquired film libraries, remaining revenues include amounts to be earned for up to twenty years from the date of acquisition. Television network and station rights for theatrical movies and other long-form programming are charged to expense primarily on an accelerated basis related to the projected usage of the programs. Development costs for projects that have been determined will not go into production or have not been set for production within three years are written off.

Estimates of total gross revenues can change significantly due to a variety of factors, including advertising rates and the level of market acceptance of the production. Accordingly, revenue estimates are reviewed periodically and amortization is adjusted, if necessary. Such adjustments could have a material effect on results of operations in future periods. The net realizable value of network television broadcast program licenses and rights is reviewed using a daypart methodology. A daypart is defined as an aggregation of programs broadcast during a particular time of day or programs of a similar type. The Company's dayparts are early morning, daytime, late night, primetime, news, children and sports (includes network and cable). The net realizable values of other cable programming are reviewed on an aggregated basis for each cable channel.

Capitalized Software Costs   The Company expenses costs incurred in the preliminary project stage of developing or acquiring internal use software, such as research and feasibility studies, as well as costs incurred in the post-implementation/operational stage, such as maintenance and training. Capitalization of software development costs occurs only after the preliminary project stage is complete, management authorizes the project, and it is probable that the project will be completed and the software will be used for the function intended. As of October 1, 2005 and September 30, 2004, capitalized software costs totaled $483 million and $433 million, respectively. The capitalized costs are amortized on a straight-line basis over the estimated useful life of the software, which ranges from 3–10 years.

Parks, Resorts and Other Property   Parks, resorts and other property are carried at historical cost. Depreciation is computed on the straight-line method over estimated useful lives as follows:

Attractions	25 – 40 years
Buildings and improvements	40 years
Leasehold improvements	Life of lease or asset life if less
Land improvements	20 – 40 years
Furniture, fixtures and equipment	3 – 25 years

Goodwill and Other Intangible Assets   The Company performs an annual impairment test at fiscal year end for goodwill and other indefinite-lived intangible assets, which include FOC licenses and trademarks. As required by Statement of Financial Accounting Standards No. 142, *Goodwill and Other Intangible Assets* (SFAS 142), goodwill is allocated to various reporting units, which are either the operating segment or one reporting level below the operating segment. For purposes of performing the impairment test for goodwill as required by SFAS 142, we established the following reporting units: Cable Networks, Television Broadcasting, Radio, Studio Entertainment, Consumer Products and Parks and Resorts.

SFAS 142 requires the Company to compare the fair value of the reporting unit to its carrying amount on an annual basis to determine if there is potential goodwill impairment. If the fair value of the reporting unit is less than its carrying value, an impairment loss is recorded to the extent that the fair value of the goodwill within the reporting unit is less than the carrying value of its goodwill.

SFAS 142 requires the Company to compare the fair value of an indefinite-lived intangible asset to its carrying amount. If the carrying amount of an indefinite-lived intangible asset exceeds its fair value, an impairment loss is recognized. Fair values for goodwill and other indefinite-lived intangible assets are determined based on discounted cash flows, market multiples or appraised values as appropriate.

To determine the fair value of our reporting units, we generally use a present value technique (discounted cash flow) corroborated by market multiples when available and as appropriate, except for the Television Network, a business within the Television Broadcasting reporting unit. The Television Broadcasting reporting unit includes the Television Network and the owned and operated television stations. These businesses have been grouped together because their respective cash flows are dependent on one another. For purposes of our impairment test, we used a revenue multiple to value the Television Network. We did not use a present value technique or a market multiple approach to value the Television Network as a present value technique would not capture the full fair value of the Television Network and there is little comparable market data available due to the scarcity of television networks. We applied what we believe to be the most appropriate valuation methodology for each of the reporting units. If we had established different reporting units or utilized different valuation methodologies, the impairment test results could differ.

Amortizable intangible assets, principally copyrights, are amortized on a straight-line basis over periods ranging from 10–31 years.

Required: (1) Discuss the strengths and weaknesses of Disney's depreciation and amortization policies.

(2) Identify the types of costs that would be included in a "movie asset" reported on Disney's balance sheet.

21-54 Yesterday, you received the following letter for your advice column in the local paper:

DR. DECISIVE

Dear Dr. Decisive:

Recently a group of us went to see a movie. And guess what we started to talk about when we got back to the dorm?! All the people whose names are listed at the end of the movie. Including the accountant. Can you get me that job? But seriously, one thing led to another, and we started to discuss how the movie company accounts for the costs of a movie. We thought we had that figured out, and we were all about to get some sleep when one of my friends asked how the company would depreciate the movie. That kept us up much too late. Then one of my friends showed me the annual report of **Devon Energy**. And you won't believe that they said that the costs of their dry holes are capitalized. How can a oil well that doesn't produce oil be an asset? Now tell me that accountants aren't weird! Please help us with these issues.

Call me "Sleepless in the Dorm."

Required: Meet with your Dr. Decisive team and write a response to "Sleepless in the Dorm."

PART 8

MANAGING, REPORTING, AND EVALUATING LONG-TERM FINANCING AND INVESTING ACTIVITIES IN A CORPORATE ENVIRONMENT

This section consists of three chapters that discuss issues involving a corporation's long-term financing and investing activities. After reading these chapters, you will be able to:

- *Identify the factors that affect interest rates*

- *Know how a corporation accounts for its bond issues and capital leases*

- *Explain how different methods of accounting for investments in stocks and bonds affect a corporation's financial statements*

- *Describe a corporation's capital structure*

- *Understand a corporation's income statement and earnings per share*

- *Use a corporation's long-term debt, investment, and earnings information for evaluating its financial position and performance*

LONG-TERM DEBT AND OTHER FINANCING ISSUES

1. How does a corporation compute the periodic payment, the interest expense, and the repayment of the principal on a loan?

2. What is a bond, what are its characteristics, and why does a corporation issue bonds?

3. What are the factors that affect long-term interest rates?

4. Why does a corporation issue bonds at less than or more than their face value?

5. How does the interest expense each period compare with the interest paid in that period when a corporation issues bonds at a discount or a premium?

6. What are zero-coupon bonds, and how does a corporation account for the interest on them?

7. How do long-term debt and interest expense disclosures help external users evaluate a corporation?

8. What is a lease? What is a capital lease, and what impact does it have on a lessee's financial statements?

9. Why do deferred income taxes arise, and how does a corporation report them in its financial statements?

10. What is a defined-benefit pension plan, and how does a corporation account for it?

On **Hershey Foods**' (maker of "Peter Paul Mounds") December 31, 2005 balance sheet, the company shows that it owes a total of $943 million of long-term debt— 22 percent of its total liabilities and stockholders' equity. On **Rocky Mountain Chocolate Factory**'s February 28, 2006 balance sheet, it had *no* long-term debt (because it retired all of its $1.655 thousand of long-term debt during 2005). These dollar amounts shown on Hershey Foods' and Rocky Mountain's balance sheets result from decisions by managers as well as the accounting methods the companies used to keep track of long-term debt.

There are various ways to understand the meaning of these disclosures. For example, if Hershey manufactures one piece of candy for an average cost of three cents, its long-term debt balances held the dollar equivalent of over 31 billion pieces! Another way to think about these amounts is to think about the business operations that create them. For example, long-term debt is used to create leverage, but since it requires interest payments and the eventual repayment of the debt, Hershey Foods' risk is increased. In their respective annual reports, Hershey Foods reported interest expense of $89.5 million and net cash flows from operating activities of $461.8 million. Rocky Mountain Chocolate Factory reported interest expense of $19.7 thousand and net cash flows from operating activities of $5,265 thousand. So Hershey Foods' net cash flows from operating activities was only 5.2 times its interest expense, while Rocky Mountain Chocolate Factory's was 267 times (because it had very little interest expense on the debt it retired during 2005).

Can you conclude whether Hershey Foods or Rocky Mountain Chocolate Factory is better at managing its long-term debt? What factors besides these amounts on the balance sheets, income statements, and cash flow statements of the two companies should you consider?

To be able to evaluate a company's liquidity and financial flexibility, as well as its ability to finance operations over the long run, both external and internal users must be familiar with how it issues and reports any long-term debt. Users also must be knowledgeable about how "market forces" affect the ability of a company to issue long-term debt. Typically, when a company borrows from a bank, the debt is called a *note payable,* whereas when it borrows from individual investors, the debt is called *bonds payable.* The primary difference between the two is that bonds can be sold on a "capital market," such as the New York Exchange, in the same way as stocks. Also, notes payable are usually

© DON COUCH PHOTOGRAPHY

If a bank asked you to list your long-term liabilities and their amounts on your loan application, what information about your long-term liabilities would you want to have with you?

issued at their face value, whereas bonds may be issued at their face value, at a premium, or at a discount, as we will discuss later in the chapter.

In Chapter 21, we explained how a company reports on its property, plant, and equipment. In this chapter, we will discuss one of the primary ways that a company finances its acquisition of those assets—the issuance of long-term debt.

 If you prepared a personal balance sheet, what would you include as long-term debt?

VALUING LONG-TERM DEBT

Make a list of a few of your long-term liabilities. Your list may include your car loan, a student loan, a mortgage, etc. Next, use your best judgment to write in a value for each liability. How did you decide which amount to use? Did you have any problems deciding what values to assign? Write down why you chose the amounts you selected for each of your liabilities.

In Exhibit 22-1, we show the list for Jennifer Book, the business student we introduced in Chapter 21. In addition to writing her list, Jennifer explained why she had some difficulty deciding on the values to assign to her liabilities. Perhaps your difficulties were similar to hers. Let's examine the problems she encountered in assigning the amounts.

As we show in Exhibit 22-1, Jennifer lists a family obligation, a "loan" from her grandparents, a car loan, and her student loan as her long-term liabilities. We see that Jennifer has doubts about the appropriate amount to list for her liabilities. For example, she lists her family obligation at the cost of the food but is unsure whether to include the costs of her time. Her grandparents gave her a check for $5,000 on her 18th birthday to help her with college, but she is unsure whether it is a loan or a gift. So

EXHIBIT 22-1	JENNIFER BOOK'S LIST OF FOUR LIABILITIES OWED AND SOME ISSUES WITH ASSIGNING DOLLAR VALUES TO THEM

Liability	Value	Issues in Deciding Dollar Value
Family	$100	We have a family tradition of alternating cooking Christmas dinner. Next year it's my turn, and I think the food will cost me $100. But it will take me a lot of time. Perhaps I should also include the cost of my time for shopping and cooking.
Grandparents	$1,000	My grandparents gave me a check for $5,000 on my 18th birthday to help me with college. They wrote "loan to help with college," but I am pretty sure they don't expect me to repay them when I get a job after graduation. I will assume there is a 20% chance of repaying them, so I will assign a value of $1,000.
Car loan	$12,000	When I bought the car two years ago for $18,000, I took out a loan for $14,000, but I just got a bank statement showing that I have paid $2,000 of principal so far. But I will still have some of the loan outstanding when I plan to sell the car in four years. What should I do about that?
Student loan	$12,000	Since I don't have to start repaying this loan until after I graduate, I decided to compute the present value. The loan is at a subsidized rate of 6%, but I know that market rates are about 10%. So I laid out a schedule of all the cash payments I will have to make and discounted them at 10%. I also know I will borrow more in my senior year, but I left those out. I don't see how I can have a liability until I have the cash.

she assumes there is a 20% chance of repaying her grandparents and assigns a value of $1,000.

Do you think that a gift to Jennifer is the equivalent of an investment in her—that is, stockholders' equity? Why or why not?

When Jennifer bought her car two years ago, she borrowed $14,000 but recently has received a bank statement showing that she has paid $2,000 of principal. She is uncertain how to handle the principal of the loan that will be outstanding when she plans to sell the car. Finally, for her student loan she schedules the cash flows so that she can compute their present value, but she is uncertain whether to use the rate on the loan of 6% or the market rate of 10%. Also she is unsure whether to include the amounts she will borrow for her senior year.

Do you agree with Jennifer's decisions? Was she consistent in her approach to valuing the liabilities? Why or why not? Did you have valuation problems similar to Jennifer's? Do you have a long-term liability that you think is worth less (or more) than its face value, but you don't know how much?

The difficulties Jennifer had in assigning dollar values for long-term liabilities illustrate why financial statement users need to understand how companies account for and report on long-term debt in order to make informed business decisions. In our example, Jennifer Book had difficulty deciding the value to assign to her liabilities. Notice that she did not use any accounting rules to help her decide. A company, however, is required to use GAAP, which for long-term debt is based on three accounting concepts we introduced earlier in the book—the *historical cost concept,* the *concept of a transaction,* and the *matching principle.* Let's review these concepts.

Recall that the historical cost concept states that a company records its transactions on the basis of the dollars exchanged (in other words, the cost) in the transaction. Once a company records a transaction, it usually retains the *cost* involved in the transaction in its accounting records. For instance, assume in July 2008, Unlimited Decadence Corporation borrowed $100,000 for five years at 11% to finance the purchase of some machinery. It is required to make a payment on the loan only once a year. At the end of 2008, interest rates on that type of loan have increased to 12%. Under the historical cost concept, Unlimited Decadence continues to show the debt on its balance sheet at $100,000.

Do you think that the present value of the payments on the loan discounted at 11% are greater or less than those same payments discounted at 12%? Explain your answer.

Many accounting and business experts are concerned about the usefulness of the historical cost concept. They ask, "How does including the $100,000 amount of the loan on Unlimited Decadence's 2008 ending balance sheet help investors and creditors evaluate its liquidity?" In other words, they question the *relevance* of reporting this historical cost amount. They believe that it would be more useful to report the current market value of the loan because if the company paid the loan off early, it would pay the market value of the loan. Supporters of the historical cost concept argue that the $100,000 *is* relevant for evaluating the company's long-term liquidity, and if the company has no intention of paying off the liability this year, then the current market value is *not* relevant.

To whom might the market value be relevant?

Supporters of historical cost also argue that the *reliability* of historical costs outweighs any potential increase in relevance that might be gained from using a measure of current value. In essence, GAAP supporters say, "We know that Unlimited Decadence borrowed $100,000 at 11%. We are not sure how reliable a measure the current interest rate is. With historical cost accounting, at least financial statement users know what they are getting." Also we know that all accountants would conclude that the amount borrowed was $100,000, whereas they would probably differ in their estimates of the value based on a current market interest rate.

 Whose side do you take on this discussion—the supporters or the critics of the historical cost concept? Explain your position.

The concept of a transaction means that a company must have engaged in a transaction in order to record a liability (or an asset). Thus, budgeted cash outflows for an amount that a company will borrow in the future do not create a liability until the amount is borrowed.

 If a company hires a new CEO and agrees to pay her $1 million per year for five years, do you think the company has a liability? Why or why not?

The matching principle states that to determine its net income for an accounting period, a company computes the total expenses involved in earning the revenues of the period and deducts them from the revenues earned in that period. Because long-term debt provides benefits every period that it is outstanding, a company includes the cost of the borrowing as an expense in determining its net income for each accounting period. For example, Unlimited Decadence borrowed $100,000 at 11%. In each accounting period during which the company has use of the money, it matches the cost of borrowing against the revenues recorded during the period. **Interest expense** is the cost to a company of borrowing money for a period. If the company has not paid the interest in the period, it records the interest expense as an end-of-period adjustment.

So, the historical cost concept, the transaction concept, and the matching principle provide the basis for how a company accounts for its long-term debt and reports this debt in its financial statements. Next we will address four important issues: (1) loan payments and interest, (2) the nature of bonds, (3) why a company issues bonds, and (4) bonds issued at face value. However, companies do not always issue bonds at their face value, because the market rate of interest may differ from the interest rate stated on the bonds. Therefore, we will also discuss the factors affecting interest rates and how the market rate of interest affects bond selling prices. In later sections, we will discuss other long-term debt issues, including leases, mortgages, deferred income taxes, and retirement benefits. In the appendix to this chapter, we discuss the accounting for bonds that are sold at a discount or premium and that pay interest semiannually.

 Do you think the fact that a company reports its long-term debt at historical cost affects the usefulness of this balance sheet information? If so, how?

LOAN PAYMENTS AND INTEREST

1 How does a corporation compute the periodic payment, the interest expense, and the repayment of the principal on a loan?

Individuals and businesses have many types of loans. For example, individuals may take out a loan to pay for college, to buy a car, or to purchase a house; a company may take out a loan to buy a specific item of property or to finance its general operations. All these loans have similar characteristics and involve many of the same issues. Since it is important for you to understand these issues, we start by explaining those related to a simple loan. Let's assume that when you graduate, you decide to buy a car and take out a loan of $20,000 to pay for it. The loan is for four years and has an interest rate of 10%. The typical loan requires equal monthly payments (an annuity), but for simplicity, we will assume that this loan requires an equal single payment at the end of each year (this is still an annuity). Don't be concerned about this simplification: it does not affect the issues we discuss—it simply means we can discuss 4 payments instead of 48! So the first issue is the amount of the annual payment. Car dealers and banks determine these payments according to the present value principles we discussed in Chapter 20. Note that since you are borrowing $20,000 today, this is the present value amount. The periodic payment is the amount of an annuity that has a present value equal to the amount borrowed. Since the present value of an annuity is computed as follows:

Present Value of Annuity = Periodic Payment × Present Value of Annuity Factor

and since the amount borrowed is the present value amount, the periodic payment is computed as follows:

Periodic Payment = Amount Borrowed ÷ $\dfrac{\text{Present Value of Annuity Factor Based on}}{\text{the Interest Rate and the Life of the Loan}}$

Each periodic payment on the loan consists of two components: (1) interest expense and (2) a portion of the principal balance. The interest expense is based on the interest rate and the balance (called the **book value**) in the liability account at the beginning of the period. The interest expense and the repayment of principle are computed as follows:

Interest Expense = Periodic Interest Rate × $\dfrac{\text{Book Value of Loan at the}}{\text{Beginning of the Period}}$

Repayment of Principal = Periodic Payment − Interest Expense

The four annual payments are an annuity, so we need to look at Table 20-2 (at the end of Chapter 20) to find the appropriate factor to use. The factor for 10% and 4 years is 3.1699. Therefore the annual payment is computed as follows:

Annual Payment = Amount Borrowed ÷ Present Value of Annuity Factor

= $20,000 ÷ 3.1699

= $6,309.35 (rounded)

The interest expense for the first year is calculated as follows:

Interest Expense = Periodic Interest Rate × $\dfrac{\text{Book Value of Loan at the}}{\text{Beginning of the Year}}$

= 10% × $20,000

= $2,000

The remaining portion of the payment is $4,309.35 ($6,309.35 − $2,000.00) and is the repayment of the principal. So at the beginning of the second year, the balance (principal) of the loan, or the *book value* of the loan, is $15,690.65 ($20,000 − $4,309.35). The interest for year 2 is 10% × $15,690.65, or $1,569.07 (rounded). The remaining portion of the payment is $4,740.28 ($6,309.35 − $1,569.07) and is the repayment of the principal. So at the beginning of the third year, the book value of the loan is $10,950.37 ($15,690.65 − $4,740.28). By now we hope you follow the process, but here are the calculations for the final two years:

Interest, year 3 = 10% × $10,950.37 = $1,095.04 (rounded)

Repayment of principal, year 3 = $6,309.35 − $1,095.04 = $5,214.31

Book value of loan, beginning of year 4 = $10,950.37 − $5,214.31 = $5,736.06

Interest, year 4 = 10% × $5,736.06 = $573.61 (rounded)

Repayment of principal, year 4 = $6,309.35 − $573.61 = $5,735.74

So you see that the balance of your loan is now eliminated because your final payment includes a repayment of principal of $5,735.74, which is equal to the book value of the loan at the beginning of Year 4 of $5,736.06 (allowing for a $0.32 rounding error).

 If the loan required monthly payments, would the monthly payment be $\frac{1}{12}$ of the annual payment?

In this example, we have not discussed how to record the loan or the asset (the car). We will discuss those issues later in the chapter, but if you prepared personal financial statements, you would record the car as an asset and the loan as a liability. Then, at the end of each year, you would record both the interest expense on the loan (as we just calculated) and the depreciation on the car (as we discussed in Chapter 21). You would report the depreciation expense and interest expense in your income statement. We now turn our discussion to situations in which companies borrow money under formal agreements, often called *bonds*.

 How would you respond if a friend asked you why you paid a total of $25,237.40 (4 × $6,309.35) for a $20,000 car (assuming you borrowed 100% of the cost of the car)?

BOND CHARACTERISTICS

2 What is a bond, what are its characteristics, and why does a corporation issue bonds?

Virtually every company borrows money. In Chapter 14 we discussed notes payable, which a company issues when it borrows money for a short time. When a company borrows a large amount of money from investors for a long time, it usually issues bonds. A **bond** is a type of note in which a company agrees to pay the holder of the bond its face value at the maturity date and to pay interest on the face value periodically at a specified rate. Thus the company that issues the bond, the *borrower,* receives money when it sells the bond to the holder (purchaser) of the bond, the *lender.* We will now explain some terms related to bonds. The **face value** (also called the *par value*) is the amount of money that the issuer promises to pay on the maturity date. The face value is the same concept as the principal of a note. The **maturity date** is the date on which the issuer of the bond agrees to pay the face value to the holder. The issuer also agrees to pay interest each period. The **contract rate** (also called the *stated* or *nominal* rate) is the rate at which the issuer of the bond pays interest on the face value each period until the maturity date. All this information is printed on a bond certificate or related documents, provided to the owner of the bond. A **bond certificate** is a serially numbered legal document that specifies the face value, the annual interest rate, and the maturity date.[1] A company usually issues bonds so that each bond has a face value of $1,000. It may sell the entire bond issue to one purchaser or to numerous individual purchasers. Thus a $100,000 bond issue will consist of 100 bonds, each with a $1,000 face value. In addition, the bond issue usually specifies that interest is paid twice each year (semiannually), although it may state the contract rate in annual terms on the bond certificate. The interest rate per semiannual period, therefore, is 1/2 of the stated annual rate. For example, a $1,000, 10% bond pays interest of $50 ($1,000 × 10% × 1/2) twice each year (every six months), for a total of $100 per year.

USER ANALYSIS PERSPECTIVE: REASONS FOR ISSUING BONDS

A company (corporation) can obtain large amounts of money (capital) for a long time in two ways. The first way is to sell common stock, which we briefly discussed in Chapter 10 and will discuss more completely in Chapter 24. Selling common stock provides a cor-

---

[1]The bond certificate may contain other provisions as well. For instance, bonds may be registered, convertible, zero-coupon, serial, and callable, to name a few. We will briefly discuss zero-coupon and callable bonds later in the chapter.

poration with permanent capital, since it has no obligation to repay the stockholders. In addition, it has no legal obligation to pay dividends, although many corporations choose to do so. Because the stockholders are the owners of a corporation, selling more stock spreads ownership rights, voting rights, and the corporation's earnings over more shares. The second way a corporation can obtain long-term capital is to borrow the money by, for example, issuing bonds, which obligate the corporation to repay the amount borrowed and also to pay interest each period. The payment of interest is a legal obligation, and if the corporation issuing the bonds (the borrower) fails to pay the interest on the face value, the holder of the bonds (the lender) can take legal action to enforce payment, which may cause the borrower to declare bankruptcy. The bondholders are creditors of the corporation; they are not the owners and therefore have no voting rights.

The main reason why the managers of a corporation may decide that it should issue bonds instead of common stock is that the earnings available to the common stockholders can be increased through leverage. **Leverage** is the use of borrowing by a corporation to increase the return to common stockholders. It also is called *trading on equity*. If a corporation can borrow money by issuing bonds and can use the money to invest in a project that provides greater income than the interest that it must pay on the bonds, the corporation and its stockholders will be better off (they will earn a higher income). One measure of the return to common stockholders is earnings per share, which we discussed in Chapter 10. When a corporation successfully uses leverage, it increases its earnings per share.

For example, assume that a corporation currently has 10,000 shares of common stock held by stockholders, income before income taxes of $100,000, and an income tax rate of 40%. The managers have decided to expand its operations by building a factory, at a cost of $300,000. They expect the factory to provide additional pretax income of $50,000 per year. The corporation is considering selling 6,000 additional shares of common stock for $50 per share or issuing bonds with a face value of $300,000 and a 10% interest rate. We show the effects of these two alternatives in Exhibit 22-2.

First, let's look at financing the expansion by issuing bonds for $300,000. In this case (the middle column of Exhibit 22-2), the corporation has interest expense of $30,000 ($300,000 × 10%), which it records as an expense on the income statement. After subtracting the income tax expense, its net income increases by $12,000 (from $60,000 to $72,000) when it uses bond financing. Since it does not increase the number of common shares with bond financing, it also reports an *increase* in its earnings per share from $6.00 to $7.20 ($72,000 ÷ 10,000).

Now suppose the corporation decides to finance the expansion by issuing common stock. In this case (the right column of Exhibit 22-2), the corporation has no additional interest expense, so it reports an increase in its income before income taxes of $50,000 and an increase in net income of $30,000 (from $60,000 to $90,000). Although its net income increases by more than it does under the bond financing alternative, the corporation

EXHIBIT 22-2	USE OF LEVERAGE THROUGH BOND FINANCING		
	Before Expansion	**Bond Financing**	**Stock Financing**
Earnings before interest and income taxes	$100,000	$150,000	$150,000
Interest expense	—	(30,000)	—
Income before income taxes	$100,000	$120,000	$150,000
Income tax expense	(40,000)	(48,000)	(60,000)
Net Income	$ 60,000	$ 72,000	$ 90,000
Number of shares of common stock	10,000	10,000	16,000
Earnings per share	$ 6.00	$ 7.20	$ 5.63

also increases the number of common shares by 6,000, to 16,000. Therefore, it reports a *decrease* in its earnings per share from $6.00 to $5.63 ($90,000 ÷ 16,000). In this situation, although financing by issuing bonds does not increase net income by as much as selling common stock, bond financing has a more favorable effect on the earnings per share of current stockholders and is of greater benefit to them.

The reason for this advantageous result is that the new factory is expected to earn a pretax return (additional earnings ÷ investment) of nearly 17% ($50,000 ÷ $300,000), whereas the pretax interest cost on the bonds is only 10%. Stockholders benefit from leverage when a corporation borrows money at 10% to earn a return of 17%.

 How much would the corporation report as net income and earnings per share under the bond and stock financing alternatives if the expansion was not as successful and the new factory provides additional pretax income of only $15,000?

Although stockholders may benefit when a corporation borrows money, there is a limit to the amount of money it can borrow. As the corporation borrows more money, its risk of default increases, so that the interest rate it will have to pay also increases. At some point the interest rate will exceed the rate that the corporation can earn from an investment (so earnings per share will decrease), lenders will refuse to lend it more money, or the managers will decide that the risk of borrowing has become too high. Thus all companies have a limit on the amount of money they can borrow.

 Explain whether you are using leverage if you borrow money to pay for your college education.

BONDS ISSUED AT FACE VALUE

If a company issues bonds for the amount of their face value, the recording and reporting are straightforward because the cash received from the sale equals the face value. For example, assume that on January 1, 2008, Unlimited Decadence issues 10%, 10-year bonds with a face value of $200,000 for $200,000 cash. When it issues these bonds, Unlimited Decadence records the face value in a liability account called Bonds Payable, as follows:

Assets	=	Liabilities	+	Stockholders' Equity
Cash		Bonds Payable		
+$200,000		+$200,000		

Interest Expense and Payment

As we discussed earlier, bonds issued by companies usually pay interest semiannually. Unlimited Decadence pays interest each June 30 and December 31. Therefore, it computes the semiannual interest expense on these dates as follows:

$$\frac{\text{Semiannual}}{\text{Interest Expense}} = \frac{\text{Face Value}}{\text{of Bonds}} \times \left(\frac{\text{Annual}}{\text{Contract Rate}} \div \frac{\text{Number of Interest}}{\text{Payments per Year}} \right)$$

Since the interest payment is based on the face value of the bonds and the company issued the bonds for the amount of the face value, the interest expense and interest payment are equal. The company computes them as follows:

$$\text{Semiannual Interest Expense and Interest Payment} = \$200,000 \times (10\% \div 2)$$

$$= \$10,000$$

Note that since the interest expense and interest payment are equal, the company does not reduce the principal amount, as we discussed earlier for the $20,000 car loan. Unlimited Decadence records each semiannual interest expense and payment as follows:

Assets	=	Liabilities	+	Stockholders' Equity		
					Net Income	
				Revenues	−	Expenses
Cash						Interest Expense
−$10,000					−	+$10,000

Accrual of Interest

Companies may issue bonds at any time during the year, but they still pay interest every six months from the date of issuance. For instance, if a company issues bonds on May 1, then it pays interest every October 31 and April 30. In this situation, the company issuing the bonds must be sure it reports the correct amount of interest expense on its annual income statement and the bond interest owed at the end of the year on its ending balance sheet. So the company *accrues* the interest it owes from the date of the last interest payment to the end of the year.

 What do you think is the primary difference between the payments on a car loan and the payments on a bond?

To illustrate, assume that Layth Company issued 12%, 10-year bonds with a face value of $300,000 for $300,000 cash on September 1, 2008. It pays interest on these bonds every February 28 and August 31. At the end of 2008, the company has not yet paid any interest, but it *owes* interest for four months (from September 1 through December 31). Therefore, the company must report four months of interest expense on its 2008 income statement and four months of interest owed on its ending 2008 balance sheet. The company computes its interest expense and interest owed to date as follows:

$$\frac{\text{Interest Expense for}}{\text{Fraction of Period}} = \frac{\text{Semiannual}}{\text{Interest Expense}} \times \frac{\text{Fraction of Period}}{\text{since Interest Last Paid}}$$

$$= [\$300,000 \times (12\% \div 2)] \times 4/6$$

$$= \$12,000$$

Note that we determine the interest expense for the four months by computing the semiannual interest amount and then multiplying this amount by the fraction of the semiannual period since the bonds were issued (since the company has not yet paid interest). In this case the company's bonds were outstanding for four months of the six-month interest period. Therefore, it records the interest expense and interest owed on December 31, 2008, as follows:

Assets	=	Liabilities	+	Stockholders' Equity		
					Net Income	
				Revenues	−	Expenses
		Interest Payable				Interest Expense
		+$12,000			−	+$12,000

When the company makes its first $18,000 semiannual interest payment on February 28, 2009, it will record interest expense of $6,000 for the two months of the interest period in 2009 and will eliminate the $12,000 interest payable recorded at the end of 2008. This pattern of accruing interest will continue every year for the life of the bonds.

 Record the February 28 entry for the $18,000 interest payment.

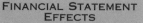

FACTORS AFFECTING BOND INTEREST RATES

3 What are the factors that affect long-term interest rates?

In the examples of a car loan and bonds issued at face value, we assumed an interest rate. Several factors affect interest rates, including the policies of the Federal Reserve Board (which affect the supply and demand for money in the national economy), federal regulations, and the budget surplus or deficit of the federal government. Long-term interest rates for corporations, however, include three *primary* factors:

- The risk-free rate
- The expected inflation rate
- The risk premium

The **risk-free rate** is the rate that a borrower would pay, and a lender would receive, when there is no risk of default by the borrower and when no inflation is expected. Borrowing by the U.S. government is considered to be risk-free because the government will not default. Since the United States is not inflation-free, most U.S. government borrowing reflects the effect of the risk-free rate plus the expected inflation rate. The interest rate includes the **expected inflation rate** so that the borrower pays additional interest to compensate for the expected inflation over the life of the borrowing. Inflation causes the value of the dollar that eventually is repaid to be worth less than the dollar that was originally lent, so the added interest compensates for this decline. Most borrowings of the federal government illustrate the risk-free rate plus the expected inflation because they are considered to be risk-free, but occur in an inflationary environment. However, in recent years the U.S. government has issued "inflation indexed" bonds whose principal amounts are adjusted to reflect inflation. Therefore, the interest rate on these borrowings is the risk-free rate. The **risk premium** is the additional interest that a borrower, such as a company, pays when there is a possibility that it will default. The higher the risk of default, the higher is the risk premium. So a company that has a higher risk of default will have to pay a higher rate of interest to its lenders.

To illustrate the nature of these three components, at the time of writing this book the following rates (called *yields,* which we explain later) existed on selected borrowings:

Borrower	Maturity Date	Yield
U.S. Government (inflation indexed)	2016	2.3%
U.S. Government	2016	4.6
Home Depot	2013	5.2
Home Depot	2016	5.5
Sprint Nextel	2016	6.2

Thus the risk-free rate until 2016 is 2.3%. The risk-free rate plus the inflation expectation until 2016 is 4.6% per year. Thus, the market is expecting inflation of 2.3% (4.6% − 2.3%) per year until 2016. Since **Home Depot** does have some risk of default, the risk premium associated with the borrowing that will mature in 2016 is 0.9% (5.5% − 4.6%). The risk premium for the 2013 borrowing of Home Depot is lower by 0.3% (5.5% − 5.2%) because there is a shorter time period in which Home Depot could have financial problems and a shorter period of potential inflation. The risk premium for **Sprint Nextel** is 1.6% (6.2% − 4.6%), which indicates that its likelihood of default is significantly higher than Home Depot. We do not expect you to compute an interest rate for a particular situation. However, an understanding of the components of long-term interest rates is helpful in understanding both general business issues and accounting for bonds that are issued at less than or more than their face value (which we will discuss in the next section and in the appendix to this chapter), as well as accounting for investments in bonds (which we will discuss in Chapter 23).

Look in a newspaper to find the current yields of each of the bonds listed above. Have expectations of inflation changed? Have any of the risk premiums changed?

BONDS ISSUED AT LESS THAN OR MORE THAN FACE VALUE

A company must follow certain steps when it issues bonds, such as receiving approval from the regulatory authorities (for example, the Securities and Exchange Commission). It also must publish the terms of the bond issue, such as the contract rate, maturity date, and interest payment dates, and must print the bond certificates. When a company decides to issue bonds, it usually deals with a securities broker(s) or investment banker(s). The broker and the company agree on a price for the bonds, and the company sells the bonds to the broker. The broker then sells the bonds to its customers and plans to make a profit on this service. The company issuing (selling) the bonds deals with a broker to avoid the problem of having to find the purchasers and having to be involved in cash transactions with each purchaser.

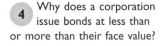

4 Why does a corporation issue bonds at less than or more than their face value?

 Do you think this is similar to the relationship among a manufacturer, a wholesaler, and a retailer?

The broker and the company base the selling price on the terms of the bond issue and the components of the long-term interest rate, as we discussed earlier. They determine the rate that they believe best reflects current market conditions. This market rate of interest is called the *yield*. The **yield** is the market rate at which the bonds are issued.[2] Although the yield is stated as a percentage, it is usually referred to as a yield instead of a yield rate. The yield is often called the *effective rate*. The yield on a bond issue may be different from the contract rate set by the company and printed on the bond certificates. The managers of the company set the contract rate, whereas the marketplace determines the yield. The difference between the contract rate and the yield may result from a difference of opinion between the broker and the company about the yield at which the bonds will be sold. It also may result from a change in economic conditions between the date the terms of the bond were set and the date the bonds are issued. Sometimes companies issue bonds for which the yield is equal to the contract rate, in which case it sells the bonds at face value, as we illustrated earlier. However, often these rates are not equal. When this is the case, a company sells the bonds at less than or more than their face value.

Bond Selling Prices

Once the broker and the company have set the terms of a bond issue and determined the yield, they calculate the selling price of the bonds. We explain the calculation in the appendix to this chapter. However, we can state some general rules now. If the yield is *more* than the contract rate, the company will receive (and the purchasers of the bonds will pay) a selling price that is *less* than the face value of the bonds; that is, the company will sell the bonds at a *discount*. Since the contract rate is less than the market rate of interest for similar bonds, the company's bonds are worth less in comparison and, therefore, sell for less. Alternatively, if the yield is *less* than the contract rate, the company will receive (and the purchasers of the bonds will pay) a selling price that is *more* than the face value of the bonds; that is, the company will sell the bonds at a *premium*.

 Why do you think purchasers are willing to pay a premium for bonds that have a contract rate greater than their yield?

The issuance price of bonds sold at a discount or a premium is usually quoted as a percentage of the face value. For example, a company issuing bonds that have a face value of $200,000 and that are quoted at 97 (i.e., 97% of the face value) sells these bonds at a

---

[2]After a company issues bonds, the yield on these bonds will fluctuate in the bond market as changes occur in the risk premium and the expected inflation rate. It is the yield at the time of issuance, however, that a company uses in accounting for its bonds payable.

discount for $194,000 ($200,000 × 0.97). Bonds that have a face value of $100,000 and that are quoted at 102 are sold at a premium for $102,000 ($100,000 × 1.02). When a company sells bonds (whether at a premium or a discount), it records the selling price in the Bonds Payable account. For example, the company selling bonds with a face value of $200,000 for $194,000 would record the sale as follows:

Assets	=	Liabilities	+	Stockholders' Equity
Cash		Bonds Payable		
+$194,000		+$194,000		

FINANCIAL STATEMENT EFFECTS

Increases current assets and total assets on *balance sheet*. Increases noncurrent liabilities and total liabilities on *balance sheet*. Increases cash flows from financing activities on *cash flow statement*.

The $194,000 is the *book value* of the bonds.

Users need to understand why bonds sell at a price different from the face value when the yield is different from the contract rate. Remember that the selling price is the amount received by the company (and paid by the purchasers) at the time it issues the bonds, and that the face value is the amount that the company will pay (and the purchasers will receive) on the maturity date. The difference between the selling price and the face value means that the company incurs a cost (and the purchasers earn a return) on the bonds' selling price equal to the yield required by the market on the date of issue. For instance, a company sells bonds at a discount because the yield is higher than the contract rate. Remember that when a company sells a bond at a discount, it borrows *less* than the face value of the bond but still must pay back the entire face value of the bond on its maturity date. The difference (the discount) between the lower selling price and the face value, combined with the contract interest paid by the company each interest period, results in a cost to the company (and return to the purchasers) equal to the higher yield. Alternatively, a company sells bonds at a premium because the yield is lower than the contract rate. When a company sells a bond at a premium, it borrows *more* than the face value of the bond but only pays back the face value of the bond on its maturity date. The difference (the premium) between the higher selling price and the face value, offset by the contract interest paid by the company each interest period, results in a cost to the company (and return to the purchasers) equal to the lower yield. We know this paragraph may be difficult to understand, but we will be explaining the issues more as we go through the chapter and in the appendix to this chapter.

 If the yield on two bonds is the same, would you prefer to buy a bond that sells at a discount or one that sells at a premium? Explain your answer.

Bond Interest Expense

5 How does the interest expense each period compare with the interest paid in that period when a corporation issues bonds at a discount or a premium?

Interest expense is the cost of borrowing money. When a company sells bonds at a discount, the amount of money it receives (borrows) is less than the face value of the bonds. But the total amount of cash the company pays (the interest and principal) is the same amount it would pay if it sold the bonds at their face value. The excess of the total amount paid over the amount borrowed is the total (lifetime) interest. When a company sells bonds at a discount, that difference is higher than it would be if the company sold the bonds for their face value. Not only the *amount* of interest but also the *rate* of interest is higher in this situation.

Because a company issuing bonds at a discount or premium incurs a cost (yield) either higher (for bonds sold at a discount) or lower (for bonds sold at a premium) than the contract rate, the interest *expense* it records each semiannual period is either higher or lower than the interest *paid* in that period (remember, the borrower pays the contract rate). A company computes the interest expense on bonds payable each period as follows:

$$\text{Interest Expense for Period} = \frac{\text{Book Value of Bonds Payable}}{\text{at Beginning of Period}} \times \text{Yield}$$

When a company sells bonds at a *discount,* its interest expense each period is *higher* than the interest it pays in that period. When a company sells bonds at a *premium,* its

© 1998 SIDNEY HARRIS

"When interest rates go up, bond prices go down. When interest rates go down, bond prices go up. But please don't ask me why."

interest expense each period is *lower* than the interest it pays in that period. The difference between the interest expense and the interest paid is the amount of the discount or premium that the company *amortizes* each period. As you will see, by the maturity date, the company will have amortized all the discount or premium so that the book value of the bonds payable equals the face value (the amount the borrower pays the lender).

We show the relationships between the yield and the contract rate, as well as the related impact on the selling price and the interest expense, in Exhibit 22-3. Because the accounting procedures for the amortization of a discount or premium on bonds that pay interest each period are complex, we do not show them here. We will illustrate the calculations and the accounting procedures for these bonds in the appendix to this chapter. We do, however, illustrate the amortization of the discount on zero-coupon bonds in the next section.

Zero-Coupon Bonds

In the previous sections, we discussed bonds on which a company pays interest *each period*. In recent years, many companies have issued a slightly different type of bond called a *zero-coupon bond.* **Zero-coupon bonds** are bonds that pay no interest each period. That is, the only cash flows associated with the bonds are the amount borrowed (which is less than the face value of the bonds) and the payment of the face value on the maturity date. The face value includes the amount borrowed plus the interest. Even though the bonds

6 What are zero-coupon bonds, and how does a corporation account for the interest on them?

EXHIBIT 22-3	RELATIONSHIPS BETWEEN BOND SELLING PRICES AND INTEREST EXPENSE	
Yield Compared to Contract Rate	**Bonds Sell at**	**Annual Interest Expense Compared to Annual Interest Payment**
Yield > Contract Rate	Discount	Interest Expense > Interest Paid
Yield = Contract Rate	Face Value	Interest Expense = Interest Paid
Yield < Contract Rate	Premium	Interest Expense < Interest Paid

pay no interest each period, the company still reports an interest *expense* each period because it has incurred interest on the amount borrowed. The selling price of zero-coupon bonds is the present value of the face value (using the *annual* yield),[3] and therefore is always less than the face value. Recall from Chapter 20 that the present value is the value today of a certain amount of dollars paid or received in the future. (You should go back to Chapter 20 if you need to review the concept of, and calculations for, present value.) The *discount* is the difference between the selling price and the face value. The company computes the annual interest expense by multiplying the annual yield by the book value of the bonds at the beginning of the year. This way of computing interest expense is called the **effective interest method**. Since the company pays no cash for interest each year, it records the annual interest expense as an increase in the book value of the bonds payable each year, so that the book value on the maturity date is equal to the face value (the amount the borrower pays the lender). Similarly, although the purchasers *receive* no interest, they earn interest *revenue* each year.

For example, suppose that, on January 1, 2008, Unlimited Decadence issues 10-year, zero-coupon bonds with a face value of $1 million. The bonds are sold to yield 10%. The selling price of the bonds is calculated by discounting the face value (a single future amount) using the 10% yield and the 10-year life of the bonds, as follows:

$$\text{Selling Price of the Bond Issue} = \text{Present Value of the Face Value}$$

$$= \text{Face Value} \times \begin{array}{c}\text{Present Value of \$1 Factor} \\ \text{for 10 Periods at 10\%}\end{array}$$

$$= \$1,000,000 \times \begin{array}{c}0.3855 \text{ (from Table 20-1 at} \\ \text{the end of Chapter 20)}\end{array}$$

$$= \$385,500$$

Notice that the $385,500 selling price of the zero-coupon bonds is much less than the $1 million face value. This is why many people refer to them as *deep discount* bonds. Unlimited Decadence records the sale of the bonds as follows:

Assets	=	Liabilities	+	Stockholders' Equity
Cash		Bonds Payable		
+$385,500		+$385,500		

The company computes the $38,550 interest expense for 2008 by multiplying the book value of the bonds payable at the beginning of the period by the annual yield, as follows:

$$\text{Interest Expense for Period} = \begin{array}{c}\text{Book Value of Bonds Payable} \\ \text{at Beginning of Period}\end{array} \times \text{Annual Yield}$$

$$= \$385,500 \times 10\%$$

$$= \$38,550$$

Since Unlimited Decadence does not *pay* any interest, on December 31, 2008, it records the amount of the interest as an increase in the book value of the liability. This is called *amortizing* a portion of the discount, and the company records the interest expense and amortization as follows:

---

[3]A zero-coupon bond may also be valued using a semiannual yield. We use the annual yield for simplicity.

Assets	=	Liabilities	+	Stockholders' Equity		
					Net Income	
				Revenues	−	Expenses
		Bonds Payable				Interest Expense
		Bal $385,500				
		+ 38,550			−	+$38,550
		Bal $424,050				

Unlimited Decadence reports the new $424,050 book value of the bonds as a non-current liability on its December 31, 2008 balance sheet as follows:

Long-term debt
   10% bonds payable (face value $1,000,000), due 12/31/17 $424,050

Unlimited Decadence computes the interest expense for 2009 as follows:

$$\text{Interest Expense for Period} = \frac{\text{Book Value of Bonds Payable}}{\text{at Beginning of Period}} \times \text{Annual Yield}$$

$$= (\$385,500 + \$38,550) \times 10\%$$

$$= \$424,050 \times 10\%$$

$$= \$42,405$$

Each year for 10 years, Unlimited Decadence increases the book value of the bonds by the amount of that year's amortization so that at the end of their 10-year life, their book value will be $1 million (the face value of the bonds). Unlimited Decadence will then pay $1 million to the bondholders to retire the liability.

Retirement of Bonds

As we mentioned earlier, whether a company issues bonds at a premium or at a discount, on the maturity date the book value of the bonds payable is equal to the face value because of the amortization process over the life of the bonds. Therefore, when the company pays the face value on the maturity date, it retires the bonds and eliminates the bond liability.

Sometimes a company retires bonds prior to their maturity date. This may occur if the bonds are traded on a "capital market" and the company purchases them from the investors at their market price on the day of the purchase. Also the bond certificate may include a provision that allows the issuer to purchase them. These bonds are called **callable bonds**. When bonds are callable, the company that issued the bonds has the right to recall (retire) the bonds before the maturity date at a *call price* that was specified when the bonds were issued, rather than at their market price. The call price is higher than the *original* selling price.

Would you buy bonds from a company if the call price was less than the face value? Why or why not?

When a company retires bonds before their maturity date, the price paid may be more, less, or the same as the current book value of the bonds. When the cash paid to retire bonds is less than the book value of the bonds, the company records a *gain* on the retirement. Or, if the cash paid to retire bonds is more than the book value of the bonds, the company records a *loss* on the retirement.

To understand the early retirement of bonds, suppose that a company pays $205,000 to retire bonds with a current book value of $198,000. In this situation, the company incurs a $7,000 ($205,000 − $198,000) loss to retire the bonds, and it records the retirement as follows:

Assets	=	Liabilities	+	Stockholders' Equity	
				Net Income	
				Revenues −	Expenses
				(Gains)	(Losses)
					Loss on Retirement of Debt
Cash		Bonds Payable			
		Bal $198,000			
−$205,000		−198,000		−	+$7,000
		Bal $ 0			

The $198,000 reduction of the Bonds Payable account eliminates the liability because the current book value was $198,000.

Similarities between Loans and Bonds Payable

Now that we have discussed loans (such as a car loan) and bonds, it is helpful to understand the similarities between the two. In both cases, the following statements apply:

1. The initial amount recorded by the company is the present value of the future cash flows.

2. The interest expense for the period is the book value of the liability at the beginning of the period multiplied by the interest rate (yield).

3. The book value of the liability at any time is the present value of the remaining cash flows.

So you see that the principles followed are the same. The differences are in the form of the agreement rather than its substance. Of course, loans and bonds can have different characteristics than the ones we discussed.

REPORTING LONG-TERM DEBT AND INTEREST

We have used the title Long-Term Debt in this chapter because that is the title many companies use in their balance sheet. You may come across titles such as Long-Term Liabilities or Noncurrent Liabilities. The types and extent of long-term debt disclosures reported in an annual report vary from one company to another. However, GAAP requires all companies to disclose information about the terms of the debt, the interest expense, and the interest paid in their financial statements or the notes accompanying those statements. We show excerpts from **PepsiCo**'s annual report for 2005 in Exhibit 22-4.

Examine PepsiCo's disclosures. Do you understand these disclosures? What do they tell you about PepsiCo's managers' decisions concerning long-term debt? What additional disclosures do you think might be useful?

Using Long-Term Debt and Interest Expense Disclosures for Evaluation

7 How do long-term debt and interest expense disclosures help external users evaluate a corporation?

So far in the chapter, we have focused on the issues involved in reporting long-term debt. Knowledge of these issues provides you with the foundation necessary to understand how external users evaluate a company's long-term debt and interest expense disclosures to assess its long-term financial flexibility, risk, and liquidity. **Financial flexibility** refers to a company's ability to adapt to change. Financial flexibility enables a company to increase

EXHIBIT 22-4	PEPSICO'S DISCLOSURES RELATED TO DEBT

Consolidated Balance Sheet (in part)

(in millions except per share amount)
PepsiCo, Inc. and Subsidiaries
December 31, 2005 and December 25, 2004

LIABILITIES AND SHAREHOLDERS' EQUITY	2005	2004
Current Liabilities		
Short-term obligations	$ 2,889	$ 1,054
Accounts payable and other current liabilities	5,971	5,599
Income taxes payable	546	99
Total Current Liabilities	9,406	6,752
Long-Term Debt Obligations	2,313	2,397
Other Liabilities	4,323	4,099
Deferred Income Taxes	1,434	1,216
Preferred Stock, no par value	41	41
Repurchased Preferred Stock	(110)	(90)
Common Shareholders' Equity		
Common stock, par value 1 2/3¢ per share (issued 1,782 shares)	30	30
Capital in excess of par value	614	618
Retained earnings	21,116	18,730
Accumulated other comprehensive loss	(1,053)	(886)
	20,707	18,492
Less: repurchased common stock, at cost (126 and 103 shares, respectively)	(6,387)	(4,920)
Total Common Shareholders' Equity	14,320	13,572
Total Liabilities and Shareholders' Equity	$31,727	$27,987

See accompanying notes to consolidated financial statements.

continued

(or reduce) its operating activities in response to changing economic conditions. For example, this concept relates to a company's ability to raise additional capital resources to adapt to a changing environment. **Risk** is a measure of the uncertainty of a company's future performance. **Long-term liquidity** relates to the amount of cash a company will generate over the long run to pay off its liabilities as they become due.

As with other parts of financial statements, external users evaluate long-term debt by performing intracompany and intercompany analysis—through the use of percentage analysis (trend analysis and ratio analysis). We will discuss only intracompany analysis in this chapter, using the disclosures from PepsiCo's 2005 annual report given in Exhibit 22-4. You can also perform intercompany analysis following the procedures we discussed in Chapter 21.

Intracompany Analysis of Long-Term Debt: PepsiCo

Listed below are three specific questions that relate to PepsiCo's long-term financial flexibility, risk, and liquidity. You can ask these same three questions (as well as others) when evaluating any company's long-term debt and interest expense using intracompany analysis. Under each question, we explain how financial analysis helps external users answer these questions.

EXHIBIT 22-4	PEPSICO'S DISCLOSURES RELATED TO DEBT, CONT'D

Consolidated Statement of Income

(in millions except per share amounts)
PepsiCo, Inc. and Subsidiaries
Fiscal years ended December 31, 2005, December 25, 2004 and December 27, 2003

	2005	2004	2003
Net Revenue	$32,562	$29,261	$26,971
Cost of sales	14,176	12,674	11,691
Selling, general and administrative expenses	12,314	11,031	10,148
Amortization of intangible assets	150	147	145
Restructuring and impairment charges	—	150	147
Merger-related costs	—	—	59
Operating Profit	5,922	5,259	4,781
Bottling equity income	557	380	323
Interest expense	(256)	(167)	(163)
Interest income	159	74	51
Income from Continuing Operations before Income Taxes	6,382	5,546	4,992
Provision for Income Taxes	2,304	1,372	1,424
Income from Continuing Operations	4,078	4,174	3,568
Tax Benefit from Discontinued Operations	—	38	—
Net Income	$ 4,078	$ 4,212	$ 3,568
Net Income per Common Share—Basic			
Continuing operations	$ 2.43	$ 2.45	$ 2.07
Discontinued operations	—	0.02	—
Total	$ 2.43	$ 2.47	$ 2.07
Net Income per Common Share—Diluted			
Continuing operations	$ 2.39	$ 2.41	$ 2.05
Discontinued operations	—	0.02	—
Total	$ 2.39	$ 2.44*	$ 2.05

* Based on unrounded amounts.

Consolidated Statement of Cash Flows Statements (in part)

Net Cash Provided by Operating Activities	$ 5,852	$ 5,054	$ 4,328

See accompanying notes to consolidated financial statements.

Notes to Consolidated Financial Statements (in part)

Note 9—Debt Obligations and Commitments (in part)

	2005	2004
Short-term debt obligations		
Current maturities of long-term debt	$ 143	$ 160
Commercial paper (3.3% and 1.6%)	3,140	1,287
Other borrowings (7.4% and 6.6%)	356	357
Amounts reclassified to long-term debt	(750)	(750)
	$ 2,889	$ 1,054

See accompanying notes to consolidated financial statements.   *continued*

EXHIBIT 22-4	PEPSICO'S DISCLOSURES RELATED TO DEBT, CONT'D

Long-term debt obligations

Short-term borrowings, reclassified	$ 750	$ 750
Notes due 2006–2026 (5.4% and 4.7%)	1,161	1,274
Zero coupon notes, $475 million due 2006–2012 (13.4%)	312	321
Other, due 2002–2014 (6.3% and 6.2%)	233	212
	2,456	2,557
Less: current maturities of long-term debt obligations	(143)	(160)
	$2,313	$2,397

The interest rates in the above table reflect weighted-average rates as of year-end.

Short-term borrowings are reclassified to long-term when we have the intent and ability, through the existence of the unused lines of credit, to refinance these borrowings on a long-term basis. At year-end 2005, we maintained $2.1 billion in corporate lines of credit subject to normal banking terms and conditions. These credit facilities support short-term debt issuances and remained unused as of December 31, 2005. Of the $2.1 billion, $1.35 billion expires in May 2006 with the remaining $750 million expiring in June 2009.

In addition, $181 million of our debt was outstanding on various lines of credit maintained for our international divisions. These lines of credit are subject to normal banking terms and conditions and are committed to the extent of our borrowings.

Long-Term Contractual Commitments

Payments Due by Period	Total	2006	2007–2008	2009–2010	2011 and beyond
Long-term debt obligations*	$2,313	$ —	$1,052	$ 876	$ 385
Operating leases	769	187	253	132	197
Purchasing commitments†	4,533	1,169	1,630	775	959
Marketing commitments	1,487	412	438	381	256
Other commitments	99	82	10	6	1
	$9,201	$1,850	$3,383	$2,170	$1,798

* Excludes current maturities of long-term debt of $143 million which are classified within current liabilities.
† Includes approximately $13 million of long-term commitments which are reflected in other liabilities in our Consolidated Balance Sheet.

The above table reflects non-cancelable commitments as of December 31, 2005 based on year-end foreign exchange rates.

Question #1: Is PepsiCo's Long-Term Financial Flexibility Reasonable?

To answer this question, we first examine PepsiCo's comparative balance sheets to see how much of its total assets (which is equal to total liabilities plus shareholders' equity) is financed by long-term debt. In Chapter 7 we discussed the debt ratio (total liabilities ÷ total assets) as a measure of a company's financial flexibility.

What is the debt ratio in 2005 and 2004 for PepsiCo, and how has the company's financial flexibility changed?

A variation of the debt ratio is the debt-to-equity ratio, which is computed by dividing total liabilities by total shareholders' equity. Yet another variation results from dividing *long-term* debt by shareholders' equity. This ratio is a better measure of a company's long-term financial flexibility because its numerator includes only long-term debt. The lower the ratio is, the more likely a company can finance needed capital by issuing long-term debt, thereby increasing its leverage (as we discussed earlier in the chapter). We compute this ratio for PepsiCo as follows:

	2005	2004
$\dfrac{\text{Long-term debt}}{\text{Shareholders' equity}}$	$\dfrac{\$2,313}{\$14,320} = 0.16$	$\dfrac{\$2,397}{\$13,572} = 0.18$

This analysis shows that PepsiCo has reduced its reliance on long-term debt in financing its activities in 2005 as compared to 2004 and, therefore, its financial flexibility has increased.

Question #2: Can PepsiCo Pay Its Interest Obligations Each Period?

External users often use the interest coverage ratio (also called the *times interest earned ratio*) to evaluate a company's ability to meet its interest obligations through its annual earnings. It is a measure of the financial risk of creditors' (especially long-term creditors') investments in the company's long-term debt. A user typically uses income before income taxes plus interest expense as the numerator of the interest coverage ratio. As a general rule, the higher the interest coverage ratio, the better able the company is to meet its interest obligations. We compute the ratio for PepsiCo as follows:

$$\text{Interest Coverage} = (\text{Income before Income Taxes} + \text{Interest Expense}) \div \text{Interest Expense}$$

$$2005: \quad (\$6,392 + \$256) \div \$256 = 26.0$$

$$2004: \quad (\$5,546 + \$167) \div \$167 = 34.2$$

So you see that PepsiCo's interest coverage has decreased significantly in 2005 as compared to 2004; therefore, this aspect of its financial risk has increased. However the company still has a very high interest coverage ratio.

Continued interest *payments* (which are legal commitments) are endangered by low earnings over an extended period of time. Because both earnings and interest *expense* are based on accrual accounting, the times interest earned ratio is slightly inaccurate, since it should include only cash outflows for interest and cash inflows from earnings. Such refinements are usually not made to this ratio, however. Note that companies are required to disclose interest paid.

Question #3: Does PepsiCo Have Sufficient Long-Term Liquidity?

One way to evaluate a company's long-term liquidity is to examine its cash flow obligations compared to its operating cash flows. From the discussion in Note 9 of Exhibit 22-4, notice that PepsiCo has total maturities of long-term contractual commitments over the next *five* years of $7.403 billion ($1,850 million + $3,383 million + $2,170 million). Its cash flows from operating activities for the past *three* years total $15.234 billion ($5,852 + $5,054 + $4,328 in Exhibit 22-4). Although we are comparing *past* cash flows to *future* obligations, these amounts suggest that PepsiCo would be able to pay off its long-term debts as they become due even if it did not borrow any additional amounts. Furthermore, in Note 9 PepsiCo discloses that it has $2.1 billion in corporate lines of credit at the end of 2005. This analysis suggests that PepsiCo has sufficient long-term liquidity and financial flexibility.

 *What information would you need to help you decide whether PepsiCo could afford to buy **Coca-Cola Company** (ignore antitrust considerations)?*

LEASES

8 What is a lease? What is a capital lease, and what impact does it have on a lessee's financial statements?

Many companies choose to lease an asset rather than buy it. A **lease** is an agreement giving the right to use property, plant, or equipment without transferring legal ownership of the item. For instance, when Unlimited Decadence leases a computer from IBM, it acquires the right to use the computer for the period of the lease, but it does not acquire legal ownership. IBM remains the legal owner of the computer. The **lessee** is the company that acquires the right to use the item. The **lessor** is the company that gives up the use of the item. For instance, Unlimited Decadence is the lessee and IBM is the lessor in this example. In a lease, the lessee agrees to make periodic lease payments to the lessor for the right to use the leased item.

There are several reasons a company might lease instead of buy. First, a lease may not require a down payment to acquire the use of an asset, so a lessee with a cash shortage may be able to save its cash. Second, a lease may allow a lessee to avoid the risk of obsolescence, since the leased item may be returned to the lessor at the end of the lease. Third, if the lessee is a corporation, it may obtain a tax benefit because it can take a tax deduction on its income tax return for the total lease payment.

Before we discuss how a company accounts for leases, you should understand the similarities between leasing an asset and purchasing an asset on credit. For example, if a company purchases a building for use in its operations by issuing a 30-year mortgage, it records an asset (the building) and a noncurrent liability (the mortgage payable). Although the company owns the building, the mortgage company has a legally secured interest in the building to protect its financial interests.

Now suppose another company leases a building for 30 years for use in its operations. It does not acquire legal ownership of the building but agrees to make lease payments for 30 years. In both the mortgage and the lease situations, the company purchasing the building and the company leasing the building will each use the building in its operations, and each is committed to making payments for 30 years. External users of financial statements usually are not concerned with the legal differences between a purchase and a lease. Rather, they are concerned about evaluating a company's operating capability and financial flexibility. In the lease situation, it is *not* appropriate for the lessee to leave the asset and the liability off its balance sheet just because it does not "legally" own the building. Instead, the lessee should report that it has an asset because it has the use of the building for 30 years, and it should report a liability because it has a 30-year commitment to make lease payments. In other words, a lessee's financial statements are more helpful to external users if the statements report on the economic substance of the transaction. That is, the purchaser of the building and the lessee of the building both have engaged in similar economic transactions. Therefore, the lessee should record both an asset (which helps users evaluate the increase in its operating capability) and a noncurrent liability (which helps users evaluate the decrease in its financial flexibility) in the same way as does the purchaser. This is an example of the accounting principle that states that **economic substance is more important than legal form**—the lessee records an asset that it does not legally own. However, some leases (such as when you rent an apartment) are short term, and the economic substance is *not* like a purchase.

There are two types of leases for financial reporting purposes: a capital lease and an operating lease. A lease is a **capital lease** if it transfers the risks and benefits of ownership from the lessor to the lessee. A lessee records an asset and a liability for a capital lease.[4] On the other hand, a lease is an **operating lease** if it does *not* transfer the risks and benefits of ownership (such as the lease on an apartment). If a lease is an operating lease, the accounting is simple. The *lessee* records each lease payment as rent expense, which it reports as an operating expense on its income statement, and as an operating cash flow. The *lessor* records each lease payment as rent revenue, which it reports on its income statement, and as an operating cash flow. Note that the *lessor* includes the asset on its balance sheet under a title such as Property Leased to Others, records depreciation expense on the asset, and reports the depreciation expense as an operating expense on its income statement.

Capital Lease

If a lease is a capital lease, the lessee records an operating asset and a noncurrent liability. It records both the asset and the liability at the present value of the lease payments agreed to in the lease. Determining the interest rate to use in the present value calculation

---

[4]A lease transfers the risks and benefits of ownership if the lease agreement meets any one of the following criteria: (1) the lease transfers ownership to the lessee at the end of the lease, (2) the lease includes a bargain-purchase option, (3) the lease is for 75 percent or more of the economic life of the property, or (4) the present value of the lease payments is 90 percent or more of the market value of the property. The specific evaluations are beyond the scope of this book.

is complex, so we will always assume a rate. For example, suppose that Unlimited Decadence signs a capital lease for a computer with HiTech Company having the following terms:[5]

Lease date	January 1, 2008
Annual lease payments at end of year	$4,000
Life of lease	5 years
Interest rate	10%
Date of first payment	December 31, 2008

Unlimited Decadence computes the amount at which to record the asset and the liability as follows:

$$\text{Present Value of Lease Payments} = \frac{\text{Periodic Lease}}{\text{Payment}} \times \frac{\text{Present Value of Annuity}}{\text{Factor for 5 Periods at 10\%}}$$

$$= \$4,000 \times 3.7908 \text{ (from Table 20-2)}$$

$$= \$15,163 \text{ (rounded)}$$

Unlimited Decadence (the lessee) records an asset and a liability on January 1, 2008, as follows:

Assets	=	Liabilities	+	Stockholders' Equity
Leased Property		Capital Lease Obligation		
+$15,163		+$15,163		

Since Unlimited Decadence records an asset, it must depreciate the cost over the life of the lease. Assuming straight-line depreciation (and no residual value), the depreciation is $3,033 ($15,163 ÷ 5, rounded) for each year of the lease. On December 31, 2008, Unlimited Decadence records the depreciation as follows:

Assets	=	Liabilities	+	Stockholders' Equity		
				Net Income		
				Revenues	–	Expenses
Leased Property						Depreciation Expense
Bal $15,163						
– 3,033					–	+$3,033
Bal $12,130						

Unlimited Decadence reports the $12,130 balance (book value) of the leased property account[6] in the property, plant, and equipment section of its December 31, 2008 balance sheet. It reports the $3,033 depreciation expense on its 2008 income statement. Each year the company reports the same amount of depreciation expense and reduces the book value of the leased asset by $3,033.

Each $4,000 lease payment includes both interest and principal. Every year when Unlimited Decadence records the payment, it must separate the payment into the interest expense portion and the portion that reduces the lease obligation. It computes the yearly interest expense by multiplying the book value of the lease obligation at the beginning of the year by the interest rate. It reduces the lease obligation by the difference between the cash payment and the interest expense.

---

[5]Most leases require payments at the beginning of the lease, and often more frequently than once a year. These issues make the accounting procedures much more complex but do not change the basic issues we discuss in this chapter.

[6]Some companies record the accumulated depreciation in a separate contra account called Accumulated Depreciation on Leased Property. The contra account balance then is subtracted from the Leased Property cost to determine the book value. Our method is less complex and conveys similar information.

At the end of 2008, Unlimited Decadence computes its interest expense and reduction of lease obligation as follows:

$$\text{Interest Expense} = \frac{\text{Book Value of Lease Obligation}}{\text{at Beginning of Year}} \times \text{Interest Rate}$$

$$= \$15,163 \times 10\%$$

$$= \$1,516 \text{ (rounded)}$$

$$\text{Reduction of Lease Obligation} = \text{Cash Payment} - \text{Interest Expense}$$

$$= \$4,000 - \$1,516$$

$$= \$2,484$$

Unlimited Decadence records the lease payment on December 31, 2008, as follows:

Assets	=	Liabilities	+	Stockholders' Equity		
					Net Income	
				Revenues	−	Expenses
		Capital Lease				Interest
Cash		Obligation				Expense
		Bal $15,163				
−$4,000		− 2,484			−	+$1,516
		Bal $12,679				

FINANCIAL STATEMENT EFFECTS

Decreases current assets and total assets on **balance sheet**. Decreases noncurrent liabilities and total liabilities on **balance sheet**. Increases expenses (in "other items"), which decreases net income on **income statement** (and therefore decreases stockholders' equity on **balance sheet**). Decreases cash flows from operating activities (by $1,516) and financing activities (by $2,484) on **cash flow statement**.

The balance (book value) of the capital lease obligation account now is $12,679. Unlimited Decadence reports the amount to be paid next year ($4,000) as a current liability and the remaining portion ($8,679) as a noncurrent liability on its December 31, 2008 balance sheet. It includes the interest paid in the cash flows from operating activities section, and reports the reduction of the capital lease obligation in the cash flows from financing activities section of its cash flow statement.

Each year, the company computes and records the interest expense and the reduction of the lease obligation in the same manner. For 2009, the interest expense is $1,268 ($12,679 × 10%, rounded), and the reduction of the lease obligation is $2,732 ($4,000 − $1,268). Using this method, the company will reduce the lease obligation to zero by the end of the lease life.

 Explain why the book value of the asset and the liability are not equal during each year (after the initial recording of the asset and the liability).

Impacts of Capital Lease Accounting

By recording a lease as a capital lease because the risks and benefits of ownership are transferred, a lessee company's financial statements provide external users with better information to assess the profitability, financial flexibility, and operating efficiency of the company.

When a company records an asset and a liability for a capital lease (instead of recording the lease as an operating lease), there is a negative effect on the company's return on stockholders' equity (net income ÷ average stockholders' equity) in the earlier years of the lease. This occurs because net income is lower for a capital lease than it would have been if the company had recorded an operating lease. The net income is lower because the total of the depreciation expense and the interest expense is higher than the rent expense that would have been reported for an operating lease. This indicates that the company is less profitable and therefore its return on stockholders' equity is lower.[7] Thus, when a company reports an asset and a liability for a capital lease, this financial reporting allows for a more valid comparison about profitability with companies that purchase their assets.

In regard to a company's financial flexibility, recording an asset and a liability for a capital lease also has a negative effect on the company's debt ratio (total liabilities ÷ total assets). The effect is negative because the numerator and the denominator increase by the same amount, thereby increasing the proportion of debt to assets. This increase indicates that the company has less financial flexibility. Again, this financial reporting allows for more valid comparisons about financial flexibility with companies that purchase their assets.

 Suppose a company has assets of $200 and liabilities of $100. It enters into a capital lease with a value of $30. Compute the debt ratio before and after recording the capital lease.

In regard to a company's operating capability, recording an asset and a liability for a capital lease provides more information about the ability of the company to use its assets to generate revenue. For example, the ratio of net revenues to net property, plant, and equipment is lower because of the larger denominator, thereby showing a lower operating efficiency. This financial reporting gives a better picture of the total property, plant, and equipment that the company uses in its operations and again helps with intercompany comparability of operating efficiency.

Lessor Accounting for a Capital Lease

Although this is a chapter on long-term debt, we will briefly discuss the lessor's accounting for the asset involved in a capital lease. The lessor in a capital lease reports the "sale" of the asset on credit and a receivable, like a "mirror image" of the lessee's "purchase" and liability. Since the lessee records the payments to be *made* as a liability, to be consistent the lessor records the payments to be *received* as an asset. Since the lessee records the payments it makes on the lease as interest expense and a reduction in its liability, the lessor records the payments received as interest revenue and a reduction in its receivable. The difference between a sale using a lease and a typical credit sale is that the lessor offers credit for the term of the lease rather than for, say, 30 days.

Business Issues and Values

Many lessees have numerous leases that fail the criteria that would make them capital leases. Therefore, these are classified as operating leases. Two industries in which this is common are airlines and retailers. For its operating leases, a company must disclose the cash flows that it is obligated to make on those leases. It must disclose the amount it will pay each year for the next five years and the total amount it must pay for all years thereafter. An external user should examine this disclosure to see if the cash flows are significant. If so, the user can compute an approximate present value of the cash flows to determine the effect on the liabilities (and assets) of the company. To illustrate, **Southwest Airlines** disclosed the following in its 2005 annual report:

[7] Later in the lease, the total of the depreciation expense and the interest expense is lower than the rent expense that would have been reported for an operating lease because the interest expense decreases as the amount of the liability decreases. The return on assets [(net income + interest expense) ÷ average total assets] is also lower in the earlier years of the lease, but we do not discuss this ratio here.

Future minimum lease payments under capital leases and noncancelable operating leases with initial or remaining terms in excess of one year at December 31, 2005, were:

	Capital Leases	Operating Leases
	(In Millions)	
2006	$16	$ 332
2007	16	309
2008	16	274
2009	16	235
2010	15	219
After 2010	12	1,164
Total minimum lease payments	91	$2,533
Less amount representing interest	17	
Present value of minimum lease payments	74	
Less current portion	11	
Long-term portion	$63	

Some aspects of this disclosure may surprise you. Southwest's operating leases (which it does not report on its balance sheet) involve much higher cash flows than its capital leases. Its operating leases also appear to have longer lives than the capital leases. Note also that Southwest reports the present value of the capital leases but not of the operating leases. To compute the present value of the operating leases, an external user has to discount the annual operating lease cash flow for each of the five years (and for the years after 2010) to its present value, and sum the present values to determine the total present value (as we did with capital budgeting in Chapter 20). To do so, the user has to assume the number of years after 2010 over which the remaining operating lease payments of $1.164 billion are to be made and also has to assume an interest rate. In its 2005 balance sheet, Southwest disclosed that it had long-term debt of $1.394 billion and total noncurrent liabilities of $3.695 billion. Therefore, no matter what life and interest rate the external user selects, the present value of the operating leases represents a significant obligation for Southwest and, if considered to be debt, would significantly affect the user's perception of the company's risk and financial flexibility.

Some companies also deliberately structure leases so that they fail the criteria for being a capital lease (thus the companies avoid recording their long-term lease liabilities). Such companies do this in the belief that external users will be "fooled" by the low amount of debt they report on their balance sheets and will therefore believe the companies have less risk. However, since each company must report the future cash flows for operating leases, external users can perform the present value analysis we just discussed and avoid being misled.

MORTGAGES PAYABLE

Earlier we compared the purchase of a building (by signing a mortgage payable) with the lease of a building. Since accounting for a mortgage payable is similar to accounting for a lease obligation (and for a loan, as we discussed earlier in the chapter), we will briefly discuss mortgages here. A **mortgage payable** is a noncurrent liability for which the lender has a specific claim against an asset of the borrower. For example, most homeowners purchase their homes by issuing a mortgage. That is, they borrow the money from a lender, and the lender is assigned a secured claim on the home. A company also may acquire an asset through a mortgage. When a company acquires an asset in this way, it records the cost of the asset and the mortgage payable. The typical mortgage requires equal monthly payments (an annuity), and these payments are determined by a present value of an annuity calculation. Each mortgage payment consists of interest and of a reduction of the mortgage obligation. The company computes and records the interest expense and the liability reduction in the same way as we discussed for lease payments, except on a monthly basis.

DEFERRED INCOME TAXES

9 Why do deferred income taxes arise, and how does a corporation report them in its financial statements?

In earlier chapters, for simplicity we assumed that the amount of a corporation's income tax expense for a period is the same as its income tax obligation for that period. The income tax *expense* is the amount that the corporation reports on its income statement, whereas the income tax *obligation* is the amount that the corporation must pay the government(s) for that year. In our discussion for some topics, we explained that the rules for computing taxable income are different from the rules for determining pretax accounting income. One of the major differences is depreciation. In Chapter 21 we explained that most corporations use the straight-line method for financial reporting but use the Modified Accelerated Cost Recovery System (MACRS), a type of accelerated depreciation, for income tax reporting. When a corporation uses these methods, its pretax accounting income is different from its taxable income in any given year. Although the two amounts of depreciation in any year are different, the *total* depreciation expense over the life of the asset is the same (assuming a zero residual value). Therefore, the yearly difference in the depreciation amounts computed by these two methods is known as a *temporary difference*.

A **temporary difference** occurs when a corporation records an expense (or a revenue) for financial reporting in a period different from that used for income tax reporting, but the total lifetime expense (or revenue) is the same for both. In the case of depreciation expense, in the early years of an asset's life the MACRS depreciation expense that a corporation reports on its income tax return is usually *greater* than the depreciation expense that the corporation reports on its income statement. This causes taxable income to be *less* than its pretax accounting income, as we discussed in Chapter 21. However, in future years the temporary difference reverses, and the corporation's MACRS depreciation expense is *less* than the income statement depreciation expense. This causes its taxable income to be *greater* than its pretax accounting income. These *future taxable amounts* will cause the corporation to owe additional taxes in future years because of the higher taxable income. **Deferred Tax Liability** is the account a corporation uses to report on its balance sheet the amount of its future additional income taxes resulting from future taxable amounts.

To determine its deferred tax liability at the end of a given year, a corporation multiplies the income tax rate times its expected future taxable amounts.[8] It then makes an adjustment to its beginning deferred tax liability. (These computations are beyond the scope of this book.) The corporation's income tax expense is the sum of its current income tax obligation (based on its taxable income for the year) and its deferred taxes for the year. For example, if for 2008 Barbre Corporation's income tax obligation is $9,000 and the increase in its deferred tax liability is $480, the corporation's income tax expense is $9,480, and it records these amounts as follows (assuming that it did not make any interim tax payments for 2008)[9]:

FINANCIAL STATEMENT EFFECTS

Increases current liabilities, noncurrent liabilities, and total liabilities on **balance sheet**. Increases expenses, which decreases net income on **income statement** (and therefore decreases stockholders' equity on **balance sheet**).

Assets	=	Liabilities		+	Stockholders' Equity	
					Net Income	
					Revenues	− Expenses
		Income Taxes Payable	Deferred Tax Liability			Income Tax Expense
		+$9,000	+$480		−	+$9,480

A corporation also may have a deferred tax asset. **Deferred Tax Asset** is the account a corporation uses to report on its balance sheet the amount by which its future income

---

[8]If the tax rate has been changed (e.g., by the U.S. Congress) for future years, a corporation uses that new rate to compute the amount of its deferred tax liability.

[9]Many other temporary differences cause deferred taxes. A corporation also may have *permanent* differences between its taxable income and its pretax accounting income; these do *not* cause deferred taxes. As a result, accounting for income taxes is very complex, and we discuss only the basic issues here.

taxes will be reduced by future deductible amounts. For example, as we discussed in Chapter 14 of Volume 1, using GAAP, a company records warranty expense in the period of the sale. However, the corporation deducts the warranty costs on its income tax return when it pays them. Therefore, the amount of the warranty expense in the period of the sale is usually *greater* than the warranties paid. However, in future years the temporary difference reverses and the corporation's warranty payments are *greater* than the income statement warranty expense, causing its taxable income to be *less* than its pretax accounting income. These *future deductible amounts* will cause the corporation to owe fewer taxes in future years because of its lower taxable income.

EXTERNAL USER PERSPECTIVE: ANALYSIS OF DEFERRED TAX REPORTING

Deferred income tax reporting is controversial. Typically, over time a corporation increases its depreciable assets either because it is growing larger or because it replaces these assets at a higher cost. When these assets increase, the MACRS depreciation expense that the corporation reports on its income tax return each year is consistently higher than the depreciation expense it reports on its income statement. Therefore, the corporation's taxable income each year is *always* less than its pretax accounting income, so that the deferred tax liability accumulates and will not be paid. Another way of saying this is that the corporation's deferred income tax liability will decrease only if its income tax obligation is greater than its income tax expense; this will occur only when its investment in depreciable assets *decreases* over time. For this reason, many external users of financial statements argue that deferred income taxes are not a "real" liability and that the deferred tax procedures should *not* be used. Instead, they suggest that the income tax expense a corporation reports on its income statement should be equal to its income tax obligation for the period. So these external users ignore a corporation's deferred income taxes in their evaluation of its profitability, financial flexibility, and liquidity.

Note also that, although a corporation reports deferred taxes as a liability (or asset) on its ending balance sheet, they are very different from any other liability (asset)—there is no other entity that claims that the corporation owes it money. Specifically, the federal government does not have a claim because the corporation has filed its tax return and has paid (or will pay) any amounts it owes for the current year.

 Use Exhibit 22-4 to find the difference in PepsiCo's debt ratio in 2005 if you exclude deferred income taxes from its liabilities.

RETIREMENT BENEFITS

A person who retires usually has three sources of retirement income: savings, social security, and a pension. Many companies, especially larger ones, have pension plans for their employees. A **pension plan** is an agreement by a company to provide income to its employees after they retire. A **defined-contribution plan** specifies the amount that the company must contribute to the plan each year while its employees work. A **defined-benefit plan** specifies the amount that the company must pay to its employees each year during their retirement. For example, a retired employee might receive an annual pension income under a defined-benefit plan based on the following formula:

10 What is a defined-benefit pension plan, and how does a corporation account for it?

$$\text{Annual Pension Income} = \frac{\text{Average of Last}}{\text{5 Years' Pay}} \times \frac{\text{Number of Years}}{\text{of Service}} \times 0.02$$

Therefore, an employee who worked for 40 years for a company and had an average salary of \$100,000 for the last 5 years of service receives \$80,000 per year (\$100,000 × 40 × 0.02) during retirement until death.

For a defined-benefit plan, to pay each employee's future pension benefits, a company must pay ("fund") an annual amount to a "funding agency" during each year that the employee works. The funding agency (e.g., insurance company) is responsible for safeguarding and investing the assets of the pension plan and for making payments to the retired employees. An *actuary*, who is trained to calculate risks and premiums, determines the amount that the company contributes. The computations involve present value analyses and are based on assumptions about future pay rates, life expectancies, and expected rates of return.

The agreement to pay future retirement benefits causes the company to incur a pension expense each year that the employee works. However, in some cases, a company pays less to the funding agency in a given year than it records as pension expense. This is because GAAP defines the amount of the expense whereas federal law specifies the amount the company must pay. When this occurs, the company records a pension obligation. For instance, if Crabtree Company computes its yearly pension expense to be $8,900 but pays only $8,000 to its funding agency, it records a $900 liability as follows:

Assets	=	Liabilities	+	Stockholders' Equity		
					Net Income	
				Revenues	−	Expenses
Cash		Pension Obligation				Pension Expense
−$8,000		+$900			−	+$8,900

Alternatively, the company could pay more than the pension expense, in which case it will decrease any previous pension obligation (or, if none, record a pension asset).

How does a defined-benefit pension plan add to the enjoyment of this couple?

© PHOTODISC/GETTY IMAGES

The computation of pension expense is very complex and beyond the scope of this book. However, it is important for external users to know that the obligation of the company to its employees for the work they have done to date is called the **projected benefit obligation** (which is computed by the company's actuary). When the projected benefit obligation is *more* than the assets of the pension plan (held by the funding agency), the pension plan is *underfunded*. When the pension plan assets are more than the projected benefit obligation, the pension plan is *overfunded*. The company reports this difference as a liability or asset (generally, noncurrent) on its balance sheet, along with related information in the notes to its financial statements. External users should look at the amount that a company's pension plan is underfunded or overfunded because it may affect their evaluation of the company's liquidity, risk, and financial flexibility. For example, if the projected benefit obligation exceeds the pension plan assets (the plan is underfunded), the company will need to increase its payments to the plan in future years, thereby increasing its risk and reducing its liquidity and financial flexibility.

Companies that provide a pension plan for their employees may also provide other retirement benefits, often referred to as OPEBs (other postemployment benefits). Healthcare benefits are the most common form of OPEB, but some companies also provide such items as dental and life insurance benefits. A company that provides OPEBs to its employees also computes and records an OPEB expense. Usually the company does not "fund" these other retirement benefits, so that its OPEB obligation exceeds the OPEB assets (zero in this case). It must also report this underfunded amount as a liability on its balance sheet.

HOW LONG-TERM DEBT TRANSACTIONS AFFECT THE CASH FLOW STATEMENT

A company generally reports long-term debt transactions involving cash in the financing activities section of its cash flow statement. It reports the cash received from the issuance of notes payable or bonds payable—whether issued at face value, at a premium, or at a discount—as a cash inflow from financing activities. It reports the cash paid to retire notes payable and bonds payable as cash outflows for financing activities. It includes the cash paid for interest, however, in the operating activities section. Even though the interest paid is related to a financing activity, GAAP requires it to be included as an operating cash flow because the interest expense is included in the company's income statement. A lease payment includes both interest and principal. Thus, a company includes the interest portion of a lease payment as a cash outflow for operating activities and the principal portion (the reduction of the lease obligation) as a cash outflow for financing activities. A company includes income tax payments and pension payments as cash outflows for operating activities.

 If a company's interest payments are less than its interest expense (because of accrued interest), explain whether the difference is added to or subtracted from net income in computing the net cash flow from operating activities under the indirect method.

SUMMARY

At the beginning of the chapter we asked you several questions. During the chapter, we asked you to STOP and answer some additional questions to build your knowledge about specific issues. Be sure you answered these additional questions. Below are the questions from the beginning of the chapter, with a brief summary of the key points relating to the answers. Use your creative and critical thinking skills to expand on these key points to develop more complete answers to the questions and to determine what other questions you have that might lead you to learn more about the issues.

How does a corporation compute the periodic payment, the interest expense, and the repayment of the principal on a loan?

The periodic payment is the amount of an annuity that has a present value equal to the amount borrowed; it is computed as follows:

$$\text{Periodic Payment} = \text{Amount Borrowed} \div \frac{\text{Present Value of Annuity Factor Based on}}{\text{the Interest Rate and the Life of the Loan}}$$

The interest expense is computed as follows:

$$\text{Interest Expense} = \text{Periodic Interest Rate} \times \frac{\text{Book Value of Loan at the}}{\text{Beginning of the Period}}$$

The repayment of principal is computed as follows:

$$\text{Repayment of Principal} = \text{Periodic Payment} - \text{Interest Expense}$$

 What is a bond, what are its characteristics, and why does a corporation issue bonds?

A bond is a type of note in which a company agrees to pay the holder the face value at the maturity date and to pay interest periodically at a specified rate on the face value. The face value (also called the *par value*) is the amount of money that the issuer promises to pay on the maturity date. The maturity date is the date on which the issuer of the bond agrees to pay the face value to the holder. The contract rate is the rate at which the issuer of the bond pays interest each period until the maturity date. A bond certificate is a legal document that shows the face value, the annual interest rate, and the maturity date. The main reason managers of a company (corporation) may decide to issue bonds instead of common stock is that the earnings available to the common stockholders can be increased through leverage. Leverage is the use of borrowing by a company to increase the return to common stockholders. If a corporation can borrow money by issuing bonds and use the money to invest in a project that provides greater income than the interest that must be paid on the bonds, the corporation and its stockholders will be better off (they will earn a higher return).

 What are the factors that affect long-term interest rates?

Several factors affect long-term interest rates, including the policies of the Federal Reserve Board (whose policies affect the supply and demand for money in the national economy), federal regulations, and the budget surplus or deficit of the federal government. Long-term interest rates for corporations, however, include three *primary* factors. First, interest rates include the risk-free rate, which is the rate that a borrower would pay, and a lender would receive, when there is no risk of default by the borrower and when no inflation is expected. Most borrowing by the U.S. government is considered to be risk-free because the government will not default. Second, interest rates include the expected inflation rate, so the borrower pays additional interest to compensate for the expected inflation over the life of the borrowing. Third, interest rates include the risk premium, which is the additional interest that the borrower pays when there is a possibility that it may default.

 Why does a corporation issue bonds at less than or more than their face value?

When a company decides to issue bonds, it usually deals with a securities broker (or an investment banker). The broker and the company agree on a price for the bonds, and the broker pays the company for them. The broker and the company base this selling price on the terms of the bond issue and the components of the long-term interest rate. They determine the rate that they believe best reflects current market conditions. This market rate of interest is called the *yield* and is the rate at which the bonds are issued. The yield on a bond issue may be different from the contract rate set by the company. The managers of the company set the contract rate, whereas the marketplace determines the yield. If the yield is more than the contract rate, the company will receive a selling price (and the purchasers of the bonds will pay) less than the face value of the bonds; that is, the company will sell the bonds at a discount. Alternatively, if the yield is less than the contract rate, the company will receive a selling price (and the purchasers of the bonds will pay) more than the face value of the bonds; that is, the company will sell the bonds at a premium.

5 **How does the interest expense each period compare with the interest paid in that period when a corporation issues bonds at a discount or a premium?**

Because a company issuing bonds incurs a cost (yield) either higher (for bonds sold at a discount) or lower (for bonds sold at a premium) than the contract rate, the interest expense recorded in each semiannual period is different from the interest paid. When a company sells bonds at a discount, its interest expense each period is higher than the interest it pays that period. When a company sells bonds at a premium, its interest expense each period is lower than the interest it pays that period. The difference between the interest expense and the interest paid is the amount of the discount or premium that the company amortizes each period.

6 **What are zero-coupon bonds, and how does a corporation account for the interest on them?**

Zero-coupon bonds are bonds that pay no interest each period. That is, the only cash flows associated with the bonds are the amount borrowed (which is less than the face value of the bonds) and the payment of the face value on the maturity date. Zero-coupon bonds always sell at a discount. The discount is the difference between the selling price and the face value. A company computes the annual interest expense by multiplying the annual yield by the book value of the bonds at the beginning of the year. Since the company pays no cash for interest each year, it records the annual interest expense as an increase in the book value of the bonds payable each year, so that the book value on the maturity date is equal to the face value (the amount the borrower pays the lender).

7 **How do long-term debt and interest expense disclosures help external users evaluate a corporation?**

External users evaluate a company's long-term debt and interest expense disclosures to help them evaluate its long-term financial flexibility, risk, and liquidity. A company's financial flexibility refers to its ability to raise additional capital. Financial flexibility enables a company to increase (or reduce) its operating activities in response to changing economic conditions. A company's risk is a measure of the uncertainty of its future performance. A company's long-term liquidity relates to the amount of cash it will generate over the long run to pay off its liabilities as they become due. As with other parts of financial statements, external users evaluate long-term debt by performing intracompany and intercompany analysis—through the use of percentage analysis (trend analysis and ratio analysis).

8 **What is a lease? What is a capital lease, and what impact does it have on a lessee's financial statements?**

A lease is an agreement giving a company the right to use property, plant, or equipment without transferring legal ownership of the item. The *lessee* is the company that acquires the right to use the item. The *lessor* is the company that gives up the use of the item. A capital lease is a lease in which the risks and benefits of ownership are transferred from the lessor to the lessee. If a lease is a capital lease, the lessee reports an operating asset and a noncurrent liability on its balance sheet at the present value of the lease payments agreed to in the lease. The company computes the amount at which to record the asset and the liability as follows:

$$\text{Present Value of Lease Payments} = \text{Periodic Lease Payment} \times \text{Present Value of Annuity Factor Based on the Interest Rate and the Life of the Lease}$$

The lessee must depreciate the cost of the asset over the life of the lease. It also must separate the lease payment into the interest expense portion and the portion that reduces the lease obligation, as follows:

$$\text{Interest Expense} = \text{Book Value of Lease Obligation at Beginning of Year} \times \text{Interest Rate}$$

$$\text{Reduction of Lease Obligation} = \text{Cash Payment} - \text{Interest Expense}$$

The lessee reports the depreciation expense and the interest expense related to the lease on its income statement.

9 Why do deferred income taxes arise, and how does a corporation report them in its financial statements?

Deferred taxes arise because a temporary difference occurs when a corporation records an expense (or a revenue) for financial reporting in a period different from that used for income tax reporting, but the total lifetime expense (or revenue) is the same for both. A common type of temporary difference involves depreciation expense. In the early years of an asset's life, the MACRS depreciation expense that a corporation reports on its income tax return is usually greater than the depreciation expense that the corporation reports on its income statement. However, in future years the temporary difference reverses and the corporation's MACRS depreciation expense is less than the income statement depreciation expense, causing its taxable income to be greater than its pretax accounting income. These future taxable amounts will cause the corporation to owe additional taxes in future years because of the higher taxable income. Deferred Tax Liability is the account that a corporation uses to report on its balance sheet the amount of its future additional income taxes resulting from taxable temporary differences. To determine its deferred tax liability at the end of a given year, a corporation multiplies the income tax rate times its expected future taxable amounts. It then makes an adjustment to its beginning deferred tax liability. A corporation also may have future deductible amounts (e.g., warranty costs). Deferred Tax Asset is the account that a corporation uses to report on its balance sheet the amount by which its future income taxes will be reduced by future deductible amounts. The corporation's income tax expense reported on its income statement is the sum of its current income tax obligation (based on its taxable income for the year) and its deferred taxes for the year.

10 What is a defined-benefit pension plan, and how does a corporation account for it?

A defined-benefit pension plan is an agreement that specifies the amount a company must pay to its employees each year during their retirement. For this plan, the company pays an annual amount to a funding agency, which is responsible for safeguarding the assets and paying the retirement benefits. The company records the difference between its annual pension expense and the amount it pays to the funding agency as an increase (decrease) in its pension obligation. When the company's projected benefit obligation is *more* than the assets of the pension plan, the pension plan is *underfunded*. When its pension plan assets are more than the projected benefit obligation, the pension plan is *overfunded*. The company reports this difference as a liability or asset (generally, noncurrent) on its balance sheet, along with related information in the notes to its financial statements.

KEY TERMS

bond *(p. 778)*
bond certificate *(p. 778)*
book value *(p. 777)*
callable bonds *(p. 787)*
capital lease *(p. 793)*
contract rate *(p. 778)*
deferred tax asset *(p. 798)*
deferred tax liability *(p. 798)*
defined-benefit plan *(p. 799)*
defined-contribution plan *(p. 799)*
economic substance is more important
  than legal form *(p. 793)*
effective interest method *(p. 786)*
expected inflation rate *(p. 782)*
face value *(p. 778)*
financial flexibility *(p. 781)*
interest expense *(p. 776)*

lease *(p. 792)*
lessee *(p. 792)*
lessor *(p. 792)*
leverage *(p. 779)*
long-term liquidity *(p. 789)*
maturity date *(p. 778)*
mortgage payable *(p. 797)*
operating lease *(p. 793)*
pension plan *(p. 799)*
projected benefit obligation *(p. 801)*
risk *(p. 789)*
risk-free rate *(p. 782)*
risk premium *(p. 782)*
temporary difference *(p. 798)*
yield *(p. 783)*
zero-coupon bonds *(p. 785)*

APPENDIX

Accounting for Bonds That Are Sold at a Discount or Premium and That Pay Interest Semiannually

In the chapter we discussed why companies issue bonds at a discount or at a premium—the yield on the bonds is different from the contract rate. We also illustrated the accounting for a zero-coupon bond, for which a company incurs interest expense each year but does not pay any interest until the maturity date. In this appendix, we discuss how a company accounts for bonds payable that it sells at a discount or a premium and that pay interest semiannually.

CALCULATING THE SELLING PRICE OF BONDS

We can calculate the selling price of a bond issue that pays interest each semiannual period using a present value computation when we know the maturity date, face value, contract rate, and yield. The **selling price** is the present value of the cash flows that the company agrees to pay under the terms of the bond issue. A bond issue has two cash flows: (1) the face value paid on the maturity date and (2) the semiannual interest paid on each interest payment date. In "present value language," the face value is a *single future amount,* and the semiannual interest payments are an *annuity.* The selling price is computed as follows:

Selling Price of Bond Issue = Present Value of Face Value + Present Value of Interest Payments

The present value of the face value is computed as follows:

Present Value of Face Value = Face Value × Present Value of $1 Factor

Remember that we list the present value of $1 factors in Table 20-1 at the end of Chapter 20. Also, you need to understand that the company pays interest payments semiannually and computes the amount of the interest paid by multiplying the face value by half the contract rate. It computes the present value of the interest payments as follows:

Present Value of Interest Payments = Periodic Interest Payment × Present Value of Annuity Factor

We list the present value of annuity factors in Table 20-2 at the end of Chapter 20. The present value factors in each of the preceding equations are based on the *yield* and the life of the bonds. Recall from our earlier discussion that the yield on the bonds is the market rate of interest when the bonds are *issued.* The yield is the cost to the company of the money it borrows, and also is the return that will be earned on the purchase price by the purchasers of the bonds. Although bond yields are stated in terms of annual rates, the actual yield for each interest period is *half* the annual yield because bonds pay interest semiannually. Since the yield is stated in terms of a semiannual rate, the life of the bonds also must be stated in semiannual periods. These items are computed as follows:

Semiannual Yield = Annual Yield ÷ 2

Number of Semiannual Periods = Life of Bonds in Years × 2

Thus, the company discounts the cash payments that it agrees to make for the bonds at the semiannual yield for the number of semiannual periods in the life of the bonds.

BONDS ISSUED AT A DISCOUNT

When a company sells bonds at a discount, the yield earned by investors is more than the contract rate. We illustrate the accounting for bonds issued at a discount by assuming that Unlimited Decadence issues bonds with the following terms:

Date of sale .... January 1, 2008
Face value $100,000
Contract rate 10%
Interest payment dates .... June 30 and December 31
Maturity date .... December 31, 2011

We use a short life of 4 years to simplify the calculations. However, companies typically issue bonds with much longer lives. For example, **IBM** has issued $850 million of bonds with a 100-year life!

The selling price of Unlimited Decadence's 10% bonds is the present value of the future cash payments that it has agreed to make. These payments are the $100,000 face value on the maturity date and a $5,000 [$100,000 × (10% ÷ 2)] interest payment every 6 months. The $100,000 is a single future amount, and the $5,000 semiannual interest payments are an annuity.

If Unlimited Decadence sells the bonds to yield 12%, it discounts the cash payments at 6% (12% ÷ 2) per semiannual period for 8 (4 years × 2) semiannual periods. The selling price of this bond issue is $93,789, computed as follows:

$$\text{Present Value of Face Value} = \text{Face Value} \times \text{Present Value of \$1 Factor for 8 Periods at 6\%}$$

$$= \$100,000 \times 0.6274 \text{ (from Table 20-1)}$$

$$= \$62,740$$

$$\begin{array}{c}\text{Present Value of} \\ \text{Interest Payments}\end{array} = \text{Periodic Interest Payment} \times \begin{array}{c}\text{Present Value of Annuity} \\ \text{Factor for 8 Periods at 6\%}\end{array}$$

$$= \$5,000 \times 6.2098 \text{ (from Table 20-2)}$$

$$= \$31,049$$

$$\begin{array}{c}\text{Selling Price of} \\ \text{Bond Issue}\end{array} = \text{Present Value of Face Value} + \begin{array}{c}\text{Present Value of} \\ \text{Interest Payments}\end{array}$$

$$= \$62,740 + \$31,049$$

$$= \$93,789$$

In this case, Unlimited Decadence sells the bonds at a discount of $6,211, the difference between the $100,000 face value and the $93,789 selling price, because the yield is *higher* than the contract rate. The company has a cost of 12% (6% semiannually) on its borrowing, and the purchasers obtain a 12% return (6% semiannually) on their investment. Unlimited Decadence records the sale of these bonds at a discount on January 1, 2008, as follows:

Assets	=	Liabilities	+	Stockholders' Equity
Cash		Bonds Payable		
+$93,789		+$93,789		

FINANCIAL STATEMENT EFFECTS

Increases current assets and total assets on *balance sheet*. Increases noncurrent liabilities and total liabilities on *balance sheet*. Increases cash flows from financing activities on *cash flow statement*.

The $93,789 is the *book value* of the bonds payable on the date of their sale.[10]

Unlimited Decadence makes its first interest payment of $5,000 on June 30, 2008. This amount is *not* the interest expense for the period. For bonds sold at a discount (or premium), the company computes the **interest expense** by multiplying the book value of the bonds payable at the beginning of the period times half the annual yield. This way of computing interest expense is called the **effective interest method**. As we discussed earlier, when a company sells bonds at a discount, the interest expense is greater than the interest paid. Remember that Unlimited Decadence will pay $100,000 at the end of 4 years, not $93,789. Unlimited Decadence computes the interest expense for the first period (January 1 through June 30, 2008) to be $5,627.34, as follows:

[10]Some companies would instead record the Bonds Payable account at the face value ($100,000) and would then create a contra account called Discount on Bonds Payable for $6,211. These companies would subtract the contra-account balance from the Bonds Payable face value to determine the $93,789 book value of the bonds. Our method is less complex and conveys similar information.

$$\text{Interest Expense for Period} = \text{Book Value at Beginning of Period} \times (\text{Yield} \div 2)$$

$$= \$93,789 \times (12\% \div 2)$$

$$= \$5,627.34$$

Since the company has interest *expense* of $5,627.34 but *pays* interest of only $5,000, it increases its bond liability by $627.34. The process of increasing the bonds payable for the difference between the interest expense and the interest paid is called *amortizing* a portion of the $6,211 discount.[11] On June 30, 2008, Unlimited Decadence records the interest expense as follows:

Assets	=	Liabilities	+	Stockholders' Equity		
					Net Income	
				Revenues	−	Expenses
Cash		Bonds Payable				Interest Expense
		Bal $93,789.00				
−$5,000		+ 627.34			−	+$5,627.34
		Bal $94,416.34				

Note that the discount amortization has *increased* the Bonds Payable book value to $94,416.34.

On December 31, 2008, Unlimited Decadence records its interest expense for the second semiannual period in the same way as we showed above. In this case, however, it computes the interest expense of $5,664.98 by multiplying the $94,416.34 book value of the bonds payable at the beginning of the second period by the 6% semiannual yield. Since it pays the interest of $5,000, it amortizes $664.98 ($5,664.98 − $5,000) of the discount as an increase in the bonds payable. Thus, the book value of the bonds payable is $95,081.32 ($94,416.34 + $664.98) at the end of 2008, and Unlimited Decadence reports this amount (rounded) as a noncurrent liability on its December 31, 2008 balance sheet as follows:

Long-term debt
10% bonds payable (face value $100,000), due 12/31/11 $95,081

Note that the company reports the face value in parentheses or in the notes to the financial statements. The company reports $11,292 ($5,627.34 + $5,664.98, rounded) interest expense for the whole year in the "other items" section on its 2008 income statement. In Exhibit 22-5 we show the calculations for the entire life of the bonds. Note that after the company has recorded its interest for the 8 semiannual periods, on the December 31, 2011 maturity date the book value is equal to the $100,000 face value. This is because Unlimited Decadence has amortized all of the discount. So the liability is equal to the amount that Unlimited Decadence must pay on that date.

BONDS ISSUED AT A PREMIUM

When a company sells bonds at a premium, the yield earned by investors is less than the contract rate. We illustrate the accounting for bonds issued at a premium by assuming the same information for the Unlimited Decadence bond issue in the previous example except that the yield now is 8%. Therefore, the company computes the $106,733.50 selling price by discounting the future cash flows using a 4% semiannual yield for 8 semiannual periods as follows:

$$\text{Present Value of Face Value} = \text{Face Value} \times \text{Present Value of \$1 Factor for 8 Periods at 4\%}$$

$$= \$100,000 \times 0.7307 \text{ (from Table 20-1)}$$

$$= \$73,070$$

Decreases current assets and total assets on *balance sheet*. Increases noncurrent liabilities, and total liabilities on *balance sheet*. Increases expenses (in "other items"), which decreases net income on *income statement* (and therefore decreases stockholders' equity on *balance sheet*). Decreases cash flows from operating activities on *cash flow statement*.

[11]Some companies amortize the discount (or premium) using the *straight-line* method. Under this method, they allocate an equal portion of the discount (or premium) to interest expense each period and increase the bonds payable by that same amount each period. Because the interest expense under this method does not reflect the actual yield, we do not discuss it further.

EXHIBIT 22-5	BOND CALCULATIONS: ISSUED AT A DISCOUNT

Date	Cash Paid*	Interest Expense†	Amortization of Discount‡	Book Value of Bonds§
1/1/08				$ 93,789.00
6/30/08	$5,000.00	$5,627.34	$627.34	94,416.34
12/31/08	5,000.00	5,664.98	664.98	95,081.32
6/30/09	5,000.00	5,704.88	704.88	95,786.20
12/31/09	5,000.00	5,747.17	747.17	96,533.37
6/30/10	5,000.00	5,792.00	792.00	97,325.37
12/31/10	5,000.00	5,839.52	839.52	98,164.89
6/30/11	5,000.00	5,889.89	889.89	99,054.78
12/31/11	5,000.00	5,945.22**	945.22	100,000.00

*Face Value × (Annual Contract Rate ÷ Number of Interest Payments Each Year), or $100,000 × (10% ÷ 2)
†(Annual Yield ÷ Number of Interest Payments Each Year) × Book Value of the Bonds at the Beginning of the Period (from previous line); at 6/30/08, (12% ÷ 2) × $93,789.00 = $5,627.34
‡Interest Expense − Cash Paid; at 6/30/08, $5,627.34 − $5,000.00 = $627.34
§Book Value of Bonds (from previous line) + Amortization of Discount; at 6/30/08, $93,789.00 + $627.34 = $94,416.34
**Adjusted for rounding error of $1.93

$$\text{Present Value of Interest Payments} = \text{Periodic Interest Payment} \times \text{Present Value of Annuity Factor for 8 Periods at 4\%}$$

$$= \$5,000 \times 6.7327 \text{ (from Table 20-2)}$$

$$= \$33,663.50$$

$$\text{Selling Price of Bond Issue} = \text{Present Value of Face Value} + \text{Present Value of Interest Payments}$$

$$= \$73,070 + \$33,663.50$$

$$= \$106,733.50$$

In this case Unlimited Decadence sells the bonds at a premium of $6,733.50, the difference between the $106,733.50 selling price and the $100,000 face value, because the yield is *lower* than the contract rate. The company has a cost of 8% (4% semiannually) on its borrowing, and the purchasers obtain an 8% return (4% semiannually) on their investment. Unlimited Decadence records the sale of these bonds at a premium on January 1, 2008, as follows:

<table>
<tr><th>Assets</th><th>=</th><th>Liabilities</th><th>+</th><th>Stockholders' Equity</th></tr>
<tr><td>Cash</td><td></td><td>Bonds Payable</td><td></td><td></td></tr>
<tr><td>+$106,733.50</td><td></td><td>+$106,733.50</td><td></td><td></td></tr>
</table>

The $106,733.50 is the book value of the bonds payable.[12]

Unlimited Decadence makes its first $5,000 interest payment on June 30, 2008. It computes the interest expense by multiplying the book value of the bonds payable at the beginning of the period by half the annual yield. As we discussed earlier, when a company sells bonds at a

FINANCIAL STATEMENT EFFECTS

Increases current assets and total assets on **balance sheet**. Increases noncurrent liabilities and total liabilities on **balance sheet**. Increases cash flows from financing activities on **cash flow statement**.

---

[12]Some companies would instead record the Bonds Payable account at the face value ($100,000) and would then create a Premium on Bonds Payable account for $6,733.50. The company adds the premium to the Bonds Payable face value to determine the $106,733.50 book value of the bonds. Our method is less complex and conveys similar information.

premium, the interest expense is less than the interest paid. For Unlimited Decadence, the interest expense for the first period is $4,269.34 ($106,733.50 × 0.04, rounded). Since the company has interest *expense* of $4,269.34 but *pays* interest of $5,000, it amortizes the $730.66 difference (premium reduction) as a decrease in bonds payable. On June 30, 2008, Unlimited Decadence records the interest as follows:

Assets	=	Liabilities	+	Stockholders' Equity	
				Net Income	
				Revenues −	**Expenses**
Cash		Bonds Payable			Interest Expense
		Bal $106,733.50			
−$5,000		− 730.66		−	+$4,269.34
		Bal $106,002.84			

FINANCIAL STATEMENT EFFECTS
Decreases current assets and total assets on **balance sheet**. Decreases noncurrent liabilities and total liabilities on **balance sheet**. Increases expenses (in "other items"), which decreases net income on **income statement** (and therefore decreases stockholders' equity on **balance sheet**). Decreases cash flows from operating activities on **cash flow statement**.

Note that the premium amortization has decreased the Bonds Payable book value to $106,002.84.

On December 31, 2008, Unlimited Decadence records its interest for the second semiannual period in the same way as we showed above. In this case, however, it computes the interest expense to be $4,240.11 by multiplying the $106,002.84 book value of the bonds at the beginning of the second period by the 4% semiannual yield. Since it pays interest of $5,000, it amortizes $759.89 ($5,000 − $4,240.11) of the premium as a decrease in the bonds payable. Thus, the book value of the bonds payable is $105,242.95 ($106,002.84 − $759.89) at the end of 2008, and Unlimited Decadence reports this amount (rounded) as a long-term liability on its December 31, 2008 balance sheet. The company reports $8,509 ($4,269.34 + $4,240.11, rounded) interest expense for the whole year on its 2008 income statement. In Exhibit 22-6, we show the calculations for the entire life of the bonds. Note that after the company has recorded its interest for the 8 semiannual periods, on the December 31, 2011 maturity date the book value is equal to the $100,000 face value. This is because Unlimited Decadence has amortized all the premium. So the liability is equal to the amount that Unlimited Decadence must pay on that date.

What is the difference between the payments on a bond issued at face value and the payments on a bond issued at a premium or discount?

EXHIBIT 22-6	BOND CALCULATIONS: ISSUED AT A PREMIUM			
Date	**Cash Paid**[*]	**Interest Expense**[†]	**Amortization of Premium**[‡]	**Book Value of Bonds**[§]
1/1/08				$106,733.50
6/30/08	$5,000.00	$4,269.34	$730.66	106,002.84
12/31/08	5,000.00	4,240.11	759.89	105,242.95
6/30/09	5,000.00	4,209.72	790.28	104,452.67
12/31/09	5,000.00	4,178.11	821.89	103,630.78
6/30/10	5,000.00	4,145.23	854.77	102,776.01
12/31/10	5,000.00	4,111.04	888.96	101,887.05
6/30/11	5,000.00	4,075.48	924.52	100,962.53
12/31/11	5,000.00	4,037.47[**]	962.53	100,000.00

[*]Face Value × (Annual Contract Rate ÷ Number of Interest Payments Each Year), or $100,000 × (10% ÷ 2)
[†](Annual Yield ÷ Number of Interest Payments Each Year) × Book Value of the Bonds at the Beginning of the Period (from previous line); at 6/30/08, (8% ÷ 2) × $106,733.50 = $4,269.34
[‡]Cash Paid − Interest Expense; at 6/30/08, $5,000.00 − $4,269.34 = $730.66
[§]Book Value of Bonds (from previous line) − Amortization of Premium; at 6/30/08, $106,733.50 − $730.66 = $106,002.84
[**]Adjusted for rounding error of $1.03

SUMMARY SURFING

Here is an opportunity to gather information on the Internet about real-world issues related to the topics in this chapter (for suggestions on how to navigate various companies' Web sites to find their financial statements and other information, see the related discussion in the Preface at the beginning of the book). Answer the following questions.

- Go on the **ExxonMobil Corporation** Web site. Find the company's notes to its financial statements. What is the book value, on December 31 of the most recent year, of the guaranteed zero-coupon notes (bonds) due 2004? How much did their book value change during the most recent year? Why did the book value change?

- Go to the **Federated Department Stores, Inc.** Web site. Find the company's notes to its financial statements. How much are the company's total future minimum lease payments for capital leases? for operating leases? What is the present value of the capital leases? What is the present value of the operating leases?

INTEGRATED BUSINESS AND ACCOUNTING SITUATIONS

Answer the Following Questions in Your Own Words.

Testing Your Knowledge

22-1 What three concepts or principles affect how a company accounts for and reports on long-term debt in its financial statements?

22-2 Define the terms *bond*, *face value*, *maturity date*, *contract rate*, and *bond certificate*.

22-3 Explain what is meant by "leverage" (or trading on equity).

22-4 Explain how a company computes interest expense when it issues bonds at face value.

22-5 How does a company determine the amount of interest expense to accrue at the end of an accounting period when it issues bonds at face value?

22-6 Identify the three components that determine the yield on a bond issue.

22-7 Under what condition will a company sell a bond at a discount? at a premium?

22-8 When a company sells bonds at a discount, is its interest expense higher or lower than the interest paid? Why? How would your answer change if the company sold the bond issue at a premium?

22-9 For bonds sold at a discount or a premium, how does a company compute its interest expense?

22-10 What is meant by the phrase "amortizing a portion of the discount (or premium)" in regard to interest expense?

22-11 What are callable bonds, and how does a company record their retirement?

22-12 What is a lease? What is the difference between a lessee and a lessor?

22-13 When does a lessee company record an asset and a liability for a lease?

22-14 What is the difference between a capital lease and an operating lease?

22-15 How does a lessee company record a capital lease?

22-16 How does a lessee company compute the interest expense for a capital lease? How does this affect the lease obligation?

22-17 How does a lessor company account for a capital lease?

22-18 For income taxes, what is a temporary difference, a deferred tax liability, and a deferred tax asset?

22-19 For retirement benefits, what is a pension plan? a defined-benefit plan? Where does a company report the projected benefit obligation and the assets of its pension plan?

22-20 How does a company report its noncurrent debt transactions on its cash flow statement?

22-21 (Appendix). How does a company compute the selling price of a bond issue?

Applying Your Knowledge

22-22 On January 1, 2008, Allen Fritz borrowed $30,000 from a bank to buy a car. The loan has an interest rate of 8% and requires equal annual payments at the end of each year for the next three years.

Required: Determine the equal annual amounts that Fritz must pay at the end of each year for the next three years to repay the loan.

22-23 On January 1, 2008, Latriece Johnson borrowed $20,000 from her uncle to help finance her college education. She and her uncle sign a "contract" that charges her 6% interest and requires her to repay the loan in equal annual payments at the end of each year for the next four years.

Required: (1) Determine the equal annual amounts that Johnson must pay at the end of each year for the next four years to repay the loan.
(2) Prepare a schedule for each of the four years to show how much of each annual payment is for interest and how much is for principal. Use the following column headings: Year, Beginning Balance, Interest, Principal, Ending Balance.

22-24 The Underhill Ski Corporation has been operating at a very stable level, consistently earning $200,000 income before income taxes. The company is evaluating the possibility of expanding its operations to include snowboards. It has calculated that building a new plant would cost $1.2 million, and it estimates that pretax income would increase by $150,000 as a result of the expansion. The company currently has 100,000 shares of common stock held by stockholders. Its income tax rate is 40%. The company is considering whether to finance the expansion by selling bonds with a face value of $1.2 million and a 10% interest rate or by selling 60,000 additional shares of common stock for $20 per share to obtain the $1.2 million.

Required: (1) Compute the company's earnings per share under each method of financing.
(2) Which method of financing would you recommend? Explain your reasoning.

22-25 On January 1, 2008, Miles Shredding Machine Company issued 10%, 20-year bonds with a face value of $600,000 for $600,000. The bonds pay interest semiannually on June 30 and December 31.

Required: (1) How much interest expense does Miles record in 2008?
(2) What is the book value of the bonds on December 31, 2008? Show how the company reports this on its December 31, 2004 balance sheet.

22-26 The Martinez Company issued 12-year, zero-coupon bonds with a face value of $250,000 on January 1, 2008. The bonds were sold to yield 8%.

Required: (1) Compute the selling price of the bonds.
(2) Compute the interest expense for 2008 and 2009.
(3) What is the book value of the bonds on December 31, 2009?

22-27 The Weimer Company issued 7-year, zero-coupon bonds with a face value of $300,000 on January 1, 2008. The bonds were sold to yield 12%.

Required: (1) Compute the selling price of the bonds.
(2) Record the interest expense for 2008 and 2009.
(3) What is the book value of the bonds on December 31, 2009?

22-28 The Porter Luggage Company has 9% bonds outstanding with a face value of $80,000. The bonds pay interest on June 30 and December 31. On July 1, 2008, when the bonds have a book value of $81,000, Porter calls them for $83,000.

Required: (1) Record the retirement of the bonds.
(2) Show how Porter would report the resulting gain or loss on its 2008 income statement.

22-29 The Duran Furniture Company shows the following items in its 2008 and 2009 financial statements:

	2008	2009
Income before income taxes	$ 98,000	$104,000
Interest expense	10,000	16,000
Long-term debt, end of year	125,000	200,000
Stockholders' equity, end of year	150,000	200,000

Required: (1) Compute the (a) long-term debt to stockholders' equity ratio and (b) interest coverage ratio, for 2008 and 2009.
(2) Briefly discuss your ratio results in regard to the company's financial risk.

22-30 On January 1, 2008, Thompson Cement Company leased a machine from Hexad Equipment Company. The lease was a capital lease, and Thompson recorded the asset and the liability at $84,000 based on a 10% interest rate and a 5-year life. Thompson makes a lease payment of $22,159 at the end of each year. The company uses the straight-line depreciation method for the leased asset, and expects the asset to have no residual value.

Required: What are (1) the interest expense and (2) the depreciation expense for Thompson Cement Company for 2008?

22-31 Use the information in 22-30 but assume that Thompson classified the lease as an operating lease.

Required: (1) How much expense related to the lease will Thompson Cement Company record in 2008?
(2) Which company will report the machine on its balance sheet at the end of 2008? Why?

22-32 On January 1, 2008, Eton Horse Breeding Company leased a Mercedes from Elite Cars for the president's use. The lease specified that $20,000 was to be paid at the end of each year for five years. Eton classified the lease as a capital lease with an interest rate of 10%. It uses the straight-line method of depreciation with a zero residual value.

Required: (1) Show how Eton would report the depreciation expense and the interest expense for the lease on its 2008 income statement.
(2) Show how Eton would report the leased asset and the lease liability on its December 31, 2008 balance sheet.
(3) Briefly discuss how this lease affects Eton's risk, financial flexibility, and liquidity.

22-33 Holliday Company purchased a hotel for $360,000 and made a 20% down payment. It financed the remainder with a 20-year mortgage at 12%, with monthly payments. The present value of an annuity of 1% for 240 periods is 90.8194.

Required: (1) Compute the amount of the monthly mortgage payment.

(2) Record the (a) purchase of the building, (b) first monthly payment, and (c) second monthly payment.

22-34 At the end of 2008, Lucero Child Care Corporation reported taxable income for the year of $27,000 on its income tax return. It is subject to a 40% income tax rate, and its 2008 income taxes will be paid in early 2009. For 2008, the company computed a $700 increase in its long-term deferred tax liability.

Required: (1) Prepare the entry to record the company's income taxes for 2008.
(2) If the company had a beginning long-term deferred tax liability of $4,800, show how it would report its income tax obligations on its December 31, 2008 balance sheet.

22-35 Mullen Rafting Company operates a pension plan for the benefit of its employees. The company computed its pension expense for 2008 to be $60,000, but paid $58,000 to its funding agency at the end of the year.

Required: (1) Prepare the entry to record the company's pension expense for 2008.
(2) Where would you find the amounts of the company's projected benefit obligation and the assets of its pension plan?
(3) What is your evaluation if its projected benefit obligation is greater than the pension plan assets?

22-36 (Appendix). Mark Paint Company issues 10-year, 10% bonds with a face value of $400,000 on January 1, 2008. The bonds pay interest semiannually.

Required: Compute the issuance price of the bonds if (1) the company sells the bonds to yield 12%, and (2) the company sells the bonds to yield 8%.

22-37 (Appendix). On January 1, 2008, Loveland Tractor Company issues 10-year, 9% bonds with a face value of $200,000. The bonds pay interest semiannually and are issued to yield 10%.

Required: (1) What is the selling price of the bonds? What is the amount of the discount?
(2) How much interest expense does the company record in 2008?
(3) Show how the company reports the book value of the bonds on its December 31, 2008 balance sheet.

22-38 (Appendix). Use the same information as in 22-37 except that Loveland Tractor Company issues the bonds to yield 6%.

Required: (1) What is the selling price of the bonds? What is the amount of the premium?
(2) How much interest expense does the company record in 2008?
(3) Show how the company reports the book value of the bonds on its December 31, 2008 balance sheet.

22-39 (Appendix). The James Wood Stove Company issued 2-year, 10% bonds with a face value of $100,000 for $96,535.50 on January 1, 2008. The bonds pay interest semiannually on June 30 and December 31, and were issued to yield 12%.

Required: (1) Prepare all the entries related to the bonds over the 2-year life.
(2) Summarize how the company would report the cash flows on this bond issue in its cash flow statements over the 2-year life.

22-40 (Appendix). The Linjo Insecticide Company issued 2-year, 8% bonds with a face value of $400,000 for $414,873.60 on January 1, 2008. The bonds pay interest semiannually on June 30 and December 31 and were issued to yield 6%.

Required: (1) Prepare all the entries related to the bonds over the 2-year life.
(2) Summarize how the company would report the cash flows on the bond issue in its cash flow statements over the 2-year life.

Making Evaluations

22-41 At a board of directors meeting of Temple Battery Company to discuss the issuance of bonds with a face value of $100,000, the following comments were made:

- "At current market rates, I think the bonds will sell to yield 10%. Therefore, we should have a contract rate of 11% so that the bonds will sell at a premium. Like anyone else, investors view premiums as favorable, and we should do anything we can to get favorable reactions."

- "I agree that the yield will be 10%, but I think we should have a contract rate of 8% so that the bonds will sell at a discount. We all know people like to get a good deal, and if they can buy the bonds for less than face value, I'm sure the bonds will sell very easily."

- "If the yield is 10%, we should have a contract rate of 10%. Since we need exactly $100,000 to finance our expansion, that is the best alternative."

Required: Critically evaluate each of the above comments.

22-42 The Byrne Bus Company is planning to acquire some machinery. It is considering three methods of acquiring the machinery, which has a 6-year life and no residual value:
(a) Buy the machinery for $50,000, pay $10,000 down, and borrow the balance from a bank at 10% for 6 years. The company will pay interest on December 31 of each year.
(b) Lease the machinery under a 6-year lease, which it would classify as a capital lease. The lease would require a payment of $15,000 at the end of each year. The leased asset would revert back to the lessor at the end of the lease.
(c) Lease the machinery under a 1-year lease, which it would classify as an operating lease. The company could renew the lease each year for 5 more years. The lease payment, which is due when the lease is signed, is $15,000.

Required: (1) Prepare an analysis (using assumptions that you think are appropriate) of the cash flows the company would pay over the 6 years under each alternative.
(2) Explain how each of the alternatives would affect the company's financial statements.
(3) Which alternative would you recommend?

22-43 **Wal-Mart** reported the following amounts in its 2006 annual report (in millions):

Jan. 31	2006	2005
Cash and cash equivalents	$ 6,414	$ 5,488
Total assets	138,187	120,154
Total shareholders' equity	53,171	49,396

	2006	2005
Interest expense	$ 1,171	$ 934
Income before income taxes	17,358	16,105
Net income	11,231	10,267
Net cash provided by operating activities	17,633	15,044
Net cash used in investing activities	(14,183)	(12,351)
Net cash used in financing activities	(2,422)	(2,609)

On January 31, 2006, annual maturities of long-term debt during the next five years and thereafter are

Fiscal years ending January 31	Annual Maturity
2007	$ 4,595
2008	3,320
2009	2,858
2010	4,639
2011	2,877
Thereafter	12,735
Total	$31,024

During the year ended January 31, 2006, Wal-Mart issued and repaid long-term debt of $7,691 and $2,724, respectively.

Required: (1) Compute Wal-Mart's long-term debt to shareholders' equity ratio at January 31, 2006 and 2005. How has its financial flexibility changed?

(2) Compute Wal-Mart's interest coverage ratio for the years ended January 31, 2006 and 2005. Explain whether you are concerned about its ability to pay its interest obligations each period.

(3) Explain whether you are concerned about Wal-Mart's ability to pay its long-term debt obligations. Explain whether you would like any additional information to help you answer this question.

22-44 **Verizon** reported the following (partial) information related to its debt in the notes to its 2005 financial statements (in millions):

Dec. 31	2005	2004
Zero coupon convertible notes net of unamortized discount of $790 and $830	$1,360	$1,320

Required: (1) What was the interest rate on the zero coupon convertible notes (bonds) in 2005? What is the annual yield on these notes? Assume that Verizon did not issue or retire any notes during 2005.

(2) What will be the interest expense on the zero coupon convertible notes in 2006? Explain how the interest will affect Verizon's financial statements.

22-45 **Wal-Mart** reported the following (partial) information in the notes to its 2006 financial statements (in millions of dollars):

Commitments
Minimum annual rentals at January 31, 2006, under non-cancelable leases are as follows:

Fiscal Year	Operating Leases
2007	$ 797
2008	751
2009	710
2010	634
2011	586
Thereafter	6,205
Total minimum rentals	$9,683

Required: (1) What would be the effects on the relevant balance sheet items at January 31, 2006, and the relevant income statement items for the 2007 fiscal year if the operating leases were recorded as capital leases instead? Assume the company makes each year's lease payments at the end of the year. Use a 10% interest rate and straight-line depreciation over 12 years with no residual value. Assume each payment is made at the end of each year, and the "thereafter" payments have a present value of $2,400 million. Round to two decimal places.

(2) Show how the company would record the leases on January 31, 2006 if they were considered capital leases. Then discuss how they would affect the January 31, 2006 balance sheet and the ratios used to evaluate the company?

(3) The company reported "long-term debt and long-term obligations under capital leases" of $30,171 at January 31, 2006. Does considering the operating leases to be capital leases have a significant effect on your understanding of the company's obligations?

22-46 The following excerpts are from **United Airlines**' 2005 financial statements (in millions):

Total assets at December 31, 2005	$19,342
Total stockholders' equity at December 31, 2005	(25,560)

Lease Obligations

At December 31, 2005, scheduled future minimum lease payments under operating leases having initial or remaining noncancellable lease terms of more than one year are as follows:

Payable during	Operating Leases
2006	$ 1,271
2007	1,244
2008	1,206
2009	1,160
2010	1,118
After 2010	6,123
Total minimum lease payments	$12,122

Required: (1) What would be the effects on the relevant balance sheet items at December 31, 2005, and the relevant income statement items for 2005 if the operating leases were recorded as capital leases instead? Assume the company makes each year's lease payments at the end of the year. Use a 10% interest rate and straight-line depreciation over an 11-year life with no residual value. Assume the "After 2010" payments have a present value of $2,300. Round to two decimal places.

(2) Are the effects of treating the operating leases as capital leases material to the December 31, 2005 balance sheet?

22-47 **PepsiCo** disclosed the following (partial) information in the income taxes note to its 2005 financial statements (in millions):

Provision for income taxes:		
Current: Federal		$1,638
Foreign		426
State		118
Deferred: Federal		137
Foreign		(26)
State		11
Deferred tax liability		
Property, plant, and equipment		$ 772
Deferred tax asset		
Various liabilities		$1,764
Income taxes paid		$1,258

Required: (1) What is the amount of PepsiCo's income tax expense for 2005?

(2) What is the amount of PepsiCo's current income tax obligation to federal, foreign, and state governments for 2005? Why is this obligation different than the income tax expense? Why is it different than the income tax paid?

(3) Explain why PepsiCo has a deferred tax liability from property, plant, and equipment.

(4) Explain why PepsiCo has a deferred tax asset from various liabilities.

22-48 In its December 31, 2005 balance sheet, **Ford Motor Company** reported total assets of $269,476 million and total stockholders' equity of $12,957 million. It reported an asset of $6,209 million for its pension plans. In its notes, it disclosed that its pension plans had projected benefit obligation of $74,595 million and plan assets of $63,784 million. The company also disclosed that the discount rate used to compute the projected benefit obligation was 5.61%, down from 5.75% in the previous year.

Required: (1) Compute Ford's debt ratio with and without considering the pension plans. How does consideration of the pension plan affect your assessment of Ford's risk and financial flexibility?

(2) Explain whether the decrease in the discount rate increased or decreased the projected benefit obligation.

22-49 On its December 31, 2005 balance sheet, **General Electric** reported total assets of $673,342 million and total stockholders' equity of $109,354 million. In its notes, it disclosed that its pension plans had a projected benefit obligation of $51,428 million and plan assets of $54,309 million. The company also disclosed that its retiree health and life benefits had an obligation of $9,084 million and plan assets of $1,619 million. The company also disclosed that it reported an asset of $14,413 million for its pension plans and a liability of $4,154 million for retiree health and life benefits on its December 31, 2005 balance sheet. It disclosed that the discount rate used to compute the pension obligations was 5.5%, down from 5.75% in the previous year.

Required: (1) Compute General Electric's debt ratio with and without considering the pension plan and the OPEBs. How does consideration of the pension plan affect your assessment of General Electric's risk and financial flexibility?

(2) Explain whether the decrease in the discount rate increased or decreased the projected benefit obligation.

22-50 Use the financial section of the 2005 annual report of **Colgate-Palmolive** in Appendix B to answer the following questions.

Required: (1) How much was Colgate-Palmolive's interest incurred for 2005?

(2) How much interest did Colgate-Palmolive pay in 2005?

(3) What will be the interest expense on the 5.8% notes (bonds) in 2006, assuming the notes are outstanding the entire year? (Use an annual yield.)

(4) How much are Colgate-Palmolive's unused credit facilities at December 31, 2005?

(5) Does Colgate-Palmolive have significant operating leases that would affect your understanding of the company's financial position?

(6) What is the amount of Colgate-Palmolive's income tax expense for 2005?

(7) What is the amount of Colgate-Palmolive's current income tax obligation for 2005? Why is this obligation different from the income tax expense? Why is it different from the income tax paid?

(8) Explain why Colgate-Palmolive has a deferred tax liability from property, plant, and equipment.

(9) Explain why Colgate-Palmolive has a deferred tax asset from accrued liabilities.

(10) Are Colgate-Palmolive's pension plan assets greater or less than its projected benefit obligation at December 31, 2005 (see Note 10)?

22-51 Yesterday, you received the following letter for your advice column in the local paper?

DR. DECISIVE

Dear Dr. Decisive:

I recently took a trip and flew on Frontier Airlines. When I got back I decided to look at the company's annual report. Was I surprised! The airline has no planes listed on its balance sheet. But I definitely flew on one. How can this be? And how can I evaluate the company's performance if it reports ticket sales on the income statement but has no assets on its balance sheet? Then I took another look at the balance sheet and I saw that the company had a liability for "accrued maintenance expense." Does that mean the company is saving money by not doing maintenance? That would be scary!

Call me "Flying without a Plane."

Required: Meet with your Dr. Decisive team and write a response to "Flying without a Plane."

CHAPTER 23

INVESTMENTS IN STOCKS AND BONDS OF OTHER COMPANIES

"COMPETITION IS A LOT LIKE CODLIVER OIL. FIRST IT MAKES YOU SICK. THEN IT MAKES YOU BETTER."

—AMD INC.
ADVERTISEMENT

1. How does a company classify its investments on its financial statements?

2. How does a company record and report its investments that are available for sale?

3. How does a company record and report its investments in companies over which it has significant influence?

4. When and why does a company prepare consolidated financial statements?

5. How does a company record and report its investments in bonds that it expects to hold until maturity?

On **Intel**'s December 31, 2005 balance sheet, the company shows that it has marketable securities of $3,990 million—8.3 percent of its total assets. On **Microsoft**'s June 30, 2005 balance sheet, its marketable securities are $32,900 million. Given that its total assets were $70,815 million, 46.5 percent of Microsoft's assets are marketable securities. These dollar amounts shown on Intel's and Microsoft's balance sheets result from decisions by managers as well as the accounting methods the companies used to keep track of marketable securities.

There are various ways to understand the meaning of these disclosures. For example, if Microsoft Office sells for an average of $400, its marketable securities were the dollar equivalent of over 82 million copies! Another way to think about these amounts is to think about the business decisions that created them. For example, marketable securities are usually purchased with excess cash generated by operating cash flows.

Intel reported gains from selling marketable securities of $96 million and $52 million in 2005 and 2004 respectively, whereas its income before income taxes in each of those years was $12,610 million and $10,417 million. Microsoft reported a net gain from selling marketable securities of $1,004 million in 2005 and a net gain of $1,642 million in 2004, whereas its income before income taxes in each of those years was $12,254 million and $8,168 million. So you can see that sales of these investments had a significant impact on the amount of income each of these companies reported.

How much cash do you think Microsoft could "come up with" on short notice?

Can you conclude whether Intel or Microsoft is better at managing its marketable securities? What factors besides these amounts on the balance sheets, income statements, and cash flow statements of the two companies should you consider?

To evaluate a company's liquidity and financial flexibility, both external and internal users must be familiar with how the company records and reports its investments. A company may make various types of investments for various reasons. For example, when a company has excess cash, it has several choices. If it wants to invest for a short time with very little risk, it may invest in cash equivalents, as we discussed in Chapter 13 of Volume 1. If the company wants to invest for a longer time and accept more risk, it may invest in securities (either stocks or bonds). A company makes this investment because it expects to receive dividends or interest and to participate in an increase in the market value of the securities.

In addition, a company may purchase long-term investments in stocks of other corporations, either because it expects them to be more profitable than investing in property, plant, and equipment, or for strategic reasons. For example, a company can obtain some influence, or even control, over the operations of its suppliers or customers by purchasing stock of these companies, voting at the stockholders' meetings, and having a member(s) on the board of directors. A company also may invest in the stocks of corporations that have an operating cycle different from its own. In doing this, the company hopes that the income earned from owning the stock will help to offset any cyclical declines in the income from its own business and thus smooth its earnings trend. A company may make a long-term investment in the bonds of other companies to develop a financial relationship with another company or to obtain a relatively safe source of continued interest revenue.

CLASSIFICATIONS OF INVESTMENTS

Recall from Chapters 10 of Volume 1 and 22 that a corporation may issue (sell) stocks and bonds to investors. Recall that **common stock** is the ownership unit of a corporation and that common stockholders are the owners of a corporation.[1] These owners have the

How does a company classify its investments on its financial statements?

---

[1]Investors also may purchase *preferred stock*. For simplicity, in this chapter we focus on investments in common stock, although the principles we discuss for investments in common stock that are available for sale also apply to preferred stock.

right to vote on corporate policies and the right to share in the corporation's net income by receiving dividends. **Bonds** are a type of note in which a company agrees to pay the holder the face value on the maturity date and to pay interest on the face value periodically at a specified rate. Bondholders are creditors of a company. Although bondholders cannot vote, they do "share" in the company's income by receiving interest.

A company (called the *investor*) may choose to invest in the common stock of another company (called the *investee)*. How the investor company accounts for its investments in stock depends on its "influence" over the investee. *Influence* is defined by the percentage ownership the investor company has in the investee; percentage ownership relates to the number of votes the investor company has. If an investor company has **no significant influence** over the investee (less than 20% ownership), it has an investment in "available-for-sale stock."[2] The investor company typically makes this investment to receive dividends and participate in an increase in the market value of the stock. The company reports this investment on its balance sheet using the *market value method*. If the investor company has **significant influence** over the investee (between 20% and 50% ownership), it has an equity investment. It has a larger ownership (equity) interest in the investee and that larger interest provides it with significant influence. The investor company reports this investment using the *equity method*. If the investor company has **control** over the investee (more than 50% ownership), the investee is no longer a separate *economic* entity from the investor company, so the investor company prepares *consolidated* financial statements.

Do you think a company could own less than 20% and have significant influence? more than 20% and not have significant influence? less than 50% and have control? more than 50% and not have control? Why or why not?

A company also may choose to invest in another company's bonds. How the investor company reports its investments in bonds depends on how long it expects to hold the bonds. If the company expects to sell the bonds before their maturity date, it calls them "available-for-sale bonds" and reports this investment using the *market value method*. If the company expects to hold the bonds for their entire life, it calls them "held-to-maturity bonds" and reports this investment using the *amortized cost method*. We summarize the method a company uses to report each type of investment in Exhibit 23-1, and we will explain these methods in later sections of this chapter.

EXHIBIT 23-1	ACCOUNTING FOR INVESTMENTS
Type of Investment	**Method**
Investments in Common Stock	
Amount of Influence	
No significant influence (less than 20% ownership)	Market value method
Significant influence (20% to 50% ownership)	Equity method
Control (more than 50% ownership)	Consolidation method
Investments in Bonds	
Available-for-sale	Market value method
Held-to-maturity	Amortized cost method

[2]Some companies, such as banks, also make investments in "trading securities." *Trading securities* are securities that a company holds for a very short time (often only a few days) to earn profits from short-term differences in the selling prices of the securities. We do not discuss trading securities in this book.

MARKET PRICES OF STOCKS AND BONDS

A company (just like an individual) usually makes an investment in stocks or bonds of publicly traded companies through a stockbroker. A **stockbroker** is a person or company that buys and sells (*trades*) stocks and bonds for other people or companies. As we discussed in Chapter 10 of Volume 1, the stocks and bonds of large corporations are traded on organized securities exchanges, such as the **New York Stock Exchange**, the **Tokyo Stock Exchange**, or the **Oslo Stock Exchange**. The stocks and bonds of other corporations are traded in the over-the-counter market, such as NASDAQ, in which brokers deal directly with each other rather than through a stock exchange.

The market prices of these stocks and bonds are quoted daily and are reported on many Internet sites and in many newspapers. For example, the stock of **Merck** was recently listed as follows:

| 52 weeks | | Yield | Price | Volume | | Net |
High	Low	%	Earnings	100s	Close	Change
46.37	31.61	3.5	19	69,876	43.27	−0.03

This information indicates that the stock has sold at a high of $46.37 per share and a low of $31.61 per share in the last 52 weeks. The annual dividend provides a yield (the dividend as a percentage of the market price) of 3.5% on the closing market price. The closing market price is 19 times the earnings per share for the last four quarters. On the date of this quotation, 6,987,600 shares were traded, and the closing price was $43.27 per share, which was a decrease in price of $0.03 over the closing price of the previous day.

Look up the listing of Merck's stock. Which items have changed? By how much have they changed?

Bonds of Merck were also listed recently, as follows:

Coupon Maturity	Last Yield	Est $ Volume (000s)	Close
5.125 Nov 15, 2011	5.051	39,500	100.311

This information indicates that the bonds have a contract rate of 5.125% and mature on November 15, 2011. The bonds currently yield 5.051% (the annual interest as a percentage of the market price), and on the date of this quotation $39.5 million bonds were traded. The closing price was 100.311% per bond. This bond price is quoted as a percentage of the face value of the bond and not as a dollar amount. Since bonds have a face value of $1,000, this quote means a price of $1,003.11 (100.311% × $1,000).

Look up the listing of Merck's bonds. Which items have changed? By how much have they changed?

These quoted market prices show the prices an investor had to pay to purchase or sell the securities on the date the prices were quoted. In addition, the investor must pay a fee to the stockbroker to make a purchase or a sale. Thus, when a company purchases securities, it records the purchase in an Investment account (asset) at the cost of acquisition, which is the quoted market price on the date of the purchase plus any commissions paid to stockbrokers, and any transfer or sales taxes that are imposed. For simplicity, in this chapter we ignore stockbroker's commissions and sales taxes. We use the term *market value* in this book, but the term *fair value* is often used also.

Is this principle different from the way other assets are initially recorded? Explain why or why not.

MARKET VALUE METHOD

2 How does a company record and report its investments that are available for sale?

As we mentioned earlier, there are several methods a company may use to account for an investment in stocks and bonds. For stocks, the choice of method depends on the amount of *influence* the investor has over the investee. For bonds, the choice depends on the *intent* of the investor.

A company uses the market value method for investments in **available-for-sale securities**. These securities may be common stock or bonds. In the case of common stock available for sale, the investor does *not* have significant influence because it owns less than 20% of the investee. In the case of bonds available for sale, the investor does *not* expect to hold the bonds until their maturity date. Available-for-sale securities sometimes are called *marketable securities*.

Three general issues arise in accounting for investments in available-for-sale securities. First, when should a company record the revenue from the investment? Second, what dollar amount should it report for the asset (Investment) on its balance sheet at the end of the year? Third, how should it compute the gain or loss when it sells the securities? The answer to the first question varies between stocks and bonds. An investor company records dividend revenue on stock paid by the investee when it receives the dividends.[3] The investor records interest revenue on bonds in the period the interest is earned. In other words, interest accrues (is earned) continuously over time, whereas dividends are discretionary periodic payments. As we discussed earlier, the answer to the second question is that an investor reports investments in available-for-sale securities (both stocks and bonds) at their *market value* at year-end. The answer to the third question is that an investor computes the gain or loss on the sale of securities by comparing the cash received from the sale with the *cost* of the securities that it sold.

For example, suppose that on January 1, 2008, Unlimited Decadence had excess cash to invest, and purchased 200 shares of Fox Company common stock for $4,000 and 8 bonds of Crow Company for $8,000. The bonds have a face value of $8,000, have a contract rate of 10%, and pay interest semiannually on June 30 and December 31. Unlimited Decadence records the investment on January 1, 2008 at a cost of $12,000, as follows:

	Assets	=	Liabilities	+	Stockholders' Equity
Cash	Investments in Available-for-Sale Securities				
−$12,000	+$12,000				

FINANCIAL STATEMENT EFFECTS

No net effect on total assets on *balance sheet*. Decreases cash flows from investing activities on *cash flow statement*.

Unlimited Decadence has exchanged one current asset, Cash, for another asset, Investments in Available-for-Sale Securities. The company reports its investment as a current asset because it intends to sell the securities within one year. However, if the company intended to keep its investment for at least one year, it would report the investment as a noncurrent asset. A company's **investments portfolio** includes all of its investments in the securities of other companies. Thus, Unlimited Decadence's $12,000 portfolio of investments in available-for-sale securities on January 1, 2008 consists of 200 shares of common stock costing $4,000 and 10 bonds costing $8,000.

Recording Dividends and Interest

A company records *dividend* revenue when it receives the cash dividend. Thus, if Unlimited Decadence receives $200 of dividends on the Fox Company common stock during 2008, it records the receipt as follows:

[3]Theoretically, a company should record dividend revenue when the investee company *declares* the dividend. We will discuss the date of declaration in Chapter 24. For simplicity, here we record dividend revenue when a company receives the cash.

Assets	=	Liabilities	+	Stockholders' Equity		
					Net Income	
				Revenues	−	Expenses
Cash				Dividend Revenue		
+$200				+$200		

A company records *interest* revenue as the interest is earned during the year. Thus, Unlimited Decadence records $400 [$8,000 face value × (10% contract rate ÷ 2)] of interest revenue semiannually on June 30 and on December 31, 2008, as follows:

Assets	=	Liabilities	+	Stockholders' Equity		
					Net Income	
				Revenues	−	Expenses
Cash				Interest Revenue		
+$400				+$400		

Reporting Ending Market Value

At the end of the year, a company reports its portfolio of investments in available-for-sale securities on its ending balance sheet at the market value of the portfolio. If the market value of the portfolio is greater than the cost, the company increases its Investments account and also increases an Unrealized *Increase* in Market Value of Investments account for the difference between the market value and the cost. If the market value of the portfolio is *less* than the cost, the company decreases its Investments account and increases an Unrealized *Decrease* in Market Value of Investments account for the difference between the cost and the market value. Both the Unrealized Increase and the Unrealized Decrease accounts are stockholders' equity accounts that represent the "gain" or "loss" from the change in market value. The "gain" or "loss" is called "unrealized" because the company has not sold the securities and has not collected cash relating to the change in market value. It is important to note that the company does not include the change in value in its income statement. Instead, these accounts are included in a section of stockholders' equity on its balance sheet, called "accumulated other comprehensive income."

To understand this concept, suppose that at the end of 2008, the Fox Company stock has a market value of $4,600 and the Crow Company bonds have a market value of $7,900. Unlimited Decadence prepares a schedule of the change in market value of its investments as we show in Exhibit 23-2.

 Why do you think the market value of the bonds decreased?

EXHIBIT 23-2	SCHEDULE TO COMPUTE MARKET VALUE OF INVESTMENTS IN AVAILABLE-FOR-SALE SECURITIES		
Security	1/1/08 Cost	12/31/08 Market Value	Increase (Decrease)
Fox stock	$ 4,000	$ 4,600	$600
Crow bonds	8,000	7,900	(100)
Totals	$12,000	$12,500	$500

Based on the schedule, Unlimited Decadence records the following information in its accounts on December 31, 2008.

Assets	=	Liabilities	+	Stockholders' Equity
				Accumulated Other Comprehensive Income (Loss)
Investments in Available-for-Sale Securities				Unrealized Increase in Market Value of Investments
Bal $12,000				
+500				+$500
Bal $12,500				

As we show, the balance of the Investments account now is $12,500, and Unlimited Decadence reports this market value as an asset on its December 31, 2008 balance sheet. Since the company intends to sell the investments during 2009, it reports the Investments account as a current asset. Otherwise, it would report the Investments account as a noncurrent asset. Note that this classification is based on the intent of the managers. A company must report the amount of the Unrealized Increase (or Decrease) for the year as "other comprehensive income" (as we discuss in Chapter 24), and the *balance* of the Unrealized Increase (or Decrease) account on its ending balance sheet, directly after retained earnings, in the "accumulated other comprehensive income (loss)" component of its stockholders' equity section.[4] So, Unlimited Decadence reports the $500 balance in the Unrealized Increase account as accumulated other comprehensive income in the stockholders' equity section of its ending 2008 balance sheet, as follows:

Stockholders' Equity (in part)

Accumulated other comprehensive income
Unrealized increase in market value of investments $500

If Unlimited Decadence holds the investments at the end of the second year, it prepares a schedule similar to the one illustrated. It then increases or decreases the Investments account and the Unrealized Increase (or Decrease) account, and reports the change in the Unrealized Increase (or Decrease) account as Other Comprehensive Income for the year, and the new *balance* in the Unrealized Increase (or Decrease) account as Accumulated Other Comprehensive Income in the stockholders' equity section of its balance sheet.

Sale of Investments

When a company sells an investment, it must record the cash received, reduce the Investments account, adjust the Unrealized Increase (or Decrease) account, and record any gain or loss on the sale. The company computes the gain or loss by comparing the cash received from the sale of the securities with the *cost* of the securities sold. For example, suppose that on October 1, 2009, Unlimited Decadence sold the 200 shares of Fox Company common stock for $4,800. It computes the $800 gain on the sale by comparing the cash received with the *cost* of the investment, as follows:

Cash received...	$4,800
Cost..	(4,000)
Gain on sale..	$ 800

---

[4]Under GAAP, a company would report its unrealized increase (decrease) after deducting income taxes. In this discussion, for simplicity we ignore income taxes. Since the company does not pay income taxes until it sells the securities, the company also would report a deferred tax liability (asset). We discussed deferred taxes in Chapter 22.

Since Unlimited Decadence reported the investment in the common stock available-for-sale securities at $4,600 (see Exhibit 23-2) at the end of 2008, it eliminates this amount from the Investments account. Also, it must reduce the Unrealized Increase account by the $600 portion related to the investment in the common stock. This $600 is now part of the $800 "real" gain from the sale of the common stock. Unlimited Decadence reports this $800 gain on its income statement for 2009. If it doesn't remove the $600 unrealized increase from stockholders' equity, it will be double-counting—it would include the amount both in retained earnings (as part of net income) and as a component of stockholders' equity (the accumulated other comprehensive income). Unlimited Decadence records this transaction on October 1, 2009, as follows:

Assets	=	Liabs.	+	Stockholders' Equity		
				Accumulated Other Comprehensive Income (Loss)	**Net Income**	
					Revenues (Gains) −	**Expenses (Losses)**
Cash		Investments in Available-for-Sale Securities		Unrealized Increase in Market Value of Investments	Gain on Sale of Investments	
		Bal $12,500		Bal +$500		
+$4,800		−4,600		−600	+$800	
		Bal $ 7,900		Bal −$100		

Note that after the sale, the Investments account has a balance of $7,900, which is the market value of the Crow Company bonds at the end of 2008. The Unrealized Increase account has a *negative* balance of $100, and so the company renames it "Unrealized Decrease in Market Value of Investments," and subtracts the balance of $100 when it computes its total stockholders' equity.

  Explain why the Unrealized account now has a negative balance.

At the end of 2009, Unlimited Decadence would prepare a schedule similar to Exhibit 23-2 to determine the change in the market value of the Crow Company bonds since December 31, 2008. It then would increase or decrease the Investments and Unrealized Decrease accounts accordingly.

How Market Value Method Investment Transactions Affect the Cash Flow Statement

A company reports the cash it paid for investments in available-for-sale securities as a cash outflow for an investing activity on its cash flow statement. It reports the cash it received from the sale of these investments as a cash inflow from an investing activity. It includes the dividends (and interest) it received as cash inflows from operating activities. If the company uses the indirect method for reporting its cash flows from operating activities, it subtracts the gain on the sale of an investment from the net income (or adds the loss to net income). It does this because the gain (loss) is included in its net income but does not affect its *operating* cash flows. It does not report adjustments of the Investments account for changes in the market value on its cash flow statement.

Why do you think a company does not report these adjustments of the Investments account in its cash flow statement?

External User Perspective: Evaluation of the Market Value Method

From an external user's perspective, there are several advantages when a company uses the market value method to report its investments in available-for-sale securities. First, the current market price is a good indicator of the cash that the company will receive if it sells the securities. This information helps both external and internal users evaluate the *liquidity* of the company. Second, the company may receive the market value of the securities easily through a sale, which is an indication of the company's *financial flexibility*. Third, changes in market value are an indicator of the success of the *investment strategy* of the company's managers. Finally, the market value is easily determined and is *reliable*.

Note that under GAAP, this is the only asset for which a company uses market (fair) value when it is *higher* than cost. For inventory, a company uses the lower-of-cost-or-market method. For property, plant, and equipment as well as intangibles, a company may record an impairment. But in both of these situations, a company records only decreases in value, whereas for available-for-sale securities it records both increases and decreases. There are two reasons for the different rule. The first reason is that the market value of securities can be obtained reliably—securities have a readily available market, whereas such a market does not exist for most other types of assets. The second reason is that the market value of the securities is relevant because the managers intend to sell the securities, and the market price can be realized immediately through a sale.

Do these arguments about the reliability and relevance of market values apply equally to inventory? property, plant, and equipment?

When the FASB was developing the rules for investments in available-for-sale securities that we have discussed, some people argued that a company should also report its liabilities at market (fair) value. However, the FASB did not allow this because the Board members believed that the market values of *most* liabilities were not *reliable* because the liabilities do not trade on established markets. So, companies would have to estimate the market values of those liabilities. But, not allowing "revaluation" of liabilities to their market value created inequities for some companies. Consider, for example, a bank that holds debt securities as assets and also has debt of its own. Now assume that interest rates rise. As interest rates increase, the present value of the future cash flows decreases. Therefore, the market value of the debt securities held as assets decreases, resulting in a "loss." However, the market value of the bank's liabilities also decreases, resulting in a "gain." Since GAAP does not allow liabilities to be revalued, the bank cannot report its liabilities at market value and therefore cannot "offset" the effects of the changes in interest rates.

Another issue that arises because changes in market value are not included in income is *gains trading*. This occurs when the managers of a company select a security to sell from its investment portfolio because the sale will result in a gain. Thus, these managers are selecting the security based on the effect the sale will have on the company's income statement (and thus "managing" earnings), and not necessarily on whether the security *should* be sold.

Suppose a company owns Security A, which cost $5,000, and Security B, which cost $15,000. Each security now has a market value of $10,000. As a manager, explain which security you would sell and why would you choose that security to sell.

EXHIBIT 23-3	CISCO SYSTEMS: DISCLOSURE OF AVAILABLE-FOR-SALE SECURITIES

Notes to Consolidated Financial Statements (in part):

7. INVESTMENTS (in part)
The following tables summarize the Company's investments (in millions):

JULY 30, 2005	Amortized Cost	Gross Unrealized Gains	Gross Unrealized Losses	Fair Value
Fixed Income Securities:				
U.S. government notes and bonds	$ 3,453	$ 2	$(25)	$ 3,430
Corporate notes, bonds, and				
asset-backed securities	6,299	3	(63)	6,239
Municipal notes and bonds	705	—	(2)	703
Total fixed income securities	10,457	5	(90)	10,372
Publicly traded equity securities	514	433	(6)	941
Total	$10,971	$438	$(96)	$11,313
Reported as:				
Short-term investments				$ 2,227
Investments				9,086
Total				$11,313

JULY 31, 2004	Amortized Cost	Gross Unrealized Gains	Gross Unrealized Losses	Fair Value
Fixed Income Securities:				
U.S. government notes and bonds	$ 4,408	$ 9	$(20)	$ 4,397
Corporate notes, bonds, and				
asset-backed securities	9,333	14	(42)	9,305
Municipal notes and bonds	710	—	(1)	709
Total fixed income securities	14,451	23	(63)	14,411
Publicly traded equity securities	755	387	(8)	1,134
Total	$15,206	$410	$(71)	$15,545
Reported as:				
Short-term investments				$ 4,947
Investments				10,598
Total				$15,545

Disclosures of Available-for-Sale Securities

To illustrate how a company reports its investments in available-for-sale securities, we show the disclosures of **Cisco Systems** in Exhibit 23-3. Note that the company owns both debt and equity available-for-sale securities which it reports at market value.

EQUITY METHOD

As we discussed earlier, a company whose investment in the common stock of another company enables it to have significant influence (but not control) over the operations of the other company uses the *equity method* to account for its investment. Significant influence generally occurs when the investor owns between 20% and 50% of the investee's common stock.

3 How does a company record and report its investments in companies over which it has significant influence?

Explain whether you think a company has significant influence at 21% ownership but not at 19%.

At this level of ownership, there are several reasons why the equity method is appropriate:

1. The market value of the common stock of the investee is not a good indicator of the total value of the investment. The price of a share of stock on the stock market on any given day is the result of supply and demand on that day. If an investor company sold over 20% of the shares of an investee company, this large number of shares would sell at a market price different from the market price of a small number of shares.

2. The dividends received are not a good indicator of the increase in the investor company's wealth. For example, suppose an investee company earns $60,000 and pays dividends of $6,000. If an investor company owns 25% of the shares, it would receive dividends of $1,500, but this amount does not represent its share of the income accumulated by the investee company. Since the investee has earned $60,000 and the investor "owns" 25% of the income, the investor's wealth has increased by $15,000 on this investment.

3. The investor may be able to influence the dividend policy and thereby affect the cash payments it receives.

For these reasons, reporting of income on the accrual basis (equity method) by the investor is preferable to reporting of income on the basis of the cash received.

The equity method approach for reporting the value of the investment and for reporting income differs from the approach used in the market value method. Under the equity method, the investor company accounts for the investment and income as follows:

$$\text{Investment} = \text{Cost} + \text{Income Earned} - \text{Dividends Received}$$

where:

$$\text{Income Earned} = \text{Investee's Net Income} \times \text{Investor's Ownership \%}$$

and:

$$\text{Dividends Received} = \text{Total Dividends Paid by Investee} \times \text{Investor's Ownership \%}$$

The investor company records as income its share of the investee company's net income (it *accrues* the income as it earns it). When the investor company records this income, it also *increases* the book value of the Investment (asset) account by the same amount. It does *not* record the receipt of dividends as income. Instead, it records the receipt as a *decrease* in the book value of the Investment account. This accounting by the investor company is a "mirror image" of the accounting by the investee company. When the *investee* company earns income, it increases its stockholders' equity, and when it pays dividends, it decreases its stockholders' equity. For the *investor* company, the book value of the Investment account increases as its share of the investee company's stockholders' equity increases (as income is earned), and decreases as its share of the investee company's stockholders' equity decreases (as dividends are received). Consequently, if the investor company were to record dividends received as income, it would double-count income because it has already recorded as income its share of the investee company's income, out of which the dividends are received.

Comprehensive Example

To understand the equity method, suppose that the managers of Unlimited Decadence wanted to obtain significant influence over a supplier, Sanchez Sugar Company.

 What reasons do you think a company might have for wanting to influence the operations of one of its suppliers?

So on January 1, 2008, Unlimited Decadence purchased 30% of Sanchez Sugar Company's common stock for $60,000. At this time Sanchez reported total assets of $300,000, total liabilities of $100,000, and total stockholders' equity of $200,000 on its beginning 2008 balance sheet. Unlimited Decadence records this investment on January 1, 2008, as follows:

Assets	=	Liabilities	+	Stockholders' Equity

Cash	Investment in Sanchez Sugar Company
−$60,000	+$60,000

Note that this $60,000 investment represents 30% of the $200,000 stockholders' equity of Sanchez. For simplicity, we assume that Unlimited Decadence is able to purchase its investment on the stock market for an amount that is equal to its share of the book value (assets minus liabilities) of Sanchez Sugar Company. As we discussed in Chapter 21, it is more likely that Unlimited Decadence would have to pay more than the book value.

At the end of 2008, Sanchez reports net income of $40,000 and pays dividends of $10,000. Since Unlimited Decadence owns 30% of Sanchez's stock, the income it has earned from its investment is $12,000, computed as follows:

$$\text{Income Earned} = \text{Sanchez's Net Income} \times \text{Unlimited Decadence's Ownership \%}$$

$$= \$40,000 \times 30\%$$

$$= \underline{\$12,000}$$

Unlimited Decadence records its share (sometimes referred to as "equity income") of Sanchez's 2008 net income as follows:

Assets	=	Liabilities	+	Stockholders' Equity
				Net Income
				Revenues − Expenses
Investment in Sanchez Sugar Company				Income from Investment in Sanchez Sugar Company
Bal $60,000 +12,000				+$12,000
Bal $72,000				

The dividends of Sanchez that Unlimited Decadence receives are computed as follows:

$$\text{Dividends Received} = \frac{\text{Total Dividends}}{\text{Paid by Sanchez}} \times \frac{\text{Unlimited Decadence's}}{\text{Ownership \%}}$$

$$= \$10,000 \times 30\%$$

$$= \underline{\$3,000}$$

Unlimited Decadence records the receipt of its share of Sanchez's 2008 dividends as follows:

Assets	=	Liabilities	+	Stockholders' Equity

| | Investment in |
Cash	Sanchez Sugar Company
	Bal $72,000
+$3,000	−3,000
	Bal $69,000

To better understand the rationale of the equity method, consider the stockholders' equity of Sanchez (the investee) after it records the preceding events. The investment by Unlimited Decadence has no effect on Sanchez's stockholders' equity because Unlimited Decadence purchased 30% of the *existing* common stock.

 Why do you think that Unlimited Decadence's purchase of existing stock did not affect Sanchez's stockholders' equity?

On the other hand, the earning of income and the payment of dividends by Sanchez do affect its stockholders' equity. By looking at the changes in the accounting equation, we can examine the effects of these events. The income and dividends have the following impact on Sanchez's stockholders' equity in its balance sheet:

	Stockholders' Equity
Earning income...	+$40,000
Payment of dividends....................................	− 10,000
Net Effect..	+$30,000

The net effect is a $30,000 increase in the stockholders' equity of Sanchez. Since Unlimited Decadence owns 30% of Sanchez, it owns 30%, or $9,000, of the increase in Sanchez's stockholders' equity. Note that Unlimited Decadence's equity investment increased by $9,000 ($12,000 share of income − $3,000 dividends received) from $60,000 to $69,000 in 2008. Also note that Unlimited Decadence reported $12,000 equity income from its investment in Sanchez, which is 30% of Sanchez's net income. So the equity method reflects a proportional financial relationship between the amounts reported by the investor and by the investee.[5]

How Equity Method Investment Transactions Affect the Cash Flow Statement

A company reports the cash it paid for equity investments as a cash outflow for an investing activity on its cash flow statement. It reports the cash it received from the sale of these investments as a cash inflow from an investing activity. The company includes dividends received as a cash inflow from operating activities. If the company uses the indirect method for reporting its cash flow from operating activities, it subtracts the gain on the sale of an investment from the net income (or adds the loss to net income). It does this because the gain (loss) is included in its net income but does not affect its *operating* cash flows. If the company uses the indirect method for reporting its cash flows from operating activities, it subtracts the increase in the book value of the equity investment from

---

[5]The total stockholders' equity of Sanchez now is $230,000 ($200,000 beginning + $30,000 increase). The value of a 30% share is $69,000 (30% × $230,000). Note that this amount is the balance (book value) in Unlimited Decadence's Investment in Sanchez Sugar Company account. These amounts are equal because Unlimited Decadence purchased its investment for a price equal to 30% of Sanchez's stockholders' equity (book value) at that time. Usually a company will pay more than its share of the book value, but this situation raises complex issues that are beyond the scope of this book.

its net income because that is the amount by which the income reported exceeds the dividends (cash) received.

Does this make sense to you? Can you explain why a company subtracts the increase in the book value of the investment from net income in its indirect-method cash flow statement?

External User Perspective: Evaluation of the Equity Method

From an external user's perspective, use of the equity method by the investor company helps to show the company's increased *profitability* due to its share in the income of the investee, as well as the company's increased *operating capability* because of the significant influence it has over the investee. Some external users of financial statements criticize the equity method because the investor company reports income that is greater than the cash it received as dividends. They argue that the cash received from dividends is a more useful measure of the investor company's income. This criticism is not consistent with the accrual concept used in accounting. In accrual accounting, a company reports income in the year in which it is earned and not necessarily when it receives cash. The equity method is another example of reporting income on an accrual basis. It is the best way to report on an investor's income from an investee when the investor has enough of an ownership percentage in the investee to significantly influence the investee's operations and dividend policy.

BUSINESS ISSUES AND VALUES

The managers of an investor company may choose to purchase more than 20% of an investee's stock so that the company can use the equity method. For example, buying 19% of a company's common stock would result in the use of the market value method, and the investor company would record dividends received as income. If the managers instead bought 21%, the investor company would use the equity method and would record 21% of the investee's income as its income. If the investee's net income was larger than the dividends it paid, then the investor company's income would be increased by use of the equity method instead of the market value method. Alternatively, the managers of the investor company could argue that they have significant influence with less than 20% ownership and then use the equity method.

Under what circumstances might the managers of a company prefer not to buy more than 20% of an investee's common stock?

CONSOLIDATED FINANCIAL STATEMENTS

When an investor company owns more than 50% of the common stock of another company, the investor has **control** over the investee.[6] In this situation, the investor company is called the **parent company**. On the other hand, the investee company that has more than 50% of its common stock owned by the investor (parent) company is called the **subsidiary company**. The parent and subsidiary companies remain separate legal entities and keep separate accounting records during the year. The reasons for this separation include income tax, legal liability, and international issues that are beyond the scope of the book. Users of financial statements, however, are interested in financial statements that report the combined activities of the parent and the subsidiaries over which it has control. Therefore, at the end of the year the parent company reports the net income, cash flows, and ending balance sheets of both companies in its financial statements as if the separate

4 When and why does a company prepare consolidated financial statements?

---

[6]The FASB is discussing the substitution of the concept of economic control for the concept of legal control currently used. This proposal would result in the preparation of consolidated financial statements at less than 50% ownership.

legal entities were one economic entity. That is, it publishes a single set of "consolidated" financial statements. **Consolidated financial statements** are the combined financial statements of the parent company and all other companies over which it has control.

Explain whether, and why, you think a company has control at 51% ownership but not at 49%.

For example, **Bristol-Myers Squibb**'s (BMS) consolidated financial statements show the combined results of over 280 separate companies! An investor who owns common stock in BMS does not want 280 different sets of financial statements that report separately on the activities of each of the companies. So instead BMS publishes one set of consolidated financial statements. *The separate legal entities are treated as a single economic entity for financial reporting purposes.* So consolidated financial statements are another example of the principle of economic substance taking precedence over legal form.

The consolidated financial statements include the sum of the information in the accounting records of the separate companies. Thus, the parent company adds the assets of the separate companies together, as well as their liabilities, to prepare the consolidated balance sheet. It adds their revenues together, as well as their expenses, to prepare the consolidated income statement. It adds their operating cash flows together, as well as their investing and financing cash flows, to prepare the consolidated cash flow statement. However, the parent and subsidiary companies often buy from and sell to one another, as well as have other "intercompany" transactions. Since the companies are separate legal and accounting entities, they record these transactions in their own accounting systems. To avoid double-counting, the parent company "eliminates" (excludes) from the consolidated financial statements those items that are recorded in both accounting systems. For example, if the parent company makes a loan to the subsidiary company, the parent's note receivable and the subsidiary's note payable (as well as any related interest revenue and interest expense) would be eliminated. So the parent company prepares consolidated financial statements at the end of the year by combining the yearly information in each company's accounting records *after* the eliminations. Also recall from Chapter 21 that a parent company reports goodwill when it has control over a subsidiary company and prepares consolidated financial statements.

When a parent buys a subsidiary, it records its cost in an Investment account. During the year, the parent company accounts for its investment in the subsidiary using the equity method we discussed earlier. At the end of the year, to prepare its consolidated financial statements, the parent company makes the various eliminations (including the elimination of the Investment account). Because these eliminations are complex and because consolidated financial statements look similar to those that are not consolidated, we do not discuss the accounting procedures for preparing consolidated financial statements. Appendix B includes the consolidated financial statements of Colgate-Palmolive Corporation.

When a company controls another company but purchases less than 100% of the common stock, the holders of the remaining shares are known as the *noncontrolling (minority) interest*. So if a parent company purchases 70% of a subsidiary's shares, the owners of the remaining 30% are the noncontrolling interest. In this case, the parent company includes 100% of the subsidiary company's revenues and expenses, and assets and liabilities, in its consolidated financial statements. The noncontrolling interest is reported in two ways. First, the noncontrolling interest percentage multiplied by the subsidiary's net income is subtracted in computing the net income on the consolidated income statement. Second, the noncontrolling interest percentage multiplied by the subsidiary's stockholders' equity is included separately in the stockholders' equity section of the consolidated balance sheet.

Why do you think the noncontrolling interest is subtracted on the consolidated income statement?

BUSINESS ISSUES AND VALUES

As we discussed above, the parent company includes the assets and liabilities of the subsidiary in its consolidated balance sheet. Note that under the equity method, the investor company includes an Investment account but does not specifically report the investee's liabilities. [The equity method is sometimes referred to as *one-line consolidation* because the Investment account contains the amount of the investor company's current investment in the *net assets* (assets − liabilities) of the investee company.] Therefore, if the managers of a parent company believe they can exercise control with less than 50% ownership, they may purchase that lower amount to avoid consolidation and avoid adding the liabilities on the parent company's balance sheet. External users must read the notes to the financial statements to learn about the investee's liabilities (and other information).

SEGMENT REPORTS

Although external users believe that consolidated financial statements are important in evaluating the overall performance of a company, they also like to know information about its operating segments. These users think that evaluations of the income and assets of the separate segments are useful in evaluating each segment's performance, including the segments' *return on investment* and *operating capability*. Because users need this information, the notes to a company's consolidated financial statements include information about its different segments. That is, to provide more useful information, GAAP requires a company to "break down" its consolidated financial statements into **segment reports**. We show a diagram of this relationship in Exhibit 23-4.

An **operating segment** is a component (e.g., department, division, or subsidiary) of a company (1) that earns revenues and incurs expenses, (2) whose performance is reviewed regularly by the company's top executive, and (3) for which financial information is available. The information that the company reports includes the following for each segment:

1. *Operating profit or loss,* including certain revenues (i.e., sales) and expenses
2. *Assets*
3. *General information* (e.g., types of products, information for geographic areas)

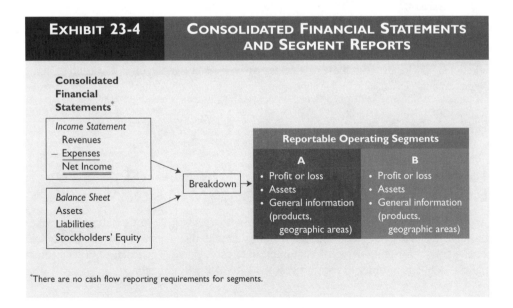

EXHIBIT 23-4   CONSOLIDATED FINANCIAL STATEMENTS AND SEGMENT REPORTS

*There are no cash flow reporting requirements for segments.

For example, three major car manufacturers reported their segments and geographic areas as we show below.

	General Motors	Ford	Toyota
Segments	General Motors Automotive General Motors Acceptance Corporation Other	Automotive Financial Services	Automotive Financial Services All Other
Geographic Areas	North America Europe Latin America All Other	United States Europe Asia Pacific & Africa All Other	Japan North America Europe Other Foreign Countries

 *Explain whether you think the segment and geographic information is useful for comparing **General Motors**, **Ford**, and **Toyota**.*

USES OF SEGMENT INFORMATION

External users can use the segment information of a company to evaluate how well each segment is doing over time or in comparison with other companies. For instance, by comparing the sales of a segment over time, users can find out which parts of the company are growing fastest. Also, by dividing a segment's operating profit by its net sales, users can compute the *profit margin* of each segment. Or, by dividing a segment's operating profit by its average total assets, they can compute the *rate of return* of the segment. They can compare these ratios with the segment's ratios in prior years or with the ratios of other companies' segments. When comparing the results with those of the segments of other companies, however, users must be sure that each company has identified its operating segments in the same way. Because each company defines its own segments, users are more likely to use segment reports for intracompany analysis than for intercompany analysis.

We do not show the procedures for preparing segment reports because they are complex. However, we show the segment reports accompanying **PepsiCo**'s consolidated financial statements in Exhibit 23-5. We recommend that you look at this exhibit now.

 For the most current year, which of PepsiCo's business segments has the highest net revenue? the highest operating profit? the highest return on assets? the highest capital spending?

In Appendix B, note that **Colgate-Palmolive** discloses two segments, which it describes as Oral, Personal and Home Care, and Pet Nutrition, in Note 14. The company also provides additional disclosures for these segments, as well as its geographic disclosures, in its Managements' Discussion and Analysis.

 Do you agree with Colgate-Palmolive's decision to have only two segments?

INVESTMENTS IN HELD-TO-MATURITY BONDS: AMORTIZED COST METHOD

5 How does a company record and report its investments in bonds that it expects to hold until maturity?

An investor company may invest in bonds that it expects to hold to maturity. It makes this investment to establish a financial relationship with the investee company or to obtain a relatively consistent source of continuing interest revenue. For instance, a bank often purchases bonds in order to earn interest for a defined period of time.

EXHIBIT 23-5	PEPSICO: SEGMENT DISCLOSURES

Note I—Our Divisions (in part)

We manufacture or use contract manufacturers, market and sell a variety of salty, sweet and grain-based snacks, carbonated and non-carbonated beverages, and foods through our North American and international business divisions. Our North American divisions include the United States and Canada. The accounting policies for the divisions are the same as those described in Note 2, except for certain allocation methodologies for stock-based compensation expense and pension and retiree medical expense, as described in the unaudited information in "Our Critical Accounting Policies." Additionally, beginning in the fourth quarter of 2005, we began centrally managing commodity derivatives on behalf of our divisions. Certain of the commodity derivatives, primarily those related to the purchase of energy for use by our divisions, do not qualify for hedge accounting treatment. These derivatives hedge underlying commodity price risk and were not entered into for speculative purposes. Such derivatives are marked to market with the resulting gains and losses recognized as a component of corporate unallocated expense. These gains and losses are reflected in division results when the divisions take delivery of the underlying commodity. Therefore, division results reflect the contract purchase price of the energy or other commodities.

Division results are based on how our Chairman and Chief Executive Officer evaluates our divisions. Division results exclude certain Corporate-initiated restructuring and impairment charges, merger-related costs and divested businesses. For additional unaudited information on our divisions, see "Our Operations" in Management's Discussion and Analysis.

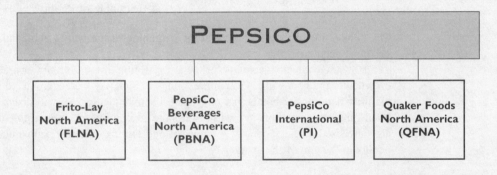

	2005	2004	2003	2005	2004	2003
	Net Revenue			Operating Profit		
FLNA	$10,322	$ 9,560	$ 9,091	$2,529	$2,389	$2,242
PBNA	9,146	8,313	7,733	2,037	1,911	1,690
PI	11,376	9,862	8,678	1,607	1,323	1,061
QFNA	1,718	1,526	1,467	537	475	470
Total division	32,562	29,261	26,969	6,710	6,098	5,463
Divested businesses	—	—	2	—	—	26
Corporate	—	—	—	(788)	(689)	(502)
	32,562	29,261	26,971	5,922	5,409	4,987
Restructuring and impairment charges	—	—	—	—	(150)	(147)
Merger-related costs	—	—	—	—	—	(59)
Total	$32,562	$29,261	$26,971	$5,922	$5,259	$4,781

Other Division Information

	2005	2004	2003	2005	2004	2003
	Total Assets			Capital Spending		
FLNA	$ 5,948	$ 5,476	$ 5,332	$ 512	$ 469	$ 426
PBNA	6,316	6,048	5,856	320	265	332
PI	9,983	8,921	8,109	667	537	521
QFNA	989	978	995	31	33	32
Total division	23,236	21,423	20,292	1,530	1,304	1,311
Corporate*	5,331	3,569	2,384	206	83	34
Investments in bottling affiliates	3,160	2,995	2,651	—	—	—
	$31,727	$27,987	$25,327	$1,736	$1,387	$1,345

*Corporate assets consist principally of cash and cash equivalents, short-term investments, and property, plant and equipment.

When a company purchases bonds as an investment and has both the *intent* and the *ability* to hold the bonds until maturity, it records the purchase price (the cost) in an Investment in Held-to-Maturity Bonds account. It may purchase the bonds for the same as, more than, or less than their face value. As we discussed in Chapter 22, if the yield is the same as the contract rate, it purchases the bonds at face value. If the yield is *more* than the contract rate, it purchases the bonds at a *discount* (less than face value). If the yield is *less* than the contract rate, it purchases the bonds at a *premium* (more than face value).

 Think back to our discussion of the sale of bonds in Chapter 22. Explain why a company purchases bonds at a discount when their yield is more than the contract rate.

If a company purchases held-to-maturity bonds at a discount or a premium, it uses the *amortized cost method* (which is another name for the effective interest method, which we discussed and illustrated in Chapter 22) to record its interest revenue each period. The company determines its interest revenue as follows:

$$\text{Interest Revenue for Period} = \frac{\text{Book Value of Investment}}{\text{at Beginning of Period}} \times \text{Yield}$$

The book value of the investment at the beginning of the period is the balance in the investment account at that time.

How the company accounts for the amortization of the discount or premium depends on whether the bonds are zero-coupon bonds (which pay the accumulated interest on the maturity date) or are bonds that pay interest semiannually. We will discuss zero-coupon bonds in the next section. We will discuss the accounting for an investment in bonds that are purchased at a discount or a premium and that pay interest semiannually in the appendix at the end of the chapter.

Zero-Coupon Bonds

Recall from Chapter 22 that **zero-coupon bonds** pay no interest each period. That is, they accrue interest each period, but *pay* interest on the maturity date. Therefore, zero-coupon bonds are always purchased at a discount. A company with an investment in zero-coupon bonds records the amount of interest it earns each period as interest revenue and as an increase in its Investment account (this is called *amortizing* the discount). In other words, this accounting is a "mirror image" of the accounting for zero-coupon bonds we discussed in Chapter 22.

For example, assume that on January 1, 2008, Beany Biscuit Company purchased for $385,500 (at a 10% yield) all of Unlimited Decadence's 10-year, $1,000,000 face value zero-coupon bonds that we discussed in Chapter 22. Beany computed the purchase price (present value) by discounting the $1,000,000 face value using the 10% yield and the 10-year life [$385,500 = $1,000,000 × 0.3855 (from Table 20-1 at the end of Chapter 20)]. Beany expects to hold the bonds until maturity and records the purchase as follows:

Assets		=	Liabilities	+	Stockholders' Equity
	Investment in				
	Held-to-Maturity				
Cash	Bonds				
−$385,500	+$385,500				

FINANCIAL STATEMENT EFFECTS
Decreases current assets and increases noncurrent assets on **balance sheet**. Decreases cash flows from investing activities on **cash flow statement**.

Since the yield is 10% annually, at the end of 2008 Beany computes the interest revenue to be $38,550 ($385,500 beginning book value × 10% yield) and records it on December 31, 2008, as follows:

Assets	=	Liabilities	+	Stockholders' Equity

				Net Income
				Revenues — Expenses

Investment in Held-to-Maturity Bonds	Interest Revenue
Bal $385,500	
+38,550	+$38,550
Bal $424,050	

Beany reports the $424,050 balance in the Investment in Held-to-Maturity Bonds account as a noncurrent asset on its balance sheet.

At the end of 2009, Beany computes its interest revenue as $42,405 ($424,050 beginning book value × 10% yield) and records the amount in the same way as in 2008. Each year it increases the Investment account so that, at the end of the 10-year life of the bonds, the book value will be $1 million. Beany will then collect $1 million from Unlimited Decadence to retire the investment.

Effects of Investments in Held-to-Maturity Bonds on the Cash Flow Statement

A company reports the cash it paid for investments in zero-coupon bonds it expects to hold until maturity as a cash outflow for investing activities on its cash flow statement. It reports the cash it received at the maturity of these investments in two places: it reports the amount it received equal to its original investment as a cash inflow from an investing activity; it reports the amount of interest it received as a cash inflow from operating activities. If the company uses the indirect method to compute its cash flows from operating activities (as we discussed in the appendix to Chapter 8 of Volume 1), each year it subtracts the increase in the book value of the investment in zero-coupon bonds (from the amortization of the discount) from net income. It does this because the increase represents the amount by which the income it reported increased due to the interest revenue although there was no cash inflow.

External User Perspective: Evaluation of Amortized Cost Method

Earlier in the chapter, we explained why the market value method is preferable for valuing available-for-sale securities. So why does a company use the amortized cost method for a held-to-maturity bond? The reason is because the bond will not be sold. As we discussed in Chapter 21, it may be argued that the market value of an asset that will not be sold is *not* relevant because the company will not receive any cash until the bond matures. However, some people argue that the market value of a bond held as an investment is relevant because its value reflects changes in the marketplace since it was purchased. Also, from an external user's perspective, use of the amortized cost method by the investor company helps to show the company's increased *profitability* due to the interest revenue it earned on the investment.

To help you review the four methods we have discussed in this chapter, we show a hypothetical balance sheet and related descriptions in Exhibit 23-6.

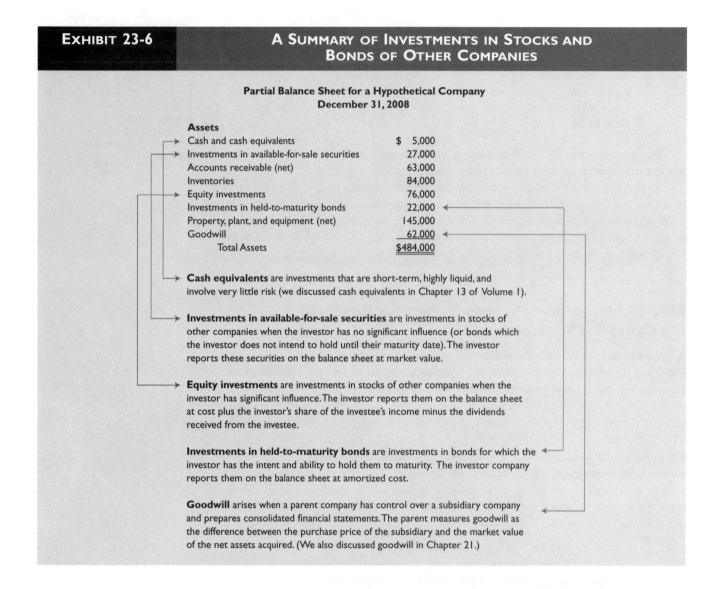

EXHIBIT 23-6   **A SUMMARY OF INVESTMENTS IN STOCKS AND BONDS OF OTHER COMPANIES**

Partial Balance Sheet for a Hypothetical Company
December 31, 2008

Assets

Cash and cash equivalents	$ 5,000
Investments in available-for-sale securities	27,000
Accounts receivable (net)	63,000
Inventories	84,000
Equity investments	76,000
Investments in held-to-maturity bonds	22,000
Property, plant, and equipment (net)	145,000
Goodwill	62,000
Total Assets	$484,000

Cash equivalents are investments that are short-term, highly liquid, and involve very little risk (we discussed cash equivalents in Chapter 13 of Volume 1).

Investments in available-for-sale securities are investments in stocks of other companies when the investor has no significant influence (or bonds which the investor does not intend to hold until their maturity date). The investor reports these securities on the balance sheet at market value.

Equity investments are investments in stocks of other companies when the investor has significant influence. The investor reports them on the balance sheet at cost plus the investor's share of the investee's income minus the dividends received from the investee.

Investments in held-to-maturity bonds are investments in bonds for which the investor has the intent and ability to hold them to maturity. The investor company reports them on the balance sheet at amortized cost.

Goodwill arises when a parent company has control over a subsidiary company and prepares consolidated financial statements. The parent measures goodwill as the difference between the purchase price of the subsidiary and the market value of the net assets acquired. (We also discussed goodwill in Chapter 21.)

SUMMARY

At the beginning of the chapter we asked you several questions. During the chapter, we asked you to STOP and answer some additional questions to build your knowledge about specific issues. Be sure you answered these additional questions. Below are the questions from the beginning of the chapter, with a brief summary of the key points relating to the answers. Use your creative and critical thinking skills to expand on these key points to develop more complete answers to the questions and to determine what other questions you have that might lead you to learn more about the issues.

1 How does a company classify its investments on its financial statements?

An investor company may choose to invest in an investee company's common stock. How the investor company accounts for its investments in stock depends on its "influence" over the investee. Influence is defined by the percentage ownership the investor company has in the investee. If an investor company has no significant influence over the investee (less than 20% ownership), it has an investment in "available-for-sale stock," and the company reports this investment on its balance sheet using the market value method. If it has significant influence over the investee (between 20% and 50% ownership) over the investee, it has an equity investment, and it reports this investment using the equity method. If it has control over the investee (more than 50% ownership), it prepares consolidated financial statements. An investor company also may choose to invest in an investee company's bonds. How the investor company reports its investments in bonds depends on how long it expects to hold the bonds. If the company expects to sell the bonds before the maturity date, it calls them "available-for-sale bonds" and reports this investment using the market value method. If the company expects to hold the bonds for their entire life, it calls them "held-to-maturity bonds" and reports this investment using the amortized cost method.

② How does a company record and report its investments that are available for sale?

A company uses the market value method for investments in available-for-sale securities. These securities may be common stock or bonds. Available-for-sale securities are sometimes called *marketable securities*. The company records dividends paid by the investee as revenue when it receives the dividends. The company records interest on bonds as revenue for each period they are owned. In other words, interest accrues continuously over time, whereas dividends are discretionary periodic payments. The company reports dividend revenue and interest revenue on its income statement and reports its investments in available-for-sale securities (both stocks and bonds) on its balance sheet at their market value at year-end. It reports the balance of the unrealized increase or decrease in the market value of its investments in available-for-sale securities in the accumulated other comprehensive income (loss) component of the stockholders' equity section on its ending balance sheet. The company computes the gain or loss on the sale of an investment in available-for-sale securities by comparing the cash it received from the sale with the cost of the securities that it sold.

③ How does a company record and report its investments in companies over which it has significant influence?

A company whose investment in the common stock of another company enables it to have significant influence over the operations of the other company uses the equity method to account for its investment. Significant influence occurs when the investor owns between 20% and 50% of the investee's common stock. Under the equity method, the investor company accounts for the investment and income as follows:

$$\text{Investment} = \text{Cost} + \text{Income Earned} - \text{Dividends Received}$$

where:

$$\text{Income Earned} = \text{Investee's Net Income} \times \text{Investor's Ownership \%}$$

and:

$$\text{Dividends Received} = \text{Total Dividends Paid by Investee} \times \text{Investor's Ownership \%}$$

The company reports the book value of the investment as a long-term asset on its balance sheet. It reports the income earned in the "other items" section on its income statement.

④ When and why does a company prepare consolidated financial statements?

When an investor company owns more than 50% of the common stock of another company, the investor has control over the investee. The investor company that owns more than 50% of the common stock of the investee is the parent company. The investee company that has more than 50% of its common stock owned by the investor (parent) company is the subsidiary company. The parent and the subsidiary companies remain separate legal entities and keep separate accounting records during the year. Users of financial statements are interested in financial statements that report the combined activities of the parent and the subsidiaries over which it has control, however. Therefore, at the end of the year the parent company reports the net income, cash flows, and ending balance sheets of both companies in its financial statements as if the separate legal entities were one economic entity. That is, the parent company publishes a single set of "consolidated" financial statements. Consolidated financial statements are the combined financial statements of the parent company and all other companies over which it has control.

 How does a company record and report its investments in bonds that it expects to hold until maturity?

When a company purchases bonds as an investment and has both the intent and the ability to hold the bonds until maturity, it records the purchase price (the cost) in an Investment in Held-to-Maturity Bonds account. It may purchase the bonds for the same as, less than, or more than their face value. If the yield is the same as the contract rate, it purchases the bonds at face value. If the yield is more than the contract rate, it purchases the bonds at a discount (less than face value). If the yield is less than the contract rate, it purchases the bonds at a premium (more than face value). When a company invests in zero-coupon bonds, it always purchases them at a discount. It determines its interest revenue for the period by multiplying the book value of the investment at the beginning of the period by the yield. It also records an increase in its Investment account of the same amount. The company reports the book value of the investment as a long-term asset on its balance sheet. It reports the interest revenue in the "other items" section of its income statement.

KEY TERMS

available-for-sale securities *(p. 822)*
bonds *(p. 820)*
common stock *(p. 819)*
consolidated financial statements
  (p. 832)
control *(pp. 820, 831)*
investments portfolio *(p. 822)*
no significant influence *(p. 820)*

operating segment *(p. 833)*
parent company *(p. 831)*
segment reports *(p. 833)*
significant influence *(p. 820)*
stockbroker *(p. 821)*
subsidiary company *(p. 831)*
zero-coupon bonds *(p. 836)*

APPENDIX

Accounting for an Investment in Held-to-Maturity Bonds That Pay Interest Semiannually

In the chapter, we discussed how a company calculates and records interest revenue on an investment in zero-coupon bonds that it intends to hold to maturity. In this appendix, we illustrate how a company calculates and records interest revenue on an investment in bonds that pay interest semiannually and that it expects to hold to maturity.

BONDS PURCHASED AT A DISCOUNT

To illustrate the accounting for an investment in bonds purchased at a discount, we assume that Baker Company, a supplier of candy ingredients, purchases bonds of Unlimited Decadence with the following terms:

Date of sale:..	January 1, 2008
Face value:..	$100,000
Contract rate:...	10%
Interest payment dates:...............................	June 30 and December 31
Maturity date..	December 31, 2011

Baker Company purchases the bonds at a yield of 12%. Therefore, it pays $93,789, which is a discount of $6,211 ($100,000 face value − $93,789 purchase price). (This is the same bond issue that we discussed in the appendix to Chapter 22, so please refer to that appendix if you want to see the present value calculations for determining the purchase/selling price.) Baker Company records the purchase on January 1, 2008, as follows:

Assets	=	Liabilities	+	Stockholders' Equity

	Investment in Held-to-Maturity
Cash	Bonds
−$93,789	+$93,789

> **FINANCIAL STATEMENT EFFECTS**
>
> Decreases current assets and increases noncurrent assets on **balance sheet**. Decreases cash flows from investing activities on **cash flow statement**.

The $93,789 is the book value of the investment at the time of purchase.

On June 30, 2008, Baker receives its first $5,000 [$100,000 face value × (10% contract rate ÷ 2)] semiannual interest receipt. It computes the interest revenue using the *amortized cost* method. For bonds purchased at a discount, the interest revenue is *more* than the interest received because the yield is *more* than the contract rate. Baker's interest revenue for the first semiannual inerest period is $5,627.34 [$93,789 book value × (12% yield ÷ 2)]. It records the $627.34 difference between the interest revenue and the interest receipt as an *increase* in the Investment in Held-to-Maturity Bonds account. This is called *amortizing* a portion of the $6,211 discount. Baker Company records the interest revenue as follows:

Assets	=	Liabilities	+	Stockholders' Equity
				Net Income
				Revenues − Expenses

	Investment in Held-to-Maturity		Interest
Cash	Bonds		Revenue
	Bal $93,789.00		
+$5,000.00	+627.34		+$5,627.34
	Bal $94,416.34		

> **FINANCIAL STATEMENT EFFECTS**
>
> Increases current assets and noncurrent assets on **balance sheet**. Increases revenues (in "other items"), which increases net income on **income statement** (and therefore increases stockholders' equity on **balance sheet**). Increases cash flows from operating activities on **cash flow statement**.

Note that the amortization of the discount increases the book value of the Investment account to $94,416.34.

On December 31, 2008, Baker records its interest revenue for the second semiannual interest period in the same way. In this case, however, the interest revenue is $5,664.98 ($94,416.34 × 6%). Since it receives interest of $5,000, it amortizes $664.98 as an increase in the investment. Thus, the book value of the investment increases to $95,081.32 ($94,416.34 + $664.98) at the end of 2008. Baker Company reports this amount as a long-term investment on its December 31, 2008 balance sheet as follows:

Long-term investments
Investment in held-to-maturity bonds ($100,000 face value)　　　　　$95,081

Baker Company reports the $11,292 ($5,627.34 + $5,664.98, rounded) interest revenue in the "other items" section on its 2008 income statement. After the company has recorded all of its interest for the 8 semiannual periods, on the December 31, 2011 maturity date the book value of the investment will equal the $100,000 face value because Baker will have amortized all the discount.

BONDS PURCHASED AT A PREMIUM

A company accounts for bonds purchased at a premium in the same way that it accounts for bonds purchased at a discount. It records the purchase price in the Investment in Held-to-Maturity Bonds account, and since it purchased the bonds at a premium, this amount is greater than the face value. It computes the interest revenue using the amortized cost method. For bonds purchased at a premium, the interest revenue is *less* than the interest received because the yield is *less* than the contract rate. A company records the difference between the interest revenue and the interest received as a *decrease* in the Investment account, because it is amortizing part of the premium.

If the yield is 8% when Baker Company purchases the Unlimited Decadence bonds, it records the purchase price of $106,733.50 in the Investment in Held-to-Maturity Bonds account. (Again, you should review the appendix to Chapter 22 for the present value calculations.) Since you should now be familiar with recording interest, we do not show the changes in the accounts and the accounting equation. On June 30, 2008, Baker records Interest Revenue of $4,269.34 [$106,733.50 × (8% ÷ 2)], an increase in Cash of $5,000, and a decrease in the Investment account of $730.66 ($5,000 − $4,269.34). On December 31, 2008, Baker records Interest Revenue of $4,240.11 [($106,733.50 − $730.66) × 4%], an increase in Cash of $5,000, and a decrease in the Investment account of $759.89. On the December 31, 2011 maturity date, the book value of the investment will equal the $100,000 face value because Baker will have amortized all the premium.

SUMMARY SURFING

Here is an opportunity to gather information on the Internet about real-world issues related to the topics in this chapter (for suggestions on how to navigate various companies' Web sites to find their financial statements and other information, see the related discussion in the Preface at the beginning of the book). Answer the following questions.

- Go to the **IBM Corporation** Web site. What was the fair value of IBM's marketable securities at December 31 of the most recent year? What was the amount of the Alliance investments under the equity method? What was the net unrealized gain (or loss) on marketable securities at December 31 of the most recent year?

- Click on the **ExxonMobil Corporation** Web site. What was Exxon's share of the net income of companies in which it had an investment accounted for by the equity method in the most recent year? its share of the total assets at the end of the most recent year? its share of the net assets at the end of the most recent year?

INTEGRATED BUSINESS AND ACCOUNTING SITUATIONS

Answer the Following Questions in Your Own Words.

Testing Your Knowledge

23-1 What method does a company use to account for its investment in common stock when it has (a) less than 20% ownership, (b) between 20% and 50% ownership, and (c) more than 50% ownership?

23-2 What method does a company use to account for its investment in bonds that it expects to be (a) available for sale and (b) held to maturity?

23-3 Under the market value method, how does a company report its investment in available-for-sale securities on its year-end balance sheet?

23-4 When a company using the market value method sells an investment, how does it compute the gain (loss)?

23-5 Under the equity method, how does a company account for its investment and income?

23-6 Under the equity method, how does a company compute the income that it has earned on its investment?

23-7 Under the equity method, how (and why) does a company account for the dividends that it receives on its investment?

23-8 Under the consolidation method, what are (a) the parent company, (b) the subsidiary company, and (c) consolidated financial statements?

23-9 What is an operating segment of a company, and what information does a company report about each of its operating segments?

23-10 What is the relationship between the yield and the contract rate when a company purchases bonds at a discount? at a premium?

23-11 How does a company compute the interest revenue on its investment in held-to-maturity zero-coupon bonds?

23-12 How does a company report its investment in held-to-maturity zero-coupon bonds on its year-end balance sheet?

23-13 How does a company report its investment transactions on its cash flow statement?

23-14 (Appendix). Under the amortized cost method, how does a company that purchases bonds at a discount record the discount amortization when it receives interest?

Applying Your Knowledge

23-15 The following information for **Harrah**'s stock and bonds was recently listed as follows:

STOCK

YTD % CHG	Symbol	Yield %	Price Earnings	Last	Net Change
2.7	HET	1.9	46	84.95	0.38

BONDS

Bonds	Current Price	One-day Change
5.625 June 1'15	85.875	-2.25

Required: Explain the meaning of each item listed.

23-16 On January 2, 2008, Castle Brush Company purchased 400 shares of Bass Company for $9,200 and 10 bonds of Trout Company for $10,000. The bonds have a $10,000 face value and an 8% contract rate, and pay interest on June 30 and December 31. Castle classifies these investments as available-for-sale securities. During 2008, it received the semiannual interest payments on the Trout Company bonds, and on December 12 it received a cash dividend of $1.50 per share on the Bass stock. At the end of 2008, the Bass stock had a market value of $9,900, and the Trout bonds had a market value of $9,800.

Required: (1) Record all of the investment transactions and events for Castle.
(2) Show how Castle would report the investment information on its December 31, 2008 balance sheet, assuming it expects to sell the investments in 2009.

23-17 At the beginning of January 2008, Belford Buckle Company held 500 shares of Wirl common stock in its investment portfolio of available-for-sale securities. These shares had cost $9,000 and had a market value of $9,500 on January 1, 2008. During 2008, Belford had several other transactions relating to its investments in available-for-sale securities, as follows. On January 8, Belford purchased 400 shares of Nirt common stock for $6,000, and on July 1, Belford purchased 10%, $10,000 bonds of Fess Company for $10,000. The bonds pay interest on June 30 and December 31. On August 6, Belford sold the 500 shares of Wirl common stock for $9,900. On December 15, Belford received cash dividends of $1 per share on the Nirt common stock, and on December 31 it received the interest on the Fess bonds. At the end of December, the Nirt shares had a market value of $5,700, and the Fess bonds had a market value of $10,200.

Required: (1) Record the 2008 investment transactions and events for Belford (keep track of the balance in the Investments account).
(2) Show how Belford would report the results of the investment transactions and events on its 2008 income statement and on its December 31, 2008 balance sheet (assuming it expects to sell the investments in 2009).

23-18 At the beginning of 2008, Morton Tile Corporation's investment in available-for-sale securities consisted of 600 shares of Teal Company common stock that had a cost of

$18,000 and a market value of $18,900. During 2008, the company engaged in the following transactions relating to this portfolio:

March 3:   Sold 400 shares of Teal stock for $31 per share
June 7:   Purchased 500 shares of Loom stock for $10,500 and 700 shares of Prat
                stock for $5,600
November 20:   Sold the remaining 200 shares of Teal stock for $29 per share
December 15:   Received dividends of $1 per share on the Loom stock and $0.50 per share
                on the Prat stock

On December 31, 2008, the Loom stock had a market value of $10,000, and the Prat stock had a market value of $6,700.

Required: (1) Record the 2008 investment transactions and events for Morton (keep track of the balance in the Investments account).
(2) Show how Morton would report the results of the investment transactions and events on its 2008 income statement and on its December 31, 2008 balance sheet (assume it expects to sell the investments in 2009).

23-19   On January 1, 2008, Jackson Pen Company purchased 10,000 shares of Rizzo Company for $50,000. This represented 40% of Rizzo's common stock selling on the stock market. On that date, the book value of Rizzo's stockholders' equity was $125,000. At the end of 2008, Rizzo reported net income of $35,000 and paid total dividends of $20,000.

Required: (1) How much does Jackson Pen Company report as income for 2008 in regard to its investment in Rizzo?
(2) What does Jackson Pen Company report as the book value of its investment in Rizzo on its December 31, 2008 balance sheet?
(3) Prepare Jackson Pen Company's entries to record its investment, income, and dividends in regard to Rizzo (keep track of the balance in the Investment account).

23-20   On January 1, 2008, Foley Aircraft Company purchased on the stock market 25% of Pet Helicopter Inc.'s 80,000 shares of common stock, paying $5.25 per share. On that date, the book value of Pet's stockholders' equity was $420,000. On December 31, 2008, Foley reported a balance in its investment account for Pet of $120,000. Pet did not pay dividends in 2008.

Required: (1) How much did Foley pay for its investment in Pet?
(2) How much did Foley report as its 2008 income in regard to its investment in Pet?
(3) What was the total net income of Pet during 2008?

23-21   Carter Company purchased, on the stock market, 48,000 of the 120,000 shares of Chavous Company on January 1, 2008 for $240,000. The condensed balance sheet of Chavous on that date is as follows:

Assets	$1,000,000	Liabilities	$ 400,000
		Stockholders' equity	600,000
			$1,000,000

At the end of 2008, Chavous reported net income of $200,000 and paid dividends of $40,000.

Required: (1) Record the preceding events in 2008 for Carter Company (keep track of the balance in the Investment account).
(2) Show how Carter Company would report the results of the preceding events on its 2008 income statement and on its December 31, 2008 balance sheet.
(3) Assuming that Chavous' liabilities remained unchanged, prepare a condensed balance sheet for Chavous on December 31, 2008.
(4) Explain the relationship between the change in the stockholders' equity of Chavous and the change in the balance of Carter's Investment account since the purchase of the investment.

23-22 On January 1, 2008, Hoffman Company purchased 12-year, zero-coupon bonds issued by Martinez Company. The bonds have a face value of $400,000 and were purchased to yield 8%. Hoffman expects to hold these bonds until maturity, so it uses the amortized cost method to account for its investment.

Required: (1) Compute the purchase price of the bonds.
(2) Compute the interest revenue for 2008 and 2009.
(3) What is the book value of the bonds on December 31, 2009?

23-23 On January 1, 2008, Courtwright Company purchased 7-year, zero-coupon bonds issued by Weimer Company. The bonds have a face value of $300,000 and were purchased to yield 12%. Courtwright expects to hold these bonds until maturity, so it uses the amortized cost method to account for its investment.

Required: (1) Compute the amount that Courtwright pays for the bonds.
(2) Record the interest revenue for 2008 and 2009.
(3) How much will Courtwright report as its investment on December 31, 2009?

23-24 During 2008, Bashor Company entered into the following investment transactions:
(a) Purchased available-for-sale securities for $57,000
(b) Purchased held-to-maturity bonds for $102,000
(c) Sold available-for-sale securities for $33,000 at a gain of $3,000
(d) Received interest of $4,600 on available-for-sale securities
(e) Received dividends of $5,000 on investments accounted for under the equity method
(f) Reported $8,000 increase in investment in available-for-sale securities because of increase in year-end market value
(g) Received dividends of $3,500 on available-for-sale securities
(h) Received interest of $9,000 on investments in held-to-maturity bonds

Required: Show how Bashor would report the preceding transactions on its 2008 cash flow statement (assuming it uses the direct method of reporting cash flows from operating activities).

23-25 (Appendix). On January 1, 2008, Robinson Steel Company purchased 12%, 10-year bonds with a face value of $100,000 for $112,463. At this price the bonds yield 10%. Interest on the bonds is paid on June 30 and December 31. The company expects to hold these bonds until maturity, so it uses the amortized cost method to account for its investment.

Required: (1) Compute the interest revenue that Robinson records in 2008 (round to the nearest dollar).
(2) What would Robinson report as the balance in its Investment in Bonds account on its December 31, 2008 balance sheet?

23-26 (Appendix). On January 1, 2008, Norel Company purchased 10%, 10-year bonds with a face value of $200,000 for $177,059. Based on this purchase price, the bonds yield 12%. Interest on the bonds is paid on June 30 and December 31. Norel expects to hold these bonds until maturity, so it uses the amortized cost method to account for its investment.

Required: (1) Compute the interest revenue that Norel records in 2008 (round to the nearest dollar).
(2) What would Norel report as the balance in its Investment in Held-to-Maturity Bonds account on its December 31, 2008 balance sheet?

23-27 (Appendix). On January 1, 2008, Nairne Gas Company purchased investments in the bonds of two companies:

	Simon Co.	Fraser Co.
Purchase price	$52,346	$37,282
Face value	$50,000	$40,000
Contract rate	9%	7%
Yield	8%	8%

Both bond issues pay interest on June 30 and December 31. The company expects to hold the bonds until maturity.

Required: (1) Prepare the entries for Nairne to record all the events for the investments during 2008 (round all calculations to the nearest dollar, use a single Investments account, and keep track of the balance in the Investments account).

(2) Show how Nairne would report its interest revenue on the bonds on its 2008 income statement.

(3) Show how Nairne would report its investments in the bonds on its December 31, 2008 balance sheet.

23-28 (Appendix). On January 1, 2008, Winfrey Silicone Company purchased investments in the bonds of two companies:

	Bates Co.	Clever Co.
Purchase price	$86,524	$74,361
Face value	$90,000	$70,000
Contract rate	9%	11%
Yield	10%	10%

Both bond issues pay interest on June 30 and December 31. The company expects to hold the bonds until maturity.

Required: (1) Prepare the entries for Winfrey to record all the events for the investments during 2008 (round all calculations to the nearest dollar, use a single Investments account, and keep track of the balance in the Investments account).

(2) Show how Winfrey would report its interest revenue on the bonds on its 2008 income statement.

(3) Show how Winfrey would report its investments in the bonds on its December 31, 2008 balance sheet.

Making Evaluations

23-29 The board of directors of Oxford Company is discussing the method that the company should use for the valuation of the company's available-for-sale securities. Some of the comments are as follows:

- "We should use cost, because until we sell the securities we don't know if we have made any money."
- "If we use cost, we are effectively misleading the users of the financial statements, and as a member of the Board of Directors, I don't feel I'm fulfilling my responsibilities."
- "Market value may also be misleading. If the price is up in one period and down in the next, we will report a loss in the second period although we may have a profit overall."

Required: Describe what the speaker of each of these comments means, and prepare a counterargument for each of them.

23-30 In its 2005 financial statements, **Starbucks** disclosed the following amounts (in thousands):

	October 2, 2005		October 3, 2004	
	Cost	Fair Value	Cost	Fair Value
Short-term investments-				
Available-for-sale securities	$95,660	$95,379	$483,704	$483,157
Cash Flow from Investing Activities, fiscal 2005				
Purchases of available-for-sale securities			$(643,488)	
Proceeds from sales and maturities of available-for-sale securities			?	

Required: (1) Recreate the entries to record the transactions and events that affected Starbucks' investments in available-for-sale securities during fiscal 2005.

Assume that the securities sold in 2005 had a fair value below cost at October 3, 2004 of $524 and were sold at a loss of $1,600.

(2) What can you assume about the intent of Starbucks' managers regarding the company's investments (available-for-sale-securities)?

23-31 In its 2005 annual report, **Hewlett-Packard** discloses the following (partial) information:

On October 31, 2005 and 2004, available-for-sale securities consisted of the following (in millions):

	Cost	Gross Unrealized Gains	Gross Unrealized Losses	Estimated Fair Value
Oct. 31, 2004				
Available for Sale	$368	$40	$(5)	$403
Oct. 31, 2005				
Available for Sale	$ 66	$38	$(4)	$100

Cash Flow from Investing Activities, 2005
Purchases of available-for-sale-investments $(1,729)
Sales of available-for-sale investments   2,066

Required: (1) Recreate the entries to record the transactions and events that affected Hewlett-Packard's available-for-sale securities during 2005. Assume that the available-for-sale securities sold in 2005 had a fair value in excess of cost at December 31, 2004 of $100.

(2) Explain how Hewlett-Packard would report the gain on the sale (disposal) of investments in the operating activities section of its cash flow statement under (a) the direct method and (b) the indirect method.

(3) Summarize the performance of Hewlett-Packard's available-for-sale securities in fiscal 2005.

23-32 Minnow Company had the following summarized balance sheet at January 2, 2008, and income statement for 2008:

Current assets	$ 250,000	Current liabilities	$ 25,000
Noncurrent assets	900,000	Noncurrent liabilities	125,000
		Stockholders' equity	1,000,000
	$1,150,000		$1,150,000

Revenue	$ 350,000
Expenses	(150,000)
	$ 200,000
Income tax expense	(80,000)
Net Income	$ 120,000

On January 2, 2008, Shark Company purchased 20% of the shares of Minnow Company on the stock market for $10 per share. Minnow Company has 100,000 shares of common stock outstanding and paid dividends of $50,000 in 2008. On December 31, 2008, the Minnow Company shares were listed on the stock market at $15 per share.

Required: (1) If Shark Company classifies the investment as an available-for-sale security, show the effects on its financial statements for 2008.

(2) If Shark Company uses the equity method, show the effects on its financial statements for 2008.

(3) How would your answers to (1) and (2) change if the market price of the shares at year-end was $8 per share?

(4) How would your answers to (1) and (2) change if Minnow Company had a net loss of $120,000 in 2008?

23-33 In its 2005 annual report, **Coca-Cola** discloses that it owns 36% of Coca-Cola Enterprises (CCE) which it accounts for under the equity method. It disclosed the following (partial) summary information for CCE, and its other equity investments, at December 31, 2005 (in millions):

	CCE	Other
Current assets	$ 3,395	$ 7,803
Noncurrent assets	21,962	20,698
Current liabilities	3,846	7,705
Noncurrent liabilities	15,868	8,395

Coca-Cola's balance sheet included the following amounts:

Current assets	$ 10,250
Equity investments	6,562
Total assets	29,427
Current liabilities	9,836
Stockholders' equity	16,355

Required: (1) Compute the current ratio for (a) Coca-Cola and (b) CCE and the other equity investments.

(2) Compute the total liabilities to total assets ratio for (a) Coca-Cola and (b) CCE and the other equity investments.

(3) Compare the liquidity and financial flexibility of Coca-Cola with CCE and the other equity investments.

(4) Explain why you think Coca-Cola may own only 36% of CCE.

(5) If Coca-Cola used the consolidation method to account for its investment in CCE and the other equity investments, evaluate the effects on its balance sheet by computing the total liabilities to total assets ratio after the consolidation. Evaluate your results.

23-34   Sheri Clark has extensive experience working in shops that sell greeting cards and small gifts. She decided that she wanted to purchase her own store, and she found two that had the appropriate characteristics. The balance sheets of the two stores at December 31, 2008 were as follows:

	Store A	Store B
Cash	$ 10,000	$ 20,000
Accounts receivable	40,000	70,000
Inventory	30,000	100,000
Furniture	62,500	125,000
Less: Accumulated depreciation	(40,000)	(25,000)
Intangible assets	10,000	0
	$112,500	$290,000
Accounts payable	$ 25,000	$ 50,000
Bank loan	40,000	80,000
Owner's equity	47,500	160,000
	$112,500	$290,000

Both owners are willing to sell their companies for 125% of the value of the net assets (assets minus liabilities) as reported on their balance sheets. An investigation of the two balance sheets reveals the following:

Accounts receivable: Store B has appropriately provided for bad debts, whereas Store A has not. It appears that $5,000 of Store A's accounts receivable may not be collectible.

Inventory: Store A uses the LIFO cost flow assumption, whereas Store B uses FIFO. The replacement cost of Store A's inventory is $20,000 higher than its balance sheet amount.

Furniture: Store A uses the MACRS depreciation method to prepare its financial statements, whereas Store B uses the straight-line method. Each store purchased its furniture two years ago.

Intangible assets: Store A's intangible asset is the cost of the promotional campaign that was undertaken when the store opened.

Required: Prepare for Sheri Clark a memo that recommends which of the two stores she should buy.

23-35 In the chapter, we discussed three methods of valuing investments in stocks: (a) the market value method, (b) the equity method, and (c) consolidation. Each method results in different amounts appearing in various sections of a company's financial statements.

Required: (1) In what situation does a company use each of the three methods?
(2) Explain how a company reports the results of the three methods on its financial statements.
(3) Explain the justification for requiring the use of each of the three different methods from the perspective of the users of the financial statements.

23-36 DuPont had a January 1, 2004 balance of $1,304 in its Investments in Affiliates account. It disclosed the following in its 2005 annual report with respect to the equity method used for its investments in affiliated companies (amounts in millions):

	2005	2004
Equity in earnings (losses) of affiliates	$(108)	$ (39)
Investments in affiliates, 12/31	844	1,034
Dividends received	107	60

Required: (1) Prepare a schedule that shows the results of the transactions that affected the Investments in Affiliates account in each year. (Hint: You need to compute the investments and/or sales the company made during each year.)
(2) Evaluate the performance of DuPont's equity investments in 2005 compared to 2004.
(3) DuPont's equity investments include three investments in which it owns 50%. Explain why DuPont may have chosen to own 50%.

23-37 Verizon disclosed the following in its 2005 annual report with respect to the equity method used for its investments in unconsolidated businesses (amounts in millions):

At December 31,	Ownership	2005 Investment	Ownership	2004 Investment
Equity Investees				
CANTV	28.5%	$ 152	28.5%	$ 199
Vodaphone Omnitel	23.1	2,591	23.1	4,642
Other	Various	772	Various	876
Total equity investees		$3,515		$5,717
Cost Investees	Various	1,089	Various	138
Total		$4,604		$5,855

Required: (1) Explain why Verizon uses the equity method for some investments and the cost method for others.
(2) For which of the equity investments did Verizon earn more income than it received dividends? Less?

23-38 On January 1, 2008, Ant Company had 100,000 shares of common stock outstanding and the balance sheet summarized on the following page.

Current assets	$ 200,000	Current liabilities	$ 100,000
Noncurrent assets	1,000,000	Noncurrent liabilities	700,000
		Stockholders' equity	400,000
	$1,200,000		$1,200,000

The market value of all Ant's assets and liabilities is equal to their book values. On January 2, 2008, Elephant Company purchased 50% of the shares of Ant Company for $10 cash per share on the stock market. Elephant Company had the following summarized balance sheet at January 1, 2008:

Current assets	$ 700,000	Current liabilities	$ 90,000
Noncurrent assets	900,000	Noncurrent liabilities	160,000
		Stockholders' equity	1,350,000
	$1,600,000		$1,600,000

Required: (1) If Elephant Company uses the equity method, prepare its balance sheet on January 2, 2008.

(2) If Elephant Company prepares consolidated financial statements instead, prepare its consolidated balance sheet on January 2, 2008. Assume the goodwill is $300,000 and the minority interest is $200,000.

(3) Compute the debt ratio for each balance sheet. Explain which debt ratio you think better measures the company's risk.

23-39   In the chapter, we showed the disclosures of **PepsiCo**'s operating segments.

Required: Write PepsiCo's shareholders a memo that evaluates the performance of Frito-Lay North America compared to Pepsi-Cola North America for 2005 and 2004. Include appropriate ratio analyses. Use ending total assets to compute the return on assets.

23-40   Yesterday, you received the following letter for your advice column in the local paper:

DR. DECISIVE

Dear Dr. Decisive:

I am becoming addicted to reading annual reports. I had no idea they could contain so much information—and that sometimes they could be so difficult to understand. I understand that accountants (in the interest of their employment opportunities?) use four methods to report on investments. Please explain to me why each of the methods is used but, more important, why there are four different methods.

Call me "Investment Curious."

Required: Meet with your Dr. Decisive team and write a response to "Investment Curious."

CORPORATE STOCK AND EARNINGS ISSUES

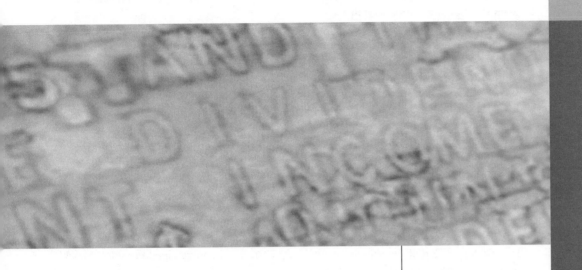

1 What are the rights of a corporation's stockholders?

2 What is important for an external user to know about a corporation's capital stock transactions?

3 What are the characteristics of a corporation's treasury stock, and how does it record and report this stock?

4 What are compensatory stock options, and how does a corporation report them?

5 How does a corporation report its results from discontinued operations and extraordinary items?

6 How does a corporation compute and report its earnings per share?

7 What kinds of dividends can a corporation distribute, and what are their characteristics?

8 How and why does a corporation report the changes in its stockholders' equity?

On **Hershey Foods**' (maker of "Bubble Yum") December 31, 2005 balance sheet, the company shows that its stockholders' equity was $1,021 million—24 percent of its total assets. On **Rocky Mountain Chocolate Factory**'s February 28, 2006 balance sheet, its stockholders' equity was $15.5 million. Given that its total assets were about $19.1 million, stockholders finance 81 percent of Rocky Mountain's assets. These dollar amounts shown on Hershey Foods' and Rocky Mountain's balance sheets result from decisions by managers as well as the accounting methods the companies used to keep track of stockholders'equity.

There are various ways to understand the meaning of these disclosures. For example, if Hershey manufactures one piece of candy for an average cost of three cents, its stockholders' equity is the dollar equivalent of over 34 billion pieces! Hershey Foods' $1,021 million of stockholders' equity is 66 times greater than Rocky Mountain Chocolate Factory's $15.5 million. Should you conclude that Hershey has operations that are about 66 times larger than those of Rocky Mountain? Another way to think about these amounts is to think about the business operations that create them. For example, as we discussed in Chapter 22, long-term debt is used to create leverage, but requires interest payments and increases the company's risk. In contrast, stockholders' equity is "permanent" capital and there is no legal requirement to pay dividends. In their respective annual reports, Hershey Foods reported paying dividends of over $221 million, whereas Rocky Mountain Chocolate Factory paid only about $1.7 million of dividends. Hershey Foods' reported contributed capital of $612 million and retained earnings of $3,646 million, and had purchased treasury stock at a cost of $3,225 million. In contrast, Rocky Mountain Chocolate Factory reported contributed capital of $10 million and retained earnings of $4.9 million, and had not purchased any treasury stock.

 Can you conclude whether Hershey Foods or Rocky Mountain Chocolate Factory have different approaches to managing their stockholders' equity? What factors besides these amounts on the balance sheets and cash flow statements of the two companies should you consider?

We began our discussion of corporations in Chapter 10 of Volume 1. There we noted that corporations are separate legal entities, and that states have enacted laws to govern how a corporation records and reports its stockholders' equity items on its balance sheet. We also briefly discussed the differences between a corporation's income statement and that of a sole proprietorship or a partnership.

To evaluate a corporation's *risk, financial flexibility,* and *return on capital,* both external and internal users must be familiar with how the corporation issues and reports on its capital stock, and with how and why it reports its nonrecurring income and related cash flows. In this chapter, we will expand on the discussion of corporations from Chapter 10 of Volume 1 by explaining different kinds of capital stock transactions, two types of nonrecurring earnings, the computation of earnings per share, the alternative forms of dividends, the impact of these items on the cash flow statement, and related issues.

CORPORATE CAPITAL STRUCTURE

A sole proprietorship has a single owner, and a partnership usually has only a few owners. In both types of company, each owner has a separate Owner's Capital account for reporting the owner's equity on the company's balance sheet. The ending balance of each Owner's Capital account includes the investments by the owner plus the owner's share of the company's net income earned to date less the owner's withdrawals. A corporation usually has many owners and frequent changes in ownership, making it almost impossible to keep separate capital accounts for each owner as is done for a sole proprietorship or a partnership. Furthermore, state laws require special accounting procedures for the owners' equity of a corporation; these laws were established to protect the absentee owners of a corporation as well as its creditors.

As we discussed in Chapter 10 of Volume 1, **stockholders' equity** is the term used for the owners' equity of a corporation. The stockholders' equity on a corporation's balance sheet includes at least two parts: contributed capital and retained earnings. Each is governed by the laws of the state in which the company is incorporated. We show the basic format (with assumed numbers of shares and dollar amounts) of the stockholders' equity section of a corporation's balance sheet as follows:

Stockholders' Equity

Contributed capital	
Capital stock, $5 par, 20,000 shares authorized,	
10,000 shares issued and outstanding..	$ 50,000
Additional paid-in capital..	70,000
Total contributed capital..	$120,000
Retained earnings...	90,000
Total Stockholders' Equity..	$210,000

A corporation includes the total amount of investments made by its stockholders in **Contributed Capital**. We discuss each of the accounts and the related transactions in the following sections. A corporation reports the balance in its **Retained Earnings** account as the second part of its stockholders' equity. The amount the corporation reports as its retained earnings is the total lifetime corporate income that it has reinvested and that it has *not* distributed to stockholders as dividends. Later in this chapter we will also discuss the accounting issues relating to retained earnings. Since the laws of each state govern some of the stockholders' equity issues that a corporation faces, we will explain only the general issues in this chapter. A particular state's laws might require another procedure or disclosure.

Capital Stock and Legal Capital

Capital stock is the ownership unit in a corporation. **Stockholders** (or **shareholders**) are the owners of a corporation, and their evidence of corporate ownership is a stock certificate. A **stock certificate** is a serially numbered legal document that indicates the number of shares of capital stock owned by a stockholder. It also may include additional information such as the legal capital and the method of transferring the capital stock to another owner.

Stockholders' Rights

Shares of stock are transferable between individuals, and the owners of a corporation may be a diverse set of stockholders who are not involved in its management. Because of this separation of ownership and management, each stockholder may have the following rights:

What are the rights of a corporation's stockholders?

1. The right to attend stockholders' meetings and to vote in setting and approving major policies and actions of the corporation. Included are policies and actions concerning such items as mergers with other companies, acquisitions of other companies, sales of major portions of the corporation, and the issuance of additional stock and bonds.

2. The right to vote in the election of the board of directors. A **board of directors** is a group of individuals that has the responsibility and authority to supervise the corporation's ordinary business activities, make future plans, and take whatever action is necessary in managing the corporation. Voting to elect the board of directors (and the *chair of the board*) also takes place at the stockholders' meetings.

3. The right to share in net income by receiving dividends from the corporation. The board of directors decides on the payment of dividends, however.

4. The right to purchase additional capital stock if it is issued—a right known as the *preemptive right*. The **preemptive right** is the right to maintain a proportionate (pro rata) share of additional capital stock if it is issued. This right often is very significant for small, privately held corporations for which control is very important, but it is less important for corporations with large numbers of shareholders who each own a relatively small number of shares. Stockholders may give up their preemptive right, for example, to allow the corporation to acquire another company by issuing a large number of additional shares of stock to obtain sufficient capital to do so.

5. The right to share in the distribution of the assets of the corporation if it is liquidated (terminated). If a corporation is terminated, creditors have first priority in the collection of their claims; stockholders receive any remaining assets.

Legal Capital

A corporation may issue capital stock in several ways: for cash, in noncash exchanges, to employees through stock options, and in other transactions. The dollar amount that a corporation reports in the Capital Stock account for each capital stock transaction depends on the laws of the state in which the corporation is incorporated. Because stockholders have a *limited liability* to protect creditors, state laws usually set a legal capital for all corporations. **Legal capital** is the amount of stockholders' equity of a corporation that it cannot distribute to stockholders (unless the corporation is liquidated). A corporation may not pay dividends or reacquire capital stock if these activities will reduce the legal capital. The definition of legal capital varies from state to state. In most states, however, the legal capital is the total par value or stated value of the issued capital stock.

 How do you think legal capital protects a corporation's creditors?

Par Value Stock

A common way a corporation establishes its legal capital is by assigning a par value to each share of capital stock. The **par value** of capital stock is a monetary amount that the corporation designates as the legal capital per share in its articles of incorporation. The par value per share is printed on each stock certificate. The total legal capital of a corporation is determined by multiplying the par value per share by the number of shares issued. Generally, states require that a corporation separately account for its legal capital. Consequently, as you will see shortly, for each issuance of capital stock, a corporation records the total dollar amount of the par value in a capital stock account.

The par value of a share of capital stock is usually very low, such as $10, $2, or even less per share. For example, the par value of **General Motors**' stock is $1⅔ per share. Since a corporation usually issues capital stock at a price much higher than the par value, the legal capital is usually only a small part of the total amount received. The total amount the corporation receives is the *market* value, the price at which the stock is issued. It is important for users to understand that the par value of capital stock has *no* direct relationship to its market value at any time.

No-Par Stock

Many states also allow the issuance of no-par capital stock. **No-par capital stock** does not have a par value. Some states require that the entire amount received by the corporation when it issues no-par stock be designated as legal capital, and the corporation records this amount in the capital stock account. Many states, however, allow the corporation's board of directors to set a stated value per share of no-par stock. The **stated value** of no-par stock is the legal capital per share of stock. The stated value per share, when multiplied by the number of shares issued, is the total amount of legal capital, and is the amount the corporation records in its capital stock account.

*Look at **Colgate-Palmolive**'s Consolidated Balance Sheet in Appendix B. Does Colgate-Palmolive have par, no-par, or stated value common stock?*

Additional Paid-In Capital

A corporation may issue capital stock in several kinds of transactions. In addition to following state laws for recording the par or stated value in a capital stock account, a corporation also records the excess value received, known as the *additional paid-in capital*. **Additional paid-in capital** is the difference between the market value (selling price) and the par (or stated) value in each stock transaction, and the corporation records it in its Additional Paid-in Capital account. Corporations may call this account *Additional Paid-in Capital on Capital Stock, Additional Paid-in Capital in Excess of Par (or Stated) Value, Premium on Capital Stock,* or *Contributed Capital in Excess of Par (or Stated) Value.* For simplicity, in this chapter we call it *Additional Paid-in Capital*. Additional paid-in capital sometimes arises from transactions not involving the original issuance of capital stock. We will discuss these transactions later in the chapter.

The concept of legal capital has a significant effect on corporate reporting, particularly as it applies to stockholders' equity. As we just described, a corporation uses a capital stock account to report its legal capital, and an additional paid-in capital account to report the remainder of the total amount of capital contributed by stockholders. However, most external users are interested in the total contributed capital.

Classes of Capital Stock

Corporations may issue two (or more) classes of capital stock—common stock and preferred stock. If a corporation issues only one class of capital stock, it refers to this stock as *common stock*. **Common stock** is capital stock that shares in all the stockholders' rights. However, some corporations issue more than one type of common stock, such as Class A and Class B common stock. Usually one type of common stock has much greater voting rights than the other in order to preserve control by the original shareholders. For example, both **Ford** and **Molson Coors** have two types of common stock, thus preserving the voting rights of members of the Ford and Coors families. A corporation also may issue **preferred stock**, which is capital stock for which stockholders receive certain additional rights in exchange for giving up some of the usual stockholders' rights. The additional rights may involve the right to receive a dividend before any dividend is paid to common stockholders, and the right to convert the preferred stock to common stock at a later date. Preferred stockholders may give up the right to vote in exchange for these additional rights. Alternatively, the preferred stock may be callable or redeemable. We will briefly discuss the conversion of preferred stock to common stock and the recall or redemption of preferred stock later in this chapter.

Does Colgate-Palmolive have preferred stock (see Appendix B)?

A corporation often issues preferred stock with a par value. When a corporation issues both common stock and preferred stock, it uses a Common Stock account and a Preferred Stock account to report the legal capital of each kind of stock. It also uses an Additional Paid-in Capital on Common Stock account and an Additional Paid-in Capital on Preferred Stock account to report the differences between the market values (selling prices) it received and the par (or stated) values of each kind of stock. We also use these titles in this book. When a corporation issues both classes of stock, it expands the contributed capital component of its stockholders' equity to include the additional items (using assumed numbers of shares and dollar amounts), as follows:

Stockholders' Equity

Contributed capital
  Preferred stock, $100 par, 2,000 shares authorized,
    600 shares issued and outstanding... $ 60,000
  Additional paid-in capital on preferred stock................................. 72,000
  Common stock, $10 par, 30,000 shares authorized,
    9,000 shares issued and outstanding.. 90,000
  Additional paid-in capital on common stock.................................... 43,000
    Total contributed capital.. $265,000
Retained earnings.. 173,000
    Total Stockholders' Equity $438,000

Now that you have this background, we will discuss recording and reporting the various types of capital stock transactions. Since most capital stock is common stock, our examples are in terms of common stock. The recording and balance sheet reporting are the same for preferred stock, however, except for the changes in the account titles from common stock to preferred stock.

CAPITAL STOCK TRANSACTIONS

2 What is important for an external user to know about a corporation's capital stock transactions?

A corporation's articles of incorporation authorize the issuance of capital stock. This authorization lists the classes of stock that the corporation may issue, their par or stated values, the number of authorized shares of each class, and in the case of preferred stock, any preference provisions. After a corporation has issued all of its authorized stock, it must obtain stockholder approval and reapply to the state if it wants to issue more shares. Hence, a corporation usually obtains authorization to issue more stock than it initially plans to sell.

Users need to understand the difference between authorized capital stock and issued capital stock. **Authorized capital stock** is the number of shares of capital stock (both common and preferred) that the corporation *may* legally issue. For example, as of December 31, 2005, **Dow Chemical Company** was authorized to issue 1.5 billion shares of common stock. On the other hand, **issued capital stock** is the number of shares of capital stock that a corporation *has* legally issued to its stockholders as of the balance sheet date. On December 31, 2005, Dow Chemical had only issued 981 million shares. As we showed earlier, a corporation reports the numbers of shares authorized and issued for each class of stock in the stockholders' equity section of its balance sheet.

How many common shares had Colgate-Palmolive issued at December 31, 2005 (see Appendix B)?

A corporation may issue common stock for cash, in noncash exchanges, and in other transactions. We will discuss each of these alternatives next.

Would you be more interested to know the number of shares a corporation is authorized to issue or the number of shares it has issued? Explain why.

Is this what a corporation means by "preferred stock"?

PREFERRED STOCK

REPRINTED BY PERMISSION OF TIAA-CREF.

Issuance for Cash

Depending on the state in which it is incorporated, a corporation may issue common stock as stock with a par value, as no-par stock with a stated value, or as true no-par stock. For simplicity, in this book we assume common stock has a par value. In most cases a corporation issues common stock for cash, at a price above the par value. For example, assume that Unlimited Decadence issues 3,000 shares of its $3 par value common stock for $20 per share. The corporation records this transaction as follows:

Assets	=	Liabilities	+	Stockholders' Equity	
				Contributed Capital	
Cash				Common Stock	Additional Paid-in Capital
+$60,000				+$9,000	+$51,000

> **FINANCIAL STATEMENT EFFECTS**
>
> Increases current assets and total assets on **balance sheet**. Increases contributed capital and total stockholders' equity on **balance sheet**. Increases cash flows from financing activities on **cash flow statement**.

If Unlimited Decadence had only this one stock transaction, it would report total contributed capital of $60,000 in stockholders' equity on its year-end balance sheet. A corporation may incur miscellaneous costs for the issuance of common stock, including legal fees, accounting fees, stock certificate costs, and other costs. When the corporation pays these costs, it reduces the Additional Paid-in Capital account, because the costs are considered to be a reduction in the amount received rather than an expense.[1]

 Why do you think these additional costs may not be recorded as an expense?

Noncash Issuance of Stock

Sometimes a corporation issues common stock for assets other than cash or for services performed. When this occurs, the corporation must use a correct value to record the transaction. Finding a correct value is particularly challenging when intangible assets such as patents or copyrights are involved, because it is difficult to value these assets. The general rule is to record the transaction at the market value of the stock issued or of the assets received (or the service performed), whichever is more *reliable*. For instance, at the time of the transaction, the stock may be selling on the stock market at a specified price. In this case the stock would have a known value (the stock market price), and therefore the corporation would use this value to record the transaction.

For example, suppose that Unlimited Decadence issues 1,000 shares of $3 par value common stock in exchange for a patent. The stock is currently selling for $18 per share on the stock market. Unlimited Decadence would use a value of $18,000 ($18 × 1,000) to record the transaction as follows:

Assets	=	Liabilities	+	Stockholders' Equity	
				Contributed Capital	
Patents				Common Stock	Additional Paid-in Capital
+$18,000				+$3,000	+$15,000

> **FINANCIAL STATEMENT EFFECTS**
>
> Increases intangible assets, total assets, contributed capital, and total stockholders' equity on **balance sheet**.

Alternatively, a corporation's stock may not trade on a stock market. In this case the market value of the asset received (or the service performed) may be more reliable, and the corporation should use it to record the transaction. The corporation may base this value on a review of recent transactions involving similar assets (or services) or on an appraisal by an independent appraiser.

Users need to understand the effect on the financial statements of an error in recording the noncash issuance of common stock. Suppose, for instance, that a corporation issued stock for equipment and that it recorded the transaction at too high a value. In this case

---

[1]At the time of the original formation of a corporation, however, it reports these costs as an expense.

the corporation would overstate both its assets and its stockholders' equity. In addition, since equipment is a depreciable asset, the initial error would cause an overstatement each year in the depreciation expense, resulting in an understatement of net income. With net income understated and assets and stockholders' equity overstated, the company's return on assets and return on stockholders' equity would be understated. The corporation's financial statements, and many of its ratios, would be correct only at the end of the asset's useful life. If the corporation initially recorded the equipment at too low a value, opposite errors would result. The managers of a corporation must use good judgment in recording noncash issuances of common stock to avoid errors in the corporation's financial statements of current and later periods.

Do you think that managers might prefer to overstate or understate the value of a noncash stock transaction? Explain why.

Transfer of Stock between Stockholders

The preceding discussions involving the sale of stock for cash and in noncash exchanges dealt only with the issuance of stock by the corporation to its stockholders. Later, stockholders may trade (i.e., purchase and sell) the corporation's stock. In this case the corporation is not directly involved in the transaction, and no stockholders' equity accounts are affected. Therefore, the corporation makes no entry in its accounts, and the value of these trades does *not* affect its financial statements. However, it must keep records of the names and addresses of the stockholders for mailing reports and dividends.

In Colgate-Palmolive's annual report in Appendix B, its stock price on December 31, 2005 was $54.85. What is the total value of the company's issued shares? By how much does that amount exceed the amount reported in the balance sheet? Why?

Convertible, Callable, and Redeemable Preferred Stock

Earlier we mentioned that a corporation may issue two classes of stock, common and preferred. One of the preferences that preferred stockholders might receive is the right to exchange (convert) the preferred stock for common stock at a later date. **Convertible preferred stock** is preferred stock that is exchangeable into common stock at the option of the individual stockholders. Usually the corporation establishes, at the time it issues the preferred stock, the number of common shares into which it will convert each preferred share. Another feature of preferred stock usually involves the right to a set dividend. For instance, in 2005, **PepsiCo, Inc.** had issued 803,953 shares of convertible, cumulative preferred stock (which we discuss later in the chapter). Each share had a right to a $5.46 annual dividend.

Both the conversion preference and the dividend feature are advantages to the preferred stockholder. Since the stockholder can convert each share of preferred stock into a specified number of shares of common stock, the market price of the convertible preferred stock tends to rise in proportion to any rise in the market price of the common stock. When the market price of the common stock falls, however, the right to a set dividend on the preferred stock tends to stabilize the market value of the preferred stock.

Would you expect the stock market price of PepsiCo's preferred stock to fluctuate more or less than the company's common stock? Why?

Preferred stock also may usually be callable. A corporation may recall (or retire) **callable preferred stock** at its option. It usually states the call price on the stock certificate, and this price is usually several dollars above the issuance price. Stockholders owning nonconvertible preferred stock must give up their shares when the shares are called by the corporation. Stockholders owning convertible preferred stock usually have the choice of conversion or recall. The primary reason a corporation issues callable preferred stock relates to dividends. Retirement of the preferred stock enables the corporation to save its preferred stock dividend payments, thereby increasing its cash available for common stock dividends or for other purposes.

When a corporation issues convertible or callable preferred stock, it records the issuance in the same manner as the issuance of common stock. After issuance, the corporation discloses the conversion, call, or redemption feature in a note to its financial statements. When the stockholder converts preferred stock to common stock, the corporation eliminates the par value of the converted preferred stock and the additional paid-in capital on the preferred stock (the total contributed capital for the converted preferred stock). Then it assigns this amount to common stock in two steps. First, it determines the par value of the common stock issued and adds that amount to the common stock account. Then it adds the remaining contributed capital from the converted preferred stock to the additional paid-in capital on the common stock. Thus, the conversion of preferred stock to common stock affects the components of contributed capital but not the total contributed capital.

For example, assume that at incorporation, Anglar Corporation issues 40 shares of $100 par value convertible preferred stock for $110 per share and 1,000 shares of $5 par value common stock for $20 per share. Each share of preferred stock is convertible into 6 shares of common stock. Later, stockholders convert all the shares of preferred stock into common stock. The effect on contributed capital before and after the conversion of all the preferred stock is shown in the following stockholders' equity sections of Anglar's balance sheet:

Before Conversion		After Conversion	
Contributed capital			
Preferred stock, $100 par	$ 4,000		
Additional paid-in capital on preferred stock	400	Contributed capital	
Common stock, $5 par	5,000	Common stock, $5 par	$ 6,200*
Additional paid-in capital on common stock	15,000	Additional paid-in capital	18,200†
Total contributed capital	$24,400	Total contributed capital	$24,400
Retained earnings (assumed)	35,000	Retained earnings (assumed)	35,000
Total Stockholders' Equity	$59,400	Total Stockholders' Equity	$59,400

*$5,000 + (40 × 6 × $5)
†$15,000 + [$4,400 − (40 × 6 × $5)]

Note that the conversion did not change the corporation's $24,400 total contributed capital because the $4,400 of contributed capital for the preferred stock was replaced by the same amount for the common stock. Also note that the corporation ignores the market value of the stock on the date of the conversion.

Why do you think that GAAP requires the corporation to ignore the market value of the stock on the date of the conversion?

Preferred stock also may be **redeemable**. Redeemable preferred stock is subject to mandatory retirement at a specified maturity date and price, or at the option of the owner.[2] The primary difference between callable preferred stock and mandatory redeemable preferred stock is that callable preferred stock *may* be retired whereas redeemable preferred stock *must* be retired at the specified date or at the stockholder's request. When a corporation issues redeemable preferred stock, it records the issuance in the same manner as the issuance of callable preferred stock. After issuance, the corporation reports mandatorily redeemable preferred stock as a liability on its balance sheet because it must pay the stockholders on the maturity date. The corporation reports

---

[2]Some redeemable preferred stock may be retired at the option of the company.

How important to the world economy is what happens on this street?

© JAMES MARSHALL/CORBIS

preferred stock that is redeemable at the option of the stockholders in stockholders' equity because it may not have to repay the stockholders.

TREASURY STOCK

3 What are the characteristics of a corporation's treasury stock, and how does it record and report this stock?

In most states a corporation may reacquire its own previously issued capital stock, after which it holds the stock in its treasury. **Treasury stock** is a corporation's own capital stock that (1) stockholders fully paid for and the corporation issued, (2) the corporation later reacquired, and (3) the corporation currently holds. For instance, at the end of 2005, **Dow Chemical** held 14.2 million shares of its own capital stock as treasury stock, for which it paid $559 million.

*What was the cost of **Colgate-Palmolive**'s treasury stock at December 31, 2005? (See Appendix B.)*

A corporation may acquire treasury stock for various reasons: (1) to have shares available to issue for employee purchase plans, (2) to have shares available to issue in the conversion of convertible preferred stock, (3) to invest excess cash (intending to later sell the shares for a higher price), (4) to have shares available to issue in the acquisition of other companies, (5) to reduce the number of shares outstanding and to increase earnings per share, in order to help maintain the market price of its stock, (6) to have shares available to use in the issuance of a stock dividend, and (7) to concentrate ownership of the shares to assist in the defense against hostile takeovers. Treasury stock transactions may be subject to legal and stock exchange regulations.

External users need to understand several features about treasury stock. Treasury stock clearly is *not* an asset of the corporation—a corporation cannot own itself. A corporation cannot report a gain or a loss from reacquiring its own stock; this restricts a corporation from influencing its net income by buying and selling its own stock. Consequently, a corporation reports treasury stock as a reduction of its stockholders' equity, as we will discuss next. Treasury stock generally does not have the stockholders' rights we discussed earlier; it has no voting or preemptive rights, cannot participate in dividends, and has no rights at liquidation.

When a corporation originally issues capital stock, it increases its stockholders' equity and the number of shares outstanding. When it acquires treasury stock, it does just the opposite. The corporation reduces its stockholders' equity and the number of shares outstanding. You should understand the difference between issued capital stock and outstanding capital stock. Recall that issued capital stock is the number of shares that a corporation has issued to stockholders. **Outstanding capital stock** is the number of shares that the corporation has issued to stockholders and that the stockholders still hold as of a specific date. Thus, the difference between *issued* capital stock and *outstanding* capital stock is the number of shares being held by a corporation as *treasury* stock. A corporation may reissue treasury stock for the reasons we mentioned earlier, in which case it increases stockholders' equity and the number of shares outstanding.

Would you be more interested to know the number of shares a corporation has issued or the number of shares it has outstanding? Explain why.

Acquisition of Treasury Stock

When a corporation reacquires its capital stock, it records the *cost* it pays as an increase in a Treasury Stock account and a decrease in Cash. It reports the cash paid as a financing activity in its cash flow statement. The corporation ignores the par value of the stock in recording the reacquisition since it already accounted for the par value when it first issued the stock. During the time between reacquisition and reissuance, the corporation treats the Treasury Stock account as a contra-stockholders' equity account. If the corporation issues a balance sheet during this period, it deducts the cost of the treasury stock from the total of contributed capital and retained earnings.

 How much did Colgate-Palmolive pay to purchase treasury stock during 2005? (See Appendix B.)

For example, suppose that Duong Corporation previously issued 5,000 shares of $10 par value common stock for $12 per share and has retained earnings of $35,000. The corporation decides to reacquire 400 shares of this common stock, and it purchases these shares on the stock market at a cost of $14 per share. The corporation records the reacquisition of the stock at $5,600 ($14 × 400) as follows:

Assets	=	Liabilities	+	Stockholders' Equity			
				Contributed Capital			
Cash				Common Stock	Additional Paid-in Capital	Retained Earnings	Treasury Stock
				Bal $50,000	Bal $10,000	Bal $35,000	
−$5,600						−	+$5,600

> **FINANCIAL STATEMENT EFFECTS**
>
> Decreases current assets and total assets on *balance sheet*. Increases treasury stock, which decreases stockholders' equity on *balance sheet*. Decreases cash flows from financing activities on *cash flow statement*.

Note that because treasury stock is a contra-stockholders' equity account, we show a minus sign (−) in the column before the account. Note also that the corporation recorded the treasury stock at its *cost* per share and that it ignored the stock's original par value. If the corporation prepared a balance sheet before reissuing these shares, it would report the stockholders' equity as follows:

Stockholders' Equity

Contributed capital	
Common stock, $10 par, 40,000 shares authorized, 5,000 shares issued, 4,600 shares outstanding	$50,000
Additional paid-in capital	10,000
Total contributed capital	$60,000
Retained earnings	35,000
Total contributed capital and retained earnings	$95,000
Less: Treasury stock (400 shares at $14 per share)	(5,600)
Total Stockholders' Equity	$89,400

In the example, Duong Corporation subtracts the $5,600 cost of the treasury stock from the $95,000 total of contributed capital and retained earnings to determine its $89,400 total stockholders' equity. Note that it also reports the numbers of shares authorized, issued, and outstanding.

Reissuance of Treasury Stock

A corporation may reissue treasury stock at a price above, below, or equal to its cost (the amount it paid when it reacquired the shares). It records the reissuance by reducing the Treasury Stock account for the *cost* of the shares reissued, and it treats the difference between the cash it receives and this cost as an adjustment of Additional Paid-in Capital. If it receives more cash than the cost of the reissued treasury stock, it records the excess as an increase in Additional Paid-in Capital. If it receives less cash than the cost, it reduces Additional Paid-in Capital by the amount of the difference. Since a corporation may reacquire treasury stock at different dates and costs, it keeps records so that it will know the cost information when it reissues the stock.

Explain why you think a corporation increases Additional Paid-in Capital for the excess of the cash it receives over the cost of the reissued treasury stock. Is this consistent with what you know about the components of the stockholders' equity section? Why or why not?

To understand the reissuance, assume that Duong Corporation reissues 300 shares of the treasury stock from our earlier example at $15 per share. It records this reissuance as follows:

FINANCIAL STATEMENT EFFECTS

Increases current assets and total assets on *balance sheet*. Increases contributed capital, decreases treasury stock, and increases total stockholders' equity on *balance sheet*. Increases cash flows from financing activities on *cash flow statement*.

Assets	=	Liabilities	+	Stockholders' Equity			
				Contributed Capital			
Cash				Common Stock	Additional Paid-in Capital	Retained Earnings	Treasury Stock
				Bal $50,000	Bal $10,000	Bal $35,000	Bal $5,600
+$4,500					+300	−	−4,200
				Bal $50,000	Bal $10,300	Bal $35,000	Bal $1,400

Note that the corporation reduces the Treasury Stock account by the $4,200 cost of the reissued shares and increases Additional Paid-in Capital by $300, the difference between the $4,500 cash received and this cost. After this transaction, the corporation reports the stockholders' equity as follows:

Stockholders' Equity

Contributed capital
  Common stock, $10 par, 40,000 shares authorized, 5,000 shares issued,
    4,900 shares outstanding... $50,000
  Additional paid-in capital.. 10,300
    Total contributed capital.. $60,300
Retained earnings 35,000
    Total contributed capital and retained earnings.. $95,300
  Less: Treasury stock (100 shares at $14 per share) .... (1,400)
    Total Stockholders' Equity... $93,900

Note that stockholders' equity of Duong Corporation has increased by $4,500 (from $89,400 before it reissued the treasury stock to $93,900), that the number of shares outstanding has increased by 300 (from 4,600 to 4,900), and that the number of shares of treasury stock has decreased to 100 shares.

When a company reissues treasury stock, why doesn't it record a gain or a loss?

STOCK OPTIONS

Another way in which corporations issue stock is through stock options. Many stock options are issued to employees as part of their compensation. A corporation's **compensatory stock options** are intended to provide additional compensation to its employees (sometimes a select group of employees, such as its top managers). Under a compensatory stock option plan, employees, in exchange for their services, receive the option to buy shares of their corporation's common stock at a fixed price for a certain period of time.[3] For example, suppose Unlimited Decadence grants an option to an employee as follows:

Date of grant:	January 1
Number of options:	10,000
Option price per share:	$20
Options first exercisable:	End of 4 years
Options expire:	End of 10 years
Price per share of common stock on 1/1	$20

4 What are compensatory stock options, and how does a corporation report them?

---

[3]Options may be granted to nonemployees, they may be noncompensatory, and they may have variable terms. These topics are beyond the scope of this book.

In this case the employee must work for Unlimited Decadence for four years (called the *service period* or *vesting period*) before he or she has the right to exercise the options and purchase the common stock. Then the employee has another six years, in which to exercise the options. It is very important to note that during those six years, the employee can purchase 10,000 shares of common stock for $20 each. This amount is referred to as the *option price, exercise price,* or *strike price.* This option price is the amount the employee pays to buy shares, *no matter what the current stock market price is.* For example, if the stock has a market price of $100 per share after four years and the employee exercises the options, he or she would pay Unlimited Decadence $200,000 (10,000 × $20) and receive shares worth $1 million (10,000 × $100). So you can see how a compensatory stock option is considered to be part of an employee's compensation!

In addition to providing compensation, compensatory stock options are designed to encourage employees to make decisions that cause the market price of the corporation's stock to increase, thereby providing a benefit to all its stockholders. These options are particularly popular in high-technology and bio-technology corporations, as well as in new corporations (called *start-up* corporations). For instance, a start-up corporation probably does not have sufficient cash available to pay high salaries to attract the best employees; therefore, it offers compensatory stock options in addition to a lower cash salary.

Prior to 2006, GAAP did not require a corporation that issued compensatory stock options to record a related expense. Instead, the corporation was required to disclose in the notes to its financial statements the effect that its stock options would have had on its net income (and earnings per share) if its income statement had included stock option expense. Therefore, if Unlimited Decadence had issued the stock option we described above on January 1, 2005, it did not have to report an expense for these options on its income statement, either on the date they were granted, during the service period, or on the date the employee exercised the options. So even though the employee was $800,000 better off in our example, the option would have had no effect on the corporation's net income. This partly explains why compensatory stock options were a popular form of compensation. They could result in significant benefits for employees but no expense, or cash outflow, for the corporation. Also, if the corporation paid its employees a *lower* cash salary when it also provided a stock option plan, its income was *higher* because of the lower salary expense!

The serious financial reporting failures that occurred in the early 2000s led external users, accountants, and even Congress to reevaluate the accounting rules for compensatory stock options. Many people felt that because no expense was reported for stock options, many corporations' income statements were misleading. In response to the need for a corporation's financial statements to provide a clearer picture of its profitability, GAAP was changed so that corporations in 2006 and thereafter are required to use a "fair value" method of recording and reporting compensatory stock option plans.

The accounting rules for compensatory stock option plans are complex, so we will just provide you with the "big picture" and not discuss them in detail. Under the fair value method, on the date of grant a corporation measures the fair value of its stock option plan using an "option pricing model." The total compensation cost is the total fair value of the stock options. However, the corporation does not record the total compensation cost on the grant date. Instead, it allocates the total compensation cost as compensation expense (and increases additional paid-in capital) to each year of the service period using the straight-line method. Thus, the corporation includes a portion of the fair value of its compensatory stock option plan as an expense on its income statement each year during the service period. This reduces the corporation's net income and presents a more relevant picture of its profitability. When an employee exercises a stock option, the corporation increases its cash and contributed capital for the amount paid by the employee.

For instance, if Unlimited Decadence had issued the stock option we previously described on January 1, 2006, it would compute the fair value of the stock option on that date. Assume it computed the fair value to be $800,000. Then it would report $200,000 as salary expense (in addition to the employee's cash salary) on its 2006, 2007, 2008, and 2009 income statements, thereby reducing its net income each of these years in the service period. It would also increase additional paid-in capital on its balance sheet by $200,000 each year, or a total of $800,000 by the end of the service period.

When the employee exercises the stock option after four years, Unlimited Decadence increases its cash and contributed capital by $200,000. Since it has already increased its additional paid-in capital by $800,000, it records a total increase in contributed capital of $1 million (the fair value of the stock option plus the cash received).

 Do you agree that a corporation that issues a stock option should record an expense? Why or why not?

As an example of the effects of these new accounting rules, **Cisco Systems** reported that its 2005 net income was $5,580 million. The disclosures in the notes reported that its expense for stock options was $1,050 million (pre-tax).

EXTERNAL USER ANALYSIS: LIABILITIES VS. STOCKHOLDERS' EQUITY

In the early chapters of this book, we explained that a corporation's liabilities are amounts it owes to creditors (creditors' equity) and that its stockholders' equity is the owners' residual interest, measured by subtracting the corporation's liabilities from its assets. In the later chapters of this book, we have seen several issues that complicate the distinction between the two categories. In this chapter, we have discussed redeemable (and callable) preferred stock, which will result in a cash outflow when the stock is redeemed. We also discussed deferred income tax liabilities (and assets), which might not be considered liabilities (and assets) if they will continue to increase in the future. We also discussed operating leases, which will require future cash payments but which are not included as liabilities on the corporation's balance sheet and are instead disclosed in the notes to its financial statements. So, an external user must be careful when looking at the equity part of a corporation's balance sheet; the user should consider the related notes and should carefully examine how much debt the corporation owes and how much stockholders' equity it reports.

CORPORATE EARNINGS

The stockholders' equity section of a corporation's balance sheet includes contributed capital and retained earnings. Contributed capital reports the total amount of investments made by stockholders into the corporation. Retained earnings is the amount of the corporation's lifetime income not distributed as dividends to stockholders. As we discussed in Chapter 10 of Volume 1, a corporation reports its net income differently from a sole proprietorship or a partnership because of the effect of income taxes, discontinued operations, extraordinary items, and the disclosure of earnings per share. A corporation may distribute dividends to both preferred and common stockholders, after "declaring" them at an earlier date. A corporation may pay cash dividends or distribute stock dividends. We will discuss each of these topics in the following sections.

Corporate Income Statement

The net income (loss) that a corporation reports on its income statement for a period is the amount of income that it transfers to retained earnings at the end of its accounting period. But, a corporation's income statement provides much more information than just net income (loss). This statement may have several major sections, as follows:

1. Income from continuing operations
    (a) Operating income
    (b) Nonoperating income (other items)
    (c) Income tax expense related to continuing operations
2. Results of discontinued operations
    (a) Income (loss) from operations of a discontinued component (net of income taxes)
    (b) Gain (loss) on disposal of discontinued component (net of income taxes)
3. Extraordinary gains or losses (net of income taxes)
4. Net income (the sum of items 1, 2, and 3)
5. Earnings per share (basic and diluted)

Not all corporate income statements contain these sections. We show Unlimited Decadence Corporation's income statement, which includes each section, in Exhibit 24-1 using assumed amounts.[4] Also included in Exhibit 24-1 is the note to the financial statements describing the computation of basic earnings per share.

Income from Continuing Operations

We discussed the income from continuing operations section of a corporate income statement in Chapter 10 of Volume 1. This section includes a corporation's *operating income*, which it determines by subtracting cost of goods sold from net sales to obtain gross profit, and then subtracting the selling expenses and general and administrative expenses. It also includes the nonoperating income (or expense), which is the sum of the *"other items."* These other items include recurring items, such as interest expense and revenue, which are not part of the corporation's primary operations, as well as ordinary (as opposed to extraordinary) gains and losses, such as those related to the sale of equipment; losses from the impairment of property, plant, and equipment (or intangibles); and "restructuring" losses.

A corporation reports the total of the operating income and the nonoperating income as "income before income taxes" *if* it does not report results of discontinued operations or extraordinary items (which we discuss later). If it does include either of these items, it reports the total of the operating income and nonoperating income as "pretax income from continuing operations." In Exhibit 24-1, Unlimited Decadence's operating income is $7,000, its nonoperating income is $1,000, and its pretax income from continuing operations totals $8,000. (Note that all amounts in Unlimited Decadence's income statement are in thousands.)

A corporation has income tax expense, which is based on its pretax accounting income. It *pays* income taxes based on its "taxable income." The difference between the income tax expense and the income tax obligation causes deferred taxes, as we discussed in Chapter 22. A corporation's pretax accounting income is the sum of its pretax income from continuing operations, results of discontinued operations, and extraordinary items.[5] To determine its *total* income taxes, the corporation multiplies its taxable income by the

[4]In this chapter, we assume that Unlimited Decadence has a vending machine component, VendoBar, that it sells in 2009.

[5]It is not necessary to understand the meaning of both *results of discontinued operations* and *extraordinary items* for computing income taxes. It may be helpful, however, to read the later sections of this chapter, which deal with these items, in conjunction with the remainder of this section.

| EXHIBIT 24-1 | INCOME STATEMENT FOR UNLIMITED DECADENCE CORPORATION |

Unlimited Decadence Corporation
Income Statement
For Year Ended December 31, 2009

(in thousands)

Sales (net)		$80,000
Cost of goods sold		(51,000)
Gross profit		$29,000
Operating expenses		
Selling expenses	$14,000	
General and administrative expenses	8,000	
Total operating expenses		(22,000)
Operating income		$ 7,000
Other Items		
Gain on sale of equipment	$ 500	
Interest revenue	700	
Interest expense	(200)	
Nonoperating income		1,000
Pretax income from continuing operations		$ 8,000
Income tax expense of continuing operations		(3,200)
Income from continuing operations		$ 4,800
Results of discontinued operations		
Loss from operations of discontinued		
VendoBar component (net of $200 income tax credit)	$ (300)	
Gain on sale of discontinued VendoBar component		
(net of $600 income tax expense)	900	600
Income before extraordinary loss		$ 5,400
Extraordinary loss from tornado (net of $800		
income tax credit)		(1,200)
Net income		$ 4,200
Basic earnings per share (see Note A)		
Income from continuing operations		$ 3.16
Results of discontinued operations		0.46
Extraordinary loss from tornado		(0.92)
Basic earnings per share		$ 2.70

Labels on left: Income from Continuing Operations; Results of Discontinued Operations; Extraordinary Loss; Net Income; Earnings per Share

Notes to the Financial Statements (in part)

Note A: Preferred dividends of $690 were deducted from net income and income from continuing operations in computing earnings per share. The weighted average number of common shares outstanding is 1,300 shares.

income tax rate. Because actual income tax computations are complex, for simplicity we assume an income tax rate of 40% for all discussion and end-of-chapter homework materials. Because GAAP requires the corporation to report on its income statement the income tax expense (or income tax credit, in the case of a loss) related to each of these sections, the corporation makes a separate income tax computation for each section.

For example, in 2009, Unlimited Decadence has a pretax income from continuing operations of $8,000, a pretax loss from operations of its discontinued VendoBar component of $500, a pretax gain on the sale of its discontinued VendoBar component of $1,500, and a pretax extraordinary loss of $2,000. It computes its total income taxes and the income taxes related to each item, as we show in the following tax schedule.[6] Note that the two items of loss *reduced* the income taxes in the amounts of $200 and $800, respectively. These amounts are income tax "savings," and are called *income tax credits*.

[6]For simplicity, in this discussion and end-of-chapter homework questions, we ignore deferred income taxes. Therefore, we assume that Unlimited Decadence has no deferred tax liability.

	Pretax Amount		Income Tax Rate		Income Taxes
Pretax income from continuing operations	$8,000	×	0.40	=	$3,200
Pretax loss from operations of discontinued component	(500)	×	0.40	=	(200)
Gain (pretax) on sale of discontinued component	1,500	×	0.40	=	600
Extraordinary loss (pretax)	(2,000)	×	0.40	=	(800)
Taxable Income and IncomeTaxes	$7,000	×	0.40	=	$2,800

As we show in Exhibit 24-1, Unlimited Decadence lists the $3,200 income tax expense for continuing operations as a separate item on the income statement and deducts this amount from the $8,000 pretax income from continuing operations to determine its $4,800 income from continuing operations.

Any items that a corporation includes in the results from discontinued operations section or as extraordinary gains and losses are reported "net of income taxes." That is, for each of these items, the corporation deducts the income tax expense (or income tax credit, in the case of a loss) *directly* from each item, and reports only the *after-tax* amount in its net income. It shows the income tax expense or credit in parentheses on the income statement, however. In Exhibit 24-1, Unlimited Decadence reports the loss from operations of its discontinued VendoBar component at the after-tax amount of $300 ($500 less the income tax credit of $200 from the tax schedule), the gain on sale of its discontinued VendoBar component at $900 ($1,500 − $600), and the extraordinary loss at $1,200 ($2,000 − $800).

Results of Discontinued Operations

Many corporations, sometimes called *conglomerates*, have several major divisions (**components**) that sell different products or services. A corporation occasionally sells one of these components—called a *sale of a discontinued component*. The corporation usually sells the component because it is not making enough profit (or is operating at a loss), or because the corporation is restructuring its activities. Examples of transactions involving the sale of a component include the sale by a communications company of all its radio stations or the sale by a food distributor of its wholesale supermarket division.

5 How does a corporation report its results from discontinued operations and extraordinary items?

 When **PepsiCo** *sold its Pizza Hut restaurants, do you think the sale was reported as the sale of a discontinued component? Why or why not?*

The sale of a discontinued component is an important event for a corporation because of the effects on its future earnings potential and on the evaluation of its past earnings. For this reason, a corporation reports certain information about the sale separately on its income statement in a section often called *results of discontinued operations*. By reporting this information separately, a corporation helps external users to evaluate the continuing part of the corporation, and thereby to assess the future potential of the corporation. That is, the current (and past) performance of the discontinued component normally is not helpful in predicting how the remaining components will perform in the future. The corporation includes two items in the discontinued operations section:

1. *The income (or loss) from the operations of the discontinued component for the year.* When a corporation operates the discontinued component for part (or all) of the year before the sale of the component, it must compute the pretax income (loss) from these operations.

2. *The gain (or loss) from the sale of the discontinued component.* When the corporation sells the assets of the discontinued component, it records a gain or loss (the difference between the selling price and the book value of the assets). It computes this gain or loss in the same way that it computes the gain or loss from the sale of an individual asset, as we discussed in Chapter 21.

The corporation deducts the related income taxes from both these pretax income (loss) amounts, and reports the after-tax income (loss) amounts related to the discontinued component on its income statement. It adds together the after-tax operating income (loss) and the after-tax gain (loss) on the sale of the discontinued component in the results of discontinued operations section of the income statement. As we discussed earlier, in Exhibit 24-1 Unlimited Decadence reported two amounts related to its discontinued VendoBar component—a $300 loss (after an income tax credit of $200) from the component's operations, and a $900 gain (after income taxes of $600) from the sale of the component.

Although we do not illustrate it here, Unlimited Decadence also adjusts its comparative income statements of the previous years to report separately the amounts of income earned by the component in those years. It also separately classifies the assets and liabilities of the component on its comparative balance sheets of previous years. Separating out these amounts allows external users to evaluate the corporation's component(s) that will continue to exist separately from the component the corporation has sold.

For instance, **General Electric Company (GE)**, reported income from continuing operations of $18,275 million for 2005 and reported that it discontinued the operations of its some of its insurance businesses. Related to this discontinued operation, GE reported an operating loss of $1,540 million and a loss on the disposal of $382 million (both amounts net of tax). GE's net income was $16,353 million for 2005.

Which income amount would you use to evaluate General Electric's performance?

Extraordinary Gains and Losses

Sometimes an event or transaction causes an extraordinary gain or loss for a corporation. An **extraordinary item** is an event or transaction that is (1) *unusual in nature* and (2) *infrequent in occurrence*. Examples of events that are likely to be extraordinary items are an earthquake, a tornado, a flood, an expropriation of assets by a foreign country, and a prohibition under a newly enacted law. These may be thought of as acts of God or acts of politicians! Extraordinary items are so abnormal in regard to a corporation's current and potential earnings that GAAP requires the corporation to report the related gains or losses separately on its income statement. They are so rare that less than one percent of companies reported extraordinary items in 2005.

Do you think that earthquake damage would be an extraordinary item in California? in Florida? Why or why not?

A corporation reports extraordinary gains or losses, net of income taxes, in a separate section of its income statement, directly below the results of discontinued operations section (or if there is no such section, after income from continuing operations). In Exhibit 24-1, Unlimited Decadence reports a $1,200 extraordinary loss from a tornado (after deducting an $800 income tax credit).

Most gains and losses are *not* considered to be extraordinary. For example, the write-down of inventories and the sale of property, plant, and equipment result in ordinary gains and losses. A corporation reports these gains and losses in the nonoperating income section as "other items" and includes them in its pretax income from continuing operations.

Like discontinued operations, a corporation reports extraordinary items separately so that external users can focus on income from continuing operations as they evaluate the corporation's performance. Although an extraordinary loss has caused a loss for the shareholders, it cannot occur again and so should be treated differently by external users in their analysis.

External User Perspective: Profitability Ratio Analysis

In Chapters 6 and 7 of Volume 1, we introduced three ratios that external users use to evaluate a company's profitability: (1) profit margin, (2) return on owners' (stockholders') equity, and (3) return on total assets. In this chapter, we discussed the various sections of a company's income statement, including income from continuing operations, results of discontinued operations, and extraordinary items. As we discussed, the latter two items are "nonrecurring" and are reported below income from continuing operations. When a user evaluates a company with these ratios, the user may make adjustments in these ratios to maintain comparability across time for that company, and across companies in the industry. Let's see how to do this by using the information for Unlimited Decadence in Exhibit 24-1 for the year 2009.

The profit margin is computed by dividing net income by net sales. So, Unlimited Decadence's profit margin is 5.3% ($4,200,000 ÷ $80,000,000). However, a user who is evaluating a corporation's profitability by computing its profit margin may omit any results of discontinued operations or extraordinary items from the numerator. Then Unlimited Decadence's profit margin is 6.0% ($4,800,000 ÷ $80,000,000).

The return on stockholders' equity is computed by dividing net income by average stockholders' equity. We will assume that Unlimited Decadence's average stockholders' equity is $18,000,000 (not shown in Exhibit 24-1). So, Unlimited Decadence's return on equity is 23.3% ($4,200,000 ÷ $18,000,000). However, a user evaluating a corporation's performance by computing its return on equity may omit any results of discontinued operations or extraordinary items from the numerator. In this case, Unlimited Decadence's return on stockholders' equity is 26.7% ($4,800,000 ÷ $18,000,000).

The return on total assets is computed by dividing net income plus interest expense by average total assets. We will assume that Unlimited Decadence's average total assets are $28,000,000 *including* the $4,000,000 average net assets of the discontinued component (not shown in Exhibit 24-1). So, Unlimited Decadence's return on total assets is 15.7% [($4,200,000 net income + $200,000 interest expense) ÷ $28,000,000]. However, a user evaluating a corporation's profitability by computing its return on total assets may omit the results of the discontinued operations and extraordinary items from the net income in the numerator, as well as the net assets of the discontinued component from the average total assets in the denominator. In this case, Unlimited Decadence's return on assets is 20.8% [($4,800,000 + $200,000) ÷ $24,000,000].

These modified calculations of the profit margin, return on stockholders' equity, and return on total assets should be better measures of Unlimited Decadence's performance and better indicators of its future performance. Also, since a company reclassifies its previous years' income statements and balance sheets to separately report the results of discontinued operations, the user can recalculate the ratios for previous years to see the trends in the performance of the company's continuing operations. Of course, users should not totally ignore the results of discontinued operations, which may indicate that the company is changing strategy or that the company's managers have made poor decisions in the past in managing the component.

A user must also be careful to examine whether the operating income section of the income statement includes "non operating" income, such as losses on the impairment of property, plant, and equipment (or intangibles), or restructuring losses. Determining the amounts of these losses may require careful reading of the notes to the financial statements. For example, **Bristal-Myers Squibb** recorded charges (reductions) against income for restructuring of $32 million and $104 million, and for litigation of $269 million and $420 million in 2005 and 2004, respectively. In those two years, it also reported gains on sales of businesses of $569 million and $320 million, respectively.

EARNINGS PER SHARE

6 How does a corporation compute and report its earnings per share?

The owners (stockholders) of a corporation hold shares of stock as evidence of ownership. Because owners can readily transfer these shares, the stock of many corporations sells on organized stock markets like the New York Stock Exchange and in the "Over The Counter" market. Stockholders invest (or sell their investments) in a corporation for many reasons, including the likelihood of receiving future dividends or participating in any future increase (or decrease) in the stock market price. The corporation's current and estimated future earnings influence both these factors.

To predict a corporation's future earnings, dividends, and stock market price, investors prepare many kinds of analyses. One of the items of financial information that they use in these analyses is the corporation's *earnings per share*. Earnings per share is probably the most frequently cited information in a financial analysis of a corporation. Each corporation reports its earnings per share (abbreviated as EPS) on its income statement, directly below the net income.

Earnings per share computations can be very complicated; here we explain the computation of "basic earnings per share," and we will discuss "diluted" earnings per share later. A corporation must report both amounts on its income statement. For instance, **PepsiCo** reported basic earnings per share of $2.43 on its income statement for 2005, based on net income available for common stockholders of $4,060 million and 1,669 million average common shares, and $2.39 diluted earnings per share based on net income available for common stockholders of $4,078 million, and 1,706 million shares. **Basic earnings per share** is a corporation's net income per share available to its common stockholders. In its simplest form, a corporation computes its basic earnings per share by dividing its net income by the number of common shares outstanding during the entire year. A corporation, however, may report several components of net income and may have preferred stock outstanding that has first priority to dividends (as we discussed earlier in the chapter). It also may have shares of common stock outstanding for only part of a year because it issued common stock during the year. Therefore, a corporation computes this basic earnings per share amount as follows:

$$\frac{\text{Basic Earnings}}{\text{per Share}} = \frac{\text{Net Income} - \text{Preferred Dividends}}{\text{Weighted Average Number of Common Shares Outstanding}}$$

Net Income and Preferred Dividends

Common stockholders are the *residual* owners of the corporation. Therefore, the earnings per share amount applies *only* to common shares, and the numerator includes only the earnings available to common stockholders. If a corporation has no preferred shares outstanding, it uses net income as the numerator. If a corporation has outstanding preferred stock, however, it deducts the preferred dividends for the current period from the net income to determine the earnings available to common stockholders. To understand the computation of the numerator, assume that Unlimited Decadence (from Exhibit 24-1) had preferred stock outstanding during 2009 and that the dividends on this preferred stock amounted to $690,000. The numerator of Unlimited Decadence's 2009 earnings per share is $3,510,000, computed by subtracting the $690,000 preferred dividends from the $4,200,000 net income. We will summarize these computations later.

Weighted Average Common Shares

Since a corporation earns its net income over the entire year, it relates the earnings to the weighted average number of common shares outstanding during the year. If a corporation has not issued any common shares during the year, it uses the common shares outstanding for the entire year as the denominator. When the corporation has issued common shares during the year, it multiplies these shares by the fraction of the year (in months) that they are outstanding. It adds the result to the beginning number of shares to determine the weighted average number of common shares outstanding during the year. It uses this number as the denominator in the earnings per share calculation.

Assume Unlimited Decadence had 1,200,000 common shares outstanding during all of 2009. On August 1, 2009, it issued an additional 240,000 common shares, so that it had a total of 1,440,000 common shares outstanding at the end of the year. Its weighted average number of common shares outstanding during 2009 is 1,300,000, determined by adding 1,200,000 + 100,000 weighted average shares (240,000 $\times$ 5/12), computed as follows:

Months Shares Are Outstanding	Shares Outstanding	×	Fraction of Year Outstanding	=	Weighted Average
January–December	1,200,000		12/12		1,200,000
August–December	240,000		5/12		100,000
Total Weighted Average Common Shares					1,300,000

 If a corporation purchases treasury stock, does its weighted average number of common shares increase or decrease? Does its basic earnings per share increase or decrease?

Computation, Reporting, and Disclosure

A corporation reports its basic earnings per share on the income statement directly below net income. In addition, it reports the earnings per share related to the major components of net income. It computes the earnings per share for the income from continuing operations by subtracting the preferred dividends from the income from continuing operations and dividing the result by the weighted average common shares. It computes the earnings per share amounts for the results of discontinued operations and extraordinary items by dividing the respective amounts (disregarding the preferred dividends) by the weighted average common shares. It discloses the amount of the preferred dividends deducted from the numerator and the weighted average number of common shares used in the denominator in the notes to its financial statements.

The basic earnings per share of Unlimited Decadence for 2009 is $2.70, as we calculate in the following schedule. We also show the earnings per share for each component of the income statement. The earnings per share amounts, of course, total $2.70, and Unlimited Decadence reports them on its income statement, as we show in Exhibit 24-1. The note to Unlimited Decadence's financial statements discloses the preferred dividends and weighted average shares.

Item	Computations	EPS
Basic earnings per share	$\dfrac{\$4,200,000 - \$690,000}{1,300,000}$	= $2.70
Components:		
Income from continuing operations	$\dfrac{\$4,800,000 - \$690,000}{1,300,000}$	= $3.16
Results of discontinued operations	$\dfrac{\$600,000}{1,300,000}$	= 0.46
Extraordinary loss from tornado	$\dfrac{\$(1,200,000)}{1,300,000}$	= (0.92)
Basic earnings per share		$2.70

Diluted Earnings per Share

A corporation has a **complex capital structure** when it has issued stock options and convertible securities (bonds or preferred stock). These securities are known as **potential common shares** because they can be used by the holder to acquire common stock. Since conversion of these securities into common stock would affect the earnings available to each common stockholder, the corporation must report its diluted earnings per share in addition to basic earnings per share. **Diluted earnings per share** includes the effects of all potential common shares that would reduce earnings per share. For example, **Goodyear Tire**'s diluted earnings per share in 2005 was $1.16 per share, as compared with its basic earnings per share of $1.30 per share, a decrease of 10.8%.

We will not illustrate the computation of diluted earnings per share because it is very complex. We will, however, explain why diluted earnings per share is lower than basic earnings per share. Two types of potential common shares affect the computation of diluted earnings per share—stock options and convertible securities.

Stock options reduce earnings per share because the computation of diluted earnings per share *assumes* that the employees exercised the options at the beginning of the year to acquire common stock.[7] These additional shares would increase the denominator of the earnings per share computation. This larger denominator would result in a lower earnings per share.

Convertible securities reduce earnings per share because the computation *assumes* that each security was converted into common stock at the beginning of the year. This assumed conversion causes two changes in the earnings per share computation—an increase in both the numerator and the denominator. The denominator increases by the number of shares that would be issued due to the assumed conversion. If convertible bonds are assumed to be converted into common stock, the numerator increases because net income would be larger, since the interest expense on the bonds would not be paid. If preferred stock is assumed to be converted into common stock, the preferred dividends would not be paid and the earnings available to common stockholders would increase.

External User Analysis: Price/Earnings Ratio

Many users consider a corporation's earnings per share to be the single most useful indicator of its performance. They look at the amount of earnings per share, the change in earnings per share from the previous period, and the trend in earnings per share as important indicators of the success, or failure, of the corporation. Since one of the important results of a corporation's performance is the market price of its common stock, another important and widely used measure is the **price/earnings ratio**, which is computed as follows:

Price/Earnings Ratio = Market Price per Share ÷ Earnings per Share

The price/earnings ratio indicates how much investors are willing to pay per dollar of *current* earnings. So a higher price/earnings ratio often is thought to mean that the

---

[7]The computation assumes that the employees paid the option price (which is *lower* than the market price) to the corporation in cash, and that the corporation issued the shares of stock to the employees. Then, the computation assumes that the corporation used the cash to purchase treasury stock at the average market price which is *higher* than the option price. Given these assumptions, the corporation would have been able to purchase fewer shares than the number that it issued due to the exercise of the options. To compute diluted earnings per share, the corporation subtracts the assumed shares reacquired as treasury stock from the assumed shares issued for the stock options and adds the difference to the denominator of the basic earnings per share computation. These assumptions are made so that all corporations compute diluted earnings per share in a consistent manner.

corporation has better prospects for *future* growth. For example, at the time of the writing of this book, the following amounts were reported for selected corporations:

Company	Market Price per Share	Earnings per Share*	Price/Earnings Ratio
PepsiCo	$52.62	$2.43	41
Coca-Cola	43.60	2.04	21
Intel	27.43	1.42	19
Microsoft	26.03	1.13	23

*Amounts computed and rounded to the nearest cent

The differences in the price/earnings ratios indicate, for example, that investors believe that **PepsiCo** will experience higher growth in earnings per share than **Coca-Cola**. Therefore, they are willing to pay a higher price per dollar of current earnings for PepsiCo's stock than for Coca Cola's stock. Similarly, investors expect **Microsoft** to grow faster than **Intel**. The price/earnings ratios also show that the expectation of growth for PepsiCo is higher than those for the two computer companies. The price/earnings ratio also can be used to predict future stock prices. For example, if an investor expects that Intel will earn $2 per share in the next year and that the price/earnings ratio will not change, the stock price should be $38 ($2 × 19).

Look up in a newspaper the market price per share and the price/earnings ratio for each of the four companies listed above. Compute the earnings per share. Which amounts have changed?

BUSINESS ISSUES AND VALUES

The accounting rule that now requires a corporation to report compensation expense on its income statement based on the fair value of its stock options was controversial. Those supporting this approach argued that stock options are a part of the employees' compensation and therefore should be an expense. Those against reporting the expense argued that a corporation does *not* have an expense because it had *no cash outflow*. They argued that corporations should continue to disclose in the notes to their financial statements the effect of their stock options on their net income and earnings per share. The controversy particularly related to executive compensation—many executives like the idea of being compensated in a way that does not affect a corporation's net income! These arguments do not mean that stock options are bad—they are designed to encourage employees to make decisions that cause the market price of a corporation's stock to increase and provide a benefit to all its stockholders.

How much is Colgate-Palmolive's basic and diluted earnings per share for 2005? How much is its pro forma basic and diluted earnings per share? Which amount would you use to evaluate the company? Why? (See Appendix B.)

Earlier we gave the example of Goodyear Tire. Goodyear reported a net income in 2005 of $228 million, or $1.30 per share. Including the effect of its stock options would reduce its net income to $212 million, or $1.20 per share. So, a stock price of, say, $14.50 would be 12 times the adjusted earnings per share amount but only about 11 times the reported amount.

Look up Goodyear's price/earnings ratio in a newspaper. How is the market evaluating Microsoft?

Another issue to understand is where the stock comes from when employees exercise options. A corporation could distribute either treasury stock or authorized but unissued common stock. For instance, **Kellogg's** chooses to use treasury stock. In 2005, it paid $664 million to purchase treasury stock primarily to issue to employees who exercised stock options! The $664 million is a cash expenditure that does not affect income—it reduces cash and stockholders' equity.

When a corporation uses authorized but unissued common stock, of course it does not pay any cash. However, the issuance of additional shares reduces the ownership interests of current shareholders and also reduces earnings per share. Therefore, *if* the price/earnings ratio remains the same, the corporation's stock price would also decrease.

 Does this make sense? Explain how the corporation's stock price would decrease if the price/earnings ratio remains the same.

CASH DIVIDENDS

7 What kinds of dividends can a corporation distribute, and what are their characteristics?

Corporations often distribute cash dividends. (We will discuss another "type" of dividend later in the chapter.) A corporation's net income increases its net assets, and it records the net income in retained earnings, but the distribution of cash dividends has the opposite effect. The corporation records the distribution as a decrease in its *assets*, and it also records this decrease in retained earnings. Thus the phrase "retained earnings paid out in dividends," which some corporations use in discussing dividends, is somewhat misleading. A corporation pays cash dividends out of *cash*, and it decreases retained earnings because the payment is a return of capital to the stockholders.

A corporation must meet legal requirements and have enough cash available to pay dividends. The board of directors is responsible for setting a corporation's dividend policy. The board determines the amount and timing of the dividends, considering legal requirements, compliance with contractual agreements, and the financial well-being of the corporation. Legal requirements vary from state to state, but most states require a corporation to have a positive balance in retained earnings before it may declare dividends. In evaluating the financial well-being of the corporation, the board of directors should consider several factors including the impact of the payment of a dividend on cash, current assets, and working capital; the corporation's ability to finance expansion projects with the remaining assets; and the effect of the dividend on the stock market price per share. The payment of dividends should be in the financial long- and short-term best interests of the corporation and its stockholders.

 Explain whether you think that a corporation that reports a loss for the year would pay dividends.

A sole proprietorship or a partnership can arrange for owner withdrawals very quickly. When the owner wants to withdraw cash, the company writes a check to the owner from its checking account, the company records the withdrawal, and the owner cashes the check for personal use. In contrast, a corporation cannot distribute dividends so quickly. The corporation may have many stockholders and therefore may require extensive record keeping. As a result, the dividend process is usually spread out over a period of several weeks.

Three dates are significant for a cash dividend (or any type of dividend): (1) the date of declaration, (2) the date of record, and (3) the date of payment. For instance in December 2006, **Bristol-Myers Squibb** declared a 28¢ per-share quarterly dividend, payable on February 1, 2007, to shareholders of record on January 5, 2007.

On the **date of declaration**, the board of directors declares that a dividend will be paid to stockholders of record on a specified future date, typically about four to six weeks later. On the declaration date, the corporation becomes legally liable to pay the future dividend. At this time, the corporation determines the total amount of the dividend liability to common stockholders, as well as any dividend liability to preferred stockholders (we will discuss this later). The corporation normally declares dividends on a *per-share basis*. That is, it sets a dollar amount per common share outstanding at the time of declaration. It determines the total amount of the dividend liability by multiplying the dividends per share by the number of common shares outstanding on the date of declaration. The corporation records the liability by reducing Retained Earnings and increasing a current liability (Dividends Payable).

It takes the corporation some time to process the dividend checks, and investors need to determine whether they want to buy or sell the stock based on the dividends. Thus, the corporation needs to specify a *cut-off* date—the date of record. On the **date of record**, only investors listed as stockholders of the corporation (the stockholders of record) can participate in the dividend. The date of record usually occurs several weeks after the declaration date and several weeks before the payment date, as specified in the dividend provisions. After the date of record, the corporation begins processing the dividend checks to the stockholders of record. On the **date of payment**, the corporation mails the dividend checks. The corporation records the payment by reducing cash and eliminating the current liability.

 Explain why you might buy or sell stock between the date of declaration and the date of record.

For example, assume that on November 15, 2008, Unlimited Decadence declared a 60¢ per-share dividend on its 1,200,000 outstanding common shares. These dividends were payable on December 29, 2008, to stockholders of record as of December 15, 2008. On November 15, Unlimited Decadence recorded the declaration of the $720,000 dividends (1,200,000 × $0.60) as follows:

Assets	=	Liabilities	+	Stockholders' Equity
		Dividends Payable		Retained Earnings
		+$720,000		-$720,000

FINANCIAL STATEMENT EFFECTS

Increases current liabilities and total liabilities on *balance sheet*. Decreases retained earnings, which decreases stockholders' equity on *balance sheet*.

On December 29, 2008, Unlimited Decadence recorded the payment of the dividends as follows:

Assets	=	Liabilities	+	Stockholders' Equity
Cash		Dividends Payable		
-$720,000		-$720,000		

FINANCIAL STATEMENT EFFECTS

Decreases current assets and total assets on *balance sheet*. Decreases current liabilities and total liabilities on *balance sheet*. Decreases cash flows from financing activities on *cash flow statement*.

If a corporation's accounting period ended between the date of declaration and the date of payment, it would report the Dividends Payable account as a current liability on its balance sheet.

Cash Dividends on Preferred Stock

As we discussed earlier in the chapter, some investors consider certain stockholder rights to be more important than others. To appeal to these investors, a corporation may issue preferred stock. The rights of preferred stockholders are included on the stock certificate. The two important rights for dividends are (1) a preference as to dividends and (2) accumulation of dividends. Preferred stock may be issued with one or both of these rights.

Preference as to Dividends

Holders of preferred stock have a preference as to dividends. A **dividend preference** is a right of preferred stockholders to receive a dividend before a corporation pays a dividend to common stockholders. A corporation usually issues preferred stock with a par value and expresses the dividends as a percentage of this value. For instance, assume that a corporation has outstanding 1,000 shares of 10%, $50 par value preferred stock. The corporation must pay $5 per share ($50 par $\times$ 10%), which totals $5,000 ($5 $\times$ 1,000 shares), as dividends to preferred stockholders before it can pay *any* dividends to common stockholders.

This preference to dividends does *not* guarantee that the corporation will pay a preferred dividend in any given year, because the board of directors can decide not to pay any dividends. To protect preferred stockholders further, the corporation may include on the preferred stock certificate a provision that requires the accumulation of dividends.

 Would you purchase preferred stock without a cumulative provision? Explain why or why not.

Cumulative Preferred Stock

Stockholders are not legally entitled to receive dividends unless the corporation's board of directors has declared these dividends. If the board of directors does not declare dividends in a given year, the corporation will never be required to pay that dividend to a holder of *non*cumulative preferred stock. For this reason, corporations rarely issue noncumulative preferred stock because investors consider this feature to be a distinct disadvantage.

Most preferred stock is cumulative. The corporation must pay the holders of **cumulative preferred stock** all dividends of the current period and the accumulated *unpaid* dividends of past periods before it can pay any dividends to common stockholders. Any dividends not declared on cumulative preferred stock in a given period become **dividends in arrears**. Dividends in arrears accumulate from period to period. The dividends in arrears are *not* a liability to the corporation because no liability exists until the dividend declaration. Any dividends in arrears, however, are very important to external users, and the corporation discloses them in a note to the financial statements.

To understand dividends in arrears, assume that a corporation has 2,000 shares of 8%, $100 par value cumulative preferred stock outstanding. Each share of stock is entitled to an $8 annual dividend (8% $\times$ $100 par value). Suppose the corporation does not declare dividends in 2006 and 2007. Preferred stockholders are entitled to dividends in arrears of $16,000 (2,000 $\times$ $8) at the end of 2006 and $32,000 (2,000 $\times$ $8 $\times$ 2 years) at the end of 2007. At the end of 2008, the corporation would have to pay dividends of $48,000 (for three years) to preferred stockholders before it could pay any dividends to common stockholders.

STOCK DIVIDENDS

Occasionally a corporation may declare and distribute a *stock* dividend. A **stock dividend** is a proportional (pro rata) distribution of additional shares of a corporation's own stock to its stockholders. For instance, in 2005, **Rocky Mountain Chocolate Factory** declared a 5% stock dividend.

 As an investor, would you generally prefer to receive a cash dividend or a stock dividend? Explain why.

Note that a stock dividend is very different from a cash dividend. A stock dividend differs from a cash dividend in that the corporation does *not* distribute assets. After a

Is this rancher participating in a stock dividend?

stock dividend, each stockholder holds the same percentage of ownership in the corporation as the stockholder held prior to the distribution. For instance, assume that a corporation has 10,000 common shares outstanding, that one stockholder owns 2,000 shares, and that the corporation issues a 10% stock dividend. After the stock dividend, the corporation has 11,000 shares outstanding (10,000 $\times$ 1.10), and the stockholder now owns 2,200 (2,000 $\times$ 1.10) shares. The stockholder owns 20% of the outstanding common stock *both prior to and after* the stock dividend. What occurs, from an accounting standpoint, is a rearrangement of stockholders' equity. Total stockholders' equity of the corporation does not change, but its retained earnings decreases by the dollar amount of the dividend and its contributed capital increases by the same amount because of the additional number of shares issued. As you will see shortly, the corporation calculates the dollar amount of the stock dividend differently depending on whether the dividend is "small" or "large."

Some stockholders view stock dividends unfavorably because, when they receive a stock dividend: (1) the stockholders receive no corporate assets; (2) theoretically, the total market value of their investment does not increase because the increased number of shares is offset by a decrease in the stock market price per share due to a larger number of shares participating in the same corporate earnings; and (3) the corporation's ability to pay future cash dividends may be limited because it decreases retained earnings by the amount of the stock dividend and most states set legal dividend restrictions based on a positive balance in retained earnings.

Some stockholders, however, welcome stock dividends because (1) they see stock dividends as evidence of corporate growth and sound financial policy; (2) other investors also may look favorably on the stock dividends and purchase the stock, causing the stock market price *not* to decrease proportionally; (3) the corporation may continue to pay the same cash dividend per share, in which case stockholders will receive higher total dividends; and (4) the market price may decrease to a lower trading range (the range of prices that investors are willing to pay for stock), making the stock more attractive to additional investors.

Explain why you think making the stock attractive to additional investors would seem positive to current stockholders.

Small Stock Dividends

For reporting purposes, GAAP distinguishes between small and large stock dividends. A **small stock dividend** is 20% or less of the previously outstanding common shares.[8] A corporation may issue a small stock dividend in order to continue a pattern of dividend *distributions* to stockholders when no cash is available for a cash dividend. For a small stock dividend, GAAP assumes that the size of the dividend does not significantly affect the stock market price of the outstanding shares. Thus, the market price at which the corporation's stock is selling is considered to be the "value" of the stock issued in the stock dividend, and the corporation records the stock dividend at this price. It reduces retained earnings and increases contributed capital by an amount equal to the current market value on the date of declaration for the additional shares of the stock dividend.

To understand the reporting of a small stock dividend, assume that Crabtree Corporation declares and issues a 10% stock dividend. Before the stock dividend, Crabtree has 10,000 shares of $10 a common stock outstanding. The common stock is selling for $19 per share, so the 1,000 share (10,000 shares × 10%) stock dividend has a current market value of $19,000. The corporation records the small stock dividend by reducing Retained Earnings by $19,000, increasing Common Stock for the $10,000 par value, and increasing Additional Paid-in Capital for $9,000 ($19,000 − $10,000). Crabtree Corporation's stockholders' equity before and after the issuance of the small stock dividend is as follows:

Stockholders' Equity

	Before Stock Dividend	Change			After Stock Dividend
Contributed capital					
Common stock, $10 par, 40,000 shares authorized, 10,000 and 11,000 shares issued and outstanding	$100,000	+	$10,000	=	$110,000
Additional paid-in capital	70,000	+	9,000	=	79,000
Total contributed capital	$170,000				$189,000
Retained earnings	140,000	−	19,000	=	121,000
Total Stockholders' Equity	$310,000				$310,000

Note that the total stockholders' equity prior to and after the stock dividend is $310,000. The components have changed, with retained earnings decreasing by $19,000 and contributed capital increasing by the same amount, and with the issued shares increasing from 10,000 to 11,000.

Large Stock Dividends and Stock Splits

Sometimes the market price of a corporation's common stock increases to the point where it is not as attractive to certain investors. Many corporations believe a wide distribution of ownership increases the demand for their stock, improves their public image, and increases their product sales to their stockholders. To reduce the market price so that it falls within the trading range of most investors, a corporation may authorize a large stock dividend or a stock split.

A **large stock dividend** is greater than 20% of the previously outstanding common shares. The size of a large stock dividend is likely to cause a substantial decrease in the stock market price of the outstanding shares. Thus, the market price at which the corporation's stock is selling cannot be considered to be the "value" of the stock issued in the dividend. Therefore, a corporation does *not* record a large stock dividend at the current market price, but uses the *par* (or *stated*) value of the stock instead. For a large stock dividend, a corporation reduces retained earnings and increases contributed capital by the

---

[8]GAAP states that a small stock dividend is less than 20% or 25%. For simplicity, we use 20%.

total par value for the additional shares of the stock dividend. Therefore, although the amount of one component decreases and the amount of the other component increases, there is no change in total stockholders' equity. To illustrate a large stock dividend, we will use the same facts for Crabtree Corporation except that now we will assume that it declares and issues a 100% stock dividend. The corporation issues an additional 10,000 (10,000 × 100%) shares and records the stock dividend at the par value of $100,000 (10,000 × $10). After the dividend, the corporation has issued a total of 20,000 shares of common stock.

Stockholders' Equity

	Before Stock Dividend	Change		After Stock Dividend
Contributed capital				
Common stock, $10 par, 40,000 shares authorized, 10,000 and 20,000 shares issued and outstanding	$100,000	+ $100,000	=	$200,000
Additional paid-in capital	70,000			70,000
Total contributed capital	$170,000			$270,000
Retained earnings	140,000	− 100,000	=	40,000
Total Stockholders' Equity	$310,000			$310,000

A stockholder who previously owned 40 shares of common stock will own 80 shares after the large stock dividend. The additional number of shares participating in the same amount of corporate earnings should cause a proportional decrease in the market price per share. Like a small stock dividend, a large stock dividend has no effect on total stockholders' equity.

A stock split is similar to a large stock dividend. A **stock split** is a decrease in the par value per share of a corporation's common stock and a proportional increase in the number of shares authorized and issued. For example, on February 15, 2005, **Rocky Mountain Chocolate Factory** authorized a four-for-three stock split payable June 13, 2005 to shareholders of record on May 31, 2005. Since a stock split affects the number of authorized shares and the legal capital, each stock split must be approved by the stockholders and the state in which the corporation is incorporated.

To illustrate a stock split, we will use the same facts for Crabtree Corporation except that now we will assume that it declares a 2-for-1 stock split with a reduction to a $5 par value. After the split, the corporation has issued a total of 20,000 shares of $5 par value common stock (still a total par value of $100,000).

Stockholders' Equity

Contributed capital	
Common stock, $5 par, 80,000 shares authorized, 20,000 shares issued and outstanding	$100,000
Additional paid-in capital	70,000
Total contributed capital	$170,000
Retained earnings	140,000
Total Stockholders' Equity	$310,000

Note that no component of stockholders' equity is changed by the stock split—but the number of shares authorized and issued has doubled and the par value is half its original amount. A stockholder who previously owned 40 shares of $10 par value common stock will own 80 shares of $5 par value common stock after the stock split. The additional number of shares participating in the same amount of corporate earnings will cause a proportional decrease in the market price per share.

As an investor, explain whether you would prefer a company to issue a large stock dividend or a stock split.

COMPREHENSIVE INCOME

Many corporations report annual *comprehensive income*. Comprehensive income is a measure of a corporation's performance that includes the corporation's (1) net income (or loss) and (2) "other" comprehensive income (or loss). A corporation's other comprehensive income (or loss) includes items such as the "unrealized increase or decrease in the value of available-for-sale securities" (which we discussed in Chapter 23) and the "gain or loss from converting the financial statements of a foreign subsidiary into U.S. dollars." These items are reported net of income taxes. GAAP requires each corporation to report its comprehensive income so that external users have more complete information to evaluate the corporation's profitability, financial flexibility, and operating capability. A corporation reporting comprehensive income has the option of including a schedule adding net income and the other items of comprehensive income either on the bottom of its income statement, in a separate statement, or in its statement of changes in stockholders' equity (which we will discuss in the next section of this chapter).

To illustrate the computation of other comprehensive income, recall from Chapter 23 that Unlimited Decadence's investments in available-for-sale securities increased from $12,000 to $12,500 in 2008. Under the market value method, Unlimited Decadence would report the $500 *increase* in its Unrealized Increase in Market Value of Investments account as its other comprehensive income for 2008. Unlimited Decadence would then add its $500 other comprehensive income to its net income, and report the total combined amount as its comprehensive income for 2008. A corporation reports the *accumulated* other comprehensive income as a separate component in the stockholders' equity section of its balance sheet. We illustrated this disclosure in Chapter 23 for the $500 *balance* of Unlimited Decadence's Unrealized Increase in Market Value of Investments account at the end of 2008.

STATEMENT OF CHANGES IN STOCKHOLDERS' EQUITY

8 How and why does a corporation report the changes in its stockholders' equity?

As you can see from the discussion in this chapter, in a single accounting period a corporation may have many transactions affecting its contributed capital. In addition, a corporation increases retained earnings by the net income and decreases it by the dividends of the accounting period. External users are interested in the changes in a corporation's stockholders' equity because these changes may have an impact on the corporation's *risk* and *financial flexibility*. To disclose its stockholders' equity activities, each corporation reports the changes in the different classes of capital stock (including the number of shares issued), in each additional paid-in capital account, in treasury stock, and in retained earnings for the accounting period.[9] Most corporations report this information on a statement of changes in stockholders' equity. A **statement of changes in stockholders' equity** is a supporting schedule to the stockholders' equity section of the balance sheet.[10]

We show the statement of changes in stockholders' equity (and the reported ending stockholders' equity) of Barth Corporation in Exhibit 24-2, using assumed amounts. In the top part of Exhibit 24-2 we list the stockholders' equity account titles across the top of the schedule, and we list the beginning balances in the respective columns. Then we briefly explain each of the transactions that affected the components of stockholders' equity in the explanation column. We include the shares issued and dollar amounts under the appropriate column. For instance, the second line indicates that the corporation

---

[9]As we discussed in the previous section, a corporation may also report its comprehensive income in this statement.

[10]When a corporation has not issued or reacquired any capital stock during the accounting period, it may choose to prepare a statement of retained earnings. A **statement of retained earnings** is a schedule that starts with the beginning balance in retained earnings, adds the amount of net income, and subtracts the amount of dividends to determine the ending balance of retained earnings. This schedule is similar to the schedule of changes in owner's equity for a sole proprietorship (see Exhibit 6-5) as well as the retained earnings column of Exhibit 24-2, and we do not illustrate it here.

EXHIBIT 24-2	REPORTING CHANGES IN STOCKHOLDERS' EQUITY AND ENDING STOCKHOLDERS' EQUITY

BARTH CORPORATION
Statement of Changes in Stockholders' Equity
Schedule A
For Year Ended December 31, 2008

| | Common Stock | | Additional | | |
Explanation	Shares Issued	$10 Par Value	Paid-in Capital	Retained Earnings	Treasury Stock
Balances, 1/1/2008	6,000	$60,000	$26,000	$67,000	$(4,500)
Issued for cash	1,000	10,000	8,000		
Reissued treasury stock					
(100 shares at $17, cost $15)			200		1,500
Net income				49,000	
Dividends (cash)				(20,000)	
Balances, 12/31/2008	7,000 (1)	$70,000 (2)	$34,200 (3)	$96,000 (4)	$(3,000) (5)

BARTH CORPORATION
Stockholders' Equity
December 31, 2008
(see Schedule A)

Contributed Capital
   Common stock, $10 par, 30,000 shares authorized,
      7,000 shares issued (1), 6,800 shares outstanding $70,000 (2)
     Additional paid-in capital   34,200 (3)

     Total contributed capital $104,200
Retained earnings   96,000 (4)

     Total contributed capital and retained earnings $200,200
Less: Treasury stock (200 shares at a cost of $15 per share)   (3,000) (5)

Total Stockholders' Equity $197,200

---

allocated the $18,000 cash received from issuing 1,000 shares of common stock as follows: $10,000 to the Common Stock account and $8,000 to Additional Paid-in Capital. Note that we list the amounts in the treasury stock column in parentheses because treasury stock is a negative component of stockholders' equity. We then total the columns, and include the column headings and totals in the stockholders' equity section of the balance sheet, as we show in the bottom part of Exhibit 24-2. Note that the items and amounts listed in stockholders' equity (which we have numbered 1 through 5 for clarity) correspond to the columns and totals in the statement of changes in stockholders' equity.

HOW CAPITAL STOCK TRANSACTIONS AFFECT THE CASH FLOW STATEMENT

A corporation generally reports capital stock transactions involving cash in the financing activities section of its cash flow statement. It reports the cash collected from the sale of stock (including sales to employees for stock options) and from the reissuance of treasury stock as cash inflows from financing activities. It reports the cash paid to acquire treasury stock and paid for cash dividends as cash outflows for financing activities.

 Why do you think a dividend that a corporation paid is a cash flow from a financing activity whereas a dividend that it received is a cash flow from an operating activity?

A corporation reports the cash flows from its income from continuing operations in the operating activities section of its cash flow statement, using either the direct or the indirect method, as we discussed in Chapter 8 of Volume 1. On the other hand, the corporation reports any cash it received from the disposal of a discontinued component as a cash inflow from investing activities because it involves the sale of property, plant, and equipment (as well as other assets). A corporation also reports any cash it received (or paid) from an extraordinary item relating to a noncurrent asset as a cash inflow (outflow) from investing activities.

Although not affecting cash, the noncash issuance of stock (e.g., issuance of stock for land) increases both a corporation's assets (an investing activity) and its stockholders' equity (a financing activity). Similarly, the conversion of preferred stock to common stock both increases and decreases a corporation's stockholders' equity (both are financing activities). A corporation discloses these types of transactions in a note accompanying its financial statements. The corporation does not disclose the issuance of a stock dividend or a stock split in this way because neither is considered by GAAP to be a financing activity.

SUMMARY

At the beginning of the chapter we asked you several questions. During the chapter, we asked you to STOP and answer some additional questions to build your knowledge about specific issues. Be sure you answered these additional questions. Below are the questions from the beginning of the chapter, with a brief summary of the key points relating to the answers. Use your creative and critical thinking skills to expand on these key points to develop more complete answers to the questions and to determine what other questions you have that might lead you to learn more about the issues.

1 What are the rights of a corporation's stockholders?

A corporation's stockholders may have the following rights: (1) the right to attend stockholders' meetings and to vote in setting and approving major policies and actions of the corporation; (2) the right to vote in the election of the board of directors; (3) the right to share in net income by receiving dividends from the corporation; (4) the right to purchase additional capital stock if it is issued—a right known as the *preemptive right;* and (5) the right to share in the distribution of the assets of the corporation if it is liquidated (terminated).

2 What is important for an external user to know about a corporation's capital stock transactions?

It is important for an external user to understand the difference between authorized capital stock and issued capital stock. Authorized capital stock is the number of shares of capital stock (both common and preferred) that the corporation may legally issue. On the other hand, issued capital stock is the number of shares of capital stock that a corporation has legally issued to its stockholders as of the balance sheet date. A corporation may issue common stock for cash, in noncash exchanges, and in other transactions. A corporation may issue common stock with a par value, as no-par stock with a stated value, or as true no-par stock. In most cases a corporation issues common stock for cash, at a price above the par value. When a corporation issues common stock for assets other than cash, or for services performed, it must use a correct value to record the transaction. The general rule is to record the transaction at the market value of the stock issued or the assets received (or services performed), whichever is more reliable.

3 What are the characteristics of a corporation's treasury stock, and how does it record and report this stock?

Treasury stock is a corporation's own capital stock that (1) stockholders fully paid for and the corporation issued, (2) the corporation later reacquired, and (3) the corporation currently holds. External users need to understand several features about treasury stock. Treasury stock is not an asset of the corporation. A corporation cannot report a gain or a loss from reacquiring its own stock; this restricts a corporation from influencing its net income. Consequently, a corporation reports treasury stock as a reduction of stockholders' equity. Treasury stock generally does not have voting or preemptive rights, cannot participate in dividends, and has no rights at liquidation. When a corporation reacquires its capital stock, it records the cost as an increase in a Treasury Stock account (which reduces stockholders' equity) and a decrease in Cash. On its balance sheet, the corporation deducts the cost of the treasury stock from the total of contributed capital and retained earnings. A corporation may reissue treasury stock at a price above, below, or equal to its cost. The corporation records the reissuance by reducing the Treasury Stock account for the cost of the shares reissued, and treats the difference between the cash received and this cost as an adjustment of Additional Paid-in Capital. If it receives more (less) cash than the cost of the reissued treasury stock, it records the excess as an increase (decrease) in Additional Paid-in Capital.

4 What are compensatory stock options, and how does a corporation report them?

A corporation's compensatory stock options are intended to provide additional compensation to its employees (sometimes a select group of employees, such as the top managers). Under a compensatory stock-option plan, employees, in exchange for their services, receive the option to buy shares of the corporation's common stock at a fixed price for a certain period of time. In addition to providing compensation, stock options are designed to encourage employees to make decisions that will increase the price of the stock and thereby provide a benefit to all stockholders. The corporation that issues compensatory stock options reports an expense on its income statement based on the fair value of the stock options on the date of grant. The corporation records compensation expense and increases additional paid-in capital by allocating the total compensation cost (the fair value) to each year of the service period using the straight-line method. This reduces the corporation's net income in each year of the service period and provides a more relevant picture of its profitability. When an employee exercises a stock option, the corporation increases its cash and contributed capital for the amount paid by the employee.

5 How does a corporation report its results from discontinued operations and extraordinary items?

Many corporations have several major divisions (components) that sell different products or services. A corporation occasionally sells one of these components—a sale of a discontinued component. The corporation reports certain information about the sale separately on its income statement in a section called results of discontinued operations. The results of discontinued operations section includes two items: (1) the income (or loss) from the operations of the discontinued component for the year and (2) the gain (or loss) from the sale of the discontinued component. The corporation deducts the related income taxes from both these pretax income (loss) amounts, and reports the after-tax income (loss) amounts related to the discontinued component in the results of discontinued operations section. The corporation also reclassifies its comparative income statements of previous periods to report separately the amounts of income generated by the component in those periods. It also separately classifies the assets and liabilities of the component on its comparative balance sheets of previous years.

An extraordinary item is an event or transaction that is (1) unusual in nature and (2) infrequent in occurrence. These extraordinary items are so abnormal in regard to a corporation's current and potential earnings that GAAP requires the corporation to report the related gains or losses separately on its income statement. A corporation reports extraordinary gains or losses, net of income taxes, in a separate section of its income statement, directly below the results of discontinued operations section.

6 How does a corporation compute and report its earnings per share?

Earnings per share is a corporation's net income per share available to its common stockholders. A corporation computes its basic earnings per share amount as follows:

$$\text{Basic Earnings per Share} = \frac{\text{Net Income} - \text{Preferred Dividends}}{\text{Weighted Average Number of Common Shares Outstanding}}$$

If a corporation has not issued any common shares during the year, it uses the common shares outstanding for the entire year as the denominator. When the corporation has issued common shares during the year, it uses the weighted average number of common shares outstanding during the year as the denominator. It reports basic earnings per share on the income statement directly below net income. In addition, it reports the earnings per share related to the major components of net income. It discloses the amount of the preferred dividends deducted from the numerator and the weighted average number of common shares used in computing earnings per share in a note to its financial statements.

A corporation has a complex capital structure when it has issued stock options and convertible securities (bonds or preferred stock). These securities are known as potential common shares because they can be used by the holder to acquire common stock. Since conversion of these securities into common stock would affect the earnings available to each common stockholder, the corporation must report its diluted earnings per share amount that includes the effects of all potential common shares that would reduce earnings per share. Two types of potential common shares affect the computation of diluted earnings per share—stock options and convertible securities.

7 What kinds of dividends can a corporation distribute, and what are their characteristics?

A corporation may distribute cash dividends, but must meet legal requirements and have enough cash available in order to pay dividends. Three dates are significant for a cash dividend (or any type of dividend): (1) the date of declaration, (2) the date of record, and (3) the date of payment. On the date of declaration, the board of directors formally declares that a dividend will be paid to stockholders of record on a specified future date, typically four to six weeks later. On the declaration date, the corporation becomes legally liable to pay the future dividend. The corporation records the liability by reducing Retained Earnings and increasing a current liability (Dividends Payable). Only investors listed as stockholders of the corporation (the stockholders of record) on the date of record can participate in the dividend. On the date of payment, the corporation mails the dividend checks and records the payment by reducing cash and eliminating the current liability.

Holders of preferred stock have a preference as to dividends. A dividend preference is a right of preferred stockholders to receive a dividend before a corporation may pay a dividend to common stockholders. This preference to dividends does not guarantee that the corporation will pay a preferred dividend in any given year, because the board of directors can decide not to pay any dividends. To protect preferred stockholders further, the corporation may include on the preferred stock certificate a provision that requires the accumulation of dividends. The corporation must pay the holders of cumulative preferred stock all dividends of the current and past periods before it can pay any dividends to common stockholders. Any dividends not declared on cumulative preferred stock in a given period become dividends in arrears. The dividends in arrears are not a liability to the corporation because no liability exists until the dividend declaration.

A stock dividend is a proportional (pro rata) distribution of additional shares of a corporation's own stock to its stockholders. For reporting purposes, GAAP distinguishes between a small and a large stock dividend. A small stock dividend is 20% or less of the previously outstanding common shares. A corporation records a small stock dividend at the current market value of the stock on the date of declaration. A large stock dividend is greater than 20% of the previously outstanding common shares. A corporation records a large stock dividend at the par (or stated) value of the stock. A stock split is similar to a large stock dividend. A stock split is a decrease in the par value per share of a corporation's common stock and a proportional increase in the number of shares authorized and issued.

8 How and why does a corporation report the changes in its stockholders' equity?

A corporation reports the effects of changes in its stockholders' equity in a statement of changes in stockholders' equity, which is a supporting schedule to the stockholders' equity section of the balance sheet. External users are interested in the changes in a corporation's stockholders' equity because these changes may have an impact on the corporation's risk and financial flexibility. To disclose its stockholders' equity activities, the corporation reports the changes in its different classes of capital stock (including the number of shares issued), in each additional paid-in capital account, in treasury stock, and in retained earnings (net income and dividends) for the accounting period in its statement of changes in stockholders' equity.

KEY TERMS

additional paid-in capital *(p. 855)*
authorized capital stock *(p. 856)*
basic earnings per share *(p. 870)*
board of directors *(p. 853)*
callable preferred stock *(p. 858)*
capital stock *(p. 853)*
common stock *(p. 855)*
compensatory stock options *(p. 862)*
complex capital structure *(p. 872)*
component *(p. 867)*
contributed capital *(p. 853)*
convertible preferred stock *(p. 858)*
cumulative preferred stock *(p. 876)*
date of declaration *(p. 874)*
date of payment *(p. 875)*
date of record *(p. 875)*
diluted earnings per share *(p. 872)*
dividend preference *(p. 876)*
dividends in arrears *(p. 876)*
extraordinary item *(p. 868)*
issued capital stock *(p. 856)*
large stock dividend *(p. 878)*

legal capital *(p. 854)*
no-par capital stock *(p. 854)*
outstanding capital stock *(p. 860)*
par value *(p. 854)*
potential common shares *(p. 872)*
preemptive right *(p. 854)*
preferred stock *(p. 855)*
price/earnings ratio *(p. 872)*
redeemable *(p. 859)*
retained earnings *(p. 853)*
small stock dividend *(p. 878)*
stated value *(p. 854)*
statement of changes in stockholders'
   equity *(p. 880)*
statement of retained earnings *(p. 880)*
stock certificate *(p. 853)*
stock dividend *(p. 876)*
stock split *(p. 879)*
stockholders' equity *(p. 853)*
stockholders or shareholders *(p. 853)*
treasury stock *(p. 860)*

SUMMARY SURFING

Here is an opportunity to gather information on the Internet about real-world issues related to the topics in this chapter (for suggestions on how to navigate various companies' Web sites to find their financial statements and other information, see the related discussion in the Preface at the beginning of the book).

- Go to the **Intel Corporation** Web site. How much was Intel's basic and diluted earnings per share for the most recent year reported? How do there compare to the previous year?

- Go to the **ExxonMobil Corporation** Web site. How many stock options did Exxon grant during the most recent year? How many stock options (shares) were outstanding at the end of the year? What is the average exercise price of the stock options? How many stock options are exercisable at the end of the year?

INTEGRATED BUSINESS AND ACCOUNTING SITUATIONS

Answer the Following Questions in Your Own Words.

Testing Your Knowledge

24-1   What are the two parts of stockholders' equity, and what is included in each part?

24-2   List the basic rights of a stockholder. Which right do you consider to be the most important?

24-3   What is legal capital? How does a corporation determine the total legal capital when its capital stock has a par value?

24-4   What is the difference between common stock and preferred stock?

24-5   What is the meaning of the following terms: (a) authorized capital stock, (b) issued capital stock, (c) outstanding capital stock, and (d) treasury stock? What is the difference between issued capital stock and outstanding capital stock?

24-6   If a corporation issues common stock for an asset other than cash, what amount does it use to record the transaction?

24-7   What is convertible preferred stock? How does the conversion of preferred stock to common stock affect a corporation's contributed capital?

24-8   What are callable preferred stock and redeemable preferred stock?

24-9   What is treasury stock? Why might a corporation acquire treasury stock?

24-10 How does a corporation report treasury stock on its balance sheet? What is the effect of the acquisition of treasury stock on the corporation's basic earnings per share?

24-11 What are the major sections (and items in each section) of a corporation's income statement?

24-12 How does a corporation report total income tax expense on its income statement?

24-13 What information for the sale of a discontinued component does a corporation report on its income statement, and where does it report it?

24-14 What is an extraordinary item? Where and how does a corporation report gains or losses from extraordinary items on its income statement?

24-15 How is basic earnings per share computed? Where and how does a corporation report this amount on its income statement?

24-16 What are the three dates of importance regarding dividends?

24-17 Define the following terms regarding preferred stock: (a) dividend preference, (b) cumulative, and (c) dividends in arrears.

24-18 What is a stock dividend? Distinguish between a small and a large stock dividend, and explain what accounts a corporation uses to record the declaration of each dividend.

24-19 How are a stock split and a large stock dividend alike? How are they different?

24-20 What is a statement of changes in stockholders' equity? What changes in specific accounts does a corporation report on this statement?

24-21 How does a corporation report the effect of its capital stock transactions on its cash flow statement?

Applying Your Knowledge

24-22 On January 8, 2008, Ryland Carpet Corporation is incorporated and is authorized to issue 20,000 shares of $7 par value common stock. On January 9, 2008, it issues 1,000 shares at $12 per share, and on July 3, 2008, it issues another 800 shares at $15 per share.

Required: (1) Record the two issuances of common stock for Ryland.
(2) Prepare the contributed capital section of Ryland's December 31, 2008 balance sheet.

24-23 On January 3, 2008, Mark Razor Corporation is incorporated and is authorized to issue 2,000 shares of $100 par value preferred stock and 25,000 shares of $3 par value common stock. During 2008, Mark issues 900 shares of preferred stock for $112 per share and 9,000 shares of common stock for $17 per share.

Required: (1) Record the two issuances of capital stock for Mark.
(2) Prepare the contributed capital section of Mark's December 31, 2008 balance sheet.

24-24 Antley Company issued 200 shares of $10 par value common stock in exchange for five acres of land.

Required: Record the acquisition of the land for each of the following independent situations: (a) the common stock is currently selling on the stock market for $80 per share and (b) the land is appraised at $15,000, but the common stock is not actively traded in the stock market.

24-25 Thompson Corporation is authorized to issue 60,000 shares of $5 par value common stock and 3,000 shares of $100 par value preferred stock. During the current period it engages in the following transactions:
(a) Sells 10,000 shares of common stock for $13 per share
(b) Sells 1,000 shares of preferred stock for $123 per share
(c) Acquires a building by paying $12,000 cash and issuing 5,000 shares of common stock and 500 shares of preferred stock. The common stock is currently selling for $15 per share; the preferred stock is selling for $125 per share. No reliable appraisal value is available for the building.

Required: (1) Record the preceding transactions for Thompson.
            (2) How would your answer to (c) change if the building was appraised at $151,000? Why?

24-26 The community of Happy Rock donated land to Jipem Window Corporation for the site of a new factory. The land was reliably appraised at $18,000.

Required: Explain how Jipem should record, if at all, the receipt of the land.

24-27 At incorporation, Gasser Furnace Corporation issued 75 shares of $100 par value preferred stock for $108 per share and 2,000 shares of $10 par value common stock for $36 per share. Each share of preferred stock was convertible into four shares of the common stock. One year later, the preferred stockholders elected to exercise the conversion option on 50 shares of preferred stock.

Required: (1) Prepare the contributed capital section of Gasser's balance sheet at the time of incorporation.
            (2) Prepare the contributed capital section of Gasser's balance sheet immediately after the conversion.
            (3) Explain the change in total contributed capital.

24-28 On January 1, Amitroy Company had 20,000 shares of $5 par value common stock outstanding. The shares were originally issued at a price of $12 per share. During the year, the following stock transactions occurred:

    March 4: The company reacquired 2,000 shares of its common stock at a cost of $12 per share.
    April 5: The company sold 1,000 shares of the treasury stock for $14 per share.
    July 9: The company sold the remaining 1,000 shares of the treasury stock for $11 per share.

Required: (1) Record all the preceding transactions in one set of accounts for Amitroy.
            (2) What is the final net effect on the accounts after these transactions are recorded? Why?

24-29 On January 1, 2008, Rollo Awning Corporation had 8,000 shares of $10 par value common stock outstanding. These shares were originally issued at $25 per share. During 2008, Rollo entered into the following transactions:
(a) Reacquired 2,500 shares of its common stock for $26 per share
(b) Sold 1,250 shares of the treasury stock for $28 per share
(c) Sold 750 shares of the treasury stock for $23 per share

Required: (1) Record all the preceding stock transactions in one set of accounts for Rollo.

(2) Prepare the stockholders' equity section of Rollo's balance sheet at December 31, 2008 (assume that 30,000 shares are authorized and that retained earnings is $40,000).

24-30   The following is a list of selected accounts and ending account balances taken from the accounting records of Dean Company on December 31, 2008:

Account Title	Amount
Additional paid-in capital on preferred stock	$11,000
Common stock	80,000
Preferred stock	50,000
Treasury stock	6,000
Retained earnings	90,000
Additional paid-in capital on common stock	33,000

Additional information:
(a) Preferred stock has a $100 par value; 1,000 shares are authorized.
(b) Common stock has a $10 par value; 10,000 shares are authorized, 8,000 shares have been issued, and 7,500 shares are outstanding.
(c) During 2008, Dean reacquired 1,500 shares of common stock at $12 per share; 1,000 shares were reissued at $13 per share.

Required: (1) Prepare the stockholders' equity section of the December 31, 2008 balance sheet for Dean Company.
(2) At what average price were the outstanding shares of preferred stock issued?
(3) At what average price were the 8,000 shares of common stock issued?

24-31   The following information is available for Teresa Textile Corporation for the year ended December 31, 2008: (1) pretax income from continuing operations, $29,000; (2) loss from operations of discontinued component B (pretax), $6,500; (3) extraordinary gain (pretax), $4,200; and (4) loss on sale of discontinued component B (pretax), $5,000. The corporation is subject to a 40% income tax rate. It had no preferred stock outstanding, and 6,000 shares of common stock were outstanding during all of 2008.

Required: Prepare the lower portion of Teresa Textile Corporation's 2008 income statement, starting with pretax income from continuing operations.

24-32   At the beginning of 2008, Deavels Corporation had 1,000 shares of 9%, $100 par value preferred stock and 16,500 shares of common stock outstanding. On June 1, Deavels issued 3,000 additional shares of common stock. On December 31, 2008, Deavels reported net income of $47,105, paid dividends for 2008 on the preferred stock, and paid a $1 per-share dividend on each share of common stock outstanding.

Required: Compute the basic earnings per share of Deavels Corporation for 2008.

24-33   The records of Stringer Cable Corporation show the following *pretax* items on December 31, 2008:

Cost of goods sold	$42,000
Extraordinary loss from tornado	1,500
General and administrative expenses	8,000
Interest revenue	700
Sales	88,000
Interest expense	200
Gain on sale of discontinued component R	1,000
Selling expenses	13,000
Loss from operations of discontinued component R	3,000

Additional information:
(a) There were 2,000 shares of common stock outstanding on January 1, 2008. On July 1, 2008, the corporation issued 4,000 additional shares of common stock.
(b) The corporation paid dividends for the current year on 200 shares of 8%, $100 par value preferred stock outstanding. No dividends were paid to common stockholders.

(c) The corporation is subject to a 40% income tax rate.

Required: Prepare the income statement of Stringer Cable Corporation for 2008.

24-34 The records of the Lundgren Chemicals Corporation show the following *pretax* items on December 31, 2008:

Cost of goods sold	$ 65,000
Extraordinary loss from flood	2,250
General and administrative expenses	12,000
Interest revenue	700
Interest expense	300
Loss on sale of discontinued component Q	250
Income from operations of discontinued component Q	800
Selling expenses	23,000
Sales	129,400

Additional information:

(a) There were 3,000 shares of common stock outstanding on January 1, 2008. On July 1, 2008, the corporation issued 6,000 common shares.

(b) The corporation paid dividends for the current year on 500 shares of 7%, $100 par preferred stock outstanding. Dividends of $6,000 were paid on common stock.

(c) The corporation is subject to a 40% income tax rate.

Required: Prepare the income statement of Lundgren Chemicals Corporation for 2008.

24-35 On October 1, Sewel Corporation declares a cash dividend on its 1,600 outstanding shares of 9%, $100 par value preferred stock. These dividends are payable on December 2, to stockholders of record as of November 15. On November 1, the company declares a $1.05 per-share cash dividend on its 9,000 outstanding shares of common stock. These dividends are payable on December 16, to stockholders of record as of November 30.

Required: Prepare entries for Sewel Corporation to record the declaration and payment of each dividend.

24-36 The stockholders' equity section of the January 1, 2008 balance sheet for Turner Tennis Corporation follows:

Contributed capital	
Common stock, $10 par, 60,000 shares authorized,	
30,000 shares issued and outstanding	$300,000
Additional paid-in capital	100,000
Total contributed capital	$400,000
Retained earnings	325,000
Total Stockholders' Equity	$725,000

Early in 2008, the corporation declared and issued a 15% stock dividend. On the date of declaration, the common stock was selling for $16 per share.

Required: (1) Prepare the stockholders' equity section of Turner's balance sheet after the issuance of the stock dividend.

(2) Explain the change(s) in the stockholders' equity section.

24-37 The stockholders' equity accounts of Quiser Corporation on January 1, 2008 were as follows:

Preferred stock, 8%, $100 par (5,000 shares authorized)	$100,000
Additional paid-in capital on preferred stock	12,000
Common stock, $10 par (80,000 shares authorized)	200,000
Additional paid-in capital on common stock	37,000
Retained earnings	172,000
	$521,000

During 2008, the company entered into the capital stock transactions on the following page.

Date	Transaction
May 15	Declared a 15% stock dividend on the common stock outstanding. The stock is to be distributed on June 28. The common stock is currently selling for $18 per share.
June 28	Issued the stock dividend declared on May 15.
Nov. 1	Declared the annual cash dividend on the outstanding preferred stock and a $1.20 annual cash dividend on the outstanding common stock. These dividends are to be paid on December 15.
Dec. 15	Paid the cash dividends declared on November 1.

Required: (1) Prepare entries to record the preceding transactions for Quiser.
(2) Prepare the stockholders' equity section of the December 31, 2008 balance sheet for Quiser (assume that 2008 net income was $121,000).
(3) Compute Quiser's return on stockholders' equity for 2008.

24-38 The Fife Office Equipment Corporation is authorized to issue 1,000 shares of 8%, $100 par value preferred stock and 20,000 shares of $10 par value common stock. The December 31, 2007 stockholders' equity accounts showed the following balances:

Common stock, $10 par	$ 80,000
Additional paid-in capital on common stock	61,000
Retained earnings	78,000
	$219,000

During 2008, the corporation engaged in the following capital stock transactions:

Date	Transaction
Jan. 3	Issued 250 shares of preferred stock at $104 per share
Mar. 1	Issued 3,000 shares of common stock for land. The common stock is selling at $22 per share.
Sept. 30	Reacquired 500 shares of common stock at $23 per share.
Nov. 1	Declared the 8% dividend on the outstanding preferred stock and a $1 per-share dividend on the outstanding common stock, to be paid on December 16.
Dec. 16	Paid the dividends on the preferred stock and common stock.

In addition, during 2008 the company earned net income of $46,000.

Required: (1) Prepare Fife's statement of changes in stockholders' equity for the year ended December 31, 2008.
(2) Prepare the stockholders' equity section of Fife's December 31, 2008 balance sheet.
(3) Compute Fife's return on stockholders' equity for 2008.

24-39 During 2008, Herley Transport Corporation entered into the following long-term debt and capital stock transactions:
(a) Issued 5,000 shares of common stock for $18 per share
(b) Issued 1,000 shares of preferred stock for $110 per share
(c) Reacquired 1,000 shares of common stock for $19 per share
(d) Issued long-term bonds for $100,000
(e) Paid interest of $10,000 on long-term bonds
(f) Paid dividends of $16,000 on preferred stock
(g) Paid dividends of $34,000 on common stock

Required: Show how Herley would report the preceding transactions on its 2008 cash flow statement (assuming it uses the direct method for reporting cash flows from operating activities).

Making Evaluations

24-40 At the beginning of the current year, Blong Chocolate Corporation issued common stock in exchange for equipment. The president of the company has asked your advice. He states, "I don't know how the company should record this transaction. However, even if the company recorded the transaction at too high or too low a price, it should not make any difference. This transaction does not affect net income for the current accounting period because it does not involve a revenue or expense account. Furthermore, since it occurs during the current accounting period, the future financial statements of the company will not be affected."

Required: Prepare a written evaluation of the president's comments. Include a suggestion for recording the transaction.

24-41 At the beginning of 2008, Zing Corporation reacquired 500 shares of its own common stock for $20 per share. During 2008 it reissued 200 of these treasury shares for $25 per share. As of December 31, 2008, the company had not yet reissued the remaining treasury stock.

    The president of Zing Corporation has suggested that the 300 shares of treasury stock be shown as an asset on the corporation's December 31, 2008 balance sheet and that the $1,000 "gain" be shown on the income statement. He also feels the treasury stock should be considered as outstanding shares and should not be distinguished from common stock issued.

Required: (1) Explain what treasury stock is.
           (2) Explain why a corporation might acquire treasury stock.
           (3) What is outstanding common stock? What is the difference between issued common stock and outstanding common stock?
           (4) Identify how the president of Zing Corporation arrived at the $1,000 gain. Explain whether you agree that treasury stock should be shown as an asset and that the gain be shown on the income statement.

24-42 In its 2005 annual report, **Best Buy** disclosed the following:

In January 2002, we sold convertible subordinated debentures having an aggregate principal amount of $402 million. The proceeds from the offering, net of $6 million in offering expenses, were $396 million. The debentures mature in 2022 and are callable at par, at our option, for cash on or after January 15, 2007. Holders may require us to purchase all or a portion of their debentures on January 15, 2007; January 15, 2012; and January 15, 2017, at a purchase price equal to 100% of the principal amount of the debentures plus accrued and unpaid interest up to but not including the date of purchase. We have the option to settle the purchase price in cash, stock, or a combination of cash and stock. Since holders may require us to purchase all or a portion of their debentures on January 15, 2007, we have classified our convertible subordinated debentures in the current portion of long-term debt at February 25, 2006. The debentures will be convertible into shares of our common stock at a conversion rate of 21.7391 shares per $0.001 principal amount of debentures, equivalent to an initial conversion price of $46.00 per share, if the closing price of our common stock exceeds a specified price for 20 consecutive trading days in a 30-trading day period preceding the date of conversion, if our credit rating falls below specified levels, if the debentures are called for redemption or if certain specified corporate transactions occur. At February 25, 2006, none of the criteria for conversion had been met. Since March 31, 2006, our closing stock price has exceeded the specified stock price for more than 20 days, therefore, holders currently have the option to convert their debentures into our common stock. As of May 9, 2006, no debentures had been converted to shares of our common stock. The debentures have an initial interest rate of 2.25% per annum. The interest rate may be reset, but not below 2.25% or above 3.25%, on July 15, 2006; July 15, 2011; and July 15, 2016.

Required: Write an owner of the debentures (bonds) a short memo explaining the alternatives that may arise.

24-43 **Starbucks** disclosed the following (partial) information about its compensatory stock options in its fiscal 2006 annual report:

	Number of Shares	Weighted Average Exercise Price per Share
Options outstanding, 10/2/05	72,458,906	$13.22
Options granted	13,357,095	30.52
Options exercised	(13,222,729)	9.02
Options cancelled	(3,173,401)	24.51
Options outstanding, 10/1/06	69,419,871	16.83
Options exercisable at 10/1/06	49,203,321	12.56

Starbucks also reported the following amounts in its fiscal 2006 annual report (all amounts in thousands except earnings per share amounts):

Earnings before income taxes	$ 906,243
Income taxes	(324,770)
Net income	$ 581,473
Basic earnings per share	$ 0.76
Diluted earnings per share	$ 0.73
Weighted average number of shares outstanding	766,114
Weighted average number of shares used to compute diluted earnings per share	799,556
Expense for stock options (pretax)	$ 105,000
Proceeds from issuance of common stock	$ 159,249
Repurchase of common stock	$(845,045)

The company does not report any treasury stock on its balance sheet. Assume that the issuance and repurchase of common stock relate to stock options and that the fiscal 2006 year-end stock price was $38 per share.

Required: (1) Explain the effects of the compensatory stock options on Starbucks' fiscal 2006 financial statements.

(2) What is the opportunity cost to Starbucks of the options exercised during fiscal 2006 (assume they were exercised at the end of fiscal 2006)?

(3) How much would the benefit be to the employees if they exercised their options at year-end?

(4) If all the exercisable options at the end of fiscal 2006 were exercised, what would be the effect on Starbucks' fiscal 2006 earnings per share? Assume that the exercise occurs at the beginning of fiscal 2006.

(5) If all the options were exercised, what would be the effect on Starbucks' fiscal 2006 earnings per share? Assume that the exercise occurs at the beginning of fiscal 2006.

(6) Explain which earnings per share amount you would use to evaluate Starbucks.

(7) Is the expense for stock options material?

24-44 **Cisco** reported the following amounts in its fiscal 2006 annual report (all amounts in millions except earnings per share amounts):

Income before income taxes	$ 7,633
Income tax expense	(2,053)
Net income	$ 5,580
Basic earnings per share	$ 0.91
Diluted earnings per share	$ 0.89
Weighted average number of shares outstanding	6,158
Weighted average number of shares used to compute diluted earnings per share	6,272

Options outstanding, 7/29/06	1,446
Expense for stock options (pretax)	$ 1,050
Repurchase of common stock	$(8,295)
Issuance of common stock	$ 1,682

Assume that the repurchase of common stock and the issuance of common stock relate to stock options.

Required: (1) How much would you use as earnings per share in your analysis of Cisco?

(2) If Cisco had a policy of using treasury stock for the exercise of stock options, how much would you use as earnings per share in your analysis of Cisco?

(3) If all employees exercised their stock options at the beginning of fiscal 2006 and the company used treasury stock for the exercise, what would be the company's earnings per share? Explain why your answer is different than Cisco's reported diluted earnings per share.

(4) Is the expense for stock options material?

(5) What was the net cash outflow during fiscal 2006 from the exercise of stock options? How could the company have avoided this outflow?

24-45 <u>**Electronic Arts**</u> disclosed in its 2005 annual report that it has a "Celebrity and Artist Stock Option Plan."

Required: (1) If you were an independent game designer or sports celebrity, explain whether you would like to be included in the Celebrity and Artist Stock Option Plan instead of receiving cash payments for your contributions to the company.

(2) If you were a shareholder of Electronic Arts, explain whether you would support the Celebrity and Artist Stock Option Plan.

24-46 <u>**Molson Coors**</u> disclosed in its 2005 annual report that it had issued 1,344,507 shares of Class A voting common stock and 61,751,615 shares of Class B non-voting common stock.

Required: (1) Why do you think the company has two classes of common stock? Would you purchase Class B common stock?

(2) Does the company include both types of shares in its computation of earnings per share?

24-47 Small Corporation shows the following items of stockholders' equity:

Common stock, $10 par (40,000 shares authorized, 10,000 shares issued and outstanding)	$100,000
Additional paid-in capital on common stock	80,000
Retained earnings	160,000
	$340,000

The company's common stock currently is selling for $30 per share on the stock market. The board of directors is considering the following *alternative* actions in regard to "dividends":

(a) Payment of a $3 per share cash dividend
(b) Distribution of a 15% stock dividend
(c) Distribution of a 40% stock dividend
(d) Distribution of a 2-for-1 stock split, reducing the par value to $5 per share

The board has always paid a cash dividend and is not very familiar with stock dividends and stock splits. It is also unsure of the effect that each of these alternatives would have on stockholders' equity and has asked for your advice.

Required: (1) Explain what is meant by a stock dividend and a stock split, including an explanation of which, if either, is really a "dividend."

(2) Explain what is likely to happen to the market price per share of common stock as a result of a stock dividend or a stock split.

(3) For each alternative, determine the amount of each item of stockholders' equity for Small Corporation immediately after the cash payment or the issuance of the common stock. Show your calculations for each amount that changed.

(4) Assume that the company's total assets before any of these transactions was $700,000. Compute the ratio of stockholders' equity to total assets for each situation. Explain the differences between the ratios.

24-48 At the end of its first year of operations, Lynn Company had a fire that destroyed many of its accounting records. It was able to save information on the following accounts and ending account balances related to stock transactions and dividends:

Amount	Balance
Cash (from stock and dividends paid)	$77,400
Equipment	77,000
8% preferred stock, $100 par	70,000
Additional paid-in capital on preferred stock	7,000
Common stock, $5 par value	35,000
Additional paid-in capital on common stock	55,000
Retained earnings	7,400

In addition, the company's managers were able to recall that during the first year, the following events occurred:

(1) The company acquired equipment with an appraised value of $77,000 by issuing 700 shares of preferred stock.
(2) Net income was $20,000.
(3) The company distributed the annual dividends on the preferred stock outstanding and on the common stock outstanding.
(4) The company sold 7,000 shares of common stock.

Required: Show how all the transactions affected Lynn Company's financial statements by preparing entries in accounts where applicable.

24-49 The bookkeeper for Cortez Company prepared the following statements for the year ended December 31, 2008:

December 31, 2008
Expense and Profits Statement

Sales (net)		$220,000
Less: Selling expenses		(27,200)
Net sales		$192,800
Add: Interest revenue		1,300
Add: Gain on sale of equipment		4,900
Gross sales revenues		$199,000
Less: Costs of operations		
Cost of goods sold	$139,100	
Dividend costs ($0.50 per share for 8,300 common shares outstanding the entire year)	4,150	
Extraordinary loss due to earthquake (net of $2,400 income tax credit)	3,600	(146,850)
Taxable revenues		$ 52,150
Less: income tax on continuing income		(14,800)
Net income		$ 37,350
Miscellaneous deductions:		
Loss from operations of discontinued component L (net of $1,200 income tax credit)	$ 1,800	
Administrative expenses	21,800	(23,600)
Net Revenues		$ 13,750

Retained Revenues Statement
For Year Ended December 31, 2008

Beginning retained earnings	$65,000
Add: Gain of sale of component L (net of $1,800 income tax expense)	2,700
Recalculated retained earnings	$67,700
Add: Net revenues	13,750
	$81,450
Less: Interest expense	(1,100)
Ending retained earnings	$80,350

You determine that the preceding account balances are correct but, in certain instances, have been incorrectly titled or classified.

Required: (1) Review both statements and indicate where each incorrectly classified item should be classified. Also indicate any other errors you find.

(2) Prepare a corrected 2008 income statement and retained earnings statement for Cortez Company.

24-50 Baker Company reports a retained earnings balance of $54,600 at the beginning of 2008. The following information is available for 2008:

(a) The company declared and paid a 62-cent cash dividend per share on the 5,000 shares of common stock that were outstanding the entire year.

(b) The company incurred a pretax $10,000 loss as a result of an earthquake, which is unusual and infrequent for the area.

(c) The company sold division P in May. From January through May, division P had incurred a pretax loss from operations of $6,000. A pretax gain of $5,500 was earned on the sale of division P.

(d) The company reported sales (net) of $99,600, cost of goods sold of $57,900, and operating expenses of $18,200.

The company is unclear how to report the various preceding items in its financial statements as well as how to compute its profit margin. It has asked for your advice.

Required: (1) Assuming that all "pretax" items are subject to a 40% income tax rate, prepare Baker Company's income statement for 2008.

(2) Prepare Baker Company's retained earnings statement for 2008.

(3) Compute the company's profit margin. Discuss your computations.

24-51 Use the financial section of the 2005 annual report for **Colgate-Palmolive** in Appendix B to answer the following questions.

Required: (1) What was Colgate-Palmolive's total shareholders' equity at December 31, 2005?

(2) How many shares of common stock are authorized? How many were issued at December 31, 2005? How many were outstanding at December 31, 2005?

(3) What is the par value per share of the common stock?

(4) What was the cost of the treasury stock at December 31, 2005?

(5) What were the basic and diluted earnings per share for the year ended December 31, 2005?

(6) What were the cash dividends declared for the year ended December 31, 2005?

(7) What were the dividends per common share for each of the last 5 years?

(8) What would Colgate-Palmolive's net income, basic earnings per share, and diluted earnings per share have been in 2005 if it had used the fair value method for stock options?

24-52 Yesterday, you received the following letter for your advice column in the local paper:

DR. DECISIVE

Dear Dr. Decisive:

My mother and father both work full time to help my sisters and me go to school. I realize they get paychecks every month, but I have just found out they get "paid" even more. My mother recently went back to work, and she is employed by a high-tech company where all employees get paid stock options. She gets 500 options every year. My father just got promoted to vice-president, and he was paid 10,000 options. Is my family rich? And what do these options cost the company?

Call me "Options for All."

Required: Meet with your Dr. Decisive team and write a response to "Options for All."

RECORDING, STORING, AND REPORTING ACCOUNTING INFORMATION

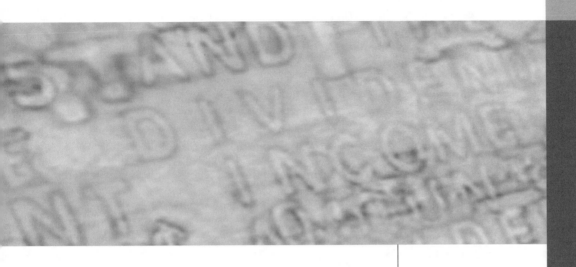

1. What is a debit entry, and what is a credit entry?

2. What are the rules for recording increases and decreases in asset and liability accounts?

3. What are the rules for recording increases and decreases in owner's equity accounts?

4. What are the major steps in a company's accounting cycle?

5. What is the difference between journalizing and posting?

6. What are adjusting entries, and what are the three types of adjusting entries?

7. What are closing entries, and how do they relate to the Income Summary account?

8. How are accounting procedures modified for corporations?

I n Chapter 5 of Volume 1, we explained transactions and source documents, as well as the entity, monetary unit, and historical cost concepts as they apply to a company's accounting process. We explained that the accounting process accumulates information and reports the results of the company's activities. We introduced a basic accounting system in terms of the accounting equation: Assets = Liabilities + Owner's Equity. The accounting system included columns for recording and retaining information from transactions related to the company's asset, liability, and owner's equity accounts, so that the company could report the information on its balance sheet. And, we explained the dual effect of recording transactions. We also discussed several accounting principles and concepts related to net income, including the concept of an accounting period, the earning process, the matching principle, and accrual accounting.

In Chapter 6 of Volume 1, we expanded the accounting system to include columns for recording and retaining information from transactions relating to each of the company's revenue and expense accounts, so the company could report the information on its income statement. From then on throughout the book, we used the accounting equation to explain the impact of transactions on a company's accounting system. We also explained the effect of each transaction on the financial statements.

The accounting equation approach for a company's accounting system worked well to explain the accounting process without getting "bogged down" in specific accounting procedures. This approach enabled you to focus more on understanding how to use the information generated by this process. However, the column method for a company's accounting system is unmanageable when the company has many transactions involving numerous accounts (sometimes hundreds!) for which it needs to keep detailed records. In this case, the company uses a more complex accounting system. Many of you will become accounting majors and will need to have a basic understanding of the specific accounting procedures a company uses in operating a more complex accounting system. Others of you also may be interested in understanding these procedures to help you better evaluate financial statements, for instance either as a manager or as an investor. The purpose of this appendix is to explain debit and credit rules, the accounting cycle, and how companies record transactions in journals, post and retain transaction information, record adjusting and closing entries, and prepare financial statements. To help explain some of these procedures, we will review what we discussed in earlier chapters. For simplicity, our discussion will focus on a sole proprietorship, but we will explain the differences for corporations later in the chapter.

ACCOUNTS

Recall that an accounting system is a means by which a company identifies, measures, records, and retains accounting information about its activities so that it can report this information in its financial statements. In an accounting system, a company uses **accounts** to record and retain the monetary information from its transactions. It uses a separate account for each asset, liability, and owner's equity item, as well as for each revenue and expense item. The number of accounts as well as the types and names of the accounts for each company depend on the particular company's operations, and on whether it is a sole proprietorship, partnership, or corporation. A **general ledger** is the entire set of accounts that a company uses. For this reason, accounts sometimes are referred to as *general ledger accounts*.

An account can take several physical forms. It might be a location on a computer disk or tape, or, in the case of a manual system, on a sheet of paper. The general ledger might be a computer file (on disk or tape), or a loose-leaf binder containing all the accounts of a manual system. Regardless of the physical form, a company uses each account for recording and accumulating accounting information about a financial statement item.

Debits and Credits

What is a debit entry, and what is a credit entry?

In a manual system, accounts may have several different forms. For convenience, in this appendix we will use the **T-account** form, as we show in the following diagram. The title of the account is written across the top of each T-account, and each T-account has a left side and a right side. The left side is called the **debit** side, and the right side is called the **credit** side. The left (debit) and the right (credit) sides of each account are used for recording and accumulating the monetary information from transactions. A **debit entry** is a monetary amount recorded (debited) on the left side of an account. A **credit entry** is a monetary amount recorded (credited) on the right side of an account.

	Title of Account
Left (debit) side	Right (credit) side

Recording Rules

Each account accumulates information about how much it has increased or decreased as a result of various transactions. Whether a company records increases or decreases on the left or the right side of an account depends on the type of account (on where the account "fits" within the accounting equation) and is based on the *debit and credit rules*. For assets, liabilities, and owner's equity accounts,[1] these rules relate to the side of the accounting equation on which the account is located. For withdrawal,[2] revenue, and expense accounts, these rules relate to whether the transactions increase or decrease owner's equity. That is, when an owner withdraws money from a company, the effect of the withdrawal is that the owner's equity in the company decreases. When the company earns revenue, the ultimate effect of the revenue increase is to increase the owner's equity. When the company incurs expenses, the ultimate effect of the expense increase is to decrease the owner's equity.

The debit and credit rules are as follows:

1. **Asset accounts (accounts on the left side of the accounting equation) are increased by debit entries (amounts recorded on the left side of a T-account) and decreased by credit entries.**

2. **Liability accounts (accounts on the right side of the equation) are increased by credit entries (amounts recorded on the right side of a T-account) and decreased by debit entries.**

3. ***Permanent* owner's equity, or capital, accounts (accounts on the right side of the equation) are increased by credit entries and decreased by debit entries. *Temporary* owner's equity accounts have the following rules:**

   (a) **Withdrawal accounts are increased by debit entries and decreased by credit entries.**

   (b) **Revenue accounts are increased by credit entries and decreased by debit entries.**

   (c) **Expense accounts are increased by debit entries and decreased by credit entries.**

Exhibit A-1 on the following page illustrates the debit and credit rules[3] as they relate to the accounting equation.

A company uses the double entry rule for recording its accounting information. The **double entry rule** states that in the recording of a transaction, the total amount of the debit entries must equal the total amount of the credit entries for the transaction. The use of

2 What are the rules for recording increases and decreases in asset and liability accounts?

3 What are the rules for recording increases and decreases in owner's equity accounts?

---

[1] Owner's equity accounts may be *permanent* or *temporary*. Permanent owner's equity accounts are those that a company reports on its balance sheet. Temporary owner's equity accounts are used only to compute a company's net income or withdrawals for the accounting period.

[2] In the earlier chapters, we recorded withdrawals as reductions in the owner's capital account column. Many companies keep track of withdrawals separately, and use a Withdrawals account to do so.

[3] The debit and credit rules for increasing and decreasing a contra account are the *opposite* of the account to which it relates. We discuss contra accounts later in this appendix.

EXHIBIT A-1	ACCOUNTING EQUATION AND DEBIT/CREDIT RULES

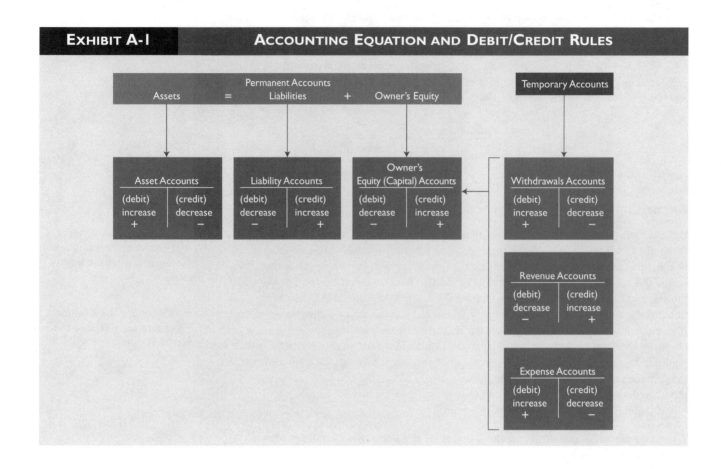

both the double entry rule and the debit and credit rules in recording transactions ensures that the accounting equation remains in balance.

At any given time, an account may have a number of debit and credit entries in it. The **balance of an account** is the difference between the total increases and the total decreases recorded in the account. Typically, total increases exceed total decreases. Therefore, each asset account normally has a debit balance because the total increases (debits) exceed the total decreases (credits) in the account. Similarly, each liability and permanent owner's equity (capital) account normally has a credit balance because the total increases (credits) exceed the total decreases (debits) in each account. For the temporary owner's equity items, revenue accounts normally have credit balances, whereas expense and withdrawal accounts normally have debit balances. The following list summarizes the normal balances in the various accounts.

Accounts	Normal Balance
Assets	Debit
Liabilities	Credit
Owner's capital	Credit
Owner's withdrawals	Debit
Revenues	Credit
Expenses	Debit

ACCOUNTING CYCLE

4 What are the major steps in a company's accounting cycle?

Now that you are familiar with the rules for recording and accumulating information in the various accounts, we will discuss the steps that a company completes during each accounting period to record, retain, and report the monetary information from its transactions. These steps are called the **accounting cycle**. The major steps include:

(1) recording (journalizing) the transactions in the general journal, (2) posting the journal entries to the accounts in the general ledger, (3) recording (and posting) adjusting entries, (4) preparing the financial statements, and (5) recording (and posting) closing entries. We will discuss and illustrate each of these steps, along with several substeps, in the following sections.

RECORDING (JOURNALIZING) TRANSACTIONS

Recall that a source document (invoice, check) is the business record from which a company obtains the information for each transaction. The company uses this information to record each transaction in a journal, after which it transfers the information to its accounts. A **general journal** includes the following information about each transaction: the date of the transaction, the accounts to be debited and credited, the amounts of the debit and credit entries, and an explanation of each transaction. In a manual system, the general journal is a book of columnar pages.

A company can use a general journal to record all types of transactions. The general journal is the kind of journal we will discuss in this appendix. However, many companies have a number of *special journals*, each of which is used to record a particular type of transaction. The common special journals are the sales (for recording credit sales), purchases (for credit purchases of inventory), cash receipts (for cash inflows), and cash payments (for cash outflows) journals. We do not discuss these special journals.

A general journal consists of a date column, a column to list the accounts affected by each transaction (and an explanation of the transaction), a column to list the account numbers of the affected accounts, and debit and credit columns to list the amount to be recorded in each account. **Journalizing** is the process of recording a transaction in a company's general journal. A **journal entry** is the recorded information for each transaction. We show an example of transactions and how they are recorded in a general journal in Exhibits A-2 and A-3 later in this appendix.

A company gains several advantages by using a general journal for initially recording its transactions. First, this process helps prevent errors. Since the company initially records the accounts and the debit and credit amounts for each transaction on a single journal page rather than directly in the many accounts, this method makes it easier to prove that the debits and the credits are equal, thus keeping the accounting equation in balance. Second, all the information about each transaction (including the explanation) is recorded in one place, thereby providing a complete "picture" of the transaction. This is useful in the auditing process, or if an error is discovered, because it is easy to review all of the transaction information. Third, the company records the transactions chronologically (day to day), so that the journal provides a "history" of its financial transactions.

Key Procedures in Journalizing

The following list outlines the journalizing procedures for each column of the general journal. Study it carefully, referring to the completed general journal in Exhibit A-3.

1. Enter the month, day, and year of the first transaction in the "Date" column. It is not necessary to repeat the month and year of later transactions until the beginning of a new journal page, a new month, or a new year.

2. Enter the title of the account to be debited at the far left of the column entitled "Account Titles and Explanations." Enter the amount of the debit to this account in the "Debit" column on the same line as the account title. Dollar signs typically are not used in the debit (or credit) columns.

3. Enter the title of the account to be credited on the next line below the title of the debited account. Indent the title of the credit account slightly to the right so that a reader looking at the journal page can easily identify which account titles are debited and which are credited. Enter the amount of the credit to this account on the same line in the "Credit" column.

4. Some transactions involve two or more debits, two or more credits, or both. (Remember that for each transaction, the *total* amount of the debit entries must equal the *total* amount of the credit entries.) In this case, the type of journal entry a company uses is called a *compound entry*. When recording a compound entry, first list all the accounts and amounts to be debited (list each account on a separate line), followed by all the accounts to be credited (indent and list each account on a separate line). The December 29, 2007 journal entry in Exhibit A-3 is an example of a compound journal entry.

5. Enter a brief explanation of the transaction on the line below the last credit entry of the transaction. Write the explanation at the far left of the column entitled "Account Titles and Explanations." Leave a blank line before beginning another journal entry, to set off each entry.

6. During the process of journalizing, do *not* record a number in the column entitled "Acct. No." (Account Number). You will enter a number in this column during the "posting" process, which we will discuss later. (When you are referring to Exhibit A-3, note that this is what the general journal page looks like *after* the posting process is complete.)

After journalizing the debit and credit entries of a transaction, journalize the next transaction for the day, and continue the process until all the transactions have been recorded. *By strictly following these journalizing procedures, you will minimize the chance of error.*

Illustration of Journal Entries

Recall from Chapter 5 of Volume 1 that Anna Cox started Sweet Temptations, a retail candy store, by investing $15,000 on December 15, 2007. During the remainder of December, the store engaged in several transactions to get ready to open for customers on January 2, 2008.

EXHIBIT A-2	SWEET TEMPTATIONS' DECEMBER 2007 TRANSACTIONS AND ANALYSIS	
Date	**Transaction**	**Analysis**
12/15	A. Cox makes initial investment in Sweet Temptations of $15,000.	Asset account Cash is increased (debited) by $15,000; owner's equity account A. Cox, Capital is increased (credited) by $15,000.
12/16	Sweet Temptations pays $6,000 for six months of rent in advance to Westwood Mall.	Asset account Prepaid Rent is increased (debited) by $6,000; asset account Cash is decreased (credited) by $6,000.
12/17	Sweet Temptations pays $700 for the purchase of supplies from City Supply Company.	Asset account Supplies is increased (debited) by $700; asset account Cash is is decreased (credited) by $700.
12/20	Sweet Temptations purchases $1,620 of inventory (candy) on credit from Unlimited Decadence Corporation.	Asset account Inventory is increased (debited) by $1,620; liability account Accounts Payable is increased (credited) by $1,620.
12/29	Sweet Temptations purchases store equipment for $2,200, paying $1,000 cash and signing a three-month note to Ace Equipment Company for $1,200.	Asset account Store Equipment is increased (debited) by $2,200; asset account Cash is decreased (credited) by $1,000; liability account Notes Payable is increased (credited) by $1,200.
12/30	Sweet Temptations sells $400 of unneeded store equipment on account to The Hardware Store.	Asset account Accounts Receivable is increased (debited) by $400; asset account Store Equipment is decreased (credited) by $400.

EXHIBIT A-3	SWEET TEMPTATIONS' GENERAL JOURNAL ENTRIES: DECEMBER 2007			

Date	Account Titles and Explanations	Acct. No.	Debit	Credit
2007 Dec. 15	Cash	101	15,000	
	A. Cox, Capital	301		15,000
	Made initial investment in Sweet Temptations.			
16	Prepaid Rent	107	6,000	
	Cash	101		6,000
	Paid 6 months' rent in advance to Westwood Mall.			
17	Supplies	106	700	
	Cash	101		700
	Purchased office supplies from City Supply Company.			
20	Inventory	105	1,620	
	Accounts Payable	201		1,620
	Purchased inventory on credit from Unlimited Decadence Corporation.			
29	Store Equipment	123	2,200	
	Cash	101		1,000
	Notes Payable	204		1,200
	Purchased store equipment from Ace Equipment Company, making cash down payment and signing 3-month note.			
30	Accounts Receivable	103	400	
	Store Equipment	123		400
	Sold unneeded store equipment (desk) on credit to The Hardware Store.			

Also recall that Sweet Temptations is a retail candy store that uses a perpetual inventory system[4] and leases store space in Westwood Mall.

We have prepared Exhibit A-2 to help you remember the December transactions of Sweet Temptations. This exhibit summarizes the six transactions and analyzes the debit and credit entries for each transaction.

To illustrate the general journal and the journalizing process, Exhibit A-3 shows the journal entries for these six transactions. In studying Exhibit A-3, you should do the following: (1) review each transaction listed in Exhibit A-2, (2) think of the source documents for the transaction, (3) understand the impact of the transactions on the accounting equation, (4) determine the debit and credit entries, (5) think of the journalizing procedures, and (6) compare these procedures with the journal entries that we made in Exhibit A-3.

To understand the journalizing process, look at the December 20, 2007 transaction in which Sweet Temptations purchased $1,620 of inventory on credit from Unlimited Decadence Corporation. The source document for the transaction is the invoice that Sweet Temptations received from Unlimited Decadence Corporation. The effect of this purchase on the accounting equation is that both an asset (Inventory) and a liability (Accounts Payable) are increased by $1,620. To record the transaction in the general journal, Sweet Temptations

---

[4]Alternatively, a company could use a *periodic inventory system*, as we discussed in Chapters 9 and 19. Under this system, the company does not keep a continuous record of the inventory on hand and sold. Instead, it determines its inventory by taking a physical inventory at the end of the period. The company derives its cost of goods sold by adding its purchases to the beginning inventory and then subtracting the ending inventory.

skipped a line after the previous transaction. It then entered the date and the account title (Inventory) and amount ($1,620) of the account to be debited. It indented the next line and entered the account title (Accounts Payable) and amount ($1,620) to be credited. On the next line it wrote a brief explanation of the journal entry. After following this process for each transaction, Sweet Temptations stored all the source documents in its files.

After a company records the journal entries, it transfers the amounts (posts them) to the related accounts. It records the number (which we discuss later) of each of these accounts in the "Acct. No." column of the general journal. To save space, we do not illustrate this posting process for Exhibit A-3. Instead, we continue our illustration of journalizing in Exhibits A-4 and A-5. Exhibit A-4 summarizes and analyzes the transactions of Sweet Temptations for January 2008. These include revenue and expense transactions, along with various other transactions.[5]

Exhibit A-5 illustrates the journal entries that Sweet Temptations made to record the January transactions. In studying this exhibit, you should review Exhibit A-4 and think through the steps of the journalizing process. Once again, note that Sweet Temptations

EXHIBIT A-4	SWEET TEMPTATIONS' JANUARY 2008 TRANSACTIONS AND ANALYSIS

Date	Transaction	Analysis
1/02	Sweet Temptations sells inventory (candy) at total cash selling price of $300.	Asset account Cash is increased (debited) by $300; revenue account Sales Revenue is increased (credited) by $300.
1/02	Sweet Temptations records cost of goods sold of $135 on cash sale.	Expense account Cost of Goods Sold is increased (debited) by $135; asset account Inventory is decreased (credited) by $135.
1/03	Sweet Temptations pays $1,620 to Unlimited Decadence Corporation for inventory purchased on 12/20/07.	Liability account Accounts Payable is decreased (debited) by $1,620; asset account Cash is decreased (credited) by $1,620.
1/04	Sweet Temptations purchases $4,320 of inventory (candy) on credit from Unlimited Decadence Corporation.	Asset account Inventory is increased (debited) by $4,320; liability account Accounts Payable is increased (credited) by $4,320.
1/06	Sweet Temptations made credit sale of $100.	Asset account Accounts Receivable is increased (debited) by $100; revenue account Sales Revenue is increased (credited) by $100.
1/06	Sweet Temptations records cost of goods sold of $45 on credit sale.	Expense account Cost of Goods Sold is increased (debited) by $45; asset account Inventory is decreased (credited) by $45.
1/07	Sweet Temptations collects $400 of accounts receivable from The Hardware Store.	Asset account Cash is increased (debited) by $400; asset account Accounts Receivable is decreased (credited) by $400.
1/20	A. Cox withdraws $50 for personal use.	Owner's equity account A. Cox, Withdrawals is increased (debited) by $50; asset account Cash is decreased (credited) by $50.
1/25	Sweet Temptations pays $200 to a consultant for promotion coordination.	Expense account Consulting Expense is increased (debited) by $200; asset account Cash is decreased (credited) by $200.
1/25	Sweet Temptations pays $300 for advertising in promotional flyer.	Expense account Advertising Expense is increased (debited) by $300; asset account Cash is decreased (credited) by $300.
1/29	Sweet Temptations purchases store equipment for $200 cash.	Asset account Store Equipment is increased (debited) by $200; asset account Cash is decreased (credited) by $200.
1/31	Sweet Temptations pays salaries totaling $2,050 to employees.	Expense account Salaries Expense is increased (debited) by $2,050; asset account Cash is decreased (credited) by $2,050.
1/31	Sweet Temptations pays telephone bill of $60.	Expense account Telephone Expense is increased (debited) by $60; asset account Cash is decreased (credited) by $60.
1/31	Sweet Temptations pays utilities bill of $190.	Expense account Utilities Expense is increased (debited) by $190; asset account Cash is decreased (credited) by $190.
1/31	Sweet Temptations records $7,700 of cash sales for 1/3/08 through 1/31/08.	Asset account Cash is increased (debited) by $7,700; revenue account Sales Revenue is increased (credited) by $7,700.
1/31	Sweet Temptations records cost of goods sold of $3,465 on cash sales.	Expense account Cost of Goods Sold is increased (debited) by $3,465; asset account Inventory is decreased (credited) by $3,465.

[5]For simplicity, on January 31 we recorded the sum ($7,700) of Sweet Temptations' January 3 through January 31 cash sales. Normally, a company records its cash sales each day.

EXHIBIT A-5	SWEET TEMPTATIONS' GENERAL JOURNAL ENTRIES: JANUARY 2008

Date	Account Titles and Explanations	Acct. No.	Debit	Credit
2008 Jan. 2	Cash Sales Revenue Made cash sales.	101 401	300	 300
2	Cost of Goods Sold Inventory To record cost of goods sold on cash sales.	501 105	135	 135
3	Accounts Payable Cash Paid Unlimited Decadence Corporation for inventory purchased on 12/20/07.	201 101	1,620	 1,620
4	Inventory Accounts Payable Purchased inventory on credit from Unlimited Decadence Corporation.	105 201	4,320	 4,320
6	Accounts Receivable Sales Revenue Made credit sale.	103 401	100	 100
6	Cost of Goods Sold Inventory To record cost of goods sold on credit sale.	501 105	45	 45
7	Cash Accounts Receivable Collected amount owed from The Hardware Store for desk sold on 12/30/07.	101 103	400	 400
20	A. Cox, Withdrawals Cash Withdrew cash for personal use.	304 101	50	 50
25	Consulting Expense Cash Paid consultant for promotion coordination.	502 101	200	 200
25	Advertising Expense Cash Paid for advertising in promotional flyer.	503 101	300	 300
29	Store Equipment Cash Purchased store equipment.	123 101	200	 200
31	Salaries Expense Cash Paid employees' salaries.	504 101	2,050	 2,050
31	Telephone Expense Cash Paid telephone bill.	505 101	60	 60
31	Utilities Expense Cash Paid utilities bill.	506 101	190	 190
31	Cash Sales Revenue To record cash sales for 1/3/08 through 1/31/08.	101 401	7,700	 7,700
31	Cost of Goods Sold Inventory To record cost of goods sold on cash sales.	501 105	3,465	 3,465

did not enter the account numbers at the time it recorded the journal entries; it entered them during the posting process, which we will discuss next.

POSTING TO THE ACCOUNTS

5 What is the difference between journalizing and posting?

In the journalizing process, a company records each transaction in its general journal. However, at this point it has not yet recorded the accounting information from each transaction in the accounts, the "storage units" for the company's accounting information. To do so, the company must *post* the amounts from the general journal to the related accounts. **Posting** is the process of transferring the debit and credit information for each journal entry to the accounts in a company's general ledger.

Account Numbers and Chart of Accounts

To help in the accounting process, a company assigns a number to each of its accounts and lists that number to the right of the account title on a T-account. The company obtains the account number from its chart of accounts. A **chart of accounts** is a numbering system designed to organize a company's accounts efficiently and to reduce errors in the recording and accumulating process. A company usually sets up its chart of accounts so that the Cash account is assigned the lowest number, followed in order by all the other asset accounts, all the liability accounts, the permanent owner's equity (capital) account, the withdrawals account, the income summary account (discussed later), the revenue accounts, and the expense accounts. The company then includes the accounts in its general ledger in the order in which they are listed in the chart of accounts. As you will see shortly, ordering the accounts in the general ledger in this way helps in preparing the financial statements.

Exhibit A-6 lists Sweet Temptations' chart of accounts. Notice that the asset account numbers begin at 101, the liabilities at 201, the owner's equity at 301, the revenues at 401, and the expenses at 501. A company uses a numbering system such as this to help identify and classify its accounts. (Some large corporations use numbers as high as six

EXHIBIT A-6	SWEET TEMPTATIONS' CHART OF ACCOUNTS

Account Titles	Account Numbers
Cash	101
Accounts Receivable	103
Inventory	105
Supplies	106
Prepaid Rent	107
Store Equipment	123
Accumulated Depreciation	124
Accounts Payable	201
Notes Payable	204
Interest Payable	205
A. Cox, Capital	301
A. Cox, Withdrawals	304
Income Summary	306
Sales Revenue	401
Cost of Goods Sold	501
Consulting Expense	502
Advertising Expense	503
Salaries Expense	504
Telephone Expense	505
Utilities Expense	506
Supplies Expense	507
Rent Expense	508
Interest Expense	509
Depreciation Expense	510

digits for classifying their accounts and even use decimals to further subclassify their accounts.) Note also that the accounts are not consecutively numbered. Sweet Temptations follows this procedure so that it can insert any new accounts into its chart of accounts (and general ledger) later and still assign account numbers in their proper order.

Key Procedures in Posting

A company with a manual accounting system usually posts at the end of each day. As with the journalizing process, the company follows a set of procedures for posting to the individual accounts. The following list outlines these procedures:

1. In the general ledger, locate the first account of the first transaction to be posted from the general journal.

2. Enter the month, day, and year of the transaction and the debit amount (as listed in the general journal) in the debit (left) side of the account.

3. Go back to the general journal and, on the same line as the account title, enter in the "Acct. No." (Account Number) column the number of the account in which the debit amount was posted. A number in the Acct. No. column indicates that the posting process has been completed for that *line* of the general journal. It also indicates to which account that amount was posted. This is the last step before continuing with the posting of the next line. (*Caution*: Remember that the company completes this procedure *after* it posts the amount in the account.)

4. For the next line of the transaction in the general journal (usually the credit entry, unless a compound entry is involved), repeat steps 2 and 3, except that the date and amount are posted to the credit (right) side of the appropriate account.

After posting the debit and credit entries for the first transaction to the related accounts, post the next journal entry for the day and continue the process until the daily postings are completed. *By strictly following these posting procedures, you will minimize the chance of error.*

Illustration of Posting Process

Exhibit A-7 illustrates the posting process for the January 2, 2008 sales transaction of Sweet Temptations. The arrows from the general journal to the general ledger indicate the debit and credit postings. Note that Sweet Temptations transferred the date of the transaction

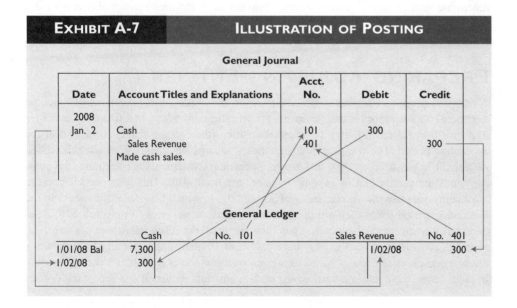

EXHIBIT A-7   ILLUSTRATION OF POSTING

General Journal

Date	Account Titles and Explanations	Acct. No.	Debit	Credit
2008 Jan. 2	Cash	101	300	
	Sales Revenue	401		300
	Made cash sales.			

General Ledger

Cash	No. 101		Sales Revenue	No. 401
1/01/08 Bal	7,300		1/02/08	300
1/02/08	300			

from the general journal to each ledger account. It posted the amount of the debit ($300) in the debit column of the Cash account, and the amount of the credit ($300) in the credit column of the Sales Revenue account in the general ledger. It then listed the account numbers (101 and 401) on the respective lines in the Acct. No. column of the general journal, as we indicate by the arrows from the general ledger to the general journal.

Note in Exhibit A-7 that the Cash account has a beginning (1/01/08) balance of $7,300. This was the ending balance from December 2007, after Sweet Temptations posted the December transactions listed in Exhibit A-3. Note also that the Sales Revenue account did not have a beginning balance. Later in this appendix, we will discuss the computation of account balances and why some accounts have beginning balances and some accounts do not have beginning balances.

Sweet Temptations completes the posting process at the end of each day in January. Exhibit A-8 shows all of the general ledger accounts of Sweet Temptations at the end of January (*before* it makes its adjusting and closing entries). They are listed according to the chart of accounts shown in Exhibit A-6. You should study the postings to the accounts, referring to the journal entries listed in Exhibit A-5. Again, note that in Exhibit A-5, the Acct. No. column had not been completed when the journal entry was made but was completed during the posting process. You should think of the account numbers that would be listed in this column based on the chart of accounts in Exhibit A-6.

TRIAL BALANCE

In discussing the journalizing and posting process, we set up procedures so that the double entry rule is followed. That is, the total amount of the debit entries equals the total amount of the credit entries in both the general journal and the general ledger accounts. By following these procedures the accounting equation remains in balance and errors are minimized.

People can make mistakes, however. Therefore, it is helpful to set up a procedure that will help to detect a journalizing or posting error. This procedure involves proving the equality of the debit and credit balances in the accounts by preparing a trial balance.

A **trial balance** is a schedule that lists the titles of all the accounts in a company's general ledger, the debit or credit balance of each account, and the totals of the debit and credit balances. Normally, a company prepares a trial balance at the end of the accounting period, before proceeding with the adjusting entries (which we discuss next). To prepare a trial balance, first compute the balance of each account and list it (along with the date on which it is computed) on the appropriate side of the account. Next, list the account titles and debit or credit balances on the trial balance in the order in which the accounts are listed in the general ledger. Finally, total the debit and credit columns to determine their equality. To save space, we do not show the trial balance of Sweet Temptations here because we will show an adjusted trial balance (which is similar to, but more extensive than, a trial balance) later in Exhibit A-11.

PREPARING ADJUSTING ENTRIES

6 What are adjusting entries, and what are the three types of adjusting entries?

A company prepares financial statements to report the results of its operations (the income statement), its cash receipts and payments for operating, investing, and financing activities (the cash flow statement), and its financial position (the balance sheet) at the end of the accounting period. The company prepares these financial statements from the balances in its general ledger accounts. To make sure its financial statements are accurate, the company must be certain that its account balances are up-to-date. This is important because most companies use the *accrual* basis of accounting, in which they record revenues in the accounting period when they sell products to, or perform services for, customers and not necessarily when they collect cash. Then they *match* all the related expenses against these revenues, regardless of whether they have paid cash. In many cases, not all of a company's revenue and expense account balances are up-to-date at the end of the accounting period. In these cases, the company must *adjust* certain amounts so that it can report the correct

EXHIBIT A-8	SWEET TEMPTATIONS' GENERAL LEDGER (JANUARY 2008)

Cash — No. 101

Date			Date	
1/01/08	Bal	7,300	1/03/08	1,620
1/02/08		300	1/20/08	50
1/07/08		400	1/25/08	200
1/31/08		7,700	1/25/08	300
			1/29/08	200
			1/31/08	2,050
			1/31/08	60
			1/31/08	190
1/31/08	Bal	11,030		

Accounts Receivable — No. 103

Date			Date	
1/01/08	Bal	400	1/07/08	400
1/06/08		100		
1/31/08	Bal	100		

Inventory — No. 105

Date			Date	
1/01/08	Bal	1,620	1/02/08	135
1/04/08		4,320	1/06/08	45
			1/31/08	3,465
1/31/08	Bal	2,295		

Supplies — No. 106

Date		
1/01/08	Bal	700

Prepaid Rent — No. 107

Date		
1/01/08	Bal	6,000

Store Equipment — No. 123

Date		
1/01/08	Bal	1,800
1/29/08		200
1/31/08	Bal	2,000

Accumulated Depreciation — No. 124

Accounts Payable — No. 201

Date			Date		
1/03/08		1,620	1/01/08	Bal	1,620
			1/04/08		4,320
			1/31/08	Bal	4,320

Notes Payable — No. 204

			Date		
			1/01/08	Bal	1,200

Interest Payable — No. 205

A. Cox, Capital — No. 301

		Date		
		1/01/08	Bal	15,000

A. Cox, Withdrawals — No. 304

Date	
1/20/08	50

Income Summary — No. 306

Sales Revenue — No. 401

	Date		
	1/02/08		300
	1/06/08		100
	1/31/08		7,700
	1/31/08	Bal	8,100

Cost of Goods Sold — No. 501

Date		
1/02/08		135
1/06/08		45
1/31/08		3,465
1/31/08	Bal	3,645

Consulting Expense — No. 502

Date	
1/25/08	200

Advertising Expense — No. 503

Date	
1/25/08	300

Salaries Expense — No. 504

Date	
1/31/08	2,050

Telephone Expense — No. 505

Date	
1/31/08	60

Utilities Expense — No. 506

Date	
1/31/08	190

Supplies Expense — No. 507

Rent Expense — No. 508

Interest Expense — No. 509

Depreciation Expense — No. 510

net income on its income statement and the correct ending financial position on its balance sheet. The company makes these adjustments by preparing adjusting entries.

Adjusting entries are journal entries that a company makes at the end of its accounting period to bring the company's revenue and expense account balances up-to-date and to show the correct ending balances in its asset and liability accounts. An adjusting entry usually affects both a permanent (balance sheet) account and a temporary (income statement) account. Adjusting entries may be grouped into three types:

1. Apportionment of prepaid items and unearned revenues
2. Recording of accrued items
3. Recording or apportionment of estimated items

We will discuss the adjusting entries for each type in the following sections.

Apportionment of Prepaid Items and Unearned Revenues

This category of adjusting entries includes adjustments of prepaid items and unearned revenues. A **prepaid item** (sometimes called a *prepaid expense*) is an economic resource for which a company has paid cash and that the company expects to use in its operating activities in the near future. When a company purchases goods or services involving a prepaid item, it records the *cost* as an asset. By the end of the accounting period, the company has used a part of the goods or services to earn revenues. Therefore, it must record the "expired" part of the cost as an *expense* to be matched against the revenues on its income statement while retaining the unexpired part of the cost as an asset on its ending balance sheet. Examples of prepaid items are supplies, prepaid rent, and prepaid insurance.

A company records the apportionment (allocation) of the cost of each prepaid item between an expense and an asset in an adjusting entry in its general journal. The adjusting entry involves a debit (increase) to an appropriately titled expense account (e.g., Rent Expense, obtained from the company's chart of accounts) and a credit (decrease) to the asset account (e.g., Prepaid Rent). The calculation of the amount of the adjusting entry depends on the type of prepaid item. For instance, in the case of supplies, the company takes a physical count of the supplies on hand (and related costs) at the end of the accounting period. In the case of prepaid rent or insurance, the company apportions the total cost evenly over the number of months of the rent agreement or insurance coverage.

For example, recall that Sweet Temptations purchased $700 of office and store supplies on December 17, 2007, and recorded an asset—Supplies—for that amount. This was the amount of supplies that was available for operations at the beginning of January 2008. At the end of January, by counting the supplies, the company determined that it had $670 of supplies on hand. Based on this information, the company must have used $30 ($700 − $670) of supplies during January. To record this expense, on January 31, 2008, Sweet Temptations debits (increases) Supplies Expense for $30 and credits (decreases) the asset Supplies for $30 in the general journal, as we show in Exhibit A-9. Note in Exhibit A-10 (which we show later) that after Sweet Temptations posts this adjusting journal entry

EXHIBIT A-9	SWEET TEMPTATIONS' ADJUSTING ENTRIES: JANUARY 31, 2008			
Date	Account Titles and Explanations	Acct. No.	Debit	Credit
	Adjusting Entries			
2008 Jan. 31	Supplies Expense	507	30	
	Supplies	106		30
	Supplies used during January.			
31	Rent Expense	508	1,000	
	Prepaid Rent	107		1,000
	Expiration of one-month's rent paid in advance on 12/16/07.			
31	Interest Expense	509	8	
	Interest Payable	205		8
	Interest accrued on note payable.			
31	Depreciation Expense	510	15	
	Accumulated Depreciation	124		15
	Depreciation on store equipment for January.			

to its general ledger accounts (as indicated by an *Adj* in the account), the Supplies Expense account has a debit balance of $30. Also note that the Supplies account has a debit balance of $670.

Sweet Temptations records its rent expense in a similar manner. Recall that Sweet Temptations paid $6,000 for six months' rent in advance on December 16, 2007, and recorded this amount as an asset, Prepaid Rent. The rental agreement stated that rent would not be charged for the last half of December. Therefore, at the end of January 2008, one month's rent has expired, and the company has incurred rent expense of $1,000 ($6,000 ÷ 6). To record this expense, on January 31 the company debits (increases) Rent Expense for $1,000 and credits (decreases) Prepaid Rent for $1,000, as we show in Exhibit A-9. After posting, the Rent Expense account has a debit balance of $1,000 and the Prepaid Rent account has a debit balance of $5,000, as we show later in Exhibit A-10.

In some cases, customers may make an advance payment to a company for goods or services that the company will provide in the future. At the time of the advance receipt, even though the company's asset Cash has increased, the company has not earned revenue because it has not yet provided the goods or services. Instead, the company has incurred a liability because it has an *obligation* to provide the future goods or services. An **unearned revenue** is an obligation of a company to provide goods or services in the future, and results from an advance receipt of cash. A company records an unearned revenue as a *liability* when it receives the cash. At the end of the accounting period, the company examines all such liabilities and related source documents to determine whether it has provided the goods or services. If it has, the company makes an adjusting entry to reduce the liability and increase its revenues of the period. The adjusting entry involves a debit (decrease) to the liability account and a credit (increase) to a related revenue account.

Sweet Temptations does not have any unearned revenues at the end of January. Therefore, to illustrate, we will use a different example. Recall that Westwood Mall collected $6,000 from Sweet Temptations on December 16, 2007, for six months' rent in advance. At that time, Westwood Mall debited (increased) an asset—Cash—for $6,000 and credited (increased) a liability—Unearned Rent—for $6,000. On January 31, 2008, since Westwood Mall earned one month of rent by providing store space to Sweet Temptations during January, Westwood Mall makes an adjusting entry to reduce the liability and increase its revenue. The journal entry is a debit (decrease) to Unearned Rent and a credit (increase) to Rent Revenue for $1,000, as follows (note that for simplicity, we do not show the "Acct. No." column in the general journal):

Date	Account Titles and Explanations	Debit	Credit
Jan. 31	Unearned Rent	1,000	
	Rent Revenue		1,000
	To record rent earned from Sweet Temptations.		

The remaining $5,000 ($6,000 − $1,000) balance in Westwood Mall's Unearned Rent account represents the obligation to provide store space to Sweet Temptations for five more months.

Accrued Items

This category of adjusting entries includes adjustments for accrued expenses and accrued revenues. A company records most of its expenses when it pays for them. At the end of an accounting period, however, it has not paid some expenses. An **accrued expense** is an expense that a company has incurred during the accounting period but that it has not paid or recorded. (Sometimes accrued expenses are called *accrued liabilities,* as we did in Chapter 14 of Volume 1 when we discussed current liabilities.) A common type of accrued expense is unpaid employees' salaries. Other common accrued expenses include unpaid interest, taxes, and utility bills. To *match* all expenses against revenues and to report all the liabilities at the end of the period, a company makes an adjusting entry to record each accrued expense. The journal entry involves a debit (increase) to an appropriately titled expense account and a credit (increase) to the related liability account.

Recall that on December 29, 2007, Sweet Temptations signed a $1,200, 3-month note payable. It agreed to pay $24 total interest, so that at the end of three months it will repay $1,224 ($1,000 + $24). Since Sweet Temptations owed the note during all of January, one month of interest, or $8 ($24 ÷ 3 months), has accrued and is an expense of doing business during January. To record this expense, on January 31, 2008, Sweet Temptations debits (increases) Interest Expense and credits (increases) the liability account Interest Payable for $8, as we show in Exhibit A-9. It would record other accrued expenses in a similar way.

A company records most revenues at the time it provides goods or services to a customer. At the end of an accounting period, however, it may not have recorded a few revenues. An **accrued revenue** is a revenue that a company has earned during the accounting period but that it has neither collected nor recorded. To report all the revenues of the period and all the assets at the end of the period, a company makes an adjusting entry for each accrued revenue. The journal entry is a debit (increase) to an asset account and a credit (increase) to a related revenue account.

There are not many types of accrued revenues, and Sweet Temptations has none. However, one common accrued revenue is the interest that has accumulated on a note *received* by a company. Recall that the $1,200, 3-month note of Sweet Temptations was issued to Ace Equipment Company. On January 31, 2008, Ace Equipment Company would record accrued interest revenue of $8. The journal entry would be a debit (increase) to the asset account Interest Receivable and a credit (increase) to the revenue account Interest Revenue for $8, as follows:

Date	Account Titles and Explanations	Debit	Credit
Jan. 31	Interest Receivable	8	
	Interest Revenue		8
	To record accrued interest revenue on note earned from		
	Sweet Temptations.		

A company would record other accrued revenues similarly.

Estimated Items

A few other adjusting entries involve estimated amounts because they are based, in part, on expected future events. Adjusting entries involving estimated amounts include the recording of (1) depreciation on buildings and equipment, (2) amortization of intangible assets, and (3) recognition of uncollectible accounts receivable. We discussed the different methods for computing the estimated amounts of depreciation and amortization in Chapter 21. We discussed the alternative ways of computing the estimated amount of uncollectible accounts receivable (bad debts) in Chapter 13 of Volume 1.

The adjusting entry for depreciation is a debit (increase) to the expense account Depreciation Expense and a credit (increase) to the contra-asset account Accumulated Depreciation. Recall from Chapter 13 of Volume 1 that a company uses a contra account to record an amount that is subtracted from the balance in a related account. Thus, the rule for increasing a contra account is the *opposite* of the rule for increasing the related account. Since Accumulated Depreciation is a contra-*asset* account, that is why it is increased by a credit entry. Also, recall from Chapter 21 that an increase in the Accumulated Depreciation account decreases the book value of the related depreciable asset account because the amount of accumulated depreciation to date is subtracted from the cost of the depreciable asset. Similarly, the adjusting entry for amortization is a debit (increase) to the expense account Amortization Expense and a credit to the related intangible asset contra-account Accumulated Amortization.

The adjusting entry for uncollectible accounts receivable is a debit (increase) to the expense account Bad Debts Expense and a credit (increase) to the contra-asset account Allowance for Bad Debts. The balance of the Allowance for Bad Debts account is subtracted from the balance of the Accounts Receivable account to determine the net realizable value of the accounts receivable, as we discussed in Chapter 13 of Volume 1.

To understand the adjustment process for an estimated item, recall that at the end of December, Sweet Temptations purchased store equipment that cost $1,800 and that it used in its operations during January.[6] Sweet Temptations estimates that this equipment will have a life of 10 years (120 months; 12 × 10), with no residual value. Using straight-line depreciation, the monthly depreciation expense is $15 ($1,800 ÷ 120 months). On January 31, 2008, Sweet Temptations records its depreciation expense for January as we show in Exhibit A-9.

Posting the Adjusting Entries

After a company prepares its adjusting entries, the company posts these entries from its general journal to the accounts in its general ledger. Sweet Temptations posts the adjusting entries that it recorded in Exhibit A-9 to its general ledger, as we show in Exhibit A-10 on the following page. Note that Exhibit A-10 is similar to Exhibit A-8, except that the adjusting entries (as indicated by an *Adj*) are included. This completes the adjusting entry process for Sweet Temptations.

ADJUSTED TRIAL BALANCE

After a company journalizes and posts its adjusting entries, the company balances its accounts and all the account balances are up-to-date for the accounting period. But before preparing the company's financial statements, it is useful to prepare an adjusted trial balance. An **adjusted trial balance** is a schedule prepared to prove the equality of the debit and credit balances in a company's general ledger accounts after it has made the adjusting entries. An adjusted trial balance is similar to a trial balance except that it also includes *all* the revenue and expense accounts. An adjusted trial balance is an accountant's *working paper* and is not a financial statement. It is used to (1) help prevent the company from including debit and credit errors in its financial statements and (2) make preparing the financial statements easier, as you will see shortly.

Exhibit A-11 on page 917 shows the adjusted trial balance of Sweet Temptations on January 31, 2008. The account balances listed were taken from the general ledger in Exhibit A-10. Note that the $28,643 total of the debits is equal to the total of the credits.

If an adjusted trial balance (or a trial balance) does not balance (i.e., the total debits do not equal the total credits), the company has made an error. To find the error, the company should re-add the debit and credit columns of the adjusted trial balance. If the column totals still do not agree, the company should check the amounts in the debit and credit columns to be sure that it did not mistakenly list a debit or credit account balance in the wrong column.

If it still does not find the error, the company should compute the difference in the column totals and divide it by 9. When the difference is evenly divisible by 9, there is a good chance that a transposition or a slide has occurred. A **transposition** occurs when two digits in a number are mistakenly reversed. For instance, if the $11,030 Cash balance in Exhibit A-11 had been listed as $11,300, the debit column would have totaled $28,913 instead of $28,643. The difference between the debit column and the correct credit column total, $270, is evenly divisible by 9. A **slide** occurs when the digits are listed in the correct order but are mistakenly moved one decimal place to the left or right. For instance, if the $1,200 Notes Payable balance in Exhibit A-11 had been listed as $120, the credit column

---

[6]Sweet Temptations purchased $200 of store equipment at the end of January. Since Sweet Temptations did not use this store equipment in January, it did not depreciate the equipment for that month. Sweet Temptations will include the depreciation on this store equipment as an expense in later months when it uses the equipment.

EXHIBIT A-10	SWEET TEMPTATIONS' GENERAL LEDGER AFTER ADJUSTING ENTRIES (JANUARY 31, 2008)

Cash   No. 101

1/01/08	Bal	7,300	1/03/08		1,620
1/02/08		300	1/20/08		50
1/07/08		400	1/25/08		200
1/31/08		7,700	1/25/08		300
			1/29/08		200
			1/30/08		2,050
			1/31/08		60
			1/31/08		190
1/31/08	Bal	11,030			

Accounts Receivable   No. 103

1/01/08	Bal	400	1/07/08		400
1/06/08	Bal	100			
1/31/08	Bal	100			

Inventory   No. 105

1/01/08	Bal	1,620	1/02/08		135
1/04/08		4,320	1/06/08		45
			1/31/08		3,465
1/31/08	Bal	2,295			

Supplies   No. 106

1/01/08	Bal	700	1/31/08	Adj	30
1/31/08	Bal	670			

Prepaid Rent   No. 107

1/01/08	Bal	6,000	1/31/08	Adj	1,000
1/31/08	Bal	5,000			

Store Equipment   No. 123

1/01/08	Bal	1,800		
1/29/08		200		
1/31/08	Bal	2,000		

Accumulated Depreciation   No. 124

		1/31/08	Adj	15

Accounts Payable   No. 201

1/03/08		1,620	1/01/08	Bal	1,620
			1/04/08		4,320
			1/31/08	Bal	4,320

Notes Payable   No. 204

		11/01/08	Bal	1,200

Interest Payable   No. 205

		11/31/08	Adj	8

A. Cox, Capital   No. 301

		11/01/08	Bal	15,000

A. Cox, Withdrawals   No. 304

1/20/08	50	

Income Summary   No. 306

Sales Revenue   No. 401

		11/02/08		300
		11/06/08		100
		11/31/08		7,700
		11/31/08	Bal	8,100

Cost of Goods Sold   No. 501

1/02/08		135	
1/06/08		45	
1/31/08		3,465	
1/31/08	Bal	3,645	

Consulting Expense   No. 502

1/25/08	200	

Advertising Expense   No. 503

1/25/08	300	

Salaries Expense   No. 504

1/31/08	2,050	

Telephone Expense   No. 505

1/31/08	60	

Utilities Expense   No. 506

1/31/08	190	

Supplies Expense   No. 507

1/31/08	Adj	30	

Rent Expense   No. 508

1/31/08	Adj	1,000	

Interest Expense   No. 509

1/31/08	Adj	8	

Depreciation Expense   No. 510

1/31/08	Adj	15	

would have totaled $27,563 instead of $28,643. The $1,080 difference between that and the correct debit column total is evenly divisible by 9.

A transposition or slide may have occurred when the company transferred the account balances from the accounts to the adjusted trial balance or when it initially computed the account balances. Thus, the company should compare the account balances listed on the adjusted trial balance with the account balances listed in the general ledger. If it properly transferred the balances, then it should recompute the ledger account balances, and if it finds no error, it should double-check the postings. Finally, if the company still does not find the error, it should review the journal entries for accuracy. As you can imagine,

EXHIBIT A-11	ADJUSTED TRIAL BALANCE

SWEET TEMPTATIONS
Adjusted Trial Balance
January 31, 2008

Account Titles	Debits	Credits
Cash	$11,030	
Accounts receivable	100	
Inventory	2,295	
Supplies	670	
Prepaid rent	5,000	
Store equipment	2,000	
Accumulated depreciation		$ 15
Accounts payable		4,320
Notes payable		1,200
Interest payable		8
A. Cox, capital		15,000
A. Cox, withdrawals	50	
Sales revenue		8,100
Cost of goods sold	3,645	
Consulting expense	200	
Advertising expense	300	
Salaries expense	2,050	
Telephone expense	60	
Utilities expense	190	
Supplies expense	30	
Rent expense	1,000	
Interest expense	8	
Depreciation expense	15	
Totals	$28,643	$28,643

detecting where an error has been made is time-consuming and frustrating. That is why it is very important to follow the set procedures in the journalizing and posting process.

PREPARING THE FINANCIAL STATEMENTS

A company prepares its financial statements for the accounting period after it completes the adjusted trial balance. It prepares the income statement first because the amount of net income (or net loss) affects the owner's capital account on the balance sheet. A sole proprietorship prepares the statement of changes in owner's equity (a supporting schedule for the balance sheet) next. Then, it prepares the balance sheet. Finally, the company completes its cash flow statement.[7]

Income Statement

An income statement is the financial statement that summarizes the results of a company's earnings activities (i.e., revenues, expenses, and net income) for its accounting period. Exhibit A-12 on the following page shows Sweet Temptations' income statement for January 2008. Sweet Temptations prepared its income statement from the accounts listed on the lower part of the adjusted trial balance in Exhibit A-11. Because the revenue and expense accounts are listed at the end of each company's chart of accounts (and, therefore,

---

[7]For simplicity, in this appendix we do not prepare a cash flow statement. Refer to Chapter 8 for an in-depth discussion of the cash flow statement.

EXHIBIT A-12	INCOME STATEMENT

SWEET TEMPTATIONS
Income Statement
For Month Ended January 31, 2008

Sales revenue		$8,100
Cost of goods sold		(3,645)
Gross profit		$4,455
Operating expenses:		
Consulting expense	$ 200	
Advertising expense	300	
Salaries expense	2,050	
Telephone expense	60	
Utilities expense	190	
Supplies expense	30	
Rent expense	1,000	
Depreciation expense	15	
Total expenses		(3,845)
Operating income		$ 610
Other item:		
Interest expense		(8)
Net Income		$ 602

its general ledger), these accounts are always listed in the lower portion of each company's adjusted trial balance. This procedure simplifies preparation of the income statement.

Statement of Changes in Owner's Equity

A statement of changes in owner's equity is a schedule that shows the impact on owner's equity of any additional investments by the owner in the company, the company's net income, and owner withdrawals during the accounting period. A company presents this statement as a supporting schedule to the owner's capital account balance listed on the balance sheet. Exhibit A-13 shows Sweet Temptations' statement of owner's equity for January 2008. A. Cox made no additional investments during January. Sweet Temptations obtained the beginning balance of the A. Cox, Capital account and the amount of the withdrawals from the middle portion of the adjusted trial balance in Exhibit A-11. It obtained the net income from the income statement in Exhibit A-12.

Balance Sheet

A balance sheet is the financial statement that reports the financial position (i.e., assets, liabilities, and owner's equity) of a company on a particular date. Exhibit A-14 shows Sweet

EXHIBIT A-13	STATEMENT OF CHANGES IN OWNER'S EQUITY

SWEET TEMPTATIONS
Statement of Changes in Owner's Equity
For Month Ending January 31, 2008

A. Cox, capital, January 1, 2008	$15,000
Add: Net income for January	602
	$15,602
Less: Withdrawals for January	(50)
A. Cox, capital, January 31, 2008	$15,552

EXHIBIT A-14 — BALANCE SHEET

SWEET TEMPTATIONS
Balance Sheet
January 31, 2008

Assets

Current Assets:

Cash		$11,030
Accounts receivable		100
Inventory		2,295
Supplies		670
Prepaid rent		5,000
Total Current Assets		$19,095
Property and Equipment:		
Store equipment	$ 2,000	
Less: Accumulated depreciation	(15)	1,985
Total Assets		$21,080

Liabilities

Current Liabilities:

Accounts payable		$ 4,320
Notes payable		1,200
Interest payable		8
Total Current Liabilities		$ 5,528

Owner's Equity

A. Cox, capital		$15,552
Total Liabilities and Owner's Equity		$21,080

Temptations' balance sheet on January 31, 2008. The company prepared the balance sheet from the accounts listed on the upper portion of the adjusted trial balance in Exhibit A-11. Use of the adjusted trial balance makes the preparation of the balance sheet very easy. The assets, liabilities, and owner's capital accounts are the first accounts in a company's chart of accounts and its general ledger. Therefore, these accounts are always listed in the upper portion of the company's adjusted trial balance. Note, however, that the amount listed as the owner's capital on the adjusted trial balance is *not* the amount the company lists on the ending balance sheet because the amount has not been updated for the company's net income or withdrawals. Instead, the company obtains the ending owner's capital account balance from the statement of changes in owner's equity. Sweet Temptations obtained the owner's capital account balance in Exhibit A-14 from the statement in Exhibit A-13.

PREPARATION OF CLOSING ENTRIES

Earlier we made two points that are relevant to our discussion of closing entries. First, the revenue, expense, and withdrawals accounts are *temporary* accounts. A company uses these accounts to determine the changes in its owner's equity in the current accounting period resulting from its net income (or net loss) and from owner's withdrawals. Second, a company does *not* use the owner's capital account listed on the adjusted trial balance in preparing its balance sheet because this account balance is not up-to-date for the net income and withdrawals of the period.

To begin the next accounting period, the company needs to (1) update the balance in the owner's capital account and (2) show zero balances in the revenue, expense, and withdrawals accounts. The owner's capital account balance should be up-to-date to show the owner's current investment in the assets of the company. The company will use the revenue, expense, and withdrawals accounts in the next accounting period to accumulate

7 What are closing entries, and how do they relate to the Income Summary account?

the company's net income and any of the owner's withdrawals *for that period*. Therefore, it is important to start with a zero balance in each of these accounts at the beginning of the period so that at the end of the period, the balances in the accounts will show the revenue, expense, and withdrawal amounts for only that period.

Closing entries are journal entries that a company makes at the end of its accounting period to create a zero balance in each revenue, expense, and withdrawals account and to transfer these account balances to the owner's permanent capital account. It makes closing entries after preparing the financial statements. Like other journal entries, a company records closing entries in the general journal and then posts them to the respective accounts. It does *not* close the revenue and expense accounts directly to the owner's capital account. Instead, it first transfers these account balances to an account entitled Income Summary. The **Income Summary** account is a temporary account a company uses in the closing process to accumulate the amount of the company's net income (or net loss) before it transfers this amount to the owner's capital account.

Closing the Revenue Accounts

Recall that each revenue account has a credit balance (prior to closing). To reduce this credit balance to zero, the company makes a debit entry in the revenue account for an amount *equal* to that of the credit balance. At the same time, it transfers the revenue amount to the Income Summary account by a credit entry to that account. It first records these debit and credit entries in the *general journal,* and then posts them to the related accounts in the general ledger. We show Sweet Temptations' closing entries in Exhibit A-15. The $8,100 journal entry of Sweet Temptations to close its revenue account is the first closing entry in Exhibit A-15. Sweet Temptations obtained the amount of the sales

EXHIBIT A-15	SWEET TEMPTATIONS' CLOSING ENTRIES: JANUARY 31, 2008			

Date	Account Titles and Explanations	Acct. No.	Debit	Credit
	Closing Entries			
2008				
Jan. 31	Sales Revenue	401	8,100	
	Income Summary	306		8,100
	To close revenue account.			
31	Income Summary	306	7,498	
	Cost of Goods Sold	501		3,645
	Consulting Expense	502		200
	Advertising Expense	503		300
	Salaries Expense	504		2,050
	Telephone Expense	505		60
	Utilities Expense	506		190
	Supplies Expense	507		30
	Rent Expense	508		1,000
	Interest Expense	509		8
	Depreciation Expense	510		15
	To close expense accounts.			
31	Income Summary	306	602	
	A. Cox, Capital	301		602
	To close net income to owner's capital account.			
31	A. Cox, Capital	301	50	
	A. Cox, Withdrawals	304		50
	To close withdrawals to owner's capital account.			

revenue from the adjusted trial balance in Exhibit A-11. It obtained the account number of the Income Summary account from the chart of accounts in Exhibit A-6. In this illustration, Sweet Temptations has only one revenue account. When a company has more than one revenue account, it makes a compound entry in which it first debits each revenue account for the amount of the balance in the account and then credits the total of the revenues to the Income Summary account.

Closing the Expense Accounts

Each expense account has a debit balance (prior to closing). To reduce each debit balance to zero, the company makes a credit entry in each expense account for an amount *equal* to that of the debit balance. It transfers this expense amount to the Income Summary account by a debit entry to that account. A company typically has many expense accounts, so it usually closes all the expense accounts by making a compound entry in the general journal in which it credits each expense account for the amount of the balance in the account and debits the Income Summary account for the *total* amount of the expenses. (Remember, however, that it always lists the debit entry first in the general journal.) The $7,498 journal entry of Sweet Temptations to close its expense accounts is the second closing entry at the end of Exhibit A-15. Sweet Temptations obtained the amounts of the various expenses from the adjusted trial balance in Exhibit A-11. (Remember that Cost of Goods Sold is an expense account.)

Closing the Income Summary Account

After a company closes the revenue and expense accounts to the Income Summary account, the balance in the account is the amount of the net income (or net loss). A credit balance indicates that the company earned a net income for the period because revenues exceeded expenses. A debit balance indicates a net loss because expenses exceeded revenues. A company transfers the amount of its net income (or net loss) to the owner's permanent capital account in the third closing entry. In the case of net income, the closing entry in the general journal is a debit to the Income Summary account for an amount equal to its balance and a credit to the owner's capital account for the same amount. The credit to the owner's capital account increases that account by the amount of the net income. (The company would handle a net loss in the opposite way, with a debit to the owner's capital account and a credit to the Income Summary account.) The $602 journal entry of Sweet Temptations to close the Income Summary account to the A. Cox, Capital account is the third closing entry at the end of Exhibit A-15.

Closing the Withdrawals Account

A company closes the debit balance of the withdrawals account *directly* to the owner's permanent capital account, since withdrawals are *disinvestments* by the owner. The closing entry in the general journal is a debit to the owner's permanent capital account and a credit to the withdrawals account for the amount of the total withdrawals of the period. The debit entry brings the owner's capital account balance up-to-date at the end of the period. The credit entry to the withdrawals account reduces the account balance to zero so that it can accumulate the withdrawals of the next period. A company *never* closes the withdrawals account to the Income Summary account because withdrawals are *not* part of net income. The $50 journal entry to close the A. Cox, Withdrawals account balance to the A. Cox, Capital account is the last closing entry at the end of Exhibit A-15. Sweet Temptations obtained the amount of the withdrawals from the adjusted trial balance in Exhibit A-11.

Posting the Closing Entries

After a company records its closing entries, the company posts these entries from its general journal to the accounts in its general ledger. Sweet Temptations posts the closing entries that it prepared in Exhibit A-15 to the appropriate accounts in its general ledger, as we show in Exhibit A-16. Note that Exhibit A-16 is similar to the right side of Exhibit A-10, except that the closing entries (as indicated by a *Cl*) are included. Also note that after the closing entries are posted, all the revenue, expense, and withdrawals accounts have zero balances. The A. Cox, Capital account has a balance of $15,552, the amount Sweet Temptations listed as the owner's equity on its January 31, 2008 balance sheet in Exhibit A-14. This completes the closing entry process for Sweet Temptations.

Post-Closing Trial Balance

After a company journalizes and posts its closing entries, the only accounts with nonzero balances should be the permanent accounts—that is, the assets, liabilities, and owner's capital accounts. As a check to make sure that no debit or credit errors were made during the closing entries, a company prepares a post-closing trial balance. A **post-closing trial balance** is a schedule a company prepares after making the closing entries to prove the equality of the debit and credit balances in its asset, liability, and owner's capital accounts. The post-closing trial balance includes only permanent accounts because all the temporary accounts have zero balances due to the closing process. After the company prepares the post-closing trial balance, the accounting cycle for the current period is complete. The company then begins the accounting cycle for its next accounting period. To save space, we do not show the post-closing trial balance of Sweet Temptations here.

EXHIBIT A-16   **SWEET TEMPTATIONS' POSTINGS OF CLOSING ENTRIES (JANUARY 31, 2008)**

A. Cox, Capital					No. 301
1/31/08	Cl	50	1/01/08	Bal	15,000
			1/31/08	Cl	602
			1/31/08	Bal	15,552

A. Cox, Withdrawals					No. 304
1/20/08		50	1/31/08	Cl	50
1/31/08	Bal	0			

Income Summary					No. 306
1/31/08	Cl	7,498	1/31/08	Cl	8,100
1/31/08	Cl	602			
			1/31/08	Bal	0

Sales Revenue					No. 401
1/31/08	Cl	8,100	1/31/08		8,100
			1/31/08	Bal	0

Cost of Goods Sold					No. 501
1/31/08	Bal	3,645	1/31/08	Cl	3,645
1/31/08	Bal	0			

Consulting Expense					No. 502
1/25/08		200	1/31/08	Cl	200
1/31/08	Bal	0			

Advertising Expense					No. 503
1/25/08		300	1/31/08	Cl	300
1/31/08	Bal	0			

Salaries Expense					No. 504
1/30/08		2,050	1/31/08	Cl	2,050
1/31/08	Bal	0			

Telephone Expense					No. 505
1/31/08		60	1/31/08	Cl	60
1/31/08	Bal	0			

Utilities Expense					No. 506
1/31/08		190	1/31/08	Cl	190
1/31/08	Bal	0			

Supplies Expense					No. 507
1/31/08	Adj	30	1/31/08	Cl	30
1/31/08	Bal	0			

Rent Expense					No. 508
1/31/08	Adj	1,000	1/31/08	Cl	1,000
1/31/08	Bal	0			

Interest Expense					No. 509
1/31/08	Adj	8	1/31/08	Cl	8
1/31/08	Bal	0			

Depreciation Expense					No. 510
1/31/08	Adj	15	1/31/08	Cl	15
1/31/08	Bal	0			

MODIFICATIONS FOR CORPORATIONS

For simplicity, earlier we discussed and illustrated the procedures in the accounting cycle of a sole proprietorship (Sweet Temptations). However, many companies are corporations, and you also should be familiar with the accounting procedures for corporations. Fortunately, the procedures we discussed for sole proprietorships need to be modified only slightly for corporations. The modifications involve differences in how a corporation records and reports investments by owners, distributions to owners, and some income statement items and balance sheet items. To illustrate, we will modify the Sweet Temptations example by assuming the company is a corporation instead of a sole proprietorship.

8 How are accounting procedures modified for corporations?

Investments by Owners

One difference between the accounting for corporations and that for sole proprietorships involves investments in the company by owners (stockholders). Assume that on December 15, 2007, Sweet Temptations was incorporated and issued 1,000 shares of $10 par value common stock to A. Cox for $15 per share. Sweet Temptations would make the following journal entry to record this transaction:

Date	Account Titles and Explanations	Debit	Credit
2007 Dec. 15	Cash	15,000	
	Common Stock, $10 par		10,000
	Additional Paid-in Capital		5,000
	Issued 1,000 shares of common stock for $15 per share.		

As we discussed in Chapter 24, the total amount received by a corporation when it issues stock is allocated between the legal capital (par value) and additional paid-in capital. Thus, a corporation has both a Common Stock account and an Additional Paid-in Capital account to record investments (contributed capital) by stockholders. Also, a corporation has a Retained Earnings account, which lists its total lifetime earnings (net income or net loss) that have not been distributed to stockholders as dividends.

Distributions to Owners

The payment of dividends to stockholders by a corporation is recorded differently than are the owner's withdrawals from a sole proprietorship. Since the Retained Earnings account includes total earnings *not* distributed to stockholders as dividends, a corporation records any dividend payments directly as a reduction in retained earnings by a debit (decrease) to Retained Earnings and a credit (decrease) to Cash. For example, assume that on January 20, 2008, Sweet Temptations Corporation declared and paid a dividend of $0.05 per share. Sweet Temptations Corporation makes the following journal entry to record the dividend of $50 (1,000 shares × $0.05):

Date	Account Titles and Explanations	Debit	Credit
2008 Jan. 20	Retained Earnings	50	
	Cash		50
	Declared and paid dividends.		

Sweet Temptations Corporation reports the dividends as a reduction of retained earnings in the statement of retained earnings (which we discussed in Chapter 24).

Income Statement Items

Another difference between a corporation and a sole proprietorship is that a corporation must pay income taxes on its earnings. These income taxes are considered an expense of doing business. Normally, a corporation *pays* its income taxes early in the next quarter after the income is earned. However, since income taxes are an expense, they should be matched against the income in the period the income is earned. Thus, in addition to the adjusting entries described earlier, a corporation also makes an adjusting entry for *accrued* income taxes at the end of each period.

Because, in this example, Sweet Temptations is a corporation, it must pay income taxes. Therefore, at the end of January 2008, Sweet Temptations Corporation must make an adjusting entry for the income taxes that it will pay early next quarter based on its January earnings. During January 2008, Sweet Temptations Corporation earned $602 of income before income taxes. If we assume a 40% tax rate, then it records the $241 ($602 × 0.40, rounded) income taxes in the following adjusting entry:

Date	Account Titles and Explanations	Debit	Credit
2008 Jan. 31	Income Tax Expense Income Taxes Payable To record income taxes for January.	241	241

Sweet Temptations Corporation reports the income tax expense on its income statement for January, and reports the income taxes payable as a current liability on its January 31, 2008 balance sheet.

A corporation's income statement is similar to that of a sole proprietorship, with two exceptions. First, the income tax expense is deducted from income before income taxes to determine net income. Second, earnings per share is shown directly below net income. The income statement of Sweet Temptations Corporation for January 2008 would look exactly like Exhibit A-12, except for the lower portion, which would appear as follows:

Income before income taxes	$602
Income tax expense	(241)
Net income	$361
Earnings per share (1,000 shares)	$0.36

Balance Sheet Items

The balance sheet of a corporation is similar to that of a sole proprietorship, with two exceptions. In addition to including income taxes payable as a current liability, a corporation's balance sheet also has a modified owners' equity section. The owners' equity of a corporation is called **stockholders' equity** and consists of two parts: contributed capital and retained earnings. The contributed capital includes both the Common Stock and the Additional Paid-in Capital account balances from the adjusted trial balance. The corporation obtains the Retained Earnings amount from the statement of retained earnings. This statement is very similar to the statement of changes in owner's equity, which we discussed earlier in this appendix. The balance sheet of Sweet Temptations Corporation on January 31, 2008, would look like Exhibit A-14, except that the liabilities and the stockholders' equity sections would appear as follows:

Liabilities

Current Liabilities:	
Accounts payable	$ 4,320
Notes payable	1,200
Interest payable	8
Income taxes payable	241
Total Liabilities	$ 5,769

Stockholders' Equity

Contributed capital:
Common stock, $10 par	$10,000
Additional paid-in capital	5,000
Total contributed capital	$15,000
Retained earnings	311
Total Stockholders' Equity	$15,311
Total Liabilities and Stockholders' Equity	$21,080

Sweet Temptations Corporation would have obtained the income taxes payable, common stock, and additional paid-in capital amounts from its adjusted trial balance. It would have obtained the $311 retained earnings amount ($0 beginning retained earnings + $361 net income − $50 dividends) from its statement of retained earnings.

There is also a slight difference in the closing entries of a corporation as compared with those of a sole proprietorship. A corporation closes the balance of the Income Summary account to the Retained Earnings account. Furthermore, since it recorded any dividends during the period directly as a reduction of retained earnings, there is no closing entry at the end of the period for dividends.

OTHER JOURNAL ENTRIES

Earlier in the appendix, we discussed the journal entries made by Sweet Temptations. As we noted in various chapters of the book, other companies may record journal entries for transactions such as sales discounts, purchases discounts, sales returns and allowances, and purchases returns and allowances. The way a company records these transactions depends on the company's accounting system and whether it uses a perpetual or a periodic inventory system. However, Exhibit A-17 shows a general framework for recording these types of transactions. We show only a few transactions in Exhibit A-17. However, by using your knowledge of the accounting equation, debit and credit rules, contra accounts, revenues and expenses, and assets, liabilities, and owner's equity, you can develop the correct journal entries for recording other transactions.

EXHIBIT A-17	ILLUSTRATIONS OF ADDITIONAL JOURNAL ENTRIES

Sales Discounts			**Purchases Discounts**		
Cash (net)	x				
Sales Discounts Taken	x		Accounts Payable (gross)	x	
Accounts Receivable (gross)		x	Inventory (or Purchases Discounts Taken*)		x
			Cash (net)		x
Sales Returns and Allowances			**Purchases Returns and Allowances**		
Sales Returns and Allowances	x				
Accounts Receivable (or Cash)		x	Accounts Payable (or Cash)	x	
			Inventory		
Inventory (at cost)	x		(or Purchases Returns and Allowances*)		x
Cost of Goods Sold		x			

*Accounts used under periodic inventory system

SUMMARY

At the beginning of the appendix we asked you several questions. Below are the questions from the beginning of the appendix, with a brief summary of the key points relating to the answers. Use your creative and critical thinking skills to expand on these key points to develop more complete answers to the questions and to determine what other questions you have that might lead you to learn more about the issues.

1 **What is a debit entry, and what is a credit entry?**

A debit entry is a monetary amount recorded (debited) in the left side of an account. A credit entry is a monetary amount recorded (credited) in the right side of an account.

2 **What are the rules for recording increases and decreases in asset and liability accounts?**

Asset accounts (accounts on the left side of the accounting equation) are increased by debit entries (i.e., amounts recorded on the left side) and decreased by credit entries. Liability accounts (accounts on the right side of the equation) are increased by credit entries (i.e., amounts recorded on the right side) and decreased by debit entries.

3 **What are the rules for recording increases and decreases in owner's equity accounts?**

Permanent owner's equity, or capital, accounts (accounts on the right side of the equation) are increased by credit entries and decreased by debit entries. *Temporary* owner's equity accounts have the following rules: (a) withdrawal accounts are increased by debit entries and decreased by credit entries, (b) revenue accounts are increased by credit entries and decreased by debit entries, and (c) expense accounts are increased by debit entries and decreased by credit entries.

4 **What are the major steps in a company's accounting cycle?**

The major steps in a company's accounting cycle include (1) recording (journalizing) the transactions in the general journal, (2) posting the journal entries to the accounts in the general ledger (3) recording (and posting) adjusting entries, (4) preparing the financial statements, and (5) recording (and posting) closing entries.

5 **What is the difference between journalizing and posting?**

Journalizing is the process of recording a transaction in a company's general journal. A journal entry is the recorded information for each transaction. Posting is the process of transferring the debit and credit information for each journal entry to the accounts in a company's general ledger.

6 **What are adjusting entries, and what are the three types of adjusting entries?**

Adjusting entries are journal entries that a company makes at the end of its accounting period to bring the company's revenue and expense account balances up-to-date and to show the correct ending balances in its asset and liability accounts. Adjusting entries may be grouped into three types: (1) apportionment of prepaid and unearned items, (2) recording of accrued items, and (3) recording or apportionment of estimated items.

7 **What are closing entries, and how do they relate to the Income Summary account?**

Closing entries are journal entries that a company makes at the end of its accounting period to create a zero balance in each revenue, expense, and withdrawals account and to transfer these account balances to the owner's permanent capital account. The Income Summary account is a temporary account used in the closing process to accumulate the amount of the company's net income (or net loss) before transferring this amount to the owner's capital account.

8 **How are accounting procedures modified for corporations?**

Accounting procedures are modified for corporations as follows: (1) investments by owners (stock-holders) are recorded in capital stock and additional paid-in capital accounts, (2) distributions (dividends) to stockholders are recorded as a decrease in the retained earnings account, (3) the income statement includes income tax expense and earnings per share, and (4) the balance sheet includes income taxes payable in the current liabilities section, and contributed capital and retained earnings in the stockholders' equity section.

KEY TERMS

accounts *(p. A-2)*
accounting cycle *(p. A-4)*
accrued expense *(p. A-15)*
accrued revenue *(p. A-16)*
adjusted trial balance *(p. A-17)*
adjusting entries *(p. A-13)*
balance of an account *(p. A-4)*
chart of accounts *(p. A-10)*
closing entries *(p. A-22)*
credit entry *(p. A-3)*
debit entry *(p. A-3)*
double entry rule *(p. A-3)*
general journal *(p. A-5)*

general ledger *(p. A-2)*
income summary *(p. A-22)*
journal entry *(p. A-5)*
journalizing *(p. A-5)*
prepaid item *(p. A-14)*
post-closing trial balance *(p. A-24)*
posting *(p. A-10)*
slide *(p. A-17)*
stockholders' equity *(p. A-26)*
T-account *(p. A-2)*
transposition *(p. A-17)*
trial balance *(p. A-12)*
unearned revenue *(p. A-15)*

QUESTIONS, EXERCISES, AND PROBLEMS

Questions

QA-1 Define an account. What are the parts of a T-account? What is a set of accounts for a company called?

QA-2 What is a debit entry? a credit entry?

QA-3 What are the debit and credit rules? How do these rules relate to the accounting equation?

QA-4 Explain the double entry rule. How (if at all) does this rule change in the case of a compound entry?

QA-5 What is a general journal (in a manual accounting system)? List the advantages of initially recording a company's transactions in a general journal.

QA-6 What is journalizing? Briefly describe the journalizing process.

QA-7 What is posting? Briefly describe the posting process.

QA-8 What are adjusting entries? Why are they necessary?

QA-9 What is an adjusted trial balance? Why is it used?

QA-10 What are closing entries? Describe how (a) revenue accounts, (b) expense accounts, and (c) the withdrawals account are closed.

QA-11 How does the lower portion of the income statement for a corporation differ from that of a sole proprietorship? Where does a corporation report its income taxes payable on its financial statements?

QA-12 How is the owners' equity of a corporation shown on its balance sheet?

Exercises

EA-1 During the month of July, Sands Insurance Company entered into the following transactions:

Date	Transaction
July 1	Nancy Sands deposited a $30,000 personal check in the company's checking account.
10	Purchased land and an office building at a cost of $2,000 and $21,000, respectively, paying $8,000 down and signing a $15,000 note due at the end of the year.
25	Purchased office supplies costing $800 on credit.

Required: (1) Prepare journal entries to record the preceding transactions.
(2) List the source documents normally used in recording each of these transactions.

EA-2 Albert Mitchell started Worldwide Travel Service on April 1 of the current year, and the company engaged in the following transactions during the month of April:

Date	Transaction
Apr. 1	Albert Mitchell opened the business by depositing a $25,000 personal check in the new company's checking account.
3	Purchased land and a small office building for $2,500 and $28,000, respectively, paying $10,500 down and signing a 1-year note for $20,000.
20	Purchased office equipment at a cost of $6,000. Half of the cost was paid in cash, and the remainder is due at the end of May.

Required: (1) Prepare journal entries to record the preceding transactions.
(2) List the source documents normally used in recording each of these transactions.

EA-3 Both Plumbing Company entered into the following transactions during the month of May:

Date	Transaction
May 4	Installed plumbing in new house under construction; contractor agreed to pay contract price of $1,800 in 30 days.
15	Made plumbing repairs for customer and collected $85 for services performed.
28	Paid $79 for May telephone bill.
31	Paid $900 to employees for May salaries.
31	Received $100 utility bill, to be paid in early June.

Required: (1) Prepare journal entries to record the preceding transactions.
(2) List the source documents normally used to record these transactions.

EA-4 Aline Taxi Service entered into the following transactions during the month of September:

Date	Transaction
Sept. 1	Paid $550 rent on garage for the month of September.
15	Cash receipts for taxi fares for the first half of the month totaled $1,640.
23	Paid $980 for September fuel bill from Wildcat Oil Company.
29	P. L. Aline withdrew $400 for personal use.
30	Paid salaries amounting to $1,200 to employees.
30	Cash receipts for taxi fares for the second half of the month totaled $1,340.

Required: (1) Prepare journal entries to record the preceding transactions.
(2) List the source documents normally used to record these transactions.

EA-5 Nomura Sales, a medical supplies wholesaler, entered into the following transactions (the company uses the perpetual inventory system):

Date	Transaction
Aug. 1	Purchased $5,300 of medical supplies on credit from Nead Company.
3	Returned $200 of defective medical supplies purchased on August 1 from Nead Company for credit.
5	Sold $2,000 of medical supplies on credit to P & H Drugs. The cost of the inventory sold was $1,200.
8	Granted $300 credit to P & H Drugs for return of medical supplies purchased on August 5. The cost of the inventory returned was $180.
9	Purchased $1,000 of medical supplies for cash.
10	Paid balance due to Nead Company for purchase of August 1.
15	Received balance due from P & H Drugs for medical supplies purchased on August 5.
30	Sold $800 of merchandise to customers for cash. The cost of the inventory sold was $500.

Required: Prepare journal entries to record the preceding transactions.

EA-6 Taylor Art Supplies Company sells various art supplies to local artists. The company uses a perpetual inventory system, and the cost of its inventory of art supplies at the beginning of August was $2,500. Its cash balance was $800 at the beginning of August, and it entered into the following transactions during August:

Date	Transaction
Aug. 1	Purchased $400 of art supplies for cash.
4	Made a $900 sale of art supplies on credit to P. Marks, with terms of n/15. The cost of the inventory sold was $550.
6	Purchased $700 of art supplies on credit from Tott Company, with terms of n/20.
10	Returned, for credit to its account, $100 of defective art supplies purchased on August 6 from Tott Company.
12	Made cash sales of $250 to customers. The cost of the inventory sold was $160.
13	Granted a $25 allowance to a customer for damaged inventory sold on August 12.
15	Received payment from P. Marks of the amount due for inventory sold on credit on August 4.
25	Paid balance due to Tott Company for purchase on August 6.

Required: (1) Prepare journal entries to record the preceding transactions.
(2) Set up appropriate T-accounts, post the journal entries to the accounts (for simplicity, it is not necessary to assign numbers to the accounts), and determine the ending account balances.

EA-7 At the end of the current year, Rulem Hair Styling provides you with the following information:
(a) Depreciation expense on styling equipment totals $1,360 for the current year.
(b) Accrued interest on a note payable issued on October 1 amounts to $850 at year-end.
(c) Unearned rent in the amount of $1,000 has been earned (the company records all receipts in advance in an Unearned Rent account).
(d) Hair styling supplies used during the year total $210 (the company records all purchases of supplies in an asset account).

Required: Prepare adjusting entries at the end of the current year based on the preceding information.

EA-8 On June 30 of the current year, Washington Background Music Company showed the following trial balance:

Account Titles	Debits	Credits
Cash	$10,150	
Office supplies	368	
Sound system	6,500	
Accounts payable		$ 295
D. L. Washington, capital		15,000
Music system revenues		3,198

continued

Account Titles	Debits	Credits
Salary expense..	1,000	
Rent expense..	300	
General expenses...	175	
Totals..	$18,493	$18,493

The following adjustments are needed:

(a) Office supplies used during the month of June totaled $62.
(b) Depreciation expense for the month of June on the sound system totaled $75.

June was the first month of operations for Washington Background Music Company.

Required: (1) Prepare adjusting entries to record the preceding adjustments.
(2) Prepare the June 30 adjusted trial balance for Washington Background Music Company.

EA-9 On October 1 of the current year, Bourdon Company paid $360 for a two-year comprehensive insurance policy on the company's building.

Required: (1) Prepare the journal entry to record each of the following:
(a) The purchase of this insurance policy
(b) The adjusting entry at the end of the year
(2) If the adjusting entry had *not* been made in (1)(b), discuss what effect this error would have on the accounts and totals listed on the income statement and balance sheet.

EA-10 On October 1 of the current year, Sagir Appraisal Company received $1,800 in advance from the Land-Ho Real Estate Agency for 6 months' rent of office space.

Required: (1) Prepare the Sagir Appraisal Company journal entries to record the following:
(a) The receipt of the payment
(b) The adjustment for rent revenue at the end of the current year
(2) If the adjusting entry had *not* been made in (1)(b), discuss what effect this error would have on the accounts and totals listed on the income statement and balance sheet.

EA-11 The Cobbler Company shows the following revenue, expense, and withdrawals account balances on December 31 of the current year, before closing:

Account Titles	Debits	Credits
A. B. Cobbler, withdrawals.............................	$1,750	
Shoe service revenues.....................................		$4,830
Salaries expense...	2,300	
Utilities expense..	226	
Supplies expense...	147	
Rent expense...	550	
Depreciation expense......................................	28	

Required: Prepare closing entries.

EA-12 The following are various accounts related to the income statement and owner's equity of Lynn Company (a sole proprietorship) for the current year:

P. Lynn, withdrawals...	$ 30,000
Salaries expense...	31,400
Delivery expense...	9,300
Utilities expense..	14,700
Sales..	189,500
Depreciation expense..	5,600
Cost of goods sold	73,800

Required: From the information given, prepare the December 31 closing entries.

EA-13 For the year ended December 31, 2008, Newhard Corporation had sales revenues of $120,000, operating expenses of $68,000, and other revenue of $2,800. The corporation is subject to a 40% income tax rate and currently has 10,000 shares of common stock held the entire year by stockholders.

Required: (1) Prepare the journal entry on December 31, 2008 to record Newhard Corporation's 2008 income taxes.
(2) Prepare a 2008 income statement for Newhard Corporation.

EA-14 On January 1, 2008, ACE Corporation showed the following account balances:

Common stock ($10 par)..................................... $100,000
Additional paid-in capital 120,000
Retained earnings... 69,700

During 2008, the following events occurred:
(a) The corporation issued 1,000 shares of additional common stock for $30,000.
(b) Net income for the year was $39,000.
(c) Dividends in the amount of $12,000 were declared and paid to stockholders.

Required: Prepare the stockholders' equity section of ACE Corporation's balance sheet on December 31, 2008.

Problems

PA-1 The Cameron Copy-Quick Company was recently set up by Joseph Cameron. The company's transactions during October, the first month of operations, were as follows:

Date	Transaction
Oct. 3	Joseph Cameron deposited $28,000 in the company's checking account.
4	Acquired land and a building for $3,000 and $42,000, respectively, paying $5,000 cash and signing a five-year mortgage for the remaining balance.
15	Copy equipment costing $8,000 was purchased on credit from Tailor Equipment Company.
20	Office supplies costing $1,600 were purchased for cash.
24	Purchased office furniture costing $2,300 from Freddy's Furniture, paying $300 cash. The balance of $2,000 is due in 30 days.
28	Purchased a three-year insurance policy for $900 cash.
31	Paid balance due to Tailor Equipment Company for copy equipment purchased on October 15.

Required: (1) Set up the following general ledger T-accounts (and account numbers): Cash (101), Office Supplies (105), Prepaid Insurance (106), Land (110), Building (112), Copy Equipment (114), Office Furniture (118), Accounts Payable (201), Mortgage Payable (220), and J. Cameron, Capital (301).
(2) Record the preceding transactions in a general journal.
(3) Post the journal entries to the general ledger accounts and determine the ending account balances.

PA-2 The Foster Tax Services Company was established on January 2 of the current year to help clients with tax planning and preparation of their tax returns. The company engaged in the following transactions during January:

Date	Transaction
Jan. 2	R. Foster set up the company by investing $33,000 cash in the company's checking account.
3	Acquired land and a building at a cost of $3,000 and $21,000, respectively. A $6,000 down payment was made, and a mortgage was signed for the remaining balance.
4	Purchased office equipment costing $7,000 by signing a note due in one year.
10	Office supplies costing $735 were purchased for cash.
21	Performed tax planning services for customer and collected $3,020.
31	Paid $1,450 for employee's salary.

continued

      31   Paid utilities bill of $88 for January.

      31   R. Foster withdrew $850 cash for personal use.

Required: (1) Set up the following T-accounts (and account numbers): Cash (101), Office Supplies (105), Land (110), Building (112), Office Equipment (115), Notes Payable (220), Mortgage Payable (221), R. Foster, Capital (301), R. Foster, Withdrawals (302), Tax Service Revenues (401), Salary Expense (501), Utilities Expense (502).

(2) Prepare journal entries to record the preceding transactions.

(3) Post the journal entries to the accounts.

(4) Prepare a trial balance at January 31.

PA-3   The Ryan Landscaping Service entered into the following transactions during March:

Date	Transaction
Mar. 1	Provided landscaping service for customer, collecting $575 cash.
2	Paid three months' rent in advance at $270 per month on storage/office building.
5	Purchased $50 of repair parts on credit from JR's, a small-engine service company; the parts are to be used immediately in repairing several of the company's mowers.
6–10	Provided landscaping service for a customer; customer agreed to pay the contract price of $2,450 in 15 days.
15	Paid $50 due to JR's for repair parts purchased on March 5.
25	Collected $2,450 from customer for service provided on March 6–10.
31	Paid $40 for March utilities bill.
31	Paid $1,800 to employees for March salaries.
31	Received $82 March telephone bill, to be paid in early April.

Required: (1) Prepare journal entries to record the preceding transactions.

(2) List the source documents normally used to record these transactions.

PA-4   Watson Heater Company sells portable heaters and related equipment. The company uses a perpetual inventory system, and the cost of its inventory at the beginning of November was $2,600. Its cash balance was $1,500 at the beginning of November, and it entered into the following transactions during November:

Date	Transaction
Nov. 1	Made $520 cash sales to customers; the cost of the inventory sold was $300.
3	Purchased $1,700 of heaters for cash from Tyler Supply Company.
5	Received $250 cash allowance from Tyler Supply Company for defective inventory purchased on November 3.
6	Paid $210 for parts and repaired defective heaters purchased from Tyler Supply Company on November 3.
8	Made $1,500 sale of heaters on credit to Nate Nursing Home, with terms of 2/10, n/20. The cost of the inventory sold was $850.
15	Purchased $1,100 of heaters on credit from Miller Supplies, with terms of n/15.
18	Received amount owed by Nate Nursing Home for heaters purchased on November 8, less the cash discount.
30	Paid for the inventory purchased from Miller Supplies on November 15.

Required: Prepare journal entries to record the preceding transactions.

PA-5   Morg Building Supplies sells building supplies and small tools to retail customers. It entered into the following transactions (the company uses the perpetual inventory system) during September:

Date	Transaction
Sept. 1	Purchased $1,900 of building supplies on credit from Doe Company, with terms 2/10, n/30.
2	Returned $150 of defective building supplies purchased on September 1 from Doe Company for credit.
5	Sold $900 of small tools (which cost $600) to customers for cash.
6	Purchased $350 of small tools for cash.

continued

6   Granted $70 cash allowance to customer for minor defects found in small tools sold on September 5.

10   Paid balance due to Doe Company for purchase of September 1.

21   Sold $1,500 of building supplies (which cost $1,000) on credit to R. Bailey, with terms 1/10, n/30.

30   Received balance due from R. Bailey for building supplies purchased on September 21.

Required: (1) Prepare journal entries to record these transactions.

(2) What were the net sales for the month?

PA-6   The trial balance of Halsey Architectural Consultants on December 31 of the current year (the end of its annual accounting period), included the following account balances before adjustments:

Note receivable	$16,000 debit
Prepaid insurance	1,560 debit
Building	92,000 debit
Drafting equipment	12,000 debit
Unearned rent	6,240 credit
Note payable	10,000 credit
Supplies	1,500 debit

In reviewing the company's recorded transactions and accounting records for the current year, you find the following information pertaining to the December 31 adjustments:

(a) On July 1, the company had accepted a $16,000, 1-year, 10% note receivable from a customer. The interest is to be collected when the note is collected.

(b) On October 1, the company had paid $1,560 for a three-year insurance policy.

(c) The building was acquired several years ago and is being depreciated using the straight-line method over a 20-year life with no residual value.

(d) The drafting equipment was purchased on December 1. It is to be depreciated using the straight-line method over an 8-year life with no residual value.

(e) On July 1, the company had received $6,240 for two years' rent in advance for a portion of its building rented to Shields Company.

(f) On November 1, the company had issued a $10,000, 3-month, 9% note payable to a supplier. The $225 total interest is to be paid when the note is paid.

(g) On January 1, the company had $200 of supplies on hand. During the year the company purchased $1,300 of supplies. A count on December 31 determined that $90 of supplies are still on hand.

Required: Prepare the adjusting entries that are necessary to bring the Halsey Architectural Consultants accounts up-to-date on December 31. Each journal entry explanation should summarize your calculations.

PA-7   Paribus Janitorial Services engaged in the following transactions during the current year and properly recorded them in its balance sheet accounts:

Date	Transaction
Jan. 1	Purchased cleaning equipment for $13,000, paying $3,000 down and issuing a 2-year, 12% note payable for the $10,000 balance. The equipment has an estimated life of 10 years and no residual value; straight-line depreciation is appropriate. The interest on the note will be paid on the maturity date.
May 24	Purchased $340 of office supplies. The office supplies on hand at the beginning of the year totaled $145.
June 1	Purchased a two-year comprehensive insurance policy for $960.
Sept. 1	Received six months' rent in advance at $350 per month and recorded the $2,100 receipt as unearned rent.
Oct. 1	Accepted a $3,000, 6-month, 10% note receivable from a customer. The $150 total interest is to be collected when the note is collected.

Additional Information

(a) On December 31, the office supplies on hand totaled $58.

(b) All employees work Monday through Friday. The weekly payroll of Paribus Janitorial Services amounts to $6,000. All employees are paid at the close of business each Friday for the previous five working days (including Friday). December 31 falls on a Thursday.

Required: On the basis of the preceding information, prepare journal entries to record whatever *adjustments* are necessary on December 31. Each journal entry explanation should show any related computations.

PA-8 The adjusted trial balance for Swire Interior Decorating Company on November 30, 2008 (the end of its monthly accounting period) is as follows:

Account Titles	Debits	Credits
Cash...	$ 7,042	
Accounts receivable	4,394	
Office supplies...	1,074	
Prepaid insurance...	1,540	
Land..	6,000	
Building	29,400	
Accumulated depreciation: building		$ 130
Office equipment..	2,880	
Accumulated depreciation: office equipment		40
Accounts payable		1,580
Mortgage payable		10,000
A. Swire, capital..		40,000
A. Swire, withdrawals	800	
Interior decorating revenues		3,105
Salaries expense	850	
Insurance expense	140	
Telephone expense...	177	
Utilities expense...	276	
Office supplies expense..	112	
Depreciation expense: building	130	
Depreciation expense: office equipment	40	
Totals..	$54,855	$54,855

Required: (1) Prepare a November income statement, statement of changes in owner's equity, and a November 30, 2008 balance sheet for Swire Interior Decorating Company.
(2) Prepare the closing entries on November 30, 2008.
(3) Prepare a post-closing trial balance.

PA-9 On May 31, 2008, the bookkeeper of Marina Boat Storage prepared the following closing entries for the month of May:

(a) Storage Revenues	4,060	
Income Summary		4,060
(b) Income Summary	2,724	
Depreciation Expense: Building		140
Depreciation Expense: Equipment		110
Supplies Expense		233
Salaries Expense		1,650
Telephone Expense		92
Utilities Expense		264
Insurance Expense		235
(c) Income Summary	1,336	
L. Marina, Capital		1,336
(d) L. Marina, Capital	830	
L. Marina, Withdrawals		830

In addition, the following *post-closing* trial balance was prepared:

Account Titles	Debits	Credits
Cash	$ 6,120	
Accounts receivable	4,989	
Supplies	1,117	
Land	16,000	
Building	25,200	
Accumulated depreciation: building		$ 140
Equipment	10,560	
Accumulated depreciation: equipment		110
Accounts payable		2,350
Notes payable (due 5/1/10)		7,000
Mortgage payable		20,000
L. Marina, capital		34,386
Totals	$63,986	$63,986

Required: (1) Prepare an income statement for the month ended May 31, 2008.

(2) Prepare a statement of changes in owner's equity for the month ended May 31, 2008.

(3) Prepare a May 31, 2008 balance sheet (report form).

PA-10 Finestein Corporation showed the following balances on January 1, 2008:

Common stock (5,000 shares, $10 par)	$50,000
Additional paid-in capital	95,000
Retained earnings	64,000

On January 4, 2008, the company issued 1,000 shares of common stock for $40,000. For the year ended December 31, 2008, the company had sales revenues of $102,000, cost of goods sold of $48,000, operating expenses of $17,000, and other revenues of $3,000. In addition, the company declared and paid dividends of $6,000 on December 31. Finestein Corporation is subject to a 40% income tax rate and uses a perpetual inventory system.

Required: (1) Prepare journal entries to record the issuance of common stock on January 4, 2008, and the declaration and payment of the cash dividends on December 31, 2008. (Assume that the company appropriately recorded the journal entries for the other transactions during the year.)

(2) Prepare the journal entry on December 31, 2008 to record the 2008 income taxes of Finestein Corporation.

(3) Prepare an income statement for the year ended December 31, 2008.

(4) Prepare the stockholders' equity section of the December 31, 2008 balance sheet.

(5) Prepare the December 31, 2008 closing entries.

COLGATE-PALMOLIVE
2005 ANNUAL REPORT:
FINANCIAL SECTION

APPENDIX
B

Management's Discussion and Analysis of Financial Condition and Results of Operations

Dollars in Millions Except Per Share Amounts

Executive Overview

Colgate-Palmolive Company seeks to deliver strong, consistent business results and superior shareholder returns by providing consumers, on a global basis, with products that make their lives healthier and more enjoyable.

To this end, the Company is tightly focused on two product segments: Oral, Personal and Home Care; and Pet Nutrition. Within these segments, the Company follows a closely defined business strategy to develop and increase market leadership positions in key product categories. These product categories are prioritized based on their capacity to maximize the use of the organization's core competencies and strong global equities and to deliver sustainable long-term growth.

Operationally, the Company is organized along geographic lines with specific regional management teams having responsibility for the financial results in each region. The Company competes in more than 200 countries and territories worldwide, with established businesses in all regions contributing to the Company's sales and profitability. This geographic diversity and balance helps to reduce the Company's exposure to business and other risks in any one country or part of the world.

The Oral, Personal and Home Care segment is operated through four reportable operating segments, North America, Latin America, Europe and Asia/Africa, which sell to a variety of retail and wholesale customers and distributors. In the Pet Nutrition segment, Hill's also competes on a worldwide basis selling its products principally through the veterinary profession and specialty pet retailers.

On an ongoing basis, management focuses on a variety of key indicators to monitor business health and performance. These indicators include market share, sales (including volume, pricing and foreign exchange components), gross profit margin, operating profit, net income and earnings per share; and measures to optimize the management of working capital, capital expenditures, cash flow and return on capital. The monitoring of these indicators, as well as the Company's corporate governance practices (including the Company's Code of Conduct), are used to ensure that business health and strong internal controls are maintained.

To achieve its financial objectives, the Company focuses the organization on initiatives to drive growth and to fund growth. The Company seeks to capture significant opportunities for growth by identifying and meeting consumer needs within its core categories, in particular by deploying valuable consumer and shopper insights in the development of successful new products regionally which are then rolled out on a global basis. Growth opportunities are enhanced in those areas of the world in which economic development and rising consumer incomes expand the size and number of markets for the Company's products.

The investments needed to fund this growth are developed through continuous, corporate-wide initiatives to lower costs and increase effective asset utilization. The Company also continues to prioritize its investments toward its higher margin businesses, specifically Oral Care, Personal Care and Pet Nutrition. In June 2004, the Company completed its acquisition of GABA Holding AG (GABA), a privately owned European oral care company headquartered in Switzerland. Also, consistent with the Company's strategy to prioritize higher margin businesses, the Company divested its North American and Southeast Asian heavy-duty laundry detergent brands in the third and fourth quarter of 2005, respectively, and certain Latin American and European laundry detergent brands during 2004 and 2003, respectively.

In December 2004, the Company commenced a four-year restructuring and business-building program to enhance the Company's global leadership position in its core businesses (the 2004 Restructuring Program). As part of the 2004 Restructuring Program, the Company anticipates the rationalization of approximately one-third of its manufacturing facilities, closure of certain warehousing facilities and an estimated 12% workforce reduction. The cost of implementing the 2004 Restructuring Program is estimated to result in cumulative pretax charges, once all phases are approved and implemented, totaling between $750 and $900 ($550 and $650 aftertax). Savings are projected to be in the range of $325-$400 ($250-$300 aftertax) annually by 2008.

Given the continued competitive marketplace and high raw and packaging material and energy costs, the Company anticipates that the near-term operating environment will remain challenging. However, the savings and benefits from the 2004 Restructuring Program along with the Company's other ongoing cost-savings and growth initiatives are anticipated to provide additional funds for investment in support of key categories and new product development while also supporting an increased level of profitability.

Dollars in Millions Except Per Share Amounts

Results of Operations

Net Sales

Worldwide sales were $11,396.9 in 2005. Sales increased 7.5% driven by volume gains of 5.5%, an increase in net selling prices of 0.5% and a positive foreign exchange impact of 1.5%. The June 2004 acquisition of GABA contributed 1.0% to worldwide sales and volume growth. Excluding the divestment of non-core product lines, sales increased 8.5% on volume growth of 6.5%.

Sales in the Oral, Personal and Home Care segment were $9,876.7, up 8.0% from 2004 on volume growth of 5.5%, increases in net selling prices of 0.5% and a 2.0% positive impact of foreign exchange. Excluding divestments, sales in this segment increased 9.0% on volume growth of 6.5%.

Sales in Pet Nutrition grew 6.0% to $1,520.2, driven by volume growth of 4.0%, an increase in net selling prices of 1.5% and positive foreign exchange of 0.5%.

In 2004, worldwide sales increased 7.0% to $10,584.2 on volume growth of 5.5%, a decrease in net selling prices of 1.5% and a positive foreign exchange impact of 3.0%.

Gross Profit

Gross profit margin was 54.4% in 2005, 55.1% in 2004 and 55.0% in 2003. The reduction in gross profit during 2005 is driven primarily by costs associated with the Company's ongoing 2004 Restructuring Program. Restructuring charges of $100.2, which related to accelerated depreciation and certain employee termination benefits under the 2004 Restructuring Program, were included in Cost of sales. These charges reduced gross profit margin by approximately 90 basis points (bps) for the year ended 2005. The benefits from higher pricing, the Company's shift towards higher margin oral care products and cost-saving programs in 2005 more than offset the impact of higher raw and packaging material costs. The increase in 2004 from the 2003 level was driven by the Company's focus on its high margin oral and personal care businesses, savings from global sourcing, the regionalization of manufacturing facilities and other cost-reduction initiatives, despite an increase in worldwide materials costs.

For additional information regarding the Company's 2004 Restructuring Program, refer to "Restructuring Activities" below and Note 4 to the Consolidated Financial Statements.

Selling, General and Administrative Expenses

Selling, general and administrative expenses as a percentage of sales were 34.4% in 2005, 34.2% in 2004 and 33.3% in 2003. Advertising expense increased by 12% in 2005, an increase of 40 bps as a percent of sales, on top of a 10% increase in 2004. Included in Selling, general and administrative expenses is advertising spending of $1,193.6, $1,063.0 and $965.6 in 2005, 2004 and 2003, respectively, supporting new product launches and helping increase market shares throughout the world. Despite the 40 bps increase in advertising, Selling, general and administrative expenses as a percentage of sales in 2005 only increased by a net 20 bps as ongoing cost-savings programs more than offset increases in shipping and handling costs (30 bps) and selling and marketing costs (10 bps). The increase as a percent of sales in 2004

as compared with 2003 resulted from increases in advertising spending (30 bps), selling and marketing costs (30 bps) and shipping and handling costs (20 bps).

Other (Income) Expense, Net

Other (income) expense, net was $69.2, $90.3 and ($15.0) in 2005, 2004 and 2003, respectively. The components of Other (income) expense, net are presented below:

	2005	2004	2003
Minority interest	$ 55.3	$ 47.9	$ 45.2
Amortization of intangible assets	15.6	14.3	12.3
Equity (income)	(2.0)	(8.5)	(0.3)
Gains on sales of non-core product lines, net	(147.9)	(26.7)	(107.2)
2004 Restructuring Program	80.8	65.3	—
2003 restructuring activities	—	2.8	59.3
Pension and other postretirement charges	34.0	—	—
Investment losses (income)	19.7	(8.7)	(39.6)
Other, net	13.7	3.9	15.3
	$ 69.2	$ 90.3	$ (15.0)

Other (income) expense, net in 2005 included a gain of $147.9 on the sale of heavy-duty laundry detergent businesses in North America and Southeast Asia, which was partially offset by charges related to the Company's 2004 Restructuring Program of $80.8 and pension and other postretirement charges of $34.0. The charges associated with certain pension and other postretirement obligations were primarily a result of the conversion of one of the Company's international pension plans to a defined contribution plan for all eligible participants and a lump sum payment of normal retirement benefits associated with a retirement plan in the U.S. as required by Statement of Financial Accounting Standard (SFAS) No. 88, "Employers' Accounting for Settlements and Curtailments of Defined Benefit Pension Plans and for Termination Benefits" (SFAS 88).

Investment losses (income) consists primarily of gains and losses on foreign currency contracts, which are economic hedges of certain foreign currency debt, but do not qualify for hedge accounting.

Other (income) expense, net in 2004 included charges of $65.3 related to the Company's 2004 Restructuring Program and a gain of $26.7 on the sale of certain detergent businesses in Latin America. Other (income) expense, net in 2003 included gains of $107.2 related to the sale of non-core brands partially offset by $59.3 of costs related to the regionalization of manufacturing facilities.

Operating Profit

In 2005, Operating profit increased 4% to $2,215.0 after a 2% decline in 2004 to $2,122.1 from $2,166.0 in 2003. All years presented benefited from sales growth and cost-savings initiatives. The gain on sale of non-core product lines recognized in 2005 and 2004 was more than offset by pretax restructuring charges related to the Company's 2004 Restructuring Program of $182.8 and $68.7 in 2005 and 2004, respectively, as well as other business realignment costs of $19.7 in 2004. For additional information regarding the Company's 2004 Restructuring Program, refer to

Dollars in Millions Except Per Share Amounts

"Restructuring Activities" below and Note 4 to the Consolidated Financial Statements.

Interest Expense, Net

Interest expense, net was $136.0 in 2005 compared with $119.7 in 2004 and $124.1 in 2003. Higher interest rates and higher average debt levels primarily to finance the GABA acquisition have resulted in increased interest expense in 2005. In 2004 low interest rates allowed the Company to lower its interest expense despite increased debt levels resulting from the GABA acquisition.

Income Taxes

The effective income tax rate was 35.0% in 2005 versus 33.7% in 2004 and 30.4% in 2003. The higher tax rate in 2005 is due to $40.9 of income taxes (200 bps) for the incremental repatriation of $780 of foreign earnings related to the American Jobs Creation Act of 2004 (the AJCA) as well as the impact (130 bps) of the lower effective benefit rate on charges incurred in connection with the Company's 2004 Restructuring Program. These increases were partially offset by the Company's global tax planning strategies which are reflected principally in overseas earnings being taxed at lower rates.

The increase in 2004 is due in part to changes in the mix of income in foreign tax rate jurisdictions and increased costs of remittances, while the effective tax rate was reduced in 2003 through the realization of tax credits and incentives, and as a result of global tax planning strategies including overseas asset revaluations.

The impact of the 2004 Restructuring Program on the effective income tax rate for an individual period will depend upon the projects and the related tax jurisdictions involved. Since the majority of restructuring costs have been incurred in low tax jurisdictions, the tax benefit derived from the charges incurred in 2005 and 2004 for the 2004 Restructuring Program was at a rate of 20.6% and 30.1%, respectively. Over its duration, charges associated with the 2004 Restructuring Program are projected to generate tax benefits at a rate between 25% and 30%.

For additional information refer to Note 11 to the Consolidated Financial Statements.

Net Income

Net income was $1,351.4 in 2005 or $2.43 per share on a diluted basis compared with $1,327.1 in 2004 or $2.33 per share and $1,421.3 in 2003 or $2.46 per share. As discussed above, Net income in 2005 was impacted by a net aftertax charge of $115.2 ($0.21 per share) resulting from restructuring charges, gains on sales of certain non-core brands, income tax expense for the incremental repatriation of foreign earnings related to the AJCA and certain pension charges. Net income in 2004 includes an aftertax charge of $48.0 ($0.09 per share) associated with the initial phase of the 2004 Restructuring Program.

Segment Results

The Company markets its products in over 200 countries and territories throughout the world in two distinct business segments: Oral, Personal and Home Care; and Pet Nutrition. Segment performance is evaluated based on several factors, including operating profit. The Company uses operating profit as a measure of operating segment performance because it excludes the impact of corporate-driven decisions related to restructuring and related costs, interest expense, income taxes, and gains and losses on sales of non-core brands and assets.

Worldwide Net Sales by Business Segment and Geographic Region

	2005	2004	2003
Oral, Personal and Home Care			
North America [1]	$ 2,509.8	$ 2,378.7	$2,356.2
Latin America	2,623.8	2,266.0	2,179.5
Europe	2,739.4	2,621.3	2,304.1
Asia/Africa	2,003.7	1,885.1	1,747.5
Total Oral, Personal and Home Care	9,876.7	9,151.1	8,587.3
Pet Nutrition [2]	1,520.2	1,433.1	1,316.1
Net Sales	$11,396.9	$10,584.2	$9,903.4

(1) Net sales in the U.S. for Oral, Personal and Home Care were $2,124.2, $2,000.3 and $1,986.9 in 2005, 2004 and 2003, respectively.
(2) Net sales in the U.S. for Pet Nutrition were $818.1, $781.0 and $752.8 in 2005, 2004 and 2003, respectively.

Worldwide Operating Profit by Business Segment and Geographic Region

	2005	2004	2003
Oral, Personal and Home Care			
North America	$ 545.7	$ 530.1	$ 547.4
Latin America	698.0	627.7	613.3
Europe	547.3	539.0	488.2
Asia/Africa	318.0	310.1	280.7
Total Oral, Personal and Home Care	2,109.0	2,006.9	1,929.6
Pet Nutrition	412.8	389.7	371.0
Corporate	(306.8)	(274.5)	(134.6)
Operating Profit	$2,215.0	$2,122.1	$2,166.0

North America

Net sales in North America increased 5.5% to $2,509.8 on volume gains of 4.0%, positive foreign exchange of 1.0% and increases in net selling prices of 0.5%. Net sales, excluding the divested heavy-duty laundry detergent business in North America, increased 8.0% on volume gains of 6.5%. Products which contributed to the growth in Oral Care included Colgate Total, Colgate Luminous and Colgate Max Fresh toothpastes and Colgate 360° manual toothbrush. New products which contributed to growth in other categories include Ajax Ruby Red Grapefruit and Palmolive Oxy Plus dish liquids, Irish Spring MicroClean bar soap, and Softsoap Kitchen Fresh Hands and Softsoap Shea Butter liquid hand soaps. In 2004, Net sales in North America increased 1.0% to $2,378.7 on volume gains of 2.5%, positive foreign exchange of 1.0% and declines in net selling prices of 2.5%.

Operating profit in North America increased 3% to $545.7 in 2005 as increased sales were partially offset by declines in gross profit margin reflecting increased raw and packaging material costs. In 2004, Operating profit in North America declined 3% to $530.1 due to increased shipping and handling costs and declines

Dollars in Millions Except Per Share Amounts

in gross profit margin reflecting increased commercial investment and higher raw material costs.

Latin America

Net sales in Latin America increased 16.0% to $2,623.8 as a result of 7.0% volume growth, increases in net selling prices of 4.0% and a positive foreign exchange impact of 5.0%. Net sales, excluding divested detergent businesses in Ecuador and Peru, increased 16.5% on volume gains of 7.5%. Sales growth was strong in Venezuela, Brazil, Mexico, the Dominican Republic, Central America, Colombia and Argentina. New products which contributed to these gains include Colgate Max Fresh and Colgate Sensitive toothpastes and the relaunch of Colgate Total toothpaste. Other new products which drove growth in Latin America are Colgate MicroSonic battery-powered toothbrush, Colgate Smiles line of manual toothbrushes for kids, Palmolive Nutri-Milk and Protex Oats bar soaps, and Lady Speed Stick and Speed Stick multiform deodorants. In 2004, Net sales in Latin America increased 4.0% to $2,266.0 on 6.0% volume growth, increases in net selling prices of 1.5% and a negative foreign exchange impact of 3.5%.

Operating profit in Latin America increased 11% to $698.0 in 2005 despite an increased level of advertising, reflecting increased sales and gross profit margins and a positive impact from foreign exchange. In 2004, Operating profit in Latin America increased 2% to $627.7 reflecting increased sales and gross profit margins partially offset by higher advertising spending and shipping and handling costs.

Europe

Net sales in Europe increased 4.5% to $2,739.4 on 6.0% volume growth, a 0.5% positive impact of stronger currencies, and a 2.0% decline in net selling prices. Excluding divestments, net sales increased 5.0% on volume gains of 6.5%. The June 2004 acquisition of GABA contributed 4.0% to European sales and volume growth. Volume gains achieved at GABA and in the United Kingdom, Ireland, Denmark, Spain, Russia, Turkey, Ukraine, Romania, the Adria region, Poland and the Baltic States more than offset challenging economic conditions in Italy, France and Germany. New products which contributed to these gains include Colgate Sensitive Plus Whitening, Colgate Oxygen and Colgate Max Fresh toothpastes, Colgate 360° manual toothbrush and Colgate MicroSonic battery-powered toothbrush. Growth in the region was also driven by strong sales of Colgate Total, Colgate Cavity Protection Extra Mint and Colgate Sensitive toothpastes and Colgate Smiles line of manual toothbrushes for kids. Products contributing to growth in other categories include Palmolive Naturals with Olive Milk, Palmolive Thermal Spa Firming shower gels, Palmolive Naturals with Olive Milk shower gel and liquid hand soap, Ajax Professional Degreaser spray cleaner and Lady Speed Stick and Speed Stick multiform deodorants. In 2004, Net sales in Europe increased 14.0% to $2,621.3 on 8.0% volume growth, a 9.0% positive impact of stronger currencies, and a 3.0% decline in net selling prices.

Operating profit in Europe increased 2% to $547.3 in 2005 and 10% to $539.0 in 2004 reflecting in both years volume growth and increased gross profit margins partially offset by an increased level of advertising. Additionally, operating profit in 2004 benefited from stronger currencies.

Asia/Africa

Net sales in Asia/Africa increased 6.5% to $2,003.7 on 6.0% volume growth, a 1.5% positive impact of foreign exchange and a 1.0% decline in net selling prices. Volume gains were achieved in Taiwan, China, India, Hong Kong, Malaysia, Australia and South Africa. New products which contributed to the oral care growth include Colgate Max Fresh and Colgate Vitamin C Fresh toothpastes, Colgate 360° manual toothbrush and Colgate MicroSonic battery-powered toothbrush. New products which contributed to growth in other categories throughout the region include Palmolive Aroma Creme shower gel and liquid hand soap, Protex Sun Care bar soap and Palmolive Naturals shampoo and conditioner. In 2004, Net sales in Asia/Africa increased 8.0% to $1,885.1 on 7.0% volume growth, a 5.5% positive impact of foreign exchange and a 4.5% decline in net selling prices.

Operating profit grew 3% in Asia/Africa to $318.0 in 2005 as a result of volume growth, which more than offset an increased level of advertising and higher shipping and handling costs. In 2004, Operating profit in Asia/Africa increased 10% to $310.1 driven by volume gains and higher gross profit margins as well as strong foreign currencies.

Pet Nutrition

Net sales for Hill's Pet Nutrition increased 6.0% to $1,520.2, driven by volume growth of 4.0%, an increase in net selling prices of 1.5% and positive foreign exchange of 0.5%. Innovative new products which contributed to growth in the U.S. specialty retail channel included Science Diet Canine Lamb & Rice Large Breed, Science Diet Canine Lamb & Rice Small Bites and Science Diet Indoor Cat pet foods. In the U.S. veterinary channel products which contributed to growth were Prescription Diet Canine j/d, a new wet form of Prescription Diet Canine z/d and Prescription Diet Feline z/d and the relaunch of Prescription Diet d/d (Canine and Feline) with an upgraded formulation. Internationally, growth was strong led by Taiwan, Russia, Australia, Spain and South Africa. New products which contributed to international growth included Science Diet Canine Large Breed, Prescription Diet Canine j/d, the wet form of Prescription Diet Canine z/d and Prescription Diet Feline z/d and the relaunch of Prescription Diet d/d. In 2004, Net sales for Pet Nutrition increased 9.0% to $1,433.1 on 3.5% volume growth, an increase of 1.5% in net selling prices and 4.0% in positive foreign currency impact.

Operating profit in Pet Nutrition grew 6% to $412.8 in 2005 on increased sales and gross profit margins partially offset by higher advertising and increased shipping and handling costs. Operating profit for 2004 increased 5% to $389.7 as a result of increased sales and ongoing cost-savings initiatives, partially offset by higher advertising spending and a decline in gross profit margin reflecting a sharp rise in commodity costs early in the year.

Dollars in Millions Except Per Share Amounts

Corporate

Operating profit (loss) for the Corporate segment was ($306.8), ($274.5) and ($134.6) for 2005, 2004 and 2003, respectively. As previously discussed in Other (income) expense, net, the change in 2005 as compared with the prior year was primarily driven by restructuring charges, gains on sales of certain non-core brands and charges relating to certain pension obligations. Corporate operating expenses in 2004 include $68.7 of pretax charges related to the Company's 2004 Restructuring Program and a $26.7 pretax gain on the sale of certain detergent businesses in Latin America.

Restructuring Activities

2004 Restructuring Program

In December 2004, the Company commenced a four-year restructuring and business-building program to enhance the Company's global leadership position in its core businesses (the 2004 Restructuring Program). As part of the 2004 Restructuring Program, the Company anticipates streamlining its global supply chain through the rationalization of approximately one-third of its manufacturing facilities and the closure of certain warehousing facilities and also plans to centralize its purchasing and other business support functions. Business-building initiatives include enhancing and reallocating resources with an increase and upgrade in the sales, marketing and new product organizations in high-potential developing and other key markets, and the consolidation of these organizations in certain mature markets. The 2004 Restructuring Program is expected to result in approximately a 12% workforce reduction.

The cost of implementing the 2004 Restructuring Program is estimated to result in cumulative pretax charges, once all phases are approved and implemented, totaling between $750 and $900 ($550 and $650 aftertax). The estimated cost in 2006 is $300-$350 ($225-$250 aftertax). Savings are projected to be in the range of $325-$400 ($250-$300 aftertax) annually by the fourth year of the program. Over the course of the four-year 2004 Restructuring Program, it is estimated that approximately 50%-60% of the charges will result in cash expenditures. While the Company's initial estimates remain unchanged, charges and savings may vary in a given year. Management's estimates of the cost and savings

associated with the 2004 Restructuring Program are forward-looking statements and are subject to revision over time.

During 2004, in connection with the initial phase of the program, the Company announced the closing or reconfiguration of eight manufacturing facilities in North America, Asia/Africa, Europe and Latin America and the realignment of marketing and sales organizations in Europe and Asia/Africa. During 2005, the Company commenced additional projects the more significant of which related to changes being implemented in its European and North American manufacturing networks. These changes will allow the Company to more cost effectively manufacture toothpaste, taking advantage of state-of-the-art technologies, and obtain cost-savings through the transfer of bar soap manufacturing to an established U.S. third party.

The Company plans to consolidate toothpaste production in Europe, which is currently located at five company sites, into a new state-of-the-art manufacturing facility in Europe. Upon completion of the consolidation project over two years, toothpaste manufacturing is expected to cease at the Company's facilities in Salford, United Kingdom; Anzio, Italy; Brasov, Romania; Gebze, Turkey; and Halinow, Poland. Other manufacturing activities will continue at these sites, except the Salford facility, which is expected to be closed. In North America, the Company plans to phase down production at its Jeffersonville, Indiana plant over the next two years, with all production expected to cease by January 2008. The plan calls for transferring production of the Company's market leading Colgate Total toothpaste to a new state-of-the-art facility to be built in Morristown, Tennessee, and the relocation of other production and administrative services currently performed at Jeffersonville to other facilities. Additionally, the Company's Kansas City, Kansas facility, where bar soap is currently produced, is expected to be closed in late 2006 after all production is transitioned to an established U.S. third party manufacturer.

Since the inception of the 2004 Restructuring Program in December 2004, the Company has incurred total charges of $251.5 ($193.1 aftertax) in connection with the implementation of various projects. The majority of costs incurred to date relate to the following significant projects: the consolidation of toothpaste production in Europe; exiting certain manufacturing activities in other categories in Portugal, Belgium, Denmark, Canada and Kansas City; and a realignment of the sales and administrative functions in Germany.

In the year ended December 31, 2005, the Company incurred $182.8 ($145.1 aftertax) of charges in connection with restructuring and implementation related activities, as detailed below:

	Year Ended December 31, 2005				
	Termination Benefits	Incremental Depreciation	Asset Impairments	Other	Total
Restructuring accrual at December 31, 2004	$ 41.7	$ —	$ —	$ 0.4	$ 42.1
Charges	45.8	65.3	30.2	41.5	182.8
Cash payments	(47.8)	—	—	(23.4)	(71.2)
Non-cash activity	—	(65.3)	(30.2)	(15.0)	(110.5)
Foreign exchange	(4.4)	—	—	(0.1)	(4.5)
Restructuring accrual at December 31, 2005	$ 35.3	$ —	$ —	$ 3.4	$ 38.7

Charges in the period related to restructuring activities in Europe (48%), North America (29%), Latin America (4%), Asia/Africa (11%), Pet Nutrition (1%) and Corporate (7%) and are reflected in the Corporate segment in the Consolidated Statements of Income in Cost of sales ($100.2), Selling, general and administrative expenses ($1.8) and Other (income) expense, net ($80.8).

Dollars in Millions Except Per Share Amounts

During 2004 the Company incurred $68.7 ($48.0 aftertax) of charges in connection with the initial phase of the 2004 Restructuring Program, as detailed below:

	Year Ended December 31, 2004				
	Termination Benefits	Incremental Depreciation	Asset Impairments	Other	Total
Charges	$41.6	$ 3.3	$ 22.0	$ 1.8	$ 68.7
Cash payments	(1.4)	—	—	(1.4)	(2.8)
Non-cash activity	—	(3.3)	(22.0)	—	(25.3)
Foreign exchange	1.5	—	—	—	1.5
Restructuring accrual at December 31, 2004	$41.7	$ —	$ —	$ 0.4	$ 42.1

Charges in the period related to restructuring activities in Europe (51%), North America (25%), Latin America (9%), Asia/Africa (7%) and Corporate (8%) and are reflected in the Corporate segment in the Consolidated Statements of Income in Cost of sales ($3.4) and Other (income) expense, net ($65.3).

2003 Restructuring Activities

In connection with the European brand divestments during 2003 and the Company's ongoing focus on the regionalization of manufacturing facilities to streamline and strengthen its operations, the Company realigned certain manufacturing operations and implemented workforce reduction programs primarily in Europe, Latin America and Asia/Africa. The Company incurred $2.8 and $59.3 of costs in 2004 and 2003, respectively, related to these restructuring activities which were substantially complete at the end of 2004. Costs for these restructuring activities are reflected in the Consolidated Statements of Income in Other (income) expense, net primarily in the Corporate segment.

Liquidity and Capital Resources

Net cash provided by operations in 2005 was $1,784.4 as compared with $1,754.3 in 2004 and $1,767.7 in 2003. The increase in 2005 reflects the Company's improved profitability and working capital management despite $38.0 of increased spending related to restructuring activities. The Company's working capital as a percentage of sales decreased to 1.7% of sales in 2005 as compared with 2.4% of sales in 2004. The Company defines working capital as the difference between current assets (excluding cash and marketable securities, the latter of which is reported in other current assets) and current liabilities (excluding short-term debt). As a result of an increased focus on working capital management, the Company's receivable days sales outstanding and inventory days coverage improved from 2004. Additionally, working capital at December 31, 2005 includes an increase of approximately $40 of accrued liabilities related to taxes and other costs associated with the Company's sale of certain non-core brands in 2005.

Investing activities used $220.7 of cash during 2005 compared with $1,090.4 and $117.6 during 2004 and 2003, respectively, with the 2004 period reflecting the Company's acquisition of GABA. In 2005, the Company increased its ownership interests in certain overseas subsidiaries to 100% at a cost of $38.5, primarily related to its Malaysia subsidiary. Investing activities in 2005 reflect $215.6

of proceeds from the sales of the Company's Southeast Asian and North American heavy-duty laundry detergent brands, as compared with 2004 which reflects $37.0 of proceeds from the sale of certain non-core detergent brands in Latin America, and with 2003 when the Company sold various detergent and certain non-core soap brands primarily marketed in Europe for an aggregate sales price of $127.6. Capital expenditures were $389.2, $348.1 and $302.1 for 2005, 2004 and 2003, respectively. Capital spending continues to be focused primarily on projects that yield high aftertax returns. As a result of the Company's multi-year restructuring and business-building program, overall capital expenditures for 2006 are expected to increase to a rate of approximately 4.0% to 4.5% of Net sales.

Financing activities used $1,524.4 of cash during 2005 compared with a use of $611.1 and $1,557.2 of cash during 2004 and 2003, respectively. Financing activities in 2005 reflect increases in the common and preference stock dividend payments as well as higher share repurchases associated with the share repurchase program authorized by the Board of Directors in October 2004. Financing activities in 2004 reflect an increased level of proceeds associated with borrowings related to the GABA acquisition. During 2005, long-term debt decreased to $3,274.7 from $3,540.8 in 2004 and total debt decreased to $3,446.2 in 2005 from $3,675.1 in 2004. The Company's long-term debt is rated AA– by Standard & Poor's and Aa3 by Moody's Investors Service.

Commercial paper outstanding was $621.8 and $844.7 as of December 31, 2005 and 2004, respectively, is denominated in U.S. dollars, Swiss francs and Canadian dollars. The maximum commercial paper outstanding during 2005 and 2004 was $1,715 and $1,519, respectively. These borrowings carry a Standard & Poor's rating of A-1+ and a Moody's rating of P-1. The commercial paper and certain current maturities of notes payable totaling $641.9 are classified as long-term debt at December 31, 2005, as the Company has the intent and ability to refinance such obligations on a long-term basis, including, if necessary, by utilizing its lines of credit that expire in 2010.

The ESOP notes guaranteed by the Company and certain credit facilities contain cross-default provisions. Noncompliance with these requirements could ultimately result in the acceleration of amounts owed. The Company is in full compliance with all such requirements and believes the likelihood of noncompliance is remote.

Dollars in Millions Except Per Share Amounts

The Company had a financing subsidiary with outside equity investors the purpose of which was to purchase some of the Company's receivables thereby giving the Company access to additional sources of capital. The subsidiary, including such receivables, was consolidated and the amounts invested by outside investors were reported as a minority interest. During 2005, the subsidiary ceased operations resulting in a cash payment to the outside investors of $89.7.

The Company repurchases common shares in the open market and in private transactions to maintain its targeted capital structure and to fulfill the requirements of its compensation and benefit plans. In October 2004, the Board of Directors authorized the Company to purchase up to 20 million shares of the Company's common stock through December 31, 2005 (the 2004 Program) and, in December 2005, the Board of Directors extended this authorization through March 31, 2006. It is anticipated that the remaining 2.5 million shares under the current program will be repurchased in the first quarter of 2006 and that the Company will implement a new stock repurchase program to take effect upon the conclusion of the 2004 Program. Aggregate repurchases for 2005, including repurchases under the 2004 Program and other Board authorizations, were 15.1 million common shares for a total purchase price of $796.2. Aggregate repurchases for 2004 were 12.4 million common shares for a total purchase price of $637.9. In 2003, 10.2 million common shares and 0.1 million shares of preferred stock were repurchased for a total purchase price of $554.9.

Dividend payments in 2005 were $607.2, up from $536.2 in 2004 and $506.8 in 2003. Common stock dividend payments increased to $1.11 per share in 2005 from $0.96 per share in 2004 and $0.90 per share in 2003. The Series B Preference Stock dividend payments were increased to $8.88 per share in 2005 from $7.68 per share in 2004 and $7.20 per share in 2003. Management currently intends to continue to pay dividends at increasing annual amounts per share from free cash flow.

The Company believes that internally generated cash flows are adequate to support business operations and capital expenditures. Free cash flow before dividends was $1,395.2, $1,406.2 and $1,465.6 in 2005, 2004 and 2003, respectively. The Company defines free cash flow before dividends as net cash provided by operations less capital expenditures. As management uses this measure to evaluate the Company's ability to satisfy current and future obligations, repurchase stock, pay dividends and fund future business opportunities, the Company believes that it

provides useful information to investors. Free cash flow before dividends is not a measure of cash available for discretionary expenditures since the Company has certain nondiscretionary obligations, such as debt service, that are not deducted from the measure. Free cash flow before dividends is not a GAAP measurement and may not be comparable with similarly titled measures reported by other companies. A reconciliation of net cash provided by operations to free cash flow before dividends follows:

	2005	2004	2003
Net cash provided by operations	$1,784.4	$1,754.3	$1,767.7
Less: Capital expenditures	(389.2)	(348.1)	(302.1)
Free cash flow before dividends	$1,395.2	$1,406.2	$1,465.6

In December 2004, the Company commenced the 2004 Restructuring Program, a four-year restructuring and business-building program, to enhance the Company's global leadership position in its core businesses. It is anticipated that cash requirements for the restructuring program will continue to be funded from operating cash flow.

The Company has additional sources of liquidity available in the form of lines of credit maintained with various banks and access to financial markets worldwide. The Company believes it has sufficient liquidity to meet its financing needs.

At December 31, 2005, the Company had access to unused domestic and foreign lines of credit of approximately $2,400 and also had $1,754.4 of medium-term notes available for issuance pursuant to effective shelf registration statements. In November 2005, the Company entered into a new five-year revolving credit facility of $1,500.0 with a syndicate of banks. The facility, which expires in November 2010, replaces existing credit facilities of $300.0 and $1,300.0 which were due to expire in December 2005 and May 2007, respectively. These domestic lines are available for general corporate purposes and to support commercial paper issuance. During 2005, the Company also issued 250 million of Swiss franc-denominated five-year bonds (approximately $190 at the year-end exchange rate) at a fixed rate of 1.9%.

Dollars in Millions Except Per Share Amounts

The following represents the scheduled maturities of the Company's contractual obligations as of December 31, 2005:

				Payments Due by Period			
	Total	2006	2007	2008	2009	2010	Thereafter
Long-term debt including current portion	$3,239.1	$ 992.8[1]	$ 701.5	$153.4	$ 95.2	$280.6	$1,015.6
Net cash interest payments on long-term debt[2]	1,263.0	176.0	104.5	79.1	72.8	64.9	765.7
Capitalized leases	35.6	5.8	6.1	6.2	6.4	6.7	4.4
Operating leases	474.7	94.6	86.0	76.5	68.6	54.2	94.8
Purchase obligations[3]	675.8	427.7	155.1	72.7	6.3	5.7	8.3
Total[4]	$5,688.2	$1,696.9	$1,053.2	$387.9	$249.3	$412.1	$1,888.8

(1) Long-term debt due in 2006 includes $6419 of commercial paper and certain current maturities of notes payable that have been classified as long-term debt as of December 31, 2005, as the Company has the intent and ability to refinance such obligations on a long-term basis, including, if necessary, by utilizing its unused lines of credit that expire in 2010.

(2) Includes the net interest payments on fixed and variable rate debt and associated interest rate swaps. Interest payments associated with floating rate instruments are based on management's best estimate of projected interest rates for the remaining term of variable rate debt.

(3) The Company has outstanding purchase obligations with suppliers at the end of 2005 for raw, packaging and other materials in the normal course of business. These purchase obligation amounts represent only those items which are based on agreements that are enforceable and legally binding and that specify minimum quantity, price and term and do not represent total anticipated purchases.

(4) Long-term liabilities associated with the Company's postretirement plans are excluded from the table above due to the uncertainty of the timing of these cash disbursements. The amount and timing of cash funding related to these benefit plans will generally depend on local regulatory requirements, various economic assumptions (the most significant of which are detailed in "Critical Accounting Policies and Use of Estimates" below) and voluntary Company contributions. Based on current information, the Company does not anticipate having to make any mandatory contributions to its qualified U.S. pension plan until 2014. Management's best estimate of cash requirements to be paid directly from the Company's assets for its postretirement plans for the year ending December 31, 2006 is $126. This estimate includes $77 of expected contributions to the Company's postretirement plans, the majority of which relate to voluntary contributions to the U.S. plans.

As more fully described in Note 13 to the Consolidated Financial Statements, the Company is contingently liable with respect to lawsuits, environmental matters, taxes and other matters arising in the ordinary course of business. While it is possible that the Company's cash flows and results of operations in a particular period could be materially affected by the one-time impacts of the resolution of such contingencies, it is the opinion of management that the ultimate disposition of these matters will not have a material impact on the Company's financial position, or ongoing results of operations and cash flows.

Off-Balance Sheet Arrangements
The Company does not have off-balance sheet financing or unconsolidated special purpose entities.

Managing Foreign Currency, Interest Rate and Commodity Price Exposure
The Company is exposed to market risk from foreign currency exchange rates, interest rates and commodity price fluctuations. Volatility relating to these exposures is managed on a global basis by utilizing a number of techniques, including working capital management, selective borrowings in local currencies and entering into certain derivative instrument transactions in accordance with the Company's treasury and risk management policies. The Company's treasury and risk management policies prohibit the use of leveraged derivatives or derivatives for trading purposes.

With operations in over 200 countries and territories, the Company is exposed to currency fluctuations related to manufacturing and selling its products in currencies other than the U.S. dollar. The major foreign currency exposures involve the markets in

Europe and certain Latin American countries, although all regions of the world are subject to foreign currency changes versus the U.S. dollar. The Company monitors its foreign currency exposures in these markets through a combination of cost-containment measures, selling price increases and foreign currency hedging of certain costs in an effort to minimize the impact on earnings of foreign currency rate movements.

The Company primarily utilizes currency forward contracts, cross currency interest rate swaps, local currency deposits and local currency borrowings to hedge portions of its exposures relating to foreign currency purchases and assets and liabilities created in the normal course of business. From time to time, the Company hedges certain of its forecasted foreign currency transactions using forward contracts with durations no greater than 18 months.

Interest rate swaps and debt issuances are utilized to manage the Company's targeted mix of fixed and floating rate debt and to minimize significant fluctuations in earnings and cash flows that may result from interest rate volatility.

The Company is exposed to price volatility related to raw materials used in production. Futures contracts are used on a limited basis to manage volatility related to anticipated raw material inventory purchases. In 2005 the results of the Company's commodity hedging activities were not material.

The Company is exposed to credit loss in the event of nonperformance by counterparties to the financial instrument contracts held by the Company; however, nonperformance by these counterparties is considered remote as it is the Company's policy to contract with diversified counterparties that have a long-term debt rating of AA–/Aa3 or higher.

Dollars in Millions Except Per Share Amounts

Value at Risk

The Company's risk management procedures include the monitoring of interest rate and foreign exchange exposures and hedge positions utilizing statistical analyses of cash flows, market value and sensitivity analysis. However, the use of these techniques to quantify the market risk of such instruments should not be construed as an endorsement of their accuracy or the accuracy of the related assumptions. Market exposures are evaluated using a value-at-risk (VAR) model and an earnings-at-risk (EAR) model that are intended to measure the maximum potential loss in interest rate and foreign exchange financial instruments, assuming adverse market conditions occur, given a 95% confidence level. Historical interest rates and foreign exchange rates are used to estimate the volatility and correlation of future rates.

The estimated maximum potential one-day loss in fair value of interest rate or foreign exchange rate instruments, calculated using the VAR model, is not material to the consolidated financial position, results of operations or cash flows of the Company in 2005 and 2004. The estimated maximum yearly loss in earnings due to interest rate or foreign exchange rate instruments, calculated utilizing the EAR model, is not material to the Company's results of operations in 2005 and 2004. Actual results in the future may differ materially from these projected results due to actual developments in the global financial markets.

For information regarding the Company's accounting policies for financial instruments and description of financial instrument activities, refer to Notes 2 and 7 to the Consolidated Financial Statements.

Recent Accounting Pronouncements

In November 2004, the Financial Accounting Standards Board (FASB) issued SFAS No. 151, "Inventory Costs—An Amendment of Accounting Research Bulletin No. 43, Chapter 4" (SFAS 151). SFAS 151 clarifies that abnormal amounts of idle facility expense, freight, handling costs and spoilage should be expensed as incurred and not included in overhead. Further, SFAS 151 requires that allocation of fixed production overhead to conversion costs be based on normal capacity of the production facilities. The provisions in SFAS 151 must be applied prospectively to the Company's inventory costs incurred on or after January 1, 2006. The adoption of SFAS 151 is not expected to have a material impact on the Company's Consolidated Financial Statements.

In December 2004, the FASB issued SFAS No. 123R, "Share-Based Payment," (SFAS 123R). SFAS 123R replaces SFAS No. 123, "Accounting for Stock-Based Compensation" (SFAS 123) by eliminating the choice to account for employee stock options under Accounting Principles Board Opinion No. 25, "Accounting for Stock Issued to Employees" (APB 25), and requires companies to recognize the cost of employee services received in exchange for awards of equity instruments, such as stock options and restricted stock, based on the fair value of those awards at the date of grant. Currently under APB 25 the value of restricted stock awards is expensed by the Company over the restriction period and, no compensation expense is recognized for stock option grants as all such grants have an exercise price not less than fair market value on the date of grant.

Additionally, certain of the Company's stock options granted to eligible participants have an accelerated vesting feature associated with employee retirement and most of the restricted stock awards specify that participants will continue to vest in the award after retirement. Currently the Company follows the nominal vesting period approach, which requires recognition of the compensation expense over the vesting period except in the instance of the participants' actual retirement. Upon the adoption of SFAS 123R, the Company's policy regarding the timing of expense recognition for new awards to employees eligible for retirement will, as required, be changed to recognize compensation cost over the period through the date that the employee first becomes eligible to retire and is no longer required to provide service to earn the award.

The Company will adopt the provisions of SFAS 123R effective January 1, 2006 using the modified prospective method which will result in an incremental expense upon adoption. The impact on earnings per share in fiscal year 2006 of these requirements is currently estimated in the range of $0.09 to $0.10. Future expense amounts for any particular quarterly or annual period could be affected by changes in the Company's assumptions or changes in market conditions. Due to the timing of the Company's equity grants the charge will not be spread evenly throughout the year. SFAS 123R also requires the benefits of tax deductions in excess of recognized compensation cost be reported as a financing cash flow, rather than as an operating cash flow as currently required, thereby potentially reducing net operating cash flows and increasing net financing cash flows in periods after adoption. Such amounts cannot be estimated for future periods with certainty because they depend largely on when employees will exercise the stock options and the market price of the Company's stock at the time of exercise.

Refer to Note 2 to the Consolidated Financial Statements for further discussion of recent accounting pronouncements.

Critical Accounting Policies and Use of Estimates

The preparation of financial statements requires management to use judgment and make estimates. The level of uncertainty in estimates and assumptions increases with the length of time until the underlying transactions are completed. Actual results could ultimately differ from those estimates. The accounting policies that are most critical in the preparation of the Company's Consolidated Financial Statements are those that are both important to the presentation of the Company's financial condition and results of operations and require significant or complex judgments and estimates on the part of management. The Company's critical accounting policies are reviewed periodically with the Audit Committee of the Board of Directors.

In certain instances, accounting principles generally accepted in the United States of America allow for the selection of alternative accounting methods. The Company's significant policies that involve the selection of alternative methods are accounting for stock options, shipping and handling costs, and inventories.

■ During 2005, two alternative methods for accounting for stock options were available, the intrinsic value method and the fair value method. The Company used the intrinsic value method of accounting for stock options, and accordingly, no compensation expense has been recognized. If the fair value method were used, diluted earnings per share for 2005, 2004 and 2003 would have decreased approximately 3%. SFAS 123R will require all companies issuing stock options to implement the fair value method and recognize compensation expense for stock options granted. As noted above, the Company will adopt SFAS 123R effective January 1, 2006 using the modified prospective method. (Refer to Note 2 to the Consolidated Financial Statements.)

■ Shipping and handling costs may be reported as either a component of cost of sales or selling, general and administrative expenses. The Company reports such costs, primarily related to warehousing and outbound freight, in the Consolidated Statements of Income as a component of Selling, general and administrative expenses. Accordingly, the Company's gross profit margin is not comparable with the gross profit margin of those companies that include shipping and handling charges in cost of sales. If such costs had been included in cost of sales, gross profit margin as a percent to sales would have decreased by 750 bps from 54.4% to 46.9% in 2005 and decreased by 720 bps and 710 bps in 2004 and 2003, respectively, with no impact on reported earnings.

■ The Company accounts for inventories using both the first-in, first-out (FIFO) method (approximately 80% of inventories) and the last-in, first-out (LIFO) method (20% of inventories). There would have been no material impact on reported earnings for 2005, 2004 and 2003 had all inventories been accounted for under the FIFO method.

The areas of accounting that involve significant or complex judgments and estimates are pensions and other postretirement benefits, asset impairment, tax valuation allowances, and legal and other contingencies.

■ In pension accounting, the most significant actuarial assumptions are the discount rate and the long-term rate of return on plan assets. The discount rate for U.S. plans was 5.50%, 5.75% and 6.25% as of December 31, 2005, 2004 and 2003, respectively. Discount rates used for the U.S. defined benefit and other postretirement plans are based on a yield curve constructed from a portfolio of high quality bonds for which the timing and amount of cash outflows approximate the estimated payouts of the U.S. plans. For the Company's international plans, the discount rates are set by benchmarking

against investment grade corporate bonds rated AA or better. The assumed long-term rate of return on plan assets for domestic plans was 8.0% as of December 31, 2005, 2004 and 2003. In determining the long-term rate of return, the Company considers the nature of the plans' investments, an expectation for the plans' investment strategies and the historical rate of return. The historical rate of return for the U.S. plans for the most recent 15-year period was 9%. In addition, the current rate of return assumption for the U.S. plans is based upon a targeted asset allocation of approximately 35% in fixed income securities (which are expected to earn approximately 6% in the long term), 61% in equity securities (which are expected to earn approximately 10% in the long term) and 4% in real estate and other (which are expected to earn approximately 6% in the long term). A 1% change in either the discount rate or the assumed rate on plan assets of the U.S. pension plans would impact Net income by approximately $10. A third assumption is the long-term rate of compensation increase, a change in which would partially offset the impact of a change in either the discount rate or the long-term rate of return. This rate was 4.0%, 4.0% and 4.25% as of December 31, 2005, 2004 and 2003, respectively. (Refer to Note 10 to the Consolidated Financial Statements.)

■ The most judgmental assumption in accounting for other postretirement benefits is the medical cost trend rate. The Company reviews external data and its own historical trends for health care costs to determine the medical cost trend rate. In 2005, the assumed rate of increase was 10.0% for 2006 and declining 1% per year until reaching the ultimate assumed rate of increase of 5% per year. The effect of a 1% increase in the assumed long-term medical cost trend rate would reduce Net income by approximately $4.5.

■ Asset impairment analysis performed for goodwill and intangible assets requires several estimates including future cash flows, growth rates and the selection of a discount rate. Since the estimated fair value of the Company's intangible assets substantially exceeds the recorded book value, significant changes in these estimates would have to occur to result in an impairment charge related to these assets. Asset impairment analysis related to certain fixed assets in connection with the 2004 Restructuring Program requires management's best estimate of net realizable value.

■ Tax valuation allowances are established to reduce tax assets such as tax loss carryforwards, to net realizable value. Factors considered in estimating net realizable value include historical results by tax jurisdiction, carryforward periods, income tax strategies and forecasted taxable income. A significant change to the Company's valuation allowances would primarily impact equity and would not materially impact reported earnings.

Dollars in Millions Except Per Share Amounts

■ Legal and other contingency reserves are based on management's assessment of the risk of potential loss, which includes consultation with outside legal counsel and advisors. Such assessments are reviewed each period and revised, based on current facts and circumstances, if necessary. While it is possible that the Company's cash flows and results of operations in a particular quarter or year could be materially affected by the one-time impacts of the resolution of such contingencies, it is the opinion of management that the ultimate disposition of these matters will not have a material impact on the Company's financial position, or ongoing results of operations and cash flows. (Refer to Note 13 to the Consolidated Financial Statements for further discussion of the Company's contingencies.)

The Company generates revenue through the sale of well-known consumer products to trade customers under established trading terms. While the recognition of revenue and receivables requires the use of estimates, there is a short time frame (typically less than 60 days) between the shipment of product and cash receipt, thereby reducing the level of uncertainty in these estimates. (Refer to Note 2 to the Consolidated Financial Statements for further description of the Company's significant accounting policies.)

Outlook

Looking forward into 2006, while the Company expects market conditions to remain highly competitive, it believes it is well positioned for continued growth. It anticipates continuing to prioritize its investments in key categories and markets in order to further strengthen its competitive position and build market share. The 2004 Restructuring Program is designed to enhance the Company's global leadership position in its core businesses. As part of the 2004 Restructuring Program, the Company anticipates streamlining its global supply chain, reallocating resources with an increase and upgrade in the sales, marketing and new product organizations in high-potential developing and other key markets and the consolidation of these organizations in certain mature markets. The savings and benefits from the 2004 Restructuring Program, along with the Company's other ongoing cost-savings and growth initiatives, are anticipated to provide additional funds for investment in support of key categories and new product development while also supporting an increased level of profitability.

However, as noted above, the Company operates in a highly competitive global marketplace that is experiencing increased trade concentration and industry consolidation. In addition, changes in economic conditions, movements in commodity prices and foreign currency exchange rates can impact future operating results as measured in U.S. dollars. In particular, economic and political uncertainty in some countries in Latin America and changes in the value of Latin American and European currencies may impact the overall results of these regions. Historically, the consumer products industry has been less susceptible to changes in economic growth than many other industries. Over the long term, Colgate's continued focus on its consumer products business and the strength of its global brand names, its broad international presence in both developed and developing markets, and its strong capital base all position the Company to take advantage of growth opportunities and to increase profitability and shareholder value.

Cautionary Statement on Forward-Looking Statements

In this report and from time to time, we may make statements that constitute or contain "forward-looking" information as that term is defined in the Private Securities Litigation Reform Act of 1995 or by the United States Securities and Exchange Commission in its rules, regulations and releases. Such statements may relate, for example, to sales or volume growth, earnings growth, financial goals, cost-reduction plans, estimated charges and savings associated with the 2004 Restructuring Program, and new product introductions among other matters. These statements are made on the basis of our views and assumptions as of the time the statements are made and we undertake no obligation to update these statements. We caution investors that any such forward-looking statements we make are not guarantees of future performance and that actual results may differ materially from anticipated results or expectations expressed in our forward-looking statements. For some of the factors that could impact our business and cause actual results to differ materially from forward-looking statements see Item 1A – Risk Factors of our annual report on Form 10-K for the year ended December 31, 2005 filed with the SEC on February 24, 2006.

Report of Independent Registered Public Accounting Firm

To the Board of Directors and Shareholders of
Colgate-Palmolive Company:

We have completed integrated audits of Colgate-Palmolive Company's 2005 and 2004 consolidated financial statements and of its internal control over financial reporting as of December 31, 2005, and an audit of its 2003 consolidated financial statements in accordance with the standards of the Public Company Accounting Oversight Board (United States). Our opinions on Colgate-Palmolive Company's 2005, 2004, and 2003 consolidated financial statements and on its internal control over financial reporting as of December 31, 2005, based on our audits, are presented below.

Consolidated financial statements

In our opinion, the accompanying consolidated balance sheets and the related consolidated statements of income, retained earnings, comprehensive income and changes in capital accounts and cash flows present fairly, in all material respects, the financial position of Colgate-Palmolive Company and its subsidiaries at December 31, 2005 and 2004, and the results of their operations and their cash flows for each of the three years in the period ended December 31, 2005 in conformity with accounting principles generally accepted in the United States of America. These financial statements are the responsibility of the Company's management. Our responsibility is to express an opinion on these financial statements based on our audits. We conducted our audits of these statements in accordance with the standards of the Public Company Accounting Oversight Board (United States). Those standards require that we plan and perform the audit to obtain reasonable assurance about whether the financial statements are free of material misstatement. An audit of financial statements includes examining, on a test basis, evidence supporting the amounts and disclosures in the financial statements, assessing the accounting principles used and significant estimates made by management, and evaluating the overall financial statement presentation. We believe that our audits provide a reasonable basis for our opinion.

Internal control over financial reporting

Also, in our opinion, management's assessment, included in the accompanying Management's Report on Internal Control over Financial Reporting, that the Company maintained effective internal control over financial reporting as of December 31, 2005 based on criteria established in *Internal Control— Integrated Framework* issued by the Committee of Sponsoring Organizations of the Treadway Commission (COSO), is fairly stated, in all material respects, based on those criteria. Furthermore, in our opinion, the Company maintained, in all material respects, effective internal control over financial reporting as of December 31, 2005, based on criteria established in *Internal Control— Integrated Framework*

issued by the COSO. The Company's management is responsible for maintaining effective internal control over financial reporting and for its assessment of the effectiveness of internal control over financial reporting. Our responsibility is to express opinions on management's assessment and on the effectiveness of the Company's internal control over financial reporting based on our audit. We conducted our audit of internal control over financial reporting in accordance with the standards of the Public Company Accounting Oversight Board (United States). Those standards require that we plan and perform the audit to obtain reasonable assurance about whether effective internal control over financial reporting was maintained in all material respects. An audit of internal control over financial reporting includes obtaining an understanding of internal control over financial reporting, evaluating management's assessment, testing and evaluating the design and operating effectiveness of internal control, and performing such other procedures as we consider necessary in the circumstances. We believe that our audit provides a reasonable basis for our opinions.

A company's internal control over financial reporting is a process designed to provide reasonable assurance regarding the reliability of financial reporting and the preparation of financial statements for external purposes in accordance with generally accepted accounting principles. A company's internal control over financial reporting includes those policies and procedures that (i) pertain to the maintenance of records that, in reasonable detail, accurately and fairly reflect the transactions and dispositions of the assets of the company; (ii) provide reasonable assurance that transactions are recorded as necessary to permit preparation of financial statements in accordance with generally accepted accounting principles, and that receipts and expenditures of the company are being made only in accordance with authorizations of management and directors of the company; and (iii) provide reasonable assurance regarding prevention or timely detection of unauthorized acquisition, use, or disposition of the company's assets that could have a material effect on the financial statements.

Because of its inherent limitations, internal control over financial reporting may not prevent or detect misstatements. Also, projections of any evaluation of effectiveness to future periods are subject to the risk that controls may become inadequate because of changes in conditions, or that the degree of compliance with the policies or procedures may deteriorate.

PricewaterhouseCoopers LLP

New York, New York
February 22, 2006

Report of Management

Management's Report on Internal Control over Financial Reporting

The Company's management is responsible for establishing and maintaining adequate internal control over financial reporting. The Company's internal control over financial reporting is a process designed under the supervision of its Chief Executive Officer and Chief Financial Officer to provide reasonable assurance regarding the reliability of financial reporting and the preparation of the Company's financial statements for external reporting in accordance with accounting principles generally accepted in the United States of America. Management evaluates the effectiveness of the Company's internal control over financial reporting using the criteria set forth by the Committee of Sponsoring Organizations of the Treadway Commission (COSO) in Internal Control—Integrated Framework. Management, under the supervision and with the participation of the Company's Chief Executive Officer and Chief Financial Officer, assessed the effectiveness of the Company's internal control over financial reporting as of December 31, 2005 and concluded that it is effective.

The Company's independent registered public accounting firm, PricewaterhouseCoopers LLP, has audited the effectiveness of the Company's internal control over financial reporting and management's assessment of the effectiveness of the Company's internal control over financial reporting as of December 31, 2005, and has expressed unqualified opinions in their report which appears on page 30.

Management's Responsibility for Consolidated Financial Statements

The management of Colgate-Palmolive Company is also responsible for the preparation and content of the accompanying consolidated financial statements as well as all other related information contained in this annual report. These financial statements have been prepared in accordance with accounting principles generally accepted in the United States of America and necessarily include amounts which are based on management's best estimates and judgments.

The consolidated financial statements included in this annual report have been audited by PricewaterhouseCoopers LLP and their report, in which they express their unqualified opinion on such financial statements, appears on page 30.

Audits

The Board of Directors engaged PricewaterhouseCoopers LLP to audit the effectiveness of the Company's internal control over financial reporting, management's assessment of the effectiveness of such internal controls over financial reporting as of December 31, 2005 and the consolidated financial statements for each of the three years ended December 31, 2005. Their report was based on an audit conducted in accordance with standards of the Public Company Accounting Oversight Board (United States of America) and included tests of accounting records and system of internal control and such other procedures to enable them to render opinions on the effectiveness of the Company's internal control over financial reporting and management's assessment of the effectiveness of the Company's such internal control over financial reporting as of December 31, 2005 and on the Company's consolidated financial statements.

The Board of Directors has an Audit Committee comprised entirely of independent directors. The Committee meets periodically and independently throughout the year with management, internal auditors and the independent public accountants to discuss the Company's internal controls, auditing and financial reporting matters. The internal auditors and independent public accountants have unrestricted access to the Audit Committee.

Reuben Mark
Chairman and
Chief Executive Officer

Stephen C. Patrick
Chief Financial Officer

Dollars in Millions Except Per Share Amounts

Consolidated Statements of Income

For the years ended December 31,	2005	2004	2003
Net sales	$11,396.9	$10,584.2	$9,903.4
Cost of sales	5,191.9	4,747.2	4,456.1
Gross profit	6,205.0	5,837.0	5,447.3
Selling, general and administrative expenses	3,920.8	3,624.6	3,296.3
Other (income) expense, net	69.2	90.3	(15.0)
Operating profit	2,215.0	2,122.1	2,166.0
Interest expense, net	136.0	119.7	124.1
Income before income taxes	2,079.0	2,002.4	2,041.9
Provision for income taxes	727.6	675.3	620.6
Net income	$ 1,351.4	$ 1,327.1	$1,421.3
Earnings per common share, basic	$ 2.54	$ 2.45	$ 2.60
Earnings per common share, diluted	$ 2.43	$ 2.33	$ 2.46

See Notes to Consolidated Financial Statements.

Dollars in Millions Except Per Share Amounts

Consolidated Balance Sheets

As of December 31,	2005	2004
Assets		
Current Assets		
Cash and cash equivalents	$ 340.7	$ 319.6
Receivables (less allowances of $41.7 and $47.2, respectively)	1,309.4	1,319.9
Inventories	855.8	845.5
Other current assets	251.2	254.9
Total current assets	2,757.1	2,739.9
Property, plant and equipment, net	2,544.1	2,647.7
Goodwill	1,845.7	1,891.7
Other intangible assets, net	783.2	832.4
Other assets	577.0	561.2
Total assets	$ 8,507.1	$ 8,672.9
Liabilities and Shareholders' Equity		
Current Liabilities		
Notes and loans payable	$ 171.5	$ 134.3
Current portion of long-term debt	356.7	451.3
Accounts payable	876.1	864.4
Accrued income taxes	215.5	153.1
Other accruals	1,123.2	1,127.6
Total current liabilities	2,743.0	2,730.7
Long-term debt	2,918.0	3,089.5
Deferred income taxes	554.7	509.6
Other liabilities	941.3	1,097.7
Shareholders' Equity		
Preference stock	253.7	274.0
Common stock, $1 par value (1,000,000,000 shares authorized,		
732,853,180 shares issued)	732.9	732.9
Additional paid-in capital	1,064.4	1,093.8
Retained earnings	8,968.1	8,223.9
Accumulated other comprehensive income	(1,804.7)	(1,806.2)
	9,214.4	8,518.4
Unearned compensation	(283.3)	(307.6)
Treasury stock, at cost	(7,581.0)	(6,965.4)
Total shareholders' equity	1,350.1	1,245.4
Total liabilities and shareholders' equity	$ 8,507.1	$ 8,672.9

See Notes to Consolidated Financial Statements.

Dollars in Millions Except Per Share Amounts

Consolidated Statements of Retained Earnings, Comprehensive Income and Changes in Capital Accounts

	Common Shares		Additional Paid in Capital	Treasury Shares		Retained Earnings	Accumulated Other Comprehensive Income	Comprehensive Income
	Shares	Amount		Shares	Amount			
Balance, January 1, 2003	536,001,784	$732.9	$1,133.9	196,873,236	$(6,152.3)	$6,518.5	$(1,865.6)	
Net income						1,421.3		$1,421.3
Other comprehensive income:								
Cumulative translation adjustment							4.0	4.0
Other							(5.2)	(5.2)
Total comprehensive income								$1,420.1
Dividends declared:								
Series B Convertible Preference Stock, net of income taxes						(25.5)		
Preferred stock						(0.2)		
Common stock						(481.1)		
Shares issued for stock options	4,928,861		(20.9)	(4,928,861)	96.9			
Treasury stock acquired	(10,146,986)			10,250,146	(554.9)			
Other	2,913,518		13.2	(3,038,518)	110.4			
Balance, December 31, 2003	533,697,177	$732.9	$1,126.2	199,156,003	$(6,499.9)	$7,433.0	$(1,866.8)	
Net income						1,327.1		$1,327.1
Other comprehensive income:								
Cumulative translation adjustment							75.4	75.4
Other							(14.8)	(14.8)
Total comprehensive income								$1,387.7
Dividends declared:								
Series B Convertible Preference Stock, net of income taxes						(25.9)		
Common stock						(510.3)		
Shares issued for stock options	2,142,895		2.1	(2,142,895)	60.5			
Treasury stock acquired	(12,383,273)			12,383,273	(637.9)			
Other	3,168,259		(34.5)	(3,168,259)	111.9			
Balance, December 31, 2004	526,625,058	$732.9	$1,093.8	206,228,122	$(6,965.4)	$8,223.9	$(1,806.2)	
Net income						1,351.4		$1,351.4
Other comprehensive income:								
Cumulative translation adjustment							17.7	17.7
Other							(16.2)	(16.2)
Total comprehensive income								$1,352.9
Dividends declared:								
Series B Convertible Preference Stock, net of income taxes						(28.2)		
Common stock						(579.0)		
Shares issued for stock options	1,533,768		(4.8)	(1,533,768)	61.2			
Treasury stock acquired	(15,126,263)			15,126,263	(796.2)			
Other	3,138,394		(24.6)	(3,138,394)	119.4			
Balance, December 31, 2005	516,170,957	$732.9	$1,064.4	216,682,223	$(7,581.0)	$8,968.1	$(1,804.7)	

See Notes to Consolidated Financial Statements.

Dollars in Millions Except Per Share Amounts

Consolidated Statements of Cash Flows

For the years ended December 31,	2005	2004	2003
Operating Activities			
Net income	$ 1,351.4	$ 1,327.1	$ 1,421.3
Adjustments to reconcile net income to net cash provided by operations:			
Restructuring, net of cash	111.6	38.3	53.8
Depreciation and amortization	329.3	327.8	315.5
Gain before tax on sale of non-core product lines and other			
investment activities	(147.9)	(26.7)	(107.2)
Deferred income taxes	30.8	57.7	(48.8)
Cash effects of changes in:			
Receivables	(24.1)	(5.6)	(14.4)
Inventories	(46.8)	(76.1)	(3.1)
Accounts payable and other accruals	193.8	109.4	188.7
Other non-current assets and liabilities	(13.7)	2.4	(38.1)
Net cash provided by operations	1,784.4	1,754.3	1,767.7
Investing Activities			
Capital expenditures	(389.2)	(348.1)	(302.1)
Payment for acquisitions, net of cash acquired	(38.5)	(800.7)	—
Sale of non-core product lines	215.6	37.0	127.6
Purchases of marketable securities and investments	(20.0)	(127.7)	(43.2)
Proceeds from sales of marketable securities and investments	10.0	147.3	85.1
Other	1.4	1.8	15.0
Net cash used in investing activities	(220.7)	(1,090.4)	(117.6)
Financing Activities			
Principal payments on debt	(2,100.3)	(753.9)	(804.0)
Proceeds from issuance of debt	2,021.9	1,246.5	229.2
Payments to outside investors	(89.7)	—	—
Dividends paid	(607.2)	(536.2)	(506.8)
Purchases of treasury shares	(796.2)	(637.9)	(554.9)
Proceeds from exercise of stock options	47.1	70.4	79.3
Net cash used in financing activities	(1,524.4)	(611.1)	(1,557.2)
Effect of exchange rate changes on cash and cash equivalents	(18.2)	1.5	4.5
Net increase in cash and cash equivalents	21.1	54.3	97.4
Cash and cash equivalents at beginning of year	319.6	265.3	167.9
Cash and cash equivalents at end of year	$ 340.7	$ 319.6	$ 265.3
Supplemental Cash Flow Information			
Income taxes paid	$ 584.3	$ 593.8	$ 498.1
Interest paid	149.9	123.2	131.5
Principal payments on ESOP debt, guaranteed by the Company	37.0	29.8	23.5

See Notes to Consolidated Financial Statements.

Dollars in Millions Except Per Share Amounts

Notes to Consolidated Financial Statements

1. Nature of Operations

The Company manufactures and markets a wide variety of products in the U.S. and around the world in two distinct business segments: Oral, Personal and Home Care; and Pet Nutrition. Oral, Personal and Home Care products include toothpaste, oral rinses and toothbrushes, bar and liquid hand soaps, shower gels, shampoos, conditioners, deodorants and antiperspirants, shave products, laundry and dishwashing detergents, fabric conditioners, cleansers and cleaners, bleaches and other similar items. These products are sold primarily to wholesale and retail distributors worldwide. Pet Nutrition products include pet food products manufactured and marketed by Hill's Pet Nutrition. The principal customers for Pet Nutrition products are veterinarians and specialty pet retailers. Principal global and regional trademarks include Colgate, Palmolive, Kolynos, Sorriso, Elmex, Mennen, Protex, Softsoap, Irish Spring, Ajax, Axion, Soupline, Suavitel, Hill's Science Diet and Hill's Prescription Diet in addition to several other regional trademarks.

The Company's principal classes of products accounted for the following percentages of worldwide sales for the past three years:

	2005	2004	2003
Oral Care	38%	35%	34%
Home Care	26	28	29
Personal Care	23	23	24
Pet Nutrition	13	14	13

2. Summary of Significant Accounting Policies

Principles of Consolidation

The Consolidated Financial Statements include the accounts of Colgate-Palmolive Company and its majority-owned subsidiaries. Intercompany transactions and balances have been eliminated. The Company's investments in consumer products companies with interests ranging between 20% and 50% are accounted for using the equity method. As of December 31, 2005 and 2004, equity method investments included in Other assets were $5.1 and $3.8, respectively. Investments with less than a 20% interest are accounted for using the cost method. Unrelated third parties hold the remaining ownership interest in these investments. Net income (loss) from such investments is recorded in Other (income) expense, net in the Consolidated Statements of Income.

Use of Estimates

The preparation of financial statements in accordance with accounting principles generally accepted in the United States of America requires management to use judgment and make estimates that affect the reported amounts of assets and liabilities and disclosure of contingent gains and losses at the date of the financial statements and the reported amounts of revenues and expenses during the reporting period. The level of uncertainty in estimates and assumptions increases with the length of time until the underlying transactions are completed. As such, the most significant uncertainty in the Company's assumptions and estimates involved in preparing the financial statements includes pension and other retiree benefit cost assumptions, asset impairment, tax valuation allowances, and legal and other contingency reserves. Additionally, the Company uses available market information and other valuation methodologies in assessing the fair value of financial instruments. Judgment is required in interpreting market data to develop the estimates of fair value, and accordingly, changes in assumptions or the estimation methodologies may affect the fair value estimates. Actual results could ultimately differ from those estimates.

Revenue Recognition

Sales are recorded at the time products are shipped to trade customers and when risk of ownership transfers. Net sales reflect units shipped at selling list prices reduced by sales returns and the cost of current and continuing promotional programs. Current promotional programs, such as product listing allowances and co-operative advertising arrangements, are recorded in the period incurred. Continuing promotional programs are predominantly consumer coupons and volume-based sales incentive arrangements with trade customers. The redemption cost of consumer coupons is based on historical redemption experience and is recorded when coupons are distributed. Volume-based incentives offered to trade customers are based on the estimated cost of the program and are recorded as products are sold.

Shipping and Handling Costs

Shipping and handling costs are classified as Selling, general and administrative expenses and were $860.2, $767.4 and $700.8 for the years ended December 31, 2005, 2004 and 2003, respectively.

Marketing Costs

The Company markets its products through advertising and other promotional activities. Advertising costs are included in Selling, general and administrative expenses and are expensed as incurred. Certain consumer and trade promotional programs, such as consumer coupons, are recorded as a reduction of sales.

Cash and Cash Equivalents

The Company considers all highly liquid investments with original maturities of three months or less to be cash equivalents.

Inventories

Inventories are stated at the lower of cost or market. The cost of approximately 80% of inventories is determined using the first-in, first-out (FIFO) method. The cost of all other inventories, predominantly in the U.S. and Mexico, is determined using the last-in, first-out (LIFO) method.

Dollars in Millions Except Per Share Amounts

Property, Plant and Equipment

Land, buildings, and machinery and equipment are stated at cost. Depreciation is provided, primarily using the straight-line method, over estimated useful lives, ranging from 3 to 15 years for machinery and equipment and up to 40 years for buildings.

Goodwill and Other Intangibles

Goodwill and indefinite life intangible assets, such as the Company's global brands, are subject to annual impairment tests. These tests were performed and did not result in an impairment charge. Other intangible assets with finite lives, such as trademarks, local brands and non-compete agreements, are amortized over their useful lives, ranging from 5 to 40 years.

Income Taxes

The provision for income taxes is determined using the asset and liability method. Under this method, deferred tax assets and liabilities are recognized based upon the differences between the financial statements and tax bases of assets and liabilities using enacted tax rates that will be in effect at the time such differences are expected to reverse. Deferred tax assets are reduced by a valuation allowance when, in the opinion of management, it is more likely than not that some portion or all of the deferred tax assets will not be realized. Provision is made currently for taxes payable on remittances of overseas earnings; no provision is made for taxes on overseas retained earnings that are deemed to be permanently reinvested.

Financial Instruments

Derivative instruments are recorded as assets and liabilities at estimated fair value based on available market information. The Company's derivative instruments that qualify for hedge accounting are primarily designated as either fair value hedges or cash flow hedges. For fair value hedges, changes in fair value of the derivative, as well as the offsetting changes in fair value of the hedged item, are recognized in earnings each period. For cash flow hedges, changes in fair value of the derivative are recorded in other comprehensive income and are recognized in earnings when the offsetting effect of the hedged item is also recognized in earnings. Cash flows related to fair value hedges and cash flow hedges are classified in the same category as the cash flows from the hedged item in the Consolidated Statements of Cash Flows.

The Company may also enter into certain foreign currency and interest rate instruments that economically hedge certain of its risks but do not qualify for hedge accounting. Changes in fair value of these derivative instruments, based on quoted market prices, are recognized in earnings each period.

Stock-Based Compensation

Stock-based compensation plans, more fully described in Note 8, are accounted for under the provisions of Accounting Principles Board Opinion No. 25, "Accounting for Stock Issued to Employees" (APB 25) and related interpretations. The value of restricted stock awards, based on market prices, is amortized over the restriction period. No compensation expense has been recognized for stock option grants as all such grants had an exercise price not

less than fair market value on the date of grant. The following illustrates the effect on net income and earnings per share if the Company had applied the fair value method of Statement of Financial Accounting Standards (SFAS) No. 123, "Accounting for Stock-Based Compensation" (SFAS 123):

	2005	2004	2003
Net income, as reported	$1,351.4	$1,327.1	$1,421.3
Less: pro forma stock option compensation expense, net of tax	42.9	42.3	44.2
Pro forma net income	$1,308.5	$1,284.8	$1,377.1
Earnings per share:			
Basic – as reported	$ 2.54	$ 2.45	$ 2.60
Basic – pro forma	2.46	2.37	2.52
Diluted – as reported	2.43	2.33	2.46
Diluted – pro forma	2.35	2.26	2.38

Pro forma stock option compensation expense above is the estimated fair value of options granted amortized over the vesting period. The weighted average estimated fair value of stock options granted in 2005, 2004 and 2003 was $9.59, $12.48 and $13.46, respectively. Fair value is estimated using the Black-Scholes option-pricing model with the following assumptions: option term until exercise ranging from 4 to 5 years, volatility ranging from 20% to 30%, risk-free interest rate ranging from 3.2% to 4.0% and an expected dividend yield of 2.0%. See Note 8 for a discussion of changes made to the Company's stock option plans in 2003.

The Company will adopt the provisions of SFAS No. 123R, "Share-Based Payment," (SFAS 123R) effective January 1, 2006 using the modified prospective method. See Recent Accounting Pronouncements for a discussion of the estimated impact in 2006.

Translation of Overseas Currencies

The assets and liabilities of foreign subsidiaries, other than those operating in highly inflationary environments, are translated into U.S. dollars at year-end exchange rates, with resulting translation gains and losses accumulated in a separate component of shareholders' equity. Income and expense items are translated into U.S. dollars at average rates of exchange prevailing during the year.

For subsidiaries operating in highly inflationary environments, inventories, goodwill and property, plant and equipment are translated at the rate of exchange on the date the assets were acquired, while other assets and liabilities are translated at year-end exchange rates. Translation adjustments for these operations are included in Net income.

Recent Accounting Pronouncements

In November 2004, the Financial Accounting Standards Board (FASB) issued SFAS No. 151, "Inventory Costs—An Amendment of Accounting Research Bulletin No. 43, Chapter 4" (SFAS 151). SFAS 151 clarifies that abnormal amounts of idle facility expense, freight, handling costs and spoilage should be expensed as incurred and not included in overhead. Further, SFAS 151 requires that allocation of fixed production overhead to conversion costs be based on normal capacity of the production facilities. The provisions in SFAS 151 must be applied prospectively to the Company's inventory costs incurred on or after January 1, 2006. The adoption of SFAS 151 is not expected to have a material impact on the Company's Consolidated Financial Statements.

In December 2004, the FASB issued SFAS 123R. SFAS 123R replaces SFAS 123 by eliminating the choice to account for employee stock options under APB 25 and requires companies to recognize the cost of employee services received in exchange for awards of equity instruments, such as stock options and restricted stock, based on the fair value of those awards at the date of grant. Currently under APB 25 the value of restricted stock awards is expensed by the Company over the restriction period and, no compensation expense is recognized for stock option grants as all such grants have an exercise price not less than fair market value on the date of grant.

Additionally, certain of the Company's stock options granted to eligible participants have an accelerated vesting feature associated with employee retirement and most of the restricted stock awards specify that participants will continue to vest in the award after retirement. Currently the Company follows the nominal vesting period approach, which requires recognition of the compensation expense over the vesting period except in the instance of the participants' actual retirement. Upon the adoption of SFAS 123R, the Company's policy regarding the timing of expense recognition for new awards to employees eligible for retirement will, as required, be changed to recognize compensation cost over the period through the date that the employee first becomes eligible to retire and is no longer required to provide service to earn the award.

The Company will adopt the provisions of SFAS 123R effective January 1, 2006 using the modified prospective method which will result in an incremental expense upon adoption. The impact on earnings per share in fiscal year 2006 of these requirements is currently estimated in the range of $0.09 to $0.10. Future expense amounts for any particular quarterly or annual period could be affected by changes in the Company's assumptions or changes in market conditions. Due to the timing of the Company's equity grants the charge will not be spread evenly throughout the year. SFAS 123R also requires the benefits of tax deductions in excess of recognized compensation cost be reported as a financing cash flow, rather than as an operating cash flow as currently required, thereby potentially reducing net operating cash flows and increasing net financing cash flows in periods after adoption. Such amounts cannot be estimated for future periods with certainty because they depend largely on when employees will exercise the stock options and the market price of the Company's stock at the time of exercise.

Reclassifications
Certain prior year amounts have been reclassified to conform to the current year presentation.

3. Acquisitions and Divestitures
Consistent with the Company's strategy to prioritize higher margin businesses, the Company sold its North American and Southeast Asian heavy-duty laundry detergent brands in 2005. The North American brands were sold in August 2005 and included the detergent brands Fab, Dynamo, Artic Power, ABC, Cold Power and Fresh Start, and the license of the Ajax brand for laundry detergents, marketed in the U.S., Canada and Puerto Rico. The Southeast Asian brands, marketed in Thailand, Malaysia, Singapore and Hong Kong, were sold effective December 31, 2005. The transaction included the sale of the detergent brands Fab, Trojan, Dynamo and Paic. These operations accounted for less than 2% of the Company's annual Net sales. The aggregate proceeds from these sales were $215.6, resulting in a gain of $147.9 ($93.5 net of tax) included in Other (income) expense, net.

The Company increased its ownership interests in certain overseas subsidiaries to 100% during 2005 at a cost of $38.5, primarily related to its Malaysia subsidiary.

On June 1, 2004, the Company completed the purchase of 100% of the outstanding shares of GABA Holding AG (GABA), a privately owned European oral care company headquartered in Switzerland. The cost of GABA, net of cash acquired, was $729 plus acquisition costs. The results of GABA's operations have been included in the Company's European segment in the Consolidated Financial Statements since the date of acquisition. The aggregate purchase price for all other acquisitions in 2004 was approximately $60. The Company did not make any significant acquisitions in 2003.

During 2004, the Company sold its detergent businesses in Ecuador and Peru resulting in a pretax gain of $26.7 included in Other (income) expense, net for the year ended December 31, 2004. The aggregate sale price of all 2003 divestitures was $127.6 related to the sale of European soap brands marketed in France, and the sale of various European detergent brands marketed primarily in France, Italy and Scandinavia, resulting in a pretax gain of $107.2 included in Other (income) expense, net for the year ended December 31, 2003.

Dollars in Millions Except Per Share Amounts

4. Restructuring Activities

In December 2004, the Company commenced a four-year restructuring and business-building program (the 2004 Restructuring Program) to enhance the Company's global leadership position in its core businesses. As part of this program the Company anticipates the rationalization of approximately one-third of the Company's manufacturing facilities, closure of certain warehousing facilities and an estimated 12% workforce reduction.

In the year ended December 31, 2005, the Company incurred $182.8 ($145.1 aftertax) of charges in connection with restructuring and implementation related activities, as detailed below:

	Termination Benefits	Incremental Depreciation	Asset Impairments	Other	Total
Year Ended December 31, 2005					
Restructuring accrual at December 31, 2004	$ 41.7	$ —	$ —	$ 0.4	$ 42.1
Charges	45.8	65.3	30.2	41.5	182.8
Cash payments	(47.8)	—	—	(23.4)	(71.2)
Non-cash activity	—	(65.3)	(30.2)	(15.0)	(110.5)
Foreign exchange	(4.4)	—	—	(0.1)	(4.5)
Restructuring accrual at December 31, 2005	$ 35.3	$ —	$ —	$ 3.4	$ 38.7

Charges in the period related to restructuring activities in Europe (48%), North America (29%), Latin America (4%), Asia/Africa (11%), Pet Nutrition (1%) and Corporate (7%) and are reflected in the Consolidated Statements of Income in Cost of sales ($100.2), Selling, general and administrative expenses ($1.8) and Other (income) expense, net ($80.8).

During 2004 the Company incurred $68.7 ($48.0 aftertax) of charges in connection with the initial phase of the 2004 Restructuring Program, as detailed below:

	Termination Benefits	Incremental Depreciation	Asset Impairments	Other	Total
Year Ended December 31, 2004					
Charges	$41.6	$ 3.3	$ 22.0	$ 1.8	$ 68.7
Cash payments	(1.4)	—	—	(1.4)	(2.8)
Non-cash activity	—	(3.3)	(22.0)	—	(25.3)
Foreign exchange	1.5	—	—	—	1.5
Restructuring accrual at December 31, 2004	$41.7	$ —	$ —	$ 0.4	$ 42.1

Charges in the period related to restructuring activities in Europe (51%), North America (25%), Latin America (9%), Asia/Africa (7%) and Corporate (8%) and are reflected in the Consolidated Statements of Income in Cost of sales ($3.4) and Other (income) expense, net ($65.3).

Since the inception of the 2004 Restructuring Program in December 2004, the Company has incurred total charges of $251.5 ($193.1 aftertax) in connection with the implementation of various projects. The majority of costs incurred to date relate to the following significant projects: the consolidation of toothpaste production in Europe; exiting certain manufacturing activities in other categories in Portugal, Belgium, Denmark, Canada and Kansas City; and a realignment of the sales and administrative functions in Germany.

Restructuring costs are recorded in the Corporate segment as these decisions are corporate-driven and are not included in internal measures of segment operating performance.

Termination benefits are calculated based on long-standing benefit practices, local statutory requirements and, in certain cases, voluntary termination arrangements. Incremental depreciation was recorded to reflect changes in useful lives and estimated residual values for long-lived assets that will be taken out of service prior to the end of their normal service period. Asset impairments have been recorded to write down assets held for sale or disposal to their fair value based on amounts expected to be realized.

In connection with the Company's announcement in October 2005 to phase down toothpaste production in Jeffersonville, Indiana, the Company announced in January 2006, its plan to construct a new state-of-the-art dental cream facility in Morristown, Tennessee.

5. Goodwill and Other Intangible Assets

The net carrying value of Goodwill as of December 31, 2005 and 2004 by segment is as follows:

	2005	2004
Oral, Personal and Home Care		
North America	$ 276.6	$ 276.9
Latin America	539.1	502.0
Europe	843.8	936.5
Asia/Africa	171.2	161.3
Total Oral, Personal and Home Care	1,830.7	1,876.7
Pet Nutrition	15.0	15.0
Total Goodwill	$1,845.7	$1,891.7

Dollars in Millions Except Per Share Amounts

Other intangible assets as of December 31, 2005 and 2004 are comprised of the following:

	2005			2004		
	Gross Carrying Amount	Accumulated Amortization	Net	Gross Carrying Amount	Accumulated Amortization	Net
Trademarks	$418.5	$(158.2)	$260.3	$432.1	$(147.0)	$285.1
Other finite life intangible assets	11.9	(10.6)	1.3	10.2	(8.4)	1.8
Indefinite life intangible assets	521.6	—	521.6	545.5	—	545.5
Total Other intangible assets	$952.0	$(168.8)	$783.2	$987.8	$(155.4)	$832.4

The changes in the net carrying amounts of Goodwill and Other intangible assets during 2005 are mainly due to the impact of foreign currency translation adjustments.

Amortization expense of the above trademarks and other finite life intangible assets was $15.6 for the year ended December 31, 2005. Annual estimated amortization expense for each of the next five years is expected to approximate $16.

6. Long-Term Debt and Credit Facilities
Long-term debt consists of the following at December 31:

	Weighted Average Interest Rate	Maturities	2005	2004
Notes	5.8%	2006-2078	$1,824.5	$1,813.3
Payable to banks	4.3	2006-2008	555.7	563.9
ESOP notes, guaranteed by the Company	8.7	2006-2009	237.1	274.1
Commercial paper	3.0	2006	621.8	844.7
Capitalized leases			35.6	44.8
			3,274.7	3,540.8
Less: current portion of long-term debt			356.7	451.3
			$2,918.0	$3,089.5

Commercial paper and certain current maturities of notes payable totaling $641.9 are classified as long-term debt as the Company has the intent and ability to refinance such obligations on a long-term basis. Scheduled maturities of long-term debt and capitalized leases outstanding as of December 31, 2005, excluding commercial paper and certain current maturities of notes payable reclassified, are as follows: 2006—$356.7; 2007—$707.6; 2008—$159.6; 2009—$101.6; 2010—$287.3 and $1,020.0 thereafter. The Company has entered into interest rate swap agreements and foreign exchange contracts related to certain of these debt instruments (see Note 7).

At December 31, 2005, the Company had unused credit facilities amounting to approximately $2,400 and also had $1,754.4 of medium-term notes available for issuance pursuant to effective shelf registration statements. In November 2005, the Company entered into a new five-year revolving credit facility of $1,500.0 with a syndicate of banks. The facility, which expires in November 2010, replaces existing credit facilities of $300.0 and $1,300.0 which were due to expire in December 2005 and May 2007, respectively. Commitment fees related to credit facilities are not material. The

weighted average interest rate on short-term borrowings, included in Notes and loans payable in the Consolidated Balance Sheets, as of December 31, 2005 and 2004, was 4.0% and 3.7%, respectively.

The ESOP notes guaranteed by the Company and certain credit facilities contain cross-default provisions. Noncompliance with these requirements could ultimately result in the acceleration of amounts owed. The Company is in full compliance with all such requirements and believes the likelihood of noncompliance is remote.

7. Fair Value of Financial Instruments
The Company uses available market information and other valuation methodologies in assessing the fair value of financial instruments. Judgment is required in interpreting market data to develop the estimates of fair value, and accordingly, changes in assumptions or the estimation methodologies may affect the fair value estimates.

Derivative Instruments
Following are the notional amounts and net recorded fair values of the Company's derivative instruments:

	2005		2004	
	Notional Amount	Fair Value	Notional Amount	Fair Value
Interest rate swap contracts	$138.0	$4.8	$152.2	$4.8
Foreign currency contracts	875.0	3.6	1,468.4	(8.5)

The Company utilizes interest rate swap contracts to manage its targeted mix of fixed and floating rate debt. Forward and swap contracts are utilized to hedge a portion of the Company's foreign currency purchases and assets and liabilities created in the normal course of business. Forward contracts used in hedging forecasted foreign currency purchases have durations no greater than 18 months. It is the Company's policy to enter into derivative instruments with terms that match the underlying exposure being hedged. As such, the Company's derivative instruments are considered highly effective and the net gain or loss from hedge ineffectiveness was not material.

Cumulative losses related to foreign currency contracts designated as cash flow hedges which are expected to be recognized in earnings over the next 12 months, when the offsetting effects of the hedged item are also recorded in earnings, are not material.

Dollars in Millions Except Per Share Amounts

Other Financial Instruments

The carrying amount of cash and cash equivalents, accounts receivables, marketable securities, long-term investments and short-term debt approximated fair value as of December 31, 2005 and 2004. The estimated fair value of the Company's long-term debt, including current portion, as of December 31, 2005 and 2004, was $3,161.1 and $3,522.7, respectively, and the related carrying value was $3,274.7 and $3,540.8, respectively.

Credit Risk

The Company is exposed to credit loss in the event of nonperformance by counterparties to the financial instrument contracts held by the Company; however, nonperformance by these counterparties is considered remote as it is the Company's policy to contract with diversified counterparties that have a long-term debt rating of AA–/Aa3 or higher.

8. Capital Stock and Stock Compensation Plans

Preferred Stock

Preferred Stock consists of 250,000 authorized shares without par value. During 2003, the Company redeemed and retired all outstanding shares of its $4.25 Preferred Stock at the stated redemption price of $100 per share.

Preference Stock

In 1988, the Company authorized the issuance of 50,000,000 shares of Series B Convertible Preference Stock (the Preference Stock), without par value. The Preference Stock is convertible into eight shares of common stock. As of December 31, 2005 and 2004, 3,902,988 and 4,215,246 shares of Preference Stock, respectively, were outstanding and issued to the Company's Employee Stock Ownership Plan.

Stock Repurchases

In October 2004 the Company announced that the Board of Directors approved a share repurchase program, under which the Company is authorized to purchase up to 20 million shares of the Company's common stock through December 31, 2005. The Board also authorized at that time share repurchases on an ongoing basis associated with certain employee elections under the Company's compensation and benefit programs. On December 1, 2005 the Board of Directors authorized the extension of the share repurchase program through March 31, 2006. Stock purchases in 2005 were $796.2.

Incentive Stock Plan

The Company has a plan that provides for grants of restricted stock awards for officers and other employees of the Company and its major subsidiaries. A committee of independent members of the Board of Directors administers the plan. The awarded shares are made in common stock and vest at the end of the restriction period, generally between three and five years. During 2005 and 2004, approximately 1,153,000 and 1,142,000 shares, respectively, were awarded to employees in accordance with the provisions of the plan. The Company recognized compensation expense for the plan of $45.1, $38.4 and $30.1 for the years ended December 31, 2005, 2004 and 2003, respectively. As of December 31, 2005, there were approximately 2,949,000 restricted shares awarded but not vested.

Stock Option Plans

The Company's Stock Option Plans (the Stock Option Plans) provide for the issuance of non-qualified stock options to officers and other employees that generally vest over three to five years. In September 2003, the Company reduced the contractual term of the grants from ten years to six years and eliminated the reload feature described below. As of December 31, 2005, approximately 35,753,000 shares of common stock were available for future stock option grants.

Prior to September 2003, the Stock Option Plans contained a reload feature that provided for the grant of new options when previously owned shares of Company stock were used to exercise existing options. The number of new options granted under this feature was equal to the number of shares of previously owned Company stock used to exercise the original options and to pay the related required U.S. income tax. The new options were granted at a price equal to the fair market value on the date of the new grant and had shorter expected lives as they had the same expiration date as the original options exercised and vested over six months.

Stock option plan activity is summarized below:

	2005		2004		2003	
	Shares (in thousands)	Weighted Average Exercise Price	Shares (in thousands)	Weighted Average Exercise Price	Shares (in thousands)	Weighted Average Exercise Price
Options outstanding, January 1	41,041	$52	40,348	$51	43,054	$46
Granted	4,666	53	4,545	54	5,458	57
Exercised	(1,607)	32	(2,270)	34	(7,315)	29
Canceled or expired	(2,325)	57	(1,582)	57	(849)	57
Options outstanding, December 31	41,775	52	41,041	52	40,348	51
Options exercisable, December 31	31,999	$52	29,702	$50	28,371	$49

Dollars in Millions Except Per Share Amounts

The following table summarizes information relating to currently outstanding and exercisable options as of December 31, 2005:

Range of Exercise Prices	Weighted Average Remaining Contractual Life (in years)	Options Outstanding (in thousands)	Weighted Average Exercise Price	Options Exercisable (in thousands)	Weighted Average Exercise Price
$20.31–$25.90	1	507	$20	507	$20
$25.91–$32.37	2	744	31	744	31
$32.38–$38.85	2	2,191	35	2,191	35
$38.86–$45.32	2	1,184	42	1,156	42
$45.33–$51.80	4	3,682	48	3,373	48
$51.81–$58.27	4	31,619	55	22,333	55
$58.28–$64.75	2	1,848	60	1,695	60
	4	41,775	$52	31,999	$52

9. Employee Stock Ownership Plan

In 1989, the Company expanded its Employee Stock Ownership Plan (ESOP) through the introduction of a leveraged ESOP that funds certain benefits for employees who have met eligibility requirements. The ESOP issued $410.0 of long-term notes due through 2009 bearing an average interest rate of 8.7%. The remaining balance of the long-term notes, which are guaranteed by the Company, is reflected in the accompanying Consolidated Balance Sheets. The ESOP used the proceeds of the notes to purchase 6.3 million shares of the Preference Stock from the Company. The Preference Stock, which is convertible into eight shares of common stock, has a minimum redemption price of $65 per share and pays semiannual dividends equal to the higher of $2.44 or the current dividend paid on eight common shares for the comparable six-month period. During 2000, the ESOP entered into a loan agreement with the Company under which the benefits of the ESOP may be extended through 2035.

Dividends on the Preference Stock, as well as on the common shares also held by the ESOP, are paid to the ESOP trust and, together with cash contributions and advances from the Company, are used by the ESOP to repay principal and interest on the outstanding notes. Preference Stock is released for allocation to participants based upon the ratio of the current year's debt service to the sum of total principal and interest payments over the life of the loans. As of December 31, 2005, 1,644,365 shares were allocated to participant accounts and 2,258,623 shares were available for future allocation.

Dividends on the Preference Stock are deductible for income tax purposes and, accordingly, are reflected net of their tax benefit in the Consolidated Statements of Retained Earnings, Comprehensive Income and Changes in Capital Accounts.

Annual expense related to the leveraged ESOP, determined as interest incurred on the original notes, plus the higher of either principal payments or the historical cost of Preference Stock allocated, less dividends received on the shares held by the ESOP and advances from the Company, was $11.9 in 2005, $14.9 in 2004 and $5.3 in 2003. Unearned compensation, which is shown as a reduction in shareholders' equity, represents the amount of ESOP debt outstanding reduced by the difference between the cumulative cost of Preference Stock allocated and the cumulative principal payments.

Interest incurred on the ESOP's notes was $21.7 in 2005, $24.7 in 2004 and $27.1 in 2003. The Company paid dividends on the shares held by the ESOP of $36.9 in 2005, $34.4 in 2004 and $34.5 in 2003. Company contributions to the ESOP were $11.9 in 2005, $14.5 in 2004 and $19.0 in 2003.

10. Retirement Plans and Other Retiree Benefits

Retirement Plans

The Company, its U.S. subsidiaries and some of its overseas subsidiaries maintain defined benefit retirement plans covering substantially all of their employees. Benefits are based primarily on years of service and employees' career earnings. In the Company's principal U.S. plans, funds are contributed to the trusts in accordance with regulatory limits to provide for current service and for any unfunded projected benefit obligation over a reasonable period. Assets of the plans consist principally of common stocks, guaranteed investment contracts with insurance companies, investments in real estate funds, and U.S. government and corporate obligations. The Company's pension plan asset allocations at December 31 are as follows:

	2005	2004	2005	2004
	United States		International	
Asset Category				
Equity securities	63%	62%	50%	46%
Debt securities	33	32	43	45
Real estate and other	4	6	7	9
Total	100%	100%	100%	100%

Equity securities in the U.S. plans include investments in the Company's common stock representing 7% of plan assets at December 31, 2005 and 2004.

Dollars in Millions Except Per Share Amounts

Other Retiree Benefits

The Company and certain of its subsidiaries provide health care and life insurance benefits for retired employees to the extent not provided by government-sponsored plans. The Company utilizes a portion of its leveraged ESOP, in the form of future retiree contributions, to reduce its obligation to provide these postretirement benefits and to offset its current service cost. Additionally, during 2005 and 2004 the Company made contributions of $5.6 and $5.1, respectively, to fund the payment of future postretirement medical benefits, the maximum permitted under U.S. tax regulations.

The Company uses a December 31 measurement date for its defined benefit retirement plans and postretirement benefit plans. Summarized information for the Company's defined benefit retirement plans and postretirement plans are as follows:

	Pension Benefits				Other Retiree Benefits	
	2005	2004	2005	2004	2005	2004
	United States		International			
Change in Benefit Obligation						
Benefit obligation at beginning of year	$1,368.3	$1,232.4	$ 675.8	$ 518.3	$ 332.9	$ 238.2
Service cost	47.4	43.8	20.0	18.0	(3.6)	(4.3)
Interest cost	76.1	75.7	33.3	31.5	26.4	22.7
Participants' contributions	2.6	2.7	3.6	3.5	—	—
Acquisitions/plan amendments	2.6	—	—	69.8	10.2	—
Actuarial loss	83.4	93.0	49.4	20.5	63.7	90.5
Foreign exchange impact	—	—	(62.5)	49.9	(0.8)	3.2
Termination benefits	11.4	—	—	—	1.4	—
Curtailments and settlements	(34.0)	—	(27.7)	(8.0)	(0.1)	—
Benefit payments	(95.4)	(79.3)	(33.1)	(27.7)	(17.1)	(17.4)
Benefit obligations at end of year	$1,462.4	$1,368.3	$ 658.8	$ 675.8	$ 413.0	$ 332.9
Change in Plan Assets						
Fair value of plan assets at beginning of year	$1,148.2	$1,059.6	$ 360.0	$ 269.1	$ 5.5	$ —
Actual return on plan assets	92.4	102.6	41.8	22.6	1.1	0.4
Company contributions	123.0	62.6	41.6	29.9	22.7	22.5
Participants' contributions	2.6	2.7	3.6	3.5	—	—
Foreign exchange impact	—	—	(33.0)	24.8	—	—
Acquisitions/plan amendments	—	—	—	41.1	—	—
Settlements	(34.0)	—	(25.1)	(3.3)	—	—
Benefit payments	(95.4)	(79.3)	(33.1)	(27.7)	(17.1)	(17.4)
Fair value of plan assets at end of year	$1,236.8	$1,148.2	$ 355.8	$ 360.0	$ 12.2	$ 5.5
Funded Status						
Funded status at end of year	$ (225.6)	$ (220.1)	$(303.0)	$(315.8)	$ (400.8)	$ (327.4)
Unrecognized net actuarial loss	470.8	430.6	150.8	148.5	198.8	148.4
Unrecognized transition/prior service costs	9.7	12.0	10.0	14.4	1.5	(2.3)
Net amount recognized	$ 254.9	$ 222.5	$(142.2)	$(152.9)	$ (200.5)	$ (181.3)
Amounts Recognized in Balance Sheet						
Prepaid benefit cost	$ 400.0	$ 368.9	$ 14.4	$ 23.5	$ —	$ —
Accrued benefit liability	(224.7)	(199.7)	(245.2)	(267.6)	(200.5)	(181.3)
Accumulated other comprehensive income	79.6	53.3	88.6	91.2	—	—
Net amount recognized	$ 254.9	$ 222.5	$(142.2)	$(152.9)	$ (200.5)	$ (181.3)
Weighted Average Assumptions Used to Determine Benefit Obligations						
Discount rate	5.50%	5.75%	4.83%	5.53%	5.50%	5.75%
Long-term rate of compensation increase	4.00%	4.00%	3.42%	3.63%	—	—
ESOP growth rate	—	—	—	—	10.00%	10.00%

The overall investment objective is to balance risk and return so that obligations to employees are met. The Company evaluates its long-term rate of return on plan assets on an annual basis. In determining the long-term rate of return, the Company considers the nature of the plans' investments, an expectation for the plans' investment strategies and the historical rates of return. The assumed rate of return for 2005 for the U.S. plans was 8.0%. Historical rates of return for the U.S. plans for the most recent 15-year period were 9%. In addition, the current rate of return assumption for the U.S. plans is based upon a targeted asset allocation of approximately 35% in fixed income securities (which are expected to earn approximately 6% in the long term), 61% in equity securities (which are expected to earn approximately 10% in the long term) and 4% in real estate and other (which are expected to earn approximately 6% in the long term). Similar assessments were performed in determining rates of returns on international pension plan assets, to arrive at the Company's current weighted average rate of return of 7.5%.

Dollars in Millions Except Per Share Amounts

The U.S. pension benefits include funded qualified plans covering most domestic employees and certain unfunded non-qualified plans. As of December 31, 2005 and 2004, the U.S. qualified pension plans had benefit obligations of $1,211.8 and $1,131.6, and plan assets of $1,233.8 and $1,145.0, respectively.

	Pension Benefits						Other Retiree Benefits		
	2005	2004	2003	2005	2004	2003	2005	2004	2003
	United States			International					
Components of Net Periodic Benefit Costs									
Service cost	$ 47.4	$ 43.8	$ 39.4	$ 20.0	$ 18.0	$ 13.7	$ 10.3	$ 8.7	$ 6.3
Interest cost	76.1	75.7	74.5	33.3	31.5	25.7	26.4	22.7	19.8
Annual ESOP allocation	—	—	—	—	—	—	(13.9)	(13.0)	(10.8)
Expected return on plan assets	(90.0)	(83.4)	(73.2)	(23.7)	(21.3)	(17.3)	(0.8)	—	—
Amortization of transition/prior service costs	4.8	3.3	3.2	1.3	1.3	0.2	(0.4)	(1.0)	(1.0)
Amortization of actuarial loss (gain)	26.6	24.2	26.4	6.6	5.2	4.3	9.5	4.5	1.1
Net periodic benefit cost	$ 64.9	$ 63.6	$ 70.3	$ 37.5	$ 34.7	$ 26.6	$ 31.1	$ 21.9	$ 15.4
Other postretirement charges	25.6	—	—	12.6	—	—	10.7	—	—
Total pension cost	$ 90.5	$ 63.6	$ 70.3	$ 50.1	$ 34.7	$ 26.6	$ 41.8	$ 21.9	$ 15.4
Weighted Average Assumptions Used to Determine Net Periodic Benefit Costs									
Discount rate	5.75%	6.25%	6.75%	5.53%	6.03%	6.51%	5.75%	6.25%	6.75%
Long-term rate of return on plan assets	8.00%	8.00%	8.00%	7.50%	8.10%	8.48%	8.00%	—	—
Long-term rate of compensation increase	4.00%	4.25%	4.25%	3.63%	3.79%	3.84%	—	—	—
ESOP growth rate	—	—	—	—	—	—	10.00%	10.00%	10.00%

Other postretirement charges include certain charges required by SFAS 88 totaling $26.9 which primarily relate to the conversion of one of the Company's international pension plans to a defined contribution plan for all eligible participants for $10.6 and a lump sum payment of normal retirement benefits associated with a retirement plan in the U.S. for $14.2. Additionally, other postretirement charges above includes $12.8 of one-time termination benefits associated with the Company's 2004 Restructuring Program and a non-cash charge of $9.2 associated with an international postretirement obligation.

The accumulated benefit obligation for the U.S. pension plans was $1,381.1 and $1,274.3, respectively, as of December 31, 2005 and 2004. The accumulated benefit obligation for the International plans was $572.5 and $587.6, respectively, as of December 31, 2005 and 2004. Plans with accumulated benefit obligations in excess of plan assets and plans with projected benefit obligations in excess of plan assets as of December 31 consist of the following:

Benefit Obligation Exceeds Fair Value of Plan Assets

Years ended December 31,	2005	2004
Projected benefit obligation	$958.0	$941.9
Fair value of plan assets	387.4	378.5
Accumulated benefit obligation	696.2	675.4
Fair value of plan assets	236.0	223.0

These amounts represent non-qualified U.S. plans and certain plans at foreign locations that are primarily unfunded; as such, liabilities equal to the unfunded amounts have been recorded.

The assumed medical cost trend rate used in measuring the postretirement benefit obligation was 10% for 2006, 9% for 2007, 8% for 2008, 7% for 2009, 6% for 2010 and 5% for years thereafter. Changes in this rate can have a significant effect on amounts reported. The effect of a 1% increase in the assumed medical cost trend rate would increase the accumulated postretirement benefit obligation by approximately $75 and increase the annual expense by approximately $7. The effect of a 1% decrease in the assumed medical cost trend rate would decrease the accumulated postretirement benefit obligation by approximately $60 and decrease the annual expense by approximately $5.

Management's best estimate of cash requirements to be paid directly from the Company's assets for its postretirement plans for the year ending December 31, 2006 is $126, including $31 for other retiree benefit plans. These estimated cash requirements include $77 of projected contributions to the Company's postretirement plans and $49 of projected benefit payments made directly to participants of unfunded plans. Expected contributions are dependent on many variables, including the variability of the market value of the assets as compared to the obligation and other market or regulatory conditions. Accordingly, actual funding may differ from current estimates.

Total benefit payments expected to be paid to participants, which include payments directly from the Company's assets to participants of unfunded plans, as discussed above, as well as payments paid from the plans are as follows:

Dollars in Millions Except Per Share Amounts

Expected Benefit Payments

| | Pension Benefits | | Other |
	United States	International	Retiree Benefits
Years ended December 31,			
2006	$106.2	$28.4	$24.8
2007	108.4	28.2	25.5
2008	99.4	29.6	26.1
2009	99.3	31.3	26.7
2010	101.6	39.7	27.3
2011–2015	576.1	186.7	142.4

11. Income Taxes

The provision for income taxes consists of the following for the three years ended December 31:

	2005	2004	2003
United States	$215.5	$164.6	$209.2
International	512.1	510.7	411.4
	$727.6	$675.3	$620.6

The components of income before income taxes are as follows for the three years ended December 31:

	2005	2004	2003
United States	$ 556.8	$ 511.1	$ 602.0
International	1,522.2	1,491.3	1,439.9
	$2,079.0	$2,002.4	$2,041.9

The difference between the statutory U.S. federal income tax rate and the Company's global effective tax rate as reflected in the Consolidated Statements of Income is as follows:

Percentage of Income Before Tax	2005	2004	2003
Tax at United States statutory rate	35.0%	35.0%	35.0%
State income taxes, net of federal benefit	0.9	1.0	0.9
Effect of American Jobs Creation Act	2.0	—	—
Effect of overseas asset revaluations	—	—	(3.1)
Earnings taxed at other than United States statutory rate	(1.5)	(1.1)	(1.4)
Other, net	(1.4)	(1.2)	(1.0)
Effective tax rate	35.0%	33.7%	30.4%

In addition, net tax benefits of $12.0 in 2005, $27.1 in 2004 and $34.3 in 2003 recorded directly through equity predominantly include tax benefits related to certain employee benefit plans, as well as exchange losses on U.S. dollar-denominated investments in foreign subsidiaries.

Temporary differences between accounting for financial statement purposes and accounting for tax purposes result in taxes currently payable being higher (lower) than the total provision for income taxes as follows:

	2005	2004	2003
Intangible assets	$(60.2)	$(46.9)	$ 22.1
Property, plant and equipment	34.2	(9.8)	(5.8)
Pension and other postretirement benefits	(19.8)	4.8	(24.5)
Other, net	8.3	(8.4)	69.5
	$(37.5)	$(60.3)	$ 61.3

The components of deferred tax assets (liabilities) are as follows at December 31:

	2005	2004
Deferred Taxes – Current:		
Accrued liabilities	$ 75.2	$ 71.7
Other, net	17.9	49.9
Total deferred taxes, current	93.1	121.6
Deferred Taxes – Long-term:		
Intangible assets	(338.1)	(278.0)
Property, plant and equipment	(257.8)	(288.9)
Tax loss and tax credit carryforwards	193.3	178.6
Other, net	(18.3)	(2.5)
Valuation allowance	(133.8)	(118.8)
Total deferred taxes, long-term	(554.7)	(509.6)
Net deferred taxes	$(461.6)	$(388.0)

The major component of the 2005 and 2004 valuation allowance relates to tax benefits in certain jurisdictions arising from net operating losses not expected to be realized.

Applicable U.S. income and foreign withholding taxes have not been provided on approximately $1,200 of undistributed earnings of foreign subsidiaries at December 31, 2005. These earnings have been and are currently considered to be permanently invested and are currently not subject to such taxes. Determining the tax liability that would arise if these earnings were remitted is not practicable.

The American Jobs Creation Act of 2004 (the AJCA) created a temporary incentive for U.S. corporations to repatriate accumulated income earned abroad by providing an 85% dividends received deduction for qualifying dividends received prior to December 31, 2005. This deduction results in an approximate 5.25% federal tax rate on qualifying repatriated earnings. During 2005, the Company's Chairman and CEO, together with the Board of Directors, approved domestic reinvestment plans as required by the AJCA to repatriate $780 in foreign earnings. The Company recorded tax expense in 2005 of $40.9 related to these dividends received. The related earnings were repatriated in the second half of 2005.

12. Earnings Per Share

	For the Year Ended 2005			For the Year Ended 2004			For the Year Ended 2003		
	Income	Shares (millions)	Per Share	Income	Shares (millions)	Per Share	Income	Shares (millions)	Per Share
Net income	$1,351.4			$1,327.1			$1,421.3		
Preferred dividends	(28.2)			(25.9)			(25.7)		
Basic EPS	1,323.2	520.5	$2.54	1,301.2	530.9	$2.45	1,395.6	537.2	$2.60
Stock options and restricted stock		3.8			3.9			4.9	
Convertible preference stock	28.2	32.2		25.9	34.5		25.5	36.7	
Diluted EPS	$1,351.4	556.5	$2.43	$1,327.1	569.3	$2.33	$1,421.1	578.8	$2.46

In determining the dilutive effect of the stock options, the number of shares resulting from the assumed exercise of the options is reduced by the number of shares that could have been purchased by the Company with the proceeds from the exercise of such options.

13. Commitments and Contingencies

Minimum rental commitments under noncancellable operating leases, primarily for office and warehouse facilities, are $94.6 in 2006, $86.0 in 2007, $76.5 in 2008, $68.6 in 2009, $54.2 in 2010 and $94.8 thereafter. Rental expense amounted to $130.6 in 2005, $124.5 in 2004 and $113.1 in 2003. Contingent rentals, sublease income and capital leases, which are included in fixed assets, are not significant. The Company has various contractual commitments to purchase raw, packaging and other materials totaling $675.8.

The Company is contingently liable with respect to lawsuits, environmental matters, taxes and other matters arising out of the normal course of business.

As a matter of course, the Company is regularly audited by the Internal Revenue Service (IRS). The IRS has completed its examination of the Company's federal income tax returns for 1996 through 2003 and has proposed an assessment that challenges the Company's tax deductions for compensation in connection with expatriate executives. During 2005 the Company and the IRS reached agreement with respect to the compensation tax deduction for 1996 through 1998, and the amount of additional tax involved did not have a material impact on the financial position, results of operations or ongoing cash flows of the Company. For the remaining years under audit, 1999 through 2003, the tax in connection with the challenged deductions is $62. Estimated incremental tax payments related to the potential disallowances for subsequent periods could be an additional $11. While the Company believes that its tax position complies with applicable tax law and intends to continue to defend its position, potential settlement discussions with the IRS for the later years are underway. It is the opinion of management that the ultimate disposition of this and other tax matters, to the extent not previously provided for, will not have a material impact on the financial position, results of operations or ongoing cash flows of the Company.

Management proactively reviews and monitors its exposure to, and the impact of, environmental matters. The Company is a potentially responsible party to various environmental matters and as such may be responsible for all or a portion of the cleanup, restoration and post-closure monitoring of several sites. Substantially all of the Company's potential liability for these matters relates to a single superfund site associated with a prior acquisition. Substantially all of the Company's potential liability that may arise in connection with this site has been acknowledged in writing as being covered by the Company's insurance carriers which are presently making all their required payments and are expected to continue to do so in the future. While it is possible that the non-performance of other potentially responsible parties or the Company's insurance carriers could affect the cash flows and results of operations in any particular quarter or year, it is the opinion of management that the ultimate disposition of these matters, to the extent not previously provided for, will not have a material impact on the financial position, or ongoing results of operations and cash flows of the Company.

In 1995, the Company acquired the Kolynos oral care business from Wyeth (formerly American Home Products) (the Seller), as described in the Company's Form 8-K dated January 10, 1995. On September 8, 1998, the Company's Brazilian subsidiary received notice of an administrative proceeding from the Central Bank of Brazil primarily taking issue with certain foreign exchange filings made with the Central Bank in connection with the financing of this strategic transaction, but in no way challenging or seeking to unwind the acquisition. The Central Bank of Brazil in January 2001 notified the Company of its decision in this administrative proceeding to impose a fine, which, at the current exchange rate, approximates $110. The Company has appealed the decision to the Brazilian Monetary System Appeals Council (the Council), resulting in the suspension of the fine pending the decision of the Council. If the fine is affirmed, interest and penalties will also be assessed. Further appeals are available within the Brazilian federal courts. Although there can be no assurances, management believes, based on the opinion of its Brazilian legal counsel and other experts, that the filings challenged by the Central Bank fully complied with Brazilian law and that the Company should either prevail on appeal (at the Council level or if necessary in Brazilian federal court) or succeed in having the fine reduced significantly. The Company intends to challenge this proceeding vigorously.

In addition, the Brazilian internal revenue authority has disallowed interest deductions and foreign exchange losses taken by the Company's Brazilian subsidiary for certain years in connection with the financing of the Kolynos acquisition. The tax assessments with interest, at the current exchange rate, approximate $90. The Company has been disputing the disallowances by appealing the assessments within the internal revenue authority's appellate process, with the following results to date:

Dollars in Millions Except Per Share Amounts

■ In June 2005, the First Board of Taxpayers ruled in the Company's favor and allowed all of the previously claimed deductions for 1996 through 1998, which represent more than half of the total exposure. It is possible the tax authorities will appeal this decision.

■ For the remaining exposure related to subsequent years, the assessment is still outstanding, and the Company is also appealing this assessment to the First Board of Taxpayers.

In the event of an adverse decision within the internal revenue authority's appellate process, further appeals are available within the Brazilian federal courts. Although there can be no assurances, management believes, based on the opinion of its Brazilian legal counsel and other experts, that the disallowances are without merit and that the Company should prevail on appeal before the First Board of Taxpayers or if necessary in the Brazilian federal courts. The Company intends to challenge these assessments vigorously.

In addition, Brazilian prosecutors reviewed the foregoing transactions as part of an overall examination of all international transfers of reais through non-resident current accounts during the 1992 to 1998 time frame, a review which the Company understands involved hundreds and possibly thousands of other individuals and companies unrelated to the Company. At the request of these prosecutors, in February 2004, a federal judge agreed to authorize criminal charges against certain current and former officers of the Company's Brazilian subsidiary based on the same allegations made in the Central Bank and tax proceedings discussed above. Management believes, based on the opinion of its Brazilian legal counsel, that these officers behaved in all respects properly and in accordance with law in connection with the financing of the Kolynos acquisition. Management intends to support and defend these officers vigorously.

In 2002, the Brazilian Federal Public Attorney filed a civil action against the federal government of Brazil, Laboratorios Wyeth-Whitehall Ltda., the Brazilian subsidiary of the Seller, and the Company, as represented by its Brazilian subsidiary, seeking to annul an April 2000 decision by the Brazilian Board of Tax Appeals that found in favor of the Seller's subsidiary on the issue of whether it had incurred taxable capital gains as a result of the divestiture of Kolynos. The action seeks to make the Company's Brazilian subsidiary jointly and severally liable for any tax due from the Seller's subsidiary. Although there can be no assurances, management believes, based on the opinion of its Brazilian legal counsel, that the Company should ultimately prevail in this action. The Company intends to challenge this action vigorously.

In December 2005, the Brazilian internal revenue authority issued to the Company's Brazilian subsidiary a tax assessment with interest and penalties of approximately $45 at the current rate of exchange, based on a claim that certain purchases of U.S. Treasury bills by the subsidiary and their subsequent sale during the period 2000 to 2001 were subject to a tax on foreign exchange transactions. The Company is disputing the assessment within the internal revenue authority's administrative appeals process. Although there can be no assurances, management believes,

based on the opinion of its Brazilian legal counsel, that the tax assessment is without merit and that the Company should prevail either through administrative appeal or if necessary through further appeal in the Brazilian federal courts. The Company intends to challenge this assessment vigorously.

French competition authorities have initiated an inquiry into potential competition law violations in France involving exchanges of competitive information and agreements on selling terms and conditions among a number of consumer goods companies in France, including the Company's French subsidiary. The Company intends to cooperate fully with the authorities in their inquiry. At this time, no formal claim for a fine or penalty has been made. The Company cannot at this time predict the financial impact of this matter.

While it is possible that the Company's cash flows and results of operations in a particular quarter or year could be materially affected by the one-time impacts of the resolution of such contingencies, it is the opinion of management that the ultimate disposition of these matters will not have a material impact on the Company's financial position, or ongoing results of operations and cash flows.

14. Segment Information

The Company operates in two product segments: Oral, Personal and Home Care; and Pet Nutrition. The operations of the Oral, Personal and Home Care segment are managed geographically in four reportable operating segments: North America, Latin America, Europe and Asia/Africa. Management evaluates segment performance based on several factors, including operating profit. The Company uses operating profit as a measure of operating segment performance because it excludes the impact of corporate-driven decisions related to interest expense and income taxes.

The accounting policies of the operating segments are generally the same as those described in Note 2. Intercompany sales have been eliminated. Corporate operations include restructuring and related costs, research and development costs, unallocated overhead costs, and gains and losses on sales of non-core brands and assets. Corporate assets primarily include benefit plan assets. Segment information regarding Net sales, Operating profit, Capital expenditures, Depreciation and amortization, and Identifiable assets is detailed below:

Net Sales	2005	2004	2003
Oral, Personal and Home Care			
North America [1]	$ 2,509.8	$ 2,378.7	$2,356.2
Latin America	2,623.8	2,266.0	2,179.5
Europe	2,739.4	2,621.3	2,304.1
Asia/Africa	2,003.7	1,885.1	1,747.5
Total Oral, Personal and Home Care	9,876.7	9,151.1	8,587.3
Pet Nutrition [2]	1,520.2	1,433.1	1,316.1
Total Net Sales	$11,396.9	$10,584.2	$9,903.4

(1) Net sales in the U.S. for Oral, Personal and Home Care were $2,124.2, $2,000.3 and $1,986.9 in 2005, 2004 and 2003, respectively.
(2) Net sales in the U.S. for Pet Nutrition were $818.1, $781.0 and $752.8 in 2005, 2004 and 2003, respectively.

Dollars in Millions Except Per Share Amounts

Operating Profit	2005	2004	2003
Oral, Personal and Home Care			
North America	$ 545.7	$ 530.1	$ 547.4
Latin America	698.0	627.7	613.3
Europe	547.3	539.0	488.2
Asia/Africa	318.0	310.1	280.7
Total Oral, Personal and Home Care	2,109.0	2,006.9	1,929.6
Pet Nutrition	412.8	389.7	371.0
Corporate	(306.8)	(274.5)	(134.6)
Total Operating Profit	$2,215.0	$2,122.1	$2,166.0

Capital Expenditures	2005	2004	2003
Oral, Personal and Home Care			
North America	$ 39.3	$ 55.4	$ 48.3
Latin America	104.1	75.4	72.9
Europe	57.3	71.2	47.4
Asia/Africa	123.7	79.9	58.1
Total Oral, Personal and Home Care	324.4	281.9	226.7
Pet Nutrition	28.5	30.4	38.3
Corporate	36.3	35.8	37.1
Total Capital Expenditures	$389.2	$348.1	$302.1

Depreciation and Amortization	2005	2004	2003
Oral, Personal and Home Care			
North America	$ 71.2	$ 74.9	$ 83.3
Latin America	67.1	58.8	55.6
Europe	70.4	76.5	65.7
Asia/Africa	55.7	54.0	49.7
Total Oral, Personal and Home Care	264.4	264.2	254.3
Pet Nutrition	30.1	31.1	31.9
Corporate	34.8	32.5	29.3
Total Depreciation and Amortization	$329.3	$327.8	$315.5

Identifiable Assets	2005	2004	2003
Oral, Personal and Home Care			
North America	$1,918.0	$2,001.4	$2,081.8
Latin America	2,084.3	1,825.1	1,757.2
Europe	2,118.9	2,544.4	1,542.2
Asia/Africa	1,337.9	1,329.8	1,123.9
Total Oral, Personal and Home Care	7,459.1	7,700.7	6,505.1
Pet Nutrition	614.3	614.0	587.2
Corporate	433.7	358.2	386.5
Total Identifiable Assets[1]	$8,507.1	$8,672.9	$7,478.8

(1) Long-lived assets in the U.S., primarily property, plant and equipment and good-will and other intangibles, represented approximately one-third of total long-lived assets of $5,225.7, $5,808.0 and $4,826.7 in 2005, 2004 and 2003, respectively.

15. Supplemental Income Statement Information

Other (Income) Expense, Net	2005	2004	2003
Minority interest	$ 55.3	$ 47.9	$ 45.2
Amortization of intangible assets	15.6	14.3	12.3
Equity (income)	(2.0)	(8.5)	(0.3)
Gains on sales of non-core product lines, net	(147.9)	(26.7)	(107.2)
2004 Restructuring Program	80.8	65.3	—
2003 restructuring activities	—	2.8	59.3
Pension and other postretirement charges	34.0	—	—
Investment losses (income)	19.7	(8.7)	(39.6)
Other, net	13.7	3.9	15.3
	$ 69.2	$ 90.3	$ (15.0)

Interest Expense, Net	2005	2004	2003
Interest incurred	$ 145.0	$ 126.0	$132.1
Interest capitalized	(2.5)	(2.3)	(4.0)
Interest income	(6.5)	(4.0)	(4.0)
	$ 136.0	$ 119.7	$124.1

Research and development	$ 246.3	$ 229.2	$204.8
Advertising	$1,193.6	$1,063.0	$965.6

16. Supplemental Balance Sheet Information

Inventories	2005	2004
Raw materials and supplies	$208.1	$212.4
Work-in-process	37.5	37.3
Finished goods	610.2	595.8
	$855.8	$845.5

Inventories valued under LIFO amounted to $191.7 and $176.5 at December 31, 2005 and 2004, respectively. The excess of current cost over LIFO cost at the end of each year was $29.5 and $26.3, respectively. The liquidations of LIFO inventory quantities had no effect on income in 2005, 2004 and 2003.

Property, Plant and Equipment, Net	2005	2004
Land	$ 134.5	$ 149.9
Buildings	896.5	919.9
Manufacturing machinery and equipment	3,540.9	3,599.8
Other equipment	775.2	782.0
	5,347.1	5,451.6
Accumulated depreciation	(2,803.0)	(2,803.9)
	$ 2,544.1	$ 2,647.7

Other Accruals	2005	2004
Accrued advertising	$ 344.9	$ 342.6
Accrued payroll and employee benefits	305.6	319.0
Accrued taxes other than income taxes	72.3	92.3
Restructuring accrual	38.7	42.1
Accrued interest	17.5	22.4
Other	344.2	309.2
	$1,123.2	$1,127.6

Other Liabilities	2005	2004
Minority interest	$103.3	$ 216.0
Pension and other retiree benefits	670.4	648.6
Other	167.6	233.1
	$941.3	$1,097.7

Dollars in Millions Except Per Share Amounts

Accumulated Other Comprehensive Income

Accumulated other comprehensive income is comprised of cumulative foreign currency translation gains and losses, minimum pension liability adjustments, unrealized gains and losses from derivative instruments designated as cash flow hedges, and unrealized gains and losses from available-for-sale securities. As of December 31, 2005 and 2004, accumulated other comprehensive income primarily consisted of cumulative foreign currency translation adjustments.

The 2005 cumulative translation adjustment reflects a weakening euro and its effect primarily on euro-denominated long-term debt, similar effects from a weakening Swiss franc, together with a strengthening Brazilian real and Mexican peso. The 2004 cumulative translation adjustment reflects stronger currencies in Brazil and South Africa, the devaluation of the Venezuelan bolivar and the impact of the strengthening euro.

17. Quarterly Financial Data (Unaudited)

	First Quarter	Second Quarter	Third Quarter	Fourth Quarter
2005				
Net sales	$2,743.0	$2,837.5	$2,911.8	$2,904.6
Gross profit	1,503.6	1,539.1	1,577.6	1,584.7
Net income	300.1[1]	342.9[2]	347.2[3]	361.2[4]
Earnings per common share:				
Basic	0.56	0.64	0.66	0.68
Diluted	0.53[1]	0.62[2]	0.63[3]	0.65[4]
2004				
Net sales	$2,513.5	$2,571.7	$2,695.7	$2,803.3
Gross profit	1,399.6	1,423.6	1,476.7	1,537.1
Net income	338.5	373.9	329.0	285.7[5]
Earnings per common share:				
Basic	0.62	0.69	0.61	0.53
Diluted	0.59	0.66	0.58	0.50[5]

(1) Net income and diluted earnings per share for the first quarter of 2005 were reduced by a net aftertax charge of $44.6 and $0.08, respectively, reflecting charges related to the 2004 Restructuring Program.

(2) Net income and diluted earnings per share for the second quarter of 2005 were reduced by a net aftertax charge of $28.7 and $0.05, respectively, reflecting charges related to the 2004 Restructuring Program.

(3) Net income and diluted earnings per share for the third quarter of 2005 were reduced by a net aftertax charge of $22.5 and $0.04, respectively, reflecting the net impact of a gain on the sale of the Company's heavy-duty laundry detergent brands in North America, charges related to the 2004 Restructuring Program, income taxes for incremental repatriation of foreign earnings related to the American Jobs Creation Act and charges related to certain pension obligations as required by SFAS 88.

(4) Net income and diluted earnings per share for the fourth quarter of 2005 were reduced by a net aftertax charge of $19.4 and $0.04, respectively, reflecting the net impact of charges related to the 2004 Restructuring Program, a gain on the sale of the Company's heavy-duty laundry detergent brands in Southeast Asia, income taxes for incremental repatriation of foreign earnings related to the American Jobs Creation Act and a non-cash charge related to an international postretirement obligation.

(5) Net income and diluted earnings per share for the fourth quarter of 2004 include an aftertax charge of $48.0 and $0.09, respectively, related to the initial phase of the 2004 Restructuring Program.

Market and Dividend Information

The Company's common stock is listed on the New York Stock Exchange. The trading symbol for the common stock is CL. Dividends on the common stock have been paid every year since 1895 and the Company's regular common stock dividend payments have increased for 43 consecutive years.

Market Price of Common Stock

Quarter Ended	2005		2004	
	High	Low	High	Low
March 31	$55.20	$48.55	$56.55	$49.62
June 30	53.95	48.60	58.92	53.56
September 30	54.06	49.55	58.73	45.15
December 31	56.39	51.78	51.26	43.06
Closing Price	$54.85		$51.16	

Dividends Paid Per Common Share

Quarter Ended	2005	2004
March 31	$0.24	$0.24
June 30	0.29	0.24
September 30	0.29	0.24
December 31	0.29	0.24
Total	$1.11	$0.96

Eleven-Year Financial Summary[1]

	2005	2004	2003	2002
Continuing Operations				
Net sales[2]	$11,396.9	$10,584.2	$9,903.4	$9,294.3
Results of operations:				
Net income	1,351.4[3]	1,327.1[4]	1,421.3	1,288.3
Per share, basic	2.54[3]	2.45[4]	2.60	2.33
Per share, diluted	2.43[3]	2.33[4]	2.46	2.19
Depreciation and amortization expense	329.3	327.8	315.5	296.5
Financial Position				
Current ratio	1.0	1.0	1.0	1.0
Property, plant and equipment, net	2,544.1	2,647.7	2,542.2	2,491.3
Capital expenditures	389.2	348.1	302.1	343.7
Total assets	8,507.1	8,672.9	7,478.8	7,087.2
Long-term debt	2,918.0	3,089.5	2,684.9	3,210.8
Shareholders' equity	1,350.1	1,245.4	887.1	350.3
Share and Other				
Book value per common share	2.67	2.43	1.71	0.69
Cash dividends declared and paid per common share	1.11	0.96	0.90	0.72
Closing price	54.85	51.16	50.05	52.43
Number of common shares outstanding (in millions)	516.2	526.6	533.7	536.0
Number of common shareholders of record	35,000	36,500	37,700	38,800
Average number of employees	35,800	36,000	36,600	37,700

Glossary of Terms

- **Category Innovation Centers:** dedicated teams of Colgate marketing and consumer insight professionals focused on identifying opportunities for new products from unmet consumer wants and needs or from unique local practices or behaviors that can be transferred to broader geographies.
- **Commercial Investment:** includes media, promotion and other consumer and trade incentives, some of which reduce reported net sales.
- **Corporate Governance:** the practices, principles and values that guide our Company and its business every day, at all levels of the organization.
- **eTeamRooms:** a centralized, virtual workplace on Colgate's intranet where Colgate teams and departments can coordinate people, tasks, project plans, documents and calendars all in one location.
- **Market Share:** the percentage of a category or segment's retail sales obtained by one brand or company. In this report, market shares are based on value share data provided primarily by ACNielsen. Global or regional shares are a weighted average of markets where Colgate competes and purchases third-party syndicated data.
- **Nutrigenomics:** an emerging field of nutritional research which focuses on the interaction between genes and nutrients.
- **SAP:** computer software that links all business processes into one integrated system that can be viewed in real time by everyone connected to it. This facilitates efficiencies and smooth running of the business. SAP is a trademark of SAP Aktiengesellschaft.
- **Shopper Marketing Initiatives:** Colgate accompanies shoppers as they shop to determine how and why they make their brand choices and then develops brand advertising messages specifically for in-store use.
- **Unit Volume Growth:** growth in product units sold, weighted to reflect price per unit.

Dollars in Millions Except Per Share Amounts

	2001	2000	1999	1998	1997	1996	1995
	$9,084.3	$9,004.4	$8,801.5	$8,660.8	$8,786.8	$8,493.1	$8,201.5
	1,146.6	1,063.8	937.3	848.6	740.4	635.0	172.0[5]
	2.02	1.81	1.57	1.40	1.22	1.05	0.26[5]
	1.89	1.70	1.47	1.30	1.13	0.98	0.25[5]
	336.2	337.8	340.2	330.3	319.9	316.3	300.3
	1.0	1.0	1.0	1.1	1.1	1.2	1.3
	2,513.5	2,528.3	2,551.1	2,589.2	2,441.0	2,428.9	2,155.2
	340.2	366.6	372.8	389.6	478.5	459.0	431.8
	6,984.8	7,252.3	7,423.1	7,685.2	7,538.7	7,901.5	7,642.3
	2,812.0	2,536.9	2,243.3	2,300.6	2,340.3	2,786.8	2,992.0
	846.4	1,468.1	1,833.7	2,085.6	2,178.6	2,034.1	1,679.8
	1.54	2.57	3.14	3.53	3.65	3.42	2.84
	.675	0.63	0.59	0.55	0.53	0.47	0.44
	57.75	64.55	65.00	46.44	36.75	23.06	17.56
	550.7	566.7	578.9	585.4	590.8	588.6	583.4
	40,900	42,300	44,600	45,800	46,800	45,500	46,600
	38,500	38,300	37,200	38,300	37,800	37,900	38,400

(1) All share and per share amounts have been restated to reflect the 1999 and 1997 two-for-one stock splits.

(2) Net sales amounts for 2001 and prior have been revised to reflect the reclassification of certain sales incentives and promotional expenses from selling, general and administrative expenses to a reduction of net sales and cost of sales in accordance with new accounting standards.

(3) Net income and earnings per share in 2005 include a gain for the sale of heavy-duty laundry detergent brands in North America and Southeast Asia of $93.5 aftertax. This gain was more than offset by $145.1 of aftertax charges associated with the 2004 Restructuring Program, $40.9 of income taxes for incremental repatriation of foreign earnings related to the American Jobs Creation Act and $22.7 aftertax of non-cash pension and other postretirement charges.

(4) Net income and earnings per share in 2004 include a provision for the 2004 Restructuring Program of $48.0 aftertax.

(5) Net income and earnings per share in 1995 include a net provision for restructured operations of $369.2 aftertax.

SOUTH AFRICA

Colgate Delivers Oral Health Education to Children Around the World

Colgate reaches millions of children annually through its sampling and oral education programs. In South Africa, these consumption building programs include free dental treatments and teach good oral care habits.

Colgate

GLOSSARY

Parentheses indicate page references.

A

Accelerated depreciation method Records the highest depreciation in the first year of an asset's service life and lower depreciation in subsequent years (728)

Accounting cycle Steps that a company completes during each accounting period to record, retain, and report the monetary information from its transactions (A-4)

Accounts Documents used to record and retain the monetary information from a company's transactions (A-2)

Accrued expense Incurred by a company during the accounting period but not paid or recorded (A-15)

Accrued revenue Earned by a company during the accounting period but neither collected nor recorded (A-16)

Accumulated depreciation Total amount of depreciation expense recorded over the life of an asset to date (722)

Activity pool Grouping of related activities involving factory overhead (622)

Activity-based costing (ABC) System which allocates factory overhead to units of product; first allocates factory overhead costs to activity pools, then assigns costs in each activity pool to jobs based on the relative number of activities needed to complete the jobs, and finally assigns the total factory overhead costs allocated to each job equally to the individual units of product in the job (622)

Activity-based management The technique of managing a company's activities to increase its customers' satisfaction and to increase its profits, either through increased revenues or reduced costs (629)

Additional paid-in capital Difference between the selling price and the par value in each stock transaction (855)

Adjusted trial balance Schedule prepared to prove the equality of the debit and credit balances in a company's general ledger accounts after it has made the adjusting entries (A-17)

Adjusting entries Journal entries that a company makes at the end of its accounting period to bring the company's revenue and expense account balances up-to-date and to show the correct ending balances in its asset and liability accounts (A-13)

Amortization expense Portion of the acquisition cost of an intangible asset that a company allocates as an expense to each accounting period over the asset's service life (749)

Amount One-time future cash flow (694)

Annuity Series of equal periodic future cash flows (695)

Appraisal costs Costs of catching product defects inside the company (614)

Authorized capital stock Number of shares of capital stock that a corporation may legally issue (856)

Available-for-sale securities Investments in common stocks where the investor does not have significant influence over the investee or bonds that the investor does not expect to hold until their maturity date (822)

Average cost flow assumption Allocates the average cost per unit for the period to both the ending inventory and the cost of goods sold (674)

Average cost method Assigns the total costs of direct materials and conversion separately to products at the average costs per equivalent unit by adding the amount of each type of cost in the beginning inventory to the amount of that cost type incurred during the month (550)

Average rate of return on investment Average return on the investment per year, per dollar invested for a capital expenditure proposal (701)

Avoidable costs Costs that must be incurred to perform an activity at a given level, but that can be avoided if that activity is reduced or discontinued (499)

B

Back-flush costing System of costing where a company records its product costs directly in cost of goods sold and then "backs out" the costs of the finished goods still on hand at the end of an accounting period (616)

Balance of an account Difference between the total increases and the total decreases recorded in the account (A-4)

Balanced scorecard A technique that links competitive strategies with specific measures of the success of the strategies (608)

Basic earnings per share   Corporation's net income per share available to its common stockholders (870)

Benchmarking   A technique that allows the company to compare its operations against its most successful competitors by measuring its own practices against the best practices (benchmarks) occurring in the industry in which it operates (611)

Board of directors   Group of individuals that has the responsibility and authority to supervise a corporation's ordinary business activities, make future plans, and take whatever action is necessary in managing the corporation (853)

Bond   Type of note in which a company agrees to pay the holder the face value on the maturity date and to pay interest on the face value periodically at a specified rate (778, 820)

Bond certificate   Serially numbered legal document that specifies the face value, the annual interest rate, and the maturity date (778)

Book value   Asset's original cost minus the related accumulated depreciation (722, 777)

C

Callable bonds   Have a provision that allows the issuer to purchase them (787)

Callable preferred stock   Corporation claims the right to recall (or retire) at its option (858)

Capital expenditure   Cost that increases the benefits a company will obtain from an asset (687, 732)

Capital lease   Transfers the risks and benefits of ownership from the lessor to the lessee (793)

Capital rationing   Occurs when a company cannot obtain sufficient cash to make all of the investments that it would like to make, and thus must choose in which of the acceptable proposals to invest (703)

Capital stock   Units of ownership in a corporation that are given to owners in exchange for capital (853)

Chart of accounts   Numbering system designed to organize a company's accounts efficiently and to reduce errors in the recording and accumulating process (A-10)

Closing entries   Entries made by a company at the end of an accounting period to create a zero balance in each revenue, expense, and withdrawals T-account, and to update the owner's equity by transferring the balances in the revenue, expense, and withdrawals T-accounts to the T-account for owner's capital (A-22)

Common stock   Ownership unit of a corporation (819, 855)

Compensatory stock options   Options to buy stock; intended to provide additional compensation to employees (862)

Complex capital structure   Structure of a corporation that has issued stock options and convertible securities (872)

Component   A major division of a company that sells products or services that are different from those of the rest of the company (867)

Compound interest   Interest that accrues on both the principal and the past (unpaid) interest (693)

Conservatism principle   Holds that a company should apply GAAP in such a way that there is little chance that it will overstate assets or income (667)

Consolidated financial statements   Combined financial statements of the parent company and all other companies over which it has control (832)

Contract rate   Rate at which the issuer of a bond pays interest on the face value each period until the maturity date (778)

Contributed capital   Total investments made by stockholders in the corporation (853)

Control over investee   More than 50% ownership of the common stock of another company (820, 831)

Conversion costs   Direct labor and factory overhead costs necessary to convert raw materials into a finished product (544)

Convertible preferred stock   Exchangeable into common stock at the option of the individual stockholders (858)

Copyright   Exclusive right granted by the U.S. government to publish or sell literary or artistic products for the life of the author plus an additional 70 years (750)

Cost accounting (Cost analysis)   Process of determining and evaluating the costs of specific products or activities of a company (527)

Cost driver   Activities on which a company bases activity pools (622)

Cost of capital   Weighted average cost (rate of return) a company must pay to all sources of capital (691)

Cost of goods sold   Major expense of a retail company consisting of the cost of the goods (merchandise) that it sells during the accounting period (650)

Credit entry   Monetary amount recorded (credited) on the right side of an account (A-3)

Cumulative preferred stock   Must receive all dividends of current period and the accumulated unpaid dividends of past periods before any common stockholders receive any dividends (876)

D

Date of declaration Date that a corporation's board of directors declares that a dividend will be paid to stockholders of record on a specified future date (874)

Date of payment Date that a corporation mails the dividend checks (875)

Date of record Only investors listed as stockholders of the corporation on this date can participate in dividends (875)

Debit entry Monetary amount recorded (debited) on the left side of an account (A-3)

Deferred tax asset Account that a corporation uses to report on its balance sheet the amount by which its future income will be reduced by deductible temporary differences (798)

Deferred tax liability Account a corporation uses to report on its balance sheet the amount of its future additional income taxes resulting from taxable temporary differences (798)

Defined-benefit plan Pension plan that specifies the amount that a company must pay to its employees each year during their retirement (799)

Defined-contribution plan Specifies the amount that a company must contribute to a pension plan each year while its employees work (799)

Depletion expense Portion of the cost (less the estimated residual value) of a natural resource asset that a company allocates as an expense to each accounting period over the asset's service life (757)

Depreciable cost Cost of a physical asset less its residual value (724)

Depreciation expense Part of the cost of property, plant, and equipment (physical asset) that a company allocates as an expense to each accounting period in which the company uses the asset (722)

Development Translation of research into a plan or design for a new or improved product or process (749)

Diluted earnings per share Includes the effects of all potential common shares that would reduce earnings per share (872)

Direct labor efficiency variance Difference between the standard cost of the direct labor hours that a company should have used for the actual number of units produced and the standard cost of the direct labor hours that it did use to produce those units (577)

Direct labor price standard Current wage rate that a company should incur per hour for a specific type of direct labor employed in production (575)

Direct labor price variance Difference between the cost that a company should have incurred for the actual labor hours worked and the actual direct labor cost it did incur for the number of actual labor hours worked (577)

Direct labor quantity standard Amount of direct labor time that a company should use to produce one unit of product (576)

Direct materials price standard Cost that a company should incur to acquire one unit of a direct material for production (570)

Direct materials price variance Difference between the standard cost that a company should have incurred to acquire the direct materials and the actual cost it did incur to acquire the direct materials (571)

Direct materials quantity standard Amount of a direct material that a company should use to produce one unit of product (570)

Direct materials quantity variance Difference between the standard cost of the quantity of direct materials that a company should have used for the actual number of units produced and the standard cost of the quantity of direct materials that it did use to produce those units (572)

Discount rate Rate used to convert a future amount to a present value (695)

Dividend preference Right of preferred stockholders to receive a dividend before a corporation pays a dividend to common stockholders (876)

Dividends in arrears Accumulated unpaid dividends of past periods on cumulative preferred stock (876)

Double entry rule In the recording of a transaction, the total amount of the debit entries must be equal to the total amount of the credit entries for the transaction (A-3)

Double-declining-balance method Computes depreciation expense by multiplying the book value of an asset at the beginning of the period by twice the straight-line rate (728)

E

Economic substance is more important than legal form In the context of a lease agreement, because a particular lease transfers the risks and benefits of ownership from the lessor to the lessee, the lessee records an asset that it does not legally own (the leased property) (793)

Effective interest method Computing annual interest expense by multiplying the annual yield by the book value of the bonds at the beginning of the year (786)

Equivalent units Physical products multiplied by their average percentage of completion (546)

Estimated residual value　Cash a company estimates it will receive from the sale or disposal of an asset at the end of its estimated service life (724)

Estimated service life　Life over which a company expects an asset to be useful (724)

Expected inflation rate　Additional interest rate paid by the borrower to compensate for the expected inflation over the life of the borrowing (782)

External failure costs　Costs to a company of flaws in products that reach the company's customers (613)

Extraordinary item　Event or transaction that is unusual in nature and infrequent in occurrence (868)

F

Face value　Stated value on a note (or bond) that must be paid on the maturity date (778)

Factor　Decimal amount in a present value table (694)

Financial flexibility　Company's ability to adapt to change (781)

First-in, first-out (FIFO)　Earliest (first) costs incurred are included in cost of goods sold as the products are sold, leaving the latest costs incurred in ending inventory (653)

Fixed overhead volume variance　Difference between the amount of applied fixed overhead and the amount of budgeted fixed overhead (590)

Flexible manufacturing system　Computerized networks of automated equipment that use computer software to control such tasks as machine setups, direct materials and parts selection, and product assembly (618)

FOB destination　Selling company transfers ownership to the buyer at the place of delivery (after transit is completed) (651)

FOB shipping point　Selling company transfers ownership to the buyer at the place of sale (shipping point), that is, before the inventory is in transit (651)

Franchise　Agreement entered into by two parties where, for a fee, one party gives the other party rights to perform certain functions or sell certain products or services over the legal life of the franchise (750)

Functional causes of depreciation　Limit the life of the asset, even though the physical life is not exhausted (722)

Future value　The value at a future date of a certain amount of dollars paid or received today (692)

G

General journal　Includes the following information about each transaction: the date of the transaction, the ac-counts to be debited and credited, the amounts of the debit and credit entries, and an explanation of each transaction (A-5)

General ledger　Entire set of accounts for a company (A-2)

Goodwill　Difference between the total price a company paid to buy another company and the market value of the identifiable net assets it acquired (752)

Gross profit method　Used to estimate the cost of ending inventory by multiplying the net sales by the historic gross profit percentage and subtracting this amount from net sales to determine the estimated cost of goods sold, and then subtracting this amount from the cost of goods available for sale (668)

H

Holding gain (inventory profit)　Artificial profit that results when a company records cost of goods sold at an historical cost that is lower than the replacement cost of the units sold (658)

I

Impairment　Occurs when the expected future cash flows from an asset are less than the book value of that asset (733)

In transit　A freight company is in the process of delivering inventory from the selling company to the buying company (651)

Income summary　Temporary account used in the closing process to accumulate the amount of net income (or net loss) before transferring it to the T-account for owner's capital (A-22)

Incremental costs　Cost increases resulting from the performance of an additional activity (499)

Initial cost　Expected cash payment to put a capital expenditure proposal into operation (688)

Intangible assets　Company's long-term assets that do not have a physical substance (748)

Interest expense　Cost to a company of borrowing money for a period (776)

Internal failure costs　Costs of reworking defective products, replacement parts and materials, and time that the factory is "down" while employees trace and fix the cause of the defects (614)

Inventory　Merchandise a retail company is holding for resale (648)

ISO 9000　Set of quality standards set up by the International Organization for Standardization (611)

Issued capital stock Number of shares of capital stock that a corporation has legally issued to its stockholders as of the balance sheet date (856)

J

Job order Unique product or group of products being manufactured (532)

Job order cost accounting system Keeps track of the costs applied to each job order (533)

Journal entry Recorded information for each transaction (A-5)

Journalizing Process of recording a transaction in a company's general journal (A-5)

Just-in-time strategies Reducing or eliminating inventories, streamlining the factory and increasing operational efficiencies, and controlling quality (615)

L

Large stock dividend Stock dividend greater than 20% of the previously outstanding common shares (878)

Last-in, first-out (LIFO) Latest costs incurred before a sale are included in cost of goods sold and the earliest costs incurred are included in ending inventory (654)

Lease Agreement giving the right to use property, plant, or equipment without transferring legal ownership of the item (792)

Legal capital Amount of stockholder's equity of a corporation that it cannot distribute to stockholders (854)

Lessee Company that acquires the right to use a leased item (792)

Lessor Company that gives up the use of a leased item (792)

Leverage Use of borrowing by a corporation to increase the return to common stockholders (779)

LIFO liquidation Occurs when a company reduces the physical quantity of inventory from the beginning of the year to the end of the year (666)

LIFO liquidation profit Extra profit that results from reporting a lower cost of goods sold than would have been reported if a LIFO liquidation had not occurred (666)

LIFO reserve Difference between LIFO and non-LIFO ending inventory amounts (663)

Long-term liquidity Relates to the amount of cash a company will generate over the long run to pay off its liabilities as they become due (789)

Lower-of-cost-or-market (LCM) method When the market value of a company's inventory falls below its cost, the company is required to reduce, or "write down," the inventory to that market value (666)

M

Maintenance and customer-support costs Computer software costs that a company incurs after it releases the software (752)

Maturity date Specific day when a company that issued a bond (or note) promises to pay the principal (and interest) amounts to the bond (or note) holder (778)

Modified Accelerated Cost Recovery System (MACRS) Accelerated depreciation method acceptable under the Internal Revenue Code and used by companies for income tax purposes (731)

Mortgage payable Long-term liability for which the lender has a specific claim against an asset of the borrower (797)

Moving average Average cost per unit is calculated after each purchase and this new average cost is assigned to items sold or held in inventory until the next purchase (when another average cost is computed) (653)

Mutually exclusive capital expenditure proposals Proposals that accomplish the same thing, so that when one proposal is selected, the others are not (702)

N

Natural resource assets Assets that are used up as they are extracted, mined, dug up, or chopped down (757)

Net asset value Cost of an asset less its accumulated depreciation (722)

Net present value Present value of the expected future net cash receipts and payments minus the initial cash payment for a capital expenditure proposal (699)

No significant influence Less than 20% ownership by an investor company in the common stock of an investee company (820)

No-par capital stock Does not have a par value (854)

Non-LIFO Costs of ending inventories under an alternative to the LIFO cost flow assumption, such as FIFO, average, current, or replacement cost (663)

Normal activity Average of a company's expected future annual production volumes (587)

O

Operating capability   Company's ability to continue a given level of operations (738)

Operating efficiency   How well a company uses its assets to generate revenue (738)

Operating expenditure   Cost that only maintains the benefits that a company originally expected from an asset (732)

Operating lease   Does not transfer the risks and benefits of ownership (793)

Operating segment   Component of a company that earns revenues and incurs expenses, whose performance is reviewed regularly by the company's top executive, and for which financial information is available (833)

Opportunity costs   Profits that a company forgoes by following a particular course of action (499)

Outstanding capital stock   Number of shares that a corporation has issued to stockholders and that the stockholders still hold as of a specific date (860)

Overhead budget variance   Difference between the total overhead budgeted and the total overhead incurred (589)

P

Par value   Monetary amount per share that must be kept in a corporation as legal capital (854)

Parent company   Investor company that has control over the investee company (831)

Patent   Exclusive right granted by the U.S. government giving the owner of an invention the control of its manufacture or sale for 20 years from the date of the patent application (750)

Payback period   Length of time required for a return of the initial investment in a capital expenditure proposal (700)

Pension plan   Agreement by a company to provide income to its employees after they retire (799)

Periodic inventory system   System that does not keep a continuous record of the inventory on hand and sold, but determines the inventory at the end of each accounting period by physically counting it (648)

Perpetual inventory system   System that keeps a continuous record of the cost of inventory on hand and the cost of inventory sold (648)

Physical causes of depreciation   Include wear and tear due to use, deterioration and decay caused by the passage of time, and damage and destruction (722)

Post-closing trial balance   Schedule a company prepares after making its closing entries to prove the equality of the debit and credit balances in its asset, liability, and owners' equity accounts (A-24)

Posting   Process of transferring the debit and credit information for each journal entry to the accounts in a company's general ledger (A-10)

Potential common shares   Securities that can be used by the holder to acquire common stock (872)

Practical capacity   Volume of activity at which the company's manufacturing facilities are capable of operating per year under practical conditions, allowing for usual levels of efficiency (587)

Predetermined overhead rate   Budgeted factory overhead cost divided by budgeted total volume of manufacturing activity for the year (539)

Preemptive right   Right to maintain a proportionate (pro rata) share of additional capital stock if it is issued (854)

Preferred stock   Type of capital stock issued for which stockholders receive certain additional rights in exchange for giving up some of the usual stockholders' rights (855)

Prepaid item   Current asset (economic resource) that a company records when it pays for goods or services before using them (A-14)

Present value   Value today of a certain amount of dollars to be paid or received in the future (697)

Prevention costs   Costs to a company of preventing flaws and defects in its products (614)

Price/earnings ratio   Market price per share divided by earnings per share (872)

Price standard   Cost that a company should incur to acquire one unit of input for its manufacturing process (568)

Price standard for factory overhead   Standard predetermined overhead rate (587)

Process cost accounting system   Keeps track of the costs applied to identical units of a product as they move through one or more manufacturing processes (543)

Product defect rates   Percentage of defective products manufactured (616)

Projected benefit obligation   Obligation of a company to its employees in regard to its pension plan for the work they have done to date (801)

Property, plant, and equipment   All of the physical (tangible), long-term assets a company uses in its operations (719)

Pull-through production   Customers' orders "pull" products through a company's production process, from the customers' orders backward through the production process to the purchase of raw materials (616)

Push-through production   Sales forecast "pushes" the products through a company's production process (615)

Q

Quantity standard   Amount of an input that a company should use to produce a unit of product in its manufacturing process (568)

Quantity standard for factory overhead   Volume of production activity (direct labor hours, machine hours, or other measure of activity) that should be used to produce one unit of product (587)

R

Rational   A characteristic of depreciation that relates it to the benefits an asset produces in any period (724)

Redeemable preferred stock   Subject to mandatory retirement at a specified maturity date and price or at the option of the owner (859)

Relevant cash flows   Future cash flows that differ, either in amount or in timing, as a result of accepting a capital expenditure proposal (689)

Relevant costs   Future costs that will change as a result of a decision (496)

Relevant revenues   Future revenues that will change as a result of a decision (496)

Replacement cost   Cost that a company would have to pay at the balance sheet date to purchase (replace) an item of inventory (657)

Required rate of return   Cutoff rate used to distinguish between acceptable and unacceptable capital expenditure proposals (691)

Research   Activity aimed at the discovery of new knowledge intended for use in developing a new or improved product or process (749)

Residual value   Estimated cash to be received from the sale or disposal of an asset at the end of its estimated service life (724)

Retail inventory method   Used to estimate the cost of ending inventory by multiplying the retail value of the ending inventory by the cost-to-retail ratio of the current period (670)

Retained earnings   A corporation's total lifetime net income that has been reinvested in the corporation and not distributed to stockholders as dividends (853)

Risk   Amount of uncertainty that exists about the future operations of a company (789)

Risk premium   Additional interest that a borrower, such as a company, pays when there is a possibility that it will default (782)

Risk-free rate   Interest rate that a borrower would pay, and a lender would receive, when there is no risk of default by the borrower and when no inflation is expected (782)

S

Segment report   Provides financial information about a company's operating segments (833)

Service life   Life over which a company expects an asset to be useful (724)

Significant influence over investee   When an investor company owns between 20% and 50% of another company's common stock (820)

Slide   Occurs when the digits are listed in the correct order but are mistakenly moved one decimal place to the left or right (A-17)

Small stock dividend   Dividend of 20% or less of the previously outstanding common shares (878)

Software production cost   Costs of designing, coding, testing, and preparing documentation and training materials (752)

Specific identification method   Allocates costs to cost of goods sold and to ending inventory by assigning to each unit sold and to each unit in ending inventory the cost to a company of purchasing that particular unit (649)

Standard costs   Costs that a company should incur in performing an activity or producing a product under a given set of planned operating conditions (567)

Standard costs of an input   Quantity standard of an input multiplied by its price standard (568)

Standard cost system   Assigns standard costs rather than actual costs to each inventory account (567)

Standard direct labor hours budgeted   Number of direct labor hours that should be used for the company's actual production level (577)

Standard direct materials quantity budgeted   Amount of direct materials that should be used for the company's actual production level (572)

Stated value   Legal capital per share of no-par stock (854)

Statement of changes in stockholders' equity   Supporting schedule that shows the changes in all the accounts in the stockholders' equity section of a corporation's balance sheet (880)

Statement of retained earnings   Schedule that starts with the beginning balance in retained earnings, adds the amount of net income, and subtracts the amount of dividends to determine the ending balance of retained earnings (880)

Stock certificate   Serially numbered legal document that indicates the number of shares of capital stock owned by a stockholder (853)

Stock dividend   Proportional (pro rata) distribution of additional shares of a corporation's own stock to its stockholders (876)

Stock split   Decrease in the par value per share of a corporation's common stock and a proportional increase in the number or shares authorized and issued (879)

Stockbroker   Person or company that buys and sells (trades) stocks and bonds for other people or companies (821)

Stockholders (Shareholders)   Owners of a corporation who hold shares of the corporation's capital stock (853)

Stockholders' equity   Owners' equity of a corporation, consisting of contributed capital and retained earnings (853, A-26)

Straight-line method   Computes depreciation expense by allocating the cost of an asset, less its estimated residual value, equally to each period of the asset's estimated service life (724)

Subsidiary company   Investee company that has more than 50% of its common stock owned by an investor company (831)

Sum-of-the-years'-digits method   Computes depreciation expense by multiplying the depreciable cost of an asset by a fraction that declines each year (729)

Systematic   Following a formula for the calculation of depreciation (724)

T

T-account   Accounts used to record transactions for individual types of assets, liabilities, and owner's equity, as well as revenues and expenses (A-2)

Temporary difference   Occurs when a corporation records an expense (or a revenue) for financial reporting in a period different from that used for income tax reporting, but the total lifetime expense (or revenue) is the same for both (798)

Total overhead variance   Difference between total factory overhead cost applied and total factory overhead cost incurred in a standard cost system (589)

Total quality management (TQM)   Management philosophy or approach that focuses on a company's customers to foster continuous improvement (611)

Trademark (Tradename)   Exclusive right granted by the U.S. government (or the government of another country) to use a name or symbol for product identification (750)

Transposition   Occurs when two digits in a number are mistakenly reversed (A-17)

Treasury stock   Corporation's own capital stock that stockholders fully paid for and the corporation issued, the corporation later reacquired, and the corporation currently holds (860)

Trial balance   Schedule that lists the titles of all accounts in a company's general ledger, the debit or credit balance of each account, and the totals of the debit and credit balances (A-12)

U

Unearned revenue   Obligation of a company to provide goods or services in the future, resulting from an advance receipt of cash (A-15)

Unit cost   Computer software cost of producing software, such as costs of the disks and the duplication of the software, packaging, documentation, and training materials (752)

Units-of-production method   Used to compute depletion (or depreciation) based on the level of an asset's physical activity (756)

Y

Yield   Market rate at which bonds are issued (783)

Z

Zero-coupon bonds   Bonds that do not pay interest each period, but pay the interest on the maturity date (785, 836)

INDEX